# The State of
# Working America

# The State of Working America

## 2002/2003

LAWRENCE MISHEL

JARED BERNSTEIN

HEATHER BOUSHEY

ECONOMIC POLICY INSTITUTE

*ILR Press*
*an imprint of*
*Cornell University Press*
*Ithaca and London*

First published 2003 by Cornell University Press
First printing, Cornell Paperbacks, 2003

Printed in the United States of America

ISBN 0-8014-4064-5 (cloth)
ISBN 0-8014-8803-6 (pbk.)

Recommended citation for this book is as follows: Mishel, Lawrence, Jared Bernstein, and Heather Boushey, *The State of Working America 2002/2003.* An Economic Policy Institute Book. Ithaca, NY: ILR Press, an imprint of Cornell University Press, 2003.

Cornell University Press strives to use environmentally responsible suppliers and materials to the fullest extent possible in the publishing of its books. Such materials include vegetable-based, low-VOC inks and acid-free papers that are recycled, totally chlorine-free, or partly composed of nonwood fibers. For further information, visit our website at www.cornellpress.cornell.edu.

Cloth printing      10 9 8 7 6 5 4 3 2 1
Paperback printing      10 9 8 7 6 5 4 3 2 1

To Fred, who worked for justice one case at a time,
and to Mom, for a lifetime of love.
– LARRY MISHEL

To the men and women who make up the statistical infrastructure at the
Bureaus of the Census, Labor Statistics, and Economic Analysis. Without
their work, ours would be impossible.
– JARED BERNSTEIN

To my parents, Mike and Bobbi.
– HEATHER BOUSHEY

To Senator Paul Wellstone, a tireless fighter
for economic justice.
– THE AUTHORS

## VISIT EPINET.ORG

The Economic Policy Institute's web site contains current analysis of issues
addressed in this book. The DataZone section presents up-to-date historical
data series on incomes, wages, employment, poverty, and other topics. The
data can be viewed online or downloaded as spreadsheets.

# Table of Contents

# Acknowledgments

The preparation of this publication requires the intensive work of many people on EPI's staff and many contributions from other researchers on the topics covered in the text.

Thacher Tiffany and Brendan Hill provided extensive and enormously valuable research assistance in all of the areas covered in this book by collecting and organizing data and creating tables and graphs. Our programming staff, headed by Danielle Gao and including Yvon Pho and Jin Dai, provided extensive computer programming and data analysis. Danielle's tireless work and deep knowledge of our data are invaluable resources. David Webster's programming work for earlier editions of the book continues to be of great value. Alyce Anderson and Debra Agostini helped to prepare the text for the wages chapter and various appendices.

Among EPI staffers (and former staffers), Jeffrey Wenger, Christian Weller, Michael Ettlinger, and Dean Baker made helpful contributions. John Schmitt, co-author of the last two versions of this book, made a lasting intellectual contribution to our work and he continues to provide extensive assistance. Vicky O'Reilly and Princess Goldthwaite provide valuable help in raising funds for our work.

It has been a pleasure to continue the partnership with Kim Weinstein and Patrick Watson in the development and production of this book. Patrick reviewed every word we wrote and effectively edited, checked, made consistent, and substantially improved the text and presentation. Patrick is a behind-the-scenes author, and we owe him a great debt for making us look like better writers and for the equanimity with which he conducts the editing process in a particularly short time period. Kim produced and designed the book. Nancy Coleman, Karen Conner, and Stephaan Harris work to provide a large audience for our work.

Many experts were helpful in providing data or their research papers for our use. We are particularly grateful to Tim Bartik and Ed Wolff for the provision of special tabulations. Others who provided data, advice, or their analysis include Josh Bivens, Al Blostin, Joe Dalaker, Howard Hayghe, David Johnson, Tom Nardone, Chuck Nelson, Steven Sabow, William Shay, Kathleen Short, Timothy Smeeding, Reid Steadman, Jay Stewart, John Stinson, Ed Welniak, and Robert Zahradnik.

We are grateful to the Ford Foundation, the Foundation for Child Development, the Joyce Foundation, the John D. & Catherine T. MacArthur Foundation, the Charles Stewart Mott Foundation, and the Rockefeller Foundation for providing support for the research and publication of this volume.

# The State of
# Working America

# Executive summary

A comprehensive review of the state of working America reveals three important developments.

First, the U.S. labor market has moved into a recession for the first time in a decade. The downturn has been underway in manufacturing since 2000, and, as of June 2002, unemployment remained high. The terrorist attacks of September 11, 2001 meant that, unlike in previous recessions, the services industry has experienced little or no employment growth, and transportation, retail trade, and wholesale trade are experiencing unusual weakness. So far (through June 2002), the unemployment levels are below those of the early 1990s, but job losses have been steep nevertheless. The percentage decline in private-sector employment is greater than that seen in the early 1990s, and the employment decline for women is double what it was then. Higher unemployment has led to losses in family income in 2001, and these losses have been largest for those at the bottom of the income scale, reversing the long-term trend toward lower poverty rates. Rising joblessness is also taking a toll on wage growth, which has begun to slow, and there are indications of an expansion in earnings inequality.

Second, this recession comes after years of persistently low unemployment. Although structural problems remained—the long-term decline in job quality and unionization, the deregulation of key industries, and the persistence of imbalanced trade and the ensuing loss of a manufacturing base—low unemployment brought rapid wage and income growth to families across the income distribution. Most notably, middle- and lower-income families, whose economic fortunes had stagnated in prior years, saw real income gains over the late 1990s. African American and Hispanic families also disproportionately benefited in terms of low unemployment and fast earnings growth during those years.

Third, the long-term trend of increased hours of paid work by America's families continued through the late 1990s. The pace slowed, however, because, as wages were rising, families could work the same hours while bringing home more income. In any case, more time at work, a reduction in paid vacation and holiday time, and the lack of legislated paid family leave mean that families are under increasing time stress.

The living standards of most American families are determined by opportunities in the labor market. The majority of family income derives from earnings, and the loss of a job poses real hardship. In this regard, the recent recession and the ensuing slow-growth recovery are serious problems that have been underappreciated by many commentators who have judged the downturn to be mild based on macroeconomic measures such as overall growth in gross domestic product. Although production has begun to increase and the recession in output may have passed, unemployment continues to rise. As in the early 1990s recession, the United States appears to be in yet another "jobless recovery." The lack of job growth during this recession is compounded by the fact that the traditional reliance on services to pull up employment has not been effective during this recession.

The data described in the following chapters provide a thorough examination of the trends affecting workers and their families over the post-World War II period. This history-in-numbers shows that falling unemployment in the late 1990s was critical for workers for two reasons. First, it provided workers with the foundations upon which to bargain with their employers over wages and working conditions. Second, it provided a counterpoint to structural changes in the U.S. economy—the long-term decline in unions, industry deregulation, and continued declines in manufacturing—that had been undermining the security and bargaining power of workers for the past two decades. The low unemployment of the late 1990s was also important because it demonstrated that the economy could reach 4% unemployment without generating inflation, contrary to the long-held wisdom of the economics profession.

## Family income: full employment reverses historic stagnation

The full-employment economy of the late 1990s made a large and positive difference in the growth of real income for low- and middle-income families. Whereas real median family income grew 2.8% annually between 1947 and 1973, growth slowed to 0.4% between 1973 and 1995. Between 1995 and 2000, though, growth accelerated to 2.2% per year. The least advantaged—younger families, minority families, and families headed by single mothers—benefited most from the tight labor markets that prevailed in the latter half of the 1990s. For example, between 1995 and 2000, the real median family income of African American and Hispanic families grew 16% and 25%, respectively, compared to 11% for white families.

The larger gains by lower-income families also meant that inequality grew more slowly in the 1990s. Inequality did not, however, stop growing, nor did it reverse course. The richest families continued to pull away from the pack over the decade: the income of the top 1% of taxpayers (including their realized capital gains) grew by 59% from 1995 to 1999 (the most recent available data of this type) while that of the bottom half grew by 9%. Thus, while full employment gave low- and middle-wage workers the bargaining power that was missing over prior decades of stagnant growth, it did not correct structural inequities that persist in the economy.

While these recent developments have lifted family incomes throughout the income scale, longer-term stagnation among low- and middle-income families led to large increases in the amount of time families spend at work. Over the last 30 years, workers in middle-income married-couple families with children have added an average of 20 weeks at work, the equivalent of five more months. Most of the increase comes from working wives, many more of whom entered the labor market over this period, adding more weeks per year and more hours per week. In fact, middle-income wives added close to 500 hours of work per year between 1979 and 2000, the equivalent of more than 12 weeks of full-time work.

Increases in family hours have been equally as large among families headed by high school graduates or minorities as they have been for high-income, highly educated families. On average, between 1979 and 2000, increases in annual hours worked were slightly greater for minorities than for white families: 14.7% and 14.4% for black and Hispanic families, respectively, compared to 11.7% for white families. Middle-income African American and Hispanic families worked significantly more hours than did white families in order to reach the same income levels (given the existing racial wage gaps, this is to be expected). By 2000, middle-income black families worked the equivalent of 12 full-time weeks more than white families.

Income losses during the recession of 2001 further underscore the importance of full employment. The increase in the unemployment rate, from 4.0% in 2000 to 4.8% in 2001, led to declines in family income that were largest (in percentage terms) at the low end of the income scale. The median family lost 1.4% ($741 in 2001 dollars), while the average income of the poorest families—those in the bottom income fifth—fell by 3.4% (about $500). Family income also fell among the top fifth of families, by 1.0%, demonstrating the broad impact of the recession on family incomes.

## Wages: broad-based gains in late 1990s

Wages make up the majority of income for most American families. Over the late 1990s, low unemployment played a critical role in boosting wage growth overall, but particularly at the bottom, by strengthening workers' bargaining power with respect to their employers. Jobs were relatively easy to find, and many employers had to compete for workers. This in turn spurred strong wage and income gains over the latter half of the 1990s economic boom.

The era of stagnant and falling wages from the early 1970s to 1995 gave way to one of strong wage growth after 1995 as wages changed course, rising strongly in response to persistent low unemployment and the faster productivity growth relative to the 1973-95 period. However, despite the strong wage improvements in recent years, it was not until 1998 that the wage level for middle-wage workers (the median hourly wage) jumped above its 1979 level. The median *male* wage in 2000 was still below its 1979 level, even though productivity was 44.5% higher in 2000 than in 1979. One reason for this divergence is increased corporate profitability, which drove a wedge between productivity and compensation growth.

The trends in average wage growth—the slowdown in the 1970s and the pick-up in the mid-1990s—can be partly attributed to corresponding changes in productivity growth, as well as to changing macroeconomic conditions. Productivity accelerated in the late 1990s, and its growth continued into the current recession, helping to spur strong growth in average wages. Even so, the benefits of the faster productivity growth went disproportionately to capital, as income shifted from labor to capital in the 1995-2000 period.

Over the late 1990s, the pattern of wage growth shifted and growth in inequality decelerated, although it did not change course. In the 1980s, wage inequality widened dramatically and, coupled with stagnant average wages, brought about widespread erosion of real wages. Wage inequality continued to grow in the 1990s but took a different shape: a continued growth in the wage gap between top and middle earners—the 90/50 gap between high-wage workers at the 90th percentile and middle-wage workers at the median—but a shrinking wage gap between middle and low earners—the 50/10 gap. The positive trend in the 50/10 wage gap owes much to several increases in the minimum wage, low unemployment, and the slight, relative contraction in low-paying retail jobs in the late 1990s. Slower growth in wage inequality at the top, relative to the 1980s, was the result of the continuing influence of globalization, deunionization, and the shift to lower-paying service industries.

Explaining the shifts in wage inequality requires attention to several factors that affect low-, middle-, and high-wage workers differently. Low unemployment benefits workers, especially low-wage earners. Correspondingly, the high levels of unemployment in the early and mid-1980s disempowered wage earners and provided the context in which other forces—specifically, a weakening of labor market institutions and globalization—could drive up wage inequality. Significant shifts in the labor market, such as the severe drop in the minimum wage and deunionization, can explain one-third of the growing wage inequality in the 1980s. Similarly, the increasing globalization of the economy—immigration, trade, and capital mobility—and the employment shift toward lower-paying service industries (such as retail trade) and away from manufacturing can explain, in combination, another third of the total growth in wage inequality.

One explanation that does not hold up is that the growth of wage inequality reflects primarily a technology-driven increase in demand for "educated" or "skilled" workers. Economists have found that the overall impact of technology on the wage and employment structure was no greater in the 1980s or 1990s than in the 1970s. Moreover, skill demand and technology have little relationship to the growth of wage inequality within the same group (i.e., for workers with similar levels of experience and education), and this within-group inequality was responsible for half of the overall growth of wage inequality in the 1980s and 1990s. Technology has been and continues to be an important force, but there was no "technology shock" in the 1980s or 1990s and no ensuing demand for "skill" that was not satisfied by the continuing expansion of the educational attainment of the workforce.

Among other noteworthy trends in wages:

- The long-term convergence of wages for men and women stalled, and the gap between men's and women's wages was about as wide at the end of the 1990s as at the beginning.

- Benefits declined in the late 1990s. Although health insurance coverage increased after falling for more than a decade, employer costs for health insurance dropped in the 1990s. Employer pension contributions also fell. Since 2000, the amount of money that employers have spent on benefits has grown, as health care costs began to rise again.

- As wages fell for the typical worker, executive pay soared. From 1989 to 2000, the wage of the typical (i.e., median) chief executive officer grew 79.0%, and average compensation grew 342%. In 1965, CEOs made 26 times more than a typical worker; this ratio had risen to 72-to-1 by 1989 and to 310-to-1 by 2000. U.S. CEOs make about three times as much as their counterparts abroad.

- Unionization provides an 11.5% wage advantage to workers. However, the union edge is even greater for benefits, with union workers far more likely than non-union workers to receive health insurance and pension coverage from their employers. Moreover, union workers have better health plans with lower deductibles and less cost sharing, and are provided more paid time off, including three more days of vacation.

## Jobs: recession leads to employment losses

Rapid economic growth combined with unemployment averaging below 5% improved the job prospects of American workers in the late 1990s. Employment opportunities expanded considerably, especially for traditionally disadvantaged groups such as women, African Americans, and Hispanics. However, the recession threatens to erode these gains. Unemployment began to rise in October 2000 and, through June 2002, it had risen by 2.0 percentage points, up to 5.9%. Both the percentage-point increase and the level of unemployment are smaller than during the recession of the early 1990s, when unemployment increased by 2.6 percentage points to 7.8%. However, the employment losses (in percentage terms) have been greater.

Typically, men's unemployment increases are larger than women's, but during this recession women and men have experienced a similar rise in unemployment. Although the total employment loss for men remains higher than for women, women's employment losses have been twice as large as their losses during the early 1990s recession. Higher job losses for women are a result of the change in the industrial composition of job losses during this recession. Usually, the employment in the service sector (employing about one-third of all workers—two out of five women but only one out of four men) rises over recessions. During the 2000-02 recession, however, services rose only slightly. The terrorist attacks of September 11, 2001 appear to have played a large role in the composition of industries that lost employment over this recession, as transportation and retail trade saw major job losses after September 11.

Jobs losses have been spread fairly equally across educational groups, but not so among racial groups. African American workers have experienced nearly twice as large an increase in unemployment as have white workers; the increase among Hispanic workers is a third larger than among white.

Nonstandard work arrangements—part-time or contingent employment— remain widespread after the 1990s boom, even though this work is generally substandard. Compared to regular full-time work, nonstandard arrangements pay less for comparable work, are much less likely to provide health or pension benefits and, almost by definition, provide far less job security. Over the 1980s and 1990s, temporary work doubled each decade, even though it remains a small proportion of nonstandard work overall. As the economy moved toward full employment in the late 1990s, the share of nonstandard workers reporting that they would rather have full-time work fell, presumably the result of dissatisfied contingent workers finding full-time regular employment.

Job security fell in the 1980s and 1990s as workers began spending less time with one employer. The long-term trend in job stability is disconcerting for a number of reasons. First, workers who are displaced from their jobs often find new ones that pay less and are less likely to offer benefits. Further, many employee benefits, such as health insurance and pensions, are tied to employers. Workers who switch jobs not only tend to start at the firm's minimal number of vacation weeks, but they may have to go through waiting periods for employer-provided health insurance or vesting of pensions. Since many employers use health maintenance organizations, job switching may also entail changing doctors. However, over the late 1990s, employment retention—whether or not a worker was able to maintain consistent employment over time—increased slightly. Thus, even though workers were switching jobs more rapidly, some of these changes may have been voluntary responses to more rewarding economic conditions.

Low unemployment was insufficient to reverse the long-term trend toward fewer fringe benefits. In 2002, workers were less likely to have employer-provided health insurance than they were 30 years ago, and those who have it pay more. Further, there has been little progress in expanding job flexibility and paid time off—vacations, holidays, and family and medical leave. Heightened job insecurity left over from the recession of the early 1990s along with lower rates of unionization may have limited workers' capacity to bargain for on-the-job benefits, even when labor was scarce.

## Wealth: deeper in debt

Like wages and incomes, wealth is a vital component of a family's standard of living. Several key features about American wealth stand out. First, wealth distribution is highly unequal. The wealthiest 1% of all households control about 38% of national wealth, while the bottom 80% of households hold only 17%. The ownership of stocks is particularly unequal. The top 1% of stock owners hold almost half (47.7%) of all stocks, by value, while the bottom 80% own just 4.1% of total stock holdings.

Second, the total wealth of the typical American household improved only marginally during the 1990s. The net worth of the average household in the middle 20% of the wealth distribution rose about $2,200 in the 1990s—from $58,800 in 1989 to $61,000 in 1998. On the asset side over the same period, the value of the

9

stock holdings of this typical household grew $5,500, and the value of non-stock assets increased $8,500. Home ownership—the most important asset for most American families—rose over the late 1990s, especially among non-white households. Meanwhile, on the liabilities side, typical household debt rose $11,800. The relatively modest gains in stock and non-stock assets combined with the explosion in household debt meant that the 1990s were far less generous to typical households than business-page headlines often suggested.

Third, only households at the very top of the income spectrum are likely to be adequately prepared for retirement. For many Americans, the 1990s boom left them less prepared for retirement than before: for two out of five Americans, income from Social Security, pensions, and defined-contribution plans will replace less than half of their pre-retirement income.

Fourth, even well into the decade-long boom in the stock market, most Americans had no economically meaningful stake in it. The most recent government data show that less than half of households hold stock in any form, including mutual funds and 401(k)-style pension plans. The same data reveal that 64% of households have stock holdings worth $5,000 or less. While this means that most Americans did not benefit from the stock market boom of the late 1990s, it also means that most have not been directly hurt by the crash of the stock market in 2000.

Finally, for the typical household, rising debt, not a rising stock market, was the big story of the 1990s. Household debt grew much more rapidly than household income in the last decade. By 2001, total household debt exceeded total household disposable income by nearly 10%. Households in the middle of the wealth distribution absorbed the largest share of this run-up in debt. While low nominal interest rates have made it easier for households to carry the greatly expanded debt, many households appear to be straining. The most recent government data show that 14% of middle-income households have debt-service obligations that exceed 40% of their income; 9% have at least one bill that is more than 60 days past due. Meanwhile, despite the robust state of the economy, personal bankruptcy rates reached all-time highs by 2001.

For many, the debt run-up begins from the day they exit college. Student loans increased substantially over the 1990s as college costs rose and grant aid declined. Most of the increase in loans was in the form of unsubsidized federal student loans—loans that accrue interest while the student is in school. Although students from lower-income families continue to take out more loans on average relative to those from higher-income families, students from higher-income families saw their loan burdens—especially their unsubsidized loan burdens—increase over the 1990s. The result is that students are graduating with historically high levels of loan debt.

## Poverty: recession reverses recent declines

Over the last five years of the 1990s boom, significant progress was made in reducing poverty, particularly rates for minorities and children. Yet in 2000, the last year of available data, the share of the nation's poor was about equal to its level in 1973. Despite positive and even robust income growth, poverty remains stuck at relatively high levels. This lack of progress occurred despite growth in productivity of 52% and growth in real per capita income of 60% over this period. By 2001, the recession reversed the recent progress against poverty, and the rate increased from 11.3% to 11.7%, adding 1.3 million more persons to the poverty rolls.

While levels of poverty are still high in historic terms, the trends of the latter 1990s were clearly positive, especially for the least advantaged. Low unemployment and slower-growing inequality helped drive poverty lower for demographic groups that have historically faced persistent high rates. While the overall poverty rate fell 2.5 percentage points from 1995 to 2000, the rate for African Americans fell 6.8 points, to a historic low of 22.5% (still twice the overall rate), and Hispanic poverty fell 8.8 points, close to two points per year. For minority children, the declines were even larger. For example, for African American children under age 6, poverty declined by 16 points from 1995 to 2000; for young Hispanic children it fell by 14 points. Poverty among single-mother families also fell steeply, by 8.5 percentage points between 1995 and 2000, though a third of these families still remained poor in 2000.

Economic growth post-1973 did not lead to as much poverty reduction as expected for a number of reasons. While demographics—the continued increase in female-headed households, in particular—and measurement issues play non-trivial roles, the more important set of factors are economic. The slower overall growth that has prevailed since 1973 (except for the 1995-2000 period) meant there was less income to be distributed throughout the income scale over this period. But equally important, especially over the 1980s, when poverty rates were particularly unresponsive to growth, was the increase in inequality. By preventing low-income families from benefiting from overall growth as they had pre-1973, higher inequality created a wedge between growth in the overall economy and the economic progress of low-income families

Various policy changes over the past decade have had a significant impact on the way we view poverty, both in terms of the problem and the solutions. Among the most important policy changes were the increase in the Earned Income Tax Credit (EITC) in the early 1990s and the vast changes in the welfare system signed into law in 1996. In both cases, the emphasis was on work in the paid labor market as the primary pathway out of poverty.

The impact of these policy shifts comes across clearly in the poverty data from this period. The poor, particularly families headed by a single parent, are working more and deriving much more of their income from the labor market than they were in prior years; work is playing a much larger role in the lives of the poor and near-poor now than at any time over the past few decades. For example, for single-mother families with incomes below the median, labor market earnings as a share of income climbed from 41% in 1979 to 73% in 2000. At the same time, considerably less government cash assistance (transfer income) is flowing to the poor.

Effective poverty reduction depends of both market forces and redistribution of economic resources. During the 1960s, when the United States most effectively lowered its share of poor, both the market and the tax and transfer system were working in tandem. Low unemployment, rising real wages, and broad-based, equally shared growth were complemented by transfers that helped to raise family incomes above the poverty line. Though some redistributive efforts were considerably expanded in the 1990s (such as the EITC), others, such as cash assistance, were sharply cut. Thus, the market and the tax and transfer system were working against each other. Market outcomes drove poverty down by 3.3 points in the latter 1990s, but the diminished effectiveness of transfers added back 1.6 points. This effect was particularly notable over the 2001 recession, when the safety net was less effective in reducing the poverty rates of single-mother families than has historically been the case.

Measuring poverty presents numerous methodological challenges, and the official U.S. poverty measure has serious shortcomings in this regard. A new measure, implemented on an experimental basis by the Census Bureau, corrects many of the shortcomings in the official measure; it estimates that 15% of the nation was poor in 1999. This rate, much higher than the official rate of 11.8%, assigns an additional 8.8 million to the ranks of the poor.

## Regional analysis: significant variation among the states

The national trends in income, wages, employment, and poverty vary extensively by state and region. For example, the 1990s boom took hold in the Midwest and South sooner than in the rest of the country, leading to faster income growth and bigger poverty declines there. Part of these gains stem from the fact that the early 1990s recession, mild by historical standards, was felt much more acutely in the Northeast and, to a lesser extent, the West.

While labor markets tightened everywhere in the 1990s (particularly in the second half), unemployment fell the most in the Midwest and the South, helping to fuel some of the impressive trends in income and poverty there. Yet middle- and low-wage workers in almost every state experienced gains in wages and income and declines in poverty in the latter 1990s, as unemployment fell throughout the country and low-wage labor markets tightened.

Still, as impressive as these gains were, they did not continue long enough to reverse the trend of rising inequality in most states. The gap between those at the top and the bottom of the income scale was significantly higher at the end of the 1990s than in the late 1970s in almost every state.

It is too early (as of this writing) to fully assess the geographical impact of the recession of 2001 and the subsequent slow-growth recovery. It appears, however, that the increase in unemployment and the loss of jobs were greater in the South and Midwest, the areas that most enjoyed the boom of the latter 1990s. In this regard, the pattern of the last recession, in which the East and West Coasts felt the brunt of the downturn, may be shifting.

## International comparisons:
## more inequality, less mobility out of poverty

Because of high productivity growth and low unemployment in the United States during the 1990s relative to Europe, many have argued that Europe should emulate key features of the U.S. economy, including weaker unions, lower mini- mum wages, less-generous social benefit systems, and lower taxes. The inter- national comparisons in this analysis can shed light on this ongoing debate about the advisability of exporting the "U.S. model."

Overall the 1990s were a period of slow growth in national income and pro- ductivity in most of the OECD economies. In the second half of the 1990s in the United States, however, both national income and productivity growth increased more so than in other OECD countries. But the recent good news for the United States must be considered along with other economic trends. First, income and productivity growth over the last decade have generally trailed the rates obtained in the 1970s and 1980s and are far below those of the "Golden Age" from the end of World War II through the first oil shock in 1973. Second, the above-average income and productivity growth in the United States in the late 1990s came after decades of consistent rankings in the middle or near the bottom among the OECD countries since the 1970s. Third, the U.S. economy has consistently produced the highest levels of economic inequality. Moreover, inequality in the United States (along with the United Kingdom) has shown a strong tendency to rise, even as inequality was relatively stable or declining in most of the rest of the OECD. Fourth, poverty is deeper and more difficult to escape in the United States than in the rest of the OECD. The lack of redistributive social policies only exacerbates the high levels of poverty and income inequality in the United States.

## Conclusion

America's working families responded to the strong economy of the latter 1990s by working harder and more productively, and, for the first time in decades, their efforts were rewarded with real gains in income and declines in poverty. Yet, while inequality grew more slowly in the 1990s than in the prior decade, the richest families continued to reap disproportionate gains. And while working harder meant higher incomes, it also came to mean increasingly more hours spent at work and away from the family. The challenge moving forward is to generate positive gains in living standards that reflect the multidimensional needs of families, both in terms of their incomes and family lives.

The historically long period of economic growth that began in 1991 ended in 2001, and many of the broad-based income gains of the latter part of that recovery have slowed or reversed during the recession. What will happen to family income as the recovery gets underway? If past is a guide, then we might anticipate a return to the experience of the 1990s recovery. But which part? The slow growth early years, when unemployment continued to rise and family income fell? Or the later years, when the economy headed toward full employment and family income grew at historic rates? Unfortunately, the early indicators suggest a slow growth recovery, with unemployment lingering at relatively high rates and family income taking its expected hit.

The turnaround of the late 1990s has been a boon for workers' wages and incomes, but now all eyes are on the future. If productivity growth continues to be strong (say, 2% or higher), even if not as strong as in recent years, then real wages may continue to expand for most of the workforce. However, unless we head back to full employment—with unemployment in the 4% neighborhood—low-wage workers are unlikely to have the needed bargaining power to claim their fair share of the added growth. As evidence, note that the increase in unemployment in 2001 led to both declining family incomes and greater inequality. Continuing pressures from globalization, more losses of manufacturing jobs, deunionization, high average unemployment, or a fall in the real value of the minimum wage could further exacerbate these trends. The near-term answers depend on the extent of the recession and the extent to which the recovery is characterized by growth too slow to lower unemployment. In the longer term, our willingness to alter these structural constraints in the labor market will determine the future living standards of working America.

# Introduction: what kind of recovery?

With the recovery of the 1990s officially at an end and a new business cycle struggling to begin, the American economy is facing considerable and unexpected challenges. The recession of 2001 appears to have been short lived, and by some measures, not particularly deep. Yet the inflation-adjusted income of the median family fell 1.4% that year, and the poverty rolls increased by 1.3 million persons. Even as the gross domestic product expanded through the first half of 2002, the unemployment rate remained well above its level of a few years back, job growth was virtually zero, wage growth was slowing, and the share of the long-term unemployed was hitting historically high rates. At the same time, corporate accounting scandals and diminished investor confidence sent financial markets tumbling. Given these trends, it is extremely likely that median income will fall further and poverty will grow higher in 2002.

With those dynamics in play, it is easy to forget that the last half of the 1990s boom was, from the perspective of working families, truly exemplary. In those years, a number of economic factors aligned in a way not seen in decades, and the results were real increases in living standards for the millions of middle- and lower-income American families who had hitherto seen their economic prospects stagnate while the American economy expanded.

In this period, lasting roughly from 1995 to 2000, full employment masked a set of structural problems in the labor market that have evolved over the past few decades. These structural imbalances—the long-term decline in job quality and unionization, the deregulation of key industries, the persistence of imbalanced trade and the ensuing loss of the manufacturing base, not to mention the erroneous belief that unemployment itself could not fall below 6% without generating spiraling inflation—served to shift bargaining power away from minority, blue-collar, and non-college-educated workers, and thus drove the fastest increase in inequality of economic outcomes since such data were collected over the last half century. Now, as full employment fades, recent data suggest that inequality's growth is resurfacing.

Our main conclusions are that:

- While the recession that officially began in March 2001 may ultimately be recorded as relatively short and mild, both the downturn and the slow growth recovery that followed have created a slack labor market. Unemployment as of mid-2002 was two percentage points above its level two years before, significant "hidden unemployment," exists, job growth is scant, and wage growth has slowed (especially at the bottom). Early signs indicate a return to the pattern of widening wage inequality seen in the 1980s.

- In the latter 1990s, the labor market reached full employment for the first time in 30 years. At the same time, productivity growth accelerated. Together, these two trends meant that more economic growth was available to be distributed and that those whose weak bargaining power had previously prevented them from receiving their fair share of growth were now in a much better position. The tight labor market meant that, for the first time in decades, employers had to raise wages to keep or expand their workforce.

- The other side of the picture is that nothing fundamental has shifted in the economy to ensure that the negative trends that loomed over the 1979-95 period won't return. By lifting the bargaining power of low- and middle-wage workers, historically low unemployment was a potent antidote against the structural imbalances noted above. But these negative forces remain, and unless they are addressed, in tandem with efforts to return to full employment, the broad-based prosperity of the 1990s is unlikely to return soon.

- Families are spending more time than ever at work. Over the last 30 years, workers in middle-income, married-couple families with children have added an average of 20 more weeks at work, the equivalent of five more months. Most of the increase comes from working wives, many more of whom entered the labor market over this period, working more weeks per year and hours per week. In fact, middle-income wives added close to 500 hours per year to their work schedules between 1979 and 2000, the equivalent of more than 12 weeks of full-time work. Contrary to any notion that increased work in the "new economy" falls mostly to busy professionals, increases in annual hours worked have been larger among middle-income families than among those at the top of the income scale, and increases in annual hours worked by middle-income families headed by a high school graduate surpass those of families headed by a college graduate.

The economic trends of the late 1990s managed at least to hold these forces at bay. What can we learn from this period about reconnecting economic growth to the progress in living standards for middle- and low-income families? To what extent did those boom years repair the damage of prior years, when growth was concentrated at the top and wages fell for large sections of the working class? The answers to these questions will be important as we evaluate developments in the current, fledgling business cycle.

## The impact of the recession

What determines whether an economy is in recession? The National Bureau of Economic Research, to which policy makers and academics turn for questions about the timing of business cycles, use a variety of indicators, including industrial production, real aggregate income growth, retail sales, and payroll employment, in making its widely accepted judgment. To best evaluate the impact of the recession from the perspective of working families, however, we employ a different dating procedure that focuses on what might be termed the "labor market recession." In this dating method, the downturn begins at the end of a recovery when unemployment begins to rise and ends when, as the new recovery takes hold in the labor market, unemployment begins to fall. Since unemployment can sometimes rise well into an official recovery, labor market recessions can last longer than NBER-measured recessions.

For example, the recession of the early 1990s was officially dated as lasting from July 1990 through March 1991, despite the fact that unemployment continued to rise until June 1992. In the current context, since unemployment began rising after October 2000 and was continuing to rise through June 2002 (the last month for which we have data), we consider the labor market recession to have begun in October 2000 and to be continuing as of this writing. By contrast, NBER's official start date is March 2001.

The fact that the unemployment rate had not yet surpassed 6% by June 2002 has served as evidence for some that the recession has been mild. But just as important as the level of unemployment is the size of the increase, which tends to influence how the downturn is perceived by working families. Since its low point of 3.9% in October 2000, the unemployment rate has climbed two percentage points, adding 2.9 million to the jobless rolls. The increase for various groups of job seekers, particularly minorities, has been more severe. For example, the unemployment rate for African Americans was in double-digits by June 2002 (10.7%), an increase of 3.3 points over this period. The increase for black women, also 3.3 points, was only slightly lower than the 3.5-point increase over the prior downturn (see Chapter 3). And, given projections for relatively slow growth throughout the rest of this year, these rates are likely to climb higher before they reverse course.

While the rates for minorities have gone up the most, it is also the case that this recession, much like that of 1990-91, has been more broad-based than prior downturns. In prior downturns, unemployment grew most among less-educated workers. However, between the fourth quarter of 2000 and the second quarter of 2002, unemployment grew fairly equally for workers with less than a high school degree (2.0 percentage points), workers with a high school degree (2.1 percentage points), and those with some college (2.3 percentage points). As usual, workers with a college degree have experienced a smaller increase in unemployment— 1.4 percentage points—but this increase is also greater than that of past recessions.

The fact that unemployment has fairly equally affected workers with different levels of education is driven largely by the industries and occupations where jobs have been lost. Unlike in previous recessions, the service industry has failed to grow over this recession, and retail and wholesale trade have both seen more job losses than usual. In addition, both this and the prior recession (1990-91) were more "white collar" than previous downturns, suggesting that one downside of the "new economy" is that higher education and occupational status provide less insulation from negative market forces.

The increase in unemployment has been considerably dampened by another factor at work in this recession: the slowing of growth in the civilian labor force. Had the trend in labor force growth continued along its path of the early 1990s, in 2002 there would be 2.2 million more workers in the labor market than was actually the case (**Figure A**). Such a gap is symptomatic of a weak labor market in which potential job seekers avoid even attempting to enter the workforce because they are pessimistic about their employment prospects. It is likely that the national unemployment rate would have been higher in 2002 if these "missing workers" had instead opted to seek work. Had the labor force continued to grow at the rate that prevailed before the slowdown, and if instead of leaving or not joining the labor force half of these missing job seekers had unsuccessfully sought work over this period, then the unemployment rate would have been 6.6% in June 2002 instead of 5.9%. This represents "hidden unemployment" of over a million workers.

Another key symptom of the slow-growth recovery is the lack of private sector job growth compared to earlier recessions and recoveries. **Figure B** plots

**FIGURE A** Effects of higher unemployment on size of civilian labor force

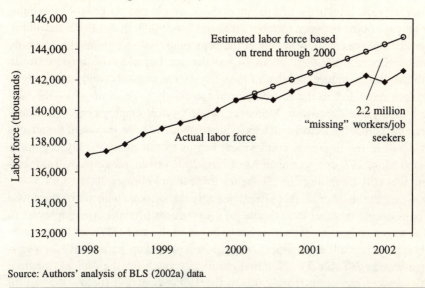

Source: Authors' analysis of BLS (2002a) data.

**FIGURE B** Payroll employment growth during three recent recessions, from unemployment's low point

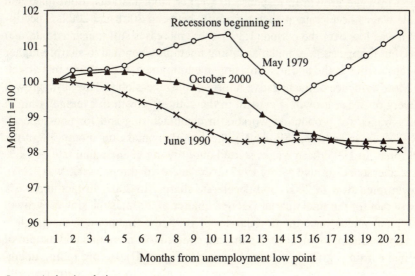

Source: Authors' analysis.

private sector employment over the last three downturns. In each case, the trend is indexed to its level in the first month of the downturn and tracked for 21 months, the length of time between October 2000 and June 2002. In the 1980s downturn, payroll employment grew slowly at the beginning, fell sharply as the economy "double-dipped," and then, about 14 months out, began to rise briskly. But in both this last downturn and that of the early 1990s, payrolls contracted initially and then stagnated, as the economy grew too slowly to generate jobs—the hallmark of a jobless recovery. Moreover, while payroll employment was clearly declining before the terrorist attacks in September 2001, the impact of the attacks is evident in the figure, as employment begins to fall more quickly beginning around Month 12, or September. As of June 2002 private sector payroll employment was still 2.2 million, or 2%, below its peak in February 2001.

Slack in the labor market affects not only the workers who are unemployed or considering whether to seek jobs; it also reduces pressures on employers to raise wages. When the economic boom began in the mid-1990s and labor markets approached full employment, wage growth picked up, particularly for lower-wage workers (**Table 1**). Nominal earnings growth for the typical (median) male worker increased from 2.0% in the 1995-96 period (below the rate of inflation) to 5.4% in 1999-2000 (2% above inflation). Low-earning males saw a similar increase, but their wages began to slow in 1999-2000. This pattern of acceleration is less clear for female workers, especially at the median

The data through the first half of 2002 show a fairly clear pattern of deceleration in wage growth in response to weaker labor markets. Both male and female wages decelerate at each percentile between 2001 and 2002. Since inflation was low over the period (1.3%), these increases still translated into real gains, but it appears that, much as falling unemployment led to sharply higher earnings earlier in the boom, increasing unemployment is reversing this effect.

More evidence of the negative impact of the recession and the slow-growth recovery on wage growth is evident in the path of growth in average nominal hourly wages for production workers in manufacturing and for non-supervisory workers in services (**Figure C**); these workers make up about 80% of the workforce. In 1995 these wages started out growing at an annual rate of 2.6% and accelerated to around 4% by 1997 (average growth through 2000 was 3.9%). Growth rates slow in 2001, and decelerate sharply in 2002. In fact, the 2.6% growth rate for the final quarter (second quarter of 2002) is the slowest growth in nominal wages since the first quarter of 1995, the first point in the graph.

Higher unemployment is also driving a return to a more unequal pattern of nominal earnings growth, at least for males (**Figure D**). Before falling unemployment boosted wages, earnings growth for males formed a staircase, with lower wages growing more slowly than those at the median, and the median

**TABLE 1** Weekly nominal earnings growth for full-time workers, age 25 and over, by gender

| Growth over first half of year | 10th | Median | 90th |
|---|---|---|---|
| **Men** | | | |
| 1995-96 | 1.6% | 2.0% | 3.4% |
| 1996-97 | 2.5 | 2.3 | 2.4 |
| 1997-98 | 3.7 | 2.6 | 5.1 |
| 1998-99 | 5.1 | 5.1 | 5.9 |
| 1999-2000 | 4.2 | 5.4 | 5.8 |
| 2000-01 | 4.2 | 3.1 | 5.1 |
| 2001-02 | 2.1 | 2.6 | 3.9 |
| **Women** | | | |
| 1995-96 | 3.9% | 3.5% | 3.9% |
| 1996-97 | 3.8 | 3.6 | 3.6 |
| 1997-98 | 4.9 | 4.5 | 3.7 |
| 1998-99 | 4.3 | 2.9 | 3.7 |
| 1999-2000 | 4.5 | 3.8 | 5.1 |
| 2000-01 | 4.3 | 6.2 | 6.2 |
| 2001-02 | 2.7 | 5.0 | 4.0 |

Source: Authors' analysis of BLS data.

growing more slowly than the top. By 1999, when the labor market was much tighter, not only were men's earnings growing faster overall, they were also growing at the same rate for low and middle earners (though still more quickly at the top). By the last period, the staircase pattern had returned.

There is no such pattern for women workers. The nominal earnings of the lowest-wage female workers grew more slowly in the first half of 2002 than it did for other wage groups, but there is no evidence of a more unequal pattern of growth accompanying the higher unemployment rates of the 2001-02 period. The extent to which the pattern of wage growth among men persists and spreads to women will be indicative of whether the factors that fueled the growth of inequality over the 1980s and early 1990s—lower minimum wages, less union coverage, loss of manufacturing employment, high unemployment—were suppressed by the tight labor market. In this sense, the lowest unemployment rates in decades acted to temporarily return bargaining power to less-advantaged workers. As the unemployment rate rises, this macroeconomic source of bargaining power dissipates. Barring a quick return to full employment, less broadly distributed growth is likely to resume as time progresses.

**FIGURE C** Growth in nominal average hourly earnings, by quarter, 1995-2002

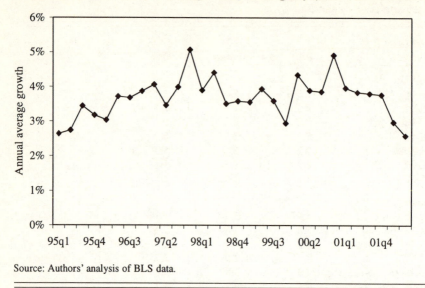

Source: Authors' analysis of BLS data.

Since most families depend on earnings as their primary income source, the lower wages and fewer hours of work that result from higher unemployment will take a toll on family income. In fact, the 0.8 point increase in unemployment from 2000 to 2001 (from 4.0% to 4.8%) led to a 1.4% fall in real median family income. Statistical analysis of this relationship finds that a 1% increase in unemployment results in a loss in family income of just about this magnitude. In addition, the pattern of income losses in 2001 was highly unequal, with larger declines among low-income families relative to middle- and upper-income families. Furthermore, the average unemployment rate for 2002 will likely be another point higher, implying further losses in real income. Rising unemployment is also associated with rising poverty, and so, after falling steeply over the latter 1990s, poverty rates increased in 2001 by 0.4 percentage points, adding 1.3 million more persons to the poverty rolls.

Thus, by the middle of 2002, evidence of the recession and the ensuing slow-growth recovery could clearly be observed in the growth of unemployment, the lack of job creation, the slowing of earnings, the decline in family income, and the return to unequal growth. These negative developments point to the further slowing of family income growth and the lack of progress against poverty in coming years. In this sense, those who look solely at GDP growth or recent gains in industrial capacity may fail to understand the much more direct

**FIGURE D**  Growth in nominal earnings, 1995-2002 (first half to first half)

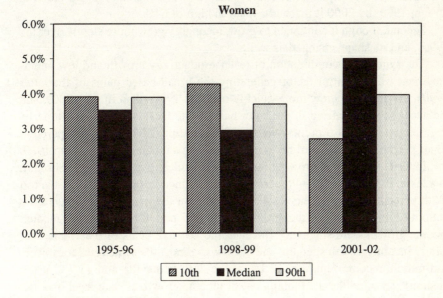

Source: Authors' analysis of BLS data.

impact of the downturn on the lives of working families, an impact that is all the more pronounced given its contrast to the positive trends that prevailed over the latter 1990s. We turn now to an analysis of this important period.

## Moving toward full employment, 1995-2000

The living standards gains of the 1990s, the latter 1990s in particular, came in two main forms. First, the key determinants of the economic well being of working families—wages, incomes, poverty rates—all improved in real terms. The real wages and incomes of families whose fortunes had stagnated reversed course around the mid-1990s, and the gains were often greatest for the least advantaged. For example, after increasing by 1.0 percentage points between 1989 and 1995, the overall poverty rate fell 2.5 points from 1995 to 2000 (**Table 2**). Poverty rates for minorities (not shown in this table, but discussed in Chapter 5) fell even more quickly over this five-year period, by 7.3 percentage points for African Americans and 9.1 points for Hispanics. Income for minorities also grew quickly at the median between 1995 and 2000, both in historical terms and relative to that of whites (though by no means fast enough to close persistent racial income gaps). The ratio of black-to-white median income stood at 56% in 1989; by 2000 it reached a historic high of 64%.

Second, though it continued to grow, inequality grew more slowly over the 1990s, and its shape changed as well.

The synergistic combination of faster productivity growth and low unemployment was a central factor generating the broad-based gains of the latter 1990s. Productivity grew more quickly over the 1990s than in the 1980s, and the acceleration occurred in the latter half of the decade (Table 2). Similarly, unemployment fell 1.3 points over the 1990s, hitting 4% in 2000, compared to a half percentage-point decline over the 1980s to a much higher 5.3% in 1989.

In terms of income, growing inequality is evident over both the 1980s and, to a lesser extent, the 1989-95 period, as family incomes grew faster at the top (95th percentile) than at the median and faster at the median than toward the bottom (20th percentile) (though in the 1989-95 period both low and median income growth were stagnant). But over the last five years of the 1990s, real family income growth sped up, and it grew at almost the same rates for lower- and middle-income families (12.1% at the 20th percentile and 11.7% at the median). Thus, unlike the fanning out of income growth at each level over the 1980s, inequality did not increase between middle- and low-income families in the 1990s, primarily because the strong economy boosted their earnings, and, as discussed below, their hours of work as well.

**TABLE 2** The benefits of full employment

|  | 1979-89 | 1989-2000 | 1989-95 | 1995-2000 |
|---|---|---|---|---|
| Productivity (annual) | 1.4% | 2.0% | 1.5% | 2.5% |
| Unemployment | -0.5 | -1.3 | 0.3 | -1.6 |
| Poverty | 1.1 | -1.5 | 1 | -2.5 |
| **Real income growth** | | | | |
| 20th percentile | -1.0% | 11.9% | -0.3% | 12.1% |
| Median | 6.6 | 10.9 | -0.6 | 11.7 |
| 95th percentile | 19.0 | 20.8 | 4.6 | 15.5 |
| **Real hourly wage growth** | | | | |
| 20th percentile | -14.1% | 13.1% | 1.8% | 11.0% |
| Median | 0.0 | 5.9 | -1.8 | 7.8 |
| 95th percentile | 8.1 | 16.6 | 5.4 | 10.6 |

Source: Productivity and unemployment, BLS; poverty and income, Census Bureau; wage growth, authors' analysis of CPS ORG data.

Income growth at the 95th percentile, however, also was faster in this period; it rose 15.5% between 1995 and 2000. In fact, growth among the wealthiest families was remarkably consistent over the 1980s and 1990s business cycles, expanding by about 20% in each period. Data presented in Chapter 1 that include realized capital gains provide further evidence that, even with the strong growth spurt at the low end of the income scale, the wealthiest American families continued to pull away from the rest of the pack throughout the 1990s.

Hourly wage growth, unsurprisingly, follows a pattern similar to that of income, though the sharp reversal toward positive real wage growth for the lowest-wage workers was even more plain. Hourly wages at the 20th percentile were down 14.1% over the 1980s and median wages were stagnant; high wages rose 8.1%. Low wages stopped falling in the first half of the 1990s (in part due to minimum wage increases in 1990-91), but they sharply accelerated in the 1995-2000 period, growing more quickly than at any point since the mid-1970s. Median wages grew less quickly; a discussed in Chapter 2, they too respond to lower unemployment, but they do not do so as quickly or dramatically as those of the lowest paid. Thus, the gap between middle- and low-wage workers narrowed in the 1990s. For the most part, high wages grew most quickly of all (the slight exception being the latter 1990s), and pulled away from median wages even more quickly in the 1990s than over the 1980s.

Along with higher wages, the 1990s saw a continued trend in rising hours in the paid labor market. The annual weeks and hours worked by married-couple families with children provide compelling evidence of some of the stresses facing families trying to manage their work and family lives. Analysts who focus exclusively on individual average weekly hours have missed this trend, because that measure fails to reflect the combined work efforts of all family members (in fact, when a part-time working wife joins the workforce, average weekly hours will fall while family hours will rise). Due to more wives working more weeks per year and more hours per week, the average middle-income, married-couple family with children is now working 660 more hours per year than in 1979, the equivalent of more than 16 extra weeks of full-time work.

Contrary to conventional wisdom, it is not the case that high-income, highly educated families are driving this trend toward more work. Rather, increases in family hours have been equally as large among families headed by high school graduates or minorities. On average, between 1979-2000 increases in annual hours worked were slightly larger for minorities than for white families: 14.7% and 14.4% for black and Hispanic families, respectively, compared to 11.7% for white families. Middle-income black and Hispanic families worked significantly more hours than did white families in order to reach the same income levels (given the fact of racial wage gaps, this is to be expected). By 2000, middle-income black families worked the equivalent of 12 full-time weeks more than white families.

The increase in wives hours of work was driven by the influx of women into the labor market since the early 1960s, as job opportunities opened up and discriminatory hiring and promotion practices were outlawed. Women not only have increased their presence in the labor market, they are also now less likely to drop out when they marry or have children. At the same time, most male workers experienced stagnant or falling real wages in the 1980s and early 1990s. Wives' contributions to family income thus grew in importance. Had wives not increased their labor supply, the real incomes of middle-income families would have declined by 2.5% between 1979 and 1989 instead of rising by 6.3%.

Increases in work were not restricted to married-couple families. The strong expansion of demand for low-wage workers, in tandem with the welfare-to-work emphasis of welfare reform, led to historically large increases in the employment rates of low-income single mothers with children. While their hours and earnings increased, their welfare benefits contracted sharply, dramatically reshaping the sources of their income. In 1979, labor market earnings and cash assistance each made up about 40% of the income of a low-income single mother (the rest came from other miscellaneous sources). By 2000, about 70% came from labor market earnings and less than 10% from cash transfers.

Clearly, the labor market, and the low-wage sector in particular, is much more of a factor in the lives of these low-income families than at any time in the recent past. Low-income families are also more exposed to market forces, for better or worse. Thus, when the market stumbles, as it did in 2001, and when the recovery is too slow to move unemployment back down, they are likely to experience both higher increases in joblessness and less protection from a safety net that has become less effective at preventing hardship among non-workers.

The United States stands apart from other advanced economies in the hours of work individuals devote to paid labor. The U.S. economy employs a greater share of its working-age population, and, in 2000, its workers worked an average of 1,877 hours per year, more than in any other rich, industrialized economy. Even as Americans work more hours, they are not seeing respite through increases in the number of vacation days or holidays. Further, the increased hours of work for families mean that there is less time available for family members to care for their families. Unlike almost every other advanced economy, the United States provides no paid family leave for mothers and fathers. Press reports indicate that the stress on working families has been palpable; the numbers reported here show that families must indeed have difficulty balancing work and family.

## Conclusion

The labor market is the primary determinant of living standards for working families. True, more families now hold stock than in the past (about half of households hold some stock, either directly or through a pension plan), but for low- and middle-income families the magnitude of these holdings is small (about $4,000 for the bottom 60% in 1998, the most recent data available), and the inherent risk in such assets is glaringly clear in the current economy. The earnings and employment opportunities in the job market will continue to be the defining factor in the economic lives of the majority of families.

Prior to the mid-1990s, many working families were struggling to avoid getting caught by an economic undertow that eroded their bargaining power and led to lower earnings and more inequality. But a unique period took hold in those years, characterized by a potent combination of low unemployment and fast productivity growth. The economic lessons of those years may well be called the most important of the past half-century: the United States can run a full-employment labor market, generating broad-based gains in living standards without fear of overheating, spiraling inflation, or whatever distortion economic theory incorrectly predicted would befall us if unemployment fell below 6%.

Of course, nothing in this lesson contradicts the precept that the economy is cyclical, and that recessions are endemic. And the recession of 2001 and the current slow-growth recovery are proving to be considerably more difficult for working families than the conventional wisdom suggests. Much of this current discussion focuses on a set of macroeconomic indicators that seem to suggest that the recession was historically mild and that the recovery is, if not particularly strong, well underway and building momentum. As the proponents of this view increasingly maintain: "the fundamentals are all in place."

Perhaps they are. But if so, the recovery they are driving is a slow-growth one, and it is a certainty that unemployment will fail to fall back anywhere near the levels of the latter 1990s within a year or even possibly two. This is problematic for two related reasons. First, the loss of the tight labor market also spells the loss of the strengthened bargaining power that lower-wage workers enjoyed for the first time in decades. And as this dissipates, so will the unique earnings gains from that period. In fact, real incomes of middle- and low-income families reversed course and fell in real terms in 2001, and earnings growth continued to decelerate through 2002.

Second, full employment masked a set of structural problems that have evolved over the past few decades in the labor market. Before the late 1990s, these imbalances served to shift bargaining power away from minority, blue-collar, and non-college-educated workers, and thus drove a historic increase in inequality. As full employment fades, growth in inequality is resurfacing, as can be seen in the unequal distribution of income losses over the recession.

These issues need to be a top concern of policy makers at all levels of government. Federal policy makers, including but not limited to central bankers, must acknowledge the importance of full employment and chart a course back as soon as possible. The Federal Reserve and other national policy makers need to recognize the difficulties inherent in a jobless recovery and consider appropriate demand stimulus and safety-net measures. State policy makers can complement these actions by avoiding contractionary spending cuts and also by pushing the federal government—which, unlike the states, can engage in deficit spending—for grants to spend on local stimulus projects.

The chapters that follow make this case in great detail. By examining hundreds of economic trends relevant to the lives of working families, we build a strong case for tapping the benefits of full employment. But our view is a historical one, and we are mindful of the limits of five years of strong growth in the context of decades of eroding institutional supports and diminished regulations. In prior decades, these protections, in tandem with full employment, helped to ensure that the benefits of growth were fairly shared with the families of working America. There is no better goal for economic policy.

# Documentation and methodology

## *Documentation*

The comprehensive portrait presented in this book of changes in incomes, taxes, wages, employment, wealth, poverty, and other indicators of economic performance and well-being relies almost exclusively on data in the tables and figures. Consequently, the documentation of our analysis is essentially the documentation of the tables and figures. For each, an abbreviated source notation appears at the bottom, and complete documentation is contained in the Table Notes and Figure Notes found at the back of the book. (In rare circumstances, however, we incorporate data in the discussion that are not in a table or figure.) This system of documentation allows us to omit distracting footnotes and long citations within the text and tables.

The abbreviated source notation at the bottom of each figure and table is intended to inform the reader of the general source of our data and to give due credit to the authors and agencies whose data we are presenting. We have three categories of designations for these abbreviated sources. In instances where we directly reproduce other people's work, we provide an "author-year" reference to the bibliography. Where we present our own computations based on other people's work, the source line reads "Authors' analysis of *author (year).*" In these instances we have made computations that do not appear in the original work and want to hold the original authors (or agencies) blameless for any errors or interpretations. Our third category is simply "Authors' analysis," which indicates that the data presented are from our original analysis of microdata (such as much of the wage analysis) or our computations from published (usually government) data. We use this source notation when presenting descriptive trends from government income, employment, or other data, since we have made judgments about the appropriate time periods or other matters for the analysis that the source agencies have not made.

## Time periods

Economic indicators fluctuate considerably with short-term swings in the business cycle. For example, incomes tend to fall in recessions and rise during expansions. Therefore, economists usually compare business cycle peaks with other peaks and compare troughs with other troughs so as not to mix apples and oranges. In this book, we examine changes between business cycle peaks. The initial year for many tables is 1947, with intermediate years of 1967, 1973, 1979, 1989 and 2000, all of which were business cycle peaks (at least in terms of having low unemployment). We also present data for the latest full year for which data are available (2001, when available) to show the changes over the current business cycle.

We also separately present trends for the 1995-2000 period in order to highlight the differences between those years and those of the early 1990s (or, more precisely, 1989-95) and earlier business cycles. This departs from the convention of presenting only business-cycle comparisons (e.g., comparing 1979-89 to 1989-2000 trends) or comparisons of recoveries. We depart from the convention because there was a marked shift in a wide variety of trends after 1995, and it is important to understand and explain these trends.

## Growth rates and rounding

Since business cycles differ in length, we usually present the annual growth rates in each period rather than the total growth. We also present compound annual growth rates rather than simple annual rates. Compound annual growth rates are just like compound interest on a bank loan: the rate is compounded continuously rather than yearly. In some circumstances, as noted in the tables, we have used log annual growth rates. This is done to permit decompositions.

While annual growth rates may seem small, over time they can amount to large changes. For example, the wages of male, blue-collar workers fell 0.7% annually between 1979 and 1989; over the full period, however, incomes declined by 7.2%.

In presenting the data we round the numbers, usually to one decimal place, but we use unrounded data to compute growth rates, percentage shares, and so on. Therefore, it is not always possible to exactly replicate our calculations by using the data in the table. In some circumstances, this leads to an appearance of errors in the tables. For instance, we frequently present shares of the population (or families) at different points in time and compute changes in these shares. Because our computations are based on the "unrounded" data, the change in shares presented in a table may not match the difference in the actual shares. Such rounding errors are always small, however, and never change the conclusions of the analysis.

### Adjusting for inflation

In most popular discussions, the Consumer Price Index for All Urban Consumers (CPI-U), often called simply the consumer price index, is used to adjust dollar values for inflation. However, some analysts hold that the CPI-U overstated inflation in the late 1970s and early 1980s by measuring housing costs inappropriately. The methodology for the CPI-U from 1983 onward was revised to address these objections. Other changes were introduced into the CPI in the mid-1990s but not incorporated into the historical series. Not all agree that these revisions are appropriate. We chose not to use the CPI-U so as to avoid any impression that this report overstates the decline in wages and understates the growth in family incomes over the last few decades.

Instead of the CPI-U, we adjust dollar values for inflation using the CPI-U-RS index. This index uses the new methodology for housing inflation over the entire 1967-2001 period and incorporates the 1990s changes into the historical series (though not before 1978, which makes economic performance in the years after 1978 falsely look better than the earlier years). The CPI-U-RS is now used by the Census Bureau in appendices to its presentations of real income data. Because it is not available for years before 1978, we extrapolate the CPI-U-RS back to earlier years based on inflation as measured by the CPI-U.

In our analysis of poverty in Chapter 5, however, we generally use the CPI-U rather than the CPI-U-RS, since Chapter 5 draws heavily from Census Bureau publications that use the CPI-U. Moreover, the net effect of all of the criticisms of the measurement of poverty is that current methods *understate* poverty. Switching to the CPI-U-RS without incorporating other revisions (i.e., revising the actual poverty standard) would lead to an even greater understatement and would be a very selective intervention to improve the poverty measurement. (A fuller discussion of these issues appears in Chapter 5.) There is discussion in Chapter 5 of the effect of using different deflators on the measured trends in poverty.

### Household heads

We often categorize families by the age or the race/ethnic group of the "household head," that is, the person in whose name the home is owned or rented. If the home is owned jointly by a married couple, either spouse may be designated the household head. Every family has a single household head.

## Hispanics

Unless specified otherwise, data from published sources employ the Census Bureau's designation of Hispanic persons. That is, Hispanics are included in racial counts (e.g., with blacks and whites) as well as in a separate category. For instance, in government analyses a white person of Hispanic origin is included both in counts of whites *and* in counts of Hispanics. In our original analyses, such as the racial/ethnic wage analysis in Chapter 2, we remove Hispanic persons from other racial (white or black) categories; using this technique, the person described above would appear only in counts of Hispanics.

## CHAPTER 1

# Family income:

# full employment reverses historic stagnation

The single most important determinant of a family's standard of living is its income. In this regard, the stagnant and unequal trend in real income growth over much of the last quarter century has posed a significant problem for America's working families. Yet, in the second half of the 1990s, family income growth reversed course, as middle- and lower-income families experienced the first persistent gains in decades. These gains were particularly notable among the least advantaged, those who had been hurt most by the negative trends that proceeded this period of broad-based growth. For example, between 1995 and 2000, the real median income of African American and Hispanic families grew 16% and 25%, respectively, compared to 11% for white families. Inequality also grew more slowly over these years, though it did not decrease, as those at the very top continued to pull far ahead of the rest.

This period was short-lived; it came to an end with the recession of 2001. But the fact that incomes sharply reversed course when unemployment rose in 2001 reinforces the point that low unemployment and the commensurate tight labor markets of the latter 1990s were a key economic determinant of these favorable trends. Fast productivity growth is also necessary, as it creates the extra income growth to be shared among the broad working class, but, by itself, it is insufficient. The added bargaining power that comes from full employment is the extra ingredient needed to ensure that the gains from faster growth are broadly shared.

The larger gains by lower-income families also meant that inequality grew more slowly in the 1990s. It did not, however, stop growing, nor did it reverse course. The fact that the income gap between middle- and lower-income families grew smaller over the 1990s led some analysts to mistakenly conclude that the inequality problem was solved. But in fact, the richest families continued to pull away from the pack over the decade. The income of the top 1% of tax-payers (including realized capital gains) grew by 59% from 1995 to 1999, while that of the bottom half grew by 9%. Thus, while full employment gave low- and middle-wage workers the bargaining power that was missing over prior decades of stagnant growth, it did not serve to correct structural inequities that persist in the economy.

While there is much to learn from these last few years, several long-term trends are still important to the analysis of income. First, even with the growth of the last half of the 1990s, median family income grew much more slowly over the last quarter of the 20th century than over the previous one. Over the 26 years from 1947 to 1973, median family income doubled in real terms. Over the next 27 years, it grew 25%. This dramatic slowing of growth relates to the slower productivity growth of the post-1973 period, the higher unemployment rates that prevailed then, and the increase in income inequality. Taken together, these changes meant that the benefits of reduced economic growth were less likely to flow to middle- and lower-income families.

Another important long-term development is the increase in time that family members are spending in the labor market. These trends reveal why the question of balancing work and family has so much currency in today's living standards discussions. Over the last 30 years, workers in middle-income married-couple families with children have added an average of 20 more weeks at work, the equivalent of five more months. Most of the increase comes from working wives, many more of whom entered the labor market over this period, added more weeks per year, and added more hours per week. In fact, middle-income wives added close to 500 hours of work per year between 1979 and 2000, the equivalent of more than 12 weeks of full-time work.

These increases in time spent working occur not simply among wealthy or highly educated families. In fact, between 1979 and 2000, middle-income families headed by someone with at most a high school degree increased their annual work hours more than did families headed by a college graduate. At the same time, the average African American family not only increased its work hours more than did white families, it also worked 64 more hours per year than did the average white family in 2000. Gains in hours were particularly dramatic for low-income minority families from 1995 to 2000, another indicator of the importance of full employment in providing expanded opportunities for these families. These opportunities come at a cost, however, and the stresses engendered by so much work need to be recognized and addressed by policy makers concerned with the quality of life for these parents and their children.

The historically long period of economic growth that began in 1991 ended in 2001, and it is likely that the income gains of the latter part of that recovery slowed, stalled, or even reversed during the recession. What will happen to family income as the recovery gets underway? If the past is any guide, then we might anticipate a return to the experience of the 1990s recovery. But which part? The slow growth early years, when unemployment continued to rise and family income fell? Or the later years, when the economy headed toward full employment and family income grew at historic rates? Unfortunately, the early indicators suggest a slow growth recovery, with unemployment lingering at relatively high rates and family income taking its expected hit.

America's working families responded to the strong economy of the latter 1990s by working harder and more productively, and, for the first time in decades, their efforts were rewarded with real gains in income. Yet, while inequality grew more slowly in the 1990s than in the prior decade, the richest families continued to reap disproportionate gains. And while working harder meant higher incomes, it also came to mean increasingly more hours spent at work and away from the family. The challenge moving forward is to generate positive gains in living standards that reflect the multidimensional needs of families, both in terms of their incomes and family lives.

## Median income: slow recovery, then strong gains

**Figure 1A** and **Table 1.1** track real median family income from the post-World War II period through 2000. There are two distinct growth periods. The first, from about 1947 to the early 1970s, was the strongest and by far the most sustained. Over the 26 years from 1947 to 1973, median family income grew 104% in real terms. Over the next 27 years, it grew 25%. But this latter period can be subdivided into the period of stagnation (growth never surpassed 1% per year) from the mid-1970s to the mid-1990s, and the short but strong growth period of 1995-2000, when family incomes expanded by 2.2% per year.

The negative impact of recessions, particularly the relatively deep back-to-back recessions of the early 1980s, is illustrated in the shaded portions of Figure 1A (which shows the early 1980s downturns as one long recession). Interestingly, even though the milder recession of 1990-91 did not lead to as large a real loss in income as in some prior downturns, income continued to fall after the recession and into the first two years of the 1990s recovery.

Typically, real median income falls in a downturn as working families lose labor market income, either due to layoffs, cutbacks in hours, or real wage cuts. Note, for example, the recession-induced 1.4% decline in 2001 illustrated in Figure 1A. Conversely, when the recovery gets underway, and labor market

**FIGURE 1A** Real median family income, 1947-2001

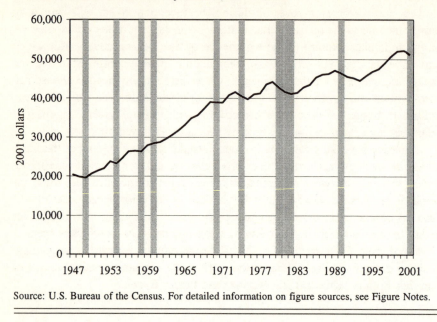

Source: U.S. Bureau of the Census. For detailed information on figure sources, see Figure Notes.

income bounces back, incomes reverse course and start to climb. One measure of how quickly families are able to make up for lost ground is shown in **Table 1.2.** The first column shows the year of the prior income peak, the second shows the year in the following recovery when the peak was surpassed, and the third shows how many years it took to regain the prior peak.

Over time, it has taken longer for real median family income to regain lost ground. Income losses over the downturns of the 1950s and 1960s were quickly replenished, in two or three years. But during the last two recoveries incomes took much longer to climb back—seven years in both cases—even though the 1980s recession was much more severe than that of the early 1990s.

**Figure 1B** examines the path of median family income over these last two business cycles in greater detail. In both cases, income is measured from peak to peak over the cycle, and indexed to the first year of the cycle. The recession of the early 1980s was more severe than that of the early 1990s, with unemployment rising almost 4 percentage points, to 9.7%, in 1982 compared to 2.2 points, to 7.5%, in 1992, and with income falling 7% four years after the peak compared to 4% in the 1990s. But incomes leveled off and began growing earlier in the 1980s recovery, and so six years after the peak both trends were equal, at 3% below the prior peak value.

**TABLE 1.1** Median family income,* 1947-2001 (2001 dollars)

| Year | Median family income* |
|------|------------------------|
| 1947 | $20,402 |
| 1967 | 35,629 |
| 1973 | 41,590 |
| 1979 | 44,255 |
| 1989 | 47,166 |
| 1995 | 46,843 |
| 2000 | 52,148 |
| 2001 | 51,407 |

| Changes | Total dollar changes | Annual growth rates |
|---------|----------------------|---------------------|
| 1947-67 | $15,228 | 2.8% |
| 1967-73 | 5,960 | 2.6 |
| 1973-79 | 2,666 | 1.0 |
| 1979-89 | 2,911 | 0.6 |
| 1989-2000 | 4,982 | 0.9 |
| 1989-95 | -323 | -0.1 |
| 1995-2000 | 5,304 | 2.2 |
| 2000-01 | -741 | -1.4 |

* Income includes all wage and salary, self-employment, pension, interest, rent, government cash assistance, and other money income.

Source: Authors' analysis of U.S. Bureau of the Census data. For detailed information on table sources, see Table Notes.

**TABLE 1.2** Length of time to recovery of median family income after recession

| Year of prior peak | Year prior peak surpassed | Number of years to recover |
|--------------------|---------------------------|----------------------------|
| 1953 | 1955 | 2 |
| 1957 | 1959 | 2 |
| 1969 | 1972 | 3 |
| 1973 | 1978 | 5 |
| 1979 | 1986 | 7 |
| 1989 | 1996 | 7 |

Source: Authors' analysis.

**FIGURE 1B** Median family income over the 1980s and 1990s

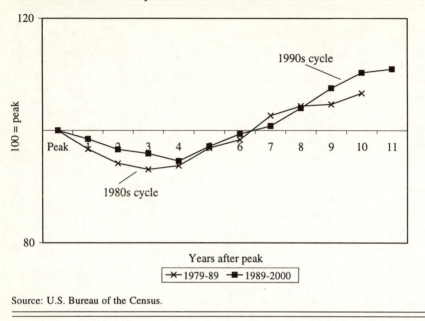

Source: U.S. Bureau of the Census.

In the second half of the 1990s, real median family income grew quickly, at 2.2% per year, and it grew for an extra year in the longer 1990s recovery (as shown below, econometric research shows that family income growth accelerates as the business cycle lengthens). Thus, by 2000, median family income was 10.6% above its 1989 level, compared to the 1980s gain of 6.6%.

Two lessons emerge from this analysis that may be relevant to the current business cycle. First, even after a relatively mild recession, it can take years for median family income to regain its prior peak if the recovery is weak. The recession that began in 2001 was probably a mild one, yet it led to a 1.4% real decline in median family income. Furthermore, most measures to date point to a weak recovery, with GDP rising too slowly to prevent further increases in unemployment. If the pattern of the last recovery is a guide, then median family income may continue to stagnate over the next few years. Second, the low unemployment of the latter 1990s led to historically fast rates of growth in median family income. Getting back to the low levels of unemployment that prevailed at the end of the 1990s must be a top goal of policy makers.

It is common practice also to examine measures of family income growth that adjust for changes in family size, since the same total family income shared

**TABLE 1.3** Annual family income growth for the middle fifth, 1967-2000, unadjusted and adjusted for family size

| Period | Unadjusted for family size* | Adjusted for family size** | Difference (adjusted minus unadjusted) |
|---|---|---|---|
| 1967-73 | 2.6% | 2.8% | 0.2% |
| 1973-79 | 0.7 | 0.5 | -0.2 |
| 1979-89 | 0.4 | 0.5 | 0.1 |
| 1989-2000 | 0.6 | 0.6 | 0.0 |
| 1989-95 | -0.6 | -0.5 | 0.1 |
| 1995-2000 | 2.1 | 2.0 | -0.1 |

\*    These data use a different price deflator than that used throughout the rest of the chapter; see table notes.
\*\*   Annualized growth rate of family income of the middle fifth, divided by the poverty line for each family size.

Source: Authors' analysis of U.S. Bureau of the Census data.

by fewer family members can be interpreted as improved economic well-being for each family member. However, trends in incomes adjusted for family size can be misleading, since the recent decline in the average family's size is partially due to lower incomes; that is, some families feel they cannot afford as many children as they could have if incomes had continued to rise at early postwar rates. As a result, a family deciding to have fewer children or a person putting off starting a family because incomes are down will appear "better off" in size-adjusted family-income measures. It also seems selective to adjust family incomes for changes in family size and not adjust for other demographic trends such as more hours of work and the resulting loss of leisure.

Nevertheless, even when income growth is adjusted for the shift toward smaller families (**Table 1.3**, column 2), the income growth of the 1970s, 1980s, and 1990s was only slightly higher than the unadjusted measure. In fact, the annual growth rates of size-adjusted income are never more than 0.2 percentage points higher than the unadjusted numbers, and are even lower than the unadjusted values in some periods (presumably due to faster income growth among larger families). Thus, these trends offer no evidence to suggest that the shrinking size of families has been an important factor explaining the slower growth of median family income since 1979.

One possible reason for the similarity in the growth of size-adjusted family income and unadjusted income is the leveling off in family size. **Figure 1C** shows the average number of persons per family from 1947 to 2000. At the

**FIGURE 1C** Average number of persons per family, 1947-2000

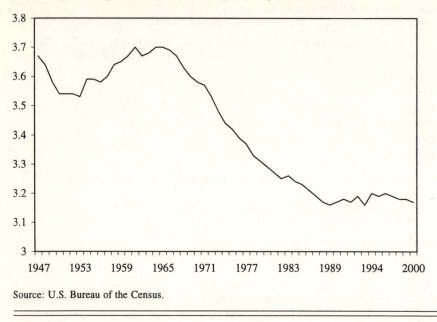

Source: U.S. Bureau of the Census.

beginning of the period, in 1947, families had on average about 3.7 members. In the mid-1960s this number began to drop, and by about 1986 had declined to 3.2. Since that time, the trend has been fairly flat, and therefore, one would not expect size adjustments to play a role in income trends. We return below to a more detailed investigation of the impact of other aspects of demographic change on family income growth and inequality.

## Latter 1990s pay off for less-advantaged family types

Growth in median income tend to vary by the race/ethnicity of the head of the family, the age of the family head, and the family type. Typically, growth rates are slower for younger and minority-headed families and for married-couple families where only one spouse works. However, some notable differences in this historical pattern appeared in the latter 1990s, where minority and younger families experienced particularly fast growth rates. Income growth for families headed by single mothers also accelerated.

Over the 1995-2000 period, the real median income of minority families grew significantly more quickly than that of white families (**Table 1.4**). In-

**TABLE 1.4** Median family income by racial/ethnic group, 1947-2001 (2001 dollars)

| Year | White | Black* | Hispanic** | Ratio to white family income of: Black | Hispanic |
|---|---|---|---|---|---|
| 1947 | $21,250 | $10,864 | n.a. | 51.1% | n.a. |
| 1967 | 36,981 | 21,895 | n.a. | 59.2 | n.a. |
| 1973 | 43,467 | 25,086 | $30,077 | 57.7 | 69.2% |
| 1979 | 46,180 | 26,151 | 32,014 | 56.6 | 69.3 |
| 1989 | 49,595 | 27,860 | 32,323 | 56.2 | 65.2 |
| 1995 | 49,191 | 29,956 | 28,341 | 60.9 | 57.6 |
| 2000 | 54,509 | 34,616 | 35,403 | 63.5 | 64.9 |
| 2001 | 54,067 | 33,598 | 34,490 | 62.1 | 63.8 |
| *Annual growth rate* | | | | | |
| 1947-67 | 2.8% | 3.6% | n.a. | | |
| 1967-73 | 2.7 | 2.3 | n.a. | | |
| 1973-79 | 1.0 | 0.7 | 1.0% | | |
| 1979-89 | 0.7 | 0.6 | 0.1 | | |
| 1989-2000 | 0.9 | 2.0 | 0.8 | | |
| 1989-95 | -0.1 | 1.2 | -2.2 | | |
| 1995-2000 | 2.1 | 2.9 | 4.6 | | |
| 2000-01 | -0.8 | -2.9 | -2.6 | | |

\* Prior to 1967, data for blacks include all non-whites.
\*\* Persons of Hispanic origin may be of any race.

Source: Authors' analysis of U.S. Bureau of the Census data.

comes for white families grew 2.1% per year compared to 2.9% for African American families and an historically exceptional 4.6% for Hispanics.

Although black and Hispanic incomes remain well below those of whites, their strong relative growth rates over this period significantly raised the ratio of minority/white incomes. The ratio of black-to-white family incomes stood at 63.5% in 2000, a historical peak. Relative incomes for Hispanics fell from 1973 to 1995 (some of this fall can probably be attributed to increased immigration of lower-income families over this period), but then reversed course sharply after 1995. These recent patterns differ from those of the 1970s and 1980s, when the family income of minorities grew either at the same rate or more slowly than that of white families.

**Figure 1D** plots the ratio of black-to-white and Hispanic-to-white family income. (Hispanic data are available only for 1972 and later. Note also that the

**FIGURE 1D** Ratio of black and Hispanic to white median family income, 1947-2001

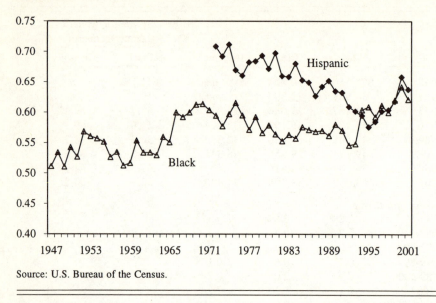

Source: U.S. Bureau of the Census.

data for white families include Hispanics who identify their race as white. Data on non-Hispanic whites are available from 1972 forward; using this series for whites does not change the trends shown in the figure.) Throughout the 1960s, the median income of black families increased relative to that of whites, with the ratio peaking in the mid-1970s. Over the 1980s black families lost ground relative to whites, but this trend was reversed in the 1990s, when blacks surpassed the relative income levels of the 1960s. (The figure reveals a large upward shift in one year: 1994. There are no obvious data reasons, such as a coding or weighting change, that would explain this one-year jump. It is, however, unusual for a trend to change this dramatically in one year, and there may be a non-economic explanation. However, blacks made relative gains in other areas over these years, including poverty and hours worked, so, while the change probably occurs more gradually than reflected in the figure, it likely did occur.)

The 1960s and the 1990s shared certain characteristics that might explain these favorable shifts in relative incomes. First, both the 1960s and the latter 1990s were periods of fast productivity growth and low unemployment. Falling unemployment in particular is generally more beneficial to minorities than to white families, in part because, as unemployment falls, labor force activity increases more for minorities than for whites (data later in this chapter show

**FIGURE 1E** Median family income by age of household head, 2000

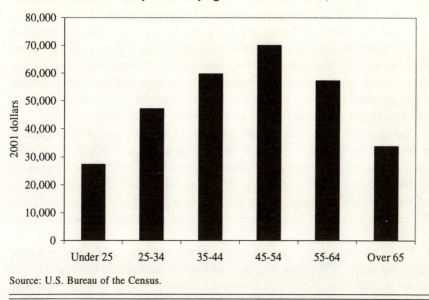

Source: U.S. Bureau of the Census.

faster gains in hours worked for black families over this period, and Chapter 3 shows relative gains in employment rates for minorities in the 1990s). One notable difference between the two periods is that the relative gains in the 1960s were also driven by geographic and industry shifts by African Americans, with many black families migrating North and finding employment in manufacturing. In fact, by 1970, the share of black men working in manufacturing surpassed that of whites. As manufacturing employment contracted over the 1980s and especially the latter 1990s, this sector ceased to be a venue for relative gains by minorities. Conversely, recessionary contractions and the associated increases in unemployment tend to lower minority income more than that of whites, as can be seen in the bottom sections of Table 1.4, which show black and Hispanic income falling further than income for whites. As Figure 1D illustrates, this result was a reversal in the trend in relative incomes.

## An income 'generation gap'

The income data examined thus far take no account of age differences. As **Figure 1E** shows, up to a point, older families tend to have higher incomes than younger families, primarily because both earning capacity and wealth expand with age. As families retire and spend down their assets, income tends to decline. This section addresses two questions related to income and age. First, how have the median incomes of different age groups moved over time? An examination of this question allows a comparison of how families of different ages are doing compared to each other over different time periods. Second, how has median family income grown within age cohorts? This analysis illustrates the lifetime income growth for a young worker starting out in, say, the 1950s and compares it to the experience of young workers starting out in later decades.

The previous section showed that minority families made relative gains in the latter 1990s. Similarly, younger families, who did worse relative to older families over the 1970s and particularly over the 1980s, made relative gains in the 1990s. While this is a positive finding for this one-half of one business cycle, longer-term analysis shows that the stagnant growth of family income after 1973 (see Figure 1A) has meant that recent age cohorts have not done as well as earlier cohorts.

**Table 1.5** reveals real income losses among the youngest families over the 1980s and early 1990s. For families headed by someone under age 25, real median family income declined at an annual rate of 2.2% from 1979 to 1989 and 1.4% from 1989 to 1995. For families headed by someone age 25-34, income growth was also negative, though less so. Over these same years, incomes grew most for families headed by someone over age 65.

These growth trends reversed sharply after 1995, especially for younger families. In fact, growth rates in 1995-2000 decline with age. Median income rose 5.1% per year for the youngest families and 2.3% for those headed by someone age 25-34.

However, even with the post-1995 boost, the youngest families in 2000 had about $1,700 less income to spend in real dollars than their 1979 counterparts had when they were starting out. In fact, families headed by someone younger than 44 experienced falling median incomes from 1989 to 1995, with the youngest families losing 1.4% per year. This experience from the slow-growth recovery of the early 1990s may be indicative of what young families can expect if the recovery from the 2001 recession is a weak one as well.

The impact of the 2001 recession can also be observed here, though no clear pattern emerges in the losses by age level. The income loss was largest for those families headed by someone age 35-44; in one year, this group lost over a third of the gains it received from 1995 to 2000. This loss may relate partly to the nature of this downturn, which has been more broadly felt throughout the age, education, and occupation scales relative to past recessions.

The last column of Table 1.5 compares the median income of families headed by someone age 45-54 to that of families headed by someone age 25-34. The

**TABLE 1.5** Median family income by age of household head, 1947-2001 (2001 dollars)

| Year | Under 25 | 25-34 | 35-44 | 45-54 | 55-64 | Over 65 | Ratio of 45-54 income to 25-34 income |
|------|----------|-------|-------|-------|-------|---------|----------------------------------------|
| 1947 | $15,784 | $19,729 | $22,165 | $23,155 | $21,553 | $12,304 | 1.17 |
| 1967 | 26,247 | 36,357 | 41,495 | 43,458 | 36,119 | 17,642 | 1.20 |
| 1973 | 27,657 | 42,125 | 49,375 | 52,537 | 44,109 | 22,177 | 1.25 |
| 1979 | 29,397 | 43,625 | 51,772 | 57,163 | 49,515 | 25,581 | 1.31 |
| 1989 | 23,525 | 42,562 | 55,423 | 63,555 | 51,895 | 31,822 | 1.49 |
| 1995 | 21,634 | 41,548 | 53,667 | 63,474 | 52,211 | 32,644 | 1.53 |
| 2000 | 27,708 | 46,639 | 59,708 | 69,736 | 56,991 | 34,282 | 1.50 |
| 2001 | 26,900 | 46,272 | 57,492 | 68,114 | 57,457 | 33,816 | 1.47 |
| *Annual growth rate* | | | | | | | |
| 1947-67 | 2.6% | 3.1% | 3.2% | 3.2% | 2.6% | 3.0% | 0.1% |
| 1967-73 | 0.9 | 2.5 | 2.9 | 3.2 | 3.4 | 6.4 | 0.7 |
| 1973-79 | 1.0 | 0.6 | 0.8 | 1.4 | 1.9 | 6.2 | 0.8 |
| 1979-89 | -2.2 | -0.2 | 0.7 | 1.1 | 0.5 | 2.5 | 1.3 |
| 1989-2000 | 1.5 | 0.8 | 0.7 | 0.8 | 0.9 | 0.7 | 0.0 |
| 1989-95 | -1.4 | -0.4 | -0.5 | 0.0 | 0.1 | 0.4 | 0.4 |
| 1995-2000 | 5.1 | 2.3 | 2.2 | 1.9 | 1.8 | 1.0 | -0.4 |
| 2000-01 | -2.9 | -0.8 | -3.7 | -2.3 | 0.8 | -1.4 | -1.6 |

Source: Authors' analysis of U.S. Bureau of the Census data.

median income of the older family was 20% greater than that of the younger family in 1967, and, due to faster income growth for older families over the 1970s and 1980s, this relative advantage grew to 53% in 1995 (i.e., their 1995 median income was 1.53 times that of the younger families). While the 1995-2000 period dented the economic "generation gap" that has grown since 1967, younger families continue to start out much lower down the income scale relative to older families.

Some income analysts have discounted the importance of the general trend toward slower income growth by noting that families receive higher real incomes as they age, as shown in Figure 1E. But this fact does not solve the problem of the slower growth of income and wages that has persisted since the mid-1970s. The slower growth of median income means that the living standards of today's working families are improving less quickly as they age compared to the experience of families in earlier periods. The next table examines how this dynamic has changed over time by tracking and comparing the progress of various cohorts. It offers clear evidence that the economic progress of recent cohorts has lagged behind that of their predecessors.

**Table 1.6** tracks various cohorts over time and compares two dimensions of real income growth. The first is how quickly one age cohort's income grows relative to a different cohort's. The top section follows five different cohorts over time, beginning in 1949. Each column contains the median family income of families headed by persons in three different age groups, 25-34, 35-44, and 45-54 (referenced as young, middle, and older, respectively). Note that these data do not track the same families over time, but this kind of analysis provides an approximation of what such families would experience.

The real median income of families in the cohort starting out in 1949 grew by more than half as they aged through each period. As they went from young to middle, their income grew by 57.4%; as they grew from middle to older, it grew by 51.4%. For the cohort starting out in 1959, income grew by 59.2% as they started out, about the same rate as for Cohort 1 (note also that the 1959 cohort started from a higher level; this is discussed below). But as the 1959 cohort passed from middle to older age, its rate of growth decelerated, to 23.1, as compared to 51.4% for the earlier cohort.

The 1969, 1979, and 1989 cohorts saw considerably slower growth as they aged, relative to earlier age groups (since the last cohort started out in 1999, there is only one observation for this group). Families in the 1979 cohort saw their median family income grow by 27.1% as they moved into middle age and by 25.2% as they entered older age. Over the full 30 years, the median income of their cohort grew by 59.1%, less than half as fast as that of the 1949 cohort. The income of the 1989 cohort can only be observed as it moved from young to middle age, and, thanks to the faster growth of the latter 1990s, income for these families grew faster as they aged than it did for either of the two previous cohorts (though slower than for the first two).

With this one exception, each cohort's real income growth has been successively slower than that of the previous cohort. The bottom panel, however, shows that, except for the 1989 cohort, the income starting line was higher for each successive cohort, but even that trend diminishes over time. For example, the 1959 cohort began its trajectory 41.6% above that of the 1949 cohort, and the 1969 cohort began its journey 37.9% ahead of the previous group. But as the 1979 cohort began, its income was only 8.5% above that of the 1969 cohort, and the next cohort, beginning in 1989, was the first to start out with lower income (by 2.4%) in real terms (though by the time the 1989 cohort reached middle age, it had caught up). The most recent cohort, which started out in 1999, began 8.1% above the previous cohort, but that is small advantage relative to the much larger gains posted by earlier cohorts.

TABLE 1.6 Median family income growth by 10-year cohorts, starting in 1949 (2001 dollars)

| Age of family head | 1949 cohort Young in '49 Middle in '59 Older in '69 | 1959 cohort Young in '59 Middle in '69 Older in '79 | 1969 cohort Young in '69 Middle in '79 Older in '89 | 1979 cohort Young in '79 Middle in '89 Older in '99 | 1989 cohort Young in '89 Middle in '99 n.a. | 1999 cohort Young in '99 n.a. n.a. |
|---|---|---|---|---|---|---|
| 25-34 (young) | $20,590 | $29,160 | $40,216 | $43,618 | $42,558 | $46,013 |
| 35-44 (middle) | 32,417 | 46,410 | 51,764 | 55,418 | 58,362 | n.a. |
| 45-54 (older) | 49,094 | 57,154 | 63,549 | 69,380 | n.a. | n.a. |
| *Percent growth:* | | | | | | |
| Young to middle | 57.4% | 59.2% | 28.7% | 27.1% | 37.1% | n.a. |
| Middle to older | 51.4 | 23.1 | 22.8 | 25.2 | n.a. | n.a. |
| Young to older | 138.4 | 96.0 | 58.0 | 59.1 | n.a. | n.a. |

**Addendum:**

| Growth between cohorts | 1949-59 (1959 cohort compared to 1949 cohort) | 1959-69 (1969 cohort compared to 1959 cohort) | 1969-79 (1979 cohort compared to 1969 cohort) | 1979-89 (1989 cohort compared to 1979 cohort) | 1989-99 (1999 cohort compared to 1979 cohort) |
|---|---|---|---|---|---|
| 25-34 (young) | 41.6% | 37.9% | 8.5% | -2.4% | 8.1% |
| 35-44 (middle) | 43.2 | 11.5 | 7.1 | 5.3 | n.a. |
| 45-54 (older) | 16.4 | 11.2 | 9.2 | n.a. | n.a. |

Source: Authors' analysis of U.S. Bureau of the Census data.

The data in Table 1.6 confirm the contention that income tend to rise as families age. The data also show that, at least through the late 1970s, each cohort started out ahead of the last. But the table also reveals that the rate of income growth of later cohorts has slowed considerably compared to that of earlier ones.

## Strong growth among dual-earner couples and single mothers

Along with age and race, it is also revealing to examine trends in family income growth by family type. In fact, some analysts argue that changes in family composition, especially the shift from married-couple families to those headed by a single person, is the primary explanation for many of the trends noted in this chapter. In a later section, we show that, while such shifts have had an important impact, the evidence does not support any dominant role for demographics in shaping income trends. While the shift to family types with lower incomes (such as mother-only families) will lower the level of overall income at any point in time, it is also important to look at how fast these families' incomes are growing relative to those of other family types, a factor that should offset some of the impact of the changing shares of family types. In fact, in both the 1970s and the second half of the 1990s, incomes of mother-only families grew more quickly than those of other families, suggesting a more complex story than that based wholly on shifts to lower-income family types.

**Table 1.7** focuses both on changes in median family income by family type and changes in the shares of different family types in the population. Since 1973, the most consistent income growth has occurred among married couples with both spouses in the paid labor force, as these families (specifically, the wives in these families) have increased their amount of time spent in paid work relative to other families (though single-mother families also made large labor force gains over the 1990s). In 1979, the share of married couples without a wife in the labor force was about equal to that of those with a wife in the labor force (41.9% versus 40.6% of married-couple families). By 2000, married couples with two earners (assuming the husband worked) made up 47.7% of all families, while one-earner married couples were proportionately fewer in number, 29.1% of the total.

While this shift toward two-earner families has been a major factor in recent income growth, the shift appears to be attenuating, since the rate at which wives have been joining the labor force and increasing their hours of work has slowed in recent years. For example, among married-couple families, the share of wives in the paid labor force increased at an annual rate of about 1% in the

**TABLE 1.7** Median family income by family type, 1947-2001 (2001 dollars)

| Year | Total | Married couples Wife in paid labor force | Wife not in paid labor force | Single Male- headed | Female- headed | All families |
|---|---|---|---|---|---|---|
| 1947 | $20,927 | — | — | $19,762 | $14,620 | $20,402 |
| 1967 | 37,911 | $44,715 | $34,183 | 30,604 | 19,286 | 35,629 |
| 1973 | 44,961 | 52,585 | 39,405 | 37,072 | 20,006 | 41,590 |
| 1979 | 48,417 | 56,171 | 40,005 | 37,976 | 22,323 | 44,255 |
| 1989 | 53,141 | 62,404 | 39,631 | 38,390 | 22,667 | 47,166 |
| 1995 | 54,284 | 64,390 | 37,344 | 35,017 | 22,713 | 46,843 |
| 2000 | 60,748 | 71,167 | 41,098 | 38,780 | 26,434 | 52,148 |
| 2001 | 60,335 | 70,834 | 40,782 | 36,590 | 25,745 | 51,407 |

*Annual growth rate*

| | | | | | | |
|---|---|---|---|---|---|---|
| 1947-67 | 3.0% | n.a. | n.a. | 2.2% | 1.4% | 2.8% |
| 1967-73 | 2.9 | 2.7% | 2.4% | 3.2 | 0.6 | 2.6 |
| 1973-79 | 1.2 | 1.1 | 0.3 | 0.4 | 1.8 | 1.0 |
| 1979-89 | 0.9 | 1.1 | -0.1 | 0.1 | 0.2 | 0.6 |
| 1989-2000 | 1.2 | 1.2 | 0.3 | 0.1 | 1.4 | 0.9 |
| 1989-95 | 0.4 | 0.5 | -1.0 | -1.5 | 0.0 | -0.1 |
| 1995-2000 | 2.3 | 2.0 | 1.9 | 2.1 | 3.1 | 2.2 |
| 2000-01 | -0.7 | -0.5 | -0.8 | -5.6 | -2.6 | -1.4 |

*Share of families*

| | | | | | | |
|---|---|---|---|---|---|---|
| 1951* | 86.7% | n.a | n.a | 3.0% | 9.9% | 100.0% |
| 1967 | 86.4 | 31.6% | 54.8% | 2.4 | 10.6 | 100.0 |
| 1973 | 85.0 | 35.4 | 49.7 | 2.6 | 12.4 | 100.0 |
| 1979 | 82.5 | 40.6 | 41.9 | 2.9 | 14.6 | 100.0 |
| 1989 | 79.2 | 45.7 | 33.5 | 4.4 | 16.5 | 100.0 |
| 2000 | 76.8 | 47.7 | 29.1 | 5.9 | 17.3 | 100.0 |

* Earliest year available

Source: Authors' analysis of U.S. Bureau of the Census data.

1960s and 1970s, 0.8% in the 1980s, and 0.4% in the 1989-2000 period. It is difficult to know the causes of this deceleration. It could be that, at 62% (47.7%/76.8%), the country is approaching the "ceiling" of the share of wives that are able or willing to spend time in the labor market. Second, wives' willingness to work has generally been found to be more sensitive to both their own and their spouses' earnings than it is among most other groups of workers, meaning that they are more likely than other groups of workers to cut back their hours when their earnings or their spouses' earnings rise, as occurred in the latter 1990s. However, while this so-called "cross income effect" has consistently been found to exist, its estimated magnitude is small and has shrunk over time. Thus, it can only explain a small part of the flatter trend in wives' labor force participation.

Married-couple families, although still predominant—representing 76.8% of all families in 2000—make up a smaller share of families than they did in the 1950s and 1960s. At the same time, the share of families headed by single women has grown; in 2000 single-mother families represented 17.3% of the total. Although this phenomenon has been the focus of increased critical attention in recent years, the share of families headed by single women grew more quickly in the 1967-79 period than it has since.

After stagnating in the first half of the 1990s, the real median income of mother-only families grew more quickly from 1995 to 2000 than it did for any other family type (3.1% annually). As will be discussed both later in this chapter and in Chapter 5 on poverty, such families sharply increased their annual weeks and hours of paid work over this period, which helped boost their incomes. Still, their income is about half that of all families in 2000, and it was slightly less than twice the poverty line that year for a family with one parent and two children. (Two times the poverty line is a benchmark for what it takes for working families to make ends meet, including child care costs). Thus, even with considerable effort in a strong economy, the median single-mother family still faces income constraints.

The increased labor market participation that helped drive the gains made by mother-only families from 1995 to 2000 makes this group more vulnerable to economic contraction than it was before (a theme explored in Chapter 5). Note that the recession of 2001 led to greater real losses for single-parent families than for two-parent families.

The fact that incomes grew quickly for single mothers over various time periods is important in another light as well. Many analysts of family income trends argue that changes in family structure of the type shown in the bottom panel of Table 1.7 are a major determinant of the overall trend in incomes. Specifically, this argument holds that, more than high unemployment or slow wage growth, the shift to lower-income family types has driven the post-1973 slowdown in income growth. Yet the data in Table 1.7 suggest that the trends in income within each family group are at least as important as the shifts in the types of families. Our more detailed analysis of this question below finds that the shift to lower-income families was a relatively minor factor explaining trends in both income growth and inequality in the 1980s and 1990s.

**FIGURE 1F** Low-, middle-, and high-income growth, 1947-2001

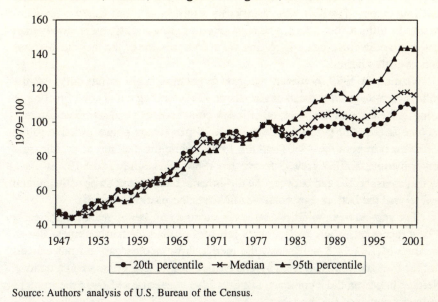

Source: Authors' analysis of U.S. Bureau of the Census.

## Growing inequality of family income

Along with the slower growth rates discussed thus far, the other important trend in the analysis of American family incomes has been increased income inequality. Even the strong, full employment economy of the late 1990s, which generated large wage gains for workers at the bottom, was unable to reverse that trend. In fact, certain measures that focus on the relative growth of income among the most wealthy suggest that the gap between those at the very top continued to pull away from the rest at least as quickly as in earlier periods. By other measures—those that focus more on changes in the middle and lower end of the income scale—inequality grew more slowly over the 1990s than over the 1980s. Ordinarily, a sustained period of low unemployment like that of the latter 1990s would have significantly lowered inequality, and it is perhaps a sign of diminished expectations about economic equity that slower growth in income inequality seems like good news.

**Figure 1F** looks at this issue by tracking three real family income percentiles—the 20th, the median (50th), and the 95th—from 1947 to 2001. The values are indexed to 100 in 1979, and thus they illustrate long-term developments between high-, middle-, and low-income families. From the beginning of the postwar period until the mid-1960s, the rate of income growth for middle- and low-income families was remarkably similar—at times the two lines appear to be almost coincident. And high incomes grew slightly more slowly than low and median incomes, suggesting some compression of the income distribution over this period.

Starting in 1979, however, the growth patterns begin to fan out, with the 95th percentile pulling ahead of the others. (This fanning out is not a function of using 1979 as the index point; other index point choices yield a similar picture). Income at the 95th percentile grew about 20 percentage points (relative to the 1979 level) in both the 1980s and the 1990s, while the incomes of middle- and lower-income families grew little over the 1980s and slightly in the 1990s. Thus, by this measure, the gap between the top-income families and those at the middle and toward the bottom expanded steadily over the past two decades.

The gap between middle- and lower-income families appeared in the early 1980s recession, when low incomes fell further than median incomes. But as the data in Table 1.8 will show, the median/low income gap did not expand further over the 1990s, at least by this particular measure of income inequality. Neither, however, did it contract, as might have been expected given the strength and persistence of the recovery.

Another useful means for assessing the pace of the overall trend in inequality is the Gini coefficient (**Figure 1G**), wherein higher numbers reveal greater inequality. In 1993, the main survey used by the Census Bureau to measure income changed in such a way as to induce a large jump in the Gini. The smooth trend line (see figure note for details), however, statistically controls for this shift and plots the underlying trend in family income inequality. The trend has been positive since the mid-1970s, rising quickly over the 1980s and decelerating in the 1990s.

Sorting families into fifths, or quintiles, of the population by income allows an examination of the percent of total national income goes to each family. Under perfect equality, each fifth would get 20%. In the U.S. economy, income shares at the top far exceed those at the bottom of the income scale (**Table 1.8**). The 20% of families with the lowest incomes are considered the lowest fifth, the next best-off 20% of families are the second fifth, and so forth. The 1993 change in Census survey methodology, noted above, has a large effect in these data as well (it leads to a sudden increase in the share of income going to the top fifth), and so the table includes 1993 to allow an examination of the change in income shares over the consistently measured 1993-2001 period.

The upper 20% of families received 47.7% of all income in 2001, and the top 5% received 21.1%, more than the families in the bottom 40% combined (they received 13.9%). In fact, the 2001 share of total income in each of the

**FIGURE 1G** Family income inequality, Gini coefficient, 1947-2001

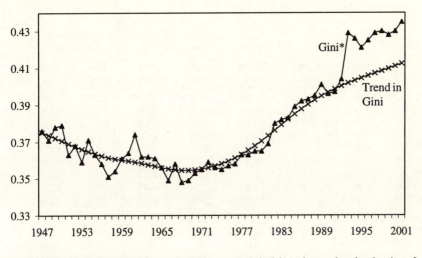

\* After 1993 the coefficients reflect a change in survey methodology that produced a showing of greater inequality.

Source: U.S. Bureau of the Census.

three lowest-income fifths—the 29.5% of total income going to the bottom 60% of families—was smaller than the 34.5% share this group received in 1979. As discussed in Chapter 7, income in the United States is distributed far more unequally than in other industrialized countries.

The changes in income shares, shown in the bottom section, show that the two decades following World War II (1947-67) were equalizing in terms of income: 1.6% of national income shifted from the top fifth to the bottom four-fifths. In contrast, over the 1980s 3.2% shifted the other way—from the bottom 80% to the top 20%—with most of this (2.6%) going to the top 5%. The change in the survey makes it difficult to look over the full 1990s cycle, but between 1993 and 2000 there is evidence of a hollowing of the middle, with share gains at the bottom and the top. Note that these data exclude income from realized capital gains, an omission that biases the inequality estimates downward both in terms of levels and, in periods of strong growth in equity prices such as the latter 1990s, trends as well. (We correct this omission in some of the data below and in the analysis of wealth in Chapter 4).

The increase in the income gap between upper- and lower-income groups is illustrated in **Figure 1H**, which shows the ratio of the average incomes of families in the bottom 20% to those of the top 5% from 1947 to 2000. The gap

**TABLE 1.8** Shares of family income going to various income groups and to top 5%, 1947-2001 (2001 dollars)

| Year | Lowest fifth | Second fifth | Middle fifth | Fourth fifth | Top fifth | Breakdown of top fifth |  |
|---|---|---|---|---|---|---|---|
|  |  |  |  |  |  | First 15% | Top 5% |
| 1947 | 5.0% | 11.9% | 17.0% | 23.1% | 43.0% | 25.5% | 17.5% |
| 1947 | 5.0 | 11.9 | 17.0 | 23.1 | 43.0 | 25.5 | 17.5 |
| 1967 | 5.4 | 12.2 | 17.5 | 23.5 | 41.4 | 25 | 16.4 |
| 1973 | 5.5 | 11.9 | 17.5 | 24.0 | 41.1 | 25.6 | 15.5 |
| 1979 | 5.4 | 11.6 | 17.5 | 24.1 | 41.4 | 26.1 | 15.3 |
| 1989 | 4.6 | 10.6 | 16.5 | 23.7 | 44.6 | 26.7 | 17.9 |
| 1993* | 4.1 | 9.9 | 15.7 | 23.3 | 47.0 | 26.7 | 20.3 |
| 2000 | 4.3 | 9.8 | 15.4 | 22.7 | 47.7 | 26.6 | 21.1 |
| 2001 | 4.2 | 9.7 | 15.5 | 22.9 | 47.7 | 26.7 | 21.0 |
| *Percentage-point change* |  |  |  |  |  |  |  |
| 1947-67 | 0.4 | 0.3 | 0.5 | 0.4 | -1.6 | -0.5 | -1.1 |
| 1967-73 | 0.1 | -0.3 | 0.0 | 0.5 | -0.3 | 0.6 | -0.9 |
| 1973-79 | -0.1 | -0.3 | 0.0 | 0.1 | 0.3 | 0.5 | -0.2 |
| 1979-89 | -0.8 | -1.0 | -1.0 | -0.4 | 3.2 | 0.6 | 2.6 |
| 1993-2000 | 0.2 | -0.1 | -0.3 | -0.6 | 0.7 | -0.1 | 0.8 |

\* In 1993, a change in Census survey methodology led to greater measured inequality, and so 1993 is included here to gauge the change in income shares over the 1993-2000 period.

Source: Authors' analysis of U.S. Bureau of the Census data.

between the top and the bottom incomes fell from 1947 to 1979 but grew to 19.1 by 2000, reversing three decades of lessening inequality.

Another way of viewing this recent surge in income inequality is to compare the "income cutoff" of families by income group, as in **Table 1.9.** These values, some of which appeared above in Figure 1F, represent the income at the top percentile of each fifth. Focusing on this measure allows an examination of income gains and losses for complete groupings of families (e.g., the bottom 40%). Also, since the cases affected by the top-coding change are typically above the 95th percentile, the 1995 and 2000 values in this table are not upwardly biased relative to earlier years.

Note that in this latter period, income growth accelerated sharply in each percentile shown in the table. For example, after falling or growing very slightly from the 80th percentile and down, real family income grew faster than 2% per year from 1995 to 2000. Still, inequality continued to grow, as income grew most quickly (2.9%) at the 95th percentile.

Over the 1980s, income growth was flat at the bottom of the income scale

**FIGURE 1H** Ratio of family income of top 5% to lowest 20%, 1947-2000

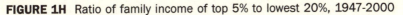

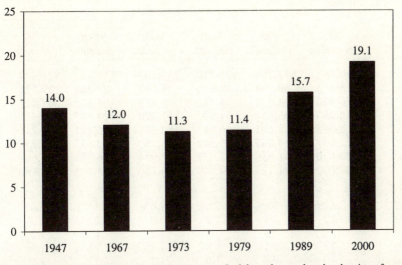

Note: The 2000 ratio reflects a change in survey methodology that produced a showing of greater inequality.

Source: Authors' analysis of U.S. Bureau of the Census.

(the 20th percentile), and was consecutively higher at each percentile; this is the only cycle in the table with this extreme pattern of inequality-inducing growth rates, suggesting that the factors that generate higher inequality (discussed in the Introduction) —were firing on all cylinders in this decade in the 1980s. As shown in the next figure, many of the postwar years followed an opposite pattern, one of widely shared growth.

**Figure 1I** presents a revealing picture of incomes growing together in the first 26 years of the postwar period and thereafter growing apart. The bars in each panel represent the growth rate of average income by income fifth over the periods 1947-73 and 1973-2000. The top panel, covering the years 1947-73, shows strong and even growth, with average incomes either doubling (i.e., growing by at least 100%) or nearly doubling for each income fifth. Note also that over this period growth was slightly faster at the bottom of the income scale than at the top, i.e., growth was equalizing. The bottom panel shows a different pattern. Since 1973, the annual growth of family income was relatively weak for the bottom fifth, rising only 10.3% through 2000. Income growth was moderate for the second and middle fifth, but much more positive for the top fifth (61.6%) and especially for the top 5% (87.5%, not shown in

**TABLE 1.9** Real family income by income group, 1947-2001, upper limit of each group (2001 dollars)

| Year | 20th percentile | 40th percentile | 60th percentile | 80th percentile | 95th percentile | Average |
|---|---|---|---|---|---|---|
| 1947 | $10,662 | $17,205 | $23,330 | $33,103 | $54,333 | $23,868 |
| 1967 | 18,455 | 30,294 | 40,624 | 55,692 | 89,484 | 39,528 |
| 1973 | 20,986 | 34,629 | 48,316 | 66,445 | 103,586 | 47,011 |
| 1979 | 22,280 | 36,637 | 51,903 | 71,470 | 114,657 | 50,421 |
| 1989 | 22,062 | 38,601 | 56,247 | 82,096 | 136,431 | 57,221 |
| 1995 | 21,997 | 38,047 | 56,503 | 83,350 | 142,633 | 59,234 |
| 2000 | 24,670 | 41,980 | 63,037 | 93,924 | 164,589 | 67,609 |
| 2001 | 24,000 | 41,127 | 62,500 | 94,150 | 164,104 | 66,863 |
| *Annual growth rate* | | | | | | |
| 1947-67 | 2.8% | 2.9% | 2.8% | 2.6% | 2.5% | 2.6% |
| 1967-73 | 2.2 | 2.3 | 2.9 | 3.0 | 2.5 | 2.9 |
| 1973-79 | 1.0 | 0.9 | 1.2 | 1.2 | 1.7 | 1.2 |
| 1979-89 | -0.1 | 0.5 | 0.8 | 1.4 | 1.8 | 1.3 |
| 1989-2000 | 1.0 | 0.8 | 1.0 | 1.2 | 1.7 | 1.5 |
| 1989-95 | 0.0 | -0.2 | 0.1 | 0.3 | 0.7 | 0.6 |
| 1995-2000 | 2.3 | 2.0 | 2.2 | 2.4 | 2.9 | 2.7 |
| 2000-01 | -2.7 | -2.0 | -0.9 | 0.2 | -0.3 | -1.1 |

Source: Authors' analysis of U.S. Bureau of the Census data.

figure; data for the top 5% are not available for the earlier period). Between 1947 and 1973 income grew 31% more slowly in the top relative to the bottom fifth; since 1973, income has grown 51% more *quickly* in the top relative to the bottom fifth. Thus, the 1947-73 equalizing pattern of growth was sharply reversed in the post-1973 period.

## Counterarguments to the evidence on income trends

A number of questions have been raised regarding the evidence presented thus far about the high levels and increasing trend of inequality. We've already noted the lifting of the Census top codes and shown that controlling for this change does not alter the finding that inequality continued to grow through the 1990s. In this section we evaluate the validity of two sets of counterarguments.

The first arguments deal with the definition of income: should it be pre-tax or post-tax, and should it include various income components such as capital

**FIGURE 1I** Family income growth by quintile, 1947-2000

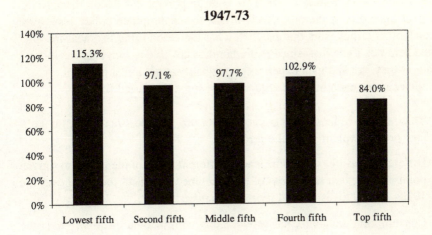

**1947-73**

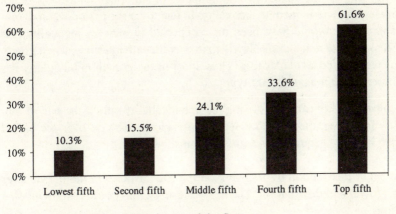

**1973-2000**

Source: Authors' analysis of U.S. Bureau of the Census.

gains or the cash value of food stamps? Also, some economists argue that consumption, a close approximation of "permanent" income, is a better measure of family well-being than annual income. This raises the question of whether the inequality of consumption has increased along with that of income.

The second set of arguments accepts the increase in inequality demonstrated thus far, but discounts its importance (at least in an economic sense) in two ways. First, critics say that demographics are the important factor, suggesting that non-economic trends, such as the shift to single-parent families over time, are the main reason for inequality's rise. This is an important distinction, because an incorrect diagnosis of the problem will lead to inappropriate policy responses. Second, other critics grant that inequality has increased using the measures presented here but argue that, since many families are able to move up the income ladder as they age and gain experience, inequality is not a real problem.

We examine each of these arguments in some detail and find:

- The increase in inequality occurred both pre- and post-tax; thus, tax policies do not explain away the problem;

- Different measures of income lead to different levels of inequality at a given point in time, but, regardless of how income is defined, the *trend* over the 1980s and 1990s is toward more inequality;

- Consumption inequality has grown along with income inequality over the 1980s; its trend flattened, however, though the mid-1990s;

- Controlling for the changing demographics of American families does not reverse the trend in income inequality. In fact, over the period when demographic shifts would have been most expected to increase inequality (the 1970s), it grew much more slowly than over the latter periods, when family structure played a smaller role. Thus, most of the growth in inequality has occurred within each family type;

- Income mobility can offset rising income inequality only if the rate of mobility increases; there is no evidence of such an increase over the period when income inequality was growing most quickly.

We begin this section by focusing on the role of taxes in the debate over income growth and distribution. The next section examines alternative income definitions.

### Are taxes the reason for rising inequality and disappointing growth in family incomes?

Some participants in the national debate over family income inequality blame the slower family income growth and widening inequality documented above on rising taxes. All the preceding data on family incomes, however, have referred to *before-tax* incomes. Since the analysis has relied on income data before taxes have been taken out, changes in the tax code cannot be directly responsible for the observed trends. Nevertheless, the tax code can act to reduce or to reinforce the income patterns documented above. For example, reductions in taxes for higher-income families increases the assets they have available for investment, and more investment can generate higher investment income.

Significant changes in federal, state, and local tax rates have been implemented since the 1970s. In general terms, over the 1980s, taxes became more regressive—higher-income families saw their tax payments fall relative to lower-income families—and more progressive during the early 1990s—higher-income families saw their tax payments rise relative to lower-income families. Changes in tax policy over the 1980s, then, reinforced the overall trend toward inequality, while changes in tax policy during the early 1990s helped to reduce inequality's growth. The tax cuts passed in 1997 and 2001 partially reversed the progressive changes introduced in the early 1990s, so that by 2001 the income tax system was closer to where it was in the 1980s.

**Table 1.10** shows the effective tax rate for and share of post-tax income received by each income quintile (including finer gradations of income for the top fifth) before and after the tax cuts of 2001 are fully implemented in 2010. The effective federal tax rate is the share of the household's total income that is actually paid out in all federal income taxes, including personal income, payroll, corporate income, and excise taxes; the data in Table 1.10, from a model developed by the Institute on Taxation and Economic Policy, also include estate taxes. Both before and after the tax cuts of 2001, the federal tax system is fundamentally progressive (primarily a function of the personal income tax, as shown below), and the effective tax rate rises with household income. The tax cut of 2001 reduced the average effective federal tax rate across the income distribution, but more so for higher-income families. Whereas families in the bottom fifth saw their tax rate fall by 0.7 percentage points, from 9.1% to 8.4%, the top 1% of families saw their tax rate fall by 4.1 percentage points, from 35.4% to 31.3%. This comes out to an average tax cut of $67 among families in the bottom fifth and a cut of $1,978 for those in the top fifth. Those in the top 1% will receive an average tax cut of $45,715.

Changes in the effective tax rate lead to changes in the share of post-tax income received by each quintile. The distribution of after-tax income (as with pre-tax income) is highly unequal: the bottom 20% receive only 3.8% of total income after the 2001 tax cuts, while the top 20% receive over half (55.9%). The regressivity of the 2001 tax cuts means that, after their implementation, higher-income families will have more of total national income and lower-income families will have less. The share going to the top 1% increases by 0.6 percentage points, from 16.8% to 17.4%, while every other income group experiences a slight decline.

The next set of tables use data from the Congressional Budget Office (CBO)

**TABLE 1.10** Distribution of tax burdens and income before and after 2001 tax law change

| Income category | Average effective federal tax rate | | | Share of post-tax income | | | Average dollar value of 2001 tax law change |
|---|---|---|---|---|---|---|---|
| | Pre-2001 law | Post-2001 law | Percentage-point change | Pre-2001 law | Post-2001 law | Percentage-point change | |
| **Bottom four-fifths** | | | | | | | |
| First | 9.1% | 8.4% | -0.7 | 3.9% | 3.8% | -0.1 | $67 |
| Second | 15.8 | 14.0 | -1.8 | 8.1 | 8.0 | -0.1 | 368 |
| Third | 20.4 | 18.8 | -1.6 | 12.8 | 12.7 | -0.1 | 570 |
| Fourth | 24.0 | 22.3 | -1.7 | 20.0 | 19.8 | -0.2 | 951 |
| **Top fifth** | | | | | | | |
| Next 15% | 27.0% | 24.9% | -2.1 | 24.9% | 24.8% | -0.1 | $1,978 |
| Next 4% | 29.5 | 27.9 | -1.6 | 13.8 | 13.7 | -0.1 | 3,326 |
| Top 1% | 35.4 | 31.3 | -4.1 | 16.8 | 17.4 | 0.6 | 45,715 |
| **All** | 26.3% | 24.1% | -2.2 | 100.0% | 100.0% | 0.0 | $1,245 |

Note: The distributional effects are examined at 2001 income levels with fully phased-in values for the tax cuts (i.e., the tax cuts that would occur in 2010) adjusted for inflation to 2001 levels.

Source: Gale (2002).

to examine tax rates from 1979 to 1997 (the most recent year available). CBO's methodology for estimating effective tax rates differs slightly from that used in Table 1.10, in two important ways. First, CBO uses a broader measure of income that includes more types of in-kind receipts, such as health benefits, as well as taxes paid by corporations in which individuals have investments and voluntary contributions to retirement accounts. Second, while Table 1.10 assigns households to quintiles based solely on income, the CBO adjusts household income based on household size. Thus, CBO assigns larger households to lower quintiles and smaller households to higher quintiles than does Table 1.10. Largely because of tax preferences for children, this method results in lower effective tax rates in lower quintiles and higher rates in higher quintiles in the CBO analysis.

**Table 1.11** puts the 2001 tax cut into historical perspective, showing effective tax rates in 1979, 1989, and 1997. The progressivity of federal taxes varied substantially over the period. In 1979, the effective federal tax rate for the top fifth of households was 3.4 times higher than the effective rate paid by the bottom fifth. Changes to the tax code implemented in the 1980s made the tax code less progressive, lowering the ratio to 3.0 by 1989. Further changes in the early 1990s made the tax code, by this measure at least, much more progressive, with the ratio rising to 4.9 by 1997. The most important reason for the rise in the ratio of effective tax rates was the steep drop—from 8.5% to 5.6%— in the effective tax rate for the bottom fifth, which resulted primarily from the expansion of the Earned Income Tax Credit (EITC), which boosts the after-tax income of low-wage earners in low-income families.

From the standpoint of progressivity, one of the most important developments over the period was the big swing, back and forth and back again, in the effective tax rates for high-income households. In 1979, the top 1% of households paid 37.3% of their income in federal taxes. By the end of the 1980s, the effective federal tax rate for this group had fallen to 28.2%. Countervailing changes to the tax code in the early 1990s pushed the effective rate for these top-earners up to 33.3%, still four percentage points lower than the 1979 level. The effective tax rates for the top 5% and the top 10% of households show similar, though less pronounced, swings.

The overall trend toward regressivity is probably understated by these data. Under a progressive income tax, increasing income inequality will increase the progressivity of tax collections, as the disproportionate additions to wealth at the top get taxed at the highest rates. Thus, much of the regressive effect of statutory changes has been offset. An analysis comparing, for example, the current distribution of taxes with what the distribution would be were 1979 law in effect (adjusting brackets, exemptions, etc., for inflation) would show a much greater increase in regressivity.

**TABLE 1.11** Effective federal tax rates for all households, by income quintile, using comprehensive household income adjusted for household size, 1979-97

| Income category | 1979 | 1989 | 1997 |
|---|---|---|---|
| **Bottom four-fifths** | | | |
| First | 8.1% | 8.5% | 5.6% |
| Second | 14.0 | 14.3 | 13.9 |
| Third | 18.2 | 17.6 | 17.5 |
| Fourth | 21.2 | 20.3 | 20.5 |
| **Top fifth** | 27.8% | 25.1% | 27.7% |
| Top 10% | 30.0 | 26.2 | 29.4 |
| Top 5% | 32.2 | 27.0 | 30.9 |
| Top 1% | 37.3 | 28.2 | 33.3 |
| **All** | 22.3% | 21.3% | 22.8% |

Source: Congressional Budget Office (2001).

The data in Table 1.11 also demonstrate how little impact the various tax changes in the 1980s and 1990s have had on typical middle-income households. The effective federal tax rate for the middle fifth of households was 18.2% in 1979, 17.6% in 1989, and 17.5% in 1997. Since taxes have fallen slightly for the middle fifth, there is no truth to the claims that government taxes (at the federal level, at least) are taking a bigger chunk out of middle-class family incomes.

**Table 1.12** decomposes (i.e., breaks down into their component parts) the changes in after-tax income shares between 1979-89 and 1989-97 into the portion due to pre-tax income shifts and the portion attributable to changes in federal tax policy. The first two columns show the change in actual after-tax income shares. The third and fourth columns show the portion of the overall change in after-tax income that was due to pre-tax income shifts in each period. The last two columns show the corresponding portion of the overall shift due to changes in the tax burden (from changes in the tax code as well as movements of families in and out of tax brackets and other factors) across the income distribution. Of the 5.1 percentage-point decline between 1979 and 1989 in the share of total after-tax income received by the bottom four-fifths of households, 4.3 points were due to a relative loss of pre-tax income and only 0.8 points were due to shifts in the distribution of the tax burden. Thus, shifts in the tax burden, though significant, were clearly not the primary mechanism of the overall redistribution of income from 1979 to 1989. Over the same period, the top 1% of households captured a 3.0-point larger share of after-tax income, but, again, most of

**TABLE 1.12** The effects of federal tax and income changes
on after-tax income shares, 1979-97

| | | | Change in shares due to: | | | |
|---|---|---|---|---|---|---|
| | Change in after-tax shares | | Change in pre-tax income shifts | | Change in relative tax burdens | |
| Income category | 1979-89 | 1989-97 | 1979-89 | 1989-97 | 1979-89 | 1989-97 |
| **Bottom four-fifths** | -5.1 | -2.2 | -4.3 | -3.2 | -0.8 | 0.9 |
| First | -1.2 | -0.2 | -1.0 | -0.4 | -0.3 | 0.2 |
| Second | -1.5 | -0.7 | -1.2 | -0.9 | -0.3 | 0.2 |
| Third | -1.2 | -0.7 | -1.1 | -0.9 | -0.2 | 0.3 |
| Fourth | -1.2 | -0.7 | -1.1 | -1.0 | -0.1 | 0.3 |
| **Top fifth** | 5.1 | 2.2 | 4.3 | 3.2 | 0.8 | -0.9 |
| Top 10% | 5.0 | 2.4 | 4.2 | 3.6 | 0.8 | -1.1 |
| Top 5% | 4.8 | 2.7 | 3.9 | 4.0 | 0.8 | -1.2 |
| Top 1% | 3.0 | 2.9 | 2.2 | 4.0 | 0.8 | -1.1 |

Source: Authors' analysis of Congressional Budget Office (2001).

this improvement (2.2 points) was due to changes in pre-tax income share and much less (0.8 points) to changes in the tax burden.

Column 2 shows that the after-tax income share for the bottom four-fifths of the population fell 2.2 percentage points over the 1989-97 period. This decline was the result of two countervailing forces. The share of pre-tax income for the bottom four-fifths fell 3.2 percentage points, indicating a further growth of pre-tax income inequality. The greater tax progressivity built into tax changes in the early 1990s, however, partially offset these declines, raising the after-tax income share for this group by 0.9 percentage points. At the top of the income distribution, the share of after-tax income going to the top 1% of households rose 2.9 percentage points during the 1990s (through 1997, the latest year available). Gains in pre-tax income shares (4.0 percentage points) drove this rise, since increased tax progressivity moved this group's income shares in the other direction (by 1.1 percentage points).

Even if we narrow the analysis to the stereotypical family of four (with two children and one earner), changes in federal taxes have had little impact on family living standards, except for those of low-income families, for whom effective federal taxes have fallen as a result, primarily, of expansions in the EITC. **Figure 1J** shows separate data from the Department of the Treasury on the effective federal tax rate for families of four with low and median incomes from 1955 to 1999 (low income is defined as one-half of median income for a

**FIGURE 1J** Effective federal tax rate for family of four, 1955-99

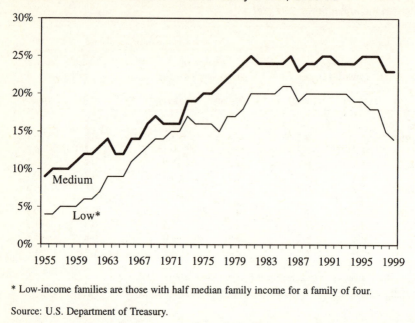

* Low-income families are those with half median family income for a family of four.

Source: U.S. Department of Treasury.

family of four). Federal taxes for the median-income family increased from just below 10% in 1955 to 25% in 1981. The effective rate hovered around 24% through the late 1990s, when it dropped closer to 20% as a result of the 1993 tax cuts. Low-income families of four saw their effective tax rates fall in the 1990s, mostly as a result of the increased EITC after 1993.

So far, the analysis of taxes has examined the combined effects of all federal taxes. In fact, federal taxes take a variety of forms, some progressive and some regressive. Changes in the relative importance of different kinds of federal taxes can have an important impact on the progressivity of the federal tax system as a whole. **Table 1.13** shows the effective tax rate for households at different income levels for the four most important types of federal taxes. The data in the table compare effective rates in 1979, before income stagnation and inequality began to rise strongly, to rates in 1997. In both 1979 and 1997, the personal income tax (first two columns) is strongly progressive, with effective rates rising smoothly with income. Refundable tax credits administered through the personal income tax actually increased the income of poorest fifth of all households in both years, though much more so in 1997. Middle-income households paid about 7.3% of their income in federal income taxes in 1979 and

**TABLE 1.13** Effective tax rates for selected federal taxes, 1979 and 1997

| Income category | Personal income tax | | Payroll tax | | Corporate income tax | | Excise tax | |
|---|---|---|---|---|---|---|---|---|
| | 1979 | 1997 | 1979 | 1997 | 1979 | 1997 | 1979 | 1997 |
| **Bottom four-fifths** | | | | | | | | |
| First | -0.4% | -5.3% | 5.3% | 7.4% | 1.0% | 0.5% | 2.1% | 2.8% |
| Second | 3.9 | 1.3 | 7.3 | 9.2 | 1.4 | 0.7 | 1.3 | 1.6 |
| Third | 7.3 | 4.8 | 8.3 | 9.7 | 1.6 | 1.1 | 1.1 | 1.1 |
| Fourth | 10.1 | 7.5 | 8.4 | 10.2 | 1.8 | 1.4 | 0.9 | 0.9 |
| **Top fifth** | 15.9% | 15.8% | 5.6% | 6.7% | 5.6% | 4.4% | 0.7% | 0.5% |
| Top 10% | 17.5 | 17.8 | 4.5 | 5.4 | 7.1 | 5.4 | 0.7 | 0.4 |
| Top 5% | 19.4 | 19.5 | 3.2 | 4.2 | 9.0 | 6.3 | 0.6 | 0.4 |
| Top 1% | 22.4 | 22.3 | 1.4 | 2.1 | 13.0 | 8.0 | 0.5 | 0.2 |
| **All** | 11.1% | 10.5% | 6.8% | 8.1% | 3.4% | 2.9% | 1.0% | 0.9% |

Source: Authors' analysis of Congressional Budget Office (2001).

4.8% in 1997. The top 1% paid, on average, substantially more than the middle fifth did in both years (22.4% in 1979 and 22.3% in 1997).

The third and fourth columns of Table 1.13 show effective rates for the payroll tax, which is used primarily to finance Social Security and Medicare. All workers pay the payroll tax at the same rate (15.3%) from their first dollar of earnings until the point in the year when they reach an income cap ($65,400 in 1997 and $80,400 in 2001). With the lowest earners paying the full rate from the first dollar earned and high earners paying no payroll tax on earnings over the cap, the payroll tax is regressive, and the effective rates in Table 1.13 bear this out. The rate rises through the bottom, second, middle, and fourth fifth of households, but falls steeply thereafter. In 1997, for example, households in the middle fifth paid 9.7% of their income in federal payroll taxes, compared to just 2.1% paid by top 1% of households. Comparing rates in 1997 with those in place in 1979 demonstrates that effective rates rose about 1.3 percentage points as a result of increases in the payroll tax implemented in the 1980s to improve the long-term finances of the Social Security and Medicare systems. Yet, while the payroll tax is regressive, the Social Security and Medicare benefits it funds are progressive. This suggests that the most appropriate way to judge the progressivity or regressivity of a particular tax or tax system should involve looking at the effect of the tax or tax system after accounting for all benefits realized from government activities.

**TABLE 1.14** Types of federal vs. state and local taxes, as a percent of revenue at each level, 2001

| Type of tax | Federal | State and local |
|---|---|---|
| **Progressive** | 58.5% | 25.9% |
| Personal income tax | 49.3 | 23.0 |
| Corporate income tax | 9.2 | 2.9 |
| **Regressive** | 39.9% | 70.2% |
| Excise/customs/sales/other* | 4.4 | 43.8 |
| Contributions for social insurance | 35.5 | 1.0 |
| Property | 0.0 | 25.3 |
| **Non-taxes*** | 1.6% | 4.0% |
| **Total** | 100.0% | 100.0% |

\* Other taxes include vehicle licenses, severance taxes, etc.
\*\* Fines, certain fees, rents, royalties, tuition, hospital fees, etc.

Source: Authors' analysis of NIPA (2002) data.

The fifth and sixth columns in Table 1.13 display the effective rates from the corporate income tax, which are portioned out to households according to their estimated income from capital. The corporate income tax is progressive, with effective rates rising sharply with income. However, between 1979 and 1997 corporate taxes declined. In practice, the progressivity of the corporate income tax simply reflects the ownership structure of corporations, with few poor and middle-income households holding any substantial amount of stock. The last two columns show effective rates of federal excise taxes (such as those on gasoline, alcohol, and cigarettes). These taxes are highly regressive, with the bottom fifth of households spending four times more of its income than did the top 1% in 1997. In fact, the poorest fifth of households paid more in federal excise taxes in both years than it did in corporate income taxes.

The mix of taxes—federal, state, and local—can have an important impact on how the tax burden is shared. Federal taxes, driven by the progressivity of the federal income tax, are far more progressive than state and local taxes, which tend to include regressive sales, excise, and property taxes. **Table 1.14** shows the share of federal and state and local tax revenues collected by progressive and regressive tax systems in 2001. Almost three-fifths (58.5%) of federal tax revenue is raised through progressive taxes, compared to just over one-quarter (25.9%) for state and local revenues.

**TABLE 1.15** Federal vs. state and local tax revenue as a percent of GDP, 1959-2001

| Year | Federal | State and local | Total |
|------|---------|-----------------|-------|
| 1959 | 17.1% | 6.9% | 24.0% |
| 1967 | 17.4 | 8.1 | 25.4 |
| 1973 | 17.9 | 9.5 | 27.5 |
| 1979 | 18.6 | 8.7 | 27.4 |
| 1989 | 18.4 | 9.5 | 27.9 |
| 2000 | 20.7 | 9.9 | 30.6 |
| 2001 | 19.9 | 10.0 | 29.9 |
| 1959-79 | 1.5 | 1.8 | 3.3 |
| 1979-89 | -0.2 | 0.7 | 0.5 |
| 1989-2000 | 2.3 | 0.4 | 2.7 |

Source: Authors' analysis of NIPA (2002) data.

Changes over time in the share of taxes collected at the federal versus the state and local level, therefore, can change the progressivity of the overall tax system. **Table 1.15** shows data on tax revenues raised at the federal and the state and local level from 1959 through 2001. Between 1959 and 1979, total tax revenue grew 3.3 percentage points of GDP, with more regressive state taxes increasing at a slightly faster rate (1.8 percentage points of GDP from a base of 6.9%, compared to a 1.5 percentage-point rise in federal tax revenue from a base of 17.1%). During the 1980s, overall tax revenues rose 0.5 percentage points of GDP, the net result of a 0.2 percentage-point decrease in more progressive federal tax revenues and a 0.7 percentage-point rise in more regressive state and local taxes. In the 1990s, tax revenues rose sharply (2.7 percentage points of GDP), mostly as a result of increases in federal revenue collection (2.3 percentage points).

The data in Tables 1.10 through 1.15 make a strong case that slower income growth and widening income inequality are primarily before-tax phenomena. Taxes exacerbated the rise in inequality in the 1980s, but important changes to the tax code in the early 1990s, especially the expansion of the EITC, helped reduce income inequality somewhat in the 1990s. The 2001 tax cuts, however, introduce more regressivity into the tax system. Although the tax cuts were accompanied by increases in child credits and reduced taxes across the board, the effective tax rates for higher-income families will fall much more than for lower-income families as the taxes are phased in through 2010.

*Is the increase in inequality sensitive to income definitions?*

Studies in income distribution, as in all areas of empirical work, have to be careful and complete as to how they define the items being analyzed. More specifically, it is important to ensure that any conclusions drawn from a data analysis are not sensitive to particular measurement decisions.

Other than the tax data just discussed, the income definition used thus far in this chapter is the Census Bureau's primary definition of income: pre-tax, post-cash-transfer money income, which includes earnings (including self-employment), interest, dividends, pensions, and rental income, as well as cash transfers from government programs such as public assistance (welfare benefits) and Social Security. This measure leaves out a variety of income components, some of which, like the cash value of publicly provided near-cash benefits like food stamps, are equalizing, while others, like capital gains, tend to increase inequality. Fortunately, the Census Bureau provides an alternative series so that we can examine the extent to which any of our conclusions are sensitive to alternative income definitions.

Before we turn to these data, however, we want to emphasize that the

## ALTERNATIVE INCOME DEFINITIONS

*Money income:* The Census Bureau's official definition of income used to compute income and poverty trends. This definition combines all labor income (wage and salary and self-employment), all government cash transfers (unemployment insurance, Temporary Assistance for Needy Families, Social Security), pensions, alimony, rent, interest, dividends, and other money income. This definition does not take account of non-cash government assistance (e.g., Medicaid), taxation, and capital gains.

*Market income, pre-tax:* This definition adjusts money income by subtracting government cash assistance and by adding market incomes excluded from the official definition: employer-provided health insurance and realized capital gains (gains from selling assets such as stock). Thus, this definition includes only income generated by the market.

*Market income, after-tax:* This definition adjusts market income to an "after-tax" basis by subtracting estimates of federal income and payroll taxes, the EITC, and state income taxes. There is no adjustment for other federal (corporate, excise), other state (sales) taxes, or any local taxes.

*Comprehensive income:* This definition adds the value of government assistance to income. It includes both cash assistance (Social Security, unemployment insurance, etc.) and the value of various subsidies and programs, such as housing subsidies, food stamps, school lunch programs, and health programs (Medicare/Medicaid). This definition is thus the most comprehensive in including both market income and government assistance as well as adjusting for most taxes.

central question under investigation here is how the *trend* in inequality is affected by the alternative definitions. These alternative series indeed typically produce different *levels* of inequality at a point in time, but we are primarily interested in whether there is some important income component missing from the above analysis that would change our conclusions about the *trend*.

*Census Bureau alternative income definitions:* The Census Bureau offers an array of household income measures (most of the tables up to this point have referred to families, i.e., two or more related persons; the data in this section are available only for households, which include persons living alone). We have selected four of the 15 available measures for analysis so that we can identify how results change as incomes become more comprehensively measured and as changes in the tax system are integrated into the analysis (see the box, "Alternative Income Definitions"). The first measure is the official Census Bureau "money income" definition used thus far. The limitations of this definition are that it excludes any effect of the tax system or employer-provided health benefits, realized capital gains (i.e., gains from selling assets such as stocks), and the value of government non-cash programs (housing subsidies, Medicaid/Medicare, food stamps). The second definition is "pre-tax market income," obtained by subtracting government cash assistance from money income and adding in realized capital gains and employer-provided health insurance. The third definition puts market incomes on an after-tax basis. The last measure, "comprehensive income," adds the value of government cash transfers, health programs (Medicare/Medicaid), food stamps, and school lunch programs in order to have the broadest measure of income (see table note for more information on how these values are derived).

**Table 1.16** presents several measures of inequality for each definition of income for the years 1979, 1989, 1995, and 2000 and the percent growth over time. No matter which measure is used, inequality increased over both the 1980s and the 1990s. The top section employs the Gini coefficient (see Figure 1F). As the last column shows, this measure of income inequality grew between 10.0% and 14.2% after 1979. Note also that the most comprehensive definition shows the greatest increase, suggesting that the income components left out of the basic Census measure lead to a downward bias in the growth of inequality (e.g., the omission of capital gains has a greater impact on inequality's growth than the omission of the cash value of food stamps). Note, for example, that while the Gini measure of household income inequality was essentially unchanged from 1995 to 2000 under the Census money income definition (0.7%), it grew 4.1% under the comprehensive measure.

The second two sections of Table 1.16 use a variation of the income ratio

**TABLE 1.16** Growth of household income inequality using different income definitions and inequality measures

| Inequality measure and income definition | Includes: | | | | Inequality measure | | | | Percent change in inequality | | | |
|---|---|---|---|---|---|---|---|---|---|---|---|---|
| | Capital gains & health insurance | Government cash transfers | Subtracts taxes | Value of non-cash government subsidies & programs | 1979 | 1989 | 1995 | 2000 | 1979-1989 | 1989-2000 | 1995-2000 | 1979-2000 |
| **Gini coefficient** | | | | | | | | | | | | |
| Census money income | No | Yes | No | No | 0.403 | 0.429 | 0.444 | 0.447 | 6.5% | 4.2% | 0.7% | 10.9% |
| All market income, pre-tax | Yes | No | No | No | 0.460 | 0.492 | 0.509 | 0.506 | 7.0 | 2.8 | -0.6 | 10.0 |
| All market income, after-tax | Yes | No | Yes | No | 0.429 | 0.465 | 0.481 | 0.486 | 8.4 | 4.5 | 1.0 | 13.3 |
| Comprehensive income | Yes | Yes | Yes | Yes | 0.359 | 0.389 | 0.394 | 0.410 | 8.4 | 5.4 | 4.1 | 14.2 |
| **Household income ratios** | | | | | | | | | | | | |
| *Top fifth/bottom fifth* | | | | | | | | | | | | |
| Census money income | No | Yes | No | No | 10.6 | 12.1 | 13.0 | 13.9 | 14.1% | 15.1% | 7.3% | 31.4% |
| All market income, pre-tax | Yes | No | No | No | 41.7 | 44.8 | 58.1 | 51.5 | 7.4 | 15.1 | -11.3 | 23.7 |
| All market income, after-tax | Yes | No | Yes | No | 33.9 | 34.9 | 43.6 | 37.2 | 2.8 | 6.6 | -14.7 | 9.7 |
| Comprehensive income | Yes | Yes | Yes | Yes | 7.7 | 8.7 | 9.0 | 10.1 | 12.6 | 15.9 | 12.4 | 30.4 |
| *Top fifth/middle fifth* | | | | | | | | | | | | |
| Census money income | No | Yes | No | No | 2.6 | 2.9 | 3.2 | 3.4 | 12.9% | 15.6% | 4.6% | 30.5% |
| All market income, pre-tax | Yes | No | No | No | 2.8 | 3.3 | 3.6 | 4.0 | 16.2 | 19.8 | 9.8 | 39.3 |
| All market income, after-tax | Yes | No | Yes | No | 2.6 | 3.0 | 3.1 | 3.4 | 12.8 | 14.0 | 8.2 | 28.6 |
| Comprehensive income | Yes | Yes | Yes | Yes | 2.4 | 2.7 | 2.7 | 3.0 | 12.9 | 12.0 | 9.6 | 26.5 |

Source: Authors' analysis of U.S. Bureau of the Census data.

approach shown in Figure 1H. Here, we use Census alternative definitions to track the incomes of the highest fifth relative to both the lowest fifth and the middle fifth of families. The second panel reveals that income inequality between the top and the bottom grew by about the same amount between 1979 and 2000 using either the basic Census measure or the comprehensive measure. In fact, under the comprehensive measure, inequality grew as quickly in the 1995-2000 period (12.4%) as over the 1980s (12.6%). Interestingly, inequality diminished between 1995 and 2000 under both market income measures, due to the fact that the earnings of low-income households grew relatively quickly over this period while their government transfers (which are excluded from these definitions) declined sharply. We provide further analysis of this phenomenon in the examination of poverty in Chapter 5.

The gap between top- and middle-income households also rose at fairly consistent rates (from about 26% to 39%) across all income definitions between 1979 and 2000. In fact, looking at the ratios themselves reveals little variation among definitions, as they range from 2.4 to 4.0 over the years shown in the table.

In sum, these data provide no basis upon which to claim that the Census Bureau money income definition, used in the first section of this chapter, distorts the trend in income inequality.

The inequality measures in these alternative income definitions offer compelling evidence on the extent to which government transfers (and certain taxes as well) dampen inequality inherent in the pre-tax distribution of income. Note the large increase in the Gini coefficient and in the top/bottom ratios when moving from definition one, which includes cash transfers, to definition two, which represents market outcomes. Market forces have generated ever-increasing inequality over the past few decades, and the federal government has needed to increase its redistributive efforts in order to offset their effect. If, in measuring inequality, one downplays the growing inequality of pretax incomes in the 1990s because after-tax income inequality grew less (compare lines two and three of the middle panel, for example), then one must concede that increasing the progressivity of the federal tax system is a useful tool against inequality.

As noted above in the section on taxes, household income data from the Congressional Budget Office allow an examination of the growth of income of the top 1%, thus yielding insight into the extent of income concentration at the very top of the income scale. This is particularly germane to the latter 1990s, a time when the top income classes continued to pull away from the rest while the gap between middle- and low-income families did not expand. Recall also that the CBO data are adjusted for differences in household size and include more income sources than the Census data generally relied upon in this chapter so far. The disadvantage of these data are that they go only through 1997. However, we also include Internal Revenue Service data on the top 1% to take the analysis through 1999.

**Table 1.17** shows the average household income for the bottom, middle, and top fifth of households, with the top 5% of the top fifth broken out into the 96-99th percentile and the top 1%. According to these data, pretax income grew at a slightly faster annual rate for the top fifth in the 1990s (2.5% a year) relative to the 1980s (2.3%). Incomes in the bottom fifth fell a bit faster in the latter period, implying faster growth in the gap between the top and the bottom in the 1990s relative to the 1980s. This pattern is not evident after taxes, due to progressive tax changes implemented in the early 1990s. In terms of market outcomes (i.e., pretax income), however, the CBO data show that the pace of inequality, at least between the top of the bottom, did not slow through 1997.

As the CBO data do not go past 1997, we can only speculate about the trend in the more complete picture of inequality through the latter 1990s. As earlier tables showed (e.g., Table 1.9), low-income families made real gains in the last few years of the 1990s, which, all else equal, would tend to slow inequality's growth. However, all else was far from equal, particularly considering the sharp run-up in asset markets over this period, along with strong gains in compensation among the highest earners.

**Figure 1K** shows two measures of the progress of the highest-income households in the 1986-99 period (the available years for these data): the average adjusted gross income (AGI) of the top 1% (left axis), and the ratio of this average to that of the bottom 50% of federal income tax payers (right axis). These IRS data differ in many ways from what we've seen so far, but they are a reliable source of information on high-income households—in fact, CBO uses these data to get a better sense of developments among the wealthiest families (the data also include realized capital gains). Note also that the AGI for those in the bottom half of taxpayers will exclude the lowest-income families who face no federal tax liability The figure shows that the highest incomes were relatively flat in the early 1990s, but grew quickly, by 59%, from 1995 to 1999. Furthermore, the rising ratio of the average AGI of the top 1% to that of the bottom 50% after 1994 indicates that inequality expanded in the latter 1990s as AGI growth at the very top outpaced growth in the bottom half.

*Inequality as measured by consumption:* Some economists express doubts about analyses of income because the incomes of families fluctuate from year to year in response to special circumstances—a layoff, a one-time sale of an asset, and so on. As a result, a family's income may partially reflect transient events and not indicate its economic well-being over the long term. For example, a family

**TABLE 1.17** Household income growth, including top 1%, CBO data  (1997 dollars)

| Income group | 1979 | 1989 | 1997 | Annualized real growth 1979-89 | 1989-97 |
|---|---|---|---|---|---|
| **Pretax** | | | | | |
| Bottom fifth | $11,800 | $11,700 | $11,400 | -0.1% | -0.3% |
| Middle fifth | 41,400 | 42,700 | 45,100 | 0.3 | 0.7 |
| Top fifth | 109,500 | 138,000 | 167,500 | 2.3 | 2.5 |
| 96-99th percentile | 136,800 | 165,800 | 199,500 | 1.9 | 2.3 |
| Top 1% | 420,200 | 694,000 | 1,016,900 | 5.1 | 4.9 |
| **After tax** | | | | | |
| Bottom fifth | $10,900 | $10,800 | $10,800 | -0.1% | 0.0% |
| Middle fifth | 33,800 | 35,200 | 37,200 | 0.4 | 0.7 |
| Top fifth | 79,100 | 103,300 | 121,000 | 2.7 | 2.0 |
| 96-99th percentile | 98,200 | 123,100 | 143,800 | 2.3 | 2.0 |
| Top 1% | 263,700 | 498,300 | 677,900 | 6.6 | 3.9 |

Source: Congressional Budget Office.

**FIGURE 1K** Average real adjusted gross income, top 1% to bottom 50%, 1986-99

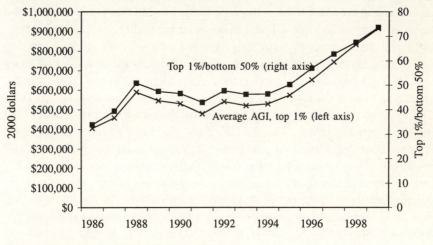

Source: Internal Revenue Service, Statistics on Income.

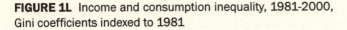

**FIGURE 1L** Income and consumption inequality, 1981-2000, Gini coefficients indexed to 1981

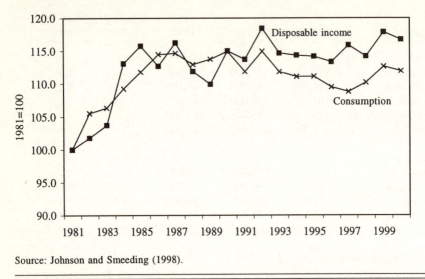

Source: Johnson and Smeeding (1998).

experiencing a bad year in terms of income may dip into its savings to continue consuming at the same level as during a better year. In this view, consumption levels of families provide a better measure of inequality, since families typically gear their consumption to their expected incomes over the long term.

**Figure 1L** shows the trend in the Gini coefficient for consumption along with the Gini ratio for disposable income (basically after-tax income) from the same data source: the Bureau of Labor Statistics' Consumer Expenditure (CE) Survey (note that these series are adjusted for differences in family size). The income inequality trends from the CPS data—the focus of most of this chapter—are considered more reliable in that they come from a larger sample and are based on a more detailed set of questions. Nevertheless, we include the CE income trend in the figure for comparative purposes (in fact, the income inequality trends from the two surveys are similar over the 1980s, while the CE data show less inequality growth over the 1990s). Both series in the figure are indexed to the starting year, 1981, to allow a comparison of their growth rates. (Note that the level of consumption inequality tends to be about 20% below that of income inequality in these data).

Both inequality measures increased over the 1980s by about 15%. Beginning in the early 1990s, disposable income inequality essentially flattened, while consumption inequality fell for a few years before beginning to climb again at the end of the decade. By the end of the series, in 2000, both measures of inequality were well above their 1981 levels. Thus, these data generally show that the growth of consumption inequality generally tracked that of income inequality over the past few decades.

## The role of mobility and demographics

*Does income mobility counteract the inequality problem?* Other critics accept the fact that inequality has grown over time but argue that the data reported so far, which are essentially snapshots of the income distribution at different points in time, miss the extent to which families move up and down the income ladder over the course of their lives (the cohort analysis in Table 1.6 is an exception). Essentially, this critique agrees that the distance from the basement to the penthouse has grown further over time, but it argues that a family that starts out in the basement has a better chance these days of making it to the top floor than it used to. In other words, these critics implicitly argue that an increase in income mobility has served to offset the increase in income inequality.

In fact, those who make the mobility argument fail to either articulate or substantiate this claim. Instead, they simply show evidence of economic mobility and leave it at that, as if mobility in and of itself should lessen the concern about increased inequality. But unless the rate of mobility is increasing relative to that of earlier decades, families are no more likely today to span the now-wider income gap. As we show below, there has been no such increase.

The economist Joseph Schumpeter derived a useful analogy to explain the concept of mobility, that of a hotel where the quality of rooms improves the higher the floor. If everyone simply ended up in the same room they started out in, society would be totally immobile, with the poor stuck in the basement and the rich ensconced in the penthouse. The reality, of course, is that some stay where they start while others move up and down.

How does this analogy help explain the interplay between increased inequality and income mobility? The fact that, as this chapter has demonstrated, the income gap between those at the top, middle, and bottom has expanded over time means that the quality of life for a resident of the basement is now worse relative to his neighbor in the penthouse than it was two decades ago.

The proponents of the mobility argument acknowledge this, but they say that this family won't always be in the basement. This is true, but unless their chance of making it to the higher floors has increased over time, the increase in inequality means that they are sure to experience more inequality over the course of their lives. The wider income gap means that the higher floors are further away, and chance of someone in the basement reaching them has not increased.

**TABLE 1.18** Income mobility, 1969-94

| 1969 income group | 1994 income group | | | | | |
| --- | --- | --- | --- | --- | --- | --- |
| | First fifth | Second fifth | Middle fifth | Fourth fifth | Top fifth | Total |
| First fifth | **41.0%** | 24.9% | 16.2% | 12.1% | 5.8% | 100.0% |
| Second fifth | 22.4 | **24.7** | 23.9 | 16.1 | 13.0 | 100.0 |
| Middle fifth | 16.9 | 21.0 | **23.5** | 22.8 | 15.9 | 100.0 |
| Fourth fifth | 11.3 | 18.5 | 19.7 | **24.2** | 26.3 | 100.0 |
| Top fifth | 9.5 | 10.6 | 16.6 | 24.5 | **38.8** | 100.0 |

Source: Unpublished tabulations of the PSID by Peter Gottschalk.

These mobility issues are best addressed with longitudinal data, or data that follow the same persons over time. Each person is assigned to an income fifth at the beginning and end of the relevant periods of observation based on his or her family's income. Different income cutoffs are used for each period, meaning that the 20th percentile upper limit in, for example, 1979 will be different than that of 1989. This approach to income mobility examines whether a family becomes better or worse off relative to other families, as opposed to better or worse off in terms of their actual incomes.

In particular, the analysis tracks how families are doing relative to others they started with at the beginning of the periods in the same age cohort and income class. If each family's income grew by the same amount (in percentage terms), there would be no change in mobility, i.e., no changes in the relative positions of families in the income distribution. If, however, a family that starts out in the bottom fifth experiences faster income growth than other low-income families, it may move into a higher fifth, i.e., this family will experience upward mobility.

**Table 1.18** presents a "transition matrix" for the period 1969-94. Going across each row in the table, the numbers reveal the percent of persons who either stayed in the same fifth or moved to a higher or lower one. For example, the first entry shows that 41.0% of persons in the bottom fifth in 1969 were also in the bottom fifth in 1994. At the other end of the income scale, 38.8% of those who started in the top fifth stayed there. The percent of "stayers" (those who did not move out of the fifth they started out in) are shown in bold.

Note that large transitions are uncommon. Only 5.8% of those who began the period in the first fifth ended up in the top fifth, while only 9.5% fell from the top fifth to the lowest. Those transitions that do occur are most likely to be a

**TABLE 1.19** Income mobility over the 1970s and 1980s*

| 1969 income group | 1979 income group | | | | | |
|---|---|---|---|---|---|---|
| | First fifth | Second fifth | Middle fifth | Fourth fifth | Top fifth | Total |
| First fifth | **61.5%** | 24.0% | 8.7% | 4.4% | 1.5% | 100.0% |
| Second fifth | 22.7 | **31.3** | 27.5 | 12.9 | 5.6 | 100.0 |
| Middle fifth | 9.6 | 22.5 | **29.6** | 26.1 | 12.2 | 100.0 |
| Fourth fifth | 3.3 | 17.3 | 22.4 | **31.6** | 25.4 | 100.0 |
| Top fifth | 2.9 | 5.0 | 11.9 | 25.1 | **55.2** | 100.0 |
| | 1989 income group | | | | | |
| First fifth | **61.0%** | 23.8% | 9.5% | 4.6% | 1.1% | 100.0% |
| Second fifth | 22.9 | **33.2** | 27.7 | 13.5 | 2.7 | 100.0 |
| Middle fifth | 8.3 | 25.2 | **29.5** | 25.7 | 11.4 | 100.0 |
| Fourth fifth | 4.6 | 13.0 | 23.0 | **33.2** | 26.2 | 100.0 |
| Top fifth | 2.7 | 4.9 | 10.8 | 22.8 | **58.8** | 100.0 |

* Unlike the previous table, this table averages family income over three years to "smooth out" temporary transitions.

Source: Unpublished tabulations of the PSID by Peter Gottschalk.

move up or down to the neighboring fifth. For example, among the middle three-fifths, slightly less than two-thirds of the transitions were to neighboring fifths.

Though Table 1.18 does not reveal a great deal of income mobility, the data do show that mobility exists and that families move up and down as their relative fortunes change. How does this fact comport with the historically large increases in inequality documented in this chapter? Has there been an increase in the rate of mobility that would serve to offset the rise in income inequality?

**Table 1.19** addresses this question. It presents two transition matrices, one for the 1970s and the other for the 1980s. (There are not yet enough years of longitudinal data available from this data source—the Panel Study of Income Dynamics—to measure the rate of income mobility over the 1990s.) These tables again show relative stability (the largest shares of persons are stayers, located along or close to the diagonal). For example, both 10-year periods reveal that about 85% of persons in families stayed in the first or second fifths. But more important in this context is the fact that mobility has not increased—the shares of both stayers and those who made transitions are similar in both periods. For example, 61.5% remained in the lowest fifth over the 1970s, and

**FIGURE 1M** Percent staying in same fifth in each pair of years, 1968-69 through 1990-91

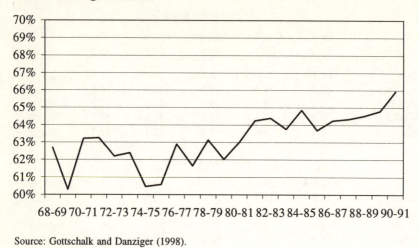

Source: Gottschalk and Danziger (1998).

61.0% remained there in the 1980s. The shares that remained in the middle were also very close (29.6% versus 29.5%), and only a slightly larger share remained in the top fifth in the 1980s. Thus, there is no evidence here of an increase in mobility to offset increased inequality.

In fact, as **Figure 1M** shows, the rate of mobility appears to have declined since the late 1960s. This figure uses the same longitudinal data source as above to plot the percent of persons who stayed in the same fifth, one year to the next. Thus, an upward trend suggests declining mobility rates, as persons are less likely over time to make the transition across income classes. For example, in 1969, 62.7% of persons ended up in the same quintile they started in one year earlier, in 1968. At the end of the period, between 1990 and 1991, 65.9% failed to move to either a lower or higher income group. The fact that the graph drifts upward implies that the rate of mobility, as measured by the probability of moving to a different income fifth in an adjacent year, has fallen.

*The impact of demographic changes on income*: It is often suggested that changes in the demographic composition of American families have been a major cause of the slow growth and rising inequality of income documented thus far, implying a lesser role for economic causes such as wage decline. While it is unquestionably the case that the increased share of economically vulnerable families has put both downward pressure on income growth and upward pressure on inequal-

**TABLE 1.20** Impact of demographic change on household income, 1969-2000

| Year | First fifth | Second fifth | Middle fifth | Fourth fifth | Top fifth | Average |
|---|---|---|---|---|---|---|
| 1969 | $7,991 | $21,553 | $34,381 | $48,100 | $82,655 | $38,936 |
| 1979 | 9,282 | 22,164 | 36,374 | 53,271 | 95,244 | 43,267 |
| 1989 | 9,707 | 23,413 | 38,789 | 58,718 | 115,446 | 49,214 |
| 2000 | 10,836 | 25,728 | 42,792 | 66,375 | 141,628 | 57,472 |
| **1969-79** | | | | | | |
| Actual change | 16.2% | 2.8% | 5.8% | 10.7% | 15.2% | 11.1% |
| *Change due to:* | | | | | | |
| Age | -1.1% | -1.6% | -1.7% | -1.8% | -2.0% | -1.8% |
| Education | 6.4 | 6.4 | 5.8 | 4.8 | 5.7 | 5.6 |
| Type of household | -16.7 | -12.2 | -8.9 | -6.0 | -4.1 | -6.8 |
| Race | -1.3 | -1.0 | -0.7 | -0.5 | -0.4 | -0.6 |
| Total demographic effect* | -9.2 | -7.2 | -5.1 | -2.5 | 1.1 | -2.2 |
| Income change, holding demographics constant | 25.4% | 10.0% | 10.9% | 13.2% | 14.1% | 13.3% |
| **1979-89** | | | | | | |
| Actual change | 4.6% | 5.6% | 6.6% | 10.2% | 21.2% | 13.7% |
| *Change due to:* | | | | | | |
| Age | 1.4% | 0.7% | 0.6% | 0.5% | -0.1% | 0.3% |
| Education | 5.1 | 5.6 | 4.9 | 4.6 | 5.4 | 5.1 |
| Type of household | -5.8 | -5.2 | -4.0 | -3.1 | -2.3 | -3.3 |
| Race | -1.5 | -1.2 | -0.9 | -0.5 | -0.4 | -0.6 |
| Total demographic effect* | -0.9 | 0.0 | 0.7 | 1.4 | 3.4 | 1.9 |
| Income change, holding demographics constant | 5.5% | 5.7% | 6.0% | 8.9% | 17.9% | 11.9% |
| **1989-2000** | | | | | | |
| Actual change | 11.6% | 9.9% | 10.3% | 13.0% | 22.7% | 16.8% |
| *Change due to:* | | | | | | |
| Age | 0.2% | 0.7% | 0.9% | 1.1% | 1.4% | 1.1% |
| Education | 6.4 | 6.6 | 6.0 | 5.3 | 5.4 | 5.6 |
| Type of household | -3.9 | -3.8 | -3.3 | -2.6 | -2.2 | -2.7 |
| Race | -1.3 | -0.9 | -0.7 | -0.6 | -0.6 | -0.7 |
| Total demographic effect* | 1.1 | 2.3 | 2.4 | 3.0 | 4.5 | 3.5 |
| Income change, holding demographics constant | 10.5% | 7.6% | 7.9% | 10.1% | 18.1% | 13.3% |

* Components do not sum to the aggregate effect due to interactions between the groups (see table note).

Source: Authors' analysis of March CPS data.

ity growth, this process is a dynamic one that has not been constant over time. In addition, some demographic factors, such as the increase in educational attainment, have led to increased family income. It is important, then, to look at the net effect of the different types of demographic shifts in various time periods.

**Table 1.20** shows the impact of age, education, family type, and race on household income (all refer to the head of the household; households, unlike families, include single persons). The challenge of this analysis is to quantify the impact of changes in these factors on income trends over time. For example, of the list of factors examined here, the two with the largest impact are family type and education level. Over time, as seen earlier in the bottom section of Table 1.7, there has been a demographic shift toward family types more likely to have low incomes, such as single-parent families or individuals living alone. A countervailing trend, however, has been the higher education levels of heads of households, a demographic trend that would lead to higher income levels over time.

Which of these two factors—educational upgrading or the shift to lower-income family types—has had a larger impact, and how has the impact varied by income level? (Race and age, while important, have played a secondary role in income trends.) Contrary to the conventional wisdom, which has typically assigned the primary role to changes in family type, there is clear evidence that educational upgrading has more than compensated for this effect. Most importantly, on net, during the 1979-2000 period, when income inequality was increasing most quickly, these demographic factors, including education, led to increasing, not falling, average household incomes. Thus, explanations that depend on demographic change to explain income decline should be discounted.

The numbers in Table 1.20 show the percent changes in real household income from 1969 to 2000, along with the changes due to specific demographic factors. For example, the first section shows that, among families in the lowest fifth by income, the shift to lower-income family types led to a 16.7% decline in income during 1969-79. Note that this effect declines further up the income scale; the negative effect of family type in the top fifth was 4.1% over this period. As expected, however, educational upgrading lifted incomes between 4.8% and 6.4%. The penultimate row of the section, which sums the impact of each demographic factor, shows that, on net, the impact of demographic change was negative for all but the highest income group over the 1970s (implying that demographic change led to higher inequality over this period).

Note, however, that the average incomes of all but the second fifth grew significantly from 1969 to 1979 (top row), and that the fastest growth was among the lowest-income households. This means that, despite the downward pressure of the negative demographic factors (primarily family type), incomes within each demographic group grew enough to offset these losses. The last row of each panel, which shows the percent of income growth within each demographic group, by income fifth, quantifies this point. These changes are net of demographic effects and thus represent the impact of economic changes such as real wage trends on household incomes.

During the 1970s, household incomes within demographic groups grew strongly, and were also equalizing in nature. Net of demographic change, the income of the bottom fifth of households grew 25.4%, while that of the top fifth grew 14.1%. Thus, over the period when demographic pressure was exerting its strongest negative effects, favorable economic growth among low-income households was great enough to more than offset the unfavorable demographic trends. (Chapter 5 finds similar dynamics regarding the impact of demographic change on poverty rates over this period.)

Over the 1980s, the impact of family type, though still negative, was less a factor than over the 1970s for each income group, particularly for the least well-off. For example, while shifts in family structure lowered the average income of the bottom fifth by 16.7% over the 1970s, continuing shifts lowered that group's average income by 5.8% in the 1980s. For the middle fifth, the comparable changes were –8.9% in the 1970s and –4.0% in the 1980s. Conversely, the positive impact of educational upgrading fell only slightly, from 6.4% in the 1970s for the bottom fifth to 5.1% in the 1980s, with similarly small declines for each income group.

Thus, in the 1980s, the net impact of demographics was notably smaller than that of the previous period, with incomes for the bottom lowered by 0.9% and raised at the top by 3.4%. Yet, this was the decade when income inequality grew most quickly. Family structure shifts, in particular, were much more disequalizing in the 1970s than in the 1980s, but income inequality expanded only slightly over the earlier decade. Clearly, many other factors are at play, and the inequality surge in the 1980s cannot be fully or even largely attributed to changes in family structure.

Unlike the prior period, however, income growth net of demographic change (i.e., within demographic groups) slowed considerably for all but the wealthiest households. For example, the last row of the middle section shows that, holding demographics constant, incomes grew by 5.5% for the bottom fifth, 6.0% for the middle fifth, and 17.9% for those at the top of the income scale. Thus, despite the smaller negative impact of changes in family type over the 1980s, economic growth shifted in such a way as to dampen the growth of income for low-income households within each demographic category.

Over the most recent period, 1989-2000, the impact of changes in family type has continued to diminish. In this period, in fact, net changes in demographics were actually *positive* for each group, though only marginally so at the bottom of the income scale. In the bottom quintile, the negative impacts of family type and race were essentially offset by the positive impact of educa-

**FIGURE 1N** Impact of demographic change on household income, by fifth, 1969-2000

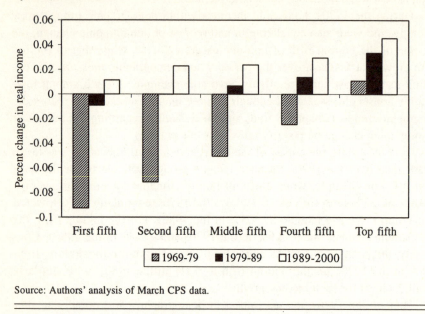

Source: Authors' analysis of March CPS data.

tion. Within-group (non-demographic) factors (bottom row), such as the wage increases that prevailed in the latter part of the period, led to real average income gains for all households, with larger gains at the bottom than in the middle. Accordingly, both net demographic and within-group trends were reinforcing in the 1990s.

**Figure 1N** shows the impact of demographic change, including educational upgrading, by fifth for each time period cited in the table. While such changes tended to lead to greater inequality in each decade, their impact diminished as time progressed. This trend stands in direct contrast to the actual time path of income inequality, which became progressively more unequal over time, particularly over the 1980s relative to the 1970s. The bars in Figure 1N also reveal that demographic change was, on net, a positive contributor to income growth over time, as the impact of educational upgrading outpaced that of the shift to lower-income family types.

The message from these data is that the impact of changing demographics, including education, cannot account for the scope of income problems that developed over the 1980s and 1990s.

## Growth in inequality narrows pathways to prosperity

Another dimension of income growth is the proportion of the population that has low, middle, and high incomes. There are two factors that determine the distribution of the population at various income levels—the rate of growth of average income and changes in income equality. As long as average income growth is faster than inflation, and income inequality does not increase, there will be a greater proportion of the population at higher income levels over time. For example, the share of families with incomes under $25,000 (adjusted for inflation) will fall under this scenario. However, if inequality grows such that the low-income population fails to receive much of the income growth and the high-income population obtains an unusually large proportion, then a rise in average income is unlikely to translate into a general upward movement of the population to higher income levels. The following table reveals that, as expected, economic growth has led to a larger share of families with higher incomes, both in absolute and relative terms. However, the post-1979 growth of inequality has mitigated that progress, meaning that fewer families reside in the middle class than would have been the case had inequality grown less.

The first section of **Table 1.21** show the proportion of families with low, low-middle ($25,000-50,000), high-middle ($50,000-100,000), and high incomes in 1969, 1979, 1989, 1995, and 2000. Over the 1969-79 period, when income inequality grew relatively little, average income growth lifted significant proportions of families from low and low-middle incomes to the two highest categories. Over this period, there was a 10.2 percentage-point shift out of the bottom two income categories (this should exactly equal the shift to the upper two categories, but, due to rounding, this is not the case). Over the 1980s, however, the share of families moving out of the lower two categories were smaller (4.7 percentage points compared to 10.2), as was the share moving into the high-middle group, which hovered around 34% over the 1979 to 1995 period. In the latter 1990s, growth was more broadly shared, as the shift out of the lower two income categories was considerably larger than in the 1980s and first half of the 1990s. Note, for example, that the lowest income share actually grew slightly between 1989 and 1995 before falling to a historic low in 2000.

Meanwhile, the share of families with incomes over $100,000 grew consistently, from 3.9% in 1979 to 17.0% in 2000. This increase in the share of higher-income households is, of course, a positive development and one that should be expected to prevail in a growing economy. But the fact that the shift from low/low-middle to high/high-middle slowed so dramatically over the last 20

**TABLE 1.21** Distribution of families and persons by income level, 1969-2000

| | 1969 | 1979 | 1989 | 1995 | 2000 | Percentage-point change | | | |
| --- | --- | --- | --- | --- | --- | --- | --- | --- | --- |
| | | | | | | 1969-79 | 1979-89 | 1989-2000 | 1995-2000 |
| **Family incomes** | | | | | | | | | |
| Under $25,000 | 27.4% | 25.0% | 24.1% | 24.8% | 21.1% | -2.4 | -0.9 | -3.0 | -3.7 |
| $25,000 to $50,000 | 42.1 | 34.3 | 30.5 | 30.1 | 27.9 | -7.8 | -3.8 | -2.6 | -2.2 |
| $50,000 to $100,000 | 26.6 | 33.6 | 33.7 | 32.8 | 34.1 | 7.0 | 0.1 | 0.4 | 1.3 |
| Over $100,000 | 3.9 | 7.0 | 11.7 | 12.2 | 17.0 | 3.1 | 4.7 | 5.3 | 4.8 |
| Total | 100.0 | 100.0 | 100.0 | 100.0 | 100.0 | | | | |
| **Persons** (income relative to the median) | | | | | | | | | |
| Less than 50% of median | 18.0% | 20.1% | 22.1% | 22.2% | 22.0% | 2.1 | 2.0 | -0.1 | -0.2 |
| 50-200% of median | 71.2 | 68.0 | 63.2 | 61.9 | 61.7 | -3.2 | -4.8 | -1.5 | -0.2 |
| Over 200% of median | 10.8 | 11.9 | 14.7 | 15.9 | 16.3 | 1.1 | 2.8 | 1.6 | 0.4 |
| Total | 100.0 | 100.0 | 100.0 | 100.0 | 100.0 | | | | |

Source: Authors' analysis of March CPS data.

years, while the share in the lowest category has remained relatively constant, means that the upward path to prosperity has been made considerably steeper by the growth in inequality.

The second section of Table 1.21 examines the incomes of individuals—single and in families—according to the per capita incomes of their families (size-adjusted), with single persons given their individual incomes. In this analysis, the income of persons is measured relative to the median. Thus, unlike the above sections, which fix the income brackets in real dollar terms, the brackets for the income categories in this section move with the median income. This approach provides more important insights into inequality, because it measures the relative, as opposed to the absolute, changes in family incomes. Thus, in the first section, the absolute income level of a low-income family may grow such that it crosses from the $25,000 category into the middle group. But if its income grows more slowly than that of the median, the family will still fall behind relative to more affluent families. The bottom panel shows evidence of precisely this pattern.

From 1979 forward, more than one-fifth of the population lived in households with income below half of the median income. Over both the 1970s and 1980s, this share grew by about two percentage points, and remained at that level in 2000. Later, in Chapter 5, we show that the poverty rate, an absolute income measure, fell significantly between 1995 and 2000 (this could also be deduced from the decline in the low-income family share over this period, shown in the top section of the table). The difference between falling poverty rates and a relatively constant share of families at half the median can be explained by increased income inequality. The poor may have made absolute gains over this period, as their real incomes increased somewhat, but they gained almost no ground relative to families with higher levels of income.

Meanwhile, the share at the top of the income distribution—above 200% of the median—grew fairly consistently over this period (though, thanks to relatively strong median income growth in the latter 1990s, less so in the 1990s than over the 1980s). Since these shares must sum to 100 in each year, and thus the changes in each of the last four columns must sum to zero, this pattern of increased shares on either side of the middle means a declining share in middle-income families (those with incomes from half to twice the median), and this share fell from 71.2% in 1979 to 61.7% in 2000. Thus, by this measure, America's broad middle class has been shrinking, with shares shifting upward and downward.

**TABLE 1.22** Sources of household income by income type, 1999

| Income group | Share of each group's income | | | | Share of income type by group | | | |
| --- | --- | --- | --- | --- | --- | --- | --- | --- |
| | Wage and salary | Capital* | Government transfer and other | Total | Wage and salary | Capital* | Government transfer and other | Total |
| **Bottom four-fifths** | 76.5% | 10.0% | 13.5% | 100.0% | 45.7% | 19.7% | 83.6% | 42.5% |
| First | 56.6 | 5.6 | 37.8 | 100.0 | 2.7 | 0.9 | 18.3 | 3.3 |
| Second | 71.7 | 8.0 | 20.3 | 100.0 | 7.4 | 2.7 | 21.7 | 7.3 |
| Middle | 76.1 | 10.9 | 13.0 | 100.0 | 12.9 | 6.1 | 23.0 | 12.1 |
| Fourth | 81.8 | 11.0 | 7.2 | 100.0 | 22.7 | 10.0 | 20.6 | 19.8 |
| **Top fifth** | 67.5% | 30.5% | 2.1% | 100.0% | 54.3% | 80.9% | 16.7% | 57.6% |
| 81-90% | 82.2 | 13.5 | 4.3 | 100.0 | 17.2 | 9.3 | 9.2 | 15.0 |
| 91-95% | 81.9 | 15.5 | 2.6 | 100.0 | 12.0 | 7.5 | 3.9 | 10.5 |
| 96-99% | 73.6 | 24.8 | 1.6 | 100.0 | 14.7 | 16.3 | 3.2 | 14.3 |
| Top 1% | 41.6 | 58.2 | 0.2 | 100.0 | 10.4 | 47.8 | 0.4 | 17.8 |
| **All** | 71.4% | 21.7% | 6.9% | 100.0% | 100.0% | 100.0% | 100.0% | 100.0% |

* Includes rent, dividends, interest income, and realized capital gains.

Source: Institute on Economic and Tax Policy (ITEP).

## Expanding capital incomes

The fortunes of individual families depend heavily on their reliance upon the particular sources of their incomes: labor income, capital income, or government assistance. For instance, one significant reason for the unequal growth in family incomes since 1979 was an increase in the share of capital income (such as rent, dividends, interest payments, and capital gains) and a smaller share earned as wages and salaries. Since most families receive little or no capital income, this shift generated greater income inequality.

**Table 1.22** presents data showing estimates of the sources of income for families in each income group in 1999. These data are from a different source than that used for the analysis of income trends above, but they are comparable to the CBO data used to analyze tax trends. The top fifth received 30.5% of its income from financial assets (capital). The top 1% received 58.2% of its income from capital assets, and the other income groups in the upper 10% received from 13.5% to 24.8% of their income from capital. In contrast, the bottom 80% of families relied on capital for 11.0% or less of their income in 1999. Turning to the share of each type of income going to different income groups,

**TABLE 1.23** Shares of market-based personal income by income type, 1959-2000

| Income type | Shares of income | | | | |
| --- | --- | --- | --- | --- | --- |
| | 1959 | 1973 | 1979 | 1989 | 2000* |
| **Total capital income** | 13.5% | 14.5% | 16.4% | 21.9% | 20.0% |
| Rent | 4.0 | 2.2 | 1.3 | 1.0 | 1.9 |
| Dividends | 3.4 | 2.9 | 3.0 | 3.6 | 5.0 |
| Interest | 6.1 | 9.4 | 12.2 | 17.3 | 13.2 |
| **Total labor income** | 72.7% | 74.4% | 74.0% | 69.6% | 70.6% |
| Wages and salaries | 69.1 | 68.3 | 65.5 | 61.1 | 63.6 |
| Fringe benefits | 3.6 | 6.1 | 8.5 | 8.5 | 7.0 |
| **Proprietor's income**** | 13.8% | 11.1% | 9.6% | 8.5% | 9.4% |
| **Total market-based personal income ***** | 100.0% | 100.0% | 100.0% | 100.0% | 100.0% |
| **Realized capital gains** | n.a. | 3.5% | 3.8% | 3.6% | 6.7% |

\*    Capital gains for 2000 are estimated based on CBO data.
\*\*   Business and farm owners' income.
\*\*\*  Total of listed income types.
Source: Authors' analysis of NIPA and IRS data.

the top fifth received 80.9% of all capital income, with nearly half (47.8%) accruing to the top 1%. Clearly, then, a fast growth of capital income will disproportionately benefit the best-off income groups.

Those with less access to capital income depend either on wages (the broad middle) or on government transfers (the bottom) as their primary source of income. As a result, any cutback in government cash assistance primarily affects the income prospects of the lowest 40% of the population by income, but particularly the bottom fifth. For instance, roughly 40% of the income of families in the bottom fifth is drawn from government cash assistance programs (e.g., welfare benefits, unemployment insurance, Social Security, Supplemental Security Income) or other income (pensions, alimony). The income prospects of families in the 20th to 99th percentiles, on the other hand, depend primarily on their wages and salaries (which make up at least 70% of their income). Thus, changes in the level and distribution of wages (see Chapter 2) are key to understanding changes in the incomes of the broad middle class.

The shift in the composition of personal income toward greater capital income is shown in **Table 1.23**. Over the 1979-89 period, capital income's share of market-based income (personal income less government transfers) shifted sharply upward, from 16.4% to 21.9%, as interest income expanded. This shift toward capital income was slightly reversed by 2000 as interest rates and, therefore, interest income fell. However, dividend income had expanded by 2000, partially offsetting the decline in interest income. Unfortunately, these data (drawn from the GDP accounts) do not capture realized capital gains as a source of income, and therefore provide only a partial picture of income trends. Adding realized capital gains to the analysis (with data drawn from the Internal Revenue Service) does not affect any conclusions about the 1970s or 1980s, as capital gains were comparably important in 1973, 1979, and in 1989. However, the share of income from capital gains grew to 7.3% of income in 1998-99 (the latest data available), and is estimated to have been 6.7% in 2000, significantly higher than 1989's 3.6% share. Thus capital income, inclusive of realized capital gains, was clearly a larger share of income in recent years than in the 1980s or 1990s, even with the large drop in interest income. Correspondingly, a smaller share of income was paid out to wages and benefits, with the compensation share falling from 74.0% in 1979 to 70.6% in 2000 (not counting any impact of capital gains).

This shift away from labor income and toward capital income is unique in the postwar period and is partly responsible for the ongoing growth of inequality since 1979. Since the rich are the primary owners of income-producing property, the fact that the assets they own have commanded an increasing share of total income automatically leads to income growth that is concentrated at the top.

It is difficult to interpret changes in proprietor's income (presented in Table 1.23) because it is a mixture of both labor and capital income. That is, the income that an owner of a business (or farmer) receives results from his or her work effort (labor income) and his or her ownership (capital income) of the business or farm. To the extent that the shrinkage of proprietor's income results from a shift of people out of the proprietary sector (e.g., leaving farming) and into wage and salary employment, there will be a corresponding increase in labor's share of income (e.g., as farm income is replaced by wage income). This shift out of proprietor's income thus helps to explain a rising labor share in some periods, such as from 1959 to 1973. However, there has not been a dramatic shift in proprietor's income over the last few decades (roughly equivalent in 1979 and 2000), so it has not been a factor that has shifted the income distribution during that time.

From the point of view of national income (incomes generated by the corporate, proprietor, and government sectors), one can also discern a clear shift away from labor income toward capital income **(Table 1.24)**. For instance, labor's share of national income fell from 73.5% in 1979 to 72.1% in 1989 and then fell further to 71.6 % in 2000. A closer look at the underlying data, however, suggests an even more significant shift away from labor income.

**TABLE 1.24** Shares of income by type and sector, 1959-2000

| Sector | Shares of domestic national income | | | | | |
|---|---|---|---|---|---|---|
| | 1959 | 1969 | 1973 | 1979 | 1989 | 2000 |
| **National income all sectors** | | | | | | |
| Labor | 68.8% | 72.5% | 72.8% | 73.5% | 72.1% | 71.6% |
| Capital | 18.6 | 17.6 | 16.9 | 17.5 | 19.6 | 19.5 |
| Proprietor's profit | 12.7 | 9.9 | 10.3 | 9.0 | 8.3 | 8.9 |
| Total | 100.0 | 100.0 | 100.0 | 100.0 | 100.0 | 100.0 |
| **Corporate and business sector** | | | | | | |
| Labor | 44.5% | 47.9% | 48.3% | 50.4% | 48.4% | 48.9% |
| Capital | 18.3 | 17.0 | 15.9 | 16.1 | 17.4 | 18.4 |
| Total | 62.7 | 64.9 | 64.1 | 66.5 | 65.8 | 67.2 |
| **Proprietor's sector** | | | | | | |
| Labor | 9.1% | 6.0% | 5.2% | 4.7% | 4.3% | 4.7% |
| Capital | 0.3 | 0.6 | 1.0 | 1.4 | 2.2 | 1.1 |
| Proprietor's profit | 12.7 | 9.9 | 10.3 | 9.0 | 8.3 | 8.9 |
| Total | 22.0 | 16.6 | 16.6 | 15.1 | 14.8 | 14.7 |
| **Government/ nonprofit sector** | | | | | | |
| Labor | 15.2% | 18.6% | 19.3% | 18.4% | 19.4% | 18.0% |
| Capital | 0.0 | 0.0 | 0.0 | 0.0 | 0.0 | 0.0 |
| Total | 15.2 | 18.6 | 19.3 | 18.4 | 19.4 | 18.0 |
| *Addendum:* **Shares of corporate sector income\*** | | | | | | |
| Labor | 78.1% | 80.3% | 81.8% | 82.3% | 81.8% | 80.5% |
| Capital | 21.9 | 19.7 | 18.2 | 17.7 | 18.2 | 19.5 |
| Total | 100.0 | 100.0 | 100.0 | 100.0 | 100.0 | 100.0 |

\* Does not include sole proprietorships, partnerships, and other private non-corporate business. The corporate sector, which includes both financial and non-financial corporations, accounted for 60% of national income in 2000.

Source: Authors' analysis of NIPA data.

First, labor's share of national income rose steadily from 1959 to 1979. One reason for the expanding share of labor income was the steady expansion of the government/nonprofit sector. When the government/nonprofit sector grows, there is a tendency for labor's share of income to grow because this sector generates *only* labor income and no capital income. For example, Table 1.24 shows that the growth of the government/nonprofit sector, from 18.4% to 19.4% of national income between 1979 and 1989, necessarily added 1.0 percentage points to labor's share of national income (other things remaining equal). On the other hand, the shrinkage of the government/nonprofit sector over the 1989-2000 period led to a smaller labor share of income. Thus, the growth of the government sector over the 1980s led to an understatement of the decline of labor's share in that decade; in the 1990s, the decline in the government/nonprofit sector had the opposite effect. The decline in labor's share of national income from 1979 to 2000, a 1.9 percentage-point decline, is not affected by any change in the size of the government/nonprofit sector, which was about as big in 2000 as in 1979.

Labor's share of national income also grows as the proprietary sector (farm and non-farm unincorporated businesses) shrinks, as it did from 1959 to 1979, because labor's share of income in that sector is relatively low (about one-third in 1979). When resources shift from a sector with a low labor share of income, such as the proprietor's sector, to sectors with a higher labor share (all of the other sectors), the share of labor income in the economy necessarily rises. The changing composition of income across organizational sectors (expanding government, shrinking proprietorships) is important to examine when studying particular decades. Changes in the proprietor's sector, however, have not materially affected the aggregate labor share over the last few decades.

The clearest way to examine the changes in income shares is to focus on the corporate sector, which accounted for 60% of national income in 2000. Such an analysis is useful because it is not muddied by income shifts among sectors (such as expanding or shrinking government or proprietors' sectors) or the difficulty in defining "proprietor's" income as either labor or capital income. The division of incomes in the corporate sector is shown in the bottom section of Table 1.24 and in **Figure 10.** Labor's share fell from 82.3% in 1979 to 81.8% in 1989 and then to 80.5% in 2000. These data suggest that there has been a strong shift away from labor income in the private corporate sector.

How important is the shift in the shares of labor and capital income? Labor's share in the corporate sector in the late 1990s (79.7%) was 2.6 percentage points below what prevailed in the 1974-89 period. It would require average hourly compensation to be 3.3% greater (82.3 divided by 79.7, less 1) to return to the previously higher labor share. Similarly, the shift of income from labor to capital lowered compensation growth by 1.6% over the 1989-2000 period. These calculations illustrate that the shift toward greater capital income shares has had non-trivial implications for wage and compensation growth.

An examination of labor and capital income shares, however, cannot fully determine whether there has been a redistribution of income from labor to capital, or vice versa. This type of analysis assumes that if labor and capital shares

**FIGURE 10** Income shares in the corporate sector, 1947-2000

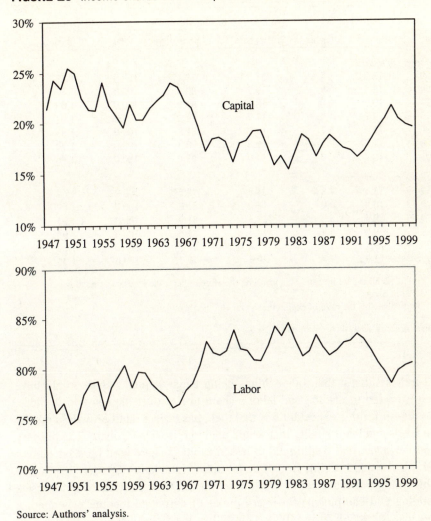

Source: Authors' analysis.

remain constant then there has been no redistribution. Such an analysis is too simple for several reasons. First, in contrast to most topics in economics, such an analysis makes no comparison of actual outcomes relative to what one might have expected to happen given a model of what drives labor and capital income shares. Accomplishing this requires looking at the current period relative to earlier periods and examining variables that affect income shares. Sev-

**TABLE 1.25** Corporate sector profit rates and shares, 1959-2001

| Year | Profit rates* Pre-tax | After-tax | Income shares Profit share** | Labor share | Total | Capital-output ratio |
|------|------|------|------|------|------|------|
| *Business cycle peaks* | | | | | | |
| 1959 | 12.0% | 6.4% | 21.9% | 78.1% | 100.0% | 1.83 |
| 1969 | 12.5 | 6.8 | 19.7 | 80.3 | 100.0 | 1.57 |
| 1973 | 10.9 | 6.0 | 18.2 | 81.8 | 100.0 | 1.67 |
| 1979 | 9.2 | 4.9 | 17.7 | 82.3 | 100.0 | 1.93 |
| 1989 | 10.0 | 5.7 | 18.2 | 81.8 | 100.0 | 1.83 |
| 2000 | 11.5 | 7.3 | 19.5 | 80.5 | 100.0 | 1.70 |
| 2001 | 10.3 | 6.7 | 17.0 | 83.0 | 100.0 | 1.66 |
| *Business cycle averages* | | | | | | |
| 1959-69 | 13.4% | 7.8% | 21.8% | 78.2% | 100.0% | 1.64 |
| 1970-73 | 10.8 | 6.0 | 18.2 | 81.8 | 100.0 | 1.69 |
| 1974-79 | 9.5 | 5.2 | 18.1 | 81.9 | 100.0 | 1.91 |
| 1980-89 | 9.0 | 5.4 | 17.4 | 82.6 | 100.0 | 1.95 |
| 1989-95 | 9.7 | 6.0 | 17.8 | 82.2 | 100.0 | 1.82 |
| 1996-2000 | 11.8 | 7.7 | 20.3 | 79.7 | 100.0 | 1.73 |

\* "Profit" is all capital income. This measure, therefore, reflects the returns to capital per dollar of assets.

\*\* "Profit share" is the ratio of capital income to all corporate income.

Source: Authors' analysis of NIPA and BEA data.

eral trends suggest that, other things being equal, capital's share might have been expected to decline and labor's share to rise over the last two decades. One reason for this expectation is that there has been a rapid growth in education levels and labor quality that would tend to raise labor's share. The primary trend, however, that would tend to lessen capital's share (and increase labor's share) is the rapid decline in the capital-output ratio since the early 1980s (see **Table 1.25**). For instance, in 1979 there was $1.93 of corporate capital assets (building and equipment) for every dollar of corporate income generated, a ratio that fell to $1.70 by 2000. This fall in the ratio of the capital stock to private-sector output implies that capital's role in production has lessened, suggesting that capital's income share might have been expected to fall in tandem.

Rather than fall, the share of capital income has risen, due to the rapid growth in the return to capital, before- and after-tax, starting in the late 1980s and continuing steadily through 1999 (Table 1.25 and **Figure 1P**). That is, the amount of before-tax profit received per dollar of assets (i.e., the capital stock) has grown to its highest levels since the mid-1960s, while the after-tax return on capital is also at historically high levels: since 1929, the only years of comparably high

## RISING PROFIT RATES, CONSTANT PROFIT SHARE

There has been some confusion as to the difference between a rise in the *profit rate*, or return to capital (which has risen dramatically in the last 15 years), and a rise in *capital's share of income*, which has grown less. The following exercise is designed to show how these two rates differ and how each can rise or fall at its own pace.

Income is the sum of the returns to capital and labor. It can be expressed in the following equation:

$$(K * r) + (W * L) = Y$$

where K is the capital stock, r is the rate of return on capital (the profit rate), W is the average hourly wage, L is the number of labor hours, and Y is income.

Capital's share of income can be calculated by dividing capital income, K * r, by total income, Y. If the capital share remains constant, then the quantity (K * r)/Y doesn't change (nor does the labor share, (W * L)/Y). Capital's share, (K * r)/Y, can also be written as (K/Y) * r, where the quantity K/Y is equal to the ratio of the capital stock to total income. If K/Y falls, as it has over the last 10 years, then r can rise a great deal, even if capital's share remains constant.

For example, if K = $2,000, r = .05, and Y = $1,000, then the capital share of income would be 10%:

$$(K * r)/Y = (\$2,000 * .05)/\$1,000 = \$100/\$1,000 = .10$$

If the capital stock fell to $1,000 (so that K′ = $1,000), the profit rate rose to 10% (so that r′ = .10), and income remained unchanged (Y′ = $1,000), the capital share would still be 10%:

$$(K' * r')/Y' = (\$1,000 * .10)/\$1,000 = \$100/\$1,000 = .10$$

In this example, the profit rate doubles, but the capital share of income remains the same because the capital stock has fallen 50%.

Over the last 15 years, the fall in the capital-output ratio has muted the rise in capital's share of income. From 1979 to 1997 the capital-output ratio fell 25% (from 2.23 to 1.68) while the "profit rate," or return to capital, rose from 6.4% to 10.4% (a 62.5% rise). The combined effect of these two trends was to raise capital's income share from 17.4% to 21.6%.

after-tax returns on capital were the booming years of the mid-1960s and the years at the end of World War II. The relationship between the return to capital and capital's share of income is illustrated in the accompanying box.

This growth in profitability has left less room for wage growth, or it might be considered the consequence of businesses successfully being able to restrain (or impose) slow wage growth as sales and profits grew in recent years, even in years of low unemployment. If the pre-tax return to capital in the 1996-2000 period (11.8%) had been at the average of the earlier period (1974-95), or 9.3%, then hourly compensation would have been 5.3% higher in the corpo-

**FIGURE 1P** Pre- and post-tax return to capital, 1947-2001

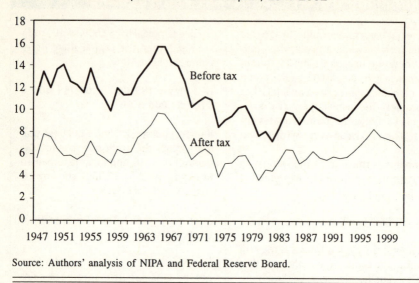

Source: Authors' analysis of NIPA and Federal Reserve Board.

rate sector. This is equivalent to an annual transfer of $205 billion dollars from labor to capital (measured for 2000), a large loss, comparable or greater in size to the loss of wages for the typical worker due to factors such as the shift to services, globalization, the drop in union representation, or any of the other prominent causes of growing wage inequality discussed in Chapter 2.

## The impact of low unemployment on family income growth

The sustained recovery of the 1990s, accompanied by fast productivity growth and low unemployment rates, were key to generating income gains in the latter part of the decade. This section broadly examines the relationship between low unemployment, income growth, and the impact of the length of the recovery on the growth in family income.

**Figure 1Q** examines the pattern of changes in unemployment and changes in the rate of real family income growth at different income levels during recent recessions and recoveries. Each set of bars represents the percentage-point change in unemployment and the percent change in real family income for low- (20th percentile), median-, and high-income (95th percentile) families (these are the same data used in Table 1.9).

In the recession of the early 1980s, unemployment increased by four per-

**FIGURE 1Q** Changes in unemployment and income during recent recessions and recoveries

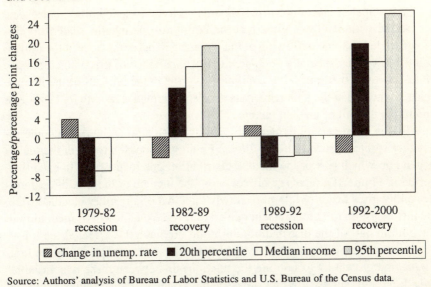

Source: Authors' analysis of Bureau of Labor Statistics and U.S. Bureau of the Census data.

centage points, and the incomes of low- and middle-income families fell by about 10% and 7%, respectively. The income of the wealthiest families was unchanged. Over the ensuing recovery of the 1980s, unemployment fell 4.4 points, from 9.7% to 5.3%, and incomes grew at each percentile shown—but at successively higher rates, leading to the growth of income inequality over this period. The milder 1990s recession saw income losses at each percentile, with larger losses again at the low end.

During the 1990s recovery, unemployment fell slightly *less* than in the much more sluggish 1980s recovery (3.5 points vs. 4.4). Yet income at the 20th percentile bounced back impressively, growing almost 20% in eight years, about 5% more than median incomes. This period of solid real growth—and most of the low-income growth occurred after 1995, when unemployment was falling to 30-year lows—translated into growth of $3,830 (in 2000 dollars) between 1992 and 2000. Growth over the 1982-89 period was about half that, at $1,990 (also in 2000 dollars).

An important difference between the two periods was the relative *levels* of unemployment: unemployment may not have fallen as much in the last recovery as over the 1980s, but it fell to—and stayed at—a lower level. In 1989, unemployment was 5.3%; in 2000, it was 4.0%. More important than the 3.5-point decline in the 1990s recovery was the movement to a sustained full-employment economy, which created enough pressure in the low-wage labor market to generate the first real advances in living standards for low-income families in decades.

Along with solid real growth at the bottom of the income scale, full employment led to some narrowing of the income gap between those at the middle and the low end, especially compared to the experience of the 1980s recovery. Note, however, that inequality continued to grow in the top half of the income scale, as income at the 95th percentile accelerated relative to both its 1980s rate and to the growth of median income.

This is an important dynamic missed by those who argue that income inequality stopped growing in the 1990s. Findings about the trend in inequality depend on which part of the income distribution one focuses on. In each time period in Figure 1Q, recovery or recession, the income of the wealthiest families either grew faster or fell more slowly than that of any other income group. By this measure, full employment helped to reverse the growth of inequality in the bottom half of the distribution, but it did not have this effect at the top.

Other research has quantified the impact of lower unemployment on family income growth by examining the relationship between these two variables over time and across different areas of the country. Two findings stand out from this research. First, the percentage gains from lower unemployment are consistently larger for families in lower income quintiles. For example, research cited in the Chapter 3 shows that, for every percentage point decline in unemployment, average income for the bottom 40% grows by 1.8%. By this measure, the 1.6-point decline in unemployment that occurred between 1995 and 2000 (from 5.6% to 4.0%) boosted incomes by about 3% for the lowest-income 40% over this period. For the top quintile, the same decline in unemployment translates into a 1.5% increase in income over what would have occurred had unemployment not fallen. Thus, the disproportionate impact of lower unemployment on lower-income families means that tight labor markets lead to slower growth in inequality.

Note, however, that income for the bottom fifth grew much faster than the 3% ascribed to the lower unemployment of 1995-2000. Clearly, other important factors were at work, including the persistence of the recovery and the acceleration in productivity growth. **Figure 1R** shows an estimate of the impact of one percentage-point lower unemployment on family income growth by year of an economic recovery. As the recovery gets underway, e.g., in the first three years, lower unemployment has little affect on family income—it grows less than 1% more than would otherwise be the case. But by the ninth year (a point reached in the 1990s expansion), a percentage-point fall in unemployment raises real income by 2.3%.

**FIGURE 1R** Impact on family income of 1% decline in unemployment, by year of recovery

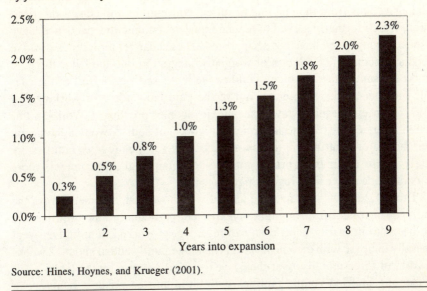

Source: Hines, Hoynes, and Krueger (2001).

## The 'time crunch': married-couple families with children working harder than ever

Family-earnings growth over the past few decades has not only been unequal, it has also come increasingly from greater work effort—from a rise in the number of earners per family and in the average weeks and weekly hours worked per earner. In this section we examine this phenomenon mostly from the perspective of married-couple families with children. The sample also focuses exclusively on families headed by someone 25-54 years of age, thus excluding families whose time spent in the paid labor market might be affected by retirement or schooling.

As the following set of tables reveals, these families have greatly increased their labor supply, giving rise to an important theme in living standards research: the "time-crunch" experienced by many working families who are spending more time than ever at work. As will be detailed in Chapter 2, over the 1980s this increased work effort occurred simultaneously with a fall in real hourly wages for men and for some groups of women. While this pattern changed in the 1990s, as husbands' wages rebounded, the fact remains that over much of the post-1979 period increases in annual earnings were primarily achieved through more work rather than through higher hourly wages.

Much of this increased work effort has, of course, come from the contribution of wives joining the paid labor force and working outside the home. This trend also stems from the fact that historical conventions and gender discrimination, which formerly served to reduce female economic independence, have lessened, though they have not disappeared. These changes represent a positive social and economic evolution of women's integration into the labor force.

At the same time, for many families the increased work effort of their female members, who were either out of the paid labor force or working few hours, has been the main way to keep their incomes growing. ("Work" in this section refers exclusively to labor market work—of course, women have long been the major contributors to non-market work.) In this regard, families are clearly worse off if their primary means to obtain higher incomes is more hours of work rather than regular pay increases.

**Table 1.26** shows the average annual weeks worked, summed across the family, by income fifth. As might be expected, particularly among prime-age families who primarily depend on earnings, weeks worked in any given year generally increase with income level. The average family added about 12 weeks of work, or three months, over the 31-year period covered by the table.

Among married-couple families with children, the greatest increase, in both absolute and percentage terms, in weeks spent in the labor market was among middle- and lower-middle-income families. Both groups added about 20 weeks—nearly five months—to their annual weeks worked per year, and these increases occurred fairly consistently over each of the last three decades.

Among lower-income, married-couple families with children, increases were concentrated in the last two decades, as their weeks worked per year fell slightly over the 1970s. Between 1979 and 2000, however, their annual weeks worked per year increased over 10 weeks, and more than half of this gain occurred just in the last five years of the 1990s. Note also that the largest increase in weeks worked over this five-year period occurred in the bottom two income fifths, another reminder of how tight labor markets provide proportionately greater opportunities for more work among the least advantaged.

There is little movement among the weeks worked of the richest families, primarily due to a "ceiling effect" present in this type of analysis, i.e., family members cannot work more than full year. Among those in the top 40%, at least two family members in both 1995 and 2000 spent the full year at work.

Another way to think about these results is to compare them to the total weeks per year that married parents can spend either in or out of the labor market, i.e., 104 (52 weeks for each parent). Thirty years ago, middle-income parents spent 75% of their weeks in the labor market (some of these weeks represent part-time work). By 2000, that share had increased to 94%.

**TABLE 1.26** Average weeks worked per year by income quintile, 1969-2000, married-couple families with children, head of household age 25-54

| Year | First fifth | Second fifth | Middle fifth | Fourth fifth | Top fifth | Average |
|------|-------------|--------------|--------------|--------------|-----------|---------|
| 1969 | 60.5 | 68.1 | 78.2 | 87.9 | 107.2 | 80.4 |
| 1979 | 58.9 | 75.4 | 83.2 | 96.7 | 109.2 | 84.7 |
| 1989 | 64.5 | 83.5 | 92.1 | 98.3 | 104.6 | 88.6 |
| 1995 | 63.3 | 85.3 | 94.8 | 101.5 | 102.1 | 89.4 |
| 2000 | 69.0 | 89.4 | 97.9 | 103.3 | 102.0 | 92.3 |
| *Weeks added* | | | | | | |
| 1969-79 | -1.6 | 7.3 | 5.0 | 8.8 | 2.0 | 4.2 |
| 1979-89 | 5.6 | 8.1 | 8.9 | 1.7 | -4.6 | 3.9 |
| 1989-2000 | 4.5 | 5.8 | 5.8 | 5.0 | -2.5 | 3.7 |
| 1989-95 | -1.2 | 1.8 | 2.8 | 3.1 | -2.4 | 0.8 |
| 1995-2000 | 5.7 | 4.0 | 3.1 | 1.9 | -0.1 | 2.9 |
| 1969-2000 | 8.5 | 21.2 | 19.7 | 15.4 | -5.2 | 11.9 |
| *Percent change* | | | | | | |
| 1969-79 | -2.7% | 10.7% | 6.4% | 10.0% | 1.8% | 5.3% |
| 1979-89 | 9.5 | 10.8 | 10.6 | 1.7 | -4.2 | 4.6 |
| 1989-2000 | 7.0 | 7.0 | 6.3 | 5.1 | -2.4 | 4.2 |
| 1969-2000 | 14.0 | 31.2 | 25.2 | 17.6 | -4.8 | 14.8 |

Source: Authors' analysis of March CPS data.

Clearly, the share of time that parents are spending in the labor market has expanded.

**Table 1.27** shows annual hours for these same families (hours data are not available for 1969), again by income fifth, with separate panels by the education level of the head of the family. As would be expected, the pattern for hours is similar to that of weeks, with proportionately large gains in the lower 60% of the income scale and a ceiling effect at the top. The largest percentage increases occurred among middle-fifth families, and they were larger for those with less education. Overall, middle-income families added 660 annual hours between 1979 and 2000, an increase of over 16 weeks of full-time work. Middle-income families headed by someone with at most a high school degree, added 21 weeks of full-time work.

Low-income families increased their hours of work by 15.9% over the 21-year period shown, with particularly large gains occurring in 1995-2000 (the 8.5% increase over this five-year period matches that of the 10-year 1979-89 period). In fact, as was the case with weeks worked, the increase in hours worked over the latter 1990s was driven by lower-income families, especially those

**TABLE 1.27** Average hours worked per year by income quintile, 1979-2000, married-couple families with children, head of household age 25-54

| Year | First fifth | Second fifth | Middle fifth | Fourth fifth | Top fifth | Average |
|---|---|---|---|---|---|---|
| *All* | | | | | | |
| 1979 | 2,354 | 3,013 | 3,272 | 3,757 | 4,256 | 3,331 |
| 1989 | 2,553 | 3,330 | 3,639 | 3,913 | 4,232 | 3,533 |
| 1995 | 2,513 | 3,440 | 3,816 | 4,066 | 4,242 | 3,616 |
| 2000 | 2,727 | 3,557 | 3,932 | 4,149 | 4,231 | 3,719 |
| | | | | | | |
| 1979-89 | 8.5% | 10.5% | 11.2% | 4.1% | -0.6% | 6.1% |
| 1989-2000 | 6.8 | 6.8 | 8.1 | 6.1 | 0.0 | 5.3 |
| 1989-95 | -1.6 | 3.3 | 4.9 | 3.9 | 0.2 | 2.3 |
| 1995-2000 | 8.5 | 3.4 | 3.0 | 2.0 | -0.3 | 2.9 |
| 1979-2000 | 15.9 | 18.1 | 20.2 | 10.5 | -0.6 | 11.7 |
| | | | | | | |
| *Head of family high school or less* | | | | | | |
| 1979 | 2,349 | 3,114 | 3,387 | 4,031 | 4,865 | 3,325 |
| 1989 | 2,517 | 3,397 | 3,801 | 4,156 | 4,893 | 3,451 |
| 1995 | 2,498 | 3,534 | 4,084 | 4,354 | 4,739 | 3,501 |
| 2000 | 2,719 | 3,729 | 4,237 | 4,605 | 4,852 | 3,675 |
| | | | | | | |
| 1979-89 | 7.1% | 9.1% | 12.2% | 3.1% | 0.6% | 3.8% |
| 1989-2000 | 8.0 | 9.8 | 11.5 | 10.8 | -0.8 | 6.5 |
| 1989-95 | -0.8 | 4.0 | 7.4 | 4.8 | -3.1 | 1.5 |
| 1995-2000 | 8.9 | 5.5 | 3.7 | 5.8 | 2.4 | 5.0 |
| 1979-2000 | 15.7 | 19.8 | 25.1 | 14.2 | -0.3 | 10.5 |
| | | | | | | |
| *Head of family some college or more* | | | | | | |
| 1979 | 2,366 | 2,835 | 3,133 | 3,489 | 3,980 | 3,337 |
| 1989 | 2,652 | 3,228 | 3,481 | 3,768 | 4,071 | 3,610 |
| 1995 | 2,548 | 3,322 | 3,643 | 3,927 | 4,163 | 3,700 |
| 2000 | 2,743 | 3,371 | 3,750 | 3,972 | 4,144 | 3,747 |
| | | | | | | |
| 1979-89 | 12.1% | 13.9% | 11.1% | 8.0% | 2.3% | 8.2% |
| 1989-2000 | 3.4 | 4.4 | 7.7 | 5.4 | 1.8 | 3.8 |
| 1989-95 | -3.9 | 2.9 | 4.6 | 4.2 | 2.3 | 2.5 |
| 1995-2000 | 7.6 | 1.5 | 2.9 | 1.2 | -0.4 | 1.3 |
| 1979-2000 | 15.9 | 18.9 | 19.7 | 13.9 | 4.1 | 12.3 |

Source: Authors' analysis of March CPS data.

with lower educational attainment. On average, annual hours worked grew 5.0% from 1995 to 2000 among those with a high school diploma or less, and grew 1.3% among those with at least some college.

Some critics have argued that the increase in inequality has been generated simply by those with higher incomes working harder, while other, less well-off families did not increase their work effort. These weeks and hours data belie this claim. Since 1979, the increases in hours and weeks are greatest in the bottom 60% of the income distribution. In addition, when low unemployment generated more and better employment opportunities, those with lower levels of education responded by increasing their average annual hours of work more than did those with higher educational attainment.

Much discussion of labor market trends has stressed the increase in demand for more highly educated workers in the so-called new, high-tech economy, suggesting that we should see significantly larger increases in hours worked among the "some college or more" group. While this was the case on average in the 1980s, it was not the case over the 1990s, either on average or for the bottom 80%. There has been considerable debate as to whether there was a new economy in the latter decade, but there definitely was persistently low unemployment, a condition absent from most of the 1980s. The fact that less-educated workers are not necessarily left behind when demand is strong is a central lesson of the 1990s.

**Table 1.28** examines hours of work by race and ethnicity for prime-age, married-couple families with children. As above, this table maintains the same income fifth cutoffs for all families in each panel. Thus, the income cutoffs for African Americans in the top section, for example, do not divide black families into five equal groups; they are the same cutoffs used for all families in the top section of the previous table. In fact, in 2000, 24% of black families were in the lowest fifth of the overall distribution, and 13% were in the top fifth; for white families, the comparable shares were 15% and 23%. Thus, the question addressed here is not, for example, how many hours an African American family must work to make it into the black middle class, but how many hours it must work to make it into the overall middle class.

Both the levels and the trends reveal interesting patterns. Average hours of work have generally grown faster among minority than white families, in both the 1980s and 1990s. This is also the case among low-income families. For example, among families in the bottom fifth of income, African American and Hispanic hours increased 22.9% and 20.4%), respectively, from 1979 to 2000, compared to 13.7% for white families. For middle-income families, Hispanic hours grew especially quickly, by just under 1,000 hours (half a year of full-time work), from 1979 to 2000.

Due to their lower average wages, both African American and Hispanic families need to work more hours in any given year to maintain a middle-class income. In 2000, middle-income African American families worked about 500 hours, or 12 full-time weeks, more than white families in the same income range; for Hispanics, the comparable number of extra hours is 584, almost 15

**TABLE 1.28** Average hours worked per year by income quintile, 1979-2000, married-couple families with children, head of household age 25-54, by race of family head

| Year | First fifth | Second fifth | Middle fifth | Fourth fifth | Top fifth | Average |
|------|-------------|--------------|--------------|--------------|-----------|---------|
| *African American* | | | | | | |
| 1979 | 2,179 | 3,227 | 3,724 | 4,008 | 4,760 | 3,313 |
| 1989 | 2,491 | 3,521 | 3,988 | 4,267 | 4,815 | 3,593 |
| 1995 | 2,426 | 3,590 | 4,008 | 4,169 | 4,679 | 3,614 |
| 2000 | 2,678 | 3,714 | 4,320 | 4,420 | 4,466 | 3,800 |
| | | | | | | |
| 1979-89 | 14.3% | 9.1% | 7.1% | 6.5% | 1.2% | 8.5% |
| 1989-2000 | 7.5 | 5.5 | 8.3 | 3.6 | -7.3 | 5.8 |
| 1995-2000 | 10.4 | 3.5 | 7.8 | 6.0 | -4.6 | 5.1 |
| 1979-2000 | 22.9 | 15.1 | 16.0 | 10.3 | -6.2 | 14.7 |
| | | | | | | |
| *Hispanic* | | | | | | |
| 1979 | 2,248 | 3,188 | 3,424 | 4,214 | 4,506 | 3,141 |
| 1989 | 2,461 | 3,605 | 3,960 | 4,242 | 4,887 | 3,359 |
| 1995 | 2,458 | 3,623 | 4,225 | 4,388 | 4,740 | 3,308 |
| 2000 | 2,707 | 3,830 | 4,421 | 4,896 | 4,583 | 3,595 |
| | | | | | | |
| 1979-89 | 9.5% | 13.1% | 15.7% | 0.7% | 8.5% | 6.9% |
| 1989-2000 | 10.0 | 6.2 | 11.6 | 15.4 | -6.2 | 7.0 |
| 1995-2000 | 10.1 | 5.7 | 4.6 | 11.6 | -3.3 | 8.7 |
| 1979-2000 | 20.4 | 20.1 | 29.1 | 16.2 | 1.7 | 14.4 |
| | | | | | | |
| *White* | | | | | | |
| 1979 | 2,412 | 2,968 | 3,225 | 3,708 | 4,214 | 3,344 |
| 1989 | 2,614 | 3,278 | 3,580 | 3,867 | 4,159 | 3,549 |
| 1995 | 2,630 | 3,381 | 3,775 | 4,019 | 4,198 | 3,672 |
| 2000 | 2,744 | 3,487 | 3,837 | 4,058 | 4,185 | 3,736 |
| | | | | | | |
| 1979-89 | 8.3% | 10.4% | 11.0% | 4.3% | -1.3% | 6.1% |
| 1989-2000 | 5.0 | 6.4 | 7.2 | 4.9 | 0.6 | 5.3 |
| 1995-2000 | 4.3 | 3.1 | 1.6 | 1.0 | -0.3 | 1.8 |
| 1979-2000 | 13.7 | 17.5 | 19.0 | 9.4 | -0.7 | 11.7 |

Source: Authors' analysis of March CPS data.

full-time weeks. Interestingly, the Hispanic/white hours gap has grown significantly since 1979, when the difference in annual hours worked for middle-income families was 199. Presumably, this increased difference is driven by the decline in relative earnings between Hispanics and whites (recall the long-term negative trend in Figure 1D).

High-income minority families consistently had hours of work above 4,400,

**FIGURE 1S** Contribution of wives' earnings to family incomes, 1970-2000

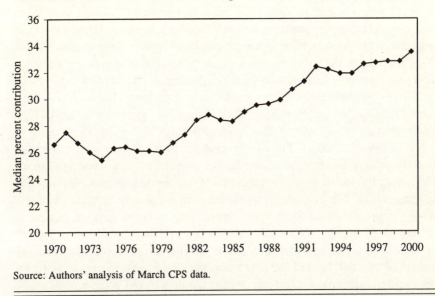

Source: Authors' analysis of March CPS data.

suggesting full-time work by both parents with contributions by other family members as well. It seems that, due to their lower wage levels, minority families have to put in extremely long hours relative to whites to make it to the top of the overall income distribution. By 2000, the highest-income minority families were working at least 280 hours (seven weeks) more per year than white families.

Thus, across education and racial groups and across the income scale, prime-age, married-couple families with children have increased their hours spent in the labor market. By 2000, the average middle-income family was spending 98 weeks and 3,932 hours at work, compared to 83 weeks and 3,272 hours in 1979. Clearly, the time crunch is a real phenomenon, and it is one experienced not just by the lawyers, money managers, or "knowledge workers" of the new economy but by families working harder to maintain their living standards.

As wives have increased their time spent in the paid labor market, their contribution to family income has also risen. Table 1.7 illustrated the increase in the share of working wives; **Figure 1S** complements that analysis by showing the growing importance of their earnings over the past three decades. The figure tracks the median percent of total family income contributed by wives' earnings for all families with working wives from 1970 to 2000 (there are no age restrictions in these data). That is, if we were to array the percent of family income contributed by working wives from the lowest to the highest, each entry in the graph would represent the median percentage for that year. After remaining relatively constant over the 1970s, the median contribution to family earnings by working wives grew from around 26% in 1979 to over 32% in 1992. Since then, the trend has been much flatter, but wives' contributions to family income have still become increasingly important over time.

These contributions have been particularly important to lower- and middle-income families. In fact, for many of these families, as shown in **Table 1.29**, family income would have fallen or grown more slowly in the absence of increased wives' earnings. The percent changes in the bottom section simulate the effect on average family income for the quintile if wives' earnings had not grown from the earlier year of comparison. Over the past two decades, middle-income families' living standards would have improved only modestly, by 7.7%, had wives not increased their weeks, hours, and earnings. Instead, income in the middle fifth grew by 25.8%. Low-income families would have experienced little or no income growth at all in the absence of wives' contributions from 1979 to 2000; instead the first and second fifths saw increases of 10.8% and 17.5%, respectively. Over the 1980s, families in the bottom 60% would have experienced real losses in the absence of wives' increased earnings. While income growth was negative over this period for families in the lowest fifth (-3.8%), their percentage loss would have been more than twice as large (-8.8%) had wives not increased their contribution to family income.

The bottom line of the table shows the percent of family income growth in 1979-2000 attributable to wives' additional earnings, by income fifth. The growth rates suggest that the faster growth at the top than at the bottom of the income scale led to greater inequality. This possibility will be addressed in more detail in the discussion of Table 1.33, below.

**Table 1.30** provides real hourly wage data for husbands and wives in prime-age families with children from 1979 to 2000. The difference in the trends between husbands and wives is pronounced, as wives' real earnings gains outpaced those of husbands in each of the bottom four income fifths. Husbands' earnings rebounded solidly over the 1990s, but wives generally continued to outpace them in terms of hourly wage growth (though not in wage levels—gender gaps persisted through the period).

Wage losses were particularly steep for low-income husbands over the 1980s: losses of 12.3% in the lowest fifth and 10.4% in the second fifth. Middle-income husbands also lost ground, while only the top fifth of husbands experienced any notable gain (8.1%). Wives above the lowest fifth saw double-digit real gains, from 11.3% in the second fifth to almost a third in the top fifth.

**TABLE 1.29** Average income, married-couple families with children, head of household age 25-54 (2000 dollars)

| Year | First fifth | Second fifth | Middle fifth | Fourth fifth | Top fifth | Average |
|------|------------|-------------|-------------|-------------|-----------|---------|
| 1979 | $22,165 | $39,471 | $51,543 | $65,773 | $108,141 | $57,431 |
| 1989 | 21,331 | 40,177 | 54,777 | 72,766 | 127,852 | 63,402 |
| 1995 | 21,499 | 41,248 | 57,408 | 77,292 | 157,543 | 71,010 |
| 2000 | 24,562 | 46,384 | 64,832 | 87,865 | 168,312 | 77,543 |
| | | | | | | |
| 1979-89 | -3.8% | 1.8% | 6.3% | 10.6% | 18.2% | 10.4% |
| 1989-2000 | 15.1 | 15.4 | 18.4 | 20.7 | 31.6 | 22.3 |
| 1979-2000 | 10.8 | 17.5 | 25.8 | 33.6 | 55.6 | 35.0 |
| *Without increase in wives earnings* | | | | | | |
| 1979-89 | -8.8% | -5.7% | -2.5% | 1.9% | 9.3% | 1.9% |
| 1989-2000 | 8.8 | 7.2 | 9.6 | 12.3 | 22.7 | 14.1 |
| 1979-2000 | -0.3 | 1.7 | 7.7 | 15.5 | 36.1 | 17.5 |

*Addendum:* Percent added to family income due to increased wives' earnings

| | | | | | | |
|------|------|------|------|------|------|------|
| 1979-2000 | 11.1% | 15.8% | 18.1% | 18.1% | 19.5% | 17.5% |

Source: Authors' analysis of March CPS data.

Wives' relatively strong gains over the 1980s were all surpassed in the 1990s (except the fourth fifth, which maintained the same pace). The lowest-income wives experienced particularly sharp acceleration of their wages in the 1990s: after growing only 1.9% in the 1980s, they grew 17.3% in the 1990s. Middle-income wives gained 19.5% over the 1990s; from 1979 to 2000 their wages rose 35.7% in real terms. Much larger gains accrued to the wealthiest husbands and wives, leading to the higher levels of income inequality discussed earlier (wage inequality is discussed further in the next chapter).

While these gains by wives are impressive, the wage levels, especially for low-income families, are less striking. By 2000, the hourly wages of those in the lowest fifth were such that, with full-time, full-year work, their combined wage income would be about $33,000, about twice the poverty line for a family of four and an income level that would only afford them basic needs. Moreover, as shown next in Table 1.31, neither of these spouses worked full-year in 2000, so their income (shown in Table 1.29) was considerably less than $33,000. Nevertheless, the gains in both their annual hours (discussed next) and hourly

**TABLE 1.30** Hourly earnings by husbands and wives, couples with children, 1979-2000, head of household age 25-54 (2000 dollars)

| Year | First fifth | Second fifth | Middle fifth | Fourth fifth | Top fifth | Average |
|------|------|------|------|------|------|------|
| **Husbands** | | | | | | |
| 1979 | $9.29 | $14.79 | $18.23 | $21.30 | $30.27 | $19.41 |
| 1989 | 8.15 | 13.25 | 17.27 | 21.41 | 32.71 | 19.34 |
| 1995 | 8.12 | 12.87 | 16.75 | 21.46 | 42.06 | 21.27 |
| 2000 | 8.99 | 14.26 | 18.46 | 24.01 | 46.99 | 23.20 |
| | | | | | | |
| **Wives** | | | | | | |
| 1979 | $5.78 | $7.61 | $9.34 | $10.97 | $14.12 | $10.34 |
| 1989 | 5.89 | 8.48 | 10.61 | 13.44 | 18.69 | 12.39 |
| 1995 | 6.19 | 8.74 | 11.37 | 14.56 | 23.56 | 14.10 |
| 2000 | 6.91 | 9.86 | 12.68 | 16.47 | 25.40 | 15.18 |
| | | | | | | |
| *Percent change* | | | | | | |
| **Husbands** | | | | | | |
| 1979-89 | -12.3% | -10.4% | -5.3% | 0.5% | 8.1% | -0.4% |
| 1989-2000 | 10.4 | 7.6 | 6.9 | 12.1 | 43.7 | 20.0 |
| 1995-2000 | 10.8 | 10.8 | 10.2 | 11.9 | 11.7 | 9.1 |
| 1979-2000 | -3.3 | -3.6 | 1.3 | 12.7 | 55.2 | 19.5 |
| | | | | | | |
| **Wives** | | | | | | |
| 1979-89 | 1.9% | 11.3% | 13.5% | 22.5% | 32.3% | 19.7% |
| 1989-2000 | 17.3 | 16.3 | 19.5 | 22.5 | 35.9 | 22.6 |
| 1995-2000 | 11.7 | 12.8 | 11.5 | 13.1 | 7.8 | 7.7 |
| 1979-2000 | 19.5 | 29.5 | 35.7 | 50.1 | 79.9 | 46.8 |

Source: Authors' analysis of March CPS data.

wages clearly demonstrate the importance of wives' contributions to family incomes over a period when, particularly for families in the bottom 60%, male wages were stagnant.

**Table 1.31** shows that the increased annual hours of work among married-couple families came mostly from working wives (the source of data in this and the next few tables uses a slightly modified dataset compared to the one used so far in this section). Even in 1979, most husbands in these prime-age families with children were already working full time year round (the average annual hours for husbands in 1979 was 2,136), and were thus unlikely to expand their hours much. But wives increased their hours 36.8% from 1979 to 2000, and middle-income wives increased their hours by 43.9%, or by more than three

**TABLE 1.31** Annual hours by husbands and wives, prime-age, married-couple families with children, 1979-2000

| Year | First fifth | Second fifth | Middle fifth | Fourth fifth | Top fifth | Average |
|------|------------|--------------|--------------|--------------|-----------|---------|
| **Husbands** | | | | | | |
| 1979 | 1,774 | 2,115 | 2,184 | 2,238 | 2,367 | 2,136 |
| 1989 | 1,781 | 2,177 | 2,225 | 2,292 | 2,428 | 2,181 |
| 2000 | 1,852 | 2,147 | 2,287 | 2,333 | 2,440 | 2,212 |
| **Wives** | | | | | | |
| 1979 | 508 | 747 | 895 | 1,110 | 1,083 | 869 |
| 1989 | 679 | 1,011 | 1,238 | 1,323 | 1,341 | 1,119 |
| 2000 | 789 | 1,221 | 1,388 | 1,452 | 1,425 | 1,255 |
| **Percent increase for wives** | | | | | | |
| *Years* | | | | | | |
| 1979-89 | 28.9% | 30.3% | 32.4% | 17.6% | 21.4% | 25.3% |
| 1989-2000 | 15.0 | 18.8 | 11.5 | 9.3 | 6.0 | 11.5 |
| 1979-2000 | 43.9 | 49.2 | 43.9 | 26.9 | 27.4 | 36.8 |

Note: Percent changes are actually log point changes.

Source: Authors' analysis of March CPS data.

months of full-time work. Wives' hours grew most quickly between 1979 and 1989 (25.3%), compared to a negligible increase (2%) for husbands. Middle- and lower-income wives experienced above-average growth rates; hours for middle-income wives rose 32.4% over the 1980s, for a total of 493 hours, or three extra months of full-time work, and for wives in the lowest fifth they rose 28.9% (though from a relatively low base of 508 annual hours in 1979).

Hours growth decelerated in the 1990s, dropping to 11.5% on average, less than half the average rate of the prior decade. Hours grew most quickly in the 1990s among lower-income families, who responded more than higher-income families to the tight labor markets of the latter 1990s.

There are competing explanations for the increase in the hours of work among wives. Rising female earnings, falling husbands' wages, and new economic opportunity all played a role. The next two tables isolate the impact of wives' earnings on family income to look more closely at this phenomenon.

As shown above in Table 1.29, wives' increased earnings and hours had a large effect on family incomes over this period. Thus, when we rank income by quintile, we are incorporating these changes into the analysis. This is often appropriate, but to get a better sense of the extent to which wives were responding to changes in family income exclusive of their own earnings, we sort families by family income minus wives' earnings (which for most families, is mostly husbands' earnings). We also break down the growth in wives' annual hours into the share who worked, their extra weeks per year, and their hours per week.

**Table 1.32** shows average annual hours of wives by income quintile. Note that both the levels and changes differ from the previous table, though the averages are the same, because these are the same wives, just sorted differently: by family income minus wives' earnings. Compared to the last table, the levels of annual hours worked are higher in the first quintile and lower in the top, meaning that wives' of low-income husbands work more hours in a given year than wives in low-income families, and wives of high-income husbands work fewer hours a year than wives in high-income families.

For middle-income families, however, there is little difference in the two tables, and wives of middle-income men had above-average gains in annual hours. But Table 1.32 also shows that hours gains were higher for wives of middle- and upper-income husbands than for wives of men in the first and second fifths over the 1980s. For example, annual hours increased by 31.6% for wives in the fourth fifth in the 1980s compared to 18.8% for those in the first fifth over this period. Since we know that earnings were falling more for lower- than for higher-income husbands over these years, we cannot assume that these faster increases in hours for wives of higher-earning men were solely driven by the need to offset husbands' lost earnings. It is likely the case that these wives were also taking advantage of new and better earnings opportunities.

As noted above, growth in hours for wives slowed considerably over the 1990s. Most of this slowdown is attributable to the decline in the growth of the share of wives who work. In the 1980s the share rose by 14.0%, accounting for more than half of the 25.3% average increase; from 1989 to 2000 the share rose by just 2.1%, meaning that increases in annual hours worked by wives in the 1990s were driven primarily by more weeks worked per year and more hours worked per week. Note, for example, that the growth in weeks worked per year (among those already employed), was only slightly slower on average over the 1990s, and actually accelerated in the bottom fifth (from 5.6% to 7.6%). Hours worked per week grew at fairly similar rates over both the 1980s and 1990s, and grew most quickly over the full period—8.9%—among wives of middle-income husbands.

Taken together, between 1979 and 2000 increased weeks and hours contributed slightly more to the increase in wives' work than did the increase in the share of wives who entered the labor force. For example, among families in

**TABLE 1.32** Annual hours, wives in prime-age, married-couple families with children, and contributions to change, 1979-2000, sorted by husband's income

| Year | First fifth | Second fifth | Middle fifth | Fourth fifth | Top fifth | Average |
|---|---|---|---|---|---|---|
| 1979 | 971 | 1,004 | 868 | 811 | 689 | 869 |
| 1989 | 1,172 | 1,242 | 1,175 | 1,113 | 892 | 1,119 |
| 2000 | 1,305 | 1,380 | 1,347 | 1,239 | 1,004 | 1,255 |
| **Years** | | | | | | |
| 1979-89 | 18.8% | 21.2% | 30.3% | 31.6% | 25.8% | 25.3% |
| 1989-2000 | 10.8 | 10.5 | 13.7 | 10.8 | 11.9 | 11.5 |
| 1979-2000 | 29.6 | 31.7 | 43.9 | 42.3 | 37.7 | 36.8 |
| **Increase in hours explained by:** | | | | | | |
| *Increase in the share of wives who worked* | | | | | | |
| 1979-89 | 11.3% | 11.1% | 16.6% | 16.1% | 15.3% | 14.0% |
| 1989-2000 | 1.5 | 0.6 | 2.8 | 3.5 | 2.3 | 2.1 |
| 1979-2000 | 12.8 | 11.6 | 19.5 | 19.6 | 17.6 | 16.1 |
| *Increase in weeks worked per year* | | | | | | |
| 1979-89 | 5.6% | 7.5% | 8.8% | 12.0% | 7.8% | 8.3% |
| 1989-2000 | 7.5 | 7.1 | 6.7 | 4.2 | 5.4 | 6.2 |
| 1979-2000 | 13.1 | 14.6 | 15.6 | 16.3 | 13.1 | 14.5 |
| *Increase in hours worked per week* | | | | | | |
| 1979-89 | 2.0% | 2.7% | 4.8% | 3.4% | 2.8% | 3.0% |
| 1989-2000 | 1.8 | 2.9 | 4.1 | 3.0 | 4.2 | 3.2 |
| 1979-2000 | 3.7 | 5.5 | 8.9 | 6.5 | 7.0 | 6.1 |

Note: Percent changes are actually log point changes.

Source: Authors' analysis of March CPS data.

the middle fifth (i.e., families of middle-income husbands), wives' hours increased by 43.9%. More than half of that increase—56%—was attributable to more weeks per year and more hours per week, with the rest due to more wives working. This pattern is consistent across the quintiles of husbands' incomes.

Have the growing hours, weeks worked, and earnings of wives contributed to or helped diminish income inequality? The notion that the growth of "two-earner" families has contributed to growing inequality is intuitively plausible if one believes that (1) there has been a growth of high-wage employed women marrying high-wage men, and (2) the increase in the hours and earnings of these women has been greater than that of their lower-income counterparts. It is true, in fact, that wives in higher-income families earn more than those in other families and that their hourly wages have grown the quickest (Table 1.30). On the other hand, when we sort families by their income, the fastest growth in work hours has been among the wives in the bottom three-fifths (Table 1.31), yet, this result reverses, to some degree, when we sort families by husbands' earnings (Table 1.32).

**Table 1.33** shows the shares of total income going to each income group, calculated with and without wives earnings. The difference between shares reveals the contribution of wives' earnings to inequality. This analysis reveals that wives' earnings have been equalizing over this period; in other words, the income distribution would have been more skewed toward the wealthy in the absence of wives' contributions to family income. This seeming contradiction with Table 1.31 is explained by the fact that the wives of low-income husbands add proportionately more to their families' incomes than do the wives of high-income husbands. It is nevertheless the case that the hours worked and wages earned by wives of high-earning husbands have increased faster than the hours and wages of wives of low-earning husbands. Thus, while wives' earnings are equalizing at a point in time, this phenomenon has made them less so as time progresses.

As shown in Table 1.33, in 1979, wives' earnings led to a more equal distribution of income, since without wives' earnings the lowest fifth would have had a 7.3% share of total income instead of the 7.9% share it had with wives' earnings. At the top end of the income scale, in the absence of wives' earnings, the income share going to the top 5% would have been 15.0%, instead of 13.6%. Overall in 1979, wives' earnings increased the income shares of the bottom four-fifths and decreased the share of income of the top fifth by 1.9 percentage points, most of which came from the top 5%. In 1989, wives' earnings had a larger effect on raising the income shares of the lowest 80% of families and on lessening the income share of the top fifth, which fell by 2.6 points; again, the largest share decline (1.8 percentage points) occurred in the top 5%. This pattern continued in 2000, as wives' contributions to the income shares of the bottom 80% continued to grow while those of the top fifth fell further.

The bottom section summarizes the results over the full period. The first line shows the actual changes in income shares by income fifth from 1979 to 2000. For example, the share of income going to the bottom fifth fell by 1.5% of total national income over the period, while that of the top fifth grew by 4.5%. As the second line shows, these changes would have been more pronounced—family income would have been further distributed away from lower-income families to families in the top fifth—in the absence of wives' earnings.

**TABLE 1.33** Effect of wives' earnings on income shares of prime-age, married-couple families with children

| Family income shares | Lowest fifth | Second fifth | Middle fifth | Fourth fifth | Top fifth | 80-95% | Top 5% |
|---|---|---|---|---|---|---|---|
| **1979** | | | | | | | |
| Actual | 7.9% | 13.9% | 18.0% | 22.9% | 37.3% | 23.6% | 13.6% |
| Without wives' earnings | 7.3 | 13.3 | 17.5 | 22.7 | 39.2 | 24.2 | 15.0 |
| Effect of wives' earning | 0.6 | 0.7 | 0.4 | 0.2 | -1.9 | -0.5 | -1.4 |
| **1989** | | | | | | | |
| Actual | 7.1% | 13.2% | 17.8% | 23.5% | 38.5% | 25.0% | 13.5% |
| Without wives' earnings | 6.2 | 12.4 | 17.2 | 23.2 | 41.0 | 25.8 | 15.2 |
| Effect of wives' earning | 0.9 | 0.8 | 0.6 | 0.3 | -2.6 | -0.8 | -1.8 |
| **2000** | | | | | | | |
| Actual | 6.4% | 12.1% | 16.9% | 22.7% | 41.8% | 26.0% | 15.8% |
| Without wives' earnings | 5.4 | 11.0 | 15.8 | 22.3 | 45.4 | 26.4 | 19.0 |
| Effect of wives' earning | 1.0 | 1.1 | 1.1 | 0.4 | -3.6 | -0.4 | -3.2 |
| *Change, 1979-2000* | | | | | | | |
| Actual | -1.5% | -1.8% | -1.1% | -0.1% | 4.5% | 2.4% | 2.1% |
| Without wives' earnings | -1.9 | -2.3 | -1.7 | -0.4 | 6.2 | 2.3 | 3.9 |
| Effect of wives' earning | 0.4 | 0.5 | 0.6 | 0.3 | -1.7 | 0.1 | -1.8 |

Source: Authors' analysis of March CPS data.

These results have several implications. First, while gender gaps persist, there is clear evidence of increased economic progress for female workers. Since 1979, more wives are in the paid labor market, working more weeks per year, and more hours per week. Unlike those of husbands, wives' real hourly wages rose in each income quintile over both the 1980s and 1990s. To a large extent, these increases in real wages and hours have more than offset the less impressive trend in the earnings of middle- and low-income husbands. Had wives earnings not increased since 1979, family income would have been stagnant in the bottom 40% of married-couple families with children. Furthermore, the pattern of these changes in wives' contributions to family income has been equalizing, i.e., the income distribution for prime-age, married-couple families would have been more skewed toward the wealthy in the absence of wives' contributions.

There are, however, at least two reasons to be concerned about these trends. First, given weak earnings by low-income husbands, wives had to sharply increase their time spent in the labor market if they wanted to raise or just maintain their families' living standards. This demand has left middle- and lower-income families in particular with fewer lifestyle choices relative to wealthier families. Wives had to go to work, and to do so for increasingly more weeks and hours per year. Higher-income wives also worked much more, but, for their lower-income counterparts, more work was a necessity. Second, an increase in time spent at work creates child care and other family challenges. In 2000 the average middle-income, married couple with children spent close to 3,700 hours per year at work, compared to about 3,100 in 1979, an increase of 600 hours a year or four added months of full-time work. It is difficult to imagine that these added hours have not had a negative effect on a parent's ability to be at home after school, help with homework, or care for an ill or aging family member.

## Conclusion

American families are working harder than ever. They are working more weeks per year and more hours per week, and these increases have occurred across the board, not simply among the wealthiest or the most highly skilled. But thanks to the positive economic conditions of the latter 1990s, particularly low unemployment, working families gained ground between 1995 and 2000. The incomes of low- and middle-income families grew quickly relative to the recent past, and the largest gains went to the least advantaged. This pattern of growth also helped to narrow the income gap between those in the middle and those at the bottom of the income scale.

Unfortunately, this was not the case at the top of income scale, where the gap between the wealthiest families and everyone else continued to expand, much as it has since the late 1970s. Though the growth period of the late 1990s had many virtues, it was neither strong enough nor long enough to reverse the tide of inequality.

The economy in 2002 appears to be entering a recovery period, albeit one characterized by slow growth. This is a potential problem for income growth for working families. In the last slow-growth recovery—the first several years of the 1990s—median family income fell for the first two years, and it did not return to its pre-recession level until 1996. One way policy makers can act to avoid this undesirable pattern is to chart a path back to full employment.

## CHAPTER 2

# Wages: broad-based gains in late 1990s

Because wages and salaries make up roughly three-fourths of total family income (the proportion is even higher among the broad middle class), wage trends are the primary determinant of income growth and income inequality trends. This chapter examines and explains the trends in wage growth and wage inequality of the last few decades up through 2001. The most recent wage trends, through mid-2002, are examined in the Introduction.

The wage story of the past quarter century has three predominant themes. First, an era of stagnant and falling wages gave way to one of strong wage growth. Wages were stagnant overall and median wages fell from the early 1970s to 1995. After 1995, wages changed course, rising strongly in response to persistent low unemployment and the faster productivity growth relative to the 1973-95 period. Second, the pattern of wage growth has shifted. In the 1980s wage inequality widened dramatically and, coupled with stagnant average wages, brought about widespread erosion of real wages. Wage inequality continued its growth in the 1990s but took a different shape: a continued growth in the wage gap between top and middle earners but a shrinking wage gap between middle and low earners. Since 1999, however, wage inequality has been growing between the top and the middle as well as between the middle and the bottom. A third theme is the critical role played by rising unemployment in raising wage inequality and the role played by low unemployment in boosting wage growth overall, but particularly at the bottom. Understanding and explaining these trends is the task of this chapter.

The trends in average wage growth—the slowdown in the 1970s and the pick-up in the mid-1990s—can be attributed to corresponding changes in productivity growth. Productivity accelerated in the late 1990s, and its growth continued into the current recession, leading to high growth in average wages. But as Chapter 1 showed, income shifted from labor to capital in 1995-2000, so the benefits of faster productivity growth went disproportionately to capital.

Explaining the shifts in wage inequality requires attention to several factors that affect low-, middle-, and high-wage workers differently. The experience of the late 1990s should remind us of the great extent to which a low unemployment rate benefits workers, especially low-wage earners. Correspondingly, the high levels of unemployment in the early and mid-1980s disempowered wage earners and provided the context in which other forces—specifically, a weakening of labor market institutions and globalization—could drive up wage inequality. Significant shifts in the labor market, such as the severe drop in the minimum wage and deunionization, can explain one-third of the growing wage inequality in the 1980s. Similarly, the increasing globalization of the economy—immigration, trade, and capital mobility—and the employment shift toward lower-paying service industries (such as retail trade) and away from manufacturing can explain, in combination, another third of the total growth in wage inequality. Macroeconomic factors also played an important role, as high unemployment in the early 1980s greatly increased wage inequality while the low unemployment of the late 1990s reduced it.

The shape of wage inequality shifted in the late 1980s as the gap at the bottom—i.e., the 50/10 gap between middle-wage workers at the 50th percentile and low-wage workers at the 10th—began to shrink. However, over the last few years, this progress against wage inequality at the bottom has been halted and wage inequality, especially among women, has resumed its growth. This reversal is partially the impact of the rise in unemployment and partially due to the drop in the real value of the minimum wage. The greatest increase in wage inequality at the bottom occurred among women and corresponded to the fall in the minimum wage over the 1980s, the high unemployment of the early 1980s, and the expansion of low-wage retail jobs. The positive trend in the wage gap over the 1990s owes much to increases in the minimum wage, low unemployment, and the slight, relative contraction in low-paying retail jobs in the late 1990s. The wage gap at the top—the 90/50 gap between high- and middle-wage earners—continued its steady growth in the 1990s and into the recession but at a slower pace than in the 1980s. The continuing influence of globalization, deunionization, and the shift to lower-paying service industries ("industry shifts") can explain the continued growth of wage inequality at the top.

There is a popular notion that the growth of wage inequality reflects primarily a technology-driven increase in demand for "educated" or "skilled" workers. Yet economists have found that the overall impact of technology on the wage and employment structure was no greater in the 1980s or 1990s than in the 1970s. Moreover, skill demand and technology have little relationship to the growth of wage inequality within the same group (i.e., workers with similar levels of experience and education), and this within-group inequality was responsible for half of the overall growth of wage inequality in the 1980s and 1990s. Technology has been and continues to be an important force, but there was no "technology shock" in the 1980s or 1990s and no ensuing demand for "skill" that was not satisfied by the continuing expansion of the educational attainment of the workforce.

The conventional story about technology leading to increased demand for skills and the erosion of wages among the less-skilled does not readily explain the pattern of growth in wage inequality. In particular, the late 1990s are seen as a period of rapid technological change, yet during that period wage inequality diminished at the bottom. Similarly, education differentials grew slowly during most of the 1990s, a trend incompatible with rapid technological change driving up demand for skills. The decline in the wage payoff for experience in the later 1990s also runs counter to the technology story. Moreover, it was the growth of wage inequality among workers of similar education and experience, not easily linked to technology, that kept wage inequality at the top growing in the 1990s and into the recession.

Despite the strong wage improvements in recent years, it was not until 1998 that the wage level for middle-wage workers (the median hourly wage) jumped above its 1979 level. The median *male* wage in 2000 was still below its 1979 level. Yet productivity was 44.5% higher in 2000 than in 1979. One reason for this divergence is increased corporate profitability (discussed in Chapter 1), which drove a wedge between productivity and compensation growth.

Another noteworthy trend is the decline in benefits in the late 1990s. Although health insurance coverage increased after falling for more than a decade, employer costs for insurance dropped in recent years. Employer pension contributions also fell. Since 2000 benefits have grown, fueled by rising health care costs.

As the wage of the typical worker fell in the early 1990s and rose in the latter 1990s, executive pay soared. From 1989 to 2000, the wage of the median chief executive officer grew 79.0%, and average compensation grew 342%. In 1965 CEOs made 26 times more than a typical worker; by 1989 the ratio had risen to 72-to-1, and by 2000 it was 310-to-1. This level of executive pay is a distinctly American phenomenon: U.S. CEOs make about three times as much as their counterparts abroad.

The turnaround of the late 1990s has been a boon for workers' wages and incomes, but will these trends continue? Fortunately, productivity growth has continued strongly through the recession, but high unemployment has knocked down wage growth, particularly at the low end. A more rapid shift to more-skilled jobs than has already occurred seems unlikely, but continuing pressures from globalization and deunionization, higher unemployment, and a continuing fall in the real value of the minimum wage could weaken wages and exacerbate inequality. The renewed across-the-board widening of wage inequality will likely continue, especially if higher unemployment persists.

The chapter's wage analysis proceeds as follows. The first half of the chapter documents changes in the various dimensions of the wage structure, i.e., changes in average wages and compensation and changes by occupation, gender, wage level, education level, age, and race and ethnicity. These shifts in the various dimensions of wage inequality are then assessed and explained by focusing on particular factors such as unemployment, industry shifts, deunionization, the value of the minimum wage, globalization and immigration, and technology.

## Contrasting hours and hourly wage growth

To understand changes in wage trends, it is important to distinguish between trends in annual, weekly, and hourly wages. Trends in annual wages, for instance, are driven by changes in both hourly wages and the amount of time spent working (weeks worked per year and hours worked per week). Likewise, weekly wage trends reflect changes in hourly pay and weekly hours. In this chapter we focus on the hourly pay levels of the workforce and its sub-groups. We do this to be able to distinguish changes in earnings resulting from more (or less) pay rather than more (or less) work. Also, the hourly wage can be said to represent the "true" price of labor (exclusive of benefits, which we analyze separately). Last, changes in the distribution of annual earnings have been predominantly driven by changes in the distribution of hourly wages and not changes in work time. Chapter 3 goes on to address employment, unemployment, underemployment, and other issues related to changes in work time and opportunities.

**Table 2.1** illustrates the importance of distinguishing between annual, weekly, and hourly wage trends. The annual wage and salary of the average worker in inflation-adjusted terms grew substantially faster than the average hourly wage in each of the last two decades. Thus, hourly wages grew 0.4% each year over the 1979-89 period and 0.9% over the 1989-2000 period. Yet annual wages grew at 0.9% and 1.4%, reflecting the hourly wage growth and the 0.5% growth in annual hours worked. The most remarkable story in Table 2.1, however, is the sharp acceleration in hourly wage growth (to 1.9%) in the 1995-2000 period, a sharp departure from the measly 0.1% growth of the ear-

**TABLE 2.1** Trends in average wages and average hours, 1967-2000 (2001 dollars)

| Year | Productivity per hour (1992=100) | Wage levels | | | Hours worked | | |
|---|---|---|---|---|---|---|---|
| | | Annual wages | Weekly wages | Hourly wages | Annual hours | Weeks per year | Hours per week |
| 1967 | 65.8 | $23,118 | $530.78 | $13.49 | 1,716 | 43.5 | 39.3 |
| 1973 | 76.6 | 26,890 | 619.03 | 16.04 | 1,679 | 43.4 | 38.6 |
| 1979 | 82.2 | 27,089 | 617.77 | 15.91 | 1,703 | 43.8 | 38.8 |
| 1989 | 94.2 | 29,653 | 653.37 | 16.63 | 1,783 | 45.4 | 39.3 |
| 1995 | 102.8 | 30,515 | 664.20 | 16.71 | 1,827 | 45.9 | 39.8 |
| 2000 | 116.6 | 34,419 | 731.84 | 18.33 | 1,878 | 47.0 | 39.9 |
| *Annual growth rate*\* | | | | | | | |
| 1967-73 | 2.5% | 2.5% | 2.6% | 2.9% | -0.4% | 0.0% | -0.3% |
| 1973-79 | 1.2 | 0.1 | 0.0 | -0.1 | 0.2 | 0.2 | 0.1 |
| 1979-89 | 1.4 | 0.9 | 0.6 | 0.4 | 0.5 | 0.3 | 0.1 |
| 1989-2000 | 1.9 | 1.4 | 1.0 | 0.9 | 0.5 | 0.3 | 0.1 |
| 1989-95 | 1.5 | 0.5 | 0.3 | 0.1 | 0.4 | 0.2 | 0.2 |
| 1995-2000 | 2.5 | 2.4 | 1.9 | 1.9 | 0.6 | 0.5 | 0.1 |

\*Log growth rates.

Source: Authors' analysis of CPS data and Murphy and Welch (1989). For detailed information on table sources, see Table Notes.

lier part of the business cycle from 1989 to 1995 and the slow growth (0.4%) of the prior business cycle of 1979-89. This pickup in wage growth, along with an even stronger pickup of wage growth at the bottom end of the wage scale (detailed below), is the main factor behind the improvements in family income in the late 1990s, discussed in Chapter 1, and the reductions in poverty, discussed in Chapter 5. Strong post-1995 wage growth is a prominent theme of our discussion throughout this chapter.

The main reason for the faster wage growth in the late 1990s—faster productivity growth—is also shown in Table 2.1. Productivity growth in 1996 and later years (2.5% annual growth from 1995 to 2000) was substantially higher than the productivity growth earlier in the business cycle (1.5% in 1989-95) or in the two prior business cycles (roughly 1.2% to 1.4%). Thus, productivity growth was 1% faster each year in the late 1990s than in the prior 22 years and comparable to the growth of the late 1960s (2.5% from 1967 to 1973). Recent productivity growth, however, is still below the pace of the 1950s and 1960s (3.0% from 1947 to 1967).

The fact that the acceleration of wage growth in the late 1990s (from 0.1% to 1.9% a year) exceeds that of the 1% productivity acceleration requires an explanation as well. One part of it is that the small 0.1% annual gain in average hourly wages over the 1989-95 period may be too pessimistic, since the wage measures more closely associated with the productivity data (shown below in Table 2.2) show a higher wage growth of 0.6% over this same period. Other wage measures discussed below, however, indicate falling average wages in the early 1990s. A better explanation is probably that the persistent low unemployment of the late 1990s allowed workers to achieve faster wage gains and share in productivity growth—after all, productivity was growing 1.5% yearly in the early 1990s while average wages were flat. Thus, there are two parts to an explanation for the faster wage growth in the late 1990s: first, persistent low unemployment enabled workers to attain a rising wage (through better jobs, better pay offers for new jobs, and greater bargaining power) that more closely reflected productivity growth; second, productivity growth accelerated (which itself requires an explanation, not discussed here). It is also worth noting that the 1.9% wage growth of the late 1990s still lags significantly behind the 2.9% growth of the late 1960s and early 1970s.

The other important story in Table 2.1 is the continuing growth in annual hours worked. For instance, the average worker worked 1,878 hours in 2000, 95 more— or about 12 additional days of work each year—than the 1,783 hours worked in 1989. This growth in hours worked was evident both in the 1989-95 and 1995-2000 parts of the current business cycle, reflecting the long-term growth in weeks worked per year and a modest growth in weekly hours.

The 1979-89 period was also characterized by growing annual hours of work (up 80, from 1,703 to 1,783). The 0.5% yearly growth in hours worked was driven by the increase in the average work year to 45.4 weeks from 43.8 weeks, a 0.3% annual growth, and a slight increase in the hours of the average work week, to 39.3 hours. In the 1973-79 period, annual hours grew more slowly, at 0.2% annually.

The growth in work hours but in terms of families rather than individual workers is discussed in Chapter 1.

## Contrasting compensation and wage growth

A worker's pay—his or her total compensation—is made up of both non-wage payments, referred to as fringe benefits, and wages. This section examines the growth of compensation using the only two available data series and finds that, in the 1980s, hourly compensation grew at the same pace as wages, while in the 1990s it grew more slowly because, although wages grew, benefits fell. Over the long term, such as from 1979 to 2000, compensation and wages have grown at similar rates. The most recent data (through March 2002) suggest that benefit costs (led by health) have grown strongly and are now growing faster than wages. One implication of compensation and wages growing in tandem is that analyses (such as ours below) that focus on wage trends are using an appropriate proxy for compensation. Analyses of wage growth sometimes overstate the corresponding growth of compensation, as in the late 1990s, and sometimes understate compensation growth, as in recent years.

**Table 2.2** examines the wage and compensation data that are developed as a major part of the National Income and Product Accounts (NIPA), the Commerce Department's effort to measure the size of the national economy, termed the gross domestic product. Compensation levels exceed wage levels because they include employer payments for health insurance, pensions, and payroll taxes (primarily payments toward Social Security and unemployment insurance).

Benefits grew much faster than wages from the 1940s to the 1970s. For instance, over the 1948-73 period real benefits grew 7.3% annually, while wages grew at a 2.6% pace. Yet total compensation (wages and benefits) grew at relatively the same rate as wages, 3.0% versus 2.6% per year. This apparent contradiction is readily explained: non-wage compensation in 1948 totaled just 5.1% of total compensation. Thus, even a faster growth of a small part of compensation (benefits) did not lead to growth in total compensation much greater than that of wages.

Another way of portraying the limited role of benefits growth is to note

**TABLE 2.2** Growth of average hourly wages, benefits, and compensation, 1948-2000 (2001 dollars)

| Year | Wages and salaries | Benefits* | Total compensation | Benefit share of compensation |
|------|------|------|------|------|
| Hourly wage** | | | | |
| 1948 | $8.52 | $0.46 | $8.99 | 5.1% |
| 1967 | 14.01 | 1.74 | 15.76 | 11.1 |
| 1973 | 16.21 | 2.66 | 18.87 | 14.1 |
| 1979 | 16.40 | 3.60 | 19.99 | 18.0 |
| 1989 | 17.64 | 4.00 | 21.65 | 18.5 |
| 1995 | 18.34 | 4.11 | 22.45 | 18.3 |
| 2000 | 20.97 | 3.82 | 24.79 | 15.4 |
| *Annual dollar change* | | | | |
| 1948-73 | $0.31 | $0.09 | $0.40 | |
| 1973-79 | 0.03 | 0.16 | 0.19 | |
| 1979-89 | 0.12 | 0.04 | 0.17 | |
| 1989-2000 | 0.30 | -0.02 | 0.29 | |
| 1989-95 | 0.12 | 0.02 | 0.13 | |
| 1995-2000 | 0.53 | -0.06 | 0.47 | |
| 1979-2000 | 0.22 | 0.01 | 0.23 | |
| *Annual percent change* | | | | |
| 1948-73 | 2.6% | 7.3% | 3.0% | |
| 1973-79 | 0.2 | 5.1 | 1.0 | |
| 1979-89 | 0.7 | 1.1 | 0.8 | |
| 1989-2000 | 1.6 | -0.4 | 1.2 | |
| 1989-95 | 0.6 | 0.4 | 0.6 | |
| 1995-2000 | 2.7 | -1.4 | 2.0 | |
| 1979-2000 | 1.2 | 0.3 | 1.0 | |

\*    Includes payroll taxes, health, pension, and other non-wage benefits.
\*\*   Deflated by personal consumption expenditure (PCE) index for all items, except health, which is deflated by PCE medical index.

Source: Authors' analysis of BEA and NIPA data.

that 1.1% annual growth over the 1979-89 period translated (in 2001 dollars) to a $0.04 per year growth in hourly benefits, boosting benefits from $3.60 an hour in 1979 to $4.00 in 1989.

Over the 1989-2000 period, benefits fell 0.4% per year. In contrast, the annual growth in average hourly wages accelerated to 1.6% per year. Consequently, the benefits share of compensation fell sharply, from 18.5% to 15.4%, and compensation grew more slowly than wages, 1.2% versus 1.6%. As Table

2.2 shows, there was a slowdown in benefits over the 1989-95 period; growth dropped to 0.4%, substantially less than the 1.1% growth in the 1979-89 period. However, there was a *reduction* in benefits of 1.4% per year over the 1995-2000 period. As shown in a later section, this benefit decline reflects a fall in employer pension contributions and a fall in employer health care costs (relative to medical inflation).

This slowdown and then fall in benefits in the 1990s tells a more complete story than one that is limited to wages. According to the wage data in Table 2.2, wage growth accelerated from 0.6% to 2.7% a year between the 1989-95 and 1995-2000 periods, a rise of 2.1 percentage points. The comparable acceleration of compensation growth, however, was a 1.4 percentage-point rise (from 0.6% to 2.0%). Taking account of the benefit reductions of the late 1990s, therefore, shows an acceleration of compensation (of 1.4%) that more closely corresponds to the 1% productivity acceleration than does the 2.1% wage acceleration.

The data in **Table 2.3** take a different look at the role of benefit growth in driving total compensation growth. These data are drawn from the Bureau of Labor Statistics' Employment Cost Index (ECI) program, which provides the value of wages and employer-provided benefits for each year since 1987. These ECI data corroborate the earlier finding that benefits, defined as pension, insurance (health and life), and payroll taxes dropped sharply in the late 1990s. The ECI data suggest a sizeable acceleration of benefits growth over the 2000-02 period, a jump of 2.2% annually. These numbers vary from the ones presented earlier because they describe only the private sector (government employment is excluded), and the definition of "hours worked" is different. We return to a discussion of benefit growth below when we examine specific benefits, such as health insurance and pensions.

Although studies of labor market trends should examine both wages and benefits, those that focus on long-term wage trends alone (usually because of a lack of benefit data) are nevertheless appropriate. Taking account of payroll taxes or pension and insurance costs (including both health and life insurance), given their small size and slow growth, would not substantively alter the picture emerging from analyses of the last few decades that use (as we do) the conventional government wage data frequently employed to track labor market trends.

## Wages by occupation

We now turn to the pattern of growth or decline in wages for the various segments of the workforce since 1973. Again, there are at least two distinct "wage regimes" over the last 30 years, one from 1973-95 that consisted of stagnant

**TABLE 2.3** Growth in private-sector average hourly wages, benefits, and compensation, 1987-2001 (2001 dollars)

| Year* | Wages and salaries | Benefits** | Total compensation | Benefit share of compensation |
|-------|--------|--------|--------|--------|
| Hourly pay*** | | | | |
| 1987 | $16.69 | $3.89 | $20.58 | 18.9% |
| 1989 | 16.34 | 3.89 | 20.23 | 19.2 |
| 1995 | 15.99 | 3.85 | 19.84 | 19.4 |
| 2000 | 16.95 | 3.58 | 20.54 | 17.4 |
| 2001 | 17.18 | 3.63 | 20.81 | 17.4 |
| 2002 | 17.65 | 3.74 | 21.39 | 17.5 |
| | | | | |
| *Annual dollar change* | | | | |
| 1989-2000 | $0.06 | $-0.03 | $0.03 | |
| 1989-95 | -0.06 | -0.01 | -0.06 | |
| 1995-2000 | 0.19 | -0.05 | 0.14 | |
| 2000-02 | 0.35 | 0.08 | 0.43 | |
| | | | | |
| *Annual percent change* | | | | |
| 1989-2000 | 0.3% | -0.7% | 0.1% | |
| 1989-95 | -0.4 | -0.2 | -0.3 | |
| 1995-2000 | 1.2 | -1.4 | 0.7 | |
| 2000-02 | 2.0 | 2.2 | 2.1 | |

\*   Data are for March.
\*\*  Includes payroll taxes, health, pension, and other non-wage benefits.
\*\*\* Deflated by CPI for all items except health, which is deflated by CPI medical care index.

Source: Authors' analysis of BLS ECI levels data.

average wage growth and real wage reductions for the vast majority, and one from 1995 to the present consisting of fast real wage growth across the board (though not equally so). In general, the workers who experienced the greatest fall in real wages in the 1973-95 period were likely to be men, workers who initially had lower wages, workers without a college degree, blue-collar or service workers, or younger workers. In the early 1990s, however, wages also eroded among male white-collar and college-educated workers. Since 1995, real wages grew most rapidly among low-wage workers, the very highest-paid workers, and younger workers.

The data in **Table 2.4** and **Figure 2A** show wage trends for the 80% of the workforce who are production and non-supervisory workers. This category includes factory workers, construction workers, and a wide variety of

**TABLE 2.4** Hourly and weekly earnings of private production and non-supervisory workers,* 1947-2001 (2001 dollars)

| Year | Real average hourly earnings | Real average weekly earnings |
|------|------------------------------|------------------------------|
| 1947 | $7.79 | $314.18 |
| 1967 | 12.32 | 467.98 |
| 1973 | 13.92 | 513.82 |
| 1979 | 13.92 | 496.79 |
| 1982 | 13.49 | 469.46 |
| 1989 | 13.32 | 460.74 |
| 1995 | 13.19 | 454.99 |
| 2000 | 14.14 | 487.72 |
| 2001 | 14.33 | 490.09 |

| | Annual growth rate | |
|------|------|------|
| **Business cycles** | | |
| 1947-67 | 2.3% | 2.0% |
| 1967-73 | 2.1 | 1.6 |
| 1973-79 | 0.0 | -0.6 |
| 1979-89 | -0.4 | -0.8 |
| 1989-2000 | 0.5 | 0.5 |
| 1989-95 | -0.2 | -0.2 |
| 1995-2000 | 1.4 | 1.4 |
| 2000-01 | 1.4 | 0.5 |
| 1979-2001 | 0.1 | -0.1 |

* Production and non-supervisory workers account for about 80% of wage and salary employment.

Source: Authors' analysis.

service-sector workers ranging from restaurant and clerical workers to nurses and teachers; it leaves out higher-paid managers and supervisors. Between 1989 and 2000, average hourly earnings for these workers rose $0.82, or 0.5% annually. As we have seen earlier, the differences in trends between the early and latter part of this period are striking: hourly wages fell 0.2% a year from 1989 to 1995 and then grew 1.4% a year from 1995 to 2000, a turnaround of 1.2 percentage points. Over the longer term, from 1979 to 2001, wages are up only slightly, from $13.92 in 1979 to $14.33 in 2001. Figure 2A also tracks an estimate of the hourly compensation of production/non-supervisory workers that shows compensation growing far faster than wages in the 1970s (see the divergence between the two series arising in the 1970s), when wages stag-

**FIGURE 2A** Hourly wage and compensation growth for production/
non-supervisory workers, 1959-2001

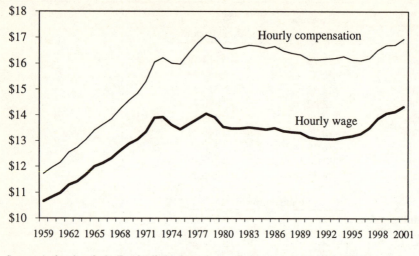

Source: Authors' analysis. For detailed information on figure sources, see Figure Notes.

nated, but otherwise shows a similar trend in compensation and wage growth.

The trend in weekly earnings corresponds closely to that of hourly earnings, with a decline in the 1980s and early 1990s and a shift to strong positive growth after 1995. Still, the weekly earnings of production and non-supervisory workers in 2001 were $490.09 per week (in 2001 dollars), $6.70 less than in 1979 and still below the $513 level of 1973.

**Table 2.5** presents post-1973 wage trends by occupation for men and women. Hourly wages declined from 1979 to 1995 among men in almost every occupational category except the highest paid white-collar occupations. For blue-collar men, who made up 39.4% of male employment in 2001, wages fell from $15.13 in 1979 to $13.41 in 1995. Men in the higher-paid white-collar occupations, on the other hand, enjoyed real wage growth in the 1980s and early 1990s but the gains were modest, up from $19.97 in 1979 to $20.77 in 1995.

The big story of the 1990s was the strong wage growth of the 1995-2000 period, which Table 2.5 shows occurred among men in every occupation. White-collar men have enjoyed roughly double the wage growth of men in blue-collar and service occupations.

Nearly three-fourths (73.9%) of women workers were white-collar workers in 2001, and their annual 1.4% wage growth over the 1989-2000 period

**TABLE 2.5** Changes in hourly wages by occupation, 1973-2001 (2001 dollars)

| Occupation* | Percent of employment 2001 | Hourly wage | | | | | | Annual percent change | | | | |
|---|---|---|---|---|---|---|---|---|---|---|---|---|
| | | 1973 | 1979 | 1989 | 1995 | 2000 | 2001 | 1973-79 | 1979-89 | 1989-2000 | 1995-2000 | 2000-01 |
| **Males** | | | | | | | | | | | | |
| *White collar* | 47.7% | $19.93 | $19.97 | $20.51 | $20.77 | $22.95 | $23.25 | 0.0% | 0.3% | 1.0% | 2.0% | 1.3% |
| Managers | 14.0 | 22.08 | 22.24 | 24.29 | 24.55 | 27.09 | 27.57 | 0.1 | 0.9 | 1.0 | 2.0 | 1.8 |
| Professional | 13.9 | 22.12 | 21.65 | 23.28 | 24.12 | 26.35 | 26.31 | -0.4 | 0.7 | 1.1 | 1.8 | -0.2 |
| Technical | 3.3 | 18.80 | 18.58 | 19.52 | 19.45 | 21.38 | 21.38 | -0.2 | 0.5 | 0.8 | 1.9 | 0.0 |
| Sales | 10.3 | 17.32 | 17.59 | 16.78 | 16.58 | 18.69 | 19.21 | 0.3 | -0.5 | 1.0 | 2.4 | 2.8 |
| Admin., clerk | 6.1 | 15.16 | 15.28 | 14.35 | 13.80 | 14.31 | 14.26 | 0.1 | -0.6 | 0.0 | 0.7 | -0.3 |
| *Service* | 10.6% | $12.49 | $11.49 | $10.70 | $10.65 | $11.30 | $11.42 | -1.4% | -0.7% | 0.5% | 1.2% | 1.1% |
| Protective | 3.1 | 16.12 | 14.59 | 14.97 | 15.18 | 16.44 | 16.28 | -1.6 | 0.3 | 0.9 | 1.6 | -1.0 |
| Other | 7.5 | 10.70 | 10.05 | 8.85 | 8.64 | 9.11 | 9.38 | -1.0 | -1.3 | 0.3 | 1.1 | 2.9 |
| *Blue collar* | 39.4% | $15.02 | $15.13 | $14.04 | $13.41 | $14.18 | $14.32 | 0.1% | -0.7% | 0.1% | 1.1% | 1.0% |
| Craft | 18.9 | 17.18 | 16.89 | 15.91 | 15.37 | 16.17 | 16.21 | -0.3 | -0.6 | 0.1 | 1.0 | 0.3 |
| Operatives | 6.8 | 13.47 | 13.97 | 13.07 | 12.28 | 12.95 | 13.05 | 0.6 | -0.7 | -0.1 | 1.1 | 0.8 |
| Trans. op. | 7.3 | 14.14 | 14.48 | 13.16 | 12.73 | 13.40 | 13.71 | 0.4 | -0.9 | 0.2 | 1.0 | 2.3 |
| Laborers | 6.3 | 12.34 | 12.26 | 10.69 | 10.10 | 10.69 | 10.75 | -0.1 | -1.4 | 0.0 | 1.2 | 0.5 |
| **Females** | | | | | | | | | | | | |
| *White collar* | 73.9% | $12.10 | $11.94 | $13.34 | $14.16 | $15.47 | $15.81 | -0.2% | 1.1% | 1.4% | 1.8% | 2.2% |
| Managers | 14.8 | 13.94 | 13.70 | 16.23 | 17.07 | 19.00 | 19.35 | -0.3 | 1.7 | 1.4 | 2.2 | 1.8 |
| Professional | 19.0 | 16.17 | 15.14 | 17.54 | 18.87 | 19.83 | 19.97 | -1.1 | 1.5 | 1.1 | 1.0 | 0.7 |
| Technical | 4.2 | 12.75 | 13.36 | 14.63 | 14.84 | 15.67 | 15.62 | 0.8 | 0.9 | 0.6 | 1.1 | -0.4 |
| Sales | 11.6 | 8.33 | 9.65 | 9.84 | 10.25 | 11.74 | 12.27 | 2.5 | 0.2 | 1.6 | 2.8 | 4.5 |
| Admin., clerk | 24.4 | 10.86 | 10.62 | 11.30 | 11.37 | 11.88 | 12.13 | -0.4 | 0.6 | 0.5 | 0.9 | 2.1 |

(cont.)

**TABLE 2.5** *(cont.)* Changes in hourly wages by occupation, 1973-2001 (2001 dollars)

| Occupation* | Percent of employment 2001 | Hourly wage | | | | | | Annual percent change | | | | |
|---|---|---|---|---|---|---|---|---|---|---|---|---|
| | 2001 | 1973 | 1979 | 1989 | 1995 | 2000 | 2001 | 1973-79 | 1979-89 | 1989-2000 | 1995-2000 | 2000-01 |
| **Females** *(cont.)* | | | | | | | | | | | | |
| *Service* | 15.5% | $7.89 | $8.16 | $7.81 | $8.01 | $8.56 | $8.91 | 0.6% | -0.4% | 0.8% | 1.3% | 4.1% |
| Protective | 0.8 | 10.78 | 10.54 | 11.67 | 12.61 | 12.46 | 12.89 | -0.4 | 1.0 | 0.6 | -0.2 | 3.5 |
| Other | 14.6 | 7.84 | 8.11 | 7.64 | 7.80 | 8.35 | 8.68 | 0.6 | -0.6 | 0.8 | 1.4 | 3.9 |
| *Blue collar* | 8.9% | $9.18 | $9.78 | $9.61 | $9.64 | $10.25 | $10.50 | 1.1% | -0.2% | 0.6% | 1.2% | 2.4% |
| Craft | 2.0 | 10.54 | 11.06 | 11.47 | 11.49 | 12.23 | 12.65 | 0.8 | 0.4 | 0.6 | 1.3 | 3.5 |
| Operatives | 4.1 | 9.00 | 9.52 | 9.03 | 9.09 | 9.73 | 9.93 | 0.9 | -0.5 | 0.7 | 1.4 | 2.1 |
| Trans. op. | 1.0 | 10.61 | 10.81 | 10.81 | 10.95 | 11.14 | 11.11 | 0.3 | 0.0 | 0.3 | 0.3 | -0.2 |
| Laborers | 1.8 | 9.06 | 9.67 | 8.90 | 8.53 | 8.83 | 9.00 | 1.1 | -0.8 | -0.1 | 0.7 | 1.9 |

* Data for private household and farming, forestry, and fishing occupations not shown and not included in wage calculations.

Source: Authors' analysis.

exceeded that of the prior decade's 1.1%. Women in every occupation (except those in which women make up less than 1% of the workforce) also enjoyed strong wage growth in the 1995-2000 period, following a period of slow growth from 1989 to 1995.

There continued to be strong wage gains in nearly every occupation in 2001 among both men and women.

## Wage trends by wage level

For any given trend in *average* wages, there will be different outcomes for particular groups of workers if wage inequality changes, as it has in recent years: it grew pervasively in the 1980s, and grew at the top and fell at the bottom through most of the 1990s. Wage trends can be described by examining groups of workers by occupation, education level, and so on, but doing so omits the impact of changes such as increasing inequality within occupation or education groups. The advantage of an analysis of wage trends by wage level or percentile (the 60th percentile, for instance, is the wage at which a worker earners more than 60% of all earners but less than 40% of all earners), as in **Table 2.6**, is that it captures all of the changes in the wage structure.

Table 2.6 provides data on wage trends for workers at different percentiles (or levels) in the wage distribution, thus allowing an examination of wage growth for low-, middle-, and high-wage earners. The data are presented for the cyclical peak years 1973, 1979, 1989, and 2000, and for the most recent year for which we have a complete year of data, 2001, as well as for 1995-2000 (so we can examine the character of the rebound in wage growth over this period). The data show that the deterioration in real wages from 1979 to 1995 was both broad and uneven. Wages were stagnant or fell for the bottom 70% of wage earners over the 1979-95 period, and grew modestly for high-wage workers—less than 1% annually—at the 90th percentile.

Wages grew strongly across the board from 1995 to 2000, rising at least 7% at every wage level. Remarkably, the fastest growth was at the two lowest wage levels (10th and 20th), where wage growth was at least 11%. However, workers with the very highest wages, at the 95th percentile, saw almost comparable wage growth of 10.6%

The pattern of wage decline differed in the 1980s and early 1990s. In the 1980s, the wage decline was greater the lower the wage, with the lowest-wage workers losing 6.2% to 14.1% and with wage stagnation at the median (50th percentile) through the 70th percentile (wage up just 1.4% over the 10 years). In the early 1990s, however, the decline in wages slowed for the bottom 40%

**TABLE 2.6** Wages for all workers by wage percentile, 1973-2001 (2001 dollars)

| Year | Wage by percentile* | | | | | | | | | |
|---|---|---|---|---|---|---|---|---|---|---|
| | 10 | 20 | 30 | 40 | 50 | 60 | 70 | 80 | 90 | 95 |
| *Real hourly wage* | | | | | | | | | | |
| 1973 | $6.30 | $7.61 | $9.04 | $10.52 | $12.06 | $13.84 | $16.07 | $18.37 | $23.09 | $28.97 |
| 1979 | 6.68 | 7.61 | 8.94 | 10.52 | 11.89 | 13.79 | 16.30 | 19.00 | 23.24 | 28.38 |
| 1989 | 5.74 | 7.14 | 8.57 | 10.24 | 11.90 | 13.89 | 16.53 | 19.76 | 24.96 | 30.68 |
| 1995 | 5.84 | 7.14 | 8.53 | 10.04 | 11.68 | 13.83 | 16.48 | 19.96 | 25.79 | 32.34 |
| 2000 | 6.48 | 7.99 | 9.34 | 10.80 | 12.59 | 14.91 | 17.67 | 21.47 | 28.06 | 35.77 |
| 2001 | 6.69 | 8.07 | 9.63 | 11.03 | 12.87 | 15.06 | 17.94 | 21.71 | 28.97 | 36.56 |
| *Dollar change* | | | | | | | | | | |
| 1973-79 | $0.37 | $0.00 | -$0.10 | $0.00 | -$0.17 | -$0.04 | $0.23 | $0.62 | $0.15 | -$0.59 |
| 1979-89 | -0.94 | -0.47 | -0.37 | -0.28 | 0.00 | 0.10 | 0.23 | 0.77 | 1.73 | 2.31 |
| 1989-2000 | 0.75 | 0.84 | 0.77 | 0.57 | 0.70 | 1.01 | 1.13 | 1.70 | 3.10 | 5.09 |
| 1989-95 | 0.10 | 0.00 | -0.04 | -0.20 | -0.21 | -0.07 | -0.05 | 0.19 | 0.82 | 1.66 |
| 1995-2000 | 0.64 | 0.85 | 0.81 | 0.77 | 0.91 | 1.08 | 1.18 | 1.51 | 2.27 | 3.43 |
| 2000-01 | 0.20 | 0.08 | 0.29 | 0.23 | 0.28 | 0.16 | 0.27 | 0.25 | 0.91 | 0.79 |
| 1979-2001 | 0.01 | 0.46 | 0.69 | 0.51 | 0.98 | 1.27 | 1.64 | 2.71 | 5.73 | 8.18 |
| *Percent change* | | | | | | | | | | |
| 1973-79 | 5.9% | 0.0% | -1.1% | 0.0% | -1.4% | -0.3% | 1.4% | 3.4% | 0.6% | -2.0% |
| 1979-89 | -14.1 | -6.2 | -4.2 | -2.7 | 0.0 | 0.7 | 1.4 | 4.0 | 7.4 | 8.1 |
| 1989-2000 | 13.1 | 11.8 | 9.0 | 5.6 | 5.9 | 7.3 | 6.9 | 8.6 | 12.4 | 16.6 |
| 1989-95 | 1.8 | -0.1 | -0.4 | -1.9 | -1.8 | -0.5 | -0.3 | 1.0 | 3.3 | 5.4 |
| 1995-2000 | 11.0 | 11.9 | 9.4 | 7.7 | 7.8 | 7.8 | 7.2 | 7.6 | 8.8 | 10.6 |
| 2000-01 | 3.2 | 1.0 | 3.1 | 2.1 | 2.2 | 1.1 | 1.6 | 1.1 | 3.2 | 2.2 |
| 1979-2001 | 0.2 | 6.0 | 7.7 | 4.9 | 8.2 | 9.2 | 10.0 | 14.3 | 24.7 | 28.8 |

* The Xth percentile wage is the wage at which X% of the wage earners earn less and (100-X)% earn more.

Source: Authors' analysis.

(wages actually grew at the 10th percentile), small gains turned into small losses for the middle, and gains diminished at the top. As mentioned above, this trend of low-wage workers experiencing more wage growth then middle-wage workers continued into the late 1990s, a change attributable to increases in the minimum wage and the drop in unemployment.

This overall picture, however, masks different outcomes for men and women. Among men in the 1980s, wages fell at nearly all parts of the wage distribution (**Table 2.7** and **Figure 2B**). In the middle, for instance, the median male hourly wage fell 7.0% between 1979 and 1989, while low-wage men lost 10.6%. In the early 1990s, across-the-board wage declines of roughly 3-4% affected the bottom 80% of male earners. Over the entire 1979-95 period the wage declines were substantial, exceeding 10%, for instance, for the median male worker. Even high-wage men at the 90th percentile, who earned about $27 per hour in 1979, did well only in relative terms, since their wage was only 6% higher in 1995 than in 1979.

As with the overall trend, the pattern of male wage deterioration shifted between the 1980s and the early 1990s. In the 1980s, wages fell most at the lower levels, while in the 1990s wages eroded in the middle and at the bottom. Thus, the wage gap between middle- and low-wage men was stable in the early 1990s, although the gap between high-wage men (at the 90th percentile) and middle- and low-wage men continued to grow.

The wage recovery among men in the 1995-2000 period corresponds to the pattern among all workers discussed earlier: strong across-the-board wage growth, with low-wage workers faring better than middle-wage workers. Among men, however, the highest-wage workers—at the 90th and 95th percentiles—clearly fared better than other male workers, excepting those at the very bottom. Over the longer term (1979-2001), the 95th percentile male wage grew faster than any other, at 26.5%, while wages at the middle and lower fell. The median male wage in 2000, for instance, was still 2.4% below its 1979 level.

The most persistent wage growth between 1979 and 1995 was among the highest-wage women (**Table 2.8** and **Figure 2C**). For instance, wages grew 19.7% for women at the 90th percentile from 1979 to 1989 and another 7.5% over 1989-95. In contrast, low-wage women saw their wages fall in the 1980s; the lowest paid at the 10th percentile experienced a decline of 16.2%. Middle-wage women saw 8.5% wage growth over that same period. For the 40th percentile and above, women's wages grew more slowly in the early 1990s than in the 1980s, with the wages in the middle falling to a stagnant 1.2% growth. A very positive development in the early 1990s was that wages for 10th percentile women rose, a market contrast to the sharp decline in the 1980s. As we will discuss below, minimum wage trends—falling in real value in the 1980s and rising in the 1990s—can explain this pattern. As with men, the far fastest wage

**TABLE 2.7** Wages for male workers by wage percentile, 1973-2001 (2001 dollars)

| Year | Wage by percentile* | | | | | | | | | |
|---|---|---|---|---|---|---|---|---|---|---|
| | 10 | 20 | 30 | 40 | 50 | 60 | 70 | 80 | 90 | 95 |
| *Real hourly wage* | | | | | | | | | | |
| 1973 | $7.44 | $9.55 | $11.26 | $12.91 | $14.63 | $16.59 | $18.25 | $21.01 | $26.76 | $32.25 |
| 1979 | 7.35 | 9.34 | 11.24 | 13.08 | 14.96 | 16.99 | 19.06 | 22.14 | 26.95 | 32.32 |
| 1989 | 6.57 | 8.23 | 10.10 | 11.95 | 13.91 | 16.38 | 18.94 | 22.19 | 27.80 | 34.52 |
| 1995 | 6.33 | 8.00 | 9.51 | 11.43 | 13.41 | 15.67 | 18.41 | 22.01 | 28.70 | 35.89 |
| 2000 | 7.07 | 8.69 | 10.36 | 12.28 | 14.37 | 16.72 | 19.66 | 23.84 | 31.74 | 39.73 |
| 2001 | 7.15 | 8.90 | 10.41 | 12.38 | 14.60 | 17.06 | 19.97 | 24.20 | 32.19 | 40.89 |
| *Dollar change* | | | | | | | | | | |
| 1973-79 | -$0.10 | -$0.21 | -$0.02 | $0.17 | $0.33 | $0.41 | $0.81 | $1.13 | $0.20 | $0.08 |
| 1979-89 | -0.78 | -1.11 | -1.14 | -1.12 | -1.05 | -0.62 | -0.13 | 0.05 | 0.85 | 2.19 |
| 1989-2000 | 0.50 | 0.46 | 0.26 | 0.33 | 0.46 | 0.34 | 0.72 | 1.65 | 3.94 | 5.21 |
| 1989-95 | -0.24 | -0.23 | -0.58 | -0.52 | -0.51 | -0.71 | -0.53 | -0.18 | 0.90 | 1.38 |
| 1995-2000 | 0.73 | 0.69 | 0.85 | 0.85 | 0.96 | 1.05 | 1.25 | 1.83 | 3.04 | 3.83 |
| 2000-01 | 0.09 | 0.21 | 0.05 | 0.10 | 0.23 | 0.34 | 0.32 | 0.36 | 0.44 | 1.16 |
| 1979-2001 | -0.19 | -0.44 | -0.82 | -0.70 | -0.36 | 0.06 | 0.91 | 2.06 | 5.23 | 8.57 |
| *Percent change* | | | | | | | | | | |
| 1973-79 | -1.3% | -2.2% | -0.2% | 1.3% | 2.3% | 2.5% | 4.4% | 5.4% | 0.7% | 0.2% |
| 1979-89 | -10.6 | -11.9 | -10.2 | -8.6 | -7.0 | -3.6 | -0.7 | 0.2 | 3.1 | 6.8 |
| 1989-2000 | 7.6 | 5.6 | 2.6 | 2.8 | 3.3 | 2.1 | 3.8 | 7.4 | 14.2 | 15.1 |
| 1989-95 | -3.6 | -2.7 | -5.8 | -4.3 | -3.6 | -4.3 | -2.8 | -0.8 | 3.2 | 4.0 |
| 1995-2000 | 11.6 | 8.6 | 8.9 | 7.4 | 7.2 | 6.7 | 6.8 | 8.3 | 10.6 | 10.7 |
| 2000-01 | 1.2 | 2.4 | 0.5 | 0.8 | 1.6 | 2.0 | 1.6 | 1.5 | 1.4 | 2.9 |
| 1979-2001 | -2.6 | -4.7 | -7.3 | -5.3 | -2.4 | 0.4 | 4.8 | 9.3 | 19.4 | 26.5 |

* The Xth percentile wage is the wage at which X% of the wage earners earn less and (100-X)% earn more.

Source: Authors' analysis.

**FIGURE 2B** Change in real hourly wages for men by wage percentile, 1973-2001

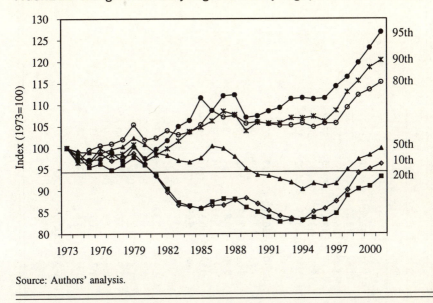

Source: Authors' analysis.

growth among women was at the highest level—the 95th percentile—where wages grew 52.1% from 1979 to 2001. This is more than double the wage growth for the median woman, 21.6%, over the same period.

As with men, women's wages rose strongly across the board in the 1995-2000 period. It is remarkable that this wage growth was fairly even among all women, from about 8.5% to 10%.

Tables 2.6 through 2.8 also include data for 2001 and the change from 2000 to 2001, the start of the current business cycle and the first part of the current downturn—unemployment rose from 4.0% in 2000 to 4.8% in 2001. It is still too early to draw any conclusions about the current downturn using annual data (such as for the full years of 2000 and 2001); this is why the wage section of the Introduction compares data from the start of the downturn (in late 2000, when unemployment started to rise) to data for mid-2002). Two aspects of the wage patterns of 2000 to 2001 are notable. One is that, even though unemployment rose, real wages continued to grow across the board among both men and women. Yet the strongest growth has been at the very highest wage levels—the 95th percentile—where wages grew 2.9% and 3.0%, respectively, for men and women. This trend reflects the seeming renewal of the wage patterns of the 1980s, where wages grew faster at the top than the middle and faster at the middle than the bottom, for an across-the-board widening of wage

**TABLE 2.8** Wages for female workers by wage percentile, 1973-2001 (2001 dollars)

| Year | \multicolumn{10}{c}{Wage by percentile*} | | | | | | | | | |
|---|---|---|---|---|---|---|---|---|---|---|
| | 10 | 20 | 30 | 40 | 50 | 60 | 70 | 80 | 90 | 95 |
| *Real hourly wage* | | | | | | | | | | |
| 1973 | $5.24 | $6.51 | $7.33 | $8.20 | $9.24 | $10.40 | $11.71 | $13.50 | $16.70 | $19.73 |
| 1979 | 6.37 | 6.90 | 7.49 | 8.36 | 9.38 | 10.66 | 11.87 | 13.81 | 17.19 | 20.32 |
| 1989 | 5.34 | 6.58 | 7.61 | 8.75 | 10.17 | 11.62 | 13.68 | 16.40 | 20.58 | 24.82 |
| 1995 | 5.59 | 6.66 | 7.79 | 8.96 | 10.29 | 11.85 | 14.08 | 17.21 | 22.12 | 27.48 |
| 2000 | 6.16 | 7.33 | 8.44 | 9.78 | 11.17 | 12.91 | 15.29 | 18.58 | 24.41 | 30.00 |
| 2001 | 6.23 | 7.49 | 8.71 | 9.97 | 11.40 | 13.20 | 15.56 | 18.89 | 24.82 | 30.90 |
| *Dollar change* | | | | | | | | | | |
| 1973-79 | $1.13 | $0.39 | $0.16 | $0.16 | $0.14 | $0.26 | $0.16 | $0.31 | $0.49 | $0.59 |
| 1979-89 | -1.03 | -0.32 | 0.12 | 0.39 | 0.79 | 0.96 | 1.81 | 2.58 | 3.39 | 4.50 |
| 1989-2000 | 0.82 | 0.75 | 0.83 | 1.03 | 1.00 | 1.29 | 1.61 | 2.18 | 3.83 | 5.18 |
| 1989-95 | 0.25 | 0.08 | 0.17 | 0.21 | 0.12 | 0.23 | 0.40 | 0.81 | 1.54 | 2.66 |
| 1995-2000 | 0.57 | 0.67 | 0.66 | 0.82 | 0.88 | 1.05 | 1.21 | 1.37 | 2.30 | 2.51 |
| 2000-01 | 0.07 | 0.15 | 0.27 | 0.20 | 0.23 | 0.29 | 0.26 | 0.31 | 0.41 | 0.90 |
| 1979-2001 | -0.14 | 0.58 | 1.22 | 1.62 | 2.02 | 2.54 | 3.68 | 5.08 | 7.63 | 10.58 |
| *Percent change* | | | | | | | | | | |
| 1973-79 | 21.5% | 5.9% | 2.2% | 2.0% | 1.5% | 2.5% | 1.4% | 2.3% | 2.9% | 3.0% |
| 1979-89 | -16.2 | -4.7 | 1.6 | 4.7 | 8.5 | 9.0 | 15.2 | 18.7 | 19.7 | 22.2 |
| 1989-2000 | 15.3 | 11.4 | 10.9 | 11.8 | 9.8 | 11.1 | 11.8 | 13.3 | 18.6 | 20.9 |
| 1989-95 | 4.6 | 1.3 | 2.3 | 2.4 | 1.2 | 2.0 | 2.9 | 5.0 | 7.5 | 10.7 |
| 1995-2000 | 10.2 | 10.0 | 8.4 | 9.1 | 8.5 | 8.9 | 8.6 | 7.9 | 10.4 | 9.1 |
| 2000-01 | 1.1 | 2.1 | 3.2 | 2.0 | 2.1 | 2.3 | 1.7 | 1.7 | 1.7 | 3.0 |
| 1979-2001 | -2.2 | 8.5 | 16.3 | 19.4 | 21.6 | 23.9 | 31.0 | 36.8 | 44.4 | 52.1 |

* The Xth percentile wage is the wage at which X% of the wage earners earn less and (100-X)% earn more.

Source: Authors' analysis.

**FIGURE 2C** Change in real hourly wages for women by wage percentile, 1973-2001

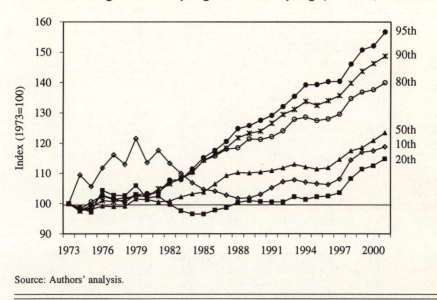

Source: Authors' analysis.

inequality. This trend is confirmed in the more recent data presented in the Introduction. Thus, high-wage earners seem to perennially enjoy strong wage growth, whether in a boom or in a downturn.

## Shifts in low-wage jobs

Another useful way of characterizing changes in the wage structure is to examine the trend in the proportion of workers earning low, middle, and high wages. These trends are presented in **Table 2.9** for all workers and for men and women. The workforce is divided into six wage groups based on multiples of the "poverty-wage level," or the hourly wage that a full-time, year-round worker must earn to sustain a family of four at the poverty threshold, which was $8.70 in 2001 (in 2001 dollars). Thus, workers are assigned to a wage group according to the degree to which they earned more (or less) than poverty-level wages.

Women are much more likely to earn low wages than men. In 2000, 31.1% of women earned poverty-level wages or less, significantly more than the share of men (19.5%). Women are also much less likely to earn very high wages. In 2000 only 7.8% of women, but 16.0% of men, earned at least three times the poverty-level wage.

**TABLE 2.9** Distribution of total employment by wage level, 1973-2001

| | Share of employment by wage multiple of poverty wage* | | | | | | | |
|---|---|---|---|---|---|---|---|---|
| | Poverty level wages: | | | | | | | |
| Year | 0-75 | 75-100 | Total** | 100-125 | 125-200 | 200-300 | 300+ | Total |
| **All** | | | | | | | | |
| 1973 | 11.7% | 18.2% | 29.9% | 13.8% | 35.0% | 14.9% | 6.4% | 100% |
| 1979 | 4.9 | 22.2 | 27.1 | 14.2 | 33.0 | 18.5 | 7.1 | 100 |
| 1989 | 13.9 | 16.5 | 30.5 | 12.6 | 30.9 | 17.2 | 8.9 | 100 |
| 2000 | 9.8 | 15.2 | 25.0 | 15.3 | 28.5 | 19.0 | 12.1 | 100 |
| 2001 | 9.3 | 14.6 | 23.9 | 14.5 | 30.0 | 18.7 | 12.8 | 100 |
| *Change* | | | | | | | | |
| 1979-89 | 9.0% | -5.7% | 3.3% | -1.6% | -2.1% | -1.4% | 1.8% | |
| 1989-2000 | -4.1 | -1.3 | -5.4 | 2.7 | -2.4 | 1.9 | 3.2 | |
| 2000-01 | -0.5 | -0.6 | -1.1 | -0.9 | 1.5 | -0.3 | 0.7 | |
| **Men** | | | | | | | | |
| 1973 | 5.6% | 11.9% | 17.4% | 11.2% | 40.2% | 21.5% | 9.7% | 100% |
| 1979 | 2.8 | 12.9 | 15.7 | 10.8 | 35.5 | 26.8 | 11.2 | 100 |
| 1989 | 9.5 | 13.2 | 22.7 | 10.7 | 31.8 | 21.7 | 13.1 | 100 |
| 2000 | 7.2 | 12.3 | 19.5 | 13.6 | 28.7 | 22.3 | 16.0 | 100 |
| 2001 | 6.8 | 11.8 | 18.6 | 12.8 | 30.1 | 21.6 | 16.9 | 100 |
| *Change* | | | | | | | | |
| 1979-89 | 6.7% | 0.3% | 7.0% | -0.1% | -3.7% | -5.1% | 1.9% | |
| 1989-2000 | -2.3 | -0.9 | -3.2 | 2.8 | -3.1 | 0.6 | 3.0 | |
| 2000-01 | -0.3 | -0.5 | -0.8 | -0.7 | 1.4 | -0.7 | 0.9 | |
| **Women** | | | | | | | | |
| 1973 | 20.5% | 27.5% | 48.0% | 17.6% | 27.5% | 5.4% | 1.6% | 100% |
| 1979 | 7.8 | 34.4 | 42.1 | 18.6 | 29.8 | 7.7 | 1.8 | 100 |
| 1989 | 19.0 | 20.3 | 39.2 | 14.8 | 29.8 | 12.0 | 4.2 | 100 |
| 2000 | 12.7 | 18.4 | 31.1 | 17.3 | 28.4 | 15.5 | 7.8 | 100 |
| 2001 | 12.1 | 17.6 | 29.7 | 16.3 | 30.0 | 15.7 | 8.4 | 100 |
| *Change* | | | | | | | | |
| 1979-89 | 11.2% | -14.1% | -2.9% | -3.8% | 0.1% | 4.3% | 2.4% | |
| 1989-2000 | -6.3 | -1.8 | -8.1 | 2.5 | -1.5 | 3.5 | 3.6 | |
| 2000-01 | -0.6 | -0.8 | -1.4 | -1.0 | 1.6 | 0.2 | 0.6 | |

\* The wage ranges are equivalent in 2001 dollars to: $6.53 and below (0-75), $6.53-$8.70 (75-100), $8.70-$10.88 (100-125), $10.88-$17.40 (125-200), $17.40-$26.10 (200-300), and $26.10 and above (300+).

\*\* Combines lowest two categories and represents the share of wage earners earning poverty-level wages.

Source: Authors' analysis.

**FIGURE 2D** Share of workers earning poverty-level wages, by gender, 1973-2001

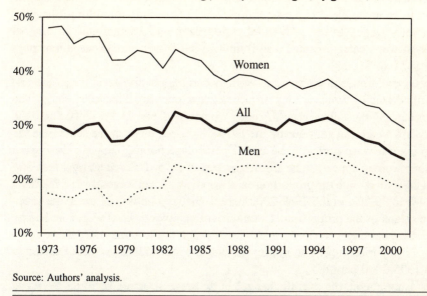

Source: Authors' analysis.

As we have seen with other dimensions of the wage structure, there is a sharp change in the trend before and after 1995. The share of workers earning at least 25% below the poverty-level wage (labeled "0-75") expanded significantly between 1979 and 1989, from 4.9% to 13.9% of the workforce. The total group earning poverty-level wages rose from 27.1% in 1979 to 30.5% in 1989. Thus, over the 1979-89 period there was not only a sizable growth (3.3% of the workforce) in the proportion of workers earning poverty-level wages, but also a shift within this group to those earning very low wages.

The share of workers earning poverty-level wages continued to expand, though more slowly, in the 1989-95 period, but then, not surprisingly given wage trends at the bottom, contracted in the 1995-2000 period (**Figure 2D**). The result was a fall in the poverty-wage employment share to 25.0% in 2000, down 5.4 percentage points from 1989 and the lowest level since 1973. Those earning very low wages still represented 9.8% of the workforce in 2000, 4.9% more than in 1979. The real wage growth at the bottom of the wage scale in the latter 1990s thus rapidly diminished the share of workers earning poverty-level wages and offset the growth in poverty-wage shares over the 1979-95 period. However, a large share of the workforce, roughly a fourth, still earns poverty-level wages.

Over the 1979-89 period, the entire wage structure shifted downward, with proportionately fewer workers in the middle- and high-wage groups in 1989 than in 1979. The only exception is the modest expansion of the share of the workforce at the very highest earnings level (exceeding three times the poverty-level wage). In the 1989-2000 period there was a larger shift to the two highest-wage categories and a shift upward into lower middle-wage jobs paying $8.70 to $10.88.

Overall trends in the share of workers earning poverty-level wages are primarily driven by trends among women, since women are disproportionately the ones earning these low wages. Among women workers, 11.2% shifted into the very-low-wage category during the 1979-89 period, while at the same time the two highest-wage groups grew by 6.7 percentage points. The shift downward among women appears to be an enlargement of the workforce earning very low wages, even though the proportion earning poverty-level wages overall fell from 42.1% to 39.2%. In the 1989-2000 period, the very bottom of the wage structure shrank as the proportion of women earning poverty-level wages, including the share earning very low wages, diminished. At the same time, the top two wage categories grew. The improvements, as Figure 2D shows, accelerated in the 1995-2000 period.

Among men, the overall changes in the wage structure between 1979 and 1989 meant proportionately fewer middle-wage workers and more low-wage workers, with very little growth in the share of very high earners. For instance, 7.0% of the male workforce shifted into the group earning less than the poverty-level wage, and the proportion of men in the other wage groups (except the highest) contracted. Over the 1989-2000 period the share of men earning poverty-level wages declined, by 3.2%. Regardless of the recent trends, the share of poverty-level earners among men was 19.5% in 2000, still 3.8% more than in 1979.

**Tables 2.10, 2.11,** and **2.12** (and **Figure 2E**) present an analysis similar to the one in Table 2.9 for white, black, and Hispanic employment. The proportion of minority workers earning low wages is substantial—31.8% of black workers and 42.5% of Hispanic workers in 2000. Minority women are even more likely to be low earners—36.5% of black women and 49.3% of Hispanic women in 2000. The wage structure for each race/gender group has shifted over the last few decades.

Table 2.10 shows the modest shift downward in the wage structure for whites in the 1970s, followed by a larger downward shift in the 1979-89 period. In the 1989-2000 period, however, whites moved from poverty level to low- to middle-wage jobs and into very-high-wage jobs. By 2000, the poverty-wage share among white workers had fallen to 21.2%, 4.9% below its 1979 level, all due to progress in the late 1990s. Over the entire period from 1979 to 2000, however, white workers shifted toward both the very bottom—the lowest earners—and the very

**TABLE 2.10** Distribution of white employment by wage level, 1973-2001

| | Share of employment by wage multiple of poverty wage* | | | | | | | |
| | Poverty level wages: | | | | | | | |
| Year | 0-75 | 75-100 | Total** | 100-125 | 125-200 | 200-300 | 300+ | Total |
|---|---|---|---|---|---|---|---|---|
| **All** | | | | | | | | |
| 1973 | 10.3% | 17.1% | 27.5% | 13.6% | 35.8% | 16.1% | 7.1% | 100% |
| 1979 | 4.5 | 20.6 | 25.1 | 13.9 | 33.5 | 19.6 | 7.9 | 100 |
| 1989 | 12.3 | 15.1 | 27.5 | 12.3 | 31.6 | 18.5 | 10.1 | 100 |
| 2000 | 8.1 | 13.1 | 21.2 | 14.3 | 29.4 | 21.1 | 14.0 | 100 |
| 2001 | 7.7 | 12.4 | 20.1 | 13.3 | 30.9 | 20.8 | 14.9 | 100 |
| *Change* | | | | | | | | |
| 1979-89 | 7.8% | -5.4% | 2.4% | -1.5% | -1.9% | -1.1% | 2.2% | |
| 1989-2000 | -4.2 | -2.0 | -6.2 | 2.0 | -2.2 | 2.5 | 4.0 | |
| 2000-01 | -0.4 | -0.7 | -1.1 | -1.0 | 1.5 | -0.3 | 0.9 | |
| **Men** | | | | | | | | |
| 1973 | 4.6% | 10.3% | 14.9% | 10.7% | 40.4% | 23.1% | 10.8% | 100% |
| 1979 | 2.4 | 11.0 | 13.4 | 10.0 | 35.7 | 28.4 | 12.4 | 100 |
| 1989 | 7.7 | 11.2 | 18.9 | 10.1 | 32.3 | 23.7 | 15.0 | 100 |
| 2000 | 5.5 | 9.7 | 15.2 | 11.7 | 29.2 | 24.9 | 18.9 | 100 |
| 2001 | 5.2 | 9.3 | 14.5 | 11.1 | 30.5 | 24.1 | 19.8 | 100 |
| *Change* | | | | | | | | |
| 1979-89 | 5.3% | 0.2% | 5.5% | 0.0% | -3.4% | -4.7% | 2.6% | |
| 1989-2000 | -2.2 | -1.5 | -3.7 | 1.7 | -3.1 | 1.2 | 3.8 | |
| 2000-01 | -0.3 | -0.4 | -0.7 | -0.7 | 1.2 | -0.8 | 1.0 | |
| **Women** | | | | | | | | |
| 1973 | 18.9% | 27.2% | 46.1% | 17.9% | 28.9% | 5.6% | 1.6% | 100% |
| 1979 | 7.4 | 33.2 | 40.6 | 18.9 | 30.7 | 8.0 | 1.9 | 100 |
| 1989 | 17.6 | 19.5 | 37.1 | 14.9 | 30.8 | 12.7 | 4.5 | 100 |
| 2000 | 11.0 | 16.7 | 27.7 | 17.1 | 29.5 | 16.9 | 8.8 | 100 |
| 2001 | 10.4 | 15.7 | 26.2 | 15.8 | 31.3 | 17.2 | 9.6 | 100 |
| *Change* | | | | | | | | |
| 1979-89 | 10.2% | -13.6% | -3.4% | -4.1% | 0.2% | 4.7% | 2.6% | |
| 1989-2000 | -6.6 | -2.8 | -9.4 | 2.3 | -1.3 | 4.1 | 4.3 | |
| 2000-01 | -0.5 | -1.0 | -1.5 | -1.3 | 1.7 | 0.3 | 0.8 | |

\* The wage ranges are equivalent in 2001 dollars to: $6.53 and below (0-75), $6.53-$8.70 (75-100), $8.70-$10.88 (100-125), $10.88-$17.40 (125-200), $17.40-$26.10 (200-300), and $26.10 and above (300+).

\*\* Combines lowest two categories and represents the share of wage earners earning poverty-level wages.

Source: Authors' analysis.

**TABLE 2.11** Distribution of black employment by wage level, 1973-2001

| | Share of employment by wage multiple of poverty wage* | | | | | | | |
| | Poverty level wages: | | | | | | | |
| Year | 0-75 | 75-100 | Total** | 100-125 | 125-200 | 200-300 | 300+ | Total |
|---|---|---|---|---|---|---|---|---|
| **All** | | | | | | | | |
| 1973 | 20.2% | 23.9% | 44.1% | 14.2% | 31.1% | 8.1% | 2.4% | 100% |
| 1979 | 7.3 | 30.2 | 37.5 | 15.6 | 31.0 | 13.0 | 3.0 | 100 |
| 1989 | 19.8 | 20.9 | 40.7 | 14.6 | 28.3 | 12.6 | 3.8 | 100 |
| 2000 | 12.3 | 19.5 | 31.8 | 18.7 | 29.0 | 15.0 | 5.6 | 100 |
| 2001 | 11.7 | 19.5 | 31.2 | 18.5 | 30.0 | 14.0 | 6.3 | 100 |
| | | | | | | | | |
| *Change* | | | | | | | | |
| 1979-89 | 12.6% | -9.4% | 3.2% | -1.0% | -2.7% | -0.4% | 2.6% | |
| 1989-2000 | -7.5 | -1.4 | -8.9 | 4.1 | 0.7 | 2.4 | 4.3 | |
| 2000-01 | -0.6 | 0.0 | -0.6 | -0.2 | 1.1 | -1.0 | 0.8 | |
| | | | | | | | | |
| **Men** | | | | | | | | |
| 1973 | 11.8% | 20.2% | 31.9% | 13.4% | 40.3% | 11.4% | 3.0% | 100% |
| 1979 | 4.9 | 22.3 | 27.2 | 14.6 | 35.2 | 18.5 | 4.5 | 100 |
| 1989 | 15.5 | 19.8 | 35.3 | 14.2 | 30.4 | 15.4 | 4.7 | 100 |
| 2000 | 10.0 | 16.3 | 26.3 | 19.2 | 30.7 | 17.1 | 6.7 | 100 |
| 2001 | 9.1 | 16.6 | 25.7 | 18.9 | 31.9 | 15.7 | 7.8 | 100 |
| | | | | | | | | |
| *Change* | | | | | | | | |
| 1979-89 | 10.6% | -2.5% | 8.1% | -0.4% | -4.8% | -3.1% | 0.2% | |
| 1989-2000 | -5.5 | -3.5 | -8.9 | 5.0 | 0.2 | 1.7 | 2.0 | |
| 2000-01 | -0.8 | 0.3 | -0.6 | -0.3 | 1.2 | -1.4 | 1.1 | |
| | | | | | | | | |
| **Women** | | | | | | | | |
| 1973 | 30.1% | 28.1% | 58.2% | 15.2% | 20.5% | 4.4% | 1.7% | 100% |
| 1979 | 9.8 | 38.7 | 48.5 | 16.6 | 26.5 | 7.1 | 1.4 | 100 |
| 1989 | 24.0 | 21.8 | 45.9 | 14.9 | 26.2 | 10.0 | 3.0 | 100 |
| 2000 | 14.3 | 22.2 | 36.5 | 18.3 | 27.5 | 13.1 | 4.6 | 100 |
| 2001 | 13.9 | 21.9 | 35.8 | 18.1 | 28.5 | 12.5 | 5.2 | 100 |
| | | | | | | | | |
| *Change* | | | | | | | | |
| 1979-89 | 14.2% | -16.9% | -2.7% | -1.6% | -0.2% | 2.9% | 1.7% | |
| 1989-2000 | -9.8 | 0.3 | -9.4 | 3.3 | 1.3 | 3.2 | 1.6 | |
| 2000-01 | -0.4 | -0.3 | -0.7 | -0.1 | 1.0 | -0.7 | 0.5 | |

\*    The wage ranges are equivalent in 2001 dollars to: $6.53 and below (0-75), $6.53-$8.70 (75-100), $8.70-$10.88 (100-125), $10.88-$17.40 (125-200), $17.40-$26.10 (200-300), and $26.10 and above (300+).

\*\*   Combines lowest two categories and represents the share of wage earners earning poverty-level wages.

Source: Authors' analysis.

**TABLE 2.12** Distribution of Hispanic employment by wage level, 1973-2001

| | Share of employment by wage multiple of poverty wage* | | | | | | | |
| | Poverty level wages: | | | | | | | |
| Year | 0-75 | 75-100 | Total** | 100-125 | 125-200 | 200-300 | 300+ | Total |
|------|------|--------|---------|---------|---------|---------|------|-------|
| **All** | | | | | | | | |
| 1973 | 16.8% | 25.4% | 42.3% | 17.4% | 30.4% | 7.7% | 2.1% | 100% |
| 1979 | 6.4 | 31.5 | 37.9 | 16.4 | 30.0 | 12.7 | 3.0 | 100 |
| 1989 | 21.8 | 24.4 | 46.2 | 13.0 | 27.2 | 10.0 | 3.6 | 100 |
| 2000 | 17.8 | 24.7 | 42.5 | 18.8 | 23.4 | 10.5 | 4.7 | 100 |
| 2001 | 16.9 | 23.5 | 40.4 | 18.1 | 25.8 | 10.9 | 4.8 | 100 |
| | | | | | | | | |
| *Change* | | | | | | | | |
| 1979-89 | 15.4% | -7.1% | 8.3% | -3.4% | -2.8% | -2.7% | 0.6% | |
| 1989-2000 | -4.0 | 0.3 | -3.7 | 5.8 | -3.8 | 0.5 | 1.2 | |
| 2000-01 | -0.9 | -1.2 | -2.1 | -0.8 | 2.4 | 0.4 | 0.1 | |
| | | | | | | | | |
| **Men** | | | | | | | | |
| 1973 | 10.6% | 21.0% | 31.7% | 16.7% | 38.0% | 10.6% | 2.9% | 100% |
| 1979 | 4.3 | 22.8 | 27.1 | 15.9 | 35.0 | 17.8 | 4.1 | 100 |
| 1989 | 18.1 | 23.0 | 41.1 | 12.9 | 29.0 | 12.5 | 4.5 | 100 |
| 2000 | 14.2 | 23.3 | 37.6 | 19.8 | 24.8 | 12.2 | 5.6 | 100 |
| 2001 | 13.8 | 22.1 | 35.9 | 18.4 | 27.5 | 12.3 | 5.9 | 100 |
| | | | | | | | | |
| *Change* | | | | | | | | |
| 1979-89 | 13.8% | 0.1% | 14.0% | -3.0% | -6.1% | -5.3% | 0.4% | |
| 1989-2000 | -3.9 | 0.4 | -3.5 | 6.9 | -4.1 | -0.3 | 1.1 | |
| 2000-01 | -0.5 | -1.3 | -1.7 | -1.4 | 2.7 | 0.2 | 0.2 | |
| | | | | | | | | |
| **Women** | | | | | | | | |
| 1973 | 27.6% | 33.0% | 60.6% | 18.7% | 17.2% | 2.8% | 0.7% | 100% |
| 1979 | 9.6 | 44.8 | 54.5 | 17.3 | 22.2 | 4.8 | 1.2 | 100 |
| 1989 | 27.2 | 26.6 | 53.8 | 13.2 | 24.6 | 6.3 | 2.1 | 100 |
| 2000 | 22.7 | 26.6 | 49.3 | 17.5 | 21.5 | 8.2 | 3.5 | 100 |
| 2001 | 21.1 | 25.5 | 46.6 | 17.6 | 23.4 | 9.0 | 3.4 | 100 |
| | | | | | | | | |
| *Change* | | | | | | | | |
| 1979-89 | 17.6% | -18.3% | -0.7% | -4.1% | 2.4% | 1.5% | 0.9% | |
| 1989-2000 | -4.5 | 0.0 | -4.5 | 4.3 | -3.1 | 1.9 | 1.4 | |
| 2000-01 | -1.6 | -1.1 | -2.7 | 0.1 | 1.9 | 0.7 | -0.1 | |

\*   The wage ranges are equivalent in 2001 dollars to: $6.53 and below (0-75), $6.53-$8.70 (75-100), $8.70-$10.88 (100-125), $10.88-$17.40 (125-200), $17.40-$26.10 (200-300), and $26.10 and above (300+).

\*\*  Combines lowest two categories and represents the share of wage earners earning poverty-level wages.

Source: Authors' analysis.

**FIGURE 2E** Share of workers earning poverty-level wages, by race/ethnicity, 1973-2001

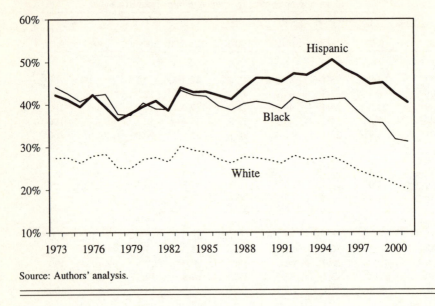

Source: Authors' analysis.

top. The white male and white female wage structures have moved in different directions. In the 1980s, white women shifted substantially into the lowest and highest earnings groups. In contrast, the share of white men eroded in the middle-wage range in the 1980s, grew in the very-high-wage category, and shifted (although less than for women) to the very bottom. Similarly, the improvements in the 1990s were far greater for white women than for white men. Over the longer term, in fact, white women have seen their share of poverty-level earners decline remarkably, from 46.1% in 1973 to 27.7% in 2000. The share of high and very high earners also grew strongly among white women.

Blacks (Table 2.11) in the 1980s saw a dramatic downward shift out of middle-wage employment into both very-low-wage employment and higher-wage employment. The shift out of poverty-level jobs in the 1990s reversed the 1980s expansion of very low earners By 2000, the share of poverty-wage earners among men, 26.3%, was about the same as in 1979 but was at a historic low of 36.5% among women. Still, though, in 2000, 31.8% of black workers were in jobs paying less than poverty-level wages. The post-1979 trends, despite the recent improvement, have left black men with fewer middle-wage jobs and more very-low-earning jobs but also some very-high-wage jobs. In contrast, among black women every share has grown except for that earning just under a poverty-level wage.

Since 1979, despite the recent turnaround, the Hispanic wage structure has generally shifted downward, for both men and women, with modest growth in the highest-wage jobs (Table 2.12). Both Hispanic women and men shifted in large numbers into the lowest-wage jobs between 1979 and 1989, and saw modest improvement over the 1990s. The growth in the percentage of Hispanic males earning poverty-level wages was substantial, up from 27.1% in 1979 to 37.6% in 2000. Roughly half (49.3% ) of Hispanic women earned poverty-level wages in 2000, a decline from the 54.5% who did so in 1979.

## Trends in benefit growth and inequality

The analysis above shows that real wages declined for a wide array of workers over both the 1980s and the early 1990s, and then rose strongly after 1995. Also, total compensation, the real value of both wages and fringe benefits, grew at the same pace as wages over the 1979-95 period. Benefits grew faster than wages during much of that time, but, since they make up a small (15-20%) share of compensation, their growth did not generate fast compensation growth overall. A new trend emerged in the 1990s, however. Benefit growth was slightly slower than wage growth in the early 1990s and then fell in the middle and late 1990s. The result was a sizable divergence between compensation and wage growth. Fast growth in health care costs caused benefits to start growing again in 2000, exceeding the pace of wage growth. In this section we explore these issues further and examine changes in benefits by type of benefit and changes in health and pension coverage for different groups of workers. This analysis allows an examination of the growing inequality of benefits. We are not able to examine the benefit of stock options, because there are no comprehensive historical data on the extent and quality of stock option programs. What evidence is available suggests that stock options are mostly provided to top managerial workers (only 1.7% of all private-sector workers and 4.6% of executives had them in 1999). Chapter 3 provides some more discussion of benefits by industry and other categories.

**Table 2.13** provides a breakdown of growth in non-wage compensation, or benefits, using the two available data series (the "aggregates" were shown already in Tables 2.2 and 2.3). The NIPA data provide a long-term perspective. In the 1948-73 and 1973-79 periods, the inflation-adjusted value of benefits grew by $0.09 and $0.29 each year, respectively, translating into annual growth rates of 7.6% and 5.0%. In contrast, the average value of non-wage compensation,

**TABLE 2.13** Growth of specific fringe benefits, 1948-2002 (2001 dollars)

| Year | Voluntary benefits | | | Payroll taxes | Total benefits and non-wage compensation |
|---|---|---|---|---|---|
| | Pension | Health* | Subtotal | | |
| **BEA NIPA**\*\* | | | | | |
| 1948 | $0.13 | $0.09 | $0.22 | $0.19 | $0.41 |
| 1967 | 0.53 | 0.53 | 1.06 | 0.59 | 1.65 |
| 1973 | 0.83 | 0.79 | 1.63 | 0.91 | 2.54 |
| 1979 | 1.18 | 1.13 | 2.31 | 1.08 | 3.39 |
| 1989 | 1.00 | 1.43 | 2.43 | 1.32 | 3.75 |
| 1992 | 1.02 | 1.61 | 2.62 | 1.39 | 4.02 |
| 1995 | 0.99 | 1.47 | 2.46 | 1.41 | 3.87 |
| 2000 | 0.79 | 1.37 | 2.16 | 1.49 | 3.65 |
| *Annual dollar change* | | | | | |
| 1948-73 | $0.03 | $0.03 | $0.06 | $0.03 | $0.09 |
| 1973-79 | 0.11 | 0.10 | 0.21 | 0.08 | 0.29 |
| 1979-89 | 0.02 | 0.06 | 0.08 | 0.04 | 0.12 |
| 1989-2000 | -0.01 | 0.04 | 0.03 | 0.03 | 0.06 |
| 1989-95 | 0.00 | 0.01 | 0.01 | 0.02 | 0.02 |
| 1995-2000 | -0.04 | -0.05 | -0.09 | 0.02 | -0.07 |
| 1979-2000 | -0.05 | -0.07 | -0.12 | -0.07 | -0.18 |
| *Annual percent change* | | | | | |
| 1948-73 | 7.8% | 9.0% | 8.3% | 6.5% | 7.6% |
| 1973-79 | 6.0 | 6.1 | 6.1 | 2.9 | 5.0 |
| 1979-89 | -1.6 | 2.3 | 0.5 | 2.0 | 1.0 |
| 1989-2000 | -2.1 | -0.4 | -1.1 | 1.1 | -0.2 |
| 1989-95 | -0.2 | 0.5 | 0.2 | 1.2 | 0.5 |
| 1995-2000 | -4.3 | -1.4 | -2.5 | 1.1 | -1.1 |
| 1979-2000 | -1.9 | 0.9 | -0.3 | 1.6 | 0.4 |
| **BLS ECI levels**\*\*\* | | | | | |
| 1987 | $0.72 | $1.47 | $2.19 | $1.70 | $3.89 |
| 1989 | 0.58 | 1.53 | 2.12 | 1.77 | 3.89 |
| 1995 | 0.60 | 1.41 | 2.01 | 1.84 | 3.85 |
| 2000 | 0.61 | 1.24 | 1.85 | 1.73 | 3.58 |
| 2001 | 0.62 | 1.28 | 1.90 | 1.73 | 3.63 |
| 2002 | 0.62 | 1.34 | 1.96 | 1.78 | 3.74 |
| *Annual dollar change* | | | | | |
| 1989-2000 | $0.00 | -$0.03 | -$0.02 | $0.00 | -$0.03 |
| 1989-95 | 0.00 | -0.02 | -0.02 | 0.01 | -0.01 |
| 1995-2000 | 0.00 | -0.03 | -0.03 | -0.02 | -0.05 |
| 2000-02 | 0.01 | 0.05 | 0.05 | 0.03 | 0.08 |
| *Annual percent change* | | | | | |
| 1989-2000 | 0.4% | -1.9% | -1.2% | -0.2% | -0.7% |
| 1989-95 | 0.5 | -1.4 | -0.9 | 0.6 | -0.2 |
| 1995-2000 | 0.3 | -2.5 | -1.6 | -1.2 | -1.4 |
| 2000-02 | 1.0 | 3.7 | 2.8 | 1.5 | 2.2 |

\*   Deflated by medical care price index.
\*\*  National Income and Product Accounts (NIPA).
\*\*\* Employment cost index (ECI) levels data for March of each year.

Source: Authors' analysis of BLS and BEA data.

including employer-provided health insurance, pension plans, and payroll taxes, grew just $0.12 per year over the 1979-89 period and was lower in 2000 than in 1989, translating into annual growth rates of 1.0% in 1979-89 and a 0.2% decline from 1989 to 2000. The decline of benefits in the 1990s took place as wages grew in the late 1990s and reflects a fall in both health insurance and pension costs. The ECI data, based on a survey of employers, confirm the decline of benefits in the late 1990s. In fact, the ECI data show a decline in benefits, from $3.98 starting in 1992 to $3.58 in 2000. Both data sources show a steep annual decline in benefits between 1995 and 2000. Even with the strong 2.2% annual benefits growth from 2000 to 2002, the value of benefits in 2002 remained below the level of 1989.

How can it be that benefits grew so slowly in the 1980s, and health care benefits fell in the late 1990s, a time when health insurance costs rose rapidly (relative to other products)? One reason is that, in Table 2.13, health insurance costs are converted to "real" dollars by a medical care price index and reflect the degree to which more health care was being bought (e.g., if medical care prices rise by 10% and health insurance expenditures rise 10%, then health care purchases did not rise). Even when health costs are adjusted by the general consumer price index, however, the results do not change significantly. More important, health care costs for employers have been contained because many workers (about a third of the workforce) do not receive health insurance coverage from their employers. Furthermore, the share of workers covered fell in the 1980s and early 1990s and is still below its 1979 level (as discussed below). Thus, even rapid increases in health costs among a small group of workers with good health plans does not necessarily mean that health costs for the workforce as a whole rose rapidly. Last, the efforts of employers to shift the costs of health care to employees has probably helped to contain the growth of benefits paid by employers (see Chapter 3). Overall, health care costs per hour worked rose from $1.13 in 1979 to $1.43 in 1989 to as high as $1.61 in 1992 before falling to $1.37 in 2000, $0.06 below the 1989 level.

The drop in pension costs over the 1980s partially offset the rise in health care costs in that time period. In 1979, employers paid $1.18 an hour for various pension and retirement schemes; by 1989 hourly pension costs were down to $1.00, and they fell to $0.79 by 2000. The drop in pension costs in the late 1990s combined with declining health care costs to drive down overall benefit costs.

The data in Table 2.13 reflect "average" benefit costs. Given the rapid growth of wage inequality in recent years, it should not be surprising to find a growing inequality of benefits. Tables 2.14 and 2.15 examine changes in health and pension insurance coverage for different demographic groups between 1979,

**TABLE 2.14** Change in private-sector employer-provided health insurance coverage, 1979-2000

| Group* | Health insurance coverage (%) | | | | Percentage-point change | | | | |
|---|---|---|---|---|---|---|---|---|---|
| | 1979 | 1989 | 1995 | 2000 | 1979-89 | 1989-2000 | 1989-95 | 1995-2000 | 1979-2000 |
| **All workers** | 70.2% | 63.1% | 59.1% | 63.4% | -7.1 | 0.3 | -4.0 | 4.3 | -6.8 |
| **Gender** | | | | | | | | | |
| Men | 75.1% | 66.8% | 61.6% | 66.6% | -8.3 | -0.3 | -5.2 | 4.9 | -8.5 |
| Women | 62.2 | 57.9 | 55.5 | 59.3 | -4.3 | 1.4 | -2.3 | 3.7 | -2.9 |
| **Race** | | | | | | | | | |
| White | 71.6% | 65.8% | 62.3% | 67.2% | -5.7 | 1.4 | -3.6 | 5.0 | -4.3 |
| Black | 64.1 | 56.9 | 53.3 | 60.2 | -7.2 | 3.3 | -3.6 | 6.9 | -3.9 |
| Hispanic | 60.9 | 46.3 | 42.3 | 44.8 | -14.5 | -1.5 | -4.1 | 2.5 | -16.1 |
| **Wage fifth** | | | | | | | | | |
| Lowest | 40.7% | 29.4% | 27.7% | 33.4% | -11.3 | 4.1 | -1.7 | 5.8 | -7.3 |
| Second | 62.8 | 54.7 | 51.3 | 57.7 | -8.1 | 3.0 | -3.3 | 6.3 | -5.1 |
| Middle | 75.9 | 69.4 | 63.6 | 68.3 | -6.5 | -1.1 | -5.8 | 4.7 | -7.6 |
| Fourth | 84.0 | 78.6 | 74.2 | 77.0 | -5.5 | -1.6 | -4.4 | 2.8 | -7.0 |
| Top | 87.9 | 83.7 | 79.1 | 81.2 | -4.2 | -2.5 | -4.6 | 2.1 | -6.7 |

* Private-sector wage and salary workers age 18-64, who worked at least 20 hours per week and 26 weeks per year.

Source: Authors' analysis.

**TABLE 2.15** Change in private-sector employer-provided pension coverage, 1979-2000

| Group* | Pension coverage (%) | | | | Percentage-point change | | | | |
|---|---|---|---|---|---|---|---|---|---|
| | 1979 | 1989 | 1995 | 2000 | 1979-89 | 1989-2000 | 1989-95 | 1995-2000 | 1979-2000 |
| **All Workers** | 51.1% | 44.3% | 45.7% | 49.6% | -6.8 | 5.3 | 1.5 | 3.9 | -1.5 |
| **Gender** | | | | | | | | | |
| Men | 56.2% | 46.4% | 47.4% | 51.1% | -9.7 | 4.7 | 0.9 | 3.7 | -5.1 |
| Women | 42.8 | 41.2 | 43.5 | 47.6 | -1.5 | 6.4 | 2.2 | 4.2 | 4.9 |
| **Race** | | | | | | | | | |
| White | 52.6% | 46.7% | 49.2% | 54.6% | -5.9 | 7.8 | 2.5 | 5.4 | 1.9 |
| Black | 46.4 | 41.3 | 43.2 | 43.1 | -5.0 | 1.8 | 1.9 | -0.1 | -3.3 |
| Hispanic | 38.3 | 26.5 | 24.6 | 28.5 | -11.8 | 2.0 | -1.8 | 3.8 | -9.8 |
| **Wage fifth** | | | | | | | | | |
| Lowest | 19.5% | 14.0% | 14.1% | 18.0% | -5.5 | 4.0 | 0.1 | 3.9 | -1.5 |
| Second | 38.0 | 30.8 | 33.1 | 38.3 | -7.2 | 7.5 | 2.4 | 5.2 | 0.3 |
| Middle | 53.3 | 46.4 | 47.6 | 53.6 | -6.9 | 7.3 | 1.3 | 6.0 | 0.3 |
| Fourth | 68.9 | 60.2 | 62.7 | 65.7 | -8.7 | 5.5 | 2.4 | 3.0 | -3.2 |
| Top | 76.5 | 70.2 | 72.0 | 73.0 | -6.3 | 2.7 | 1.8 | 1.0 | -3.5 |

* Private-sector wage and salary workers age 18-64, who worked at least 20 hours per week and 26 weeks per year.

Source: Authors' analysis.

1989, 1995, and 2000. The share of workers covered by employer-provided health care plans dropped a steep 7.1 percentage points, from 70.2% to 63.1%, in the 1980s (Table 2.15). As **Figure 2F** shows, health care coverage eroded in the 1990s until 1993-94 and then started growing, another reflection of improved pay in the late 1990s. Still, health insurance coverage in 2000 was roughly at its 1989 level and far below 1979. This growth in coverage in the late 1990s does not contradict the earlier finding of declining health benefit costs; rather, it probably means that the cost of those previously covered are not keeping up with inflation and that newly covered workers have modest benefits. Unfortunately, there are no data available to show the degree to which the quality of coverage has changed, i.e., whether health plans are more inclusive or more restricted.

Over the 1979-2000 period, health care coverage has declined more among men than women but similarly among both whites and blacks; Hispanics, though, suffered a large drop—16.1 percentage points. The pattern in the erosion of health insurance coverage by wage level shows a growth in inequality in the 1980s, with greater erosion the lower the wage. In the 1990s, however, there were modest extensions of coverage for the bottom 40% (including a 3.0 percentage-point expansion for the second fifth), while erosion continued for middle- and high-wage workers. Consequently, over the longer period, 1979-2000, health insurance coverage declined sizably, and comparably, across the wage spectrum.

Pension plan coverage (Table 2.15) declined as quickly as health care coverage in the 1980s: it dropped from 51.1% in 1979 to 44.3% in 1989. This decline is one of the reasons for the lessening of pension costs for employers over that period. In the 1989-95 period, however, pension coverage expanded slightly to 45.7%. By 2000, however, coverage had grown to 49.6%, just 1.5% shy of 1979's level. Over the 1979-2000 period, lower pension coverage occurred primarily among men, for whom it fell from 56.2% to 51.1%. Women's pension coverage, on the other hand, rose from 42.8% to 47.6%. Women workers by 2000 were only slightly less likely than men to be covered by an employer's pension plan. Both black and white workers saw pension coverage erode in the 1980s, but Hispanics experienced a large decline—an 11.8 percentage-point drop from 1979 to 1989. In the late 1990s, however, whites expanded their pension coverage and attained a level, 54.6%, 2 percentage points above the 1979 level of 52.6%. Hispanics also increased their coverage in the 1990s but still have coverage—28.5% in 2000—far below the 1979 level. Black workers saw a modest 1.8% percentage-point increase in coverage in the 1990s. Surprisingly, black workers saw no increase in pension coverage during the late 1990s recovery. Only whites had pension coverage higher in 2000 than in 1979.

The pattern of decline in pension coverage by wage level shows coverage

**FIGURE 2F** Private-sector employer-provided health insurance coverage, 1979-2001

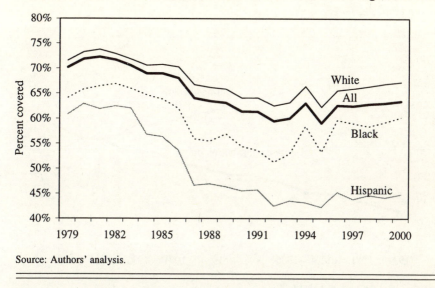

Source: Authors' analysis.

dropping relatively evenly across wage groups in the 1980s and broadening across-the-board in the 1990s, with coverage expanding most in the middle. Nevertheless, lower-wage workers are unlikely to have jobs with employer-provided pension plans (just 18.0% were covered in 2000), and only about half of all workers have pension coverage.

The widening coverage of employer-provided pension plans in the 1990s is most likely due to the expansion of 401(k) and other "defined-contribution" pension plans. These plans need to be distinguished from defined-benefit plans, which guarantee a worker a fixed payment in retirement based on pre-retirement wages and years of service regardless of stock market performance; these are generally considered the best plans from a worker's perspective. In contrast (as shown in **Figure 2G**), a larger share of workers are now covered by defined-contribution plans, in which employers make contributions (to which employees often can add) each year. With this type of plan, a worker's retirement income depends on his or her success in investing these funds, and investment risks are borne by the employee rather than the employer. Therefore, the shift from traditional defined-benefit plans to defined-contribution plans represents an erosion of pension quality. The expenditures data from Table 2.13 suggest a long-term cutback in pension costs, mirroring other indicators of lessened pension quality. Chapter 4 provides further discussion of pensions and retirement assets and income.

**FIGURE 2G** Share of pension participants in defined-contribution and defined-benefit plans, 1979-98

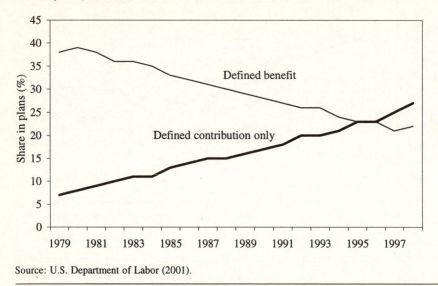

Source: U.S. Department of Labor (2001).

## Explaining wage inequality

In this section we shift the discussion from a descriptive presentation of wage and benefit trends overall and for sub-groups to an examination of explanations for the pattern of recent wage growth. It is important to understand the average performance of wage growth and why particular groups fared well or poorly compared to others.

The data presented above have shown the stagnation of wages and overall compensation between 1973 and 1995 and strong wage growth thereafter. **Table 2.16** presents indicators of a variety of dimensions (excluding race and gender differentials) of the wage structure that have grown more unequal over the 1973-2001 period. Any explanation of growing wage inequality must be able to explain the movement of these indicators. (These inequality indicators are computed from our analysis of the Current Population Survey (CPS) outgoing rotation group (ORG) data series. These trends, however, parallel those in the other major data series, the March CPS.)

The top panel shows the trends, by gender, in the 90/10 wage differential and its two components, the 90/50 and 50/10 wage differential (whose annual values are shown in **Figures 2H** and **2I**), over the 1973-2001 period. These

**TABLE 2.16** Dimensions of wage inequality, 1973-2001

| | Log wage differentials | | | | | | Percentage-point change | | | |
|---|---|---|---|---|---|---|---|---|---|---|
| | 1973 | 1979 | 1989 | 1995 | 2000 | 2001 | 1973-79 | 1979-89 | 1989-2000 | 2000-01 |
| **Total wage inquality** | | | | | | | | | | |
| *90/10* | | | | | | | | | | |
| Men | 128.0% | 130.0% | 144.3% | 151.1% | 150.2% | 150.4% | 2.0 | 14.3 | 5.9 | 0.2 |
| Women | 115.9 | 103.2 | 134.9 | 137.6 | 137.7 | 138.3 | -12.7 | 31.8 | 2.8 | 0.5 |
| *90/50* | | | | | | | | | | |
| Men | 60.3% | 58.8% | 69.2% | 76.1% | 79.2% | 79.0% | -1.5 | 10.4 | 10.0 | -0.2 |
| Women | 59.2 | 60.6 | 70.5 | 76.5 | 78.2 | 77.8 | 1.4 | 9.9 | 7.7 | -0.4 |
| *50/10* | | | | | | | | | | |
| Men | 67.6% | 71.1% | 75.1% | 75.0% | 71.0% | 71.3% | 3.5 | 3.9 | -4.1 | 0.3 |
| Women | 56.7 | 42.5 | 64.4 | 61.1 | 59.5 | 60.5 | -14.2 | 21.9 | -4.9 | 0.9 |
| **Between-group inequality*** | | | | | | | | | | |
| *College/H.S.* | | | | | | | | | | |
| Men | 25.3% | 20.1% | 33.9% | 37.1% | 42.0% | 42.7% | -5.2 | 13.9 | 8.1 | 0.7 |
| Women | 37.7 | 26.5 | 41.0 | 46.7 | 47.9 | 47.9 | -11.2 | 14.5 | 6.9 | 0.0 |
| *Less than H.S./H.S.* | | | | | | | | | | |
| Men | -18.2% | -18.0% | -18.1% | -21.0% | -20.6% | -21.1% | 0.2 | 0.0 | -2.5 | -0.5 |
| Women | -20.8 | -17.6 | -20.9 | -23.0 | -22.8 | -21.6 | 3.2 | -3.3 | -1.8 | 1.1 |
| *Experience\*\** | | | | | | | | | | |
| *Middle/young* | | | | | | | | | | |
| Men | 22.0% | 21.5% | 25.7% | 27.0% | 22.9% | 22.1% | -0.5 | 4.1 | -2.8 | -0.8 |
| Women | 8.0 | 9.5 | 17.8 | 21.8 | 18.4 | 18.0 | 1.5 | 8.3 | 0.6 | -0.4 |

*(cont.)*

**TABLE 2.16** *(cont.)* Dimensions of wage inequality, 1973-2001

| | Log wage differentials | | | | | | Percentage-point change | | | |
|---|---|---|---|---|---|---|---|---|---|---|
| | 1973 | 1979 | 1989 | 1995 | 2000 | 2001 | 1973-79 | 1979-89 | 1989-2000 | 2000-01 |
| **Between-group inequality** *(cont.)* | | | | | | | | | | |
| *Old/middle* | | | | | | | | | | |
| Men | 3.4% | 8.2% | 12.4% | 12.7% | 8.8% | 7.6% | 4.7 | 4.3 | -3.6 | -1.2 |
| Women | -2.0 | 0.4 | 2.1 | 5.4 | 4.6 | 5.6 | 2.4 | 1.7 | 2.5 | 1.0 |
| **Within-group inequality*** | | | | | | | | | | |
| Men | 0.423 | 0.428 | 0.467 | 0.478 | 0.481 | 0.484 | 1.4% | 9.0% | 3.0% | 0.6% |
| Women | 0.418 | 0.402 | 0.447 | 0.467 | 0.458 | 0.462 | -3.8 | 11.4 | 2.4 | 0.9 |

\* Differentials based on a simple human capital regression of log wages on four education categorical variables, age as a quartic, race, marital status, region and ethnicity (Hispanic).

\*\* Age differentials between 25- and 35-year-olds and 35- and 50-year-olds.

\*\*\* Mean square error from same regressions used to estimate experience and education differentials. Changes measured as percent change.

Source: Authors' analysis.

**FIGURE 2H**  Men's wage inequality, 1973-2001

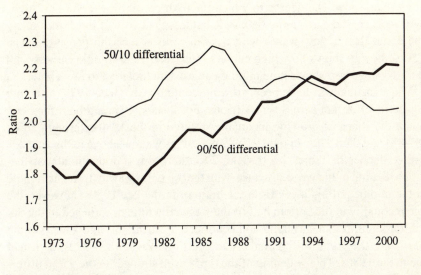

Source: Authors' analysis.

**FIGURE 2I**  Women's wage inequality, 1973-2001

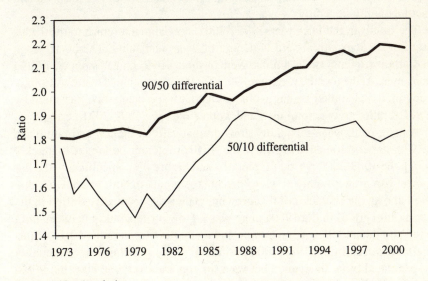

Source: Authors' analysis.

differentials reflect the growth in overall wage inequality. The 90/10 wage gap, for instance, shows the degree to which the 90th percentile worker—a "high-wage" worker who earns more than 90% but less than 10% of the workforce—fared better than a "low-wage" worker, who earns at the 10th percentile. The 90/50 wage gap shows how high earners fared relative to middle earners, and the 50/10 wage gap shows how middle earners fared relative to low earners.

Wage inequalities have been growing continuously since 1979, although the pattern of differs across time periods. For instance, among both men and women the shape of growing inequality differed in the 1980s (through about 1987-88) and the 1990s. In the 1979-89 period (as we saw above in the analysis of wage deciles in Tables 2.6 through 2.8), there was a dramatic across-the-board widening of the wage structure, with the top pulling away from the middle and the middle pulling away from the bottom. In the late 1980s, however, the wage inequality in the bottom half of the wage structure, as reflected in the 50/10 differential, began shrinking and continued to shrink through 1999. On the other hand, the 90/50 differential continued to widen in the 1990s, as it had done in the 1980s. This widening of the top is even stronger in the 95/50 differential (**Figure 2J**; the 95th percentile is the highest wage we feel can be tracked in our data with technical precision). These disparate trends between high- versus middle-wage growth and middle- versus low-wage growth should motivate explanations that focus on how causal factors affect particular portions of the wage structure—top, middle, or bottom—rather than on how causal factors affect inequality generally.

The trends in the later years, 1999-2001, may signal a return to the 1980s pattern of an across-the-board widening of wage inequality. The 50/10 wage gap started growing again among women after 1999, and it stopped falling among men. At the top, the wage gap (95/50 or 90/50) continued to grow strongly among men, but stalled among women. Overall wage inequality, measured by the 90/10 ratio, grew among men and women over the 1999-2001 period.

Among men, wage inequality grew dramatically at the top and bottom in the 1979-89 period, and the growth in the 90/50 differential continued as quickly through the 1989-2000 period (Table 2.16 and Figure 2H). Specifically, the 90/50 wage gap grew roughly 10 (log) percentage points in both periods. As discussed above, the character of this growing male wage inequality shifted in the most recent period. In the 1980s there was a growing separation between both the top and the middle and the middle and the bottom (seen in the 50/10 differential). However, in the 1989-2000 period, all of the growing wage inequality was generated by a divergence between the top and everyone else: the 90/50 differential grew while the 50/10 differential actually fell until 1999. The drop in the 50/10 wage gap actually began in 1986 (Figure 2H).

**FIGURE 2J** 95/50 percentile wage ratio, 1973-2001

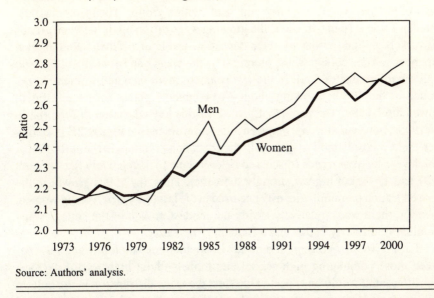

Source: Authors' analysis.

Among women, the wage inequality trends across time periods correspond to those of men. The 90/10 ratio dropped significantly between 1973 and the late 1970s, primarily because of the strong equalization in the 50/10 wage gap. In the 1980s, however, there was a tremendous growth in the 50/10 wage gap (up 21.9 percentage points) that reversed the 1970s compression and increased the gap another 8 percentage points over 1973. One conclusion that can be reached about women's wage inequality is that it has been driven much more than was the change for men by what happened at the bottom—the 10th percentile. This is likely due to the importance of the legal minimum wage to low-wage women, as we will discuss in a later section. Among women, the growth of the 90/50 differential was comparable to that of men in the 1980s but somewhat less in the 1990s. As with men, there was an actual decline of the 50/10 wage gap in the 1990s (which Figure 2I shows started about 1987). As mentioned above, the wage gap at the bottom among women started rising again after 1999.

The 95/50 wage gap among women followed approximately the same track as for men (Figure 2J). Wage inequality between the very top earners and those in the middle has been growing strongly, and steadily, since about 1980, confirming the continuous widening of wages at the top over the last two decades. The only exception is the flattening of the 95/50 gap among women since 1999.

Analysts decompose, or break down, growing wage inequality into two types of inequality—"between-group" and "within group." The former is illustrated in Table 2.16 in two ways: the growing wage differentials between groups of workers defined either by their education levels or by their labor market experience. The "college wage premium"—the wage gap between college and high school graduates—fell in the 1970s among both men and women but exploded in the 1980s, growing about 14 percentage points for each. Growth slowed after 1989. The pattern of growth of this key education differential in the 1990s, however, differed between men and women (see **Figure 2K**). Among men there was only modest growth in the education premium in the early 1990s, which year-by-year trends (discussed below) show to be relatively flat between 1987 and 1996, but it grew strongly thereafter. Thus, the 1990s growth in the male education premium primarily occurred in the last few years. Among women, however, there was a relatively steady but modest growth of the college wage premium in the early 1990s and a flattening thereafter.

Table 2.16 also presents the trends in another education differential—between those completing high school and those without high school degrees; this differential would be expected to affect the wage distribution in the bottom half, as about 10% of the workforce has less than a high school education, and high school graduates make up about a third of the workforce (see discussion of Tables 2.17 through 2.19). In 1973 as in 2000, those without a high school degree earned about 20% less than those with a degree. This wage differential has grown very modestly over the last 28 years, remaining at about a 20% gap. Thus, changing wage differentials at the bottom have had only a weak relationship to changing education differentials.

Experience, or age, is another way of categorizing "skill." The growth of experience differentials reflect the wage gap between older and middle-age and younger workers. The wage gap between middle-age and younger workers grew in the 1980s but not in the 1990s, particularly because the 1995-2000 wage boom, characterized by relatively faster wage growth among younger workers, markedly reduced this differential. The wage gap between older and middle-age women workers grew modestly over the entire 1973-2001 period; it grew as well for men until 1995, then declined.

Within-group wage inequality—wage dispersion among workers with comparable education and experience—has been a major dimension of growing wage inequality. The growth of within-group wage inequality is presented in the last section of Table 2.16, with changes measured in percent. These data show that within-group inequality grew slightly among men in the 1970s and 1990s, but grew strongly, by 9.0%, over the 1980s. Among women, within-group inequality fell in the 1970s, grew by 11.4% in the 1980s, and then grew

**FIGURE 2K** College/high school wage premium, 1973-2001

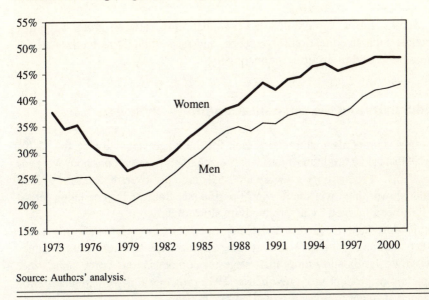

Source: Authors' analysis.

a modest 2.4% in the 1990s. However, within-group wage inequality fell among women in the 1995-2000 period, while rising slightly among men.

This measure of within-group wage inequality is a "summary measure" describing changes across the entire wage distribution. Unfortunately, such a measure does not help us understand changes in particular measures of wage inequality, such as the 90/50 and 50/10 differentials presented in Table 2.16. This is particularly troublesome for an analysis of the 1989-2000 period in which inequalities were expanding at the top (i.e., the 90/50) but shrinking at the bottom (i.e., the 50/10). A summary measure of inequality by definition reflects the net effect of the two disparate shifts in wage inequality in the 1990s, and explains the small change of within-group wage inequality from 1989 to 2000.

Since changes in within-group wage inequality have been a significant factor in various periods, it is important to be able to explain and interpret these trends. In a later section, we show that about half of the growth of wage inequality since 1979 has been from growing within-group wage inequality. Unfortunately, the interpretation of growing wage inequality among workers with similar "human capital" has not been the subject of much research. Some analysts suggest it reflects growing premiums for skills that are not captured by traditional human capital measures available in government surveys. Others

155

suggest that changing "wage norms," employer practices, and institutions are responsible.

We now turn to a more detailed examination of between-group wage differentials such as education, experience, and race/ethnicity as well as an examination of within-group wage inequality.

## Productivity and the compensation/productivity gap

The most commonly mentioned reason for the wage stagnation of the 1970s and 1980s is slow productivity growth (i.e., changes in output per hour worked) since 1973. Productivity grew about 1.5% annually over the entire 1973-95 period, slower than over the pre-1973 period (see Table 2.1). The latter period has thus been marked by a "productivity slowdown."

Slow productivity growth was a major problem, but it provides only a partial explanation for the slow average wage trends in this period, since productivity grew significantly more than wages or compensation. At the same time, the pickup of productivity growth after 1995 provides a major explanation for the much stronger real wage growth in recent years.

The relationship between hourly productivity and compensation growth is portrayed in **Figure 2L**, which shows the growth of each relative to 1973 (i.e., each is indexed so that 1973 equals 100). As the figure shows, productivity grew 55.1% from 1973 to 2001, enough to generate broadly shared growth in living standards and wages. But growth in both average and median compensation lagged behind productivity growth, and, likewise, median hourly compensation grew less than average compensation, reflecting growing wage and benefit inequality. Thus, a major reason why median compensation (or wages) lags behind productivity is that growing inequality creates a "wedge" that prevents the typical worker from enjoying the average growth of national output or income.

There are several possible interpretations of the gap between average compensation and productivity. One is that prices for national output have grown more slowly than prices for consumer purchases. Therefore, the same growth in nominal, or current dollar, wages and output yields faster growth in real (inflation-adjusted) output (which is adjusted for changes in the prices of investment goods, exports, and consumer purchases) than in real wages (adjusted for changes in consumer purchases only). That is, workers have suffered a worsening "terms of trade," in which the prices of things they buy (i.e., consumer goods) have risen faster than the items they produce (consumer goods but also capital goods). Thus, if workers consumed microprocessors and machine tools as well as groceries, their real wage growth would have been better.

**FIGURE 2L** Productivity and hourly compensation growth, 1973-2001

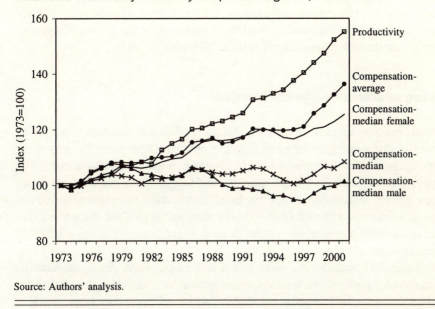

Source: Authors' analysis.

This terms-of-trade scenario is actually more of a description than an ex-planation. A growing gap between output and consumer prices has not been a persistent characteristic of the U.S. economy, and the emergence of this gap requires an exploration of what economic forces are driving it. Once the causes of the price gap are known (not simply accounted for), it can be interpreted. In the meantime, there are two ways to look at the divergence of compensation and productivity created by the terms-of-trade- shift of prices. One is to note that, regardless of cause, the implication is that the "average" worker is not benefiting fully from productivity growth. Another is to note that the price di-vergence does not simply reflect a redistribution from labor to capital; the gap between compensation and productivity growth reflects, at least in part, differ-ences in price trends rather than a larger share of productivity growth going to capital incomes.

This leaves open the question of whether wages are being squeezed by higher profits. In other words, has the growth in rates of profit (defined broadly as profits and interest per dollar of assets) meant that wages have grown less than they would have otherwise? As discussed in Chapter 1, the share of in-come going to capital has grown significantly, driven by a large increase in "profitability," or the return to capital per dollar of plant and equipment. Labor's share of corporate sector income has dropped correspondingly, thus providing evidence of a redistribution of wages to capital incomes. As discussed in Chapter 1, had growth in profitability been more modest up to the 1996-2000 period, hourly compensation would have been 5.3% higher in 2000.

## Rising education/wage differentials

Changes in the economic returns to education affect the structure of wages by changing the wage gaps between different educational groups. The growth in "education/wage differentials" has led to greater wage inequality in the 1980s and 1990s (see Table 2.16 and Figure 2K) and helps explain the relatively faster wage growth among high-wage workers. This section examines wage trends among workers at different levels of education and begins the discussion, carried on through the remainder of the chapter, of the causes of rising education/ wage differentials.

**Table 2.17** presents the wage trends and employment shares (percentage of the workforce) for workers at various education levels over the 1973-2001 period. It is common to point out that the wages of "more-educated" workers have grown faster than the wages of "less-educated" workers since 1979, with the real wages of less-educated workers falling sharply (or rising more slowly in the 1995-99 period). This pattern of wage growth is sometimes described in terms of a rising differential, or "premium," between the wages of the college-educated and high-school-educated workforces (as shown earlier in Table 2.16).

The usual terminology of the less educated and more educated is misleading. Given that workers with some college education (from one to three years) also experienced falling real wages (down 4.1% from 1979 to 1995), it is apparent that the "less-educated" group—those with less than a four-year college degree—makes up nearly three-fourths of the workforce. Moreover, it is notable that the "college-educated" group consists of two groups: one, with just four years of college, enjoyed a modest 8.6% wage gain over the 1979-95 period, while the other, the more-educated ("advanced degree") but smaller group (8.6% of the workforce in 1999), enjoyed 17.2% wage growth.

Table 2.17 also shows, however, that the strong real wage growth of the 1995-2000 period was evident among all education groups, with fastest wage growth among the college-educated workers.

The increased wage differential between college-educated and other workers is frequently ascribed to a relative increase in employer demand for workers with greater skills and education. This interpretation follows from the fact that the wages of college-educated workers increased relative to others despite an

**TABLE 2.17** Change in real hourly wage for all by education, 1973-2001 (2001 dollars)

| Year | Less than high school | High school | Some college | College | Advanced degree |
|---|---|---|---|---|---|
| *Hourly wage* | | | | | |
| 1973 | $11.66 | $13.36 | $14.39 | $19.49 | $23.56 |
| 1979 | 11.62 | 13.04 | 13.94 | 18.27 | 22.31 |
| 1989 | 9.99 | 12.17 | 13.67 | 19.16 | 24.71 |
| 1995 | 9.04 | 11.95 | 13.37 | 19.84 | 26.18 |
| 2000 | 9.40 | 12.65 | 14.36 | 22.10 | 27.94 |
| 2001 | 9.50 | 12.81 | 14.60 | 22.58 | 28.14 |
| *Annualized percentage change* | | | | | |
| 1973-79 | -0.1% | -0.4% | -0.5% | -1.1% | -0.9% |
| 1979-89 | -1.5 | -0.7 | -0.2 | 0.5 | 1.0 |
| 1989-2000 | -0.5 | 0.4 | 0.4 | 1.3 | 1.1 |
| 1989-95 | -1.6 | -0.3 | -0.4 | 0.6 | 1.0 |
| 1995-2000 | 0.8 | 1.1 | 1.4 | 2.2 | 1.3 |
| 1979-2000 | -1.0 | -0.1 | 0.1 | 0.9 | 1.1 |
| 2000-01 | 1.1 | 1.3 | 1.6 | 2.2 | 0.7 |
| *Share of employment* | | | | | |
| 1973 | 28.5% | 38.3% | 18.5% | 10.1% | 4.5% |
| 1979 | 20.1 | 38.5 | 22.8 | 12.7 | 6.0 |
| 1989 | 13.7 | 36.9 | 26.0 | 15.6 | 7.9 |
| 1995 | 10.8 | 33.3 | 30.5 | 17.3 | 8.0 |
| 2000 | 10.8 | 31.9 | 29.8 | 18.8 | 8.7 |
| 2001 | 10.5 | 31.4 | 30.2 | 19.0 | 8.9 |

Source: Authors' analysis.

increase in their relative supply, from 12.7% of the workforce in 1979 to 19.0% in 2001. That is, given the increased supply of college-educated workers, the fact that their relative wages were bid up implies a strong growth in employer demand for more-educated workers, presumably reflecting technological and other workplace trends.

Yet an increased relative demand for educated workers is only a partial explanation, especially if ascribed to a benign process of technology or other factors leading to a higher value for education, thus bidding up the wages of more-educated workers. Note, for instance, that the primary reason for an increased wage gap between college-educated and other workers is the precipi-

**TABLE 2.18** Change in real hourly wage for men by education, 1973-2001 (2001 dollars)

| Year | Less than high school | High school | Some college | College | Advanced degree |
|---|---|---|---|---|---|
| Hourly wage | | | | | |
| 1973 | $13.63 | $16.16 | $16.52 | $22.29 | $24.76 |
| 1979 | 13.40 | 15.71 | 16.34 | 21.35 | 24.29 |
| 1989 | 11.32 | 14.13 | 15.58 | 21.98 | 27.33 |
| 1995 | 9.96 | 13.49 | 15.05 | 22.31 | 29.02 |
| 2000 | 10.36 | 14.29 | 16.26 | 25.10 | 31.37 |
| 2001 | 10.34 | 14.37 | 16.48 | 25.71 | 31.41 |
| *Annualized percentage change* | | | | | |
| 1973-79 | -0.3% | -0.5% | -0.2% | -0.7% | -0.3% |
| 1979-89 | -1.7 | -1.1 | -0.5 | 0.3 | 1.2 |
| 1989-2000 | -0.8 | 0.1 | 0.4 | 1.2 | 1.3 |
| 1989-95 | -2.1 | -0.8 | -0.6 | 0.3 | 1.0 |
| 1995-2000 | 0.8 | 1.2 | 1.6 | 2.4 | 1.6 |
| 1979-2000 | -1.2 | -0.4 | 0.0 | 0.8 | 1.2 |
| 2000-01 | -0.2 | 0.6 | 1.4 | 2.4 | 0.1 |
| *Share of employment* | | | | | |
| 1973 | 30.6% | 34.4% | 19.2% | 10.3% | 5.4% |
| 1979 | 22.3 | 35.0 | 22.4 | 13.2 | 7.1 |
| 1989 | 15.9 | 35.2 | 24.4 | 15.7 | 8.8 |
| 1995 | 12.6 | 33.2 | 28.3 | 17.3 | 8.6 |
| 2000 | 12.6 | 32.1 | 27.8 | 18.5 | 9.1 |
| 2001 | 12.3 | 31.7 | 28.1 | 18.7 | 9.2 |

Source: Authors' analysis.

tous decline of wages among the non-college-educated workforce in the 1979-95 period and not any strong growth in the college wage. Moreover, as discussed below, there are many important factors (that may not reflect changes in the relative demand for skill), such as high unemployment, the shift to low-wage industries, deunionization, a falling minimum wage, and import competition, that can also lead to a wage gap between workers with more and less education. Below, we argue that technological change has not been the driving force behind growing wage inequality.

**Tables 2.18** and **2.19** present trends in wage and employment shares for the various education groups for men and women. Among men, the wages of

**TABLE 2.19** Change in real hourly wage for women by education, 1973-2001 (2001 dollars)

| Year | Less than high school | High school | Some college | College | Advanced degree |
|------|------|------|------|------|------|
| *Hourly wage* | | | | | |
| 1973 | $8.22 | $10.17 | $10.99 | $15.22 | $20.16 |
| 1979 | 8.60 | 10.20 | 10.95 | 13.87 | 17.76 |
| 1989 | 7.86 | 10.16 | 11.77 | 15.93 | 20.76 |
| 1995 | 7.59 | 10.27 | 11.77 | 17.12 | 22.53 |
| 2000 | 7.92 | 10.84 | 12.57 | 18.95 | 23.90 |
| 2001 | 8.21 | 11.08 | 12.84 | 19.29 | 24.35 |
| *Annualized percentage change* | | | | | |
| 1973-79 | 0.8% | 0.0% | -0.1% | -1.5% | -2.1% |
| 1979-89 | -0.9 | 0.0 | 0.7 | 1.4 | 1.6 |
| 1989-2000 | 0.1 | 0.6 | 0.6 | 1.6 | 1.3 |
| 1989-95 | -0.6 | 0.2 | 0.0 | 1.2 | 1.4 |
| 1995-2000 | 0.9 | 1.1 | 1.3 | 2.1 | 1.2 |
| 1979-2000 | -0.4 | 0.3 | 0.7 | 1.5 | 1.4 |
| 2000-01 | 3.8 | 2.3 | 2.1 | 1.8 | 1.9 |
| *Share of employment* | | | | | |
| 1973 | 25.6% | 44.0% | 17.5% | 9.9% | 3.1% |
| 1979 | 17.2 | 43.0 | 23.4 | 12.0 | 4.4 |
| 1989 | 11.2 | 38.8 | 27.8 | 15.4 | 6.8 |
| 1995 | 8.8 | 33.6 | 32.8 | 17.4 | 7.4 |
| 2000 | 8.8 | 31.6 | 32.0 | 19.1 | 8.4 |
| 2001 | 8.6 | 31.0 | 32.5 | 19.3 | 8.6 |

Source: Authors' analysis.

non-college-educated workers fell steadily from 1979 to 1995. The decline in wages was sizable even among men with "some college"—7.9% from 1979 to 1995. The wage of the average high-school-educated male fell more, 14.1% from 1979 to 1995, while the wages of those without a high school degree fell 25.7%. By contrast, the wages of male college graduates actually rose just 0.3% from 1979 to 1989 and over the 1989-95 period. Year-by-year data show male college wages in the 1979-95 period peaked in 1987. The period from 1995 to 2000 was one of strong real wage growth among men in every education category, although stronger for the higher-education groups.

This 1979-95 pattern of modestly growing wages for college-educated males and declining wages for non-college-educated males meant a rise in the relative wage or premium for male college graduates in this period. As shown in Table 2.16, the estimated college/high school wage premium (where experience, race, and other characteristics are controlled for) grew from 20.1% in 1979 to 33.9% in 1989 and to 42.7% in 2001. As Figure 2K shows, however, there was a flattening of the male college/high school premium over the 1988-95 period, particularly in the early 1990s. Since there has not been an acceleration of the supply of college-educated men (as shown in a later section), this implies, within a conventional demand-supply framework, that there was a slowdown in the growth of relative demand for college workers in that period. Since 1995, however, there has been modest growth in this key education differential among men.

A somewhat different pattern has prevailed among women (Table 2.19). In the 1979-89 and 1989-95 periods wages were stagnant among high-school-educated women but fell significantly among those without a high school degree (11.7%). Women with some college saw wage gains in the 1980s (unlike their male counterparts), but not in the early 1990s. College-educated women saw strong wage growth throughout the 1979-95 period (23.4% overall). This pattern of wage growth resulted in growth of the college/high school wage differential equivalent to that of men (Table 2.16), from 26.5% in 1979 to 41.0% in 1989 and to 46.7% in 1995 (the 1990s increase being more than among men). Thus, the education/wage gap grew as quickly among women as among men in the 1979-95 period but the relative losers—non-college-educated women—saw stagnant, not declining wages.

Wage growth was strong over the 1995-2000 period among women at all education levels. As with men, wage growth was strongest among those with a college degree.

Even though the wages of college-educated women have grown rapidly since 1979, a female college graduate in 2000 still earned $6.42, or 25%, less than a male college graduate in 2001.

**Table 2.20** shows a breakdown of the workforce in 2001 by the highest degree attained. Only about one-fourth (27.9%) of the workforce had at least a four-year college degree (19.0% have no more than a college degree and 8.9% also have a graduate or professional degree). Roughly three-fourths (72.1%) of the workforce has less than a college degree, with 10.5% never completing high school; 31.4% completing high school; and another 21.0% having attended college but earning no degree beyond high school; an additional 9.2% held associate degrees. These data reinforce the earlier discussion that the wage reductions experienced by the "less educated" (frequently defined by economists as those without a college degree) between 1979 and 1995 affected roughly three-fourths of the workforce.

**TABLE 2.20** Educational attainment of the workforce, 2001

| Highest degree attained | Percent of workforce | | |
|---|---|---|---|
| | All | Men | Women |
| Less than high school | 10.5% | 12.3% | 8.6% |
| High school/GED | 31.4 | 31.7 | 31.0 |
| Some college | 21.0 | 19.9 | 22.1 |
| Assoc. college | 9.2 | 8.2 | 10.4 |
| College B.A. | 19.0 | 18.7 | 19.3 |
| Advanced degree* | 8.9 | 9.2 | 8.6 |
| **Total** | 100.0 | 100.0 | 100.0 |
| *Memo* | | | |
| High school or less | 41.9% | 44.0% | 39.6% |
| Less than B.A. degree | 72.1 | 72.1 | 72.1 |
| College B.A. or more | 27.9 | 27.9 | 27.9 |
| Advanced degree | 8.9 | 9.2 | 8.6 |

\* Includes law degrees, Ph.D.s, M.B.A.s, and similar degrees.

Source: Authors' analysis.

## Young workers' wages

The most dramatic erosion of wages over the 1973-1995 period was among young workers. However, young workers experienced the fastest wage growth over the 1995-2000 period. As a result, there have been significant changes—up and down—in the wage differentials between younger and older workers, as shown earlier in Table 2.16. Young workers' prospects, therefore, seem to be an apt barometer of the strength of the labor market—when the labor market is strong for workers the prospects for young workers are very strong, and when the labor market is weak their prospects are very weak.

The adverse wage trends among young workers in the 1979-95 period were strongest among men. **Table 2.21** presents trends in wages for entry-level (one to five years of experience) for high school and college graduates. Since the wages of both younger and non-college-educated workers fell most rapidly in the 1979-95 period, it should not be surprising that entry-level wages for men and women high school graduates in 2001 were still below their levels in 1979 or 1973. The entry-level hourly wage of a young male high school graduate in 1995 was 24.7% less than that for the equivalent worker in 1979, a drop of $3.02 per hour. Among women, the entry-level high school wage fell 13.3% in this period. Entry-level wages for high school graduates rebounded strongly after 1995, growing over 9% among both men and women. The dramatic de-

**TABLE 2.21** Hourly wages of entry-level and experienced workers by education, 1973-2001 (2001 dollars)

| Education/experience | Hourly wage | | | | | | Percent change | | | | |
|---|---|---|---|---|---|---|---|---|---|---|---|
| | 1973 | 1979 | 1989 | 1995 | 2000 | 2001 | 1973-79 | 1979-89 | 1989-2000 | 1995-2000 | 2000-01 |
| **High school** | | | | | | | | | | | |
| *Men* | | | | | | | | | | | |
| Entry* | $12.43 | $12.23 | $9.91 | $9.21 | $10.09 | $10.25 | -1.6% | -19.0% | 1.8% | 9.6% | 1.6% |
| 34-40 | 17.76 | 17.51 | 15.32 | 14.70 | 15.32 | 15.30 | -1.4 | -12.5 | 0.0 | 4.2 | -0.1 |
| 49-55 | 18.72 | 18.68 | 17.28 | 16.61 | 16.46 | 16.66 | -0.2 | -7.5 | -4.7 | -0.9 | 1.2 |
| *Women* | | | | | | | | | | | |
| Entry* | $9.10 | $9.04 | $8.11 | $7.84 | $8.60 | $8.65 | -0.7% | -10.3% | 6.1% | 9.7% | 0.5% |
| 34-40 | 10.45 | 10.56 | 10.63 | 10.76 | 11.42 | 11.42 | 1.1 | 0.6 | 7.5 | 6.2 | 0.0 |
| 49-55 | 10.89 | 10.87 | 11.18 | 11.28 | 11.99 | 12.30 | -0.2 | 2.9 | 7.3 | 6.3 | 2.6 |
| **College** | | | | | | | | | | | |
| *Men* | | | | | | | | | | | |
| Entry** | $16.48 | $16.12 | $16.58 | $15.38 | $18.54 | $19.33 | -2.2% | 2.9% | 11.8% | 20.5% | 4.3% |
| 34-40 | 26.60 | 25.05 | 24.53 | 25.15 | 27.90 | 28.99 | -5.8 | -2.1 | 13.8 | 11.0 | 3.9 |
| 49-55 | 27.42 | 27.77 | 27.58 | 27.88 | 28.76 | 28.98 | 1.3 | -0.7 | 4.3 | 3.2 | 0.7 |
| *Women* | | | | | | | | | | | |
| Entry** | $13.81 | $12.75 | $14.43 | $14.13 | $15.77 | $16.01 | -7.7% | 13.2% | 9.3% | 11.6% | 1.5% |
| 34-40 | 16.48 | 14.61 | 16.67 | 18.79 | 20.53 | 21.17 | -11.3 | 14.0 | 23.2 | 9.2 | 3.1 |
| 49-55 | 15.72 | 14.79 | 16.18 | 18.96 | 19.82 | 20.59 | -5.9 | 9.4 | 22.5 | 4.5 | 3.9 |

*  Entry-level wage measured as wage of those age 19-25.
** Entry-level wage measured as wage of those age 23-29.

Source:  Authors' analysis.

**FIGURE 2M** Entry-level wages of male and female high school graduates, 1973-2001

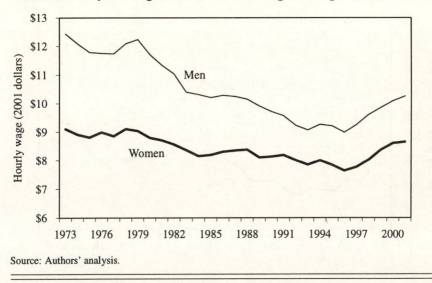

Source: Authors' analysis.

cline in entry-level wages among high school graduates and their recent recovery is illustrated in **Figure 2M**.

Entry-level wages among male college graduates were stagnant over the 1973-89 period and fell 7.2% from 1989 to 1995, as shown in **Figure 2N**. Thus, new male college graduates earned $1.10 less per hour in 1995 than their counterparts did in 1973. A decline in entry-level wages of college graduates also took place among women in the early 1990s, when the wage fell 2%. Wages for young college graduates grew very strongly—20.5% among men and 11.6% among women—in the 1995-2000 wage boom. This solid wage growth boosted entry-level male college graduates to a wage 11.8% higher than in 1989, offsetting the early 1990s decline; young women college graduates attained wages in 2000 that were 9.3%% higher than in 1989. This astounding growth of wages for young college graduates continued in 2001, where wages grew 4.3% among men and 1.5% among women.

## The importance of within-group wage inequality

The data presented so far illustrate the various dimensions of wage inequality. The "between-group" inequality for workers by both education and experience (or age) can be characterized as a growth in differentials in education and expe-

**FIGURE 2N** Entry-level wages of male and female college graduates, 1973-2001

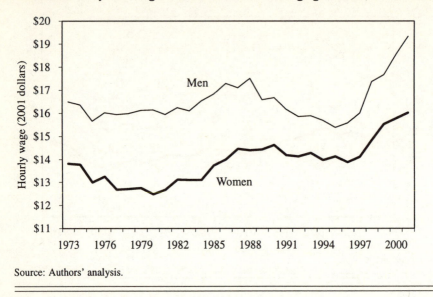

Source: Authors' analysis.

rience, which are sometimes labeled as an increase in the "returns to education and experience" or as a shift in the rewards or price of "skill." We now examine in greater depth the growth of "within-group" wage inequality, the inequality among workers with similar education and experience.

This growth in within-group wage inequality was shown earlier in Table 2.16. The analysis in **Table 2.22** illustrates the growth of this type of inequality by presenting wage trends of high-, middle-, and low-wage workers among high school and college graduates. In other words, the data track the wages of 90th, 50th (median), and 10th percentile high-school-educated and college-educated workers by gender and show a growing wage gap among college graduates and high school graduates.

Because of rising within-group inequality, the wage growth of the median or "typical" worker within each group has been less than that of the "average" worker. For instance, the wage of the median male high school graduate fell 14.4% over the 1979-2000 period, compared to the 9.0% wage drop of the "average" male high school graduate (Table 2.18). Similarly, the wage growth of male college graduates in the 1979-2000 period was 17.6% at the average (Table 2.18) but only 14.0% at the median (Table 2.22)

The growing disparity of wages within groups is amply demonstrated in Table 2.22. While the high (90th percentile) wage among female college gradu-

**TABLE 2.22** Hourly wages by decile within education groups, 1973-2001 (2001 dollars)

| Education/ gender decile | Hourly wage | | | | | | Percent change | | | | | |
|---|---|---|---|---|---|---|---|---|---|---|---|---|
| | 1973 | 1979 | 1989 | 1995 | 2000 | 2001 | 1973-79 | 1979-89 | 1989-2000 | 1995-2000 | 1979-2000 | 2000-01 |
| **High school** | | | | | | | | | | | | |
| *Men* | | | | | | | | | | | | |
| Low* | $8.25 | $7.66 | $6.63 | $6.43 | $7.03 | $7.14 | -7.2% | -13.5% | 6.1% | 9.3% | -8.2% | 1.6% |
| Median | 14.88 | 14.60 | 12.86 | 11.86 | 12.50 | 12.70 | -1.9 | -11.9 | -2.8 | 5.3 | -14.4 | 1.6 |
| High | 24.31 | 23.83 | 22.67 | 21.82 | 22.90 | 23.15 | -2.0 | -4.9 | 1.0 | 4.9 | -3.9 | 1.1 |
| *Women* | | | | | | | | | | | | |
| Low | $5.59 | $6.39 | $5.26 | $5.49 | $6.01 | $6.06 | 14.3% | -17.7% | 14.4% | 9.6% | -5.9% | 0.7% |
| Median | 9.24 | 9.04 | 9.09 | 8.96 | 9.58 | 9.85 | -2.1 | 0.6 | 5.4 | 6.9 | 6.0 | 2.8 |
| High | 15.28 | 15.43 | 16.38 | 16.56 | 17.22 | 17.48 | 1.0 | 6.2 | 5.1 | 4.0 | 11.6 | 1.5 |
| **College** | | | | | | | | | | | | |
| *Men* | | | | | | | | | | | | |
| Low | $10.19 | $9.88 | $9.39 | $8.98 | $10.26 | $10.04 | -3.1% | -5.0% | 9.3% | 14.2% | 3.9% | -2.2% |
| Median | 19.13 | 18.62 | 19.47 | 19.23 | 21.23 | 21.45 | -2.7 | 4.5 | 9.1 | 10.4 | 14.0 | 1.1 |
| High | 35.67 | 34.21 | 35.29 | 37.56 | 41.15 | 43.30 | -4.1 | 3.2 | 16.6 | 9.5 | 20.3 | 5.2 |
| *Women* | | | | | | | | | | | | |
| Low | $7.84 | $7.10 | $7.41 | $7.56 | $8.38 | $8.65 | -9.4% | 4.3% | 13.2% | 10.9% | 18.1% | 3.2% |
| Median | 13.54 | 12.32 | 14.31 | 15.22 | 16.47 | 17.01 | -9.0 | 16.1 | 15.1 | 8.2 | 33.6 | 3.3 |
| High | 21.39 | 20.94 | 24.92 | 28.25 | 31.62 | 31.84 | -2.1 | 19.0 | 26.9 | 11.9 | 51.0 | 0.7 |

* Low, median, and high earners refer to, respectively, the 10th, 50th, and 90th percentile wage.

Source: Authors' analysis.

167

ates grew 51.0% from 1979 to 2000, the low (10th percentile) wage in this group rose 18.1%, a 33 percentage-point divergence. Similarly, there was a large divergence between wage trends at the top of the college male wage ladder (20.3% growth) and the bottom (a 3.9% growth) over the 1979-2000 period.

The question remains, however, as to how much the growth in overall wage inequality in particular time periods has been driven by changes in between-group versus within-group wage inequality. It would also be useful to know the role of the growth of between- and within-group inequality on growing wage inequality at the top (the 90/50 differential) versus the bottom (the 50/10 differential), but measurement techniques for answering this question are not readily available.

**Table 2.23** presents the trends in overall wage inequality, as measured by the standard deviation of log hourly wages, and the trends in within-group wage inequality. These measures allow an examination of how much of the change in overall wage inequality in particular periods was due to changes in within-group wage inequality and between-group wage inequality (primarily changes in the differentials from education and experience).

The data in Table 2.23 indicate that half or more of the growth of wage inequality since 1979 has been driven by the growth of within-group wage inequality. Among women, for instance, overall wage inequality grew 0.107 over the 1979-2000 period, of which 0.056 was due to the growth of within-group wage inequality. Similarly, 0.053 of the 0.089 increase in overall male wage inequality over the 1979-2000 period was due to growing within-group inequality.

Wage inequality over the 1995-2000 period was essentially unchanged among men and declined among women, the latter a result of a decline in within-group wage inequality. Thus, Table 2.23 makes clear that any explanation of growing wage inequality must go beyond explaining changes in skill, education, experience, or other wage differentials and be able to explain growing inequalities within each of these categories.

It is also noteworthy that between-group wage inequality did not rise in the 1995-2000 technology-related productivity and wage boom. This finding is inconsistent with a story that technology has generated greater wage inequalities by expanding skill differentials—primarily by education and experience. These data show that, while it is true that the college/high school wage differential grew in the 1995-99 period, experience differentials fell and education differentials between high school and less-than-high-school workers were stable (see Table 2.16).

**TABLE 2.23** Decomposition of total and within-group wage inequality, 1973-2001

| | Women | | | | Men | | | |
|---|---|---|---|---|---|---|---|---|
| Year | Overall wage inequality* (1) | Between-group inequality** (2) | Within-group inequality*** (3) | Contribution of within-group inequality (3)/(1) | Overall wage inequality* (1) | Between-group inequality** (2) | Within-group inequality*** (3) | Contribution of within-group inequality (3)/(1) |
| 1973 | 0.478 | 0.061 | 0.418 | | 0.506 | 0.083 | 0.423 | |
| 1979 | 0.446 | 0.044 | 0.402 | | 0.506 | 0.078 | 0.428 | |
| 1989 | 0.529 | 0.082 | 0.447 | | 0.579 | 0.112 | 0.467 | |
| 1995 | 0.562 | 0.095 | 0.467 | | 0.595 | 0.118 | 0.478 | |
| 2000 | 0.552 | 0.094 | 0.458 | | 0.595 | 0.114 | 0.481 | |
| 2001 | 0.557 | 0.094 | 0.462 | | 0.597 | 0.113 | 0.484 | |
| *Change* | | | | | | | | |
| 1973-79 | -0.033 | -0.017 | -0.016 | 49.1% | 0.000 | -0.005 | 0.006 | n.a.**** |
| 1979-89 | 0.083 | 0.038 | 0.046 | 54.7 | 0.073 | 0.034 | 0.038 | 52.8% |
| 1989-2000 | 0.023 | 0.012 | 0.011 | 46.6 | 0.016 | 0.002 | 0.011 | 86.3 |
| 1989-95 | 0.033 | 0.013 | 0.019 | 59.5 | 0.016 | 0.006 | 0.011 | 65.5 |
| 1995-2000 | -0.009 | -0.001 | -0.009 | 91.8 | 0.000 | -0.003 | 0.003 | n.a.**** |
| 1979-2000 | 0.107 | 0.050 | 0.056 | 53.0 | 0.089 | 0.037 | 0.053 | 59.0 |

\*      Measured as standard deviation of log wages.
\*\*     Reflects changes in education, experience, race/ethnicity, marital status, and regional differentials.
\*\*\*    Measured as mean square error from a standard (log) wage regression.
\*\*\*\*   Not applicable beause denominator is zero or too small.

Source: Authors' analysis.

169

**TABLE 2.24** Hourly wage growth among men by race/ethnicity,
1989-2001 (2001 dolllars)

| | Hourly wage | | | | Changes | | | |
|---|---|---|---|---|---|---|---|---|
| | 1989 | 1995 | 2000 | 2001 | 1989-2000 | 1989-1995 | 1995-2000 | 2000-01 |
| **Median** | | | | | | | | |
| White | $14.96 | $14.40 | $15.62 | $15.90 | 4.4% | -3.7% | 8.5% | 1.8% |
| Black | 10.82 | 10.52 | 11.46 | 11.83 | 5.9 | -2.8 | 8.9 | 3.2 |
| Hispanic | 10.06 | 9.17 | 10.11 | 10.11 | 0.4 | -8.9 | 10.2 | 0.0 |
| Asian | 13.98 | 13.86 | 15.59 | 16.17 | 11.5 | -0.8 | 12.5 | 3.7 |
| **By education** | | | | | | | | |
| *High school** | | | | | | | | |
| White | $14.69 | $14.11 | $15.06 | $15.13 | 2.5% | -4.0% | 6.7% | 0.5% |
| Black | 11.74 | 11.29 | 12.08 | 12.24 | 2.9 | -3.8 | 7.0 | 1.3 |
| Hispanic | 12.17 | 11.64 | 12.22 | 12.43 | 0.4 | -4.4 | 5.0 | 1.7 |
| Asian | 12.85 | 12.55 | 13.37 | 12.93 | 4.1 | -2.3 | 6.5 | -3.3 |

* Average wage.

Source: Authors' analysis.

## Wage growth by race and ethnicity

Race and ethnicity have long played an important role in shaping employment opportunities and labor market outcomes. **Tables 2.24** and **2.25** present the wage trends by gender for two indicators of the wage structure (the median wage and the high school wage) for four populations: white, black, Hispanic, and Asian. (A finer breakdown of groups was not possible in the 1990s because of sample size limitations and, for the same reason, the trends for the 1980s are not available. Also, note that our definitions of race/ethnicity categories exclude Hispanics from the white, black, and Asian groups.)

The male median wage trends show that all groups experienced declining wages during the 1989-95 period, followed by strong wage growth between 1995 and 2000 (Table 2.24). With the strong wage growth after 1995, the median male wage among each group returned to and exceeded its 1989, pre-recession level. A similar pattern is evident among high-school-educated male workers: wages declined significantly over the 1989-95 period, then grew in 1995-2000.

Wage trends among women correspond to those of men except for slightly faster wage growth. For instance, the median or typical white, black, Hispanic, or Asian woman worker lost ground or had modest wage growth in 1989-95 but

**TABLE 2.25** Hourly wage growth among women by race/ethnicity, 1989-2001 (2001 dollars)

| | Hourly wage | | | | Changes | | | |
|---|---|---|---|---|---|---|---|---|
| | 1989 | 1995 | 2000 | 2001 | 1989-2000 | 1989-1995 | 1995-2000 | 2000-01 |
| **Median** | | | | | | | | |
| White | $10.47 | $10.73 | $11.71 | $12.07 | 11.8% | 2.5% | 9.1% | 3.0% |
| Black | 9.33 | 9.23 | 10.26 | 10.16 | 9.9 | -1.1 | 11.1 | -1.0 |
| Hispanic | 8.33 | 8.16 | 8.69 | 9.04 | 4.3 | -2.0 | 6.4 | 4.0 |
| Asian | 10.84 | 11.04 | 12.53 | 12.38 | 15.5 | 1.8 | 13.5 | -1.2 |
| **By education** | | | | | | | | |
| *High school** | | | | | | | | |
| White | $10.32 | $10.49 | $11.09 | $11.39 | 7.5% | 1.7% | 5.7% | 2.7% |
| Black | 9.52 | 9.47 | 10.19 | 10.27 | 7.0 | -0.5 | 7.5 | 0.8 |
| Hispanic | 9.57 | 9.65 | 10.08 | 10.24 | 5.2 | 0.8 | 4.4 | 1.7 |
| Asian | 9.82 | 9.93 | 10.68 | 10.91 | 8.8 | 1.2 | 7.5 | 2.1 |

* Average wage.

Source: Authors' analysis.

recovered strongly during 1995-2000. By 2000, women's median wages were at least 9% above their 1989 levels for whites, blacks and Asians, but were just 4.3% improved among Hispanics. Wage growth among high-school-educated women showed a similar pattern.

## The gender wage gap

As discussed above in several sections, women's wages have generally fared better than men's over the last few decades. For instance, in 1973 the ratio of the median woman's wage to the male median wage was 63.1% but rose to 78.1% by 2001 (See **Table 2.26** and **Figure 2O**). The rapid closing of the gender gap occurred between 1979 and 1995, primarily as the result of a fall in the male median wage and the modest growth of the female median wage. The gender wage gap at other points in the wage distribution—e.g., the 20th and the 90th percentiles—shows a similar trend.

Unfortunately, there is no research that explains these trends or examines how changes in skills, the gender composition of work, and other factors have contributed to the closing and then flattening of the gender gap.

**TABLE 2.26** Gender wage ratio, 1973-2001

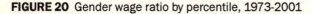

|      | Median Wage | | Ratio |
|      | Women | Men | Women/Men |
|------|-------|-----|-----------|
| 1973 | $9.24 | $14.63 | 63.1% |
| 1979 | 9.38 | 14.96 | 62.7 |
| 1989 | 10.17 | 13.91 | 73.1 |
| 1995 | 10.29 | 13.41 | 76.7 |
| 2000 | 11.17 | 14.37 | 77.7 |
| 2001 | 11.40 | 14.60 | 78.1 |

Source: Authors' analysis.

**FIGURE 20** Gender wage ratio by percentile, 1973-2001

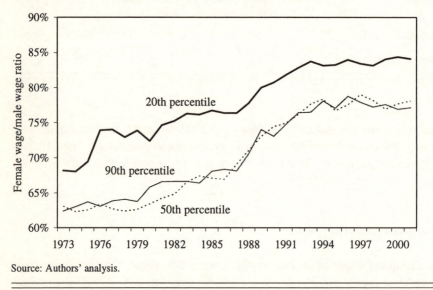

Source: Authors' analysis.

## Unemployment and wage growth

One category of factors shaping wage growth can be labeled "macroeconomic." These factors reflect the overall health of the economy and determine whether it is producing less than it has the capacity to do—as indicated by high unemployment and excess production capacity. Generally, "slack" in the economy is driven by monetary policy (the growth of the money supply, interest rates), fiscal policy (the size of the government surplus/deficits, with increasing deficits adding to demand and thereby lessening slack), and the U.S. international position (trade deficits, the flow of investment dollars abroad or from abroad to the U.S.). Factors that affect growth include those that limit or generate slack but also those that shape productive potential, such as public and private investment, technological change, workforce skills, and work organization (how factors of production are combined).

Macroeconomic conditions greatly affect wage growth and wage inequality. The issue of productivity and wage growth was discussed in an earlier section, so here we focus on how macroeconomic factors affect wage inequality. The burden of an underperforming economy and high employment is not equally shared, with lower- and middle-income families more likely to experience unemployment, underemployment, and slower wage growth because of a weak economy (see Chapter 3 for a discussion of unemployment and family income). For many years, until recently, white-collar workers and high-wage workers were relatively unaffected by unemployment and recessions. Not surprisingly, therefore, high unemployment is a factor that widens wage and income inequality.

There are a number of mechanisms through which high unemployment affects wages, and, especially, affects them differently for different groups of workers. The wages of groups that have lower wages, less education or skill, and less power in the labor market are generally more adversely affected by high unemployment. Or, in other words, those already disadvantaged in the labor market become even more disadvantaged in a recession or in a weak economy. Conversely, as unemployment falls in a recovery and stays low, the greatest benefit accrues to those with the least power in the labor market—non-college-educated, blue-collar, minority and low-wage workers. How does this happen? First, these groups experience the greatest unemployment growth in a downturn and the greatest fall in unemployment in a recovery. This greater-than-average drop in unemployment boosts demand for these workers and consequently provides them with greater leverage with employers, generating higher wages. Second, as unemployment drops, more opportunities arise for upward mobility for these workers, as they switch jobs either to a new employer or within the same firm. Third, unions are able to bargain higher wages when unemployment is low. Fourth, there is an important interaction between macroeconomic conditions and the impact of other institutional and structural factors. For instance, the early 1980s saw a surge of imports and a growing trade deficit, a decline in manufacturing, a weakening of unions, and a large erosion of the minimum wage that coincided with (and partly caused) the rising unemployment at that time. The impact of these factors on wage inequality was probably greater because of high unemployment. So, for example, the impact of

**TABLE 2.27** Impact of rising and falling unemployment on wage levels and wage ratios, 1979-2000

|  | 1979-85 | | 1995-2000 | |
| --- | --- | --- | --- | --- |
|  | Men | Women | Men | Women |
| **Actual changes** | | | | |
| *Unemployment rate* | 1.4 | 1.4 | -1.6 | -1.6 |
| 50/10 (log) | 9.6 | 17.0 | -3.9 | -1.8 |
| 90/50 (log) | 8.7 | 8.0 | 3.8 | 1.1 |
| **Simulated effect of change** | | | | |
| **in unemployment on:** | | | | |
| *Hourly wages* | | | | |
| 10th percentile | -15.2% | -17.2% | 10.2% | 7.0% |
| 50th percentile | -9.4 | -8.0 | 4.1 | 2.3 |
| 90th percentile | -8.9 | -8.3 | 3.1 | 3.7 |
| *Wage ratios (log)* | | | | |
| 50/10 | 6.6 | 10.5 | -5.7 | -4.5 |
| 90/50 | 0.6 | -0.3 | -0.9 | 1.4 |
| **Unemployment** | | | | |
| **contribution to change** | | | | |
| 50/10 (log) | 68% | 62% | 145% | 257% |
| 90/50 (log) | 6 | -4 | -25 | 131 |

Source: Authors' analysis.

trade on wages (discussed below) was greater because the recession had already induced a scarcity of good jobs.

Estimates of the effect on wages of increases in unemployment in the 1979-85 period and decreases in unemployment in the 1995-2000 period are presented in **Table 2.27**. These estimates focus on the effect of unemployment trends on the 10th, 50th, and 90th percentile wages and the 90/50 and 50/10 wage ratios for each gender.

**Figure 2P** shows the course of unemployment in these two periods—the sharp rise in unemployment in the early 1980s and the persistent drop in unemployment to roughly 4% in the late 1990s. During the 1980s recession wage inequality rose sharply, both at the top (the 90/50 ratio) and the bottom (the 50/10 ratio), with low-wage women being most adversely affected. Correspondingly, during the 1995-2000 boom the 50/10 wage ratios became smaller among both men and women while the 90/50 ratio continued to grow.

**FIGURE 2P** Unemployment, 1973-2002*

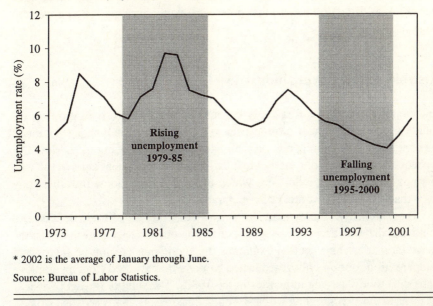

* 2002 is the average of January through June.
Source: Bureau of Labor Statistics.

How much of these shifts in wage inequality are due to unemployment trends? Table 2.27 presents the results of simulations that estimate the effect of unemployment trends during the 1979-85 and 1995-2000 periods on the wages in the final year of each period—1985 and 2000, respectively. For instance, the early 1980s recession lowered the wages (relative to what they otherwise would have been) of workers at the 10th percentile in 1985 by 15.2% among men and 17.2% among women. The drop in unemployment in the 1995-2000 period raised wages for low-wage (10th percentile) men and women by 10.2% and 7.0%, respectively. Unemployment had a sizable but lesser effect on the wages of middle- and high-wage workers; surprisingly, unemployment seems to affect middle- and high-wage workers to the same extent—about an 8-9% reduction in the 1980s and a 3-4% improvement in the late 1990s. Thus, unemployment did not greatly affect the 90/50 wage ratio, which grew in both periods. However, the very large impact of unemployment on the wages at the bottom led to large changes in the 50/10 wage ratio—a roughly 5-percentage point reduction in the late 1990s and a 6.6-point increase for men and a 10.5-point increase for women in the early 1980s. Consequently, the higher unemployment in the early 1980s can account for over 60% of the growth in the 50/10 wage ratio in that period. Moreover, lower unemployment can account for more than all of the diminution of wage inequality at the bottom in the late 1990s, indicating that unemployment offset other factors (such as immigration, trade and so on, as discussed below) that otherwise would have generated growth in wage inequality.

## The shift to low-paying industries

One causal factor that is frequently considered in any analysis of growing inequality is a changing mix of industries in the economy. Such changes include the continued shift from goods-producing to service-producing industries. The consequence for the labor market results from the consequent shift in the mix of employment among industries, which matters because some industries pay more than others (for workers of comparable skill).

These industry employment shifts are a consequence of trade deficits and deindustrialization as well as stagnant or falling productivity growth in service sector industries. This section examines the significant erosion of wages and compensation for non-college-educated workers that resulted from an employment shift to low-paying industries in the 1980s. The smaller impact of industry shifts in the 1990s among women is one of the reasons that low-wage women saw some economic gains in the 1990s.

Despite a common perception, this industry-shift effect is not the simple consequence of some natural evolution from an agricultural to a manufacturing to a service economy. For one thing, a significant part of the shrinkage of manufacturing is trade related. More important, industry shifts would not provide a downward pressure on wages if service sector wages were more closely aligned with manufacturing wages, as is the case in other countries. Moreover, since health coverage, vacations, and pensions in this country are related to the specific job or sector in which a worker is employed, the sectoral distribution of employment matters more in the United States than in other countries. An alternative institutional arrangement found in other advanced countries sets health, pensions, vacation, and other benefits through legislation in a universal manner regardless of sector or firm. Therefore, the downward pressure of industry shifts on pay can be said to be the consequence of the absence of institutional structures that lessen inter-industry pay differences.

Trends in employment growth by major industry sector and the hourly compensation in 2001 of each sector are presented in **Table 2.28**. The 18.1 million (net) jobs created between 1979 and 1989 involved a loss of manufacturing (1.6 million) and mining (266,000) jobs and an increase (19.3 million) in the service-producing sector. The largest amount of job growth (14.2 million) occurred in the two lowest-paying service sector industries—retail trade and ser-

**TABLE 2.28** Employment growth and compensation by sector, 1979-2001

| Industry sector | Employment (000) | | | | Job growth | | Industry share of job growth | | Hourly compensation |
|---|---|---|---|---|---|---|---|---|---|
| | 1979 | 1989 | 2000 | 2001 | 1979-89 | 1989-2000 | 1979-89 | 1989-2000 | 2001 |
| **Goods producing** | 26,461 | 25,254 | 25,709 | 25,122 | -1,207 | 455 | -6.7% | 1.9% | $24.40 |
| Mining | 958 | 692 | 543 | 563 | -266 | -149 | -1.5 | -0.6 | 31.44 |
| Construction | 4,463 | 5,171 | 6,698 | 6,861 | 708 | 1,527 | 3.9 | 6.4 | 24.08 |
| Manufacturing | 21,040 | 19,391 | 18,469 | 17,698 | -1,649 | -922 | -9.1 | -3.9 | 24.30 |
| Durable goods | 12,730 | 11,394 | 11,138 | 10,638 | -1,336 | -256 | -7.4 | -1.1 | 25.63 |
| Nondurable goods | 8,310 | 7,997 | 7,331 | 7,060 | -313 | -666 | -1.7 | -2.8 | 22.25 |
| **Service producing** | 63,363 | 82,630 | 106,050 | 107,092 | 19,267 | 23,420 | 106.7% | 98.1% | $19.74 |
| Trans., comm., util. | 5,136 | 5,614 | 7,019 | 7,070 | 478 | 1,405 | 2.6 | 5.9 | 27.70 |
| Wholesale | 5,221 | 6,187 | 7,024 | 7,014 | 966 | 837 | 5.3 | 3.5 | 22.83 |
| Retail | 14,972 | 19,475 | 23,307 | 23,488 | 4,503 | 3,832 | 24.9 | 16.1 | 11.49 |
| Fin., ins., real est. | 4,975 | 6,668 | 7,560 | 7,624 | 1,693 | 892 | 9.4 | 3.7 | 27.29 |
| Services | 17,112 | 26,907 | 40,460 | 41,024 | 9,795 | 13,553 | 54.2 | 56.8 | 21.11 |
| Government | 15,947 | 17,779 | 20,681 | 20,873 | 1,832 | 2,902 | 10.1 | 12.2 | 30.64 |
| Federal | 2,773 | 2,988 | 2,777 | 2,616 | 215 | -211 | 1.2 | -0.9 | 34.69 |
| State and local | 13,174 | 14,791 | 17,904 | 18,257 | 1,617 | 3,113 | 9.0 | 13.0 | 30.06 |
| Total | 89,823 | 107,884 | 131,759 | 132,213 | 18,061 | 23,875 | 100.0% | 100.0% | $22.36 |

Source: Authors' analysis.

vices (business, personnel, and health). In fact, these two industries accounted for 79% of all the net new jobs over the 1979-89 period.

The shift toward low-paying industries continued in the 1990s, although at a much slower pace. Low-wage retail jobs have played a smaller role in overall job creation, contributing 16.1% of the new jobs, but the services industry (primarily health and temporary services) became somewhat more important, supplying 56.8% of the net new jobs. Together, these low-wage industries accounted for 72.9% of all new jobs in 1989-2000. Manufacturing job loss was only 56% as great in the 1990s as in the 1980s, and higher-wage industries such as construction and transportation/communications expanded more in the 1990s than in the 1980s. Thus, industry shifts were less adverse in the 1990s.

The extent of the shift to low-wage industries in the 1980s is more evident in an analysis of changes in the shares of the workforce in various sectors (**Table 2.29**). Several high-wage sectors, such as construction, transportation, wholesale, communications, and government, increased employment in the 1980s but ended up providing a smaller or similar share of overall employment over time. A lower share of employment in these high-wage sectors puts downward pressure on wages. Overall, the share of the workforce in low-paying services and in retail trade was 7.3 percentage points higher in 1989 than in 1979. The parallel trend was the roughly 8 percentage-point drop in the share of the workforce in high-paying industries, such as manufacturing, construction, mining, government, transportation, communications, and utilities.

The data in Table 2.29 illustrate the different, and less adverse, shifts in industry employment in the 1990s relative to the 1980s. Although durable manufacturing's share of employment declined in the 1990s (by 2.1 percentage points), this was less than the decline of the 1980s (3.6 percentage points). The low-wage retail trade sector expanded by 1.4 percentage points in the 1980s but shrank in the 1990s. Similarly, higher-wage sectors such as construction and transportation/communications expanded in the 1990s but contracted in the 1980s. In general, high-wage sectors fared better in terms of employment growth in the 1990s than the 1980s. Correspondingly, the 1990s contraction of retail trade, by far the lowest-wage sector, helped wages grow. Thus, one reason that median wages eroded less and low wages did better in the early 1990s than in the 1980s might be related to this different pattern of industry employment growth.

**Table 2.30** presents an analysis of the impact of the shift in the industry mix of employment on the growth of the college/high school wage premium, providing some systematic evidence of how industry shifts affect the growth of wage inequality, at least on this one wage premium. The analysis uses wage data on individuals to determine the growth of the college/high school wage

**TABLE 2.29** Employment growth by sector, 1979-2001

| | Employment shares | | | | Change | | |
|---|---|---|---|---|---|---|---|
| Industry sector | 1979 | 1989 | 2000 | 2001 | 1979-89 | 1989-2000 | 2000-01 |
| **Goods producing** | 29.5% | 23.4% | 19.5% | 19.0% | -6.1 | -3.9 | -0.5 |
| Mining | 1.1 | 0.6 | 0.4 | 0.4 | -0.4 | -0.2 | 0.0 |
| Construction | 5.0 | 4.8 | 5.1 | 5.2 | -0.2 | 0.3 | 0.1 |
| Manufacturing | 23.4 | 18.0 | 14.0 | 13.4 | -5.4 | -4.0 | -0.6 |
| Durable goods | 14.2 | 10.6 | 8.5 | 8.0 | -3.6 | -2.1 | -0.4 |
| Nondurable goods | 9.3 | 7.4 | 5.6 | 5.3 | -1.8 | -1.8 | -0.2 |
| **Service producing** | 70.5% | 76.6% | 80.5% | 81.0% | 6.0 | 3.9 | 0.5 |
| Trans., comm., util. | 5.7 | 5.2 | 5.3 | 5.3 | -0.5 | 0.1 | 0.0 |
| Wholesale | 5.8 | 5.7 | 5.3 | 5.3 | -0.1 | -0.4 | 0.0 |
| Retail | 16.7 | 18.1 | 17.7 | 17.8 | 1.4 | -0.4 | 0.1 |
| Fin., ins., real est. | 5.5 | 6.2 | 5.7 | 5.8 | 0.6 | -0.4 | 0.0 |
| Services | 19.1 | 24.9 | 30.7 | 31.0 | 5.9 | 5.8 | 0.3 |
| Government | 17.8 | 16.5 | 15.7 | 15.8 | -1.3 | -0.8 | 0.1 |
| Federal | 3.1 | 2.8 | 2.1 | 2.0 | -0.3 | -0.7 | -0.1 |
| State and local | 14.7 | 13.7 | 13.6 | 13.8 | -1.0 | -0.1 | 0.2 |
| Total | 100.0% | 100.0% | 100.0% | 100.0% | | | |

Source: Authors' analysis.

premium when one does and does not control for industry shifts—the "constant" and "actual" under "industry composition." Comparing the growth of the education premium in the first two columns provides information on the impact of changes in the industry composition of employment, or industry shifts. This analysis suggests that the employment shift to low-wage industries accounted for almost 20% of the growth of education premiums over the 1979-89 period among men and women. Among men, for instance, the college/high school wage premium grew 13.9 percentage points from 1979 to 1989, but would have grown by 11.4 percentage points had industry composition not changed. Therefore, 2.5 percentage points of the 13.9 percentage-point growth, equivalent to 18% of the total growth in the college/high school differential in the 1980s, can be accounted for by industry shifts.

Among men, the industry shift effect was smaller in 1989-2000 than in 1979-89, 1.7% versus 2.5%, and was especially slow during the 1995-2000 period. Among women, industry shifts were actually inequality reducing in the 1990s due to the trends over the 1995-2000 boom. Thus, the industry shift effect went from inducing a 2.7% increase in the college wage premium in the 1980s to reducing this premium by 0.7% in the 1990s, a 3.4% turnaround in

**TABLE 2.30** The effect of industry shifts on the growth of the college/high school wage differential, 1973-2000

| | College/high school wage differential | | Industry shift: | |
| | Industry composition: | | | Explanatory |
| | Actual* | Constant** | Effect | contribution*** |
|---|---|---|---|---|
| **Men** | | | | |
| 1973 | 25.3% | 30.3% | | |
| 1979 | 20.1 | 24.8 | | |
| 1989 | 33.9 | 36.2 | | |
| 1995 | 37.1 | 38.3 | | |
| 2000 | 42.9 | 43.4 | | |
| *Change* | | | | |
| 1979-89 | 13.9% | 11.4% | 2.5% | 18.0% |
| 1989-2000 | 9.0 | 7.2 | 1.7 | 19.5 |
| 1989-95 | 3.2 | 2.1 | 1.1 | 33.6 |
| 1995-2000 | 5.8 | 5.1 | 0.7 | 11.6 |
| **Women** | | | | |
| 1973 | 37.7% | 35.2% | | |
| 1979 | 26.5 | 25.2 | | |
| 1989 | 41.0 | 37.1 | | |
| 1995 | 46.7 | 42.1 | | |
| 2000 | 48.2 | 45.0 | | |
| *Change* | | | | |
| 1979-89 | 14.5% | 11.9% | 2.7% | 18.4% |
| 1989-2000 | 7.2 | 7.9 | -0.7 | -10.0 |
| 1989-95 | 5.7 | 5.1 | 0.7 | 11.5 |
| 1995-2000 | 1.5 | 2.9 | -1.4 | -91.7 |

\*    Estimated with controls for experience as a quartic, marital status, race, and four regions.
\*\*   Adds 12 industry controls to the regression reported in first column, thereby holding industry "constant."
\*\*\*  Share of the rise in "actual" that is explained by industry shifts, calculated from the difference between "actual" and "constant" relative to "actual."

Source: Authors' analysis.

trend. It is likely that this reversal is due to the corresponding reversal of retail trade employment (which disproportionately comprises women) in the 1990s—its employment share contracted rather than expanded, as it had in the 1980s. On the other hand, industry shifts have remained a persistent factor in the 1990s, causing rising wage inequality among men.

## Trade and wages

The process of globalization in the 1980s and 1990s has been an important factor in both slowing the growth rate of average wages and reducing the wage levels of workers with less than a college degree. The increase in international trade and investment flows affects wages through several channels. First, increases in imports of finished manufactured goods, especially from countries where workers earn only a fraction of what U.S. workers earn, reduces manufacturing employment in the United States. While increases in exports create employment opportunities for some domestic workers, imports mean job losses for many others. Large, chronic trade deficits over the last 17 years suggest that the jobs lost to import competition have outnumbered the jobs gained from increasing exports. Given that export industries tend to be less labor intensive than import-competing industries, even growth in "balanced trade" (where exports and imports both increase by the same dollar amount) would lead to a decline in manufacturing jobs.

Second, imports of intermediate manufactured goods (used as inputs in the production of final goods) also help to lower domestic manufacturing employment, especially for production workers and others with less than a college education. The expansion of export platforms in low-wage countries has induced many U.S. manufacturing firms to outsource part of their production processes to low-wage countries. Since firms generally find it most profitable to outsource the most labor-intensive processes, the increase in outsourcing has hit non-college-educated production workers hardest. The growth of outsourcing is shown in **Figure 2Q**. For all of manufacturing, the share of intermediate inputs into the production process that were imported, i.e., outsourced, rose from 4.1% in 1974 to 8.2% in 1993. In transportation equipment, the outsourcing share rose from 6.4% in 1974 to 15.7% by 1993.

Third, low wages and greater world capacity for producing manufactured goods can lower the prices of many international goods. Since workers' pay is tied to the value of the goods they produce, lower prices internationally can lead to a reduction in the earnings of U.S. workers, even if imports themselves do not increase.

Fourth, in many cases the mere threat of direct foreign competition or of the relocation of part or all of a production facility can lead workers to grant wage concessions to their employers.

Fifth, the very large increases in direct investment (i.e., plant and equipment) flows to other countries have meant reduced investment in the domestic manufacturing base and significant growth in the foreign manufacturing capacity capable of competing directly with U.S.-based manufacturers.

**FIGURE 2Q** Outsourcing, 1974-93

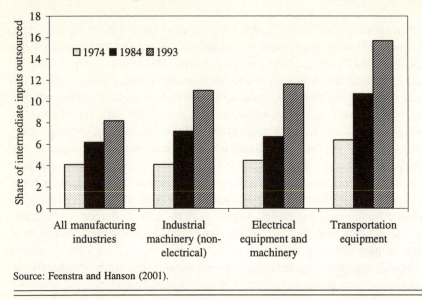

Source: Feenstra and Hanson (2001).

Finally, the effects of globalization go beyond those workers exposed directly to foreign competition. As trade drives workers out of manufacturing and into lower-paying service jobs, not only do their own wages fall, but the new supply of workers to the service sector (from displaced workers plus young workers not able to find manufacturing jobs) also helps to lower the wages of those already employed in service jobs.

This section briefly examines the role of international trade and investment in recent changes in the U.S. wage structure. Since even the preceding list of channels through which globalization affects wages is not complete and not yet quantified, this analysis will *understate* the impact of globalization on wages in the 1980s and 1990s. This topic is a relatively new area of inquiry in empirical labor economics and international trade; as befits a new area of investigation, it is beset with considerable controversy and confusion. Unfortunately, no studies are yet available that analyze trade's impact on the wage structure over the 1990s, although some do analyze the early 1990s.

**Table 2.31** provides information on the growth of the manufacturing trade deficit (the excess of imports over exports) from 1973 to 1993 by region and type of industry—industries that heavily use unskilled labor, skilled labor, or capital. The trade deficit grew to $130.7 billion in 1993 (and has grown further since), whereas U.S. manufacturing trade was balanced in 1973 and mildly

**TABLE 2.31** Net trade in U.S. manufactures by skill intensity and trading partner, 1973-93 ($ millions)

| Country/region | Skilled-intensive manufactures | | | Unskilled-intensive manufactures | | | Capital-intensive manufactures | | | Total | | |
|---|---|---|---|---|---|---|---|---|---|---|---|---|
| | 1973 | 1984 | 1993 | 1973 | 1984 | 1993 | 1973 | 1984 | 1993 | 1973 | 1984 | 1993 |
| **Advanced** | $2,648 | -$8,249 | -$27,531 | -$5,863 | -$26,078 | -$18,728 | $3,941 | -$36,550 | -$45,746 | -$7,156 | -$70,877 | -$92,006 |
| Japan | -2,088 | -19,999 | -45,284 | -1,903 | -10,772 | -4,703 | -2,005 | -17,596 | -26,076 | -5,997 | -48,367 | -76,063 |
| Other | 4,736 | 11,750 | 17,753 | -3,960 | -15,306 | -14,026 | -1,936 | -18,955 | -19,671 | -1,159 | -22,510 | -15,943 |
| **OPEC** | $1,207 | $5,029 | $6,070 | $206 | $79 | -$2,044 | $718 | $2,921 | $5,847 | $2,131 | $8,030 | $9,872 |
| **Eastern Europe** | $285 | $174 | $1,587 | -$236 | -$469 | -$1,355 | $101 | $19 | $496 | $149 | -$276 | $728 |
| **Developing** | $3,375 | $337 | -$17,407 | -$2,713 | -$24,971 | -$57,812 | $3,594 | $8,643 | $25,918 | $4,256 | -$15,991 | -$49,301 |
| Latin America | 2,422 | 4,420 | 6,136 | -41 | -2,656 | -872 | 2,091 | 4,178 | 8,981 | 4,472 | 5,942 | 14,245 |
| Asia-Four Tigers | -311 | -8,699 | -23,431 | -2,322 | -18,640 | -33,013 | 354 | 788 | 7,900 | -2,278 | -26,551 | -48,545 |
| Other Asia | 464 | 2,167 | -2,603 | -244 | -3,148 | -20,854 | 344 | 1,773 | 6,148 | 564 | 792 | -17,309 |
| **Other** | $799 | $2,449 | $2,491 | -$106 | -$527 | -$3,073 | $804 | $1,904 | $2,889 | $1,498 | $3,826 | $2,308 |
| **Total** | $7,515 | -$2,709 | -$37,281 | -$8,606 | -$51,438 | -$79,940 | $471 | -$24,968 | -$13,486 | -$620 | -$79,114 | -$130,708 |

Source:  Cline (1997).

183

unbalanced in the late 1970s. This growing trade deficit reflects the fast growth of imports in the 1980s and 1990s and the much slower growth of exports.

A sizable deterioration in the U.S. trade balance with Asian developing countries (Singapore, Taiwan, Korea, and Hong Kong), China (in "other Asia"), and Japan has driven the rising trade deficit. In contrast, the deficit with other advanced (and higher-wage) countries grew less than $15 billion over this period.

Much of the growth in the trade deficit from 1973 to 1993—about $70 billion of the $130 billion growth—occurred in industries that intensively use unskilled labor. However, there was also a roughly $45 billion deterioration (from $7.5 to -$37.3 billion) in skill-intensive industries and a $14 billion erosion in capital-intensive industries. More recent data would show a large deterioration with China, Canada, and Mexico fueling a historically high trade deficit.

These data suggest not only a large increase in the trade deficit but a growing exposure of a broad range of industries to foreign competition from the most advanced, developing countries. This growth in the trade deficit and increased global competition can, and would be expected to, adversely affect the wages of non-college-educated workers relative to others. In fact, any potential gains from trade would be created precisely through such a mechanism—a redeployment of workers and capital into more highly skilled or capital-intensive industries, a movement that lessens the need for non-college-educated workers.

We now turn to an examination of the types of jobs that were lost as the trade deficit grew, as job losses in import-sensitive industries exceeded job gains in export industries. In periods of low unemployment, it may be the case that a trade deficit does not cause actual job loss because workers displaced by rising imports have found employment in non-traded sectors such as services. Nevertheless, even at low unemployment a trade deficit will affect the composition of jobs (less manufacturing, more services), thereby affecting wage inequality. In this light, **Table 2.32** indicates how trade flows affect the composition of employment by wage level and education relative to a situation in which the ratios of imports and exports to output remained at 1979 levels.

Of the 2,366,000 jobs lost over the 1979-94 period, college-educated workers lost 290,000 and high-wage workers lost 230,000. The impact of the growing trade deficit, nevertheless, was disproportionately borne by non-college-educated workers, especially those with no more than a high school degree. Likewise, trade-deficit-related job losses fell disproportionately on the lowest-wage workers and lower-middle-wage workers, the 62.5% of the workforce with the lowest pay. Consequently, non-college-educated and middle- and lower-wage workers disproportionately bear the costs and pressures due to trade deficits and the global competition they reflect.

**TABLE 2.32** Trade-deficit-induced job loss by wage and education level, 1979-94

| Job characteristic | Share of total employment, 1989 | Trade-deficit-related job loss (thousands) | | |
|---|---|---|---|---|
| | | 1979-89 | 1989-94 | 1979-94 |
| **Education level** | | | | |
| College graduate* | 18.6% | -215 | -31 | -290 |
| Non-college | 81.4 | -1,550 | -356 | -2,076 |
| Some college | 31.3 | -403 | -55 | -519 |
| High school | 31.2 | -653 | -148 | -867 |
| Less than high school | 18.9 | -495 | -153 | -690 |
| | 100.0 | | | |
| **Wage level**** | | | | |
| Highest wage | 9.7% | -163 | -34 | -230 |
| High wage | 11.2 | -186 | -27 | -244 |
| Upper-middle | 16.6 | -269 | -36 | -345 |
| Lower-middle | 26.4 | -478 | -96 | -631 |
| Lowest wage | 36.1 | -670 | -194 | -916 |
| | 100.0 | | | |
| **Total** | | -1,765 | -387 | -2,366 |

\* Four years of college or more.
\*\* Corresponding to jobs that paid in the following wage percentile ranges in 1979:
   90-99; 75-89; 50-74; 21-49; 0-20.

Source: Scott et al. (1997), Tables 1 and 2.

Taken together, Tables 2.31 and 2.32 suggest that trade, particularly with low-wage developing countries, accelerated the long-term decline in manufacturing employment. The data also suggest that the fall in employment opportunities was especially severe for non-college-educated manufacturing production workers. Since production workers in manufacturing on average earn substantially more than workers with similar skills in non-manufacturing jobs, these trade-induced job losses contributed directly to the deterioration in the wage structure. Since millions of trade-displaced workers sought jobs in non-manufacturing sectors, trade also worked to depress wages of comparable workers employed outside manufacturing.

As discussed earlier, international trade can also affect U.S. wages through the prices of internationally traded manufactured goods without any change in the quantity of exports or imports. The expansion of manufacturing capacity in low-wage countries since the 1970s has significantly increased the supply of less-skill-intensive manufactured goods, inducing a reduction in the U.S. price of these goods. Since workers' earnings reflect changes in the prices of the goods they produce, a lower price for less-skill-intensive goods drives down the wages of less-skilled workers. **Table 2.33** presents results from some simple calculations designed to estimate the effect of trade-induced price changes on U.S. wages. It examines whether prices grew more slowly in the manufacturing industries most reliant on non-college-educated or unskilled and semi-skilled workers—the industries most affected by low-wage imports. Two measures of skill intensity are shown. The first section shows that between 1979 and 1989 the prices in college-worker-intensive industries increased by 2.9% relative to non-college-worker-intensive industries. The second section shows that the prices in non-production-intensive industries rose by 5.4% relative to those in production-worker-intensive industries over the same period.

These relative price changes require the wages of non-college-educated and production workers to fall. The size of the wage declines depends on the importance of labor costs in overall manufacturing costs. If labor were a small share of total manufacturing costs, say 10%, then a 1% decline in the relative prices of less-skill-intensive goods would require a large fall (10%) in the less-skilled workers' wage in order to leave the overall industry costs unchanged (a 10% fall in something that is 10% of total costs represents a 1% savings on overall costs). If labor were a large share of total manufacturing costs, or value-added (say, 100%), then a 1% decline in the relative prices of less-skill-intensive industries would require a much smaller (1%) decline in the costs of less-skilled labor (a 1% fall in the costs of something that is 100% of total costs represents a 1% savings on overall costs). Since labor costs are, on average, 70% of total manufacturing value-added, then a 1% fall in the relative less-skill-intensive industry price requires about a 1.4% fall in the wage of the relatively less-skilled worker. If we assume that the average real wage for college-educated and non-production workers was unchanged between 1979 and 1989 (as was generally the case), then the 2.9% fall in the relative prices in non-college-educated-intensive industries should have lowered the non-college wage by 4.1% over the period. The 5.4% relative fall in production-worker-intensive prices should have lowered production worker wages by 7.7%. Since the wages of non-college-educated relative to college-educated workers actually fell 13.9% over the period, trade appears to have contributed about 30% of the decline in the college/non-college wage over the 1979-89 period. By this measure, trade was entirely responsible for the 7.7% fall in production worker wages relative to those of non-production workers.

The preceding tables document the rise in trade deficits and the decline in

**TABLE 2.33** Effect of changes in prices of internationally traded manufactured goods on wage inequality

| Industry price changes* | 1959-69 | 1969-79 | 1979-89 |
|---|---|---|---|
| College weighted | 12.9% | 159.5% | 61.4% |
| Non-college weighted | 15.1 | 142.8 | 58.5 |
| Difference | -2.2 | 16.7 | 2.9 |
| Non-production weighted | 16.1% | 13.7% | 62.0% |
| Production weighted | 16.2 | 137.5 | 56.6 |
| Difference | -0.1 | -0.5 | 5.4 |
| Labor share in value-added | | | 70.0% |
| **Implied decline in wages**** | | | |
| Non-college | | | 4.1% |
| Production | | | 7.7 |
| **Actual change in relative wages** | | | |
| College/non-college*** | | | 13.9% |
| Non-production/production | | | 7.7 |
| **Share of change in relative wages caused by change in relative prices** | | | |
| College/non-college | | | 29.8% |
| Non-production/production | | | 110.2 |

\* Change in value-added producer price indexes over the period.
\*\* Assuming no change in the real wage of non-production and college workers.
\*\*\* Change between 1979 and 1989 in regression-based college/non-college wage differential, controlling for workers' experience and region of residence.

Source: Authors' analysis of Schmitt and Mishel (1996).

prices of less-skill-intensive, internationally traded manufactured goods. These channels have contributed to the long-term decline in manufacturing employment and directly and indirectly to the deterioration in the U.S. wage structure. Little concrete evidence is available on the other channels discussed at the beginning of this section—the "threat effect" of imports and plant relocation on U.S. manufacturing wages and the reality of large-scale international direct investment flows. Nevertheless, these effects are likely to be as large or larger than those that are more readily quantifiable.

Another aspect of globalization is immigration. After six decades of decline in the percentage of immigrants in the total population of the United States, the immigrant share began to grow in the 1970s (**Table 2.34**). The annual in-

**TABLE 2.34** Legal immigrant flow to the United States, fiscal years 1881-2000

| Decade | Number (000s) Total | Number (000s) Annual | As percentage of change in population | Foreign-born as share of population* |
|--------|------|------|------|------|
| 1881-1890 | 5,247 | 525 | 41.0% | 14.7% |
| 1891-1900 | 3,688 | 369 | 28.3 | 13.6 |
| 1901-1910 | 8,795 | 880 | 53.9 | 14.6 |
| 1911-1920 | 5,736 | 574 | 40.8 | 13.2 |
| 1921-1930 | 4,107 | 411 | 24.6 | 11.6 |
| 1931-1940 | 528 | 53 | 5.9 | 8.8 |
| 1941-1950 | 1,035 | 135 | 5.3 | 6.9 |
| 1951-1960 | 2,515 | 252 | 8.7 | 5.4 |
| 1961-1970 | 3,322 | 332 | 13.7 | 4.7 |
| 1971-1980 | 4,493 | 449 | 20.7 | 6.2 |
| 1981-1990 | 7,338 | 734 | 33.1 | 7.9 |
| 1991-2000 | 9,095 | 910 | 27.8 | 11.1 |

* At end of period.

Source: Immigration and Naturalization Service (2000) and U.S. Bureau of the Census.

crease in legal immigrants (no data are available on undocumented, or "illegal," immigrants) has grown significantly, nearly 1 million each year in the 1990s, up from less than half that much in the 1970s (449,000 annually). As a result, the foreign-born share of the population rose to 11.1 in 2000, with legal immigrants making up 27.8% of the population growth in the 1990s.

Holding all else constant, a rise in immigration increases the available labor supply in the United States and thus tends to reduce wages. **Table 2.35** shows that a large share of recent immigrants have less than the equivalent of a high school education (although immigrants, at least until 1990, also were more likely than natives to have a college degree). These numbers suggest that immigrants compete disproportionately with the least-skilled U.S. workers and therefore have generated pressure to lower wages for those without a high school degree since the end of the 1970s.

Given this downward pressure on low-wage workers from increased immigration, it is surprising that wages at the bottom have done better in the 1990s than in the 1980s, and that the 50/10 wage gap has been stable or declining since the late 1980s. However, the 1990s have also seen two increases in the minimum wage and many years of persistent low unemployment. These factors may have offset the impact of immigration.

**TABLE 2.35** Educational attainment of immigrant and native men, 1960-98

| | Less than high school | | College educated | |
|---|---|---|---|---|
| Year | Native | Immigrants | Native | Immigrants |
| 1960 | 53.0% | 66.0% | 11.4% | 10.1% |
| 1970 | 39.7 | 49.0 | 15.4 | 18.6 |
| 1980 | 23.3 | 37.5 | 22.8 | 25.3 |
| 1990 | 11.9 | 31.4 | 26.4 | 26.6 |
| 1998 | 9.0 | 33.6 | 29.8 | 28.3 |

Source: Authors' analysis of Borjas (1999).

## The union dimension

The percentage of the workforce represented by unions was stable in the 1970s but fell rapidly in the 1980s and continued to fall in the 1990s, as shown in **Figure 2R**. This falling rate of unionization has lowered wages, not only because some workers no longer receive the higher union wage but also because there is less pressure on non-union employers to raise wages (a "spillover" or "threat effect" of unionism). There are also reasons to believe that union bargaining power has weakened, adding a qualitative shift to the quantitative decline. This erosion of bargaining power is partially related to a harsher economic context for unions because of trade pressures, the shift to services, and ongoing technological change. However, analysts have also pointed to other factors, such as employer militancy and changes in the application and administration of labor law, that have helped to weaken unions.

**Table 2.36** shows the union wage premium—the degree to which union wages exceed non-union wages—by type of pay (benefits or wages) for all workers and for blue-collar workers in 2001. The union premium is larger for total compensation (39.1%) than for wages alone (28.4%), reflecting the fact that unionized workers are provided insurance and pension benefits that are more than double those of non-union workers. For blue-collar workers (where the comparison is more of an "apples to apples" one), the union premium in insurance and benefits is even larger: union blue-collar workers receive 137.5% and 359.5% more in health and pension benefits, respectively, than do their non-union counterparts.

The bottom section provides a more refined analysis of the union wage premium by comparing the pay in unionized occupations to non-union pay in comparable occupations and establishments (factories or offices). Specifically,

**FIGURE 2R** Union membership in the United States, 1973-2001

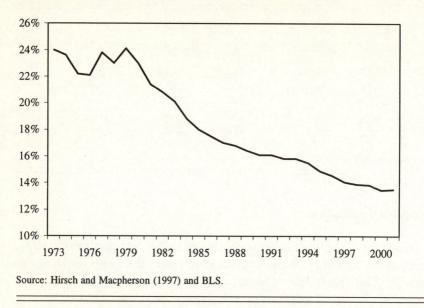

Source: Hirsch and Macpherson (1997) and BLS.

the estimated union premium controls for the sector (public or private) in which the establishment is located, the establishment's size, full-time or part-time status of its employees, and its detailed industry and region. In this analysis, the union wage premium is 21.0%, while the union compensation premium (combining the effect on wages and benefits) is 27.8%. Similarly, the employers of unionized workers pay 51.3% more in insurance costs (health and life) per hour and 20.3% more for retirement/savings/pension plans

This analysis also shows that unionized workers are 16.0% more likely to be in an employer-provided insurance plan (the "incidence" effect); among workers who are in these plans, unionized employers pay 44.2% more per hour for the plan (the "expenditure" effect). Similarly, unionized workers are 26.7% more likely to be in a pension plan, and unionized employers pay 16.0% more into these plans than do comparable non-union employers who provide pension plans.

**Table 2.37**, using a different data source and methodology (and year), presents another set of estimates of the union wage premium. Specifically, the premium is computed so as to reflect differences in hourly wages between union and non-union workers who are otherwise comparable in experience, education, region, industry, occupation, and marital status. This methodology yields

**TABLE 2.36** Union wage and benefit premium, 2001 (2001 dollars)

| | Hourly pay | | | |
| --- | --- | --- | --- | --- |
| | Wages | Insurance | Pension | Compensation |
| **All workers** | | | | |
| Union | $21.40 | $2.48 | $1.52 | $27.80 |
| Non-union | 16.67 | 1.14 | 0.51 | 19.98 |
| *Union premium* | | | | |
| Dollars | $4.73 | $1.34 | $1.01 | $7.82 |
| Percent | 28.4% | 117.5% | 198.0% | 39.1% |
| **Blue collar** | | | | |
| Union | $21.10 | $2.66 | $1.70 | $28.07 |
| Non-union | 13.72 | 1.12 | 0.37 | 16.93 |
| *Union premium* | | | | |
| Dollars | $7.38 | $1.54 | $1.33 | $11.14 |
| Percent | 53.8% | 137.5% | 359.5% | 65.8% |
| **Regression-adjusted union effect*** | | | | |
| Union effect | 21.0% | 51.3% | 20.3% | 27.8% |
| Incidence | | 16.0 | 26.7 | |
| Expenditure | | 44.2 | 16.0 | |

\* Controlling for full-time, industry (74), occupation (47), public sector, region (9), establishment size in 1994.

Note: Wage defined differently in panels (top includes paid leave and supplemental pay).

Source: Authors' analysis of BLS data and Pierce (1998).

a lower but still sizable union premium of 11.5% overall—11.9% for men and 10.0% for women. The differences in union wage premiums across demographic groups are relatively small, ranging from 9.5% to 16.9%. Hispanics and blacks, especially men, tend to reap the greatest wage advantage from unionism. Because black workers have higher-than-average rates of unionization and enjoy higher union premiums, unionization works to close the racial wage gap with whites.

**Table 2.38** provides information on the union premium for various non-wage dimensions of compensation related to health insurance, pensions, and paid time off. The first two columns present the characteristics of compensation in union and non-union settings. The difference between the union and non-union compensation packages are presented in two ways, unadjusted (sim-

**TABLE 2.37** Union wage premium by demographic group, 2001

| Demographic group | Percent union* | Union premium** | |
| --- | --- | --- | --- |
| | | Dollars | Percent |
| **Total** | 15.4% | $1.01 | 11.5% |
| Men | 17.1 | 1.24 | 11.9 |
| Women | 13.7 | 0.91 | 10.0 |
| **Whites** | 15.2% | $0.93 | 11.0% |
| Men | 17.2 | 1.22 | 11.5 |
| Women | 13.1 | 0.79 | 9.5 |
| **Blacks** | 20.5% | $1.52 | 12.7% |
| Men | 22.8 | 1.75 | 13.6 |
| Women | 18.8 | 1.34 | 11.3 |
| **Hispanics** | 12.9% | $1.79 | 16.0% |
| Men | 13.3 | 1.96 | 16.9 |
| Women | 12.3 | 1.38 | 12.8 |

\* Union member or covered by a collective bargaining agreement.
\** Regression-adjusted union premium advantage controlling for experience, education, region, industry, occupation, and marital status.

Source: Authors' analysis.

ply the difference between the first two columns) and adjusted (for differences in characteristics other than union status such as industry, occupation, and established size). The last column presents the union premium, the percentage difference between union and non-union compensation, calculated using the "adjusted" difference.

These data show that a union premium exists in every dimension of the compensation package. Unionized workers are 28.2% more likely to be covered by employed-provided health insurance. Unionized employers also provide better health insurance—they pay an 11.1% higher share of single-worker coverage and a 15.6% higher share of family coverage. Moreover, deductibles are $54, or 18.0%, less for union workers. Consequently, unionized employers pay $0.43 more per hour for health insurance, or 30.1% more. Finally, union workers are 24.4% more likely to receive health insurance coverage in their retirement.

Similarly, 71.9% of union workers have employer-provided pensions, compared to only 43.8% of nonunion workers. Thus, union workers are 28.1% more

**TABLE 2.38** Union premiums for health, retirement, and paid leave

| Benefit | Union | Non-union | Difference | | Union premium* |
|---|---|---|---|---|---|
| | | | Unadjusted | Adjusted* | |
| **Health insurance** | | | | | |
| Percent covered | 83.5% | 62.0% | 21.5% | 17.5% | 28.2% |
| Employer share (%) | | | | | |
| Single | 88.3% | 81.8% | 6.5% | 9.1% | 11.1% |
| Family | 76.3 | 64.9 | 11.4 | 10.1 | 15.6 |
| Deductible ($) | $200 | $300 | -$100 | -$54 | -18.0% |
| Employer costs (per hour) | - | - | - | $0.43 | 30.1% |
| Retiree health coverage (%) | 76.6% | 59.8% | 16.7% | 14.6% | 24.4% |
| **Pension** | | | | | |
| Percent covered | 71.9% | 43.8% | 28.1% | 23.6% | 53.9% |
| Employer costs (per hour) | - | - | | | |
| Defined benefit | - | - | - | $0.39 | 36.1% |
| Defined contribution | - | - | - | -0.11 | -17.7 |
| **Time off** | | | | | |
| Vacation weeks | 2.98 | 2.35 | 0.63 | - | 26.6% |
| Paid holiday/ vacation (hours) | - | - | - | 22.2 | 14.3% |

* Adjusted for establishment size, occupation, industry, and other factors.

Source: Buchmueller, DiNardo, and Valletta (2001).

likely to have pension coverage. Union employers spend 36.1% more on de-fined-benefit plans but 17.7% less on defined-contribution plans. As defined-benefit plans are preferable, as discussed earlier, these data indicate that union workers are more likely to have the better form of pension plans.

Union workers also get more paid time off. Their three weeks of vacation is about three days more than non-union workers receive. Including both vacations and holidays, union workers enjoy 14.3% more paid time off.

The effect of the erosion of unionization on the wages of a segment of the workforce depends on the degree to which deunionization has taken place and the degree to which the union wage premium among that segment of the workforce has declined. **Table 2.39** shows both the degree to which unionization and the union wage premium have declined by occupation and education level over the 1978-97 period (1979 data were not available). These data, which

**TABLE 2.39** Effect of deunionization on male wage differentials, 1978-97

**Effect of union decline on wages**

|  | Percent union | | | Union wage premium* | | | Union effect** | | |
|---|---|---|---|---|---|---|---|---|---|
|  | 1978 | 1989 | 1997 | 1978 | 1989 | 1997 | 1978 | 1989 | 1997 |
| **By occupation** | | | | | | | | | |
| White collar | 14.7% | 12.1% | 10.4% | 1.1% | -0.3% | 2.2% | 0.2% | 0.0% | 0.2% |
| Blue collar | 43.1 | 28.9 | 23.6 | 26.6 | 23.3 | 22.2 | 11.5 | 6.7 | 5.3 |
| Difference | -28.4 | -16.7 | -13.2 | -25.6 | -23.6 | -20.1 | -11.3 | -6.8 | -5.0 |
| **By education** | | | | | | | | | |
| College | 14.3% | 11.9% | 11.6% | 6.3% | 4.2% | 5.1% | 0.9% | 0.5% | 0.6% |
| High school | 37.9 | 25.5 | 20.8 | 21.7 | 21.5 | 20.8 | 8.2 | 5.5 | 4.3 |
| Difference | -23.6 | -13.6 | -9.2 | -15.3 | -17.3 | -15.8 | -7.3 | -5.0 | -3.8 |

**Contribution of union decline on wage differentials**

|  | Change in wage differential*** | | | Change in union effect | | | Contribution of lower union effect | | |
|---|---|---|---|---|---|---|---|---|---|
| Differential | 1978-89 | 1989-97 | 1978-97 | 1978-89 | 1989-97 | 1978-97 | 1978-89 | 1989-97 | 1978-97 |
| White collar/ blue collar | 9.3% | 2.4% | 11.6% | 4.6% | 1.7% | 6.3% | 49.2% | 74.3% | 54.3% |
| College/ high school | 13.4 | 2.3 | 15.8 | 2.3 | 1.2 | 3.5 | 17.2 | 52.8 | 22.5 |

\* Estimated with a simple human capital model plus industry and occupation controls.
\*\* Calculated as the product of percent union and the union wage premium.
\*\*\* Estimated with a simple human capital model.

Source: Authors' update of Freeman (1991).

are for men only, are used to calculate the effect of weakened unions (less representation and a weaker wage effect) over the 1978-97 period on the wages of particular groups and the effect of deunionization on occupation and education wage differentials.

Union representation fell dramatically among blue-collar and high-school-educated male workers from 1978 to 1997. Among the high-school-graduate workforce, unionization fell from 37.9% in 1978 to 20.8% in 1997, almost by half. This decline obviously weakened the effect of unions on the wages of both union and non-union high-school-educated workers. Because unionized high school graduates earned about 21% more than equivalent non-union workers (a premium that did not change over the 1978-97 period), unionization raised the wage of the average high school graduate by 8.2% in 1978 (the "union

**TABLE 2.40**  Effect of unions on wages, by wage fifth, 1973-87

|  | Lowest fifth | Second fifth | Middle fifth | Fourth fifth | Top fifth | Average |
|---|---|---|---|---|---|---|
| **Percent union** | | | | | | |
| 1973 | 39.9% | 43.7% | 38.3% | 33.5% | 12.5% | 33.7% |
| 1987 | 23.5 | 30.3 | 33.1 | 24.7 | 17.7 | 26.4 |
| *Change, 1973-87* | -15.4 | -13.4 | -5.2 | -8.8 | 7.2 | -7.3 |
| **Effect of union on:** | | | | | | |
| Union wage, 1987 | 27.9% | 16.2% | 18.0% | 0.9% | 10.5% | 15.9% |
| Average wage, 1987 | 6.6 | 4.9 | 6.0 | 2.1 | 2.1 | 4.2 |
| **Wage effect of deunionization** | | | | | | |
| 1973-87 | -4.3% | -2.2% | -0.9% | -0.1% | 0.8% | -1.1% |

Source: Card (1991).

effect"). Unions had a 0.9% impact on male college graduate wages in 1978, leaving the net effect of unions to narrow the college/high school gap by 7.3 percentage points in that year. The decline in union representation from 1978 to 1997, however, reduced the union effect for high school male workers to 4.3% in 1997 while hardly affecting college graduates; thus, unions closed the college/high school wage gap by only 3.8 percentage points in 1997. The lessened ability of unions to narrow this wage gap (from a 7.3% to a 3.8% narrowing effect) contributed to a 3.5 percentage-point rise in the college/high school wage differential, an amount equal to 22.5% of the total rise in this wage gap.

The weakening of unionism's wage impact had an even larger effect on blue-collar workers and on the wage gap between blue-collar and white-collar workers. The 43.1% unionization rate among blue-collar workers in 1978 and their 26.6% union wage premium boosted blue-collar wages by 11.5%, thereby closing the blue-collar/white-collar wage gap by 11.3 percentage points in that year. The union impact on this differential declined as unionization and the union wage premium declined, such that unionism reduced the blue-collar/white-collar differential by 5.0 rather than 11.3 percentage points in 1997, a 6.3 percentage-point weakening. This lessened effect of unionism can account for about half (54.3%) of the 11.6 percentage-point growth of the blue-collar/white-collar wage gap over the 1978-97 period.

**Table 2.40** presents the results of a study that examines the effect of lower unionization on workers at various wage levels. It thus analyzes the impact of deunionization on overall wage inequality (between low-, middle-, and high-wage workers), not just between groups (e.g., high school versus college educated). The data show that unions have their largest effect on the wages of lower-wage workers, raising the wages of union members in the lowest and second-lowest fifths by 27.9% and 16.2%, respectively. Because workers in the bottom three-fifths have higher unionization rates and higher union wage premiums, the effect of unions on average wages for these groups is largest, increasing the average wage from 4.9% to 6.6%.

Unionization declined more among low-wage than high-wage workers from 1973 to 1987, at the same time that unionization actually increased among the top fifth. The impact was to increase the wage gap between high- and low-wage workers. For instance, an increase in union representation lifted the wages of the top fifth by 0.8%, but deunionization lowered the wages in the bottom fifth by 4.3%, creating a roughly 5 percentage-point divergence between high- and low-wage earners.

The decline of union coverage and power affects men more than women and adversely affects middle-wage men more than lower-wage men. Consequently, deunionization has its greatest impact on the growth of the 90/50 wage gap among men. In this light, it is not surprising that the period of rapid decline of union coverage from 1979 to 1984 (during a deep recession, and at a time that the manufacturing sector was battered by the trade deficit) was also one where the male 90/50 wage gap grew the most. Recall from Table 2.39 that male blue-collar unionization fell from 43.1% in 1978 to just 28.9% in 1989, contributing to the rapid growth of male wage inequality in the 1980s. The decline of unionization in the 1990s put continued downward pressure on middle-wage men and contributed to the continued growth of the 90/50 wage gap.

## An eroded minimum wage

The real value of the minimum wage has fallen considerably since its high point in the late 1960s (**Figure 2S**). The decline was particularly steep and steady between 1979 and 1989, when inflation whittled it down from $6.55 to $4.62 (in 2001 dollars), a fall of 29.5% (**Table 2.41**). Despite the legislated increases in the minimum wage in 1990 and 1991 and again in 1996 and 1997, the value of the minimum wage in 2001 was still 21.4% less than in 1979. The increases in the 1990s raised its 2001 value 14.7% over 1989.

It has been argued that the minimum wage primarily affects teenagers and others with no family responsibilities. **Table 2.42** examines the demographic composition of the workforce that benefited from the 1996-97 increases in the

**FIGURE 2S** Real value of the minimum wage (2001 dollars), 1960-2002*

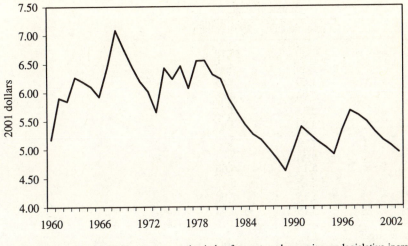

* Calculated using the CBO's consumer price index forecast, and assuming no legislative increases.

Source: Authors' analysis.

minimum wage. In fact, only 28.6% of the affected 9.9 million minimum wage workers were teenagers, suggesting that many minimum wage workers have important economic responsibilities. The information at the bottom of the table shows that minimum wage earners contribute 54% of their family's weekly earnings. Although the majority work part time (less than 35 hours weekly), 46.0% worked full time and another 33.3% worked more than 20 hours each week. While minorities are disproportionately represented among minimum wage workers, almost two-thirds are white. These workers also tend to be women (58.2% of the total). Table 2.42 also shows that minimum wage and other low-wage workers are heavily concentrated in the retail trade industry but are underrepresented in manufacturing industries and among unionized employers.

An analysis of only those earning between the old and the new minimum wage would be too narrow, since a higher minimum wage affects workers who earn more than but close to the minimum; they will receive increases when the minimum wage rises. For these reasons, Table 2.42 also presents the demographic breakdown of those workers who earned within a dollar of the new minimum wage level ($5.15-$6.14) at that time, a group labeled "other low-wage workers." This more broadly defined minimum wage workforce includes

**TABLE 2.41** Value of the minimum wage, 1960-2001

| | Minimum wage | |
| --- | --- | --- |
| Year | Current dollars | 2001 dollars |
| 1960 | $1.00 | $5.18 |
| 1967 | 1.40 | 6.43 |
| 1973 | 1.60 | 5.65 |
| 1979 | 2.90 | 6.55 |
| 1989 | 3.35 | 4.62 |
| 1990 | 3.80 | 4.99 |
| 1991 | 4.25 | 5.39 |
| 1996 | 4.75 | 5.34 |
| 1997 | 5.15 | 5.66 |
| 2001 | 5.15 | 5.15 |
| 2002* | 5.15 | 5.06 |
| 2003* | 5.15 | 4.94 |
| *Period averages* | | |
| 1960s | $1.29 | $6.17 |
| 1970s | 2.07 | 6.26 |
| 1980s | 3.33 | 5.44 |
| 1990s | 4.53 | 5.27 |
| 1979-2001 | 3.99 | 5.40 |
| *Percent change* | | |
| 1979-89 | | -29.5% |
| 1989-2000 | | 14.7 |
| 1979-2001 | | -21.4 |

* Inflation adjusted dollars are calculated using the CBO's consumer price index forcast.

Source: Authors' analysis.

an additional 9.6 million workers, or an additional 8.7% of the total workforce. Thus, any significant change in the minimum wage would affect a substantial group, as much as 18% of the workforce. The demographic breakdown of these other low-wage workers is more inclusive of full-time and adult workers but has proportionately fewer minority workers compared to the group of directly affected minimum wage earners.

**Table 2.43** assesses the impact of the lowering of the real value of the minimum wage on key wage differentials. The analysis is limited to women, who are affected most by the minimum wage. As the bottom of Table 2.43 shows, 20.1% of women workers in 1989 earned less than the real 1979 value

**TABLE 2.42** Characteristics of minimum wage and other workers, Oct. '95-Sep. '96

| Characteristic | Workers directly affected by new minimum ($4.25-$5.14) | Other low-wage workers ($5.15-$6.14) | Workers above minimum wage ($6.15+) | All workers |
|---|---|---|---|---|
| Average wage | $4.73 | $5.72 | $14.64 | $12.73 |
| Employment | 9,886,158 | 9,610,926 | 89,079,931 | 110,999,085 |
| Share of total | 8.9% | 8.7% | 80.3% | 100.0% |
| **Demographics** | | | | |
| Male | 41.8% | 41.9% | 54.9% | 52.3% |
| *16-19* | 13.7 | 8.1 | 1.0 | 2.9 |
| *20+* | 28.2 | 33.8 | 53.9 | 49.4 |
| Female | 58.2 | 58.1 | 45.1 | 47.7 |
| *16-19* | 14.9 | 7.9 | 0.7 | 2.8 |
| *20+* | 43.2 | 50.2 | 44.0 | 44.9 |
| White | 62.8 | 67.7 | 77.9 | 75.4 |
| *Male* | 24.6 | 26.2 | 42.8 | 39.4 |
| *Female* | 38.2 | 41.5 | 35.1 | 36.0 |
| Black | 16.1 | 13.8 | 10.4 | 11.3 |
| *Male* | 6.4 | 5.5 | 5.1 | 5.3 |
| *Female* | 9.8 | 8.3 | 5.3 | 6.0 |
| Hispanic | 17.5 | 14.8 | 7.9 | 9.5 |
| *Male* | 9.3 | 8.6 | 4.9 | 5.7 |
| *Female* | 8.2 | 6.2 | 3.0 | 3.8 |
| Teens (16-19) | 28.6% | 16.0% | 1.7% | 5.6% |
| **Work hours** | | | | |
| Full time (35+) | 46.0% | 62.7% | 87.7% | 81.1% |
| Part time | | | | |
| *20-34 hours* | 33.3% | 25.4% | 9.0% | 13.0% |
| *1-19 hours* | 20.7 | 11.9 | 3.3 | 5.9 |
| **Industry** | | | | |
| Manufacturing | 8.8% | 12.7% | 19.7% | 17.8% |
| Retail trade | 42.6 | 35.8 | 12.2 | 17.3 |
| **Union*** | | | | |
| Union | 4.4% | 6.3% | 19.1% | 16.4% |
| Non-union | 95.6 | 93.7 | 80.9 | 83.6 |

**Share of weekly earnings contributed by minimum wage workers, 1997**

| | Average | Median |
|---|---|---|
| All families with affected worker | 54% | 41% |
| excluding one-person families | 44 | 27 |

* Includes both union members and non-members covered by union contracts.

Source: Bernstein and Schmitt (1998).

**TABLE 2.43** Impact of lower minimum wage on key wage differentials among women, 1979-97

| Wage differential | Actual wage differentials | | | Simulated wage differentials at 1979 minimum wage | | 1979-89 | | | | 1979-97 | | | |
|---|---|---|---|---|---|---|---|---|---|---|---|---|---|
| | | | | | | Change in wage differential | | | Minimum wage effect | Change in wage differential | | | Minimum wage effect |
| | 1979 | 1989 | 1997 | 1989 | 1997 | Actual | Simulated | Difference | | Actual | Simulated | Difference | |
| *Wage ratios (logs)* | | | | | | | | | | | | | |
| 50/10 | 0.39 | 0.64 | 0.63 | 0.41 | 0.41 | 0.26 | 0.02 | 0.23 | 91.1% | 0.24 | 0.02 | 0.21 | 89.5% |
| 90/10 | 1.00 | 1.35 | 1.39 | 1.12 | 1.18 | 0.35 | 0.12 | 0.23 | 66.4 | 0.39 | 0.18 | 0.21 | 54.3 |
| *Education differentials* | | | | | | | | | | | | | |
| College/high school | 0.31 | 0.46 | 0.51 | 0.42 | 0.48 | 0.15 | 0.11 | 0.04 | 28.1% | 0.20 | 0.17 | 0.03 | 15.8% |
| College/less than high school | 0.49 | 0.69 | 0.75 | 0.60 | 0.67 | 0.20 | 0.11 | 0.09 | 44.2% | 0.26 | 0.18 | 0.08 | 29.4 |
| *Percent earning less than 1979 minimum* | | | | | | | | | | | | | |
| Less than high school | 43.4% | | 53.7% | | | | | | | | | | |
| High school | 23.6 | | 26.2 | | | | | | | | | | |
| College | 6.1 | | 7.0 | | | | | | | | | | |
| All | 20.1 | | 21.5 | | | | | | | | | | |

Source: Authors' analysis.

of the minimum wage; in other words, they were directly affected by its erosion in value after 1979. Women without a high school degree were hit hardest, with 43.4% and 53.7% earning below the 1979 minimum wage level in 1989 and 1997, respectively.

The analysis in Table 2.43 of the impact of a lower minimum wage on the wage structure is based on a simple simulation. Data on individual workers' wages in recent years are used to construct what the wage structure would have been in 1989 and 1997 if the 1979 minimum wage (again, inflation adjusted) had prevailed. Drawing on these simulated counterfactuals, the analysis compares the actual growth in wage differentials to the growth that would have occurred if the 1979 minimum wage had been maintained. The difference between "actual" and "simulated" is a measure of the impact of the lowering of the real value of the minimum wage on particular wage differentials.

The minimum wage most affects women at the 10th percentile and women with the least education, so it should not be surprising that wage differentials between middle- and low-wage women (the 50/10 differential) and college/less-than-high-school wage differentials are greatly affected by a decline in the minimum wage. For instance, the 50/10 differentials (in logs, which approximate percentage differences) would have grown from 0.39 in 1979 to only 0.41, rather than to 0.64, in 1989 if the minimum wage had been maintained. Thus, 0.23 of the 0.26 rise in the 50/10 differential in the 1980s among women, or 91.1% of the rise, can be attributed to the declining real value of the minimum wage. Similarly, the devaluing of the minimum wage can explain 44.2% of the growth in the college/less-than-high-school wage gap among women in the 1980s. A lower minimum wage also greatly affected the college/high school wage gap, explaining 28.1% of its growth in the 1980s. This analysis confirms the importance of the erosion of a key labor market institution, the minimum wage, on the growth of women's wage inequality at the bottom of the wage scale.

Because there is substantial evidence (with some controversy, of course) that a moderately higher minimum wage does not significantly lower employment (or reduce it at all), there has been an increased focus on which groups of low-wage workers benefit from a higher minimum wage. In other words, because a higher minimum may not have much of an effect on efficiency or output, the merit of such a policy will depend greatly on its fairness.

**Table 2.44** presents a computation of which families benefited from the higher minimum wage legislated over the 1996-97 period. The analysis calculates the annual gain to each worker based on the amount of his or her wage increase (i.e., based on the distance to the new minimum) and annual hours worked. Given this information, it is possible to calculate the share of the ag-

**TABLE 2.44** Distribution of minimum wage gains and income shares by fifth for various household types

| Income fifth | Share of gain from increase | Share of income | Average income |
|---|---|---|---|
| **Prime-age working households,\* 1997** | | | |
| Lowest | 35.3% | 5.4% | $15,728 |
| Second | 22.8 | 11.0 | 32,547 |
| Middle | 15.2 | 15.9 | 47,699 |
| Fourth | 14.5 | 22.3 | 66,104 |
| Highest | 12.2 | 45.3 | 134,128 |
| **All prime-age households (including non-working), 1997** | | | |
| Lowest | 28.0% | 3.8% | $10,518 |
| Second | 22.8 | 9.8 | 26,965 |
| Middle | 20.2 | 15.6 | 42,848 |
| Fourth | 15.8 | 22.7 | 62,502 |
| Highest | 13.3 | 48.0 | 131,991 |

\* Prime-age households are headed by a person age 25-54. One-person households are included. The top panel excludes households with no earners.

Source: Bernstein and Schmitt (1997).

gregate wage gain generated from the higher minimum wage that accrues to each household income fifth. As shown in Table 2.44, 35.3% of the gains generated by the higher minimum wage were received by the poorest 20% of working households; 58.1% of the gains were received by the poorest 40%.

The minimum wage generates the most help to those with the least income and the least help to those with the most income. For instance, as Table 2.44 also shows, the poorest fifth of working households had 5.4% of all income but received 35.3% of the gains from the higher minimum wage. In contrast, the best-off families received 45.3% of all income but received only 12.2% of the benefits of the higher minimum wage. The results are comparable when the analysis is repeated for all households, including those with no workers.

What happens to the minimum wage level strongly affects the wage gains of low-wage workers, particularly low-wage women whose wage is essentially set by the legislated minimum. Thus, the erosion of the minimum wage's value led to a precipitous drop in the wages of low-wage women in the 1980s and to a large increase in the 50/10 wage gap. The level of women's low wages (i.e., the 10th percentile) stabilized in the late 1980s when the wage level descended to its lowest possible level (at which employers could still hire) and as unemployment dropped. Thereafter, the 50/10 gap was flat or declined as unemployment fell to low levels in the late 1990s and as two increases in the minimum wage were implemented. Between 1999 and 2001, as the value of the minimum wage eroded and unemployment rose, the wages of low-wage women once again weakened and the 50/10 wage gap grew.

## The technology story of wage inequality

Technological change can affect the wage structure by displacing some types of workers and by increasing demand for others. Given the seemingly rapid diffusion of microelectronic technologies in recent years, many analysts have considered technological change a major factor in the recent increase in wage inequality. Unfortunately, because it is difficult to measure the extent of technological change and its overall character (whether it requires less skill from workers or more, and by how much), it is difficult to identify the role of technological change on recent wage trends. More than a few analysts, in fact, have simply assumed that whatever portion of wage inequality is unexplained by measurable factors can be considered to be the consequence of technological change. This type of analysis, however, only puts a name to our ignorance.

It is easy to understand why people might consider technology to be a major factor in explaining recent wage and employment trends. We are often told that the pace of change in the workplace is accelerating, and there is a widespread visibility of automation and robotics; computers and microelectronics provide a visible dimension evident in workplaces, such as offices, not usually affected by technology. Perhaps even more important is that technology has provided advances in products used by consumers, including home computers, CD players, VCRs, microwaves, electronic games, advanced televisions, cell phones, and so on. Equally visible is the use of the Internet among both consumers and business people. Given these advances, it is not surprising for non-economists to readily accept that technology is transforming the wage structure. It needs to be noted, however, that technological advances in consumer products are not related to changes in labor market outcomes—it is the way goods and services are produced and changes in the relative demand for different types of workers that affect wage trends. Since many high-tech products are made with low-tech methods, there is no close correspondence between advanced consumer products and an increased need for skilled workers. Similarly, ordering a book over the Internet rather than at a downtown bookstore does not necessarily change the types of jobs available in the economy—truckers, warehouse workers, and so on still do the work of getting the book to the buyer.

The economic intuition for a large role for technology in the growth of wage inequality is that the growth of wage inequality and the employment shift to more-educated workers has occurred within industries and has not been caused primarily by shifts across industries (i.e., more service jobs, fewer manufacturing jobs). Research has also shown that technological change has traditionally been associated with an increased demand for more-educated or "skilled" workers. As we have noted, the wage premium for "more-educated" workers, exemplified by college graduates, has risen over the last two decades. This pattern of change suggests, to some analysts, an increase in what is called "skill-biased technological change" that is thought to be generating greater wage inequality.

Because wages have risen the most for groups whose supply expanded the fastest (e.g., college graduates), most economists have concluded that non-supply factors (i.e., shifts in demand or institutional factors, such as those discussed in earlier sections) are the driving force behind growing wage inequality. These economists reason that those groups with the relatively fastest growth in supply would be expected to see their wages depressed relative to other groups unless there were other factors working strongly in their favor, such as rapid expansion in demand. Rapid technological change favoring more-educated groups could logically explain demand side shifts leading to wider wage differences.

There are many reasons to be skeptical of a technology-led increase in demand for "skill" as an explanation for growing wage inequality. Unfortunately, the "skills/technology" hypothesis frequently is presented as if evidence that technological change is associated with a greater need for skills or education is sufficient to show that technological change has led to the growth in wage inequality since 1979. This is not the case, since the impact of technology must have "accelerated" in order to explain why wage inequality started to grow in the 1980s and 1990s and did not grow in the prior decades. For instance, it is generally true that investment and technological change are associated with the need for more workforce skill and education—but this has been true for the entire 20th century, and it therefore does not explain why wage inequality began to grow two decades ago. Moreover, the skills and education level (and quality) of the workforce have been continually improving. Thus, the issue is whether technology's impact on skill demand was significantly greater in the 1980s and 1990s than in earlier periods.

The skills/technology story is also, unfortunately, frequently presented as a single-cause explanation of the growth in wage inequality. On this account, however, it fails to explain the pattern and timing of the growth in wage inequality over the last two decades. Specifically, there seems to be no consistent technology explanation for the relationship over time between productivity (presumably technologically driven) and wage inequality; the shifts over time in the various dimensions of wage inequality—within-group wage inequality, education differentials, and experience differentials; or the shifts in wage inequality at various parts of the wage structure, such as between the 90th and 50th or 90th and 10th percentiles. We now turn to an exploration of the various patterns documented earlier in this chapter and whether a technology story can explain them.

First consider the correspondence, or lack thereof, between productivity growth and wage inequality. It is plausible to assume that technological change that is radically shifting the demand for skills in the workplace would also raise productivity growth. Yet the greatest period of rising wage inequality, the early and mid-1980s, was a period in which productivity growth (measured as multifactor or labor productivity growth) was no faster than in the "stagnant" 1970s. Overall, wage inequality continued to grow through the mid-1990s, but productivity continued its slow pace. However, when productivity accelerated after 1995, there was no accompanying growth of wage inequality (see Table 2.23). Perhaps a process began in the 1979-95 period that led to a radical restructuring of skill demand and that ultimately led to the post-1995 productivity growth, but we are not aware of any such explanation.

Second, as we discussed above, there are two dimensions of wage inequality—the between-group wage differentials, such as those relating to education and experience, and the within-group wage inequality that occurs among workers of similar education and experience— and the technology story does not readily fit either pattern. The growth of within-group inequality, which accounts for half the growth of overall wage inequality in both the 1980s and 1990s, may be related to technological change if it is interpreted as a reflection of growing economic returns to worker skills (motivation, aptitudes for math, etc.) that are not easily measured. However, there are no signs that the growth of within-group wage inequality has been fastest in those industries where the use of technology grew the most. It is also unclear why the economic returns for measurable skills (e.g., education) and unmeasured skills (e.g., motivation) should not grow in tandem. In fact, between-group and within-group inequality have failed to move together in the various sub-periods since 1973.

The timing of the growth of within-group wage inequality does not easily correspond to a technology story. For instance, consider what happened during the 1995-2000 period associated with a technology-led productivity boom: within-group wage inequality actually declined among women and failed to grow among men. In the early 1990s, the so-called early stages of the new economy, within-group wage inequality grew moderately, whereas it grew rapidly in the 1980s.

Nor does the pattern of growth of education and experience differentials correspond easily to a technology story. Before reviewing these patterns, however, it is worth noting that these skill differentials are affected by much more than technology. For instance, we have shown in earlier sections that changes in labor market institutions such as the minimum wage and unionization are responsible for some of the rise in education wage differentials. Other factors, such as trade and industry shifts, also affect education and other skill differentials, and so, of course, there is not a complete correspondence of technology with skill differentials.

Again, the timing of change in skill differentials does not easily match the simple technology story. Among men, for instance, the college/high-school wage gap (see Table 2.16 and Figure 2K) grew most rapidly in the early 1980s but grew hardly at all in the early and mid-1990s, when technological change is thought to have been more rapid. The college wage premium did, however, grow faster in the 1995-2000 period, which is consistent with a "new economy" story (but also consistent with other stories, such as low unemployment). Among women, the growth in the college wage premium has been relatively steady since 1979, but with hardly any growth after 1995, when technology might have been expected to have its greatest impact.

The education differential pattern most in conflict with a technology story is the one between high school graduates and those without a high school degree. This wage gap (Table 2.16) rose modestly over the 1979-95 period and was stable thereafter. Thus, if those without a high school degree can be considered "unskilled," then the wage structure has not shifted much against these unskilled workers, especially during the 1995-2000 technology-led boom. It is apparent, therefore, that shifts in education differentials do not drive the changes in wage inequality at the bottom, since the 50/10 wage gap rose markedly in the 1980s and has fallen since, all while the education gap at the bottom was relatively stable.

The wage gap by age—experience differentials—is frequently considered a skill gap driven by technological change. And it is true that experience and education differentials both grew in the 1980s, giving the impression they both were affected by a common factor, such as technology. Among men, experience differentials grew only modestly in the early 1990s, as did the college wage premium, but they *fell* after 1995 as the college premium grew faster (Table 2.16). The consequence is that overall between-group inequality was stable or falling in the 1995-2000 period—a pattern true among both men and women. How can technology be driving wage inequality when between-group wage inequality (the dimension of inequality most closely corresponding to a technology-related skill) was flat or down during the 1995-2000 technology-led boom?

The experience since the mid- to late 1980s does not accord with the conventional technology story, whose imagery is of computer-driven technology bidding up the wages of more-skilled and more-educated workers, leaving behind a small group of unskilled workers with inadequate abilities. The facts are hard to reconcile with the notion that technological change grew as fast or faster in the 1990s, especially in the later 1990s, than in earlier periods. If technology were adverse for unskilled or less-educated workers, then we would expect a continued expansion of the wage differential between middle-wage and low-wage workers (the 50/10 differential). Yet, the 50/10 differential has been stable or declining among both men and women from 1986 or 1987 to 1997. Instead, we are seeing the top earners steadily pulling away from nearly all other earners—reflected in the 90/50 or 95/50 wage gap. Therefore, there seem to be factors driving a wedge between the top 10% and everyone else, rather than a skill-biased technological change aiding the vast majority but leaving a small group of unskilled workers behind. Further confirmation of the breadth of those left behind is that wages were stable or in decline for the bottom 80% of men and the bottom 70% of women over the 1989-95 period, with wages falling for the entire non-college-educated workforce (roughly 73% of workers).

Finally, the notion that technology has been bidding up the wages of the skilled relative to the unskilled does not accord with many of the basic facts presented earlier. Or, it holds true in a relative but not an absolute sense. The wages of skilled men, defined as white-collar, college-educated, or 90th percentile workers, were flat or in decline from the mid-1980s to the mid-1990s. As described in Chapter 3, white-collar men were increasingly becoming displaced and beset by employment problems in the early 1990s. High-wage women have continued to see their wages grow, but is it likely that technology is primarily affecting skilled women but not skilled men? The dramatic fall of entry-level wages for all college graduates, in the early 1990s, for both men and women, reinforces this point.

We now turn to other challenges to the technology story by examining which occupations are driving up education differentials and whether there has been an acceleration of technology's impact on the labor market.

One way of gaining insight into the role of technology in generating a widening of the education wage gap is to examine which occupations, in terms of their employment expansion and relative wage improvements, have contributed to the growth of education differentials. Such an analysis is presented in **Tables 2.45** and **2.46** for men and women, respectively. In these analyses, the workforce is divided into 11 specific white-collar occupations (from among the aggregate managerial, professional, technical, and sales groups) and three more aggregate, lower-paid occupations (blue-collar, service, and clerical). This breakdown permits an examination of which occupations within the white-collar workforce experienced the greatest growth in demand in the 1980s and 1990s, as reflected by their fast growth in employment and wages.

**TABLE 2.45** Decomposition of growth of male college/non-college wage premium by occupation, 1979-97

| | 1979-89 Growth due to: | | | | 1989-97 Growth due to: | | | | 1979-97 Growth due to: | | | |
|---|---|---|---|---|---|---|---|---|---|---|---|---|
| Occupation | Higher relative wage* | Increased relative employment** | Combined effect | Share of aggregate change | Higher relative wage* | Increased relative employment** | Combined effect | Share of aggregate change | Higher relative wage* | Increased relative employment** | Combined effect | Share of aggregate change |
| Managers | 2.9 | 1.7 | 4.6 | 58.3% | 1.2 | -0.2 | 0.9 | 27.6% | 4.1 | 1.5 | 5.6 | 49.2% |
| Engineers | 1.0 | -0.1 | 0.8 | 10.5 | 0.1 | -0.4 | -0.3 | -7.6 | 1.1 | -0.5 | 0.6 | 5.1 |
| Math/computer | 0.5 | -0.4 | 0.1 | 1.5 | 0.2 | 1.0 | 1.2 | 34.9 | 0.6 | 0.6 | 1.3 | 11.5 |
| Nat. science | 0.1 | 0.0 | 0.0 | 0.5 | 0.0 | 0.1 | 0.1 | 2.8 | 0.1 | 0.1 | 0.1 | 1.2 |
| Health prof. | 0.2 | 0.0 | 0.2 | 3.1 | 0.2 | 0.3 | 0.5 | 14.1 | 0.4 | 0.3 | 0.7 | 6.3 |
| Soc. sci./law | 0.0 | 0.0 | 0.0 | -0.6 | 0.0 | 0.0 | 0.0 | -0.5 | 0.0 | 0.0 | -0.1 | -0.5 |
| Other professional | -0.4 | -2.5 | -2.9 | -36.2 | 1.0 | 0.4 | 1.4 | 42.6 | 0.6 | -2.0 | -1.4 | -12.7 |
| Hlth., eng., sci. tech. | 0.1 | 0.0 | 0.1 | 1.4 | 0.1 | 0.0 | 0.1 | 4.2 | 0.2 | 0.0 | 0.3 | 2.2 |
| Other tech. | -0.1 | 1.4 | 1.3 | 16.7 | 0.3 | -0.2 | 0.1 | 3.4 | 0.2 | 1.2 | 1.4 | 12.7 |
| Other sales | 1.1 | 1.5 | 2.6 | 32.7 | 0.1 | -0.3 | -0.1 | -3.5 | 1.3 | 1.2 | 2.5 | 21.9 |
| Sales, fin. | 0.6 | 0.1 | 0.7 | 9.4 | -0.2 | -0.2 | -0.4 | -11.3 | 0.4 | -0.1 | 0.4 | 3.2 |
| Clerks | 0.1 | 0.0 | 0.1 | 0.9 | 0.2 | -0.1 | 0.1 | 4.4 | 0.3 | -0.1 | 0.2 | 2.0 |
| Service | 0.1 | 0.0 | 0.1 | 1.2 | 0.2 | -0.1 | 0.2 | 4.5 | 0.3 | -0.1 | 0.2 | 2.2 |
| Blue collar, farm | 0.1 | -0.1 | 0.1 | 0.7 | -0.4 | -0.1 | -0.5 | -15.7 | -0.3 | -0.2 | -0.5 | -4.2 |
| Growth of college/non-college wage premium*** | 6.3 | 1.6 | 7.9 | 100.0% | 3.1 | 0.2 | 3.4 | 100.0% | 9.4 | 1.9 | 11.3 | 100.0% |

\* Measures whether college graduates (four-year only) in this occupation had a greater (than other college graduates) increase in wages relative to non-college-educated workers, controlling for other human capital characteristics.

\*\* Measures whether college graduates in this occupation had a greater growth in employment relative to other college graduates.

\*\*\* Sample excludes those with more than four years of college.

Source: Authors' analysis.

**TABLE 2.46** Decomposition of growth of female college/non-college wage premium by occupation, 1979-97

| | 1979-89 | | | | 1989-97 | | | | 1979-97 | | | |
| | Growth due to: | | | | Growth due to: | | | | Growth due to: | | | |
| Occupation | Higher relative wage* | Increased relative employment** | Combined effect | Share of aggregate change | Higher relative wage* | Increased relative employment** | Combined effect | Share of aggregate change | Higher relative wage* | Increased relative employment** | Combined effect | Share of aggregate change |
|---|---|---|---|---|---|---|---|---|---|---|---|---|
| Managers | 1.6 | 4.0 | 5.6 | 67.7% | 1.6 | 1.4 | 3.0 | 53.8% | 3.2 | 5.4 | 8.6 | 62.1% |
| Engineers | 0.1 | 0.6 | 0.7 | 8.4 | -0.1 | 0.0 | -0.1 | -1.9 | 0.0 | 0.6 | 0.6 | 4.2 |
| Math/computer | 0.1 | -0.1 | 0.0 | -0.1 | 0.2 | 0.4 | 0.5 | 9.4 | 0.2 | 0.3 | 0.5 | 3.7 |
| Nat. science | 0.1 | 0.0 | 0.1 | 1.4 | 0.0 | 0.0 | 0.0 | 0.6 | 0.1 | 0.0 | 0.1 | 1.1 |
| Health prof. | 1.9 | 0.5 | 2.4 | 29.2 | 0.6 | -0.3 | 0.3 | 4.6 | 2.4 | 0.2 | 2.7 | 19.3 |
| Soc. sci./law | 0.0 | 0.0 | 0.0 | 0.5 | 0.0 | 0.1 | 0.1 | 1.7 | 0.1 | 0.1 | 0.1 | 1.0 |
| Other prof. | 0.2 | -4.8 | -4.6 | -55.5 | 1.8 | 0.2 | 2.0 | 35.0 | 2.0 | -4.6 | -2.6 | -18.9 |
| Hlth., eng., sci. tech. | 0.1 | 0.1 | 0.3 | 3.1 | 0.0 | -0.2 | -0.2 | -3.6 | 0.1 | -0.1 | 0.1 | 0.4 |
| Other tech. | 0.1 | 1.0 | 1.2 | 14.1 | 0.1 | -0.3 | -0.2 | -4.0 | 0.2 | 0.7 | 0.9 | 6.8 |
| Other sales | 0.8 | 1.1 | 1.8 | 22.2 | 0.5 | 0.0 | 0.5 | 9.5 | 1.3 | 1.0 | 2.4 | 17.0 |
| Sales, fin. | 0.1 | 0.0 | 0.0 | 0.5 | 0.3 | 0.0 | 0.3 | 5.7 | 0.4 | 0.0 | 0.4 | 2.6 |
| Clerks | 0.8 | -0.3 | 0.5 | 5.7 | -0.1 | -0.3 | -0.4 | -7.8 | 0.7 | -0.7 | 0.0 | 0.2 |
| Service | 0.0 | 0.1 | 0.1 | 1.0 | -0.1 | 0.1 | 0.0 | -0.9 | -0.1 | 0.2 | 0.0 | 0.3 |
| Blue collar, farm | 0.2 | 0.0 | 0.2 | 1.8 | -0.1 | 0.0 | -0.1 | -2.1 | 0.1 | 0.0 | 0.0 | 0.2 |
| Growth of college/non-college wage premium*** | 5.9 | 2.3 | 8.2 | 100.0% | 4.7 | 0.9 | 5.6 | 100.0% | 10.6 | 3.2 | 13.8 | 100.0% |

* Measures whether college graduates (four-year only) in this occupation had a greater (than other college graduates) increase in wages relative to non-college-educated workers, controlling for other human capital characteristics.

** Measures whether college graduates in this occupation had a greater growth in employment relative to other college graduates.

*** Sample excludes those with more than four years of college.

Source: Authors' analysis.

As Table 2.45 shows, the wage premium of college-educated male workers (excluding those with degrees beyond college) relative to non-college-educated males (including those with some college, a high school degree, or less) rose 7.9 percentage points from 1979 to 1989. This wage premium grew because of a 6.3 percentage-point "relative wage" effect (the wages of college graduates within particular occupations growing relatively faster than those of non-college-educated workers) and a 1.6 percentage-point "relative employment" effect (the occupations in which college graduates expanded their employment relatively faster). The analysis in Table 2.45 identifies the "relative wage" effect and "relative employment" effect overall and for specific occupations, thus allowing a computation of the share of the aggregate change in the premium associated with trends in each occupation.

The results show that it was the fast growth in the wages and employment of managers and sales workers ("other sales" and "financial sales") that drove up the education wage differential among men; it accounted for all of the increase. In contrast, engineers, scientists, mathematicians, and computer science professionals (and associated technical workers) played a very small role in driving up education differentials.

As we have noted, the college wage premium grew only modestly over the 1989-97 period (and hardly at all in 1990-97). Table 2.45 suggests this small growth was due to white-collar occupations increasing their employment relative to other occupations only slightly; white-collar wage gains were smaller as well.

Over the entire 1979-97 period, managers were responsible for half (49.2%) of the entire 11.3 percentage-point rise in the college/non-college wage premium among men, with another fourth (25.1%) associated with sales workers.

Table 2.46, which presents the occupational decomposition of the growth of the education wage gap among women, generally shows the same pattern as among men: increased wages and employment of managers and sales workers accounting for more than 80% of the 13.8 percentage-point growth in the education wage premium, with very little role for scientists, engineers, computer professionals, or technical workers. Again, this pattern seems hard to reconcile with the conventional technology story.

What does this analysis tell us about a technology story of wage inequality? Basically, if technology is responsible for bidding up the education wage gap by increasing the demand for skilled or educated workers, then the particular skills associated with technological change in this period were those of managers and sales workers. Such a portrait of technology's role is at odds with the conventional one, which tends to focus on the role of computers and microelectronics. It may be that information-age technology transforms workplaces by generating fast wage and employment growth for managers and sales workers. Nevertheless, managers and sales workers are not the usual occupations associated with the mastery of the new skills associated with an information technology era.

Table 2.47 presents data on trends from 1984 to 1997 in the use of computers at work both overall and by gender, race, age, and education. These data facilitate a test of a common version of the technology story of wage inequity: the increased use of computers at work by some groups (e.g., the college-educated) has led them to be more skilled and productive relative to other groups (e.g., non-college educated) thereby enlarging the wage gap between these groups. By using Table 2.47, we can compare the change in wage gaps by education, gender, race, and age to see whether they correspond to changes in the intensity of computer use. The data reveal that trends in computer usage are generally poor predictors of wage trends.

The use of computers at work doubled from 1984 to 1997, rising from 24.5% to 49.9% of the workforce. Computer use grew more rapidly (looking annually) in the 1984-89 period than in the 1989-97 period. The faster pace of technological change in the 1980s does correspond to the faster growth of wage inequality in that period compared to the 1990s.

Table 2.47 also shows that computer use is greater among those with more education. However, the relative use of computers did not change much, with high-school-educated workers half as likely to use computers as college graduates in both 1984 and in 1997 (47.7 % and 48.1% respectively). Of course this does not accord with the trends in the college/high school wage premium, which rose a great deal in the 1980s and rose modestly in the 1990s. Among women, the relative rate of computer use between high school and college graduates fell from 69.4% in 1984 to 62.7% in 1997, moving opposite to the upward shift in the college wage premium among women.

Women use computers at work more than men, a fact that does not, of course, accord with the higher level of men's wages. This gender computer gap, however, closed modestly in the 1990s, as use of computers by men grew more rapidly. The opposite occurred with wages, however, with women's wages faring better than men's. (Table 2.26). Likewise, the black/white gap in computer usage narrowed in the 1990s, yet the racial wage gap was little changed (Table 2.24 and 2.25). So neither gender nor racial wage gaps correspond well to technology intensity trends.

The change in computer use by age in the 1980s does accord with changes in the wage gap by age (or by experience—see Table 2.16). For instance, in the 1984-89 period computer use rose more among those in their thirties or forties than for younger workers, a time when younger workers also fared worse in wage growth. Nevertheless, the far-better wage growth by younger rather than older workers in the 1990s is not associated with any catch-up in computer

**TABLE 2.47** Use of computers at work (1984-97)

|  | 1984 | 1989 | 1993 | 1997 |
|---|---|---|---|---|
| All workers | 24.5% | 36.8% | 46.0% | 49.9% |
| **By education** |  |  |  |  |
| Less than high school | 4.8% | 7.4% | 8.9% | 11.3% |
| High school | 19.8 | 29.2 | 34.0 | 36.1 |
| Some college | 31.9 | 46.4 | 53.5 | 56.3 |
| College or more | 41.5 | 57.9 | 69.1 | 75.2 |
| *High school/college* | 47.7% | 50.5% | 49.1% | 48.1% |
| Men | 30.2 | 34.2 | 34.2 | 35.5 |
| Women | 69.4 | 69.3 | 66.9 | 62.7 |
| **By gender** |  |  |  |  |
| Men | 21.1% | 31.6% | 40.3% | 44.1% |
| Women | 29.0 | 43.2 | 52.7 | 56.7 |
| *Male/female* | 73.0% | 73.2% | 76.5% | 77.8% |
| **By race** |  |  |  |  |
| Whites | 25.3% | 37.9% | 47.3% | 51.3% |
| Blacks | 18.2 | 27.2 | 36.2 | 39.9 |
| Other | 23.7 | 36.0 | 42.3 | 48.2 |
| *Black/white* | 72.1% | 71.7% | 76.7% | 77.7% |
| **By age** |  |  |  |  |
| Under 30 | 24.7% | 34.9% | 41.4% | 44.5% |
| 30-39 | 29.5 | 42.0 | 50.5 | 53.8 |
| 40-49 | 24.6 | 40.6 | 51.3 | 54.9 |
| 50 and older | 17.6 | 27.6 | 38.6 | 45.3 |

Note: Entries display percentage of employed individuals who answer that that they "directly use a computer at work."

Source: Card and DiNardo (2002).

use—in fact, they fell further behind. Thus, computer use trends do not help very much in understanding changes in the wage gaps by age.

It may be the case that there was a large increase in overall computer usage at work that corresponds to the growth of overall wage inequality in the 1980s. However, when one examines what happened for particular subgroups by gender, education, race, or age, there does not seem to be any strong link between the increase in computer use and the growth of the associated dimensions of wage inequality.

## Executive pay soars

Another cause of greater wage inequality has been the enormous pay increases received by chief executive officers (CEOs) and the spillover effects (the pay of other executives and managers rising in tandem with CEO pay) of these increases. These large pay raises go far beyond those received by other white-collar workers.

The 1980s and 1990s have been prosperous times for top U.S. executives. **Table 2.48** presents the trends in CEO pay over the 1989-2001 period. For instance, the median wage (cash payments including bonuses of CEOs) grew 79.0% from 1989 to 2000, far exceeding the growth in any other occupation. CEO wages grew 69% in just the recovery years from 1992 to 2000. In contrast, the median hourly wage for all workers grew just 5.9% from 1989 to 2000 (Table 2.6). Moreover, CEO wage increases were probably larger if measured as averages rather than at the median.

The growth in CEO pay can also be measured by including all of the components of direct compensation: salaries, bonuses, incentive awards, stock options exercised, stock granted, and so on. By this measure, the full compensation of CEOs increased more than threefold over the 1989-2000 period, growing 342% from 1989 to 2000 and 150% in the 1992-2000 recovery. Even lesser-paid CEOs at the 25th percentile saw 38% compensation growth in the recovery. Higher-paid executives at the 75th percentile saw their compensation grow by 101% in the recovery from 1992 to 2000.

The increased divergence between the growth of CEO pay and an average worker's pay is captured in the growth of the ratio of CEO to worker pay, shown in **Figure 2T**. In 1965, U.S. CEOs in major companies earned 26.0 times more than an average worker; this ratio grew to 36.5 in 1978 and to 71.7 in 1989. The ratio surged in the 1990s and hit 310.0 at the end of the recovery in 2000. In other words, in 2000, a CEO earned more in one workday (there are 260 in a year) than what an average worker earned in 52 weeks. In 1965, by contrast, it took a CEO two weeks to earn a worker's annual pay.

Not only are U.S. executives paid far better than U.S. workers, they also earn substantially more than CEOs in other advanced countries. **Table 2.49** presents CEO pay in 13 other countries in 1988 and 2001 and an index (in the last two columns) that sets U.S. compensation equal to 100 (any index value less than 100 implies that that country's CEOs earn less than U.S. CEOs). The index shows that U.S. CEOs earn more than three times the average of the 13 other advanced countries for which there are comparable data (note the non-U.S. average of 28%). In fact, there is no country listed whose CEOs are paid even as much as 50% that of U.S. CEOs. This international pattern does not

**TABLE 2.48** Executive annual pay, 1989-2001 (2001 dollars)

| Pay category and percentile | Compensation ($000) | | | | | Dollar change ($000) | Percent change | | |
|---|---|---|---|---|---|---|---|---|---|
| | 1989 | 1992 | 1995 | 2000 | 2001 | 1992-2001 | 1989-2000 | 1992-2000 | 1995-2000 |
| **Realized direct compensation\*** | | | | | | | | | |
| 25th percentile | n.a. | $1,189 | $1,400 | $1,643 | $1,486 | $297 | n.a. | 38% | 17% |
| Median | n.a. | 1,916 | 2,299 | 2,985 | 2,959 | 1,043 | n.a. | 56 | 30 |
| 75th percentile | n.a. | 3,655 | 4,123 | 7,352 | 5,820 | 2,165 | n.a. | 101 | 78 |
| Average | $2,436 | 4,315 | 3,441 | 10,775 | 8,626 | 4,311 | 342% | 150 | 213 |
| **Cash compensation\*\*** | | | | | | | | | |
| Index, 1989=100 | | | | | | | | | |
| Median | 100.0 | 105.9 | 129.6 | 179.0 | 174.0 | n.a. | 79.0% | 69.0% | 38.1% |

\* Sum of salary, bonus, gains from options exercised, value of restricted stock at grant, and other long-term incentive award payments.

\*\* Salary and cash bonuses.

Source: Authors' analysis of *Wall Street Journal*/Mercer survey (2002).

**FIGURE 2T** Ratio of CEO to average worker pay, 1965-2001

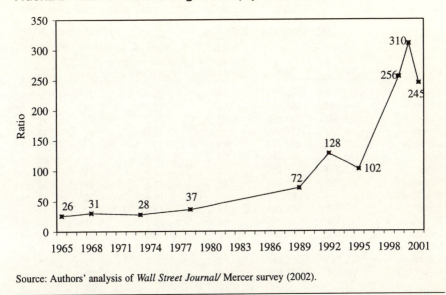

Source: Authors' analysis of *Wall Street Journal/* Mercer survey (2002).

hold true for the pay of manufacturing workers, for whom an index is also presented in Table 2.49. Workers in other advanced countries earn 65% of what U.S. workers earn. Not surprisingly, the ratio of CEO-to-worker pay was far larger in the United States in 1999 than in other countries, 153.7 versus 18.1. (Note that these cross-country comparisons employ different data (and definitions) than those used for historical U.S. trends in Table 2.49 and Figure 2T and therefore yield a different CEO/worker pay ratio.) Last, Table 2.49 shows that CEO pay in other countries has tended to grow rapidly over the 1988-2001 period, but in all but one country not as rapidly as the 165% growth in the U.S. (the non-U.S. average was a 59% growth in CEO pay).

## Conclusion

The wage structure has changed dramatically over the last two decades or so. From 1979 to 1995, the real hourly wages of most workers fell, with non-college-educated workers, especially new entrants to the labor force, experiencing the greatest wage decline. Given that nearly three-fourths of the workforce has not earned a four-year college degree, the wage erosion of high school graduates (whose wages fell somewhat less than those of high school dropouts but

**TABLE 2.49** CEO pay in advanced countries, 1988-2001 (2001 dollars)

| Country | CEO compensation ($000) | | Percent change 1988-2001 | Ratio of CEO to worker pay, 2001* | Foreign pay relative to U.S. pay, 2001 U.S. = 100 | |
|---|---|---|---|---|---|---|
| | 1988 | 2001 | | | CEO | Worker |
| Australia | $163,955 | $546,914 | 234% | 22.5 | 28% | 52% |
| Belgium | 348,044 | 696,697 | 100 | 18.7 | 36 | 79 |
| Canada | 383,999 | 787,060 | 105 | 23.2 | 41 | 72 |
| France | 366,741 | 519,060 | 42 | 16.0 | 27 | 69 |
| Germany | 373,932 | 454,974 | 22 | 13.2 | 24 | 74 |
| Italy | 310,651 | 600,319 | 93 | 21.4 | 31 | 60 |
| Japan | 455,909 | 508,106 | 11 | 11.6 | 26 | 93 |
| Netherlands | 359,550 | 604,854 | 68 | 22.2 | 31 | 58 |
| New Zealand | — | 287,345 | — | 19.8 | 15 | 31 |
| Spain | 319,280 | 429,725 | 35 | 18.8 | 22 | 49 |
| Sweden | 212,854 | 413,860 | 94 | 14.7 | 21 | 60 |
| Switzerland | 463,100 | 404,580 | -13 | 9.5 | 21 | 91 |
| United Kingdom | 411,325 | 668,526 | 63 | 25.4 | 35 | 56 |
| United States | 730,606 | 1,932,580 | 165 | 153.7 | 100 | 100 |
| Non-U.S. average | $347,445 | $552,890 | 59% | 18.1 | 28% | 65% |

* Ratio of CEO compensation to the compensation of manufacturing production workers.

Source: Authors' analysis of Towers, Perrin (1988 and 2001).

somewhat more than those of workers with some college) meant that the vast majority of men and many women were working at far lower wages in 1995 than their counterparts did a generation earlier. In the early 1990s, wages were falling or stagnant, even among college graduates and white-collar workers, especially men. New college graduates in the mid-1990s earned less than their counterparts did in the late 1980s.

Since 1995, however, there has been a very different, and far better, wage performance as real wages grew rapidly for nearly all segments of the workforce. Wage growth at the bottom, in particular, has been strong, and wage inequality at the bottom declined, as it has since the late 1980s. Faster productivity growth, persistent low unemployment, and increases in the minimum wage are responsible for this turnaround.

The current recession is challenging these positive trends. As the Introduction shows, wage growth lessened as unemployment grew. Moreover, wage inequality has been broadening across the board since 1999.

# Jobs: recession leads to employment losses

Rapid economic growth combined with unemployment averaging below 5% improved the economic prospects of American workers in the late 1990s. Employment opportunities expanded considerably, especially for traditionally disadvantaged groups, including women, African Americans, and Hispanics. Overall, low unemployment over the second half of the 1990s strengthened workers' bargaining power with respect to their employers. Jobs were relatively easy to find, and many employers had to compete for workers. This in turn spurred strong wage and income gains over the latter half of the 1990s economic boom, as discussed in Chapters 1 and 2.

The year 2001 marked the official beginning of a recession, a time of higher unemployment and lower labor force participation. But unemployment actually began to rise in October 2000 and, through June 2002, it had risen by 2.0 percentage points, to 5.9%. Both the percentage-point rise and the level of unemployment are smaller than occurred during the recession of the early 1990s, when unemployment increased by 2.6 percentage points to 7.8%. However, the employment losses (in percentage terms) have been greater.

The recession has been harder on women than previous recessions. The employment decline among women is higher than they have experienced in prior recessions, and the increase in women's unemployment is now much closer to men's, although women's unemployment is still lower. This trend has been driven by the change in the industrial composition of the job losses during this recession. Usually, the service sector (employing about one-third of all workers, two out of five women but only one out of four men) shows rising employment over recessions. During the latest recession, however, employment in services has increased only slightly. Further, the aftermath of the September 2001 terrorist attacks appears to have played a large role in the composition of industries that lost employment over this recession, as transportation and trade lost employment especially after September 11.

The recession has been more equitably distributed than past downturns in that unemployment losses have been felt more equally across educational groups. African American workers, however, have experienced nearly twice as large an increase in unemployment as have white workers, and Hispanic workers have experienced a third larger increase in unemployment compared to white workers.

The gains to workers and their families described in this and earlier chapters depended on the lower unemployment rates achieved in the late 1990s. Higher labor force participation, rising employment rates, increased job security and stability, and less involuntary participation in nonstandard working arrangements were all associated with the lower unemployment rates of the late 1990s. However, low unemployment was insufficient to reverse the long-term trend toward fewer fringe benefits. At the turn of the century, workers are less likely to have employer-provided health insurance than they were 30 years ago, and those who have it pay more. Further, there has been little progress on expanding job flexibility and paid time off—vacations, holidays, and family and medical leave. Heightened job insecurity left over from the recession of the early 1990s along with lowered rates of unionization may have limited workers' capacity to bargain for on-the-job benefits, even when labor was scarce.

## Unemployment

The economic expansion of the 1990s led to the longest period of sustained declines in unemployment in the post-World War II era (**Figure 3A** and **Table 3.1**). The smoothed unemployment line shows the average unemployment rate over the business cycle. At 4.8%, the average level of unemployment during the late 1990s came close to that achieved during the 1950s and 1960s. At the business cycle peak in 2000, the national unemployment rate was 4.0%, lower than at any cyclical peak in the last three decades and close to the 3.8% rate achieved in 1967. Even as unemployment began to rise in 2001 during the recession, it remains far below the peaks of earlier recessions. The separate unemployment rates for men, women, whites, African Americans, and Hispanics, shown in Table 3.1, were all lower in 2000 than they were during any peak year since the early 1970s. During three months of 2000 (March, April, and September), at the peak of the business cycle, the unemployment rate for African Americans fell to 7.3%, the lowest since the Bureau of Labor Statistics began tabulating unemployment separately by race in

**FIGURE 3A** Unemployment rate and its trend, 1947-2000

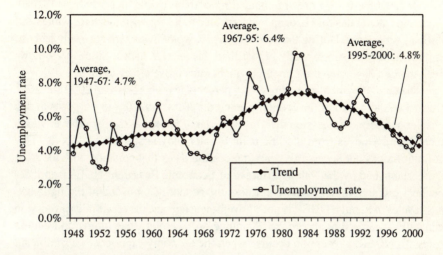

Source: Authors' analysis of BLS (2002a) data.

**TABLE 3.1** Unemployment rates, 1947-2001

| Business cycle peaks | Total | Male | Female | White | African American | Hispanic* |
|---|---|---|---|---|---|---|
| 1947 | 3.9% | 4.0% | 3.7% | n.a. | n.a. | n.a. |
| 1967 | 3.8 | 3.1 | 5.2 | 3.4% | n.a. | n.a. |
| 1973 | 4.9 | 4.2 | 6.0 | 4.3 | 9.4% | 7.7% |
| 1979 | 5.8 | 5.1 | 6.8 | 5.1 | 12.3 | 8.3 |
| 1989 | 5.3 | 5.2 | 5.4 | 4.5 | 11.4 | 8.0 |
| 2000 | 4.0 | 3.9 | 4.1 | 3.5 | 7.6 | 5.7 |
| 2001 | 4.8 | 4.8 | 4.7 | 4.2 | 8.7 | 6.6 |
| *Annual averages* | | | | | | |
| 1947-67 | 4.7% | 4.5% | 5.0% | n.a. | n.a. | n.a. |
| 1967-73 | 4.6 | 4.0 | 5.7 | 4.1% | n.a. | n.a. |
| 1973-79 | 6.5 | 5.8 | 7.5 | 5.8 | 12.5% | 9.5% |
| 1979-89 | 7.1 | 7.0 | 7.3 | 6.2 | 14.7 | 10.3 |
| 1989-2000 | 5.6 | 5.6 | 5.5 | 4.9 | 10.8 | 8.6 |

*Hispanic category includes blacks and whites.

Source: Authors' analysis of BLS (2002a) data. For detailed information on table sources, see Table Notes.

1972. Even so, over 2000, as has historically been the case, the unemployment rate for African Americans (7.6%) remained more than double that of whites (3.5%). Unemployment rates for Hispanic workers tend to lie between those for whites and African Americans. During the period 1947-79, women workers generally had unemployment rates substantially higher than the rate for males. Since 1979, however, women have seen their unemployment rates move closer to men's.

The unemployment rate climbed 0.8 percentage points between 2000 and 2001 (from 4.0% to 4.8%) as the economy entered a recession. For our purposes in this chapter, we define a recession in terms of the labor market as the period over which the economy moves from the low point of unemployment to its high point. This definition does not necessarily lead to recession dates that coincide with the standard established by the National Bureau of Economic Research (NBER), an independent research organization that tracks the economy's movement through business cycles. Although NBER is not a government agency, the economics profession generally regards it as the "official" source on recessions' beginning and ending dates. To NBER, a recession occurs "when the economy experiences a significant decline in activity across the entire economy, visible in industrial production, employment, real income, and wholesale-retail trade, and lasting more than a few months." Because they look at a number of economic indicators, this recession-dating system does not necessarily coincide with a labor market recession and recovery, which is our focus here. Unemployment is often referred to as a "lagging indicator," since it generally falls after output falls. Firms tend to run down inventories and slow output before laying off workers, and that falling output can occur prior to rising unemployment. Unemployment may continue to increase when the economy is expanding if job growth is insufficient to employ new labor market entrants and offset productivity gains, and it and may still be rising after the recession is declared over by the NBER. In the 1990-92 recession, unemployment continued to rise for 18 months after the recession had "officially" ended. Calculating in the period of rising unemployment makes the 1990s recovery a bit shorter than the official measure. Whereas by NBER's definition the 1990s expansion was exactly 10 years long, beginning in March 1991 and ending in March 2001, the unemployment rate fell consistently for only eight years and four months, from June 1992 to October 2000.

Tracking recessions from the low point of the unemployment rate to its peak allows us to see how much unemployment changes over the recession. **Table 3.2** shows the total increase in unemployment from its low point to its high point over the past five recessions. The percentage-point increase in unemployment has been smaller and the level of unemployment achieved is lower during the 2000-02 labor market recession (through June 2002, which may not be the end of unemployment's rise) relative to the previous one. During the recession of 1990-92, the unemploy-

**TABLE 3.2** Change in monthly unemployment rates over recessions

| | Percentage-point increase in unemployment from low point to high point | | | | |
|---|---|---|---|---|---|
| | May 1969-<br>Aug 1971 | Oct 1973-<br>May 1975 | May 1979-<br>Dec 1982 | June 1990-<br>June 1992 | Oct 2000-<br>June 2002 |
| **Total** | 2.7 | 4.4 | 5.2 | 2.6 | 2.0 |
| Male | 2.9 | 4.5 | 6.4 | 3.0 | 2.2 |
| Female | 2.4 | 4.1 | 3.7 | 2.1 | 1.8 |
| **White** | 2.6 | 4.3 | 4.9 | 2.4 | 1.8 |
| Male | 2.7 | 4.2 | 5.8 | 2.8 | 2.0 |
| Female | 2.2 | 4.2 | 3.5 | 1.7 | 1.4 |
| **African American** | n.a. | 6.3 | 8.5 | 4.1 | 3.3 |
| Male | n.a. | 6.8 | 11.7 | 4.8 | 3.3 |
| Female | n.a. | 5.5 | 5.0 | 3.5 | 3.3 |
| **Hispanic** | n.a. | 6.3 | 7.8 | 4.4 | 2.4 |
| Male | n.a. | n.a. | 8.9 | 5.9 | 2.0 |
| Female | n.a. | n.a. | 5.3 | 2.5 | 3.0 |

Source: Authors' analysis of BLS (2002a).

ment rate increased by 2.6 percentage points, from 5.2% to 7.8%; during the recession of 2000-02, it increased by 2.0 percentage points through June 2002, from 3.9% to 5.9%. Although unemployment rose by 1 percentage point (from 3.9% to 4.9%) between October 2000 and August 2001, it began to climb rapidly after the events of September 11. Since the unemployment rate was at such a low level at the end of the 1990s expansion, it is likely to remain below the 7.8% experienced in 1992 and far below rates of unemployment seen in the early 1980s, even if it rises as much as it did during the 1990-92 recession.

In good times and in bad, workers' experiences with unemployment differ markedly by race/ethnicity and sex. The 2000-02 recession has hit African American workers harder than other demographic groups: African American unemployment increased by 3.3 percentage points between October 2000 and June 2002 while increasing by only 1.8 percentage points among white workers. Among whites, men have seen a larger increase in unemployment than have women, although there is no difference by gender among African Americans. Among Hispanics, the unemployment rate has increased most for women, unlike in previous recession when Hispanic men's unemployment increased nearly twice as much as Hispanic women's.

**FIGURE 3B** Percentage-point change in unemployment during recession, by educational status

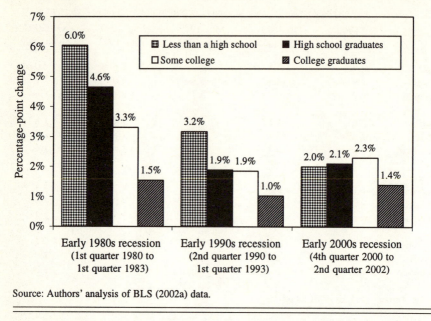

Source: Authors' analysis of BLS (2002a) data.

Historically, women's unemployment has grown less than men's during recessions. However, as women's labor force participation (the share of women who are working or seeking work) increased over the past 30 years (see Figure 3E below), their unemployment patterns have begun to look more like those of male workers. Unlike the recessions of 1979-82 and 1990-92, when men's unemployment grew by 2.7 and 0.9 percentage points more than women's, respectively, during the 2000-02 recession women and men have experienced similar percentage-point increases in unemployment (1.8 and 2.2, respectively). Men have seen a smaller increase in their unemployment rate during the 2000-02 recession relative to prior ones, whereas women have seen an increase similar to the 1990-92 recession. The relatively large increase in African American and Hispanic women's labor force participation in the late 1990s (see Figure 3F below) may explain the relatively large jump in their unemployment rates compared to those of white women during the 2000-02 recession. As more African American and Hispanic women joined the labor market, due in part to the implementation of welfare reform that pushed low-income, disproportionately minority women into the labor market, they became more vulnerable to unemployment when the economy began to slide into recession.

One remarkable thing about the current recession is that it has been more evenly

**TABLE 3.3** Underemployment in 2000 and 2002 (second quarter)

| | Second quarter of year | | |
| --- | --- | --- | --- |
| | 2000 | 2002 | Percent change |
| **Civilian labor force (thousands)** | 140,977 | 142,603 | 1.2% |
| Unemployed | 5,521 | 8,237 | 49.2 |
| Discouraged* | 282 | 285 | 1.2 |
| Other marginally attached* | 846 | 998 | 18.0 |
| Involuntary part time | 3,101 | 3,993 | 28.7 |
| Total underemployed | 9,750 | 13,513 | 38.6% |
| | | | Percentage-point change |
| Underemployment rate** | 6.9% | 9.5% | 2.6 |
| Unemployment rate | 3.9 | 5.8 | 1.9 |

\* Discouraged workers are the subset of the marginally attached who have given a job market-related reason for not currently looking for a job. Marginally attached workers are persons who currently are neither working nor looking for work, but who indicate that they want and are available for a job and have looked for work in the last 12 months.
\*\* Total underemployed workers divided by the sum of the labor force plus discouraged and other marginally attached workers.

Source: Authors' analysis of BLS (2002a).

spread across workers of different educational levels than prior recessions. **Figure 3B** shows the percentage-point change in unemployment across educational groups over the 2000-02, 1990-92, and 1980-83 recessions. In the 2000-02 recession, the percentage-point change in unemployment is nearly the same across workers with less than a high school degree, a high school degree, or some college. Only college-educated workers experience a substantially smaller increase in unemployment. This is markedly different from the prior two recessions, when workers with less education experienced larger increases in unemployment than did higher-educated workers.

Unemployment data include only workers who report that they are willing and able to work, overlooking workers who are not fully employed or who would like to be employed but are not actively seeking a job. A broader measure of "underemployment" in the economy is presented in **Table 3.3**. This alternative measure includes unemployed workers as well as: (1) those working part time but who want to work full time ("involuntary" part-timers); (2) those who want to work but have been discouraged from searching by their lack of success ("discouraged" workers);

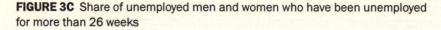

**FIGURE 3C** Share of unemployed men and women who have been unemployed for more than 26 weeks

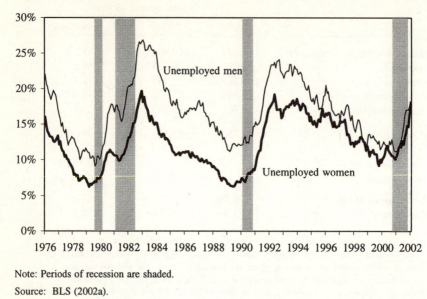

Note: Periods of recession are shaded.

Source: BLS (2002a).

and (3) others who are neither working nor seeking work at the moment but who indicate that they want and are available to work and have looked for a job in the last 12 months. (The second and third categories together are described as "marginally attached" workers.) Table 3.3 shows that the underemployment rate increased more than the unemployment rate during the 2000-02 recession. In the second quarter of 2000, the peak of the business cycle, the underemployment rate was 6.9%, 3.0 percentage points higher than the unemployment rate of 3.9%. By the second quarter of 2002, fully into the recession, the underemployment rate had increased by 2.6 percentage points to 9.5% (affecting 13.5 million workers), while unemployment had increased by 1.9 percentage points to 5.8%. Much of this was driven by increases in involuntary part-time work, as firms typically cut back workers' hours when demand falls during a recession.

Workers who have lost their jobs during the 2000-02 recession are spending more time unemployed than in prior recessions, even though this recession seems to be less severe than previous ones in terms of unemployment increases. **Figure 3C** shows that the proportion of the unemployed who remain without work for more than 26 weeks is higher in the 2000-02 recession than in earlier recessions, following a long-term trend toward increasing unemployment duration. There has

**FIGURE 3D** Effects of higher unemployment on size of civilian labor force

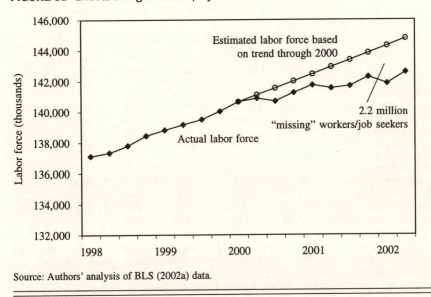

Source: Authors' analysis of BLS (2002a) data.

also been a convergence between men and women in the proportion of long-term unemployment. Changes in labor force participation within families may explain some of this trend; women are now firmly ensconced in the labor market and may be staying in the labor force (i.e., continuing to look for work) during spells of unemployment. As family income stalled over the first half of the 1990s (as documented in Chapter 1), wives' wages became more of a critical component of family income. Whereas in prior recessions, laid-off women workers may have chosen to stay out of the labor force for a while, they may in this recession be choosing to begin their job search immediately.

Even though the 2000-02 recession has not caused job losses as large as previous recessions, the labor market has seen slower growth in labor force participation. **Figure 3D** shows the extent to which the recession potentially has affected the labor market overall. If the economy had not moved into a labor market recession in 2000, 2.2 million more workers potentially still would be in the labor market. The labor force grew by 8.7% between the third quarter of 1993 and the third quarter of 2000, but it has grown by only 1.9% since the third quarter of 2000.

*Unemployment and the earnings distribution*
Data on unemployment generally show that disadvantaged groups experience the most gains from a recovery and the greatest losses during a recession. The pro-

**TABLE 3.4** Effect of a 1% higher unemployment rate on mean annual earnings, mean annual income, and share of total family income, by family income quintile, 1973 to 2000 (in 2000 dollars).

| | Lowest fifth | Second fifth | Middle fifth | Fourth fifth | Highest fifth | All families |
|---|---|---|---|---|---|---|
| **Family earnings** | | | | | | |
| Average family earnings | $2,659 | $13,235 | $27,992 | $46,874 | $90,573 | $36,266 |
| Earnings decline | -$108 | -$437 | -$501 | -$698 | -$815 | -$512 |
| (Standard error) | (47) | (53) | (68) | (78) | (173) | (59) |
| Implied percentage effect | -4.1% | -3.3% | -1.8% | -1.5% | -0.9% | -1.4% |
| **Family income** | | | | | | |
| Average family income | $7,590 | $20,563 | $34,722 | $52,855 | $100,587 | $43,263 |
| Family income decline | -$140 | -$370 | -$478 | -$636 | -$959 | -$517 |
| (Standard error) | (24) | (49) | (59) | (74) | (180) | (62) |
| Implied percentage effect | -1.8% | -1.8% | -1.4% | -1.2% | -1.0% | -1.2% |

Note: Standard errors are in parentheses. Observations are on region-year cells, with the United States divided into 21 groupings of states. Quintiles are defined by family income, with an "unrelated individual" included as a "family." All regressions and calculations are weighted by 2000 population for region. All regressions include year and regional dummies.

Source: Bartik (2002).

longed economic recovery, which brought steep declines in unemployment, disproportionately benefited the bottom 60% of families; the recession, in turn, disproportionately affects those same families. **Table 3.4** shows how changes in the unemployment rate affect earnings and income across the income distribution by estimating the effect of a 1% increase in unemployment on the annual earnings and income in each income quintile (estimated over the 1973-2000 period). The last column shows the effect of a 1% increase in the unemployment rate on the "average" family: among all persons, annual earnings decrease $512 (in 2000 dollars), about 1.4% of the corresponding family's total earnings, and annual family income decreases by $517, about 1.2% of family income. (Family income includes government cash assistance, such as unemployment compensation and welfare payments.) Higher unemployment hurts low-income families the most: families in the lowest fifth experience a 4.1% decrease in earnings with a 1% fall in unemployment, whereas families in the highest fifth experience only a 0.9% decrease. The effects on family income are more evenly distributed: families in the bottom fifth experience a 1.8% decrease in average family income, while those in the top fifth experience a 1.0% decrease. **Figure 3E** shows estimates of the gains in income attributable to lower unemployment in the late 1990s. The figure charts the income gains by quintile

**FIGURE 3E** Family income gained by quintile due to lower unemployment (falling to 4.0% rather than remaining at 5.6%) between 1995 and 2000

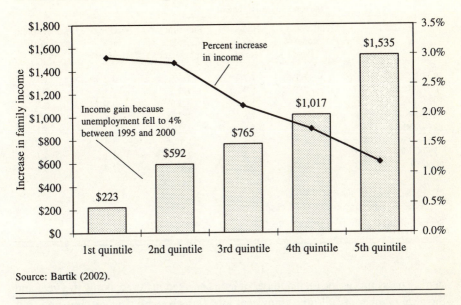

Source: Bartik (2002).

due to unemployment's fall from 5.6% to 4.0% between 1995 and 2000. Lower-income families gained the most percentage-wise, although they gained the least in terms of actual dollars since their incomes start off at a lower level.

## Employment

Unemployment is only one way of looking at the U.S. jobs picture. The level of employment in the economy—the proportion of people who are working—also indicates whether there are enough jobs in the economy for all who want (and need) to work. Over the long term, employment rates have been steadily rising, although the recession of 2000-02 has led to slower employment growth more recently.

**Table 3.5** looks at employment growth over the last three business cycles (1973-79, 1979-89, and 1989-2000) relative to the earlier postwar period and the current business cycle so far (2000-01). The table presents four measures of employment growth. The first two examine job creation—non-farm payroll employment (from a national survey of business establishments) and civilian employment (from a national survey of households). The second two indicators track the total "volume" of

**TABLE 3.5** Employment growth, 1947-2001 (annual percentage rates of growth)

| | Measures of employment | | | | | |
|---|---|---|---|---|---|---|
| | Non-farm payroll | Civilian employ- ment | Hours of work* | Full-time equivalent employment* | Working- age population | Labor-force participation rate** |
| 1947-67 | 2.0% | 1.3% | 1.7% | 1.8% | 1.2% | 0.1% |
| 1967-73 | 2.6 | 2.3 | 1.7 | 1.9 | 2.1 | 0.2 |
| 1973-79 | 2.6 | 2.5 | 1.9 | 2.3 | 1.9 | 0.5 |
| 1979-89 | 1.8 | 1.7 | 1.6 | 1.7 | 1.2 | 0.3 |
| 1989-2000 | 1.8 | 1.3 | 1.6 | 1.7 | 1.1 | 0.1 |
| 1989-95 | 1.4 | 1.0 | 1.1 | 1.1 | 1.1 | 0.0 |
| 1995-2000 | 2.4 | 1.6 | 2.3 | 2.4 | 1.1 | 0.2 |
| 2000-01 | 0.3 | -0.1 | n.a. | n.a. | 1.0 | -0.4 |

\*   1948-67 used in place of 1947-67.
\*\* Average annual percentage-point change.

Source: Authors' analysis of BLS (2002a, 2002b) and NIPA (2002) data.

work—measured as the total number of hours worked in the economy in a year and the total number of full-time equivalent jobs (which combines part-time and full-time work according to common practices in each industry).

The last two business cycles differ in important ways from the earlier postwar period. Net job creation rates over the entire period 1989-2000, whether measured using non-farm payrolls or counts of civilian employment based on household surveys, were slower than in earlier periods. Non-farm payrolls grew at a 1.8% annual rate between 1989 and 2000, equal to the annual rate for 1979-89 but well below the rates for 1967-73 and 1973-79 (both 2.6% per year). Civilian employment grew 1.3% per year in the 1990s, about three-fourths the rate for 1979-89 and just over half the rates achieved in 1967-73 (2.3%) and 1973-79 (2.5%). Relatively slow job creation during the 1990s is attributable to the slow start of the economic recovery in the early 1990s. Between 1989 and 1995, non-farm payrolls grew at an annual rate of only 1.4%, but the rate increased to 2.4% per year between 1995 and 2000 as the economy heated up.

Despite these lower job creation rates in the 1980s and 1990s, the growth in the volume (total hours) of work has been almost as rapid in the last business cycle as it was during the 1960s, 1970s, and 1980s. The average growth in annual hours worked was 1.6% per year in the period 1989-2000, equal to the preceding business cycle and not far below the rates in the earlier cycles. Full-time-equivalent employment grew at about the same rate as hours (1.7%) between 1989 and 2000, which was about the same as 1979-89 but slower than the 2.3% rate in 1973-79 and the 1.9% rate in 1967-

73. As with employment growth, hours increased substantially during the second half of the 1990s, more than doubling from 1.1% annually between 1989 and 1995 to 2.3% annually between 1995 and 2000. This is consistent with Chapter 1's finding that families' total hours worked have been rising in the 1980s and 1990s, and Chapter 2's finding that annual hours per worker have been growing. Given the deceleration in net job creation rates, the relatively constant growth rate in total hours worked between 1967 and 2000 implies that, on average, Americans are working more hours per year. In the earlier postwar period, American workers and their families took some of the benefits of higher productivity growth in the form of more hours of leisure. Between 1967 and 1979, payrolls increased more than total hours, suggesting that new workers began with fewer hours than those already employed and/or those employed were working fewer hours. Slower growth and rising inequality since the mid-1970s, however, seem to have pushed more workers to work longer hours, as total hours have continued to rise while fewer workers have joined the payrolls.

The data on job growth rates in the 1990s raise an important question: how were unemployment rates in the late 1990s below those of the 1970s and 1980s if job creation rates were below those achieved in the earlier two decades? The last two columns of Table 3.5 provide the answer. Slower job creation rates can still produce lower unemployment rates because the portion of the population seeking employment is growing much more slowly than before. There are two reasons for this decline in the share of the population seeking work. The first is that, in the 1990s, the working-age population (see the next-to-last column) was growing at only about half the rate of the late 1960s and 1970s. The two principal determinants of the size of the working-age population are native population growth and immigration. The current generation entering the labor force is smaller in numbers than the baby boomers that preceded them. While immigration rates grew in the 1980s and again in the 1990s, they were not sufficient to offset a deceleration in the growth of the native working-age population.

The second factor affecting the supply of available workers is a slowdown in the rate at which women join the paid labor force and the decline in male labor force participation. The last column of Table 3.5 and **Figures 3F, 3G,** and **3H** show the change in the labor force participation rate (the share of the population that is in work or seeking work). Since the labor force participation rate for men was falling continuously over this period (in part, because of increased time in school and early retirement), the rise in the overall labor force participation rate in the 1960s, 1970s, and 1980s reflects the large increase in women's work outside the home (see also Chapter 1). In the 1990s, the U.S. economy was able to achieve low unemployment rates despite the deceleration in job creation rates partially because women's labor force participation rates stabilized and the economy did not have to absorb as many new workers as in the 1960s, 1970s, and 1980s.

**FIGURE 3F** Labor force participation rates by gender, 1947-2001

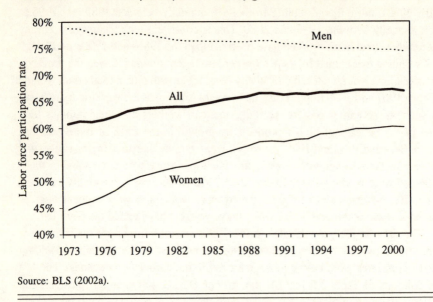

Source: BLS (2002a).

**FIGURE 3G** Labor force participation rates for women by race/ethnicity, 1973-2001

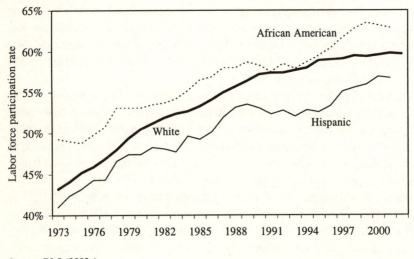

Source: BLS (2002a).

**FIGURE 3H** Labor force participation rates for men by race/ethnicity, 1973-2001

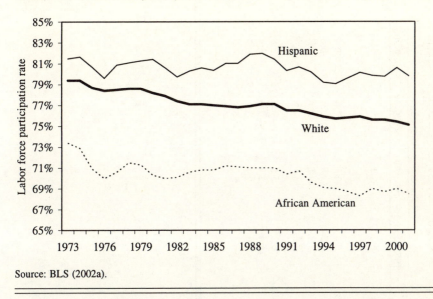

Source: BLS (2002a).

Another important gauge of employment opportunities is the share of the working-age population that has a job at any particular time. Employment rates can differ over time and across age, sex, and race for many reasons. Rising employment rates generally indicate rising opportunities, as, for example, was the case for women in the postwar period. When employment rates rise, it often means that more people are able to find work. Declining employment rates, though, may simply indicate individuals' choices, such as a decisions to stay in school or to take early retirement, both developments that presumably reflect improvements in the economic circumstances of workers and their families. (Although increased school applications and involuntary early retirement can also indicate a slack labor market.) Alternatively, rising employment rates might respond to falling wages: families facing declining real wages for current workers might send additional family members to the labor market to make up for lost earnings. For these reasons, higher employment rates do not necessarily indicate greater economic well being.

One should keep these caveats in mind when looking at **Table 3.6**, which shows the share of the working-age population employed in selected years from 1973 to 2001. These employment rates vary considerably across different groups. In 2001, for example, men had much higher employment rates (73.2%) than did women (58.4%). Among men, Hispanics had the highest employment rate (78.9%), followed by whites (74.0%), with African Americans trailing considerably (66.4%).

**TABLE 3.6** Employment rates, 1973-2001 (percent)

| | 1973 | 1979 | 1989 | 2000 | 2001 | Percentage-point change | | | |
| | | | | | | 1973-2001 | 1973-79 | 1979-89 | 1989-2000 |
|---|---|---|---|---|---|---|---|---|---|
| All (16 and over) | 57.8% | 59.9% | 63.0% | 64.5% | 63.8% | 6.0 | 2.1 | 3.1 | 1.5 |
| **Adults (age 20 and over)** | | | | | | | | | |
| *Men* | | | | | | | | | |
| White | 78.6% | 76.5% | 74.5% | 74.1% | 73.2% | -5.4 | -2.1 | -2.0 | -0.4 |
| | 79.2 | 77.3 | 75.4 | 74.8 | 74.0 | -5.2 | -1.9 | -1.9 | -0.6 |
| African American | 73.7 | 69.1 | 67.0 | 67.6 | 66.4 | -7.3 | -4.6 | -2.1 | 0.6 |
| Hispanic | 81.3 | 80.3 | 79.4 | 80.7 | 78.9 | -2.4 | -1.0 | -1.0 | 1.4 |
| *Women* | 42.2% | 47.7% | 54.9% | 58.7% | 58.4% | 16.2 | 5.5 | 7.2 | 3.8 |
| White | 41.6 | 47.3 | 54.9 | 58.3 | 58.0 | 16.4 | 5.7 | 7.6 | 3.4 |
| African American | 47.2 | 49.3 | 54.6 | 61.5 | 60.8 | 13.6 | 2.1 | 5.3 | 6.9 |
| Hispanic | 38.3 | 43.7 | 50.5 | 55.2 | 54.6 | 16.3 | 5.3 | 6.9 | 4.7 |

Source: Authors' analysis of BLS (2002a) data.

**TABLE 3.7** Change in monthly employment rate over recessions

| | Percentage-point change in employment rate from unemployment's low point to high point | | | | |
|---|---|---|---|---|---|
| | May 1969-<br>Aug 1971 | Oct 1973-<br>May 1975 | May 1979-<br>Dec 1982 | June 1990-<br>June 1992 | Oct 2000-<br>June 2002 |
| **Total** | -1.2 | -2.1 | -2.6 | -1.4 | -1.7 |
| Male | -2.6 | -4.0 | -5.8 | -2.3 | -2.1 |
| Female | -0.1 | -0.5 | 0.3 | -0.7 | -1.4 |
| **White** | -1.0 | -1.9 | -2.3 | -1.5 | -1.5 |
| Male | -2.3 | -3.6 | -5.5 | -2.4 | -2.1 |
| Female | -0.1 | -0.5 | 0.5 | -0.7 | -1.0 |
| **African American** | n.a. | -5.1 | -4.6 | -1.9 | -2.8 |
| Male | n.a. | -7.6 | -8.8 | -3.0 | -2.4 |
| Female | n.a. | -2.9 | -1.3 | -1.1 | -3.2 |
| **Hispanic** | n.a. | -2.0 | -3.9 | -3.4 | -2.2 |
| Male | n.a. | n.a. | -8.3 | -4.5 | -2.5 |
| Female | n.a. | n.a. | -0.9 | -2.8 | -2.0 |

Source: Author's analysis of BLS (2002a).

Among women, however, African Americans had the highest employment rate (60.8%), followed by whites (58.0%), and then Hispanics (54.6%). Trends in employment rates also differ across demographic groups. Employment rates for men fell between 1973 and 2001 across all racial and ethnic groups, with the largest declines in the years 1973-79 and 1979-89. In the 1990s, however, the long-term decline in male employment rates decelerated noticeably—and rates even rose over the period for African American and Hispanic men—illustrating yet another implication of the long 1990s boom. As unemployment fell, the ability of minority workers to find employment increased, reflected in their higher employment rates. For women, employment rates climbed steadily over the entire 1973-2001 period, increasing by 16.2 percentage points overall, with whites, African Americans, and Hispanics all experiencing roughly equal increases. Between 2000 and 2001, employment declined across all groups as the economy moved into recession.

Although long-term trends for women have been toward increasing employment while men have seen decreasing employment, during economic contractions all groups tend to experience employment declines. **Table 3.7** looks at changes in employment rates over the past five recessions. (As with Table 3.2, the dating sys-

**TABLE 3.8** Percent change in monthly employment by industry over recessions

| Industry | Percent change in employment from unemployment's low point to high point | | | | |
|---|---|---|---|---|---|
| | May 1969-<br>Aug 1971 | Oct 1973-<br>May 1975 | May 1979-<br>Dec 1982 | June 1990-<br>June 1992 | Oct 2000-<br>June 2002 |
| **Total** | 1.5% | -1.3% | -1.1% | -1.2% | -1.0% |
| **Total private** | 0.5% | -2.9% | -1.3% | -1.5% | -1.7% |
| *Goods producing* | -6.2% | -11.0% | -13.7% | -7.1% | -7.0% |
| Mining | 1.0 | 14.9 | 6.0 | -11.1 | 0.5 |
| Construction | 4.0 | -16.1 | -14.0 | -13.1 | -1.9 |
| Manufacturing | -8.2 | -10.7 | -14.5 | -5.4 | -9.1 |
| *Service producing* | 5.6% | 3.3% | 4.2% | 0.5% | 0.5% |
| Trans., comm.,<br>  and public utilities | 1.2% | -3.6% | -1.8% | -1.3% | -4.1% |
| Wholesale trade | 2.8 | 1.5 | 0.3 | -2.9 | -3.4 |
| Retail trade | 6.0 | 0.9 | 1.7 | -1.4 | -0.3 |
| Fin., ins., and<br>  real estate | 8.5% | 1.8% | 8.2% | -1.7% | 1.7% |
| Services | 6.0 | 6.1 | 12.4 | 3.7 | 0.9 |
| Government | 6.3% | 6.0% | -0.4% | 0.4% | 3.0% |

Source: Authors' analysis of BLS (2002b).

tem uses the period when unemployment was falling, rather than NBER-defined periods.) Men tend to lose more employment than do women in recessions, although the gap has been closing as women's labor force participation has increased. In the recession of 1979-82, the male employment rate fell by 5.8 percentage points while the women's employment rate increased by 0.3 percentage points. However, during the 2000-02 recession (through June 2002), the male employment rate fell by 2.1 percentage points (smaller than the 2.3 percentage point fall during the 1990-92 recession) while the female employment rate fell by 1.4 percentage points (double its 0.7 percentage point fall during the 1990-92 recession). African American workers tend to experience larger employment declines during recessions relative to white and Hispanic workers. During the 2000-02 recession, the African American employment rate fell by 2.8 percentage points, compared to only 1.5 percentage points for white workers and 2.2 percentage points for Hispanic workers. At 3.2 percentage points, African American women experienced the largest declines in their employment rate during the 2000-02 recession—one-and-a-half times that of African American men (2.4 percentage points) and over three times that of white women (1.0 percentage points).

**FIGURE 3I** Employment losses by industry in three most recent recessions

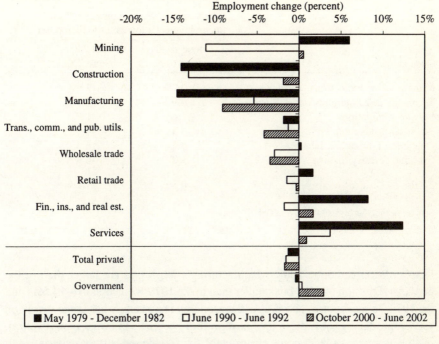

Source: Authors' analysis of BLS (2002b).

The economy's shift away from manufacturing toward service-producing industries over the past few business cycles has dampened the cyclicality of the economy overall. Total payroll employment has fallen less in the 2000-02 recession than in previous recessions (**Table 3.8** and **Figure 3I**). (The data reported in Table 3.8 differ from those reported in Table 3.7 and 3.9 because they come from different government surveys. The data in Table 3.8 come from the Bureau of Labor Statistics' Current Employment Statistics, which surveys establishments, while the data in Table 3.7 come from the Census Bureau's Current Population Survey, which surveys households.) In the 2000-02 recession, total payroll employment fell by 1.0%, compared to 1.2% in the 1990-92 recession. Smaller overall employment losses were driven by larger increases in government employment (3.0% in the 2000-02 recession compared to 0.4% in the 1990-92 recession) and slightly larger increases in private sector employment in the 2000-02 recession, relative to 1990-92 (–1.7% versus –1.5%). As has been common during recent recessions, manufacturing lost the most jobs, losing 9.1% of payroll employment between

235

**TABLE 3.9** Percent change in monthly employment by occupation over business cycle

| Occupation | Percent change in employment from unemployment's low point to high point | |
| --- | --- | --- |
| | June 1990-<br>June 1992 | Oct 2000-<br>June 2002 |
| Managerial & professional specialty | 0.7% | 2.2% |
| Technical, sales, administrative support | 0.9 | -2.1 |
| Service occupations | 1.6 | 1.7 |
| Precision production, craft, repair | -4.3 | -4.1 |
| Operators, fabricators, laborers | -4.5 | -6.3 |
| Farming, forestry, fishing | -1.2 | -0.8 |
| Total | -0.5% | -1.1% |

Source: Authors' analysis of BLS (2002a).

October 2000 and June 2002. Manufacturing's job losses are larger than in the previous recession (–.4%), but smaller than in the 1979-82 recession (–14.5%) and the 1973-75 recession (–10.7%). As the economy increasingly has come to rely on service-producing jobs, these jobs have in turn become somewhat more cyclical, relative to previous recessions. Historically, the service industry has continued to grow during recessions, rising by 4.2% during the 1979-82 recession and by 3.3% during the 1973-75 recession, but it has grown by only 0.5% during the 2000-02 recession, consistent with the 0.5% growth experienced during the 1990-92 recession. This weak growth is critical, as services make up nearly one-third of total employment, compared to about one-eighth for manufacturing. The shift to service-producing industries also has implications on recessionary job losses in specific occupations. The 2000-02 recession is different from the 1990-92 recession in that technical, sales, and administrative support saw a 3.6% employment loss compared to small but positive growth during the 1990-92 recession (**Table 3.9**).

The recession had already begun prior to the terrorist attacks of September 11, 2001, but these events wreaked havoc on certain segments of the economy—air travel, hotels, and retail, in particular—and played a role in the composition of job losses over the remainder of the recession. **Figure 3J** shows how employment declined across industries pre- and post-September 2001. In the first 11 months of the labor market recession (October 2000 through September 2001), services continued to grow, adding 0.9% to payrolls, and transportation fell only slightly. However, since September 2001, services have not grown, and transportation and wholesale and retail trade have seen sharp drops in employment, much more than in the

**FIGURE 3J** Employment change over 2000-02 recession (through June 2002)

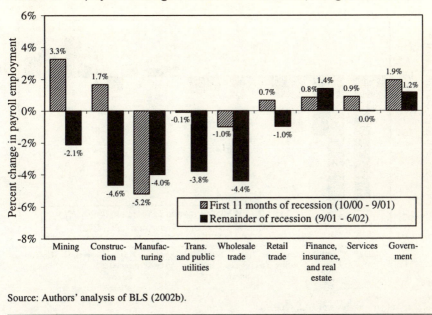

Source: Authors' analysis of BLS (2002b).

first 11 months of the recession. Compare this to **Figure 3K**, which also breaks the 1990-92 recession into the first 11 months and the remainder of the recession. Unlike the second part of the 2000-02 recession, during the second part of the 1990-92 recession services grew by 2.8% and transportation and wholesale trade fell about the same as in the first 11 months. Retail trade actually grew in the latter part of the 1990-92 recession, rather than fall as it did during the latter part of the 2000-02 recession. The hit to services, transportation, and retail trade as a result of the terrorist attacks of September 11 led to a deepening of the recession in sectors of the economy that usually provide more employment growth during recessions (or at least smaller employment losses, in the case of transportation). These trends have made the recession harder on women, as they are more likely than men to be employed in retail trade and services.

Strong economic growth in the late 1990s created a tight labor market in which many, if not most, who wanted a job had one. The evidence on the number of jobs created, however, tells us little about the characteristics of jobs. In Chapter 2, we saw that the hourly wages for most men and many women declined over most of the last two decades, but improved during the latter 1990s. Fringe benefits increased slightly in the latter 1990s, but workers are paying more out-of-pocket for the em-

**FIGURE 3K** Employment change over 1990-92 recession

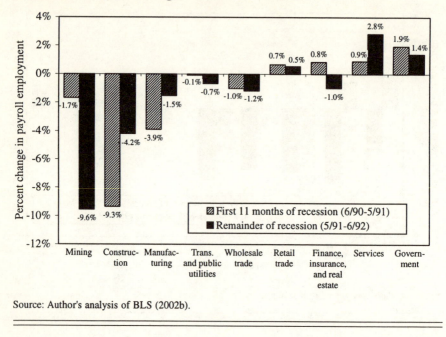

Source: Author's analysis of BLS (2002b).

ployer-provided health insurance that they do receive. Over the 1990s boom, other job quality measures, such as job stability and the ability of workers to work the number of hours they wanted, showed improvement.

## Work hours

Decelerating employment growth over past business cycles combined with constant growth in hours implies that Americans are working more hours per year. Among families, increased hours of work are due to both the entry of more family members into the labor force and longer hours of work among family members already in the labor market. Figure 3F showed that labor force participation among women has been rising steadily since the 1970s, increasing families' labor supply. Chapter 1 showed how American families are working more hours, and Table 3.5 showed that hours of work increased at an annual rate of 1.6% for the past two business cycles.

Another way of measuring increased hours of work is to look at the extent to which workers are working overtime. Over the past three business cycles in

**FIGURE 3L** Peak overtime hours and change in employment level in manufacturing across recent economic expansions

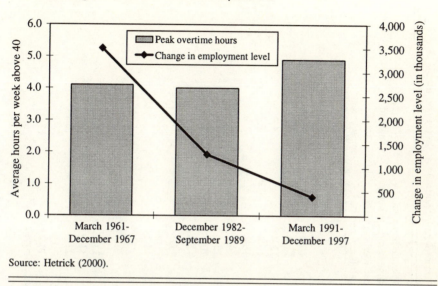

Source: Hetrick (2000).

manufacturing, hours of overtime have increased more than employment (**Figure 3L**). Thus it appears that employers have chosen to meet demand through increasing employees' hours on the job, rather than hiring more workers. Although manufacturing employs only 15.9% of all workers (9.7% in durables and 6.2% in non-durables), workers in this industry are more likely to work overtime than workers overall (**Table 3.10**). Contrary to the notion of an eight-hour day, average hours per week are above 40 hours in most industries, and hours of work are above 35 hours per week in all but two, entertainment and recreation services (34.2) and private households (29.7). The 10 industries where more than 20% of employees work overtime (with a weighted average of 24.7% of employees working overtime) employ 45.4% of all workers, indicating that overtime is widespread and not relegated to only a few industries. In those top-10 industries, average hours are 41.3, and average hours of weekly overtime among those who work more than 40 hours per week are 11.5. In the remaining industries, average hours are 37.2, and average weekly hours of overtime for those who work overtime are 12.0. On average, one in five workers (19.4%) works 11.8 hours a week over 40 hours each week, the equivalent of nearly six-and-a-half eight-hour days per week.

Increased multiple job holding is not as widespread as overtime and does not appear to be a reason why families are working more hours (**Table 3.11**).

**TABLE 3.10** Hours worked, part time and overtime, by industry, 2000 (employed individuals at their main jobs)

| Industry | Percentage working more than 40 hrs/week | Average weekly hours | Average hours of overtime worked among those working more that 40 hours per week | Share of total employment |
|---|---|---|---|---|
| *Industries with more than 20% of workers working overtime* | | | | |
| Mining | 40.0% | 48.0 | 19.0 | 0.4% |
| Wholesale trade | 30.1 | 42.2 | 11.4 | 4.0 |
| Other service professions | 27.4 | 40.0 | 12.4 | 4.4 |
| Manufacturing, durable | 26.0 | 42.2 | 10.4 | 9.7 |
| Communications | 25.3 | 41.9 | 10.8 | 1.6 |
| Agriculture | 25.2 | 40.3 | 14.5 | 1.5 |
| Transportation | 25.1 | 41.6 | 13.6 | 4.7 |
| Manufacturing, non-durable | 22.5 | 41.2 | 10.5 | 6.2 |
| Business and repair services | 22.2 | 40.3 | 11.3 | 6.5 |
| Finance, insurance, and real estate | 20.8 | 40.4 | 11.1 | 6.3 |
| Share of all employment | | | | 45.4 |
| Average (weighted) | 24.7 | 41.3 | 11.5 | |
| *Industries with less than 20% of workers working overtime* | | | | |
| Construction | 18.9% | 41.2 | 11.8 | 6.0% |
| Educational services | 18.0 | 37.3 | 11.9 | 9.0 |
| Forestry and fisheries | 17.6 | 42.6 | 21.8 | 0.1 |
| Utilities and sanitation | 17.3 | 41.3 | 10.8 | 1.2 |
| Retail trade | 15.4 | 35.3 | 11.4 | 17.0 |
| Public administration | 14.4 | 40.3 | 11.1 | 5.0 |

*(cont.)*

**TABLE 3.10** (cont.) Hours worked, part time and overtime, by industry, 2000 (employed individuals at their main jobs)

| Industry | Percentage working more than 40 hrs/week | Average weekly hours | Average hours of overtime worked among those working more than 40 hours per week | Share of total employment |
|---|---|---|---|---|
| *Industries with less than 20% of workers working overtime (cont.)* | | | | |
| Personal services | 13.2 | 37.3 | 13.6 | 2.3 |
| Entertainment and recreation services | 13.1 | 34.2 | 12.4 | 1.9 |
| Hospitals | 12.2 | 38.7 | 14.3 | 4.1 |
| Medical services | 11.5 | 37.0 | 12.0 | 4.9 |
| Social services | 9.6 | 35.7 | 12.0 | 2.5 |
| Private households | 8.7 | 29.7 | 16.7 | 0.8 |
| Share of all employment | | | | 54.6 |
| Average (weighted) | 15.1 | 37.2 | 12.0 | |
| All workers (weighted) | 19.4 | 39.1 | 11.8 | 100.0 |

Source: Golden and Jorgensen (2001).

**TABLE 3.11** Multiple job holding, 1973-2001

| Year | Number of multiple job holders (000) | Multiple-job-holding rate | Percent of workforce who hold multiple jobs because of: | |
|---|---|---|---|---|
| | | | Economic hardship* | Other reasons** |
| 1973 | 4,262 | 5.1% | n.a. | n.a. |
| 1979 | 4,724 | 4.9 | 1.8% | 3.1% |
| 1985 | 5,730 | 5.4 | 2.2 | 3.2 |
| 1989 | 7,225 | 6.2 | 2.8 | 3.4 |
| 2000 | 7,556 | 5.6 | n.a. | n.a. |
| 2001 | 7,319 | 5.4 | n.a. | n.a. |
| *Change* | | | | |
| 1973-79 | 462 | -0.2 | n.a. | n.a. |
| 1979-85 | 1,006 | 0.5 | 0.4 | 0.1 |
| 1985-89 | 1,495 | 0.8 | 0.6 | 0.2 |
| 1989-2000*** | 331 | -0.6 | n.a. | n.a. |

\*    To meet regular household expenses or pay off debts.
\*\*   Includes savings for the future, getting experience, helping a friend or relative, buying
      something special, enjoying the work, and so on.
\*\*\*  Data for 2000 and 2001 not strictly comparable with data for earlier years because of
      survey design changes.

Source: Authors' analysis of BLS (2002b) data.

Between 1989 and 2000, multiple job holding decreased by 0.6 percentage points, from 6.2% of job holders to 5.6%. For the 1979-89 period the Current Population Survey, which is the underlying source of the data presented here, also asked multiple job holders why they held more than one job. In 1989, just under half (2.8 percentage points of the 6.2% of multiple job holders) cited economic hardship (to meet regular household expenses or to pay off debts). Workers citing economic hardship for their multiple jobs accounted for most (1.0 percentage points) of the 1.3 percentage-point increase in multiple job holders between 1979 and 1989. These data support the view that multiple job holding has been one method for coping with declining real wages. Unfortunately, no data on the reasons people work multiple jobs exist after 1991, but improvements in wages and employment opportunities over the 1990s have most likely been an important reason for the fall in multiple job holdings in the 1990s.

Many workers choose to work overtime or multiple jobs and appreciate the extra income that it brings. Increased hours of work incurs costs, however, both

**TABLE 3.12** Workers feeling overworked, 1997

Percent who have high levels of feeling overworked among:

| | |
|---|---|
| Part-time workers | 19% |
| Full-time workers | 37 |
| Those working | |
|    1-19 hours/week | 6% |
|    20-34 hours/week | 23 |
|    35-49 hours/week | 34 |
|    50+ hours/week | 45 |
| Those who work *the same or fewer* hours than they prefer | 26% |
| Those who work *more* hours than they prefer | 44 |

Source: Galinsky, Kim, and Bond (2001).

to workers and to their families. **Table 3.12** reports on the extent to which individuals feel "overworked." At 45%, those who work the most (50-plus hours per week) are most likely to report feeling overworked; at 6%, those who work the least (1-19 hours per week) are least likely to report feeling overworked. Workers who are full time are more likely to report feeling overworked relative to part-timers. Not surprisingly, those working more hours than they prefer are more likely to report feeling overworked relative to those working the same or fewer hours than they prefer (44% versus 26%).

More employment, whether in the form of adding more family members to the labor market or increasing the hours of work for those already employed, adds to individual and family stress levels. Increasingly, workers must do a "double duty" at work and at home. Benefit trends—in particular, paid time off and flexible workplaces—have failed to generate more time outside work over the past few decades. At the turn of the century, workers are less likely to have paid time off than they were 30 years ago.

## Benefits

A defining characteristic of employment relations in the U.S. that distinguishes it from most other advanced countries is that benefits—health insurance, vacation, workplace flexibility—are tied generally to jobs, rather than legislated. (See Chapter 7 for a discussion of benefits in other advanced economies.) Whereas Chapter 2 discussed the level of benefits within the context of overall compensation, this section explores the extent to which workers receive benefits and the kinds of jobs that provide them.

**Table 3.13** documents the extent to which workers received retirement and health care benefits through their employer by industry in 1999, the latest year available. (Later, we show how these benefits have changed over time.) Overall, less than half of all workers receive any retirement benefits (48%), and slightly more than half (53%) receive any employer-provided health insurance. Retirement and health insurance *coverage* is much higher than this because many workers receive these benefits through a spouse or purchase them directly. Workers in the goods-producing sector (which is more heavily unionized) are most likely to have retirement (61%) and health care benefits (69%). Workers in this sector are least likely to have to contribute to their health insurance costs, and, when they do contribute, their average flat monthly contribution is lower than in the service-producing sector. Conversely, workers in lower-paying industries are less likely to have both retirement benefits and employer-provided health insurance. Retail workers, for example, who work in the lowest-paid industry, are the least likely to have employer-provided health insurance (31%), are the most likely to have to make employee contributions if they are offered health care benefits (78% for self-coverage), and have higher levels of contributions required (an average of $59.32 per month). The services industry, which makes up the fastest-growing share of employment, also has lower-than-average health care coverage (50%) and higher-than-average contributions for self- or family coverage when workers have to contribute to their health benefits.

Retirement and health insurance are only two of the kinds of benefits tied to employment in the United States. Paid-time off—vacations and holidays—is not regulated by the government but is part of the employment contract between workers and their employers. **Table 3.14** shows access to leave and family-related benefits by industry in 1999. Most workers have access to paid vacations and paid holidays: 79% receive paid vacations and 75% receive paid holidays. However, as with retirement and health care benefits, the lowest paid industry, retail trade, is also the least likely to offer any paid vacations (64%) or holidays (50%).

Employers became less likely to provide fringe benefits, which are increasingly important to American families as more family members work more hours, over the 1980s and 1990s. (Although coverage did increase during the 1995-2000 period, it was not enough to overcome the long-term decline in coverage.) **Table 3.15** shows a time series for fringe benefits for workers in large (250 employees or more) and medium (100-249 employees) establishments for 1979, 1989, and 1997 (the latest year available, and these are the only establishment sizes available in this time series). About two out of five workers is employed

**TABLE 3.13** Worker participation in retirement and health care benefits by industry, 1999

| | Retirement benefits | | | Health care benefits | | | Health care benefit costs | | | |
| | | | | | | | Employee-only coverage | | Family coverage*** | |
| Industry | All | Defined benefit | Defined contribution | Medical care | Dental care | Vision care | Percent of employees with any co-payments | Average monthly payment** | Percent of employees with any co-payments | Average monthly payment** |
|---|---|---|---|---|---|---|---|---|---|---|
| Total | 48% | 21% | 36% | 53% | 32% | 18% | 67% | $48.30 | 81% | $169.84 |
| **Goods producing*** | 61% | 36% | 43% | 69% | 39% | 21% | 61% | $42.08 | 75% | 149.73 |
| Construction | 39 | 18 | 25 | 55 | 26 | 14 | 35 | 56.66 | 51 | 256.00 |
| Manufacturing | 68 | 42 | 49 | 74 | 44 | 24 | 68 | 40.49 | 82 | 132.84 |
| **Service producing** | 44% | 17% | 34% | 48% | 30% | 17% | 70% | $50.92 | 83% | 178.94 |
| Transportation and public utilities | 59 | 39 | 46 | 57 | 40 | 22 | 70 | 57.87 | 81 | 179.49 |
| Wholesale trade | 53 | 18 | 44 | 67 | 36 | 19 | 64 | 40.95 | 73 | 161.91 |
| Retail trade | 30 | 11 | 22 | 31 | 17 | 8 | 78 | 59.32 | 83 | 212.70 |
| Finance, insurance, and real estate | 62 | 32 | 53 | 66 | 51 | 23 | 72 | 45.41 | 84 | 164.62 |
| Services | 45 | 14 | 33 | 50 | 32 | 19 | 67 | 50.54 | 86 | 175.28 |

\*   Includes data for mining not shown separately.

\*\*  The average monthly payment is for all covered workers and excludes workers without the plan provision. Averages are for plans stating a flat monthly cost.

\*\*\* Family coverage costs are not weighted for family size.

Source: Authors' analysis of BLS (2001) and BLS (2002b).

**TABLE 3.14** Percent of workers with access to leave and family-related benefits by industry, 1999

| Industry | Paid vacations | Paid holidays | Flexible workplace | Employer-provided funds | Employer assistance for child care | | |
|---|---|---|---|---|---|---|---|
| | | | | | On-site child care | Off-site child care | Total |
| Total | 79% | 75% | 3% | 4% | 3% | 2% | 6% |
| **Goods producing*** | 84% | 84% | 3% | 2% | 1% | 1% | 2% |
| Construction | 63 | 68 | 1 | 1 | 1 | 1 | 1 |
| Manufacturing | 91 | 90 | 4 | 2 | 1 | 2 | 3 |
| **Service producing** | 77% | 73% | 3% | 4% | 3% | 2% | 7% |
| Transportation and public utilities | 92 | 86 | 1 | 1 | - | - | 1 |
| Wholesale trade | 89 | 91 | 8 | 3 | - | 1 | 4 |
| Retail trade | 64 | 50 | 1 | 3 | - | - | 4 |
| Finance, insurance, and real estate | 86 | 91 | 10 | 6 | 4 | 3 | 9 |
| Services | 79 | 77 | 2 | 5 | 6 | 2 | 10 |

*Includes data for mining not shown separately.

Source: BLS (2001) data.

**TABLE 3.15** Fringe benefits for workers in medium and large private establishments, 1979-97

| Benefit | Percent of workers covered in medium and large private establishments* | | |
|---|---|---|---|
| | 1979 | 1989 | 1997 |
| **Employer-provided retirement plans** | | | |
| Participants in defined-benefit pension plans | 87% | 63% | 50% |
| Participants in defined-contributions plans | 53** | 48 | 57 |
| Participants in plans with tax-deferred savings arrangements | 26** | 41 | 55 |
| **Employer-provided health insurance plans** | | | |
| Participants in medical care plans | 97% | 92% | 76% |
| Participants with employee contribution required for: | | | |
| Self coverage | 27 | 47 | 69 |
| Average monthly contribution | $39.04** | $45.12 | $45.40 |
| Family coverage | 46%** | 66% | 80% |
| Average monthly contribution | $125.28** | $128.54 | $150.88 |
| **Time-off plans** | | | |
| Paid holidays | 99% | 97% | 89% |
| Average days per year | 10.1** | 9.2 | 9.3 |
| Paid personal leave | 19% | 22% | 20% |
| Average days per year | 3.8** | 3.1 | 3.5 |
| Paid vacations | 100% | 97% | 95% |
| Paid sick leave | 56 | 68 | 56 |
| Unpaid maternity leave | —— | 37 | —— |
| Unpaid paternity leave | —— | 18 | —— |
| Unpaid family leave*** | —— | —— | 93 |
| **Other benefits** | | | |
| Flexible benefits plans | —— | 9 | 13 |
| Reimbursement accounts | —— | 23 | 32 |

\* Medium-sized firms have 100-249 employees. Large firms have more than 250 employees.

\*\* Reported first available year: data for average paid holidays off per year from 1980; data for average personal leave days off per year from 1982; data for family coverage from 1980; data for defined-contribution and tax-deferred retirement plans from 1985.

\*\*\* Under the Family and Medical Leave Act of 1993, firms with more than 50 workers are required to provide unpaid family and medical leave.

Source: BLS (1997).

in these two kinds of establishments, which are more likely than smaller establishments to offer benefits. Even so, between 1979 and 1997, the prevalence of benefits in medium and large establishments generally decreased. Employer-sponsored retirement plans have become less common overall, and, further, workers who do receive this benefit are increasingly in defined-contribution or tax-deferred savings plans as opposed to defined benefit plans. Table 3.15 and **Figure 3M** show that the proportion of workers in medium and large establishments who participate in employer-sponsored health care plans has fallen from 97% to 76% between 1979 and 1997. Over this same time period, the proportions in those plans who have some type of co-payment for self- and family coverage have increased from 27% to 69% for self-coverage and 46% to 80% for family coverage. The average monthly contributions for those who must pay them have also risen for both self- and family coverage. This decline in employer-sponsored health care coverage is not simply due to employers refusing to pay for it, since, as noted in Chapter 2, over this time period employers' costs for health coverage have increased as well. The problem is that health care has become increasingly expensive, outpacing inflation.

Workers are not only working more hours per year, they have less paid time off from their jobs. Table 3.15 shows that between 1979 and 1997, the proportion of workers with paid holidays and paid vacations decreased, as did the number of average paid holiday and paid vacations days per year. The percent of workers in medium and large establishments with paid holidays or vacations in Table 3.15 is much higher than that in Table 3.14, which looks at all establishments. Even among these better-off workers, however, 10% lost their benefit of paid holidays, and the average worker lost eight-tenths of a day of a paid holiday over the 1980s and 1990s. The proportions of workers with paid personal leave and paid sick leave were about the same in 1997 as they were in 1979, with only one in five (20%) having any paid personal leave and a little over half (56%) with any paid sick leave. Given that the likelihood of having paid time off is greater in medium and large establishments, it is likely that most workers in small establishments do not have paid sick or personal leave. Almost all (93%) of workers in medium and large establishments have access to unpaid family leave because of the Family and Medical Leave Act passed in 1993, which requires that all establishments with more than 50 employees offer unpaid family and medical leave to qualified workers. As more family members work and as workers become older, on average, this lack of paid time off becomes an increasingly critical problem.

With workers putting in more hours on the job, workplace flexibility has become an increasingly important fringe benefit. Flexible workplaces offer an array of benefits to workers, and could include allowing workers to telecommute,

**FIGURE 3M** Employer-provided health insurance and monthly employee contribution for workers in medium and large establishments

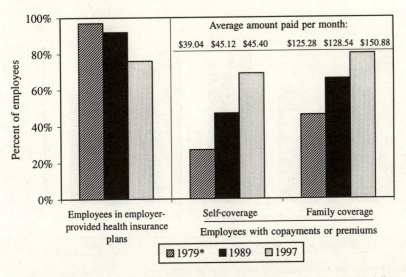

* For family coverage, the 1979 data are from 1980. Average amount paid is in 2001 dollars (consumer price index-research series (CPI-RS) for medical care).

Source: Authors' analysis of BLS (1997) data.

to work at home regularly or occasionally, to set their own hours (usually within boundaries established by the employer, such as "core" hours when everyone must be at work), or to bank flextime (work longer one day in order to leave early the next). Looking back to Table 3.14, across all industries, flexible workplace practices and employer assistance for child care are minimal. The finance, insurance, and real estate industry (along with the services industry) is most likely to offer workplace flexibility and child care assistance, but even in this industry only 10% of workers have workplace flexibility and only 9% have access to any kind of child care assistance.

Workers with familial responsibilities are the ones who perhaps are most likely to need workplace flexibility, yet, not only are flexible workplaces not generally established, but it is single mothers who are least likely to have control over their work hours (**Figure 3N**).

Over the 1980s and 90s, health care has become increasingly expensive for American workers and, more and more workers are unable to find jobs that

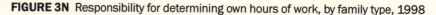

**FIGURE 3N** Responsibility for determining own hours of work, by family type, 1998

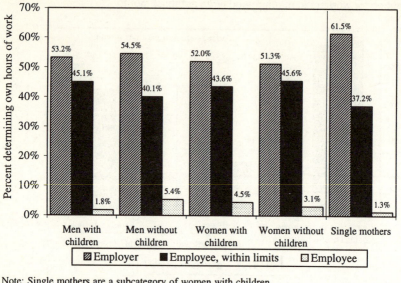

Note: Single mothers are a subcategory of women with children.

Source: McCrate (2002).

offer this benefit. Older workers and workers with young families, who tend to have more health care needs, are especially burdened by these increasing costs and lower coverage levels. At the same time, paid time off has decreased, and many workers have no access to paid sick leave. Faced with less paid time off, many workers may think about whether nonstandard employment—i.e., less than full-time work schedules or non-traditional work—may help them balance their work lives and their personal lives. However, one of the difficulties with the way that the American labor market distributes paid time off and health care, is that working full time is still the most likely way of accessing these benefits.

## Nonstandard work

Broadly defined, nonstandard work consists of employment arrangements that are not regular, full time. These include temporary work, part-time jobs, on-call jobs, and self-employment. Many workers—students, older workers, workers with families—prefer jobs that offer more flexibility than the traditional "9-to-5" job. Busi-

**TABLE 3.16** Employed workers by work arrangement, 1995-2001 (February)

| Work arrangement | Percent of women employed | | Percent of men employed | |
|---|---|---|---|---|
| | 1995 | 2001 | 1995 | 2001 |
| Regular part time | 21.3% | 19.7% | 7.1% | 6.8% |
| Temporary help agency | 1.1 | 1.1 | 0.8 | 0.7 |
| On-call/day laborer | 1.7 | 1.6 | 1.5 | 1.7 |
| Self-employed | 4.8 | 3.2 | 6.1 | 4.9 |
| Independent contractor (wage & salary) | 0.9 | 0.7 | 0.9 | 0.8 |
| Independent contractor (self-employed) | 3.7 | 4.1 | 7.3 | 6.7 |
| Contract company | 0.8 | 0.6 | 1.6 | 1.2 |
| All nonstandard arrangements | 34.3% | 31.0% | 25.3% | 22.8% |
| Regular full time | 65.3% | 69.1% | 74.7% | 77.1% |
| All | 100.0% | 100.0% | 100.0% | 100.0% |

Source: Kalleberg et al. (1997) and Wenger (2002).

nesses hire contingent workers in a variety of ways. Some put workers directly on their payrolls but assign them to an internal temporary worker pool. Others hire on-call workers and day laborers. Employers also use temporary help agencies and contracting firms to obtain workers on a temporary basis, sometimes for long periods. Some businesses hire independent contractors to perform work that would otherwise be done by direct-hire employees.

In this section, we report results from special analyses of nonstandard work arrangements, the Contingent Work Supplements to the Current Population Survey (the monthly government household survey that has provided much of the information on wages and employment presented in this book). These data allow an examination of the different types of nonstandard work, their prevalence, and their associated pay and working conditions. While the surveys provide a comprehensive look at nonstandard work arrangements from the mid-1990s to 2001, no comparable, earlier surveys exist. After reviewing the most recent data, therefore, we will turn to other, less comprehensive data that can give some indication of longer-term trends in the growth of nonstandard work arrangements.

**Table 3.16** shows the distribution of employment by type of work arrangement. Women are more likely to be in nonstandard employment than men: in 2001, 69.1% of women and 77.1% of men held regular full-time jobs (these figures exclude some self-employed workers). Among women, by far the largest nonstandard category was regular part-time work (19.7%), followed by independent contracting/self-employed (4.1%). Men in nonstandard employment are also most likely to be regular part-time workers (6.8%) or self-employed independent contractors (6.7%). The proportion of women and men in other categories of nonstandard employment are relatively similar, except that twice as many men work for a contract company (1.2% of men and 0.6% of women). During economic expansions, when unemployment falls, the proportion of workers in nonstandard arrangements also tends to fall, as workers find stable, full-time employment if they want it. This was true over the late 1990s: between 1995 and 2001, the percent of women employed in nonstandard work decreased by 3.3 percentage points, from 34.3% to 31.0%; among men it decreased by 2.3 percentage points, from 25.3% to 23.0%.

Workers who have been traditionally disadvantaged in the labor market are more likely to be in nonstandard employment (**Table 3.17**). In 2001, women made up less than half (46.9%) of the total work force, but were well over half (58.5%) of temporary workers. Women, however, were notably underrepresented (35.1%) among self-employed independent contractors, the category of nonstandard work that offers the highest pay and benefits as well as the greatest reported satisfaction rates. (see Tables 3.18 and 3.21 below). African American and Hispanic workers and workers with less than a high school degree are overrepresented in the typically least remunerative kind of nonstandard arrangements—temp and on-call work—and underrepresented in independent contracting.

Nonstandard workers generally earn less and receive fewer fringe benefits than workers with similar skills in regular full-time jobs, as shown in **Table 3.18**. For example, as illustrated in the top section, which controls for key worker characteristics such as the level of education and years of work experience, regular part-time women workers—who make up about one-fifth of the female workforce—earn, on average, 14.8% less than similar women in full-time employment; self-employed women earn 25.3% less. Men who regularly work part time experience a higher wage penalty, 24.9%, than do women. The gap between men and women who worked as temps and their regular full-time counterparts was about 10%. Not all nonstandard workers, however, earn less than regular full-timers. For example, women who are independent contractors/self-employed (3.9% of all women workers in 1999) earn 25.0% more than their full-time counterparts, and men working with contract companies (1.2% of all male workers in 1999) earn 16.2% more than comparable standard workers.

One reason that nonstandard wages are lower than those for regular full-time work is that nonstandard workers tend to be concentrated in low-paying industries and occupations. The second section of the table shows results that control for both workers' personal characteristics and the characteristics of the jobs they perform. In this analysis, the wage "penalty" for working in nonstandard jobs is smaller than

**TABLE 3.17** Characteristics of nonstandard workers, 2001

| Characteristic | Nonstandard work arrangement | | | | | | | | Regular full time | All workers |
|---|---|---|---|---|---|---|---|---|---|---|
| | Regular part time | Temporary help agency | On-call/ day laborer | Self-employed other | Independent contractor (wage & salary) | Independent contractor (self-employed) | Contract company | All nonstandard arrangements | | |
| **Gender** | | | | | | | | | | |
| Women | 71.8% | 58.5% | 45.0% | 36.7% | 41.7% | 35.1% | 30.5% | 54.5% | 44.2% | 46.9% |
| Men | 28.2 | 41.5 | 55.0 | 63.3 | 58.3 | 64.9 | 69.5 | 45.5 | 55.8 | 53.1 |
| **Race** | | | | | | | | | | |
| White | 77.8% | 52.8% | 70.7% | 87.2% | 73.4% | 81.9% | 71.8% | 78.5% | 72.1% | 73.8% |
| African American | 9.3 | 24.5 | 11.8 | 2.8 | 11.0 | 6.3 | 9.9 | 8.4 | 11.7 | 10.8 |
| Hispanic | 9.2 | 17.8 | 14.5 | 5.5 | 10.9 | 7.1 | 12.6 | 9.0 | 11.6 | 10.9 |
| Other | 3.7 | 4.9 | 3.0 | 4.5 | 4.7 | 4.8 | 5.6 | 4.2 | 4.6 | 4.5 |
| **Education** | | | | | | | | | | |
| Less than high school | 13.8% | 14.8% | 11.9% | 6.6% | 8.5% | 8.7% | 8.1% | 11.2% | 9.4% | 9.9% |
| High school | 27.1 | 30.8 | 28.7 | 29.5 | 27.7 | 30.6 | 26.9 | 28.4 | 31.7 | 30.8 |
| Some college | 40.2 | 36.9 | 36.9 | 27.8 | 24.3 | 27.7 | 29.8 | 34.6 | 28.6 | 30.2 |
| Bachelor's degree | 13.6 | 14.1 | 17.9 | 21.7 | 27.7 | 21.7 | 21.8 | 17.5 | 20.8 | 19.9 |
| Graduate degree | 5.3 | 3.4 | 4.6 | 14.4 | 11.8 | 11.2 | 13.4 | 8.3 | 9.6 | 9.2 |

Source: Wenger (2002).

253

**TABLE 3.18** Wages of nonstandard workers, compared to regular full-time workers, by sex and work arrangement, 1999

| Work arrangement | Women | Men |
|---|---|---|
| **Controlling for personal characteristics** | | |
| Regular part time | -14.8%* | -24.9%* |
| Temporary help agency | -10.7* | -9.6 |
| On-call/day laborer | -20.0* | -12.1* |
| Self-employed | -25.3* | -11.5* |
| Independent contractor (wage & salary) | 0.3 | 2.1 |
| Independent contractor (self-employed) | 25.0* | 13.6* |
| Contract company | 5.9 | 16.2* |
| **Controlling for personal and job characteristics** | | |
| Regular part time | -1.2% | -11.0%* |
| Temporary help agency | 1.5 | 3.2 |
| On-call/day laborer | -8.1* | -4.7 |
| Self-employed | -7.2* | 9.4* |
| Independent contractor (wage & salary) | 14.8* | 10.7 |
| Independent contractor (self-employed) | 22.3* | 7.0* |
| Contract company | 8.6 | 14.9* |

* Statistically significant at the .05 level.

Source: Wenger (2002).

when we ignore job characteristics. In half the cases, nonstandard workers appear to earn more than do regular full-time workers with similar personal skills in the same kinds of jobs. This evidence supports the view that nonstandard workers tend to work in less-well-paid industries and occupations.

Nonstandard workers are not only often paid less, but they also are less likely to receive benefits from their employer (**Table 3.19**). Compared to nonstandard workers, those in standard employment are more likely to have health care through their employer and are more likely to have health insurance overall. Among regular, full-time workers, 66.8% of women and 70.8% of men have employer-provided health insurance, compared to only 14.8% of women and 12.4% of men in non-standard employment. (The share of all workers with health insurance is lower than in Table 3.15 because these data include all establishments, not only medium and large ones.) Part-time workers—the largest share of nonstandard workers—are most likely to go without health insurance through their employer. A common argument

**TABLE 3.19** Health and pension coverage by nonstandard work arrangement, 2001

| | Share with health insurance | | | | Share eligible for pension | | | |
| --- | --- | --- | --- | --- | --- | --- | --- | --- |
| | Women | | Men | | Women | | Men | |
| | Any coverage | Through own employer | Any coverage | Through own employer | Any coverage | Through own employer | Any coverage | Through own employer |
| **All workers** | 86.0% | 50.7% | 83.8% | 57.4% | 59.3% | 52.4% | 61.5% | 53.3% |
| **All full-time workers** | 88.3% | 61.9% | 85.1% | 61.7% | 66.6% | 61.4% | 65.2% | 56.7% |
| Regular full time | 89.6 | 66.8 | 87.0 | 70.8 | 68.9 | 66.5 | 67.9 | 66.0 |
| **All nonstandard arrangements** | 77.7% | 14.8% | 73.0% | 12.4% | 37.7% | 20.1% | 39.6% | 11.1% |
| **Full time and nonstandard** | | | | | | | | |
| Temporary help agency | 49.9% | 11.0% | 43.0% | 15.2% | 24.9% | 10.2% | 23.0% | 12.7% |
| On-call/day laborer | 76.4 | 39.8 | 66.3 | 52.5 | 48.2 | 40.4 | 53.3 | 50.4 |
| Self-employed | 80.1 | n.a. | 83.0 | n.a. | 38.8 | n.a. | 57.0 | n.a. |
| Independent contractor, WS* | 65.4 | 17.6 | 67.5 | 25.8 | 36.7 | 15.8 | 37.5 | 18.7 |
| Independent contractor, SE** | 75.2 | n.a. | 72.5 | n.a. | 44.4 | n.a. | 44.5 | n.a. |
| Contract company | 88.8 | 54.9 | 83.3 | 59.4 | 68.7 | 64.0 | 63.3 | 53.2 |
| **All part-time workers** | 78.7% | 16.2% | 70.2% | 13.6% | 36.6% | 23.2% | 23.9% | 14.0% |
| Regular part time | 78.5 | 19.4 | 72.0 | 15.9 | 36.1 | 28.0 | 21.4 | 17.1 |
| **Part time and nonstandard** | | | | | | | | |
| Temporary help agency | 70.0% | 0.9% | 36.9% | 0.0% | 11.5% | 3.3% | 0.0% | 14.0% |
| On-call/day laborer | 69.9 | 10.6 | 60.8 | 12.0 | 33.6 | 18.7 | 25.5 | 14.4 |
| Self-employed | 88.0 | n.a. | 78.5 | n.a. | 42.7 | n.a. | 47.2 | n.a. |

*(cont.)*

**TABLE 3.19** (cont.) Health and pension coverage by nonstandard work arrangement, 2001

| | Share with health insurance | | | | Share eligible for pension | | | |
|---|---|---|---|---|---|---|---|---|
| | Women | | Men | | Women | | Men | |
| | Any coverage | Through own employer | Any coverage | Through own employer | Any coverage | Through own employer | Any coverage | Through own employer |
| **Part time and nonstandard** (cont.) | | | | | | | | |
| Independent contractor, WS* | 77.8 | 4.7 | 64.5 | 19.0 | 28.0 | 4.3 | 40.1 | 15.9 |
| Independent contractor, SE** | 81.5 | n.a. | 61.4 | n.a. | 44.9 | n.a. | 34.0 | n.a. |
| Contract company | 80.5 | 12.7 | 82.0 | 19.0 | 28.3 | 17.1 | 26.1 | 9.6 |

\* Wage and salary.
\*\* Self-employed.

Source: Wenger (2002).

is that nonstandard workers receive health insurance through their spouses, so that lack of employer-provided health insurance is not a significant problem. However, this argument is not consistent with the data. Nonstandard workers are less likely than regular, full-time workers to have *any* health insurance coverage: 89.6% of all women and 87.0% of all men in regular, full-time employment have health insurance, compared to 77.7% of women and 73.0% of men in nonstandard employment. This indicates that many nonstandard workers are not making up for lower employer-provided health insurance with spousal benefits. Nonstandard workers are also less likely to receive pensions through their employer or through any source. Among women, only 20.1% of nonstandard workers have pension coverage from their employer compared to 66.5% among regular, full-time women workers.

Some workers choose nonstandard employment because the flexibility it offers allows then to pursue other goals, such as having a family or acquiring an education. **Table 3.20** shows that women who are in nonstandard employment are only slightly more likely to have children, while men are slightly less likely to have children. The low proportions of nonstandard women workers with young children may be due to the fact that women who do not want to work full time when they have young children choose to drop out of the labor market for a period rather than work in nonstandard jobs. However, another explanation may be that the low wages and relatively few occupations that offer nonstandard employment (the majority of part-time women workers are concentrated in just 10 occupations) limit the opportunity for mothers to have this kind of employment flexibility.

Nonstandard workers are far more likely than regular, full-time workers to be in school (either high school or college): two-thirds of men and 19.4% of women who work part time also attend school (41.5%), compared to 1.7% of women and 1.4% of men in regular full-time jobs.

Workers may appreciate the flexibility that nonstandard work arrangements provide, but a substantial share of these workers would prefer to have regular full-time employment. (**Table 3.21**). In 2001, over half of women (56.3%) and two-fifths of men (43.7%) with temporary jobs said that they would rather have a standard job; similar levels of on-call workers also expressed that preference. Self-employed independent contractors, who generally enjoy pay and benefits comparable to standard workers, strongly prefer their nonstandard arrangements to standard work. As the economy improved between 1995 and 2001, the share of workers in each category that prefers standard work declined, suggesting that many nonstandard workers unhappy with their arrangements were able to find full-time employment as jobs became more plentiful; at the same time, those left in nonstandard arrangements may have been those who most enjoyed the flexibility and other benefits their type of work provided. Another possible explanation for the decline in dissatisfaction with nonstandard arrangements is that the abundance of

**TABLE 3.20** Common reasons for nonstandard employment, 2001

| | Percent of nonstandard workers with children, by work arrangement | | | |
| | Women | | Men | |
| Work arrangement | Child under 5 | Child 6-17 | Child under 5 | Child 6-17 |
|---|---|---|---|---|
| Regular part time | 10.1% | 21.3% | 4.3% | 10.6% |
| Temporary help agency | 11.4 | 21.6 | 1.8 | 15.3 |
| On-call/day labor | 9.1 | 19.8 | 8.2 | 14.7 |
| Self-employed | 8.6 | 26.1 | 8.6 | 24.0 |
| Independent contractor, WS* | 9.4 | 19.9 | 8.5 | 18.6 |
| Independent contractor, SE** | 8.7 | 23.8 | 7.8 | 21.5 |
| Contract company | 11.3 | 18.5 | 11.6 | 17.7 |
| | | | | |
| Total nonstandard | 9.8% | 22.0% | 7.0% | 17.8% |
| Regular full time | 7.1 | 19.8 | 10.1 | 19.6 |

| | Percent of nonstandard workers in school (high school or college), by work arrangement | |
| | Women | Men |
|---|---|---|
| Regular part time | 19.4% | 41.5% |
| Temporary help agency | 4.2 | 6.4 |
| On-call/day laborer | 11.4 | 7.6 |
| Self-employed other | 0.3 | 0.2 |
| Independent contractor, WS* | 3.5 | 2.3 |
| Independent contractor, SE** | 0.1 | 0.5 |
| | | |
| Total nonstandard | 13.2% | 13.7% |
| Regular full time | 1.7 | 1.4 |

\* Wage and salary.
\*\* Self-employed.

Source: Wenger (2002).

work near the end of the 1990s economic boom reduced the inherent uncertainty of nonstandard arrangements.

The most recent evidence on nonstandard work shows that such arrangements are widespread, varied, and generally substandard. Nonstandard work pays less, is much less likely to provide health or pension benefits, and, almost by definition, provides far less job security than regular full-time employment. Unfortunately, the kind of detailed survey that has allowed us to sketch the main features of nonstandard work in the mid-1990s does not exist for earlier periods. As a result, we have some difficulty gauging the growth in nonstandard work over the last two decades

**TABLE 3.21** Workers preferring standard employment by type of nonstandard work arrangement, 1995 and 2001

| | Women | | | Men | | |
|---|---|---|---|---|---|---|
| | 1995 | 2001 | Percentage-point change | 1995 | 2001 | Percentage-point change |
| Regular part time | 24.9% | 23.4% | -1.5 | 35.5% | 17.4% | -18.1 |
| Temporary help agency | 66.4 | 56.3 | -10.1 | 79.2 | 43.7 | -35.5 |
| On-call | 59.4 | 55.1 | -4.3 | 72.9 | 44.2 | -28.7 |
| Self-employed | 10.8 | 7.3 | -3.5 | 6.0 | 8.1 | 2.1 |
| Independent contractor, WS* | 23.9 | 22.8 | -1.1 | 22.3 | 23.6 | 1.3 |
| Independent contractor, SE** | 9.2 | 7.7 | -1.5 | 8.6 | 6.8 | -1.8 |

\* Wage and salary.
\** Self-employed.

Source: Kalleberg et al. (1997) and Wenger (2002).

of substantial economic change. The following sections look at the data that do exist on the growth of three kinds of nonstandard work: regular part-time employment, temporary work, and self-employment.

### Part-time work

The most pervasive form of nonstandard employment is part-time work. Many workers prefer a part-time schedule because it allows time to pursue education, family responsibilities, or more leisure. Nevertheless, part-timers generally have lower pay, less-skilled jobs, poor chances of promotion, less job security, inferior benefits (such as vacation, health insurance, and pension), and lower status overall within their places of employment. For these and other reasons, some part-timers would prefer to work full time. Even those who work part-time schedules by choice would prefer to receive the same compensation (hourly pay rate and prorated benefits) in exchange for performing work done by their full-time coworkers.

According to the data in **Table 3.22**, 16.9% of employees worked part time in 2001. (These numbers differ slightly from those in Tables 3.14 and 3.15 because here the definition of part-time includes all part-time workers; Tables 3.14 and 3.15 looked at "regular" part time, which did not include part-time workers in other kinds of nonstandard employment.) Between 1973 and 1989, part-time work increased 1.5 percentage points, from 16.6% to 18.1% of all employees, and the increase resulted almost entirely from the rise in *involuntary* part-time work, which expanded 1.2 per-

**TABLE 3.22** Non-agricultural employment by full-time and part-time status, 1973-2001

| Year | Percent part time | | | Percent full time | Total |
| | Total | Involuntary | Voluntary | | |
| --- | --- | --- | --- | --- | --- |
| 1973 | 16.6% | 3.1% | 13.5% | 83.4% | 100.0% |
| 1979 | 17.6 | 3.8 | 13.8 | 82.4 | 100.0 |
| 1989 | 18.1 | 4.3 | 13.8 | 81.9 | 100.0 |
| 2000* | 16.6 | 2.4 | 14.2 | 83.4 | 100.0 |
| 2001 | 16.9 | 2.8 | 14.1 | 83.1 | 100.0 |

\* Data for 2000 and after are not strictly comparable with earlier years because of survey changes.

Source: Authors' analysis of BLS (2002b) data.

centage points, from 3.1% to 4.3% of employment. By 1989, nearly one-fourth of all part-time workers were involuntary part-timers. The rise in part-time work over the 1970s and 1980s, therefore, did not reflect workers' preferences for shorter hours.

Part-time employment declined between 1989 and 2000 (the economic peak), from 18.1% to 16.6% of all workers, with the share of involuntary part-time employment falling even more (1.9 percentage points). As employment opportunities expanded during the 1990s, workers seeking full-time work were more able to find it, meaning that fewer part-time workers were involuntarily working less than full-time. By 2000, the share of involuntary part-time workers was below its 1973 level. Between 1989 and 2000, voluntary part-time employment increased by 0.4 percentage points, from 13.8% to 14.2%. This rise highlights the somewhat complicated nature of nonstandard employment: on the one hand, part-time workers are paid less than their similarly skilled full-time colleagues (as shown in Table 3.18), but, for many workers, nonstandard employment provides the flexibility that they need to balance work with their personal life. As unemployment fell during the late 1990s, voluntary part-time employment may have risen because employers, seeking to lure reticent workers into employment during a tight labor market, were more likely to offer nonstandard arrangements. Another reason may have been that the strong wage growth of the late 1990s softened the blow of the part-timers' wage penalty. Even so, as the recession began, the incidence of part-time work increased slightly, from 16.6% to 16.9%, and the increase was driven entirely by increases in involuntary part-time employment. As Table 3.3 showed, the growth in involuntary part-time employment continued through 2002, increasing by nearly one-third (28.7%) between the second quarter of 2000, when the labor market recession began, and the second quarter of 2002, when output began to grow again.

**TABLE 3.23** Employment in personnel services industry, 1973-2001

| | Number (thousands) | | | As share of total employment | | |
|---|---|---|---|---|---|---|
| Year | All | Men | Women | All | Men | Women |
| 1973 | 247 | 118 | 128 | 0.3% | 0.2% | 0.2% |
| 1979 | 508 | 210 | 298 | 0.6 | 0.2 | 0.3 |
| 1989 | 1,455 | 581 | 874 | 1.3 | 0.5 | 0.8 |
| 2000 | 3,887 | 1,857 | 2,030 | 3.0 | 1.4 | 1.5 |
| 2001 | 3,532 | 1,725 | 1,807 | 3.2 | 1.6 | 1.6 |

Source: Authors' analysis of BLS (2002b) data.

*Temping*

As we saw earlier, temps and workers with contract agencies are an important part of the nonstandard workforce. Unfortunately, the government did not gather data on temporary work before 1982, and even the data that the government has collected on a regular basis since 1982 are not directly comparable to the detailed information in Table 3.16. **Table 3.23**, however, reports the number of workers employed in personnel services industries, which include temporary help agencies, between 1973 and 2001. The last three columns show employment as a percent of the total workforce. In 2001, 3.2% of all workers were employed in the personnel services industry, up from 0.3% in 1973. This represents a doubling over each economic cycle since that year. Government data have tracked employment in the narrower category of temporary help agencies since 1982 (see **Figure 30**). Employment there doubled between 1982 and 1989 and again between 1989 and 2001.

The data suggest that temporary and related employment arrangements were more important in 2001 than they were at any earlier time. Earlier, more detailed, information on temps from the Contingent Work Survey indicated that temporary employment flattened out during the economic recovery of 1995-2001. However, the long-term trend captured in these two tables suggests that economic forces may be pushing the economy toward ever greater use of temporary workers as firms increasingly use contract labor rather than hire their own employees.

*Self-employment*

A significant portion of total employment consists of self-employed workers, those whose primary job is working in their own business, farm, craft, or profession. Individual independent contracting, mentioned earlier, is one form of self-employment.

261

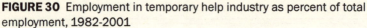

**FIGURE 30** Employment in temporary help industry as percent of total employment, 1982-2001

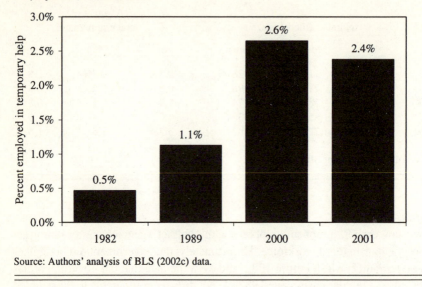

Source: Authors' analysis of BLS (2002c) data.

In 2000, 6.4% of all workers were self-employed (**Table 3.24**). This is the lowest level of self-employment during a business cycle peak since 1973 (6.4%). Self-employment was substantially higher (7.2%) in the middle of the last recession (1992) than it was during the boom year of 2000, and the decline between 1992, when the unemployment rate was high (7.5%), and 2000, when the unemployment rate was much lower (4.2%), suggests that, for some workers, self-employment is a refuge against the inability to find regular employment. The data also show that men are consistently more likely to be self-employed than are women. Research suggests that one factor in the different rates of self-employment is that women often lack the kinds of access that men have to the capital and networks necessary to start and sustain small businesses.

## Job stability and job security

As the economy moved through the recession of 2000-02, job security became a paramount issue for workers. But job stability and security are not related only to economic booms and busts, as there are indications that the long-term trends, regardless of the ups-and-downs of the business cycle, have been toward increasing levels of job insecurity and reduced job tenure.

**TABLE 3.24** Self-employment, 1948-2001 (percent of employment by gender*)

| Year | All | Men | Women |
|------|------|------|------|
| 1948 | 10.5% | n.a. | n.a. |
| 1967 | 7.0 | 8.8% | 4.4% |
| 1973 | 6.4 | 8.2 | 4.9 |
| 1979 | 6.9 | 8.3 | 4.8 |
| 1989 | 7.3 | 8.6 | 5.7 |
| 1992 | 7.2 | 8.7 | 5.5 |
| 2000 | 6.4 | 7.3 | 5.4 |
| 2001 | 6.4 | 7.2 | 5.4 |

*Non-agricultural industries.

Source: Authors' analysis of BLS (2002b) data.

Job stability and security are critical issues not only because they provide workers with a dependable paycheck, but also because longer job tenure is often associated with increased vacation time, vesting in retirement plans, and promotions and wage gains. The available evidence suggests that job stability and job security increased along with wages and job opportunities during the late 1990s, but that job instability remains high given the 30-year lows in the level of unemployment.

Throughout the review of these data, it is important to keep in mind the distinction, as enunciated by economists Daniel Aaronson and Daniel Sullivan, between *job stability*—"the tendency of workers and employers to form long-term bonds"—and *job security*—"workers' ability to remain in an employment relationship for as long as their job performance is satisfactory." From a social perspective, our primary concern should be with job security. We would not necessarily be worried, for example, if job stability had declined primarily because workers found that they could improve wages, benefits, and working conditions by frequently changing jobs. Much of the available evidence—the number of job changes in a period of time, the duration of the typical job, and the share of workers in long-term jobs—deals more directly with job stability than job security. Given the well-documented tendency of wages to rise with a worker's tenure (the time spent with a particular employer), and given the apparently widespread anxiety over the perceived decline in long-term jobs, any evidence of declining job stability would tend to support the view that job security is falling. In some cases, we can link declining job stability with falling earnings for affected groups, and this indicates declining job security. While workers could be trading their old, better-paying jobs for new, lower-paying jobs that they prefer for other reasons, these kinds of job changes are the exception,

**TABLE 3.25** Job stability of white men

| Cohort | Two-year job separation rate | Median hourly wage increase between age 16 and age 36 (1997 dollars) |
|---|---|---|
| 1966-81 | 46.4% | $9.90 |
| 1979-94 | 52.7 | 7.65 |
| Change | 13.6% | -22.7% |

Source: Bernhardt, Morris, Handcock, and Scott (2001).

not the rule. The presence of falling earnings is interpreted as evidence of diminished job security. However, trends in employment transitions and employment retention can also provide insight into job security; this is perhaps a better way of examining overall job security because it explores the extent to which workers are able to maintain consistent employment over time. Finally, job stability need not fall for job security to decline. When job insecurity rises, workers may become less likely to quit their current jobs to look for or even accept new ones. This reluctance to change would contribute to rising job stability even as job security was falling.

*Declining job stability*

**Table 3.25** presents the results of a unique analysis of job stability among young, white men during the late 1960s through the 1970s, a period that mostly predates stagnating wages and incomes, and the 1980s and early 1990s, which covers most of the period when economic inequality grew sharply. Researchers followed the labor market experiences of two cohorts of white men as they progressed from ages 16 to 21 to ages 30 to 37. (The data include individuals as young as 14, but the analysis does not look at job stability until the individual turns 16.) The first cohort was born between 1944 and 1952, and the second between 1957 and 1965. The researchers measured job instability for the two groups by counting the share of workers in a given year that were no longer with the same employer two years later. In the 1966-81 period, an average of 46.4% of young white men were not with the same employer two years later; in 1979-94, the average rose to 52.7%, a 13.6% proportional increase in job switching for the later cohort. The rise in job instability coincided with a steep decline in real wage growth across the two cohorts. As cohorts aged from 16 to 21 to 30 to 37, those in the first group saw their after-inflation wages rise an average of $9.90 between 1966 and 1981, while those in the later, less stable, group saw their wages rise only $7.65 between 1979 and 1994.

**TABLE 3.26** Median years of job tenure by age, 1963-2000

| | | | | | Change | |
|---|---|---|---|---|---|---|
| Group | 1963 | 1981 | 1987 | 2000 | 1963-2000 | 1987-2000 |
| **Age 25-34** | | | | | | |
| All | 3.0 | 3.1 | 2.9 | 2.6 | -0.4 | -0.3 |
| Men | 3.5 | 3.1 | 3.1 | 2.7 | -0.8 | -0.4 |
| Women | 2.0 | 3.0 | 2.6 | 2.5 | 0.5 | -0.1 |
| **Age 35-44** | | | | | | |
| All | 6.0 | 5.1 | 5.5 | 4.8 | -1.2 | -0.7 |
| Men | 7.6 | 7.1 | 7.0 | 5.4 | -2.2 | -1.6 |
| Women | 3.6 | 4.1 | 4.4 | 4.3 | 0.7 | -0.1 |
| **Age 45-54** | | | | | | |
| All | 9.0 | 9.1 | 8.8 | 8.2 | -0.8 | -0.6 |
| Men | 11.4 | 11.1 | 11.8 | 9.5 | -1.9 | -2.3 |
| Women | 6.1 | 6.1 | 6.8 | 7.3 | 1.2 | 0.5 |

Source: Authors' analysis of Aaronson and Sullivan (1998) and BLS (2002d) data.

Young workers typically experience significant wage increases in their first years in the labor force, and so the 22.7% decline in wage gains for the second cohort indicates a possible long-term shift in the job prospects of young white males.

No comparable data exist for women over the same period, nor are more recent, comparable data yet available for men. For a more comprehensive and up-to-date picture of job stability, therefore, we turn to a broader set of measures. Unlike the data in Table 3.25, which followed the same workers over time, the following data are "snapshots" of the employment circumstances of different workers at different points in time.

**Table 3.26** provides the most basic information on job stability—the median number of years of tenure for men and women from the early 1960s through 2000 (tenure data are not available for all business cycle peak years, so we use those closest to them). Since the tenure distribution is sensitive to the age distribution in the population (younger workers' job tenure is necessarily shorter than that of older workers, regardless of the underlying employment relationships), 25-34-year-olds, 35-44-year-olds, and 45-54-year-olds are presented separately by gender. Between 1963 and 2000, tenure declined among men while it rose among women. Declines in male tenure were largest for the middle and older age groups. For 35-44-year-old men, median tenure dropped 2.2 years, from 7.6 years in 1963 to 5.4 years in 2000;

most of the decline (1.6 years) occurred between 1987 and 2000. The pattern is similar for 45-54-year-old men, who saw median tenure fall 1.9 years between 1963 and 2000, with an even steeper decline between 1987 and 2000. Tenure fell only slightly for the youngest group of men, eight-tenths of a year between 1963 and 2000, with half of that occurring between 1987 and 2000.

For women, the tenure story looks different: women consistently have lower tenure than men of the same age. In 2000, for example, 35-44-year-old women had a median tenure of 4.3 years, while a man in the same age range had a median tenure of 5.4 years with his current employer. While women still have lower tenure than men, a combination of rising tenure for women and declining tenure for men allowed women to narrow the tenure gap between 1963 and 2000. Changes in the job tenure of women and men are reflected in the changes in the labor force participation rates: as women increasingly stay in the labor market, they are likely to also stay longer on any given job. Overall, the declining tenure for men and the rising tenure for women have come close to canceling each other out. The overall distribution at all three age levels generally changes much less than either of the corresponding male or female distributions.

The median job tenure sheds important light on job stability, but the share of jobs that are "long-term" may be more relevant to workers' perceptions of job security. Long-term jobs (ones that last, say, at least 10 years) typically are the kinds of employment situations that provide workers with the best potential for sustained wage growth, good fringe benefits, and a feeling of employment security. **Table 3.27** shows the share of workers in 1979, 1988, and 1996 that had been in their jobs for 10 or more and 20 or more years. The data show a significant decline during the 1980s and 1990s in the share of men in long-term jobs and little change in the share of women in such jobs. In 1979, just under half (49.8%) of all men had been in their jobs for 10 years or longer; by 1996, the share had fallen 9.8 percentage points to 40.0%. In 1979, far fewer women (29.1%) than men had tenure of 10 years or more, and the share increased only slightly by 1996 (to 30.3%). The data for men and women with 20 years on the job tell a similar story. The share of men with these very-long-tenure jobs fell 6.8 percentage points between 1979 and 1996, from 33.8% to 27.0%. Meanwhile, the share of women in these posts rose 1.2 percentage points, from 13.1% to 14.3%. The data by education level, which include both men and women, suggest that the declines in job tenure cut across all education levels. Declines in 10-year-tenure jobs between 1979 and 1996, for example, were almost as large among college-educated workers (−6.9 percentage points) as they were for those with less than a high school degree (−7.3 percentage points). The decline in long-term tenure is especially important as the population ages and workers have longer potential labor market experience.

One weakness of the job tenure data presented above is that it accounts for

**TABLE 3.27** Share of employed workers in long-term jobs, 1979-96

|  | 1979 | 1988 | 1996 | Percentage-point change 1979-88 | 1988-96 | 1979-96 |
|---|---|---|---|---|---|---|
| **More than 10 years on current job** | | | | | | |
| All | 41.0% | 39.1% | 35.4% | -1.9 | -3.7 | -5.6 |
| Male | 49.8 | 45.7 | 40.0 | -4.1 | -5.7 | -9.8 |
| Female | 29.1 | 31.2 | 30.3 | 2.1 | -0.9 | 1.2 |
| Less than high school | 38.6% | 39.8% | 31.3% | 1.2 | -8.5 | -7.3 |
| High school | 41.9 | 40.2 | 37.2 | -1.7 | -3.0 | -4.7 |
| Some college | 38.8 | 34.8 | 33.3 | -4.0 | -1.5 | -5.5 |
| College and beyond | 43.6 | 40.4 | 36.7 | -3.2 | -3.7 | -6.9 |
| **More than 20 years on current job** | | | | | | |
| All | 25.1% | 23.7% | 20.9% | -1.4 | -2.8 | -4.2 |
| Male | 33.8 | 31.4 | 27.0 | -2.4 | -4.4 | -6.8 |
| Female | 13.1 | 14.5 | 14.3 | 1.4 | -0.2 | 1.2 |
| Less than high school | 22.5% | 21.8% | 19.8% | -0.7 | -2.0 | -2.7 |
| High school | 26.3 | 23.8 | 22.0 | -2.5 | -1.8 | -4.3 |
| Some college | 25.5 | 21.5 | 19.2 | -4.0 | -2.3 | -6.3 |
| College and beyond | 26.6 | 26.7 | 21.7 | 0.1 | -5.0 | -4.9 |

Source: Farber (1997b).

between-employer but not within-employer job changes. Workers change jobs either through changing employers—which may mean doing the same job for different employers—or through changing jobs while working for one employer (e.g., being promoted). An example of an employer change but not a job change would be an administrative assistant moving from working in a dentist's office to a doctor's office and performing the same tasks of scheduling patients. On the other hand, workers in large firms often receive promotions or move into different jobs without switching employers. For example, the line worker may be promoted to foreman or manager. Employment retention data supplement the above measures on job stability by analyzing the ability of workers to maintain consistent employment.

Examining job transitions illuminates the employment stability aspect of job security. **Table 3.28** shows that, over the 1980s and 1990s, workers were more likely to move from one job to another than to move from a job to either unemployment or non-employment. In this sense, *employment* stability increased, even as *job* stability decreased. This was true for both men and women, although the increase in job-to-job transitions was greater for women than for men. The share of job

**TABLE 3.28** Labor market transitions, 1979-2000

| | 1979 | 1989 | 2000 | Percentage-point change | |
| | | | | 1979-89 | 1989-2000 |
|---|---|---|---|---|---|
| **Percent of workers** | | | | | |
| **with any job transition** | | | | | |
| All | 27.5% | 24.9% | 22.9% | -2.5 | -2.1 |
| Men | 25.5 | 24.1 | 22.1 | -1.4 | -2.0 |
| Women | 30.5 | 26.1 | 23.9 | -4.4 | -2.2 |
| | | | | | |
| **From job to job*** | | | | | |
| All | 11.8% | 12.8% | 13.7% | 1.0 | 0.9 |
| Men | 12.0 | 12.6 | 13.3 | 0.7 | 0.7 |
| Women | 11.5 | 13.0 | 14.3 | 1.6 | 1.2 |
| | | | | | |
| **From job to** | | | | | |
| **unemployment** | | | | | |
| All | 9.9% | 8.3% | 5.7% | -1.7 | -2.5 |
| Men | 2.6 | 2.2 | 2.5 | -0.4 | 0.2 |
| Women | 8.5 | 6.9 | 5.0 | -1.6 | -2.0 |
| | | | | | |
| **From job to** | | | | | |
| **non-employment** | | | | | |
| All | 5.8% | 3.8% | 3.4% | -1.9 | -0.4 |
| Men | 10.9 | 9.2 | 6.3 | -1.6 | -2.9 |
| Women | 10.5 | 6.1 | 4.7 | -4.4 | -1.4 |

* Job change occurred with less than two weeks of unemployment.

Source: Stewart (2002).

transitions among women that were from a job to non-employment fell sharply over the 1980s (4.4 percentage points). Men saw a larger fall in job-to-non-employment transitions over the 1990s relative to women (2.9 versus 1.4 percentage points). Among all workers, the share moving from job to non-employment fell over the 1990s, from 6.1% to 4.7%; the share moving from job to unemployment fell among women, from 6.9% to 5.0%, but increased slightly among men, from 2.2% to 2.5%. Again, the strong economy and low unemployment rates of the 1990s helped to reduce labor market exits or moves into unemployment among workers, even as the length of time a worker spent with one employer (job tenure) fell.

The strong economy of the late 1990s also helped to increase employment tenure, especially among those traditionally most disadvantaged in the labor market. **Table 3.29** shows the proportion of workers who remained employed over one and two years during the early and late 1990s. Employment retention is measured once an individual begins employment, so that the 73.6% one-year employment

**TABLE 3.29** Employment retention over the 1990s

| | Early 1990s (1993-95) | | Late 1990s (1996-99) | | Percentage-point difference | |
|---|---|---|---|---|---|---|
| | 1 year | 2 years | 1 year | 2 years | 1 year | 2 years |
| **Women** | | | | | | |
| All women | 73.6% | 47.5% | 74.6% | 48.1% | 1.1 | 0.6 |
| *Race/ethnicity* | | | | | | |
| White | 75.3% | 49.5% | 76.1% | 50.2% | 0.9 | 0.7 |
| African American | 70.6 | 45.6 | 72.0 | 46.1 | 1.4 | 0.5 |
| Hispanic | 61.3 | 32.2 | 65.6 | 35.3* | 4.3 | 3.2 |
| Other | 71.0 | 46.7 | 75.5 | 49.0 | 4.5 | 2.3 |
| *Citizenship* | | | | | | |
| Native | 74.8% | 49.5% | 75.9% | 50.0% | 1.1 | 0.5 |
| Naturalized | 70.2 | 44.9 | 76.1 | 51.0** | 6.0 | 6.2 |
| Foreign | 58.4 | 28.2 | 61.3 | 31.7** | 2.9 | 3.5 |
| *Education* | | | | | | |
| Less than high school | 51.3% | 19.5% | 59.1% | 26.3%* | 7.8 | 6.8 |
| High school degree | 73.1 | 45.6 | 72.1 | 43.5** | -1.0 | -2.2 |
| Some college | 75.2 | 50.2 | 75.3 | 49.3 | 0.1 | -0.9 |
| College degree | 80.1 | 60.2 | 81.7 | 61.9 | 1.6 | 1.8 |
| **Men** | | | | | | |
| All men | 82.7% | 63.5% | 81.8% | 63.5% | -0.8 | 0.0 |
| *Race/ethnicity* | | | | | | |
| White | 84.8% | 66.8% | 84.2% | 67.7%* | -0.6 | 0.9 |
| African American | 72.7 | 49.6 | 74.3 | 49.9 | 1.7 | 0.3 |
| Hispanic | 71.3 | 46.3 | 73.7 | 50.5* | 2.3 | 4.2 |
| Other | 80.2 | 63.0 | 76.6 | 55.7* | -3.7 | -7.3 |
| *Citizenship* | | | | | | |
| Native | 83.8% | 66.3% | 83.5% | 66.2% | -0.4 | -0.1 |
| Naturalized | 82.5 | 65.1 | 81.4 | 66.5 | -1.1 | 1.4 |
| Foreign | 70.6 | 46.2 | 75.4 | 52.8* | 4.8 | 6.6 |
| *Education* | | | | | | |
| Less than high school | 65.7% | 35.3% | 73.3% | 48.7%* | 7.7 | 13.4 |
| High school degree | 80.6 | 60.8 | 76.9 | 55.1* | -3.8 | -5.7 |
| Some college | 84.5 | 67.6 | 83.8 | 66.5 | -0.7 | -1.1 |
| College degree | 90.3 | 77.8 | 88.8 | 77.6 | -1.5 | -0.2 |

All results across *groups* are statistically significant at the 1% level.
* Results across *years* are statistically significant at the 1% level.
** Results across *years* are statistically significant at the 5% level.
Sample includes workers 25-54.

Source: Authors' analysis of Survey of Income and Program Participation (SIPP) 1993 and 1996 panel data.

retention among all women in the early 1990s indicates that nearly three-fourths of women who were employed between 1993 and 1995 still had a job one year later. Among both men and women, workers with less than a high school degree and Hispanics were most likely to remain employed in the later 1990s, relative to the early 1990s, indicating that the economic boom of the 1990s boosted the employment prospects of these traditionally disadvantaged groups. The data indicate that, even as job stability decreased generally among men in the past decades, employment retention has increased among women (especially minority, foreign-born, and less-educated women) and African American, Hispanic, foreign, and less-educated men over the economic boom of the 1990s. Low unemployment, which brought workers into the labor market (as shown above through the increases in employment rates and labor force participation), also helped workers stay employed once they got there, even if staying there meant job switching.

### Displacement

Job stability can decline because workers change jobs more frequently in order to take advantage of other opportunities, or it can fall because employers lay off or fire workers in greater numbers. The evidence of poor wage-growth for those with weak job stability argues that much of the increase in job instability was probably involuntary. This section focuses special attention on involuntary job loss or displacement.

**Table 3.30** reports data for the 1980s and 1990s on the share of workers that have experienced involuntary job loss during four different three-year periods. The data show that, in any given three-year period over the last two decades, 8-12% of workers suffered at least one involuntary job loss. The 1981-83 period, which included the 1982 recession, had an average unemployment rate of 9.0% and, at 12.8%, the highest proportion of job losses over the last two decades. The job loss rate fell to 8.5% during the economic recovery years of 1987-89, when the average unemployment rate was a much lower 5.7%. Job displacement rates rose again in the 1990s, to 10.9% in 1991-93, when the average unemployment rate was 7.1%. Despite the economic recovery that lowered the average unemployment rate to 4.6% between 1997 and 1999, the job loss rate fell only to 8.6%, comparable to that during the 1987-89 recovery, even though unemployment was 1.1 percentage points less in the later period.

Table 3.30 also summarizes how the reasons for job loss have changed over time. Plant closings and "slack work" both declined between the two recessionary periods, 1981-83 and 1991-93, reflecting in part the much lower unemployment rates in the second recession and the steeper manufacturing downturn in the 1980s recession. Over the same period, however, "position abolished," a term that may reflect the downsizing phenomenon, rose sharply, from 1.4% to 2.2%. Displace-

**TABLE 3.30** Rate of job loss by reason,* 1981-99

| | | | | | Percentage-point change | | |
|---|---|---|---|---|---|---|---|
| Reason | 1981-83 | 1987-89 | 1991-93 | 1997-99 | 1981-83/ 1987-89 | 1991-93/ 1997-99 | 1987-89/ 1997-99 |
| Plant closing | 4.5% | 3.6% | 3.6% | 2.9% | -0.9 | -0.7 | -0.7 |
| Slack work | 5.4 | 2.4 | 3.7 | 2.3 | -3.0 | -1.4 | -0.1 |
| Position abolished | 1.4 | 1.1 | 2.2 | 1.7 | -0.3 | -0.5 | 0.6 |
| Other | 1.5 | 1.3 | 1.4 | 1.8 | -0.2 | 0.4 | 0.5 |
| All reasons | 12.8% | 8.5% | 10.9% | 8.6% | -4.3 | -2.3 | 0.1 |
| Unemployment rate | 9.0% | 5.7% | 7.1% | 4.6% | -3.3 | -0.9 | -1.1 |

* Data are adjusted for change in recall period; "other" response has been discounted in all years.

Source: Farber (2001).

ments due to "position abolished" remained relatively high through 1997-99 (1.7%), despite the economic recovery.

When workers leave their jobs voluntarily, they generally move on to better circumstances in a new job with better pay or working conditions. (They may also choose to leave work to pursue other activities such as education, childrearing, or retirement.) When workers lose their jobs involuntarily, however, they typically pay a large economic price. **Table 3.31** provides estimates of some of the principal economic costs associated with involuntary job loss. The first obvious cost is the difficulty finding a new job. Among all workers who reported losing their jobs in the previous three years (the data cover the period 1981-95), 35.1% (see last column) were out of work at the time they were interviewed about their experience of job loss. While not all of these displaced, out-of-work workers were looking for a job at the time they were interviewed, if they were, then the 35.1% out-of-work rate would translate to an unemployment rate five times the average rate for the 1981-95 period (6.9%). Among the 65% or so of workers that did manage to find new jobs, average wages at the new job were lower than wages at the old one. Among the workers who moved from full-time to full-time work, their new positions paid, on average, 9.2% less than the old jobs. Many previous full-timers, however, were not able to find full-time work (though some displaced part-timers did manage to find new full-time positions). Therefore, the average decline in hourly wages for all workers, including those who went from full-time to part-time work and vice versa, was even steeper (14.2%). With both lower wages and fewer hours, workers who

**TABLE 3.31** The costs of job loss, averages for 1980s and 1990s

| | Reason for job loss | | | | |
| --- | --- | --- | --- | --- | --- |
| Post-loss outcome | Plant closing | Slack work | Position abolished | Other | All |
| Out of work* | 30.2% | 40.9% | 29.7% | 37.2% | 35.1% |
| Average wage change | | | | | |
| All job changes | -13.0% | -14.3% | -19.2% | -11.4% | -14.2% |
| Full time to full time | -9.3 | -8.7 | -12.0 | -6.5 | -9.2 |
| Average wage loss,** compared to continuously employed | -13.2% | -13.0% | -16.3% | -9.2% | -13.0% |
| Health benefits before loss/no health benefits after loss | n.a. | n.a. | n.a. | n.a. | 28.7% |
| No health benefits after loss including those with no coverage at lost job | n.a. | n.a. | n.a. | n.a. | 14.0% |

\* Of those who lost job in the last three years, the share out of work at time of interview.
\*\* Full-time to full-time job changes only.

Sources: Authors' analysis of Farber (1997a) and Gardner (1995).

lost full-time jobs and managed only to find part-time replacement jobs were hit especially hard.

The preceding figures for wage loss compare displaced workers' wages on their new jobs with those earned on their old jobs. These estimates of the wage costs of job loss, however, almost certainly underestimate the true wage loss. Some of these workers lost their jobs as many as three years before they were asked about the wages at their new job. If they had not lost their old jobs and had been able to continue at that same job for one to three years longer, many would have received further nominal pay increases. When we compare displaced workers with similar workers who did not lose their jobs, the average decline in wages for those who went from full-time to full-time jobs grows from 9.2% to 13.0% (see row 4).

Moreover, wages are only part of the story. Many displaced workers also lose the non-wage benefits provided through their previous employers. Of those workers who had health benefits on the job they lost, 28.7% (see row 5) had no employer-provided health benefits on their new jobs. Some displaced workers, of course, had no health insurance coverage at their old jobs but found new jobs that did provide insurance. When these workers are included in the calculation, job displacement reduced health insurance coverage by 14.0 percentage points (see row 6). Both health insurance figures paint an overly rosy picture, however, because, as noted above, many displaced workers (35.1%) were unable to find any work at all.

## Job security

The preceding sections on job stability and job displacement examined statistical measures of the economy's tendency to create and destroy long-term relationships with one employer. That discussion emphasized the importance of differentiating between objective measures of job stability and more subjective, and probably more important, measures of job security—workers' perceptions of their ability to remain in their current jobs as long as they perform satisfactorily. Much of the evidence presented on job stability and displacement suggests that the underlying level of job instability is higher in the 1990s than it was in the 1980s and earlier periods. Since the decline in job stability and the rise in job displacement appear to be linked to worsening economic circumstances for affected workers, we believe that this evidence on instability supports the conclusion that job insecurity has also increased in the 1990s. In this section, we turn to direct evidence on job security, based on workers' evaluations of the security of their current jobs.

**Table 3.32** presents results on reported levels of job security from a nationally representative survey of workers in the years 1978, 1989, and 1996 (no survey data exist for 1979, our normal comparison year). The share of workers who said that they thought they were very or fairly likely to lose their jobs in the next 12 months was 8.0% in both 1978 and 1989 (despite a slight decline in the national unemployment rate between the two years). Between 1989 and 1996, however, the share of workers who thought they faced a significant chance of losing their jobs in the next year rose 3.2 percentage points to 11.2%. Perceived job security fell over the period even though the national unemployment rate was essentially identical in the two years (5.3% in 1989 compared to 5.4% in 1996). The same polling data also show a large drop between 1978 and 1996 in the share of workers who thought that they were not at all likely to lose their job in the next 12 months. In 1978, 71.0% of workers thought that they faced very little chance of losing their job; by 1996, the figure had fallen 10.7 percentage points to 60.3%. As before, most of the decline in perceived job security took place in the 1990s, with 8.9 percentage points of the decline occurring between 1989 and 1996, compared to only a 1.8 percentage-point drop between 1978 and 1989.

Workers also appear less optimistic about their employment prospects in the event that they do lose their jobs. In all three years, just under 40% of workers thought that it would not be at all easy to find another job with the same pay and benefits as their current job. The share of pessimists increased slightly (1.6 percentage points) from 1989 to 1996, from 37.8% to 39.4% of all workers. Over the same

**TABLE 3.32** Perceptions of job security, 1978-96 (percent)

| | | | | Percentage-point change | |
|---|---|---|---|---|---|
| | 1978* | 1989 | 1996 | 1978-89 | 1989-96 |
| How likely are you to lose your job or be laid off in next 12 months? | | | | | |
| Very or fairly likely | 8.0% | 8.0% | 11.2% | 0.0 | 3.2 |
| Not at all likely | 71.0 | 69.2 | 60.3 | -1.8 | -8.9 |
| How easy is it to find a job with another employer with about the same income and benefits? | | | | | |
| Not easy at all | 38.7% | 37.8% | 39.4% | -0.9 | 1.6 |
| Very easy | 28.1 | 34.2 | 27.1 | 6.1 | -7.1 |
| Unemployment rate | 6.1% | 5.3% | 5.4% | -0.8 | 0.1 |

* No data available for 1979.

Source: Aaronson and Sullivan (1998) analysis of GSS data.

period, the share of optimists—those who thought it would be very easy to find a new job with the same pay and benefits—fell sharply, from 34.2% to 27.1% of all workers.

The data on workers' perceptions show a high and growing level of job insecurity in the 1990s, and these subjective impressions are consistent with the increases in job instability over the last two decades. They also support the conclusion that rising job instability does not respond to workers' desires to enter more "flexible" employment relationships, but rather represents an additional psychological and financial burden on workers.

As mentioned earlier, little information is available on job stability and job security after the mid-1990s. **Figure 3P** presents one, imperfect, indicator of job security that is available through 2001. The data in the figure show the share of all unemployed workers who are unemployed because they quit their previous jobs to look for new ones. When times are good and unemployment falls, the share of job leavers among all unemployed workers rises, reflecting both lower levels of layoffs and workers' greater confidence about their ability to find new, better jobs. When times are bad and the unemployment rate rises, the share of job leavers in total unemployment falls, reflecting both an influx of involuntarily displaced workers and the general unwillingness of workers to give up their jobs to search for new ones. As has historically been the case, the decline in the unemployment rate during the 1990s economic recovery led to a rise in the job-leavers rate, suggesting that

**FIGURE 3P** Job leavers as share of unemployed, 1967-2001

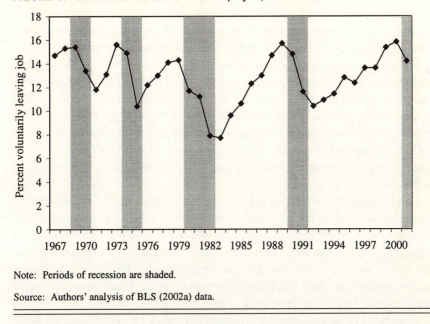

Note: Periods of recession are shaded.

Source: Authors' analysis of BLS (2002a) data.

workers' insecurity abated during the recovery. At the same time, the job-leavers data also suggest that underlying job insecurity may have been higher at the end of the 1990s than it was in earlier periods. In 2000, with the national unemployment rate at 4.0%, the job-leavers rate had risen only to the same level it reached in 1989, when the unemployment rate was 5.3%, more than a full percentage point higher. If the historical relationship between unemployment and the job-leavers rate had been present at the end of the 1990s, we would expect to have seen a higher job-leavers rate than we actually observed. The economic developments of the 1980s and 1990s appear to have raised the level of insecurity that workers feel at any given level of unemployment.

## Conclusion

The jobs picture worsened as the economy moved through the labor market recession that began in 2000. Unemployment did not increase as much as in the 1990-92 recession, but private sector employment has fallen more. Women have lost more employment, relative to previous recessions, although men have still lost more jobs than women overall. African American and Hispanic workers have been especially hard hit by the recession, although increased unemployment has been more evenly distributed across educational groups than in prior recessions. The terrorist attacks of September 11 played a role in deepening the recession and in increasing job losses in transportation and retail sales.

The strong wage and income gains of the latter half of the 1990s were contingent on a strong labor market and plenty of employment opportunities. With the recession and its ensuing job losses, the wage gains of the late 1990s may be eroded, especially if the recovery turns out to be a "jobless" one" as in 1990-92, when unemployment continued to increase for 18 months after the NBER had declared the recession officially over. As this chapter has shown, higher unemployment hurts lower-income families more than higher-income families.

Employment is the foundation for family income, wages, and economic well being. When jobs are plentiful, workers are in a better position to search for higher-paid employment and are in a better bargaining position with respect to their employer when they want higher pay. However, even with the strong economy of the late 1990s, the level of fringe benefits fell relative to earlier decades. Workers are now less likely to have paid time off, and the much-touted "flexible workplace" has taken hold in only a handful of firms.

Over the 1990s, employment retention increased for women, as did labor force participation and employment rates. For men, however, the 1990s saw a continued decline in labor force participation and employment rates, as well as employment retention. Job stability has been declining for the past few decades, and this trend may indicate a decline in job security overall. The recession has increased feelings of job insecurity, and, until unemployment falls back to its pre-recession levels, workers will continue to wonder whether they will be able to maintain their current employment situations.

# Wealth: deeper in debt

The main focus of the preceding chapters has been on the wages and incomes of American families. This chapter examines wealth in the United States and its distribution among households. Like wages and incomes, wealth is a vital component of a family's standard of living. Over the long term, families accumulate wealth in order to finance education, purchase a house, start a small business, and finance retirement. In the short term, wealth—particularly financial assets such as checking account balances, stocks, and bonds—can help families cope with financial emergencies related to unemployment or illness. Families that do not have sufficient wealth for short-term or long-term expenses accumulate debt to purchase these goods and services. For example, young people take out student loans to finance their education, families take on mortgages to finance their homes, and individuals use credit cards when they have an unexpected expense.

Several key features about American wealth stand out. First, wealth distribution is highly unequal. The wealthiest 1% of all households control about 38% of national wealth, while the bottom 80% of households hold only 17%. The ownership of stocks is particularly unequal. The top 1% of stock owners hold almost half (47.7%) of all stocks, by value, while the bottom 80% own just 4.1% of total stock holdings.

Second, the total wealth of the typical American household improved only marginally during the 1990s. The net worth of the average household in the middle 20% of the wealth distribution rose about $2,200 in the 1990s—from $58,800 in 1989 to $61,000 in 1998. Over the same period, the value of the stock holdings of this typical household grew $5,500, and the value of non-stock assets increased $8,500. Home ownership—the most important asset for most American families—rose over the late 1990s, especially among non-white households. Meanwhile, typical household debt rose $11,800. The relatively modest gains in stock and non-stock assets combined with the explosion in household debt meant that the 1990s were far less generous to typical households than business-page headlines often suggested.

Third, only households at the very top of the income spectrum are likely to be adequately prepared for retirement. For many Americans, the 1990s boom left them less prepared for retirement than before: for two out of five Americans, income from Social Security, pensions, and defined-contribution plans will replace less than half of their pre-retirement income.

Fourth, even well into the decade-long boom in the stock market, most Americans had no economically meaningful stake in it. The most recent government data show that less than half of households hold stock in any form, including mutual funds and 401(k)-style pension plans. The same data reveal that 64% of households have stock holdings worth $5,000 or less. While this means that most Americans did not benefit from the stock market boom of the late 1990s, it also means that most have not been directly hurt by the crash of the stock market in 2000.

Finally, for the typical household, rising debt, not a rising stock market, was the big story of the 1990s. Household debt grew much more rapidly than household income in the last decade. By 2001, total household debt exceeded total household disposable income by nearly 10%. Households in the middle of the wealth distribution absorbed the largest share of this run-up in debt. While low nominal interest rates have made it easier for households to carry the greatly expanded debt, many households appear to be straining. The most recent government data show that 14% of middle-income households have debt-service obligations that exceed 40% of their income; 9% have at least one bill that is more than 60 days past due. For many, the debt run-up begins from the day they exit college: college debt loads have risen substantially over the 1990s. Meanwhile, despite the robust state of the economy, personal bankruptcy rates reached all-time highs by 2001.

## Net worth

The concept of wealth used in this chapter is net worth, which is the sum of all of a family's assets—house, checking and savings account balances, stock holdings, retirement funds (such as 401(k) plans and individual retirement accounts), and other assets—minus the sum of all of the family's liabilities—mortgage, credit-card debt, student loans, and other debts. The concept of net worth excludes assets in defined-benefit contribution plans because workers do not le-

**TABLE 4.1** Distribution of income and wealth, 1998 (percent)

|  | Distribution of: | | |
| --- | --- | --- | --- |
|  | Household income | Net worth | Net financial assets |
| All | 100.0% | 100.0% | 100.0% |
| Top 1% | 16.6 | 38.1 | 47.3 |
| Next 9% | 24.6 | 32.9 | 32.4 |
| Bottom 90% | 58.8 | 29.0 | 20.2 |

Source: Unpublished analysis of 1998 Survey of Consumer Finance data by Wolff. For detailed information on table sources, see Table Notes.

gally own the assets held in these plans and thus do not necessarily benefit from improvements in the value of assets used to pay the defined benefit. (Their companies do benefit, however, because higher asset values lower the contributions companies have to pay to meet future defined benefits). Nor do workers suffer financially if the underlying assets underperform expectations. For similar reasons, this analysis also excludes Social Security and Medicare from the net worth calculations (although the section below projecting retirement income does include expected income from Social Security).

A key feature of the wealth distribution is that it is much more unequal than either the distribution of wages or incomes. **Table 4.1** shows income and wealth data from the most recent Survey of Consumer Finances (SCF), conducted by the Federal Reserve Board. The first column shows that, in 1998 (the latest year available), the 1% of households with the highest incomes received 16.6% of all income. By comparison, the wealthiest 1% of households, in the same year, owned 38.1% of all wealth. At the other end of the distribution, the 90% of households with the lowest incomes received 58.8% of all income, but the 90% with the lowest net worth held only 29.0% of all wealth.

Over the 1990s, household net worth increased substantially. (We examine the growth in net worth primarily through 1999, rather than 2000 as we do in the rest of the book, because 1999 was the peak of the stock market). **Table 4.2** shows that between 1989 and 1999, net worth increased at an annual rate of 5.9%, substantially more than in previous decades. The growth was led by the rapid growth in the value of stock (at an annual rate of 12.7%) and mutual funds (at an annual rate of 16.8%). However, between 1999 and 2001, net worth decreased dramatically, at an annual rate of 10.8%. Stock values alone dropped 23.1% each year.

**TABLE 4.2** Growth of household wealth, 1949-2001

| Type of wealth | Annual growth for average household | | | | | | |
| --- | --- | --- | --- | --- | --- | --- | --- |
| | 1949-67 | 1967-73 | 1973-79 | 1979-89 | 1989-99 | 1999-2001 | 1989-2001 |
| Total net worth* | 2.3% | -0.8% | -0.8% | 2.3% | 5.9% | -10.8% | 2.9% |
| Net tangible assets** | 2.7 | -0.6 | -0.2 | 2.5 | 5.5 | -8.3 | 3.0 |
| Net financial assets*** | 1.9 | 3.9 | 2.1 | 1.2 | -0.7 | 5.2 | 0.2 |
| **Financial assets:** | | | | | | | |
| Stock | 7.0% | -8.8% | -7.4% | 4.0% | 12.7% | -23.1% | 5.7% |
| Mutual funds | 11.7 | -8.3 | -9.0 | 19.9 | 16.8 | -5.5 | 12.7 |
| Stock and mutual funds | 7.2 | -8.7 | -7.5 | 5.6 | 13.6 | -18.3 | 7.5 |

\*      Includes all households, personal trusts, and nonprofit organizations.
\*\*    Consumer durables, housing, and land assets less home mortgages.
\*\*\*  Financial assets less nonmortgage debt.

Source: Authors' analysis of Federal Reserve Board (2001a) and Census Bureau (2001b) data.

**TABLE 4.3** Share of aggregate net worth by income quintile, 1992 and 2000

| Income category | 1992 | 2000 | Difference between 1992 and 2000 |
| --- | --- | --- | --- |
| **Total** | 100.0% | 100.0% | 0.0 |
| 81-100% | 59.6 | 62.9 | 3.3 |
| 61-80% | 17.4 | 16.5 | -0.9 |
| 41-60% | 11.7 | 9.8 | -1.9 |
| 21-40% | 7.4 | 7.2 | -0.2 |
| 0-20% | 3.9 | 3.7 | -0.2 |

Source: Maki and Palumbo (2001).

As noted earlier, the distribution of wealth is highly unequal, and the decline in financial assets in the late 1990s did not alter this inequality. **Table 4.3** shows that the distribution of wealth by household income became more unequal between 1992 and 2000 (which includes the period of stock market decline in 2000). While the bottom 80% of households saw their share of aggregate net worth fall between 1992 and 2000, households in the top 20% of income saw their share increase from 59.6% to 62.9%.

**Tables 4.4** and **4.5** use data from the six SCF surveys conducted between

**TABLE 4.4** Changes in the distribution of household wealth,* 1962-98 (percent)

| | | | | | | | Percentage-point change | | |
|---|---|---|---|---|---|---|---|---|---|
| Wealth class | 1962 | 1983 | 1989 | 1992 | 1995 | 1998 | 1962-83 | 1983-89 | 1989-98 |
| **Top fifth** | 81.0% | 81.3% | 83.5% | 83.8% | 83.9% | 83.4% | 0.4 | 2.2 | -0.1 |
| Top 1% | 33.4 | 33.8 | 37.4 | 37.2 | 38.5 | 38.1 | 0.3 | 3.6 | 0.7 |
| Next 4% | 21.2 | 22.3 | 21.6 | 22.8 | 21.8 | 21.3 | 1.2 | -0.8 | -0.2 |
| Next 5% | 12.4 | 12.1 | 11.6 | 11.8 | 11.5 | 11.5 | -0.2 | -0.5 | -0.1 |
| Next 10% | 14.0 | 13.1 | 13.0 | 12.0 | 12.1 | 12.5 | -0.9 | -0.1 | -0.5 |
| **Bottom four-fifths** | 19.1% | 18.7% | 16.5% | 16.2% | 16.1% | 16.6% | -0.4 | -2.2 | 0.1 |
| Fourth | 13.4 | 12.6 | 12.3 | 11.5 | 11.4 | 11.9 | -0.8 | -0.3 | -0.4 |
| Middle | 5.4 | 5.2 | 4.8 | 4.4 | 4.5 | 4.5 | -0.2 | -0.4 | -0.3 |
| Second | 1.0 | 1.2 | 0.8 | 0.9 | 0.9 | 0.8 | 0.2 | -0.3 | -0.1 |
| Lowest | -0.7 | -0.3 | -1.5 | -0.5 | -0.7 | -0.6 | 0.4 | -1.2 | 0.9 |
| **Total** | 100.0% | 100.0% | 100.0% | 100.0% | 100.0% | 100.0% | | | |

* Wealth defined as net worth (household assets minus debts).

Source: Unpublished analysis of Survey of Consumer Finance data by Wolff.

**TABLE 4.5** Change in average wealth* by wealth class, 1962-98 (thousands of 1998 dollars)

| | | | | | | | Annualized growth (percent) | | |
|---|---|---|---|---|---|---|---|---|---|
| Wealth class | 1962 | 1983 | 1989 | 1992 | 1995 | 1998 | 1962-83 | 1983-89 | 1989-98 |
| **Top fifth** | $587.4 | $864.5 | $1,017.1 | $991.9 | $917.8 | $1,126.7 | 1.9% | 2.7% | 1.1% |
| Top 1% | 4,851.8 | 7,175.1 | 9,101.7 | 8,796.4 | 8,422.5 | 10,203.7 | 1.9 | 4.0 | 1.3 |
| Next 4% | 768.1 | 1,186.8 | 1,313.4 | 1,351.4 | 1,192.9 | 1,441.2 | 2.1 | 1.7 | 1.0 |
| Next 5% | 359.1 | 516.2 | 565.5 | 559.3 | 504.5 | 623.5 | 1.7 | 1.5 | 1.1 |
| Next 10% | 202.9 | 278.7 | 315.9 | 283.9 | 263.9 | 344.9 | 1.5 | 2.1 | 1.0 |
| **Bottom four-fifths** | $34.6 | $49.6 | $50.2 | $48.0 | $44.0 | $56.1 | 1.7% | 0.2% | 1.3% |
| Fourth | 97.2 | 133.6 | 150.0 | 135.7 | 124.9 | 161.3 | 1.5 | 1.9 | 0.8 |
| Middle | 39.4 | 55.5 | 58.8 | 51.9 | 49.1 | 61.0 | 1.6 | 1.0 | 0.4 |
| Second | 6.9 | 12.5 | 10.2 | 10.5 | 9.6 | 11.1 | 2.9 | -3.3 | 0.9 |
| Lowest | -5.3 | -3.2 | -18.4 | -6.0 | -7.6 | -8.9 | n.a. | n.a. | n.a. |
| Average | $145.1 | $212.6 | $243.6 | $236.8 | $218.8 | $270.3 | 1.8% | 2.3% | 1.2% |
| Median | 38.8 | 54.6 | 58.4 | 49.9 | 48.8 | 60.7 | 1.6 | 1.1 | 0.4 |

* Wealth defined as net worth (household assets minus debts).

Source: Unpublished analysis of Survey of Consumer Finance data by Wolff.

1962 and 1998, the latest year available, to provide a more detailed analysis of the distribution of wealth. In 1998, the top fifth of households held 83.4% of all wealth; the middle fifth held a mere 4.5%; and the bottom fifth actually had negative net worth—they owed more than they owned. Table 4.5 puts dollar figures to these wealth shares. In 1998, the average net worth of the top 1% of households was about $10.2 million. Wealth holdings, while still substantial, drop off sharply for the rest of the top fifth of households. The loss of assets between 1999 and 2001 decreased the holdings among the wealthiest households, but probably did not change the distribution of wealth.

The data in Table 4.5 also illustrate how the absolute level of wealth changed over time for households at different points in the distribution. Over the 1990s, the average wealth of the top 1% of households grew over $1 million, from $9.1 million in 1989 to $10.2 million in 1998. Meanwhile, the average wealth of the middle 20% of households grew only marginally, from $58,800 in 1989 to $61,000 in 1998. Wealth levels among the poorest households improved considerably in the 1990s, but the poorest 20% of households still finished the decade with negative net worth (–$8,900 in 1998, up from –$18,400 in 1989).

Inequality has also increased among the very wealthy. **Figure 4A** shows the minimum, average, and maximum levels of wealth of the members of the Forbes 400, an annual, unrepresentative but carefully constructed list of the 400 wealthiest people in the United States. The graph shows wealth holdings on a log scale, which compresses large differences and helps fit the three lines on the same graph. The gap between the wealthiest and the least wealthy members of the Forbes 400 grew significantly in the 1990s, especially after 1995. However, as the stock market began to slide, the net worth began to fall for the very rich fell (after 1999) and for the average rich (after 2000). Even so, the average net worth of the Forbes 400 in 2001 was still above its 1998 level. Overall, these data suggest that inequality at the very top (above the level captured by the SCF, which, by design, excludes members of the Forbes 400) grew more rapidly in the 1990s than it did in the 1980s.

Across almost all levels of wealth, wealth grew more slowly in the period 1989-98 than it did in the periods 1962-83 and 1983-89. Average wealth grew at a 1.2% annual rate between 1989 and 1998, below the 1.8% rate for 1962-83 and the 2.3% rate for 1983-89. The same was true for the median household, whose wealth grew at only a 0.4% annual rate in the 1990s, far lower than the rate for 1962-83 (1.6%) or 1983-89 (1.1%). The apparent slowdown in wealth accumulation in the 1990s, however, blurs the very different experience between 1989 and 1995—when net worth fell across most of the wealth distribution—and 1995-98, when wealth grew rapidly by historical standards.

**FIGURE 4A** Annual net worth of "Forbes 400" wealthiest individuals

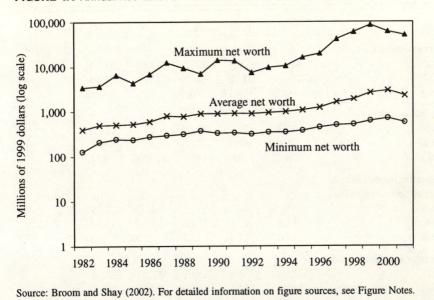

Source: Broom and Shay (2002). For detailed information on figure sources, see Figure Notes.

### Racial divide

The data presented so far mask an important feature of the wealth distribution: wealth is very unequally distributed by race. **Table 4.6** presents wealth data separately for blacks and whites. The first section shows average wealth by race. In 1998, the latest year available, the average black household had a net worth equal to about 18% of the average white household. This ratio remained relatively constant over the period 1983-98, suggesting that economic growth over those two decades did little to narrow the wealth gap between the two races.

The second section of Table 4.6 gives the median wealth holdings for blacks and whites. The most striking aspect of this data is the extremely low level of median wealth of black households. In 1998, the median black household had a net worth of $10,000, about 12% of the corresponding figure for whites. Since the median wealth of black families is so low, relatively small dollar movements have a large impact on the ratio of the black median to the white median. The 12% figure in 1998 was far better than the 3% ratio in 1989, but below the 17% figure for 1992. (In fact, the absolute level of wealth in the median black household was $2,000 lower in 1998 than in 1992).

**TABLE 4.6** Wealth* by race, 1983-98 (thousands of 1998 dollars)

| Race | 1983 | 1989 | 1992 | 1995 | 1998 |
|---|---|---|---|---|---|
| **Average wealth** | | | | | |
| Black | $46.8 | $49.3 | $52.9 | $43.6 | $58.3 |
| White | 248.4 | 293.9 | 284.4 | 259.2 | 320.9 |
| Ratio | 0.19 | 0.17 | 0.19 | 0.17 | 0.18 |
| **Median wealth** | | | | | |
| Black | $4.8 | $2.2 | $12.0 | $7.9 | $10.0 |
| White | 71.5 | 84.9 | 71.3 | 65.2 | 81.7 |
| Ratio | 0.07 | 0.03 | 0.17 | 0.12 | 0.12 |
| **Households with zero or negative net wealth (%)** | | | | | |
| Black | 34.1% | 40.7% | 31.5% | 31.3% | 27.4% |
| White | 11.3 | 12.1 | 13.8 | 15.0 | 14.8 |
| Ratio | 3.01 | 3.38 | 2.28 | 2.09 | 2.09 |
| **Average financial wealth** | | | | | |
| Black | $23.6 | $24.1 | $30.1 | $22.7 | $37.6 |
| White | 183.0 | 222.2 | 219.0 | 201.5 | 254.8 |
| Ratio | 0.13 | 0.11 | 0.14 | 0.11 | 0.15 |
| **Median financial wealth** | | | | | |
| Black | $0.0 | $0.0 | $0.2 | $0.2 | $1.2 |
| White | 19.9 | 26.9 | 21.9 | 19.3 | 37.6 |
| Ratio | 0.00 | 0.00 | 0.01 | 0.01 | 0.03 |

* Wealth defined as net worth (household assets minus debts).

Source: Unpublished analysis of Survey of Consumer Finance data by Wolff.

*Low net worth*

Another important feature of the wealth distribution is the large share of households with low, zero, or negative net worth. **Table 4.7** reports the share of all households with zero or negative net worth or net worth of less than $10,000. In 1998, 18% of all households had a net worth that was zero or negative; just over 30% had net worth of less than $10,000. As before, the experience of black households differs significantly from that of white households. As Table 4.6 (third section) shows, in 1998 almost twice as many black households (27.4%) as white households (14.8%) had zero or negative net worth. Half of black households had a net worth of $10,000 or less, compared to 30% for the population as a whole.

**TABLE 4.7** Households with low net wealth, 1962-98 (percent of all households)

| | | | | | | Percentage-point change | | |
|---|---|---|---|---|---|---|---|---|
| Net worth | 1962 | 1983 | 1989 | 1995 | 1998 | 1962-83 | 1983-89 | 1989-98 |
| Zero or negative | 23.6% | 15.5% | 17.9% | 18.5% | 18.0% | -8.1 | 2.4 | 0.1 |
| Less than $10,000* | 34.3 | 29.7 | 31.8 | 31.9 | 30.3 | -4.6 | 2.1 | -1.5 |

\* Constant 1998 dollars.

Source: Unpublished analysis of Survey of Consumer Finance data by Wolff.

The overall share of households with low net worth remained relatively constant over the 1990s. The circumstances of black households, however, appeared to improve substantially over the period, with the share having zero or negative net worth falling from 40.7% in 1989 to 27.4% in 1998.

To summarize, the data on net worth reveal the highly unequal distribution of wealth. A large share of the population has little or no net worth, while, over the last 40 years at least, the wealthiest 20% has consistently held over 80% of all wealth and the top 1% has controlled close to 40%. Wealth inequality increased sharply during the 1980s and showed no signs of improving over the 1990s. The loss of paper assets between 1999 and 2001 led to sharp declines in net worth, but did not likely change the distribution of wealth assets overall.

## Assets

The preceding section summarized the overall distribution of net worth—the sum of each household's assets and liabilities. This section focuses on the first major component of net worth, assets. Households hold a variety of assets, from houses and boats to stocks and bonds. The distribution of assets among wealth classes, however, differs significantly by asset. Some assets, such as stocks and bonds, are highly concentrated; other assets, such as houses, are more widely held. The differences in these distributions are strongly related to overall wealth. Wealthy households, for example, tend to have much of their wealth in stocks and bonds, while the less-well-to-do typically hold most of their wealth in housing equity.

**Table 4.8** shows the distribution of several types of household assets in 1998. The top 0.5% of stock-owning households held 37.0% of all stock, while the bottom 80% of households owned just 4.1%. By contrast, the top 0.5% of

**TABLE 4.8** Distribution of asset ownership across households, 1998

| | Percentage of all holdings of each asset: | | | | |
|---|---|---|---|---|---|
| Percentage of owners | Common stock excluding pensions | All common stock | Non-equity financial assets | Housing equity | Net worth |
| Top 0.5% | 41.4% | 37.0% | 24.2% | 10.2% | 25.6% |
| Next 0.5% | 11.8 | 10.7 | 7.8 | 4.6 | 8.4 |
| Next 4% | 27.7 | 27.2 | 26.2 | 20.5 | 23.4 |
| Next 5% | 10.3 | 11.3 | 14.0 | 15.4 | 11.4 |
| Next 10% | 7.2 | 9.8 | 13.9 | 20.1 | 12.8 |
| Bottom 80% | 1.7 | 4.1 | 14.0 | 29.3 | 18.5 |

Source: Poterba (2000) analysis of Survey of Consumer Finances data.

home-owning households held only 10.2% of total housing equity, while the bottom 80% held 29.3%. While housing equity is unequally distributed, it is more equally distributed than stocks.

*Stocks*

The 1990s witnessed a breathtaking run-up in the price of stocks, followed by a stock market crash in 2000. As **Figure 4B** illustrates, the inflation-adjusted value of the Standard & Poor's 500 index of stocks increased 234% between 1990 and 2000, then fell 19% between 2000 and 2001. However, data on stock ownership show that the stock market is of little or no importance to the wealth holdings of the vast majority of U.S. households. Thus, few Americans actually benefited from the increase in stocks over the 1990s and, similarly, few suffered when the stock market fell in 2001.

The last year of data available on the distribution of stock ownership is 1998, near the peak of the stock market bubble. (The distribution of stock ownership in 2001 is not likely to have changed a great deal since 1998.) Even in 1998, when so much media attention was directed at the booming market, a majority of U.S. households had no stock holdings of any form, direct (owning shares in a particular company) or indirect (owning shares through a mutual fund or through a 401(k)-style, defined-contribution pension plan). **Table 4.9** summarizes data on the share of households with direct or indirect stock holdings. In 1998, just under half (48.2%) of households owned stock in any form. Only about one-third (36.3%) held stock worth $5,000 or more.

Black households were especially unlikely to hold financial assets such as stocks and bonds (government and corporate debt). In 1998, the average finan-

**FIGURE 4B** Growth of U.S. stock market, 1955-2001 (2001 dollars)

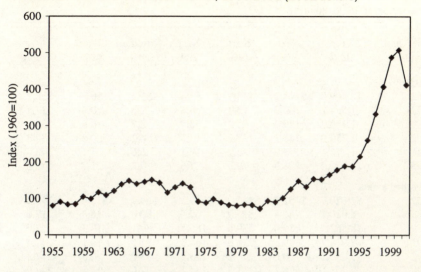

Source: Authors' analysis of data from ERP.

**TABLE 4.9** Share of households owning stock (percent), 1962-98

| Stock holdings | 1962 | 1983 | 1989 | 1992 | 1995 | 1998 | Percentage-point change 1989-98 |
|---|---|---|---|---|---|---|---|
| **Any stock holdings** | | | | | | | |
| Direct holdings | 10.7% | 13.7% | 13.1% | 14.8% | 15.2% | 19.2% | 6.1 |
| Indirect holdings | | | 24.7 | 28.4 | 30.2 | 43.4 | 18.7 |
| Total | | | 31.7 | 37.2 | 40.4 | 48.2 | 16.5 |
| **Stock holdings of $5,000 or more*** | | | | | | | |
| Direct holdings | | | 10.0% | 11.4% | 12.3% | 13.6% | 3.6 |
| Indirect holdings | | | 16.9 | 21.5 | 22.7 | 32.2 | 15.3 |
| Total | | | 22.6 | 27.3 | 28.8 | 36.3 | 13.7 |

* Constant 1998 dollars.

Source: Unpublished analysis of Survey of Consumer Finance data by Wolff.

cial wealth of black households (see the fourth section of Table 4.6) was only about 15% of the average for white households. The median financial wealth for blacks (see the last section of Table 4.6) was just $1,200, about 3% of the corresponding figure for whites.

**TABLE 4.10** Household assets and liabilities by wealth class (thousands of 1998 dollars)

| Assets and liabilities | Top 1.0% | Next 9% | Next 10% | Next 20% | Middle 20% | Bottom 40% | Average |
|---|---|---|---|---|---|---|---|
| **Stocks*** | | | | | | | |
| 1962 | $2,409.0 | $123.2 | $13.7 | $4.4 | $1.1 | $0.3 | $38.3 |
| 1983 | 1,564.2 | 100.9 | 12.1 | 4.6 | 1.6 | 0.4 | 27.7 |
| 1989 | 1,180.7 | 129.7 | 25.4 | 8.9 | 3.7 | 0.6 | 29.2 |
| 1992 | 1,350.0 | 185.1 | 37.2 | 13.8 | 4.2 | 0.8 | 38.4 |
| 1995 | 1,772.1 | 197.9 | 35.2 | 14.1 | 5.6 | 1.1 | 43.9 |
| 1998 | 2,525.2 | 291.5 | 79.5 | 27.6 | 9.2 | 1.7 | 71.8 |
| **All other assets** | | | | | | | |
| 1962 | $2,620.7 | $452.5 | $215.0 | $119.5 | $64.7 | $15.4 | $130.7 |
| 1983 | 6,020.1 | 781.4 | 315.9 | 162.5 | 80.0 | 16.8 | 217.0 |
| 1989 | 8,367.1 | 859.0 | 339.6 | 185.5 | 89.1 | 19.3 | 257.0 |
| 1992 | 7,978.7 | 849.4 | 298.3 | 164.3 | 81.5 | 19.1 | 242.4 |
| 1995 | 7,037.1 | 710.0 | 275.2 | 153.2 | 88.0 | 20.6 | 217.3 |
| 1998 | 7,961.1 | 826.2 | 331.3 | 181.1 | 97.6 | 23.8 | 246.0 |
| **Total debt** | | | | | | | |
| 1962 | $177.9 | $34.8 | $25.8 | $26.7 | $26.4 | $14.8 | $23.8 |
| 1983 | 409.1 | 68.1 | 49.2 | 33.5 | 26.1 | 12.5 | 32.1 |
| 1989 | 446.1 | 90.8 | 49.1 | 44.4 | 34.0 | 24.0 | 42.7 |
| 1992 | 532.2 | 123.2 | 51.6 | 42.5 | 33.9 | 17.6 | 44.0 |
| 1995 | 386.8 | 90.2 | 47.5 | 42.5 | 44.6 | 20.7 | 42.5 |
| 1998 | 282.6 | 104.9 | 66.0 | 47.4 | 45.8 | 24.4 | 47.5 |
| **Net worth** | | | | | | | |
| 1962 | $4,851.8 | $540.9 | $202.9 | $97.2 | $39.4 | $0.8 | $145.1 |
| 1983 | 7,175.1 | 814.2 | 278.7 | 133.6 | 55.5 | 4.7 | 212.6 |
| 1989 | 9,101.7 | 897.9 | 315.9 | 150.0 | 58.8 | (4.1) | 243.6 |
| 1992 | 8,796.4 | 911.3 | 283.9 | 135.7 | 51.9 | 2.2 | 236.8 |
| 1995 | 8,422.5 | 817.7 | 262.8 | 124.8 | 49.1 | 1.0 | 218.8 |
| 1998 | 10,203.7 | 1,012.7 | 344.9 | 161.3 | 61.0 | 1.1 | 270.3 |

* All direct and indirect stock holdings.

Source: Unpublished analysis of Survey of Consumer Finance data by Wolff.

The first panel of **Table 4.10** provides a more detailed description of the distribution of stock ownership. In 1998, the wealthiest 1% of households owned an average of $2.5 million in stocks. The holdings of the next 9% of households averaged $291,500. By comparison, the average direct and indirect stock holdings of the middle 20% of households were small, at $9,200, and the average for the bottom 40% of households was just $1,700. The value of stock holdings grew across the board in the 1990s, but in dollar terms—and relative to the typical household's needs during retirement—the increases were small for 80% of households. The total value of stocks owned by the middle 20% of households, for example, grew only $5,500 between 1989 and 1998—less than the average $11,800 rise in indebtedness for the same group over the same period (see the third section).

Stocks are also highly concentrated by household income. **Table 4.11** reports the share of all stock owned by households at different income levels. In 1998, the 1.6% of all households with annual incomes of $250,000 or more owned 36.1% of all stocks (see the bottom section). Households with annual incomes of $100,000 or more—about 8.5% of all households—controlled 63.9% of all stock. By contrast, the 29% of households with annual incomes in the $25,000-50,000 range owned just 8.5% of all stocks by value. The high degree of concentration of stocks across income levels holds true even for stocks in pension plans, such as 401(k)s. The main difference between stock holdings in pension plans and other (direct) stock holdings is that pension assets are more evenly distributed *among high-income households*. While the highest-income group—households with an annual income above $250,000—controls 48.1% of all publicly traded stock, these high earners own only 16.7% of stocks in pension plans, leaving a bigger share for households in the $100,000-250,000 range. At the same time, the bottom three-fourths of households—those with annual incomes of $50,000 or less—still hold only 13% of all stocks in pension plans (compared to 11.6% of publicly traded stock).

The high concentration of stock ownership means that the gains associated with the recent stock boom have also been highly concentrated. **Figure 4C** uses the information in Table 4.11 to illustrate the distribution of growth in stock market holdings between 1989 and 1998. Almost 35% of the growth over the period went to the wealthiest 1% of households, and almost 38% went to the next 9% of households. The middle 20% of households received only 2.8% of the rise in the overall value of stock holdings over the period.

### Home ownership

While most media analyses of wealth focus on stocks, housing equity is actually a far more important form of wealth for most households. The second section of Table 4.10, which shows the distribution of all non-stock assets by overall household wealth, makes this point indirectly. In 1998, the total value of all non-stock assets held by the middle 20% of households—overwhelmingly housing equity—was $97,600, more than 10 times larger than the average stock holdings for the same group ($9,200).

**TABLE 4.11** Concentration of stock ownership by income level, 1998 (percent)

| Income level | Share of households | Percent who own | Percent of stock owned Shares | Percent of stock owned Cumulative |
|---|---|---|---|---|
| **Publicly traded stock** | | | | |
| $250,000 and above | 1.6% | 73.8% | 48.1% | 48.1% |
| $100,000-249,999 | 6.9 | 53.0 | 24.7 | 72.8 |
| $75,000-99,999 | 7.7 | 31.4 | 8.2 | 81.0 |
| $50,000-74,999 | 17.4 | 25.9 | 8.4 | 89.4 |
| $25,000-49,999 | 29.0 | 17.7 | 7.0 | 96.5 |
| $15,000-24,999 | 16.1 | 8.6 | 2.5 | 98.9 |
| Under $15,000 | 21.3 | 4.3 | 1.1 | 100.0 |
| *Total* | 100.0 | 19.2 | 100.0 | 0.0 |
| **Stocks in pension plans*** | | | | |
| $250,000 and above | 1.6% | 44.3% | 16.7% | 16.7% |
| $100,000-249,999 | 6.9 | 51.7 | 29.7 | 46.4 |
| $75,000-99,999 | 7.7 | 51.2 | 18.4 | 64.8 |
| $50,000-74,999 | 17.4 | 41.5 | 22.2 | 87.0 |
| $25,000-49,000 | 29.0 | 28.0 | 12.0 | 99.1 |
| $15,000-24,999 | 16.1 | 10.2 | 0.8 | 99.9 |
| Under $15,000 | 21.3 | 3.6 | 0.1 | 100.0 |
| *Total* | 100.0 | 26.0 | 100.0 | 0.0 |
| **All stock**** | | | | |
| $250,000 and above | 1.6% | 93.3% | 36.1% | 36.1% |
| $100,000-249,999 | 6.9 | 89.0 | 27.7 | 63.9 |
| $75,000-99,999 | 7.7 | 80.7 | 10.8 | 74.7 |
| $50,000-74,999 | 17.4 | 70.9 | 13.1 | 87.8 |
| $25,000-49,999 | 29.0 | 52.0 | 8.5 | 96.3 |
| $15,000-24,999 | 16.1 | 29.2 | 2.6 | 98.9 |
| Under $15,000 | 21.3 | 10.6 | 1.1 | 100.0 |
| *Total* | 100.0 | 48.2 | 100.0 | 0.0 |

\*   All defined contribution stock plans including 401(k) plans.
\*\*  All stock directly or indirectly held in mutual funds, IRAs, Keogh plans, and defined-contribution pension plans.

Source: Unpublished analysis of Survey of Consumer Finance data by Wolff.

Census data graphed in **Figure 4D** indicate that, in 2001, over two-thirds (67.8%) of households owned their own homes. White households were much more likely than were black households to own their own homes (71.6% compared to 47.7%). More detailed data collected through the biennial American Housing Survey, however, show that home ownership rates vary considerably

**FIGURE 4C** Distribution of growth in stock market holdings, by wealth class, 1989-98

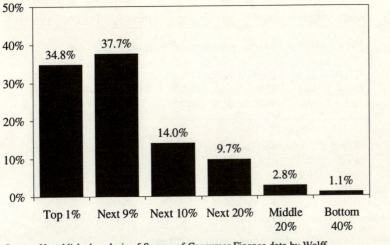

Source: Unpublished analysis of Survey of Consumer Finance data by Wolff.

**FIGURE 4D** Average homeownership rates, 1965-2001

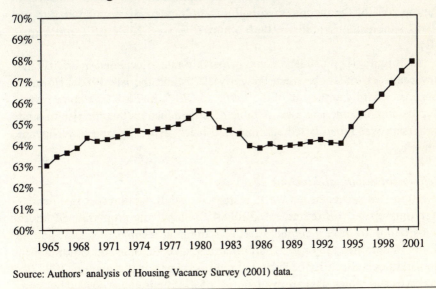

Source: Authors' analysis of Housing Vacancy Survey (2001) data.

291

**TABLE 4.12** Home ownership rates, by race and income, 1973-2001

| | Home ownership rate | | | | | Percentage-point change | | |
|---|---|---|---|---|---|---|---|---|
| | 1973 | 1979 | 1989 | 1999 | 2001 | 1979-89 | 1989-99 | 1979-2001 |
| All | 64.4% | 65.4% | 64.0% | 66.8% | 67.8% | -1.4 | 2.8 | 2.4 |
| White | 67.1% | 68.4% | 69.4% | 70.5% | 71.6% | 1.0 | 1.1 | 3.2 |
| Black* | 43.4 | 44.4 | 42.9 | 46.3 | 47.7 | n.a. | 3.4 | 3.3 |
| Hispanic | n.a. | n.a. | 40.3 | 45.5 | 47.3 | n.a. | 5.2 | n.a. |
| **Income** | | | | | | | | |
| Top 25% | 81.1% | 87.0% | 84.5% | 87.4% | n/a | -2.5 | 2.9 | n.a. |
| Next 25% | 69.2 | 72.3 | 68.6 | 73.1 | n/a | -3.6 | 4.5 | n.a. |
| Next 25% | 55.9 | 56.2 | 56.3 | 57.8 | n/a | 0.0 | 1.5 | n.a. |
| Bottom 25% | 51.3 | 46.2 | 46.4 | 49.4 | n/a | 0.2 | 2.9 | n.a. |

* Black includes all nonwhite in 1973 and 1979.

Source: Authors' analysis of American Housing Survey (2001) data.

by income. In 1999 (the most recent year available), 87.4% of households in the top 25% of the income distribution were homeowners, compared to just 49.4% among households in the bottom 25% (see **Table 4.12** and **Figure 4E**).

As Figure 4D illustrates, home ownership rates fluctuated in a fairly narrow band—64-65%—between the early 1970s and the late 1980s. However, rates rose sharply at the end of the 1990s, to 67.8% in 2001. The home ownership data by income and race in Table 4.12 demonstrate that the rise in home ownership was broad based and included black, Hispanic, and lower-income households.

### Retirement wealth and income adequacy

Over the 1990s, even as net worth increased overall, families became increasingly unprepared for retirement. **Table 4.13** shows the proportion of households failing to meet a common test of retirement income adequacy, i.e., the ability in retirement to replace half of current income, based on expected pension and Social Security benefits and returns on personal saving. In 1998 (the latest year for which data are available), 42.5% of households headed by someone age 47-64 can expect an inadequate retirement income. This share is an increase of 12.6 percentage points since1989, perhaps surprising given the long

**FIGURE 4E** Average rate of homeownership, by income quartile, 1999

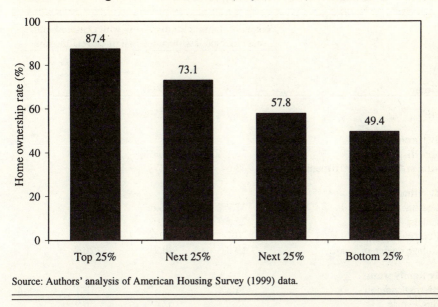

Source: Authors' analysis of American Housing Survey (1999) data.

run-up in stock values in the 1990s. African American households are more likely to have low incomes in retirement: 52.7% will be unable to replace half of current income, compared to 40.3% of white households. The education of the household head is also a factor—higher-educated households are more likely than less-educated households to be able to replace half of current income— yet retirement income adequacy has eroded the most among households headed by someone with some college or a college degree. The past decade showed slight improvement in the retirement-preparedness of households headed by single women, as the share unable to replace half of current income fell from 46.1% to 45.0%.

**Figure 4F** shows changes in mean retirement wealth by wealth class over the 1980s and 1990s. Households with the least wealth (under $25,000) saw the largest decline in retirement wealth over the 1980s, a drop of 25.5%. Most of the households also experienced declines, except for those with wealth between $500,000 and $999,999, who saw a slight increase (4.8%) over the 1980s. Between 1989 and 1998, households with the most wealth (over $1 million), saw their retirement wealth increase by 48.3%, while most other households saw their retirement wealth fall. Households at the very bottom saw their retirement wealth rise (by 11.9%), though not enough by to compensate for the drop during the 1980s.

**TABLE 4.13** Retirement income adequacy, 1989-98

| Group | Percent of households age 47-64 with expected retirement income less than one half of current income | | |
| | 1989 | 1998 | Percentage-point change, 1989-98 |
|---|---|---|---|
| **All** | 29.9% | 42.5% | 12.6 |
| **By race/ethnicity*** | | | |
| Non-Hispanic white | 26.1% | 40.3% | 14.1 |
| African American or Hispanic | 43.6 | 52.7 | 9.1 |
| **By education**** | | | |
| Less than high school | 37.7% | 48.6% | 10.9 |
| College degree | 25.5 | 40.9 | 15.4 |
| Some college | 20.2 | 42.4 | 22.3 |
| College degree or more | 19.8 | 40.7 | 20.9 |
| **By family status** | | | |
| Married couple | 24.2% | 37.3% | 13.1 |
| Single male | 25.5 | 62.4 | 36.9 |
| Single female | 46.1 | 45.0 | -1.1 |
| **By homeowner status** | | | |
| Owns a home | 23.5% | 39.5% | 15.9 |
| Renter | 52.1 | 52.8 | 0.7 |

\*   Asian and other races are excluded from the table because of small sample sizes.
\*\*  Households are classified by the education level of the head of household.

Note: A 7% real return on assets is assumed for financial wealth and net worth. Households are classified by the age of the head of household. Retirement income is based on marketable wealth holdings and all expected pension and Social Security benefits.

Source: Wolff (2002).

## Liabilities

An examination of the other side of the balance sheet—liabilities—reveals the sizeable scale of household debt in 2001. As **Table 4.14** indicates, in 2001 the total value of all forms of outstanding household debt was nearly 10% greater than the total disposable income of all households. Mortgage debt equaled nearly three-quarters of total disposable income and consumer debt (mostly credit-card debt) equaled over one-fifth.

**FIGURE 4F** Change in mean retirement wealth by wealth class, age 47 and over, 1983-98

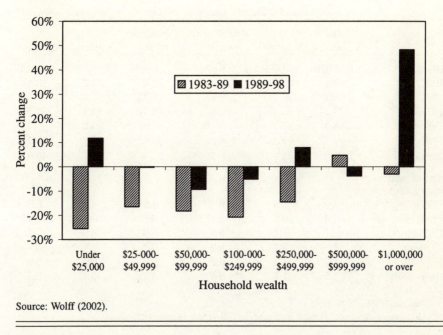

Source: Wolff (2002).

Debt levels in 2001 were at historic highs. **Figure 4G** graphs all debt and mortgage debt as a share of disposable personal income from 1947 to 2001. All debt rose from about 20% of disposable personal income at the end of World War II to over 60% by the early 1960s. Overall debt levels then remained roughly constant through the early 1980s, when they began to increase rapidly again. By 2001, overall debt was 109% of annual disposable income. Mortgage debt has declined in importance in overall debt over this period, but home equity loans have increased along with consumer credit, indicating that households are increasingly spending their accumulated equity rather than saving it.

At the aggregate level, debt is a more important feature of the household economy than at any time in modern history. The aggregate data, however, do not tell anything about the distribution of the debt; that can be seen in Table 4.10. The debt distribution (see the third section) has several striking features. First, debt is more equally distributed than are either assets or net worth. In 1998, for example, the average household in the top 1% had a net worth 167 times greater than that of a household in the middle 20%. In the same year, however, the average debt held by the top 1% was only six times greater than

**TABLE 4.14** Household debt, by type, 1949-2001 (percent)

| | As a share of disposable personal income | | | | As a share of assets** | |
|---|---|---|---|---|---|---|
| | All debt | Mortgage | Home equity loans* | Consumer credit | All debt | Mortgage |
| 1949 | 32.9% | 19.6% | n.a. | 10.2% | 6.1% | 15.0% |
| 1967 | 69.1 | 42.5 | n.a. | 18.8 | 12.0 | 30.8 |
| 1973 | 66.9 | 39.6 | n.a. | 19.7 | 12.6 | 26.3 |
| 1979 | 73.2 | 46.1 | n.a. | 19.5 | 13.7 | 27.5 |
| 1989 | 86.4 | 57.1 | 7.2% | 19.8 | 14.8 | 31.4 |
| 1995 | 94.3 | 62.4 | 6.2 | 20.7 | 15.8 | 40.2 |
| 2001 | 109.0 | 73.2 | 9.5 | 22.8 | 16.7 | 40.9 |
| *Annual percentage-point change* | | | | | | |
| 1949-67 | 2.0 | 1.3 | n.a. | 0.5 | 0.3 | 0.9 |
| 1967-73 | -0.4 | -0.5 | n.a. | 0.1 | 0.1 | -0.7 |
| 1973-79 | 1.1 | 1.1 | n.a. | 0.0 | 0.2 | 0.2 |
| 1979-89 | 1.3 | 1.1 | n.a. | 0.0 | 0.1 | 0.4 |
| 1989-2001 | 1.9 | 1.3 | 0.2 | 0.3 | 0.2 | 0.8 |
| 1995-2001 | 2.5 | 1.8 | 0.6 | 0.3 | 0.1 | 0.1 |

\* Data for 1989 refer to 1990.
\*\* All debt as a share of all assets; mortgage debt as a share of real estate assets.

Source: Authors' analysis of Federal Reserve Board (2001a) and Economagic (2002).

the average for the middle 20%. Second, for typical households, debt levels are high compared to the value of assets. In 1998, the average outstanding debt of households in the middle 20% was $45,800 (typically mortgage debt plus credit card debt). This debt level is about nine times greater than the corresponding $9,200 average for stock holdings and about half the total value of other assets (overwhelmingly the family home). Third, as noted earlier, the increase between 1989 and 1998 in the average household debt held by the middle 20% (up $11,800) was much larger than the corresponding increase in stocks (up $5,500). The run-up in debt at the middle was also larger than the corresponding increase in the value of all non-stock assets (up $8,500). These data suggest that, as far as the wealth of typical households is concerned, the real story of the 1990s was not the stock market boom, but the debt explosion.

The debt data in Table 4.10 also illustrate how the run-up in household debt during the 1990s was shared among households at different wealth levels.

**FIGURE 4G** Debt as a percentage of disposable personal income, 1947-2001

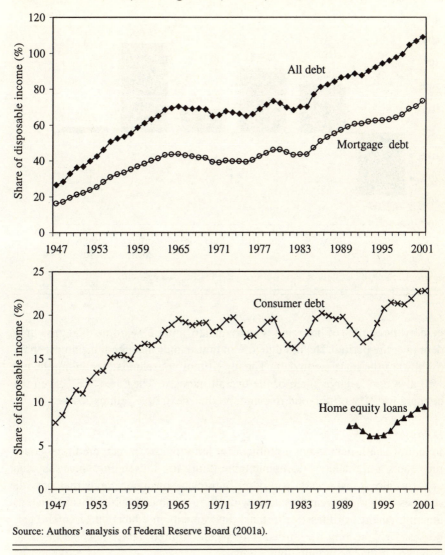

Source: Authors' analysis of Federal Reserve Board (2001a).

**Figure 4H** divides the total increase in debt between 1989 and 1998 among households at different points in the wealth distribution. (The approach here is identical to that used in Figure 4D, which looked at the distribution of growth in stock holdings.) As overall household debt ballooned during the 1990s, the share of debt held by the top 1% of households actually fell. The decline in debt

**FIGURE 4H** Distribution of growth in debt, 1989-98

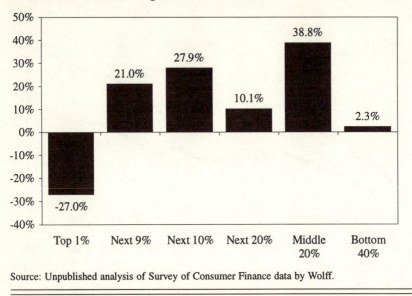

Source: Unpublished analysis of Survey of Consumer Finance data by Wolff.

held by the top 1% of households was equal to about 27% of the total growth in debt over the period. The middle 20% of households absorbed the largest share (38.8%) of the increase in debt. The top fifth of households (excluding the top 1%) also bore a large share of the overall increase. The "next 9%" group accounted for 21% of the total rise in debt; the "next 10%" almost 28%.

*Debt service*

In and of itself, debt is not a problem for households. In fact, credit generally represents a tremendous economic opportunity for households, since they can use it to buy houses, cars, and other big-ticket consumer goods that provide services over many years; to cope with short-term economic setbacks such as unemployment or illness; or to make investments in education or small businesses. Debt becomes a burden only when required debt payments begin to crowd out other economic obligations.

**Table 4.15** reproduces estimates from the Federal Reserve Board on the average household debt service burden (minimum required payments on outstanding debt, as a share of household disposable income) from 1980 through 2001. In 2001, minimum debt payments totaled about 14.1% of all household disposable income, and about half of these payments (7.9% of disposable personal income) were for mortgages. (Note that many households rent, and oth-

**TABLE 4.15** Household debt service burden,* 1980-2001
(percent of disposable personal income)

|                              | All debt | Mortgage | Consumer |
| ---------------------------- | -------- | -------- | -------- |
| 1980                         | 12.9%    | 8.4%     | 4.5%     |
| 1989                         | 13.6     | 7.6      | 6.0      |
| 1995                         | 12.7     | 6.8      | 5.9      |
| 2001                         | 14.1     | 7.9      | 6.3      |
| *Percentage-point change*    |          |          |          |
| 1980-89                      | 0.7      | -0.8     | 1.5      |
| 1989-2001                    | 0.6      | 0.3      | 0.3      |
| 1995-2001                    | 1.4      | 1.0      | 0.4      |

* Federal Reserve Board's estimate of minimum required payments on outstanding mortgage and consumer debt.

Source: Federal Reserve Board (2000).

ers have paid off their mortgages). Minimum consumer debt payments made up another 6.3% of disposable income. Over the full period 1980-2001, the debt service burden varied by only a small margin, perhaps surprising given that household debt levels rose so much over the same period. The main reason for the relatively constant debt service burden is the low nominal interest rates at the end of the 1990s compared to the early 1980s. But with debt levels substantially higher now than they were 20 years earlier, the household sector is more vulnerable now than in the past to rising interest rates.

Of course, the aggregate debt service figures in Table 4.15 do not show how debt service varies across households. **Table 4.16** shows household debt payments as a share of income for households at different income levels. (These numbers, also from the Federal Reserve Board, use a different underlying source of data than that used in Table 4.15. The definitions of payments and incomes also differ slightly. As a result, the aggregate numbers in Tables 4.15 and 4.16 do not match exactly.) Debt service takes the biggest share of income from lower-income households. In 1998 (the latest year available), households with annual incomes of $100,000 or more spent 10.0% of their income meeting minimum-required debt payments, compared to 19.4% of income for those in households with less than $10,000 in annual income and 17.4% for middle-income groups (those in the $25,000-49,999 and $50,000-99,999 range). The Federal Reserve Board data also show that debt service payments rose during the 1990s,

**TABLE 4.16** Household debt service as a share of income, by income level, 1989-98 (percent)

| Household income* | 1989 | 1992 | 1995 | 1998 | Percentage-point change 1989-98 | 1995-98 |
|---|---|---|---|---|---|---|
| $100,000 or more | 8.0% | 10.7% | 8.7% | 10.0% | 2.0 | 1.3 |
| $50,000 - 99,999 | 16.5 | 15.3 | 16.0 | 17.4 | 0.9 | 1.4 |
| $25,000 - 49,999 | 16.0 | 16.5 | 16.2 | 17.4 | 1.4 | 1.2 |
| $10,000 - 24,999 | 12.5 | 14.8 | 16.1 | 16.2 | 3.7 | 0.1 |
| Less than $10,000 | 16.2 | 16.8 | 19.5 | 19.4 | 3.2 | -0.1 |
| Average | 12.7% | 14.1% | 13.6% | 14.5% | 1.8 | 0.9 |

* In 1998 dollars.

Source: Federal Reserve Board (2000b).

especially among lower-income households. Between 1989 and 1998, for example, debt service payments by households in the $10,000-24,999 income range increased by 3.7 percentage points of total income.

*Hardship*

**Table 4.17** takes a slightly different look at the distribution of debt service payments by showing the share of each household income group that has debt service payments equal to more than 40% of household income, a level that is generally considered to represent economic hardship. In 1998, 13.8% of households in the middle-income range ($25,000-49,999) were making debt service payments in excess of 40% of their income, as were almost 20% of those in the $10,000-24,999 range and almost one-third of those with incomes below $10,000. Despite the strong recovery of 1995-99, the share of households with high debt service payouts increased significantly in the 1990s. Between 1989 and 1998, for example, the share of households facing high debt burdens increased 4.7 percentage points among households in the $25,000-49,999 range and 4.9 percentage points among households in the $10,000-24,999 range.

**Table 4.18** shows another measure of the impact of debt on economic hardship: the share of households, by income, that are late paying bills. In 1998, 8.1%—about one in 12—of all households were 60 days or more late in paying at least one bill. Not surprisingly, the share of households behind on their bills is strongly related to income. Very few (1.5%) of the highest income group were late in paying bills, while about one in 11 (9.2%) of those in the middle-

**TABLE 4.17** Households with high debt burdens, by income level, 1989-98 (percent of households)

| Household income* | 1989 | 1992 | 1995 | 1998 | Percentage-point change | |
|---|---|---|---|---|---|---|
| | | | | | 1989-98 | 1995-98 |
| $100,000 or more | 1.8% | 2.2% | 1.7% | 2.1% | 0.3 | 0.4 |
| $50,000 - 99,999 | 4.9 | 4.4 | 4.2 | 5.7 | 0.8 | 1.5 |
| $25,000 - 49,999 | 9.1 | 9.6 | 8.0 | 13.8 | 4.7 | 5.8 |
| $10,000 - 24,999 | 15.0 | 15.5 | 17.3 | 19.9 | 4.9 | 2.6 |
| Less than $10,000 | 28.6 | 28.4 | 27.6 | 32.0 | 3.4 | 4.4 |
| Average | 10.1% | 10.9% | 10.5% | 12.7% | 2.6 | 2.2 |

* Constant 1998 dollars.

Source: Federal Reserve Board (2000b).

**TABLE 4.18** Households late paying bills, by income level, 1989-98 (percent of households)

| Household income* | 1989 | 1992 | 1995 | 1998 | Percentage-point change | |
|---|---|---|---|---|---|---|
| | | | | | 1989-98 | 1995-98 |
| $100,000 or more | 1.2% | 0.5% | 1.3% | 1.5% | 0.3 | 0.2 |
| $50,000 - 99,999 | 4.5 | 2.2 | 2.7 | 4.5 | 0.0 | 1.8 |
| $25,000 - 49,999 | 4.8 | 6.3 | 8.6 | 9.2 | 4.4 | 0.6 |
| $10,000 - 24,999 | 12.2 | 9.4 | 11.3 | 12.3 | 0.1 | 1.0 |
| Less than $10,000 | 20.9 | 11.6 | 8.4 | 15.1 | -5.8 | 6.7 |
| Average | 7.3% | 6.0% | 7.1% | 8.1% | 0.8 | 1.0 |

* Constant 1998 dollars.

Source: Federal Reserve Board (2000).

income range and about one in seven (15.1%) in the lowest income range were behind on at least one bill. Another troubling feature of the data in Table 4.18 is the large rise (4.4 percentage points) during the 1990s in the share of middle-income households falling behind on their bills.

The ultimate indicator of debt-related difficulties is personal bankruptcy.

**FIGURE 4I** Consumer bankruptcies per 1,000 adults, 1980-2001

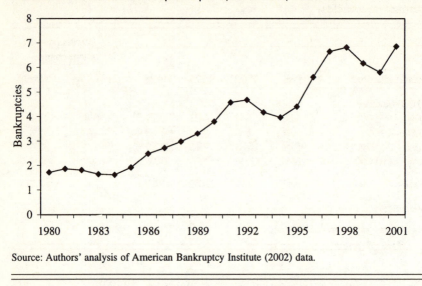

Source: Authors' analysis of American Bankruptcy Institute (2002) data.

**Figure 4I** graphs the rate of personal bankruptcies from 1980 through 2001. In 2001, seven out of every 1,000 adults declared personal bankruptcy, a rate almost twice as high as in the last business cycle peak in 1989. Despite the strong economic recovery during the second half of the 1990s, personal bankruptcies grew almost continuously during the period.

### *Student loans*
The debt burden has grown especially among recent college graduates because of large increases in the amount that students borrow to pay for college. Over the 1990s, loans not subsidized by the government grew, while grants to students and subsidized loans remained stagnant.

Over the 1980s and 1990s, the number of students attending college rose while college costs increased substantially: they nearly doubled between the early 1970s and 2000-01. Costs rose most among private, four-year colleges during the 1980s but then most among public institutions during the 1990s (**Figure 4J**). These increases are adjusted for inflation, meaning that costs consistently rose more than the cost of living overall. Rising college costs have hit lower-income families harder than higher-income families (**Figure 4K**), particularly during the 1980s.

Available student aid has increased, but not by as much as college costs, and the composition of aid has shifted from grants to (increasingly unsubsidized)

**FIGURE 4J** Annual growth rates in average tuition and fee charges, 1971-2002

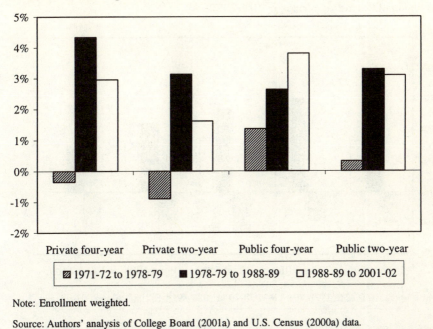

Note: Enrollment weighted.

Source: Authors' analysis of College Board (2001a) and U.S. Census (2000a) data.

loans (**Figure 4L**). There are two kinds of student loans, subsidized and unsubsidized. Under a subsidized loan, the government pays the interest until the student graduates from college (after a grace period) and also during periods of unemployment. Interest rates are capped below the market rate for personal loans. Unsubsidized loans have higher interest rate caps than subsidized loans, and interest accrues from the time of disbursement. Unsubsidized student loans increased during the 1990s as a direct result of higher education legislation that increased the amount of money students could borrow, changed the definition of need so that it was easier for dependent students to qualify, and made unsubsidized loans available to dependent students for the first time.

Cumulative amounts borrowed by fourth- and fifth-year college seniors skyrocketed in the mid- and late 1990s across the family income spectrum (**Figure 4M**). A college senior from a family in the lowest income quartile had a debt burden of $15,133 in 1999-2000, up from about $10,000 in 1992-93, and a senior from the top quartile had an average debt of $13,844, up from about $9,000. The important issue with student loan debt burdens, however, is not just the size of the loans, but whether students can pay them off in a reasonable

**FIGURE 4K** Annual growth rates in the share of family income required to pay for tuition at the average college, 1971-2002.

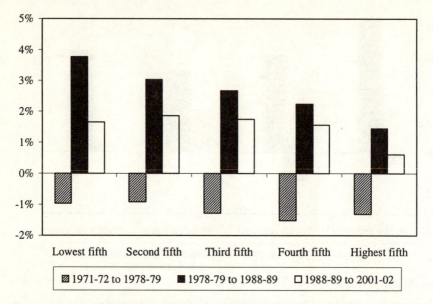

Source: Authors' analysis of National Center for Public Policy and Higher Education (2002), College Board (2001a), and U.S. Census (2002) data.

amount of time once they begin working. **Table 4.19** shows the average debt burden among 1992-93 graduates in 1994 and 1997 (the latest year available). The more income students made after graduating, the more likely they were to pay off their loans more quickly and lower their overall debt burden. Among graduates who had taken out student loans and who were earning $50,000 or more in 1997, only 58.6% still had debt, compared to 71.7% of those earning less than $20,000. The average debt was only slightly smaller among the lower-paid graduates: among those earning $50,000 or more, average debt was $8,668 in 1997, compared to $7,559 for those earning less than $20,000.

Student loan debt has not yet posed significant problems, but burgeoning debt may pose problems in the future, for a variety of reasons. First, students with high debt burdens may not save as much over the long term and thus be less adequately prepared for future expenses such as a home or retirement. Second, the rise in the debt burden in the late 1990s occurred during a period of low interest rates; higher interest rates could make it more difficult for current

**FIGURE 4L** Financial aid awarded to postsecondary students (per student), 1970-71 to 2000-01

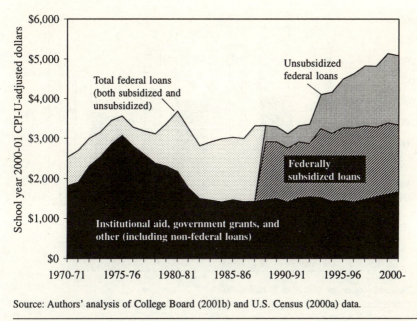

Source: Authors' analysis of College Board (2001b) and U.S. Census (2000a) data.

and future graduates to service their debt. Third, the late 1990s were also a period of rising wages. A turnaround in wages would also leave future graduates with more difficult debt burdens.

Overall, household debt grew rapidly in the 1990s, reaching historically high levels by the end of the decade. This growth in debt was disproportionately concentrated in the middle of the wealth distribution. Thanks, however, to low nominal interest rates throughout most of the 1990s, debt service did not rise as much as debt levels, and the debt burden has remained lighter than it otherwise would have been. Nevertheless, many households still experienced difficulties. Even as wages rose during the late 1990s, the share of households—especially low- and middle-income households—experiencing real economic hardships, including excessive debt service burdens and problems paying bills, increased substantially. Student loan burdens also expanded as college costs increased and more students became eligible for student loans. And by the end of the 1990s, personal bankruptcy rates stood at historically high levels, despite the strong recovery.

**FIGURE 4M** Cumulative amount borrowed by seniors who ever received student loans (subsidized or unsubsidized)

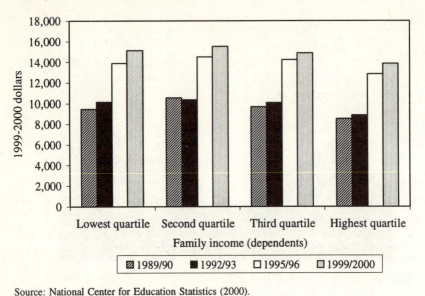

Source: National Center for Education Statistics (2000).

**TABLE 4.19** Debt burdens among bachelor's degree graduates from 1992-93 who took out student loans

|  | Percent who still owed | | Average debt burden | | Average amount still owed | |
|---|---|---|---|---|---|---|
|  | 1994 | 1997 | 1994 | 1997 | 1994 | 1997 |
| All | 83.7% | 66.4% | 9.1% | 6.4% | $10,756 | $7,791 |
| Income by 1996: | | | | | | |
| Less than $20,000 | 87.0% | 71.7% | 12.0% | 11.7% | $10,148 | $7,559 |
| $20,000-24,999 | 86.0 | 67.4 | 9.8 | 7.0 | 9,888 | 7,153 |
| $25,000-34,999 | 85.7 | 68.0 | 9.1 | 5.9 | 10,947 | 7,593 |
| $35,000-49,999 | 81.9 | 65.3 | 7.5 | 5.1 | 10,814 | 8,168 |
| $50,000 or more | 76.7 | 58.6 | 7.0 | 3.0 | 11,304 | 8,668 |

Note: Sample includes only those with no further enrollment beyond bachelor's degree. Dollar values are annual CPI-RS 2001 dollars.

Source: Choy and Carroll (2000).

## Conclusion

The data presented here establish that the distribution of wealth is highly un-equal, much more so than the distribution of wages and income that were the main focus of earlier chapters. Stocks and other financial assets are particularly concentrated, but even housing equity varies substantially by income and race. The last years of the 1990s saw large increases in net worth and, in particular, financial assets. Even after the stock market crash, the value of the stock market remained at near-record highs, and much of the gains went to the wealthiest households. Homeownership increased sharply in the late 1990s, however, especially among non-white households.

For most households rising debt, not a rising stock market, was the real story of the 1990s. Burgeoning debt has squeezed the net worth of the typical household, which saw only small gains in wealth in the 1990s. This growth in debt has put real economic strains on a significant number of low- and middle-income families, leading, in extreme cases, to personal bankruptcy. Increases in student loans over the 1990s mean that younger people are increasingly bur-dened with debt even before they buy a home or build up financial assets. The unprecedented levels of household debt suggest caution in evaluating the state of the economy at the turn of the century: much of America's current prosperity is borrowed against the future.

# Poverty: historic progress, but high rates persist

Over the last five years of the 1990s boom, significant progress was made in reducing poverty, particularly for minorities and children. Yet in 2000, the share of the nation's poor was about equal to its level in 1973. This lack of progress occurred despite growth in productivity of 52% and growth in real per capita income of 60% over this period. To the extent that we link progress as a society to progress against poverty, we have not moved far in the last 30 years.

This chapter examines why, despite periods of positive and even robust growth, poverty remains stuck at relatively high levels. We begin by focusing on both long- and short-term trends in order to understand why poverty could be cut by half between 1959 to 1973 but then hold its ground thereafter. The candidates for explaining this lack of progress include economic changes, such as slower growth, higher unemployment, and more inequality; demographic changes, such as family structure (including the shift to economically vulnerable single-parent families), and measurement (whether different measures of poverty show more or less progress). The analyses in this chapter will show that, while demographics and measurement play a non-trivial role, the more important set of factors are economic, particularly the increase in inequality that, over the past few decades, has created a wedge between growth in the overall economy and income growth among low-income families.

The experience of the latter 1990s demonstrates how a strong economy may—and perhaps may not—affect poverty. Growth sped up in the 1990s, but growth was not enough. Given the presence of inequality, other factors needed to be aligned so that the least advantaged could benefit. Among these factors, very low unemployment and slower-growing inequality helped drive poverty lower for demographic groups who historically face persistently high rates.

For example, while the overall poverty rate fell 2.5 percentage points from 1995 to 2000, the rate for African Americans fell 6.8 points, to a historic low of 22% (still twice the overall rate), and Hispanic poverty fell 8.8 points, just below two points per year. For minority children, the declines were even larger. For example, for black children under age 6, poverty declined by 16 points from 1995 to 2000; for young Hispanic children it fell by 14 points. Poverty among single-mother families also fell steeply, by 9 percentage points between 1995 and 2000, though a third of these families still remained poor in 2000. Thus, while levels of poverty are still unacceptably high in a rich economy like that of the United States, the trends of the latter 1990s were clearly beneficial, especially to the least advantaged.

These positive trends occurred at a time in which policy changes are having a significant impact on the way we view and confront poverty. Among the most important policy changes were the increase in the Earned Income Tax Credit (EITC) in the early 1990s and the vast changes in the welfare system signed into law in 1996. Both policies addressed poverty by focusing on work in the paid labor market as the primary pathway out. The impact of these policy shifts comes across clearly in the data presented below. The poor, particularly families headed by a single parent, are working more and deriving much more of their income from the labor market than they were in prior years. Work is playing a much larger role in the lives of the poor and near poor now than at any time over the past few decades. For example, for single-mother families with incomes below the median, labor market earnings as a share of income climbed from 41% in 1979 to 73% in 2000. At the same time, considerably less government cash assistance *not* tied to work is flowing to poor families.

In this regard, a major conclusion of this analysis is that truly effective poverty reduction depends on both market forces and the redistribution of economic resources. During the 1960s, when the U.S. most effectively lowered the share of the nation's poor, both the market and the tax and transfer system were working in tandem. Low unemployment, rising real wages, and broad-based, equally shared growth were complemented by transfers that helped to raise family incomes above the poverty line. But though some redistributive efforts expanded considerably in the 1990s (by increases in the EITC), others, such as cash assistance, fell sharply. The net effect of these actions was that the market and the tax and transfer system were working against each other. Accounting for the full effect of taxes and transfers, poverty fell 1.7 points over the second half of the decade. Market outcomes alone drove poverty down by 3.3 points. But the diminished effectiveness of transfers added 1.6 points back to the trend.

These insights are particularly germane when the economy is contracting or growing weakly. Even though unemployment remained historically low in

2001, the 0.8 percentage-point increase that year—from 4.0% in 2000 to 4.8% in 2001—contributed to a significant increase in poverty. The fact that the U.S. system of public support for the poor is now geared more toward work means that it is less effective when work disappears.

Measuring poverty presents numerous methodological challenges, and this chapter discusses some of them and critiques the accuracy of the official U.S. poverty measure. A new measure, implemented on an experimental basis by the Census Bureau, corrects many of the shortcomings in the official measure; it estimates that 15% of the nation was poor in 1999. This rate, much higher than the official rate of 11.8%, would consign an extra 8.8 million to the ranks of the poor. However, poverty declined even more quickly over the 1990s under this alternative measure than under the official measure. Clearly, there are important lessons to be learned by studying these years.

## The course and composition of poverty, 1959-2000

The basis for most analyses of economic deprivation in the United States over the long term (in this case, over the last 40 years) is the federal government's definition of poverty: families or individuals whose annual pretax, post-cash-transfer income (cash transfers come from various government programs, such as welfare or Social Security) falls below the federal poverty thresholds. For example, a family with two parents, two children, and income below $17,960 in 2001 would be considered poor. This threshold is adjusted each year to reflect changes in the cost of living.

The official approach to measuring poverty has been widely criticized, and in fact one would be hard-pressed to find a poverty analyst who supports the current measure. In response, social scientists have derived much improved thresholds (we present these findings in a later section). However, the trends in the new measures are quite similar to those in the official series (i.e., the new thresholds have a greater impact on the level of poverty—tending to show higher rates—than on the trend), and so the official series holds much value for historical analysis.

**Table 5.1** provides poverty rates at various cyclical peaks, and **Figure 5A** shows the historical series from 1959 to 2000. The figure shows two fairly distinct periods over the long term. The first runs from 1959 to 1973, when the poverty rate fell by half, from about 22% to about 11%. From 1973 on, however, the poverty rate moves in a broadly cyclical manner, ending up in 2000 just about where it started, at 11.3% (the recession of 2001 increased poverty by 0.4 percentage points, adding 1.3 million to the ranks of the poor). While

**TABLE 5.1** Percent and number of persons in poverty, 1959-2001

| Year | Poverty rate | Number in poverty (000) |
|------|--------------|-------------------------|
| 1959 | 22.4% | 39,490 |
| 1967 | 14.2 | 27,769 |
| 1973 | 11.1 | 22,973 |
| 1979 | 11.7 | 26,072 |
| 1989 | 12.8 | 31,528 |
| 1995 | 13.8 | 36,425 |
| 2000 | 11.3 | 31,581 |
| 2001 | 11.7 | 32,907 |

| *Averages over business cycles* | |
|------|------|
| 1959-67 | 19.0% |
| 1967-73 | 12.4 |
| 1973-79 | 11.6 |
| 1979-89 | 13.6 |
| 1989-2000 | 13.4 |
| 1989-95 | 14.1 |
| 1995-2000 | 12.8 |

Source: U.S. Bureau of the Census. For detailed information on table sources, see Table Notes.

there are important distinctions to be made regarding poverty's response to each business cycle post-1973, this lack of long-term progress against poverty is a conspicuous and unsettling feature of the U.S. economy over the past generation, especially when we consider that per capita income grew 60% between 1973 and 2000. The next section turns to an explanation of why these periods differ so much.

Table 5.1 shows that poverty rates grew successively higher in the business cycle peaks of 1973, 1979, and 1989, implying a structural (as opposed to cyclical) increase in poverty over time. The bottom part of the table shows that poverty rates averaged two percentage points higher in the 1980s than over the 1973-79 period, and they maintained about the same average over the 1990s. The pattern was different in the two halves of the decade, however, with rising poverty rates in 1989-95 giving way to a steep decline in 1995-2000.

**Figure 5B**, which plots the poverty rate from peak-to-peak over the 1980s and 1990s, takes a closer look at the differences between the two business cycles. The poverty rate was below 12% in 1979, and the deep recession of the early 1980s drove the rate higher by at least one point per year through 1981. Poverty

**FIGURE 5A** Poverty rate, 1959-2001

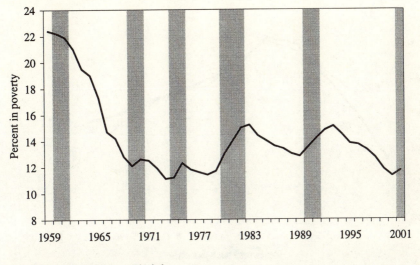

Note: Periods of recession are shaded.

Source: U.S. Bureau of the Census. For detailed information on figure sources, see Figure Notes.

rates began falling as the recovery took hold, but by the end of the recovery, in 1989, they remained a point above their 1979 level, consigning an extra 2.5 million persons to the ranks of the poor.

The 1990s business cycle began with the 12.8% poverty rate of 1989. Despite the fact that the early 1990s recession was shorter and shallower than the early 1980s recession, poverty grew relatively quickly, not only during the recession but in the first few years of the slow growth early-1990s recovery, until it reached 15% (as in the 1980s). The decline in poverty in the 1990s followed the path of the 1980s up until about 1997, when the stronger recovery of the 1990s kicked in and drove down poverty rates. The persistence of the recovery also made a difference, with the extra year of fast growth helping to drive the poverty rate down to a level below that of 1989 and about equal to that of 1979.

The next few tables examine poverty rates by personal and family characteristics. **Table 5.2**—poverty rates for persons by race—shows that poverty rates for minorities are higher at any given point in time than those for whites. Rates for African Americans are historically the highest, though Hispanic rates (unavailable for 1959 and 1967) rose more quickly than the other groups during the 1980s, in part due to increased immigration of low-income Hispanic

**FIGURE 5B** Poverty rate over 1980s and 1990s business cycles

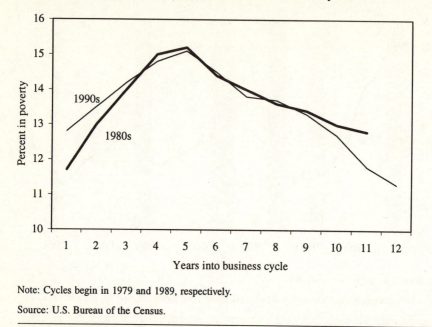

Note: Cycles begin in 1979 and 1989, respectively.

Source: U.S. Bureau of the Census.

families over this period. Yet the gains made by minorities over the 1990s, particularly the latter 1990s, were extraordinary. Between 1995 and 2000, poverty fell by 6.8 points among African Americans and by 8.8 points among Hispanics. **Figure 5C** plots poverty rates for non-Hispanic whites (note that the overall rate for whites shown in Table 5.2 includes white Hispanics), blacks, and Hispanics from 1973 to 2000 (the years for which we have data for each group). While rates among whites fell only slightly over the 1990s (by about 2 points), those of Hispanics and blacks fell by about 10 points, by far the largest decline in poverty since these data have been collected.

Note also that the large decline among Hispanics occurred over a period of high Hispanic immigration. This trend is important because it suggests that, while an increasing share of low-income immigrant families typically puts upward pressure on poverty rates (because their poverty rates are well above average), rising immigration does not automatically lead to a higher poverty rates over time. While more low-income immigrants will raise the poverty rate at a point in time, they may not have this same effect on the overall trend if their own poverty rates fall quickly enough. Thus, one cannot simply write-off persistent poverty as a function of increased immigration.

**TABLE 5.2** Persons in poverty, by race/ethnicity, 1959-2001

| Year | Total | White | Black | Hispanic |
|------|-------|-------|-------|----------|
| 1959 | 22.4% | 18.1% | n.a. | n.a. |
| 1967 | 14.2 | 11.0 | 39.3% | n.a. |
| 1973 | 11.1 | 8.4 | 31.4 | 21.9% |
| 1979 | 11.7 | 9.0 | 31.0 | 21.8 |
| 1989 | 12.8 | 10.0 | 30.7 | 26.2 |
| 1995 | 13.8 | 11.2 | 29.3 | 30.3 |
| 2000 | 11.3 | 9.5 | 22.5 | 21.5 |
| 2001 | 11.7 | 9.9 | 22.7 | 21.4 |
| *Percentage-point changes* | | | | |
| 1959-67 | -8.2 | -7.1 | n.a. | n.a. |
| 1967-73 | -3.1 | -2.6 | -7.9 | n.a. |
| 1973-79 | 0.6 | 0.6 | -0.4 | -0.1 |
| 1979-89 | 1.1 | 1.0 | -0.3 | 4.4 |
| 1989-2000 | -1.5 | -0.5 | -8.2 | -4.7 |
| 1989-95 | 1.0 | 1.2 | -1.4 | 4.1 |
| 1995-2000 | -2.5 | -1.7 | -6.8 | -8.8 |

Source: U.S. Bureau of the Census.

**FIGURE 5C** Poverty rates by race/ethnicity, 1973-2001

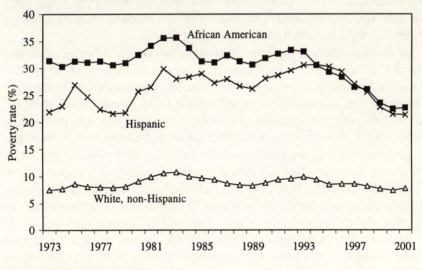

Source: U.S. Bureau of the Census.

The larger-than-average decline in minority poverty has led to a closing of the gap between poverty rates for whites and minorities (Figure 5C). In 1989, the incidence of black poverty was 3.7 times that for non-Hispanic whites; for Hispanics, the ratio was 3.2-to-1. By 2000, the gap had closed to 2.9-to-1 for blacks (the lowest on record) and 2.8-to-1 for Hispanics.

These poverty trends for minorities in the latter 1990s mirror the income trends for these groups (discussed in Chapter 1). But while these results represent dramatic gains, they also stand as a reminder of the large income gulf separating whites and minorities. The favorable economic conditions lowered minority poverty and narrowed the gap between minorities and whites, but, even after the strongest recovery in decades, more than one-fifth of these populations were poor and the gap with whites was only narrowed; it was far from closed.

Given the importance of adequate income during a child's formative years, the high poverty rates for children in the U.S. has long been considered more of a socioeconomic problem here than in other advanced nations, where child poverty is lower (**Table 5.3**; see Chapter 7 for international poverty comparisons). Here again the data reveal positive recent trends but disappointingly high levels. Even with the historically large declines in black poverty from 1995 to 2000, close to a third of African American children remain poor. In 2000, child poverty rates were 16.2% for all children and 17.2% for children under 6. Poverty among African American and Hispanic children fell by 10.7 and 11.6 percentage points from 1995 to 2000, with even faster declines among younger children. The rate for black children in 2000—31.2%—is the lowest recorded rate for this group since these data were first collected in the mid-1970s. For Hispanic children, the large decline after 1995 brought them back to their 1979 rate.

Of course, child poverty rates are fully a function of a family's income. **Table 5.4** shifts the unit of observation from persons to families, which in Census terminology refers to two or more persons related through blood, marriage, or adoption (i.e., one-person units are excluded). In general, family poverty rates are lower than poverty rates for persons, reflecting both the relatively high number of poor children and unrelated individuals included in the person counts. The patterns over time are similar to those shown in the previous tables, with consistently increasing rates of family poverty at business cycle peaks from 1973 to 1989. By 2000, family poverty had fallen to its 1973 level. Note again that progress against family poverty over the 1990s was concentrated in the latter half of the decade; family poverty rose slightly between 1989 and 1995.

At the cyclical peaks between 1973 and 1989, the poverty rates for African American families were essentially unchanged at about 28%. Over the 1990s, however, they fell by 8.5 percentage points; their 2000 rate of 19.3% is the lowest on record and the first time poverty for black families fell below 20%.

**TABLE 5.3** Percent of children in poverty, by race, 1979-2001

| Year | Total | White | Black | Hispanic |
|------|-------|-------|-------|----------|
| **Children under 18** | | | | |
| 1979 | 16.4% | 11.8% | 41.2% | 28.0% |
| 1989 | 19.6 | 14.8 | 43.7 | 36.2 |
| 1995 | 20.8 | 16.2 | 41.9 | 40.0 |
| 2000 | 16.2 | 13.1 | 31.2 | 28.4 |
| 2001 | 16.3 | 13.4 | 30.2 | 28.0 |
| | | | | |
| *Percentage-point change* | | | | |
| 1979-89 | 3.2 | 3.0 | 2.5 | 8.2 |
| 1989-2000 | -3.4 | -1.7 | -12.5 | -7.8 |
| 1989-95 | 1.2 | 1.4 | -1.8 | 3.8 |
| 1995-2000 | -4.6 | -3.1 | -10.7 | -11.6 |
| | | | | |
| **Children under 6** | | | | |
| 1979 | 18.1% | 13.3% | 43.6% | 29.2% |
| 1989 | 22.5 | 16.9 | 49.8 | 38.8 |
| 1995 | 24.1 | 18.6 | 49.2 | 42.8 |
| 2000 | 17.2 | 14.1 | 32.9 | 28.9 |
| 2001 | 18.4 | 15.1 | 35.5 | 29.1 |
| | | | | |
| *Percentage-point change* | | | | |
| 1979-89 | 4.4 | 3.6 | 6.2 | 9.6 |
| 1989-2000 | -5.3 | -2.8 | -16.9 | -9.9 |
| 1989-95 | 1.6 | 1.7 | -0.6 | 4.0 |
| 1995-2000 | -6.9 | -4.5 | -16.3 | -13.9 |

Source: U.S. Bureau of the Census.

Poverty among Hispanic families grew sharply through 1995, but thereafter reversed course and fell even more quickly than the rate for blacks; by 2000, they too posted the lowest rate on record.

The last two columns show the poverty rates of two family types with very different probabilities of being poor: married couples with children and mother-only families with children. (We exclude the other family type—father-only with children—as they represent a small share of families with children—6% in 2000.) Single-mother families are most vulnerable to poverty: about three-fifths of them were poor in 1959. As we saw in Chapter 1, many married-couple families have increased their time spent in the paid labor market since the late 1970s, mostly through the sharp increase in wives' work outside the

**TABLE 5.4** Family poverty, by race/ethnicity of family head and for different family types, 1959-2001

| Year | All | Race/ethnicity of family head: White | Black | Hispanic | Families with children: Married couples | Female head |
|------|-----|-------|-------|----------|---------|------|
| 1959 | 18.5% | 15.2% | n.a. | n.a. | n.a. | 59.9% |
| 1967 | 11.4 | 9.1 | 33.9% | n.a. | n.a. | 44.5 |
| 1973 | 8.8 | 6.6 | 28.1 | 19.8% | n.a. | 43.2 |
| 1979 | 9.2 | 6.9 | 27.8 | 20.3 | 6.1% | 39.6 |
| 1989 | 10.3 | 7.8 | 27.8 | 23.4 | 7.3 | 42.8 |
| 1995 | 10.8 | 8.5 | 26.4 | 27.0 | 7.5 | 41.5 |
| 2000 | 8.7 | 7.1 | 19.3 | 19.2 | 6.0 | 33.0 |
| 2001 | 9.2 | 7.4 | 20.7 | 19.4 | 6.1 | 33.6 |
| *Percentage-point changes* | | | | | | |
| 1959-73 | -9.7 | -8.6 | n.a. | n.a. | n.a. | -16.7 |
| 1973-79 | 0.4 | 0.3 | -0.3 | 0.5 | n.a. | -3.6 |
| 1979-89 | 1.1 | 0.9 | 0.0 | 3.1 | 1.2 | 3.2 |
| 1989-2000 | -1.6 | -0.7 | -8.5 | -4.2 | -1.3 | -9.8 |
| 1989-95 | 0.5 | 0.7 | -1.4 | 3.6 | 0.2 | -1.3 |
| 1995-2000 | -2.1 | -1.4 | -7.1 | -7.8 | -1.5 | -8.5 |
| 2000-01 | 0.5 | 0.3 | 1.4 | 0.2 | 0.1 | 0.6 |

Source: U.S. Bureau of the Census.

home, a strategy unavailable to single parents. They can, of course, increase their own hours, and they have done so, but have no other adult to make a major contribution to family income.

Nevertheless, thanks to the expansion of cash transfers over the 1960s, the increased labor force participation of women, and the expansion of this family type among more affluent women, the poverty rate among families headed by single women fell through 1979 to about two-fifths. As was the case for all families, including married couples, the poverty rates of female-headed families rose in the 1980s, from 39.6% to 42.8%. In the 1990s, poverty rates for single-mother families fell by 9.8 points, more than for any other family type shown in the table. Yet even after this considerable progress, about one-third of these families were poor in 2000.

Increased work and increased real wages at the low end of the wage scale help explain these advances against poverty among single-mother families. Nevertheless, as discussed later in this chapter, more work at low wages (even with recent gains) is a limited strategy for many of these families, as can be seen by their relatively high poverty rate in 2000. Part of the difficulty they face is that, while their increased earnings have lifted their incomes, the loss of cash welfare benefits has simultaneously reduced income.

This difficulty is particularly notable in a downturn, where less work and fewer welfare benefits are available to offset the loss of labor income. As Table 5.4 shows, poverty rose one-half of a percentage point between 2000 and 2001— 1.4 points for African American families—signaling a clear reversal of the dramatic gains produced by the full-employment economy of the latter 1990s.

## Alternative approaches to measuring poverty

An accurate assessment of poverty requires a reliable and representative measure of how much income it takes for a family to meet its most basic needs—an income threshold. Second, it requires a comprehensive measure of a family's resources. If the former is higher than the latter, then the family is poor. Determining and assembling the data for this simple equation is nowhere as easy as it sounds, and the development of these measures of income and need is fraught with many choices.

Unfortunately, the current measure fails on both of the above counts. The thresholds are outdated, and a substantial number of studies (which form the basis for much of what follows—see table notes for references) find that the poverty thresholds no longer accurately represent what even poor families need to make ends meet. And on the income side, the current approach fails to accurately take account of the resources available to families.

Almost all the alternative definitions raise the level of poverty at a point in time, suggesting that the official measure understates the extent of poverty. If our preferred definition were currently the official measure, the poverty rate would have been 15.0% in 1999 instead of the official rate of 11.8%. (The alternative measures we use, derived by the Census Bureau, are available only through 1999.) Yet, though the *level* of the official measure is probably not accurate, the alternative measures follow the same *trend* as the official series. Moreover, regarding the composition of the poor, we find that, when the costs associated with working are subtracted from available family resources, the share of the poor who work increases (and conversely, the share who do not work falls). Given the increased prevalence of work among the poor and near-poor, this finding is important.

### *What's wrong with the current poverty measure?*
Almost since they were derived by Mollie Orshansky of the Social Security Administration in the early 1960s, the U.S. poverty thresholds have been subject

to extensive criticism. The original thresholds were based on two factors: the costs deemed necessary to meet the basic food needs of low-income families of differing sizes and types, and the share of income spent on food by all families. The costs of meeting food needs came from the U.S. Department of Agriculture's low-cost food plan. Since it was believed that families of three or more persons (all such families, not just low-income families) spent about one-third of their after-tax money income on food in 1955, Orshansky multiplied the costs of the food plan for different family sizes by three to come up with the thresholds.

The first major problem with the thresholds is that they have failed to reflect changes in consumption and relative spending since the early 1960s. For example, the current measure is based on the assumption that one-third of family income is spent on food. But, over time, the prices of the items that families consume have changed considerably. Families spend relatively more (as a budget share) on housing, health care, and transportation than they used to, and less on food. (As early as 1965, Orshansky herself recognized the deficiencies in using the food plan and its multiplier for all other expenditures. At that time, she judged that the percentage of income dedicated to food had fallen closer to one-fourth of total expenditures. In addition, she also believed that the food plan used to cost out the poverty thresholds was often insufficient to feed even a poor family.) Thus, applying the original method to today's consumption bundle would yield poverty thresholds higher than those currently in use. When an academic panel updated the Orshansky method to 1992, using the lower share of food consumption, the result was a poverty threshold 45% higher than the official one ($20,659 for a two-adult, two-child family, compared with the official threshold that year of $14,228).

Second, the current approach leaves out the value of publicly provided non-cash resources that clearly increase the buying power of low-income families; leaving out these income sources actually leads to an overstatement of poverty. For example, food stamps are generally considered to be much like cash, and thus should be factored into family income, as are welfare benefits. Health care benefits, such as Medicaid, are much less fungible (i.e., harder to value), and to price them at market rates would generally overstate their value to low-income families, particularly those without significant health needs. Yet, even for these families, access to Medicaid lessens deprivation.

In addition, despite the fact that it is post-tax income that determines how much a family can consume (aside from borrowing), official poverty measures compare the thresholds to pre-tax income (including cash transfers, such as Social Security benefits and welfare payments). The EITC is particularly important in this regard, as it can now easily represent a quarter of income for low-income, working families. While this was less important decades ago, today's poor both pay more taxes (e.g., payroll taxes have increased, affecting the working poor) and receive more tax-related benefits, like the EITC and the refundable child tax credit.

At the same time, it is insufficient to just add these resources to the income side without reflecting new expenses on the outlay side. Such expenses reflect the many economic changes that have occurred over the years since the creation of the poverty thresholds, the most important being the increased number of women participating in the paid labor force. This factor alone has added significant work-related expenses, such as child care and transportation, to working families' outlays.

A final critique of the official measure is that it neglects geographic differences in the cost of living across regions, localities, and urban/rural areas. This is a significant omission, since the prices of housing, health care, and child care vary significantly across place.

A panel of poverty experts examined these issues and released a study in 1995 under the aegis of the National Research Council (NRC). The panel found that changes in consumption, work patterns, taxes, and government benefits all suggested the need for an updated measure of poverty. The panel's alternative measure incorporates these factors. It reflects contemporary consumption patterns, adds the cash value of food stamps and housing benefits, and subtracts out-of-pocket medical, child care, and work-related expenses. The next step in this evolution was undertaken by analysts at the Census Bureau and the Bureau of Labor Statistics, who implemented the panel's recommendations, added a few of their own variations, and presented a detailed analysis of the implications of the panel's approach.

The data in **Figure 5D** and **Table 5.5** use one of the Census Bureau's alternative definitions. This measure differs considerably from the current approach on both the threshold and income sides. The threshold is updated using actual expenditure on basic items (food, clothing, housing, and utilities) along with a bit more for other necessities such as household supplies and personal care items. It also adjusts the thresholds for the difference in housing costs across the country. On the resource side, it adds various cash and near-cash benefits (such as the value of food stamps) to income, and subtracts out-of-pocket medical costs. It also adjusts income for federal and state taxes, including both tax liabilities and tax credits, such as the EITC. Finally, for working parents, this measure subtracts work-related expenses such as child care and transportation.

Figure 5D plots this alternative against the current measure for the years included in the Census analysis: 1990-99. The alternative measure is higher than that of the current, official measure in each year. On average, the difference is 3.5 percentage points, though the gap is larger at the beginning than at the end of the

**FIGURE 5D** Official versus alternative poverty measures, 1990-99

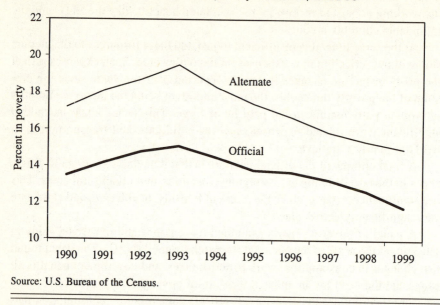

Source: U.S. Bureau of the Census.

series, perhaps due to the inclusion of taxes—and thus the poverty reduction effect of the increased EITC over this period—in the alternative measure. Thus, while both series peak in 1993, the official measure falls 3.3 percentage points through 1999 and the alternative rate falls 4.5 points. Nevertheless, by 1999, 8.8 million more persons were classified as poor under the alternative measure.

Table 5.5 shows the impact of the alternative measure on poverty rates for various demographic groups, family types, and geographic areas (top section) and for the composition of the poor within those categories (bottom section). The top section shows the two rates and their differences, while the bottom section shows the share of the poor in the categories listed (note that each sub-section in the bottom section sums to 100%). Poverty rates are 3.2 percentage points higher for all persons under the alternative rates, with larger differences for the elderly (mostly due to the subtraction of out-of-pocket medical costs from their income), married couples (medical costs and work expenses), and persons in the Northeast, West, and central cities (higher housing prices relative to the other regions and areas).

Regarding the composition of the poor (bottom section), the largest differences are for family structure, where the alternative measure leads to a 6.8-point smaller share of poor single-mother families, and for work status, where the alternative measure generates a 5.2-point larger share of working poor. The

**TABLE 5.5** Poverty rates and distribution of the poor, official and alternative measures, 1999

| | Official | Alternative | Alternative minus official |
|---|---|---|---|
| **Poverty rates** | | | |
| *All persons* | 11.8% | 15.0% | 3.2 |
| Children | 16.9 | 19.7 | 2.8 |
| Non-elderly adults | 10.0 | 12.7 | 2.7 |
| Elderly | 9.7 | 16.6 | 6.9 |
| *Persons in:* | | | |
| Married-couple families | 5.8% | 9.2% | 3.4 |
| Male-headed families | 14.9 | 17.5 | 2.6 |
| Female-headed families | 27.5 | 30.4 | 2.9 |
| *No workers* | 32.7% | 35.8% | 3.1 |
| *One or more workers* | 8.6 | 11.9 | 3.3 |
| *Regions* | | | |
| Northeast | 10.9% | 16.2% | 5.3 |
| Midwest | 9.8 | 11.8 | 2.0 |
| South | 13.1 | 14.9 | 1.8 |
| West | 12.6 | 17.4 | 4.8 |
| *Metropolitan status* | | | |
| Central city | 16.4% | 20.5% | 4.1 |
| Not central city | 8.3 | 12.1 | 3.8 |
| Non-metro area | 14.3 | 14.6 | 0.3 |
| **Distribution of the poor** | | | |
| *All persons* | 100.0% | 100.0% | 0.0 |
| Children | 37.5 | 34.4 | -3.1 |
| Non-elderly adults | 52.6 | 52.4 | -0.2 |
| Elderly | 9.8 | 13.2 | 3.4 |
| *Persons in:* | | | |
| Married-couple families | 32.3% | 40.3% | 8.0 |
| Male-headed families | 14.8 | 13.7 | -1.1 |
| Female-headed families | 52.8 | 46.0 | -6.8 |
| *No workers* | 36.3% | 31.1% | -5.2 |
| *One or more workers* | 63.7 | 68.9 | 5.2 |
| *Regions* | | | |
| Northeast | 17.6% | 20.5% | 2.9 |
| Midwest | 19.2 | 18.3 | -0.9 |
| South | 38.9 | 34.8 | -4.1 |
| West | 24.3 | 26.5 | 2.2 |
| *Metropolitan status* | | | |
| Central city | 40.7% | 39.9% | -0.8 |
| Not central city | 36.2 | 41.6 | 5.4 |
| Non-metro area | 23.1 | 18.5 | -4.6 |

Source: U.S. Bureau of the Census, P60-216, Table 4-1 and 4-2, using alternative rate DCM1/U.

former result is due to the addition of more transfer income to the resources of single-mother families relative to the official measure. The larger share of workers under the alternative measure is due to the subtraction of work-related expenses, especially child care, from resources.

There is no perfect way to measure poverty, and reasonable persons could find arguments with the experimental alternatives presented by the Census Bureau. And there is room for improvement in these measures in the way price differences, child care costs, and medical costs are estimated (note that the value of publicly provided health insurance is excluded, primarily because it remains unclear how to appropriately value this component). Nevertheless, the alternative measures represent a vast improvement in poverty measurement, successfully addressing and correcting the range of inadequacies embedded in the current measure. The corrections lead to a rate above that of the official measure, but, regardless of this difference, our understanding of poverty in this country would be advanced if we were to adopt some version of this alternative as the official measure.

Examining some other alternative ways of measuring poverty can yield additional insights.

As noted above, the official poverty lines are indexed for inflation. However, some analysts claim that the price index used to adjust the poverty lines overstated inflation in the 1970s and early 1980s and thereby overestimated real poverty rates. **Figure 5E** tracks poverty rates from 1968 to 2000 using two alternative price indexes, the CPI-U-X1, and the CPI-U-RS, both of which are considered more conservative measures of inflation (see the Methodology section for a discussion of the differences in these deflators).

Since slower price growth leads to slower-growing poverty thresholds, one would expect these alternative price indexes to generate lower measured poverty rates. The X1 index grows at the same rate as the CPI-U beginning in 1983, so poverty rates derived from the X1 index will be parallel to the official rates from that year forward. Prices in the RS index, however, grow more slowly over the full 1980s and early 1990s, so this rate will diverge over this period (the RS is consistently measured only back to 1978 and matches the CPI-U after 1998). While either of these deflators may measure price change more accurately than the CPI-U (note the use of RS throughout much of this analysis), the trends in Figure 5E generally track that of the overall rate. While the official measure and the measure against the X1 index end up at about their 1979 level in 2000, the RS measure ends up 1.3 points below that level (9.5% in 2000 compared to 10.8% in 1979).

**Figure 5F** presents three other measures that show important and different dimensions of poverty's evolution over time. These are: (1) the share of the

**FIGURE 5E** Poverty rates by price index, 1968-2000

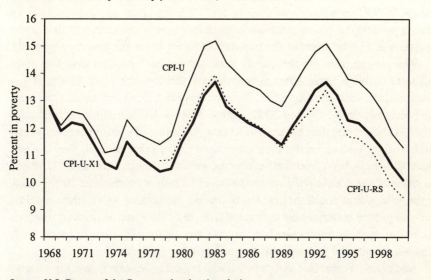

Source: U.S. Bureau of the Census and authors' analysis.

**FIGURE 5F** Various measures of poverty, 1969-2000

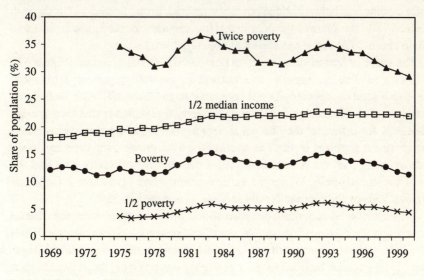

Source: U.S. Bureau of the Census.

population who are deeply poor, with income no more than half the poverty line, or $8,800 for a family of four in 2000; (2) the share of the population in relative poverty, i.e., those whose household income is less than half that of the median; and (3) the share of the population below twice the poverty threshold.

The poverty rate for the deeply poor shows less variation than the other measures through time. After rising slightly through the early 1980s, it has hovered since then at around 5%. Deep poverty did, however, fall 0.9 percentage points between 1995 and 2000, from 5.3% to 4.4%. Research on the deeply poor has shown that they have come to face two new difficulties in recent years. First, as they tend to be the least connected to the labor market, they are unlikely to benefit even from fast economic growth (though their share is small, the ranks of the deeply poor comprised over 12 million persons in 2000). Also, to the extent that social policy shifts toward supporting work, they are less likely to get the material help they need from the safety net. Moreover, research has shown that the safety net has become less likely over time to reach these persons, despite the fact that they remain eligible for benefits.

Since poverty status is assigned without regard to how far below the poverty threshold a particular family is, the rate itself reveals little about the depth of poverty. In fact, over time the deeply poor represent a larger share of the poor. This trend is implied by Figure 5F, which shows that, while overall poverty fell somewhat over the 1980s and 1990s, the share of the deeply poor changed little. **Figure 5G** confirms this, showing an increase in the share of the poor whose family income was below half the poverty threshold. From the mid-1970s through the mid-1980s, the share of the poor in this low-income category grew from about 30% to about 40%, and it has stayed at about that level since.

The share of households living on one-half the median income (Figure 5F) provides a relative, as opposed to an absolute, measure of poverty (this measure is also used in the international comparisons in Chapter 7). As noted above, a conceptual shortcoming of the official poverty thresholds is that they are adjusted only for inflation; they do not reflect overall income growth. This omission creates a problem in that, as average income grows over time and standards of living rise, the economic distance between the officially poor and the rest of society expands. While the earliest poverty line (1959) for a family of four was 55% of the median family income, it is now just 35%.

This concept of economic distance shows up as a gap between the official measure and the relative measure. When official poverty fell both over the 1980s and 1990s, relative poverty did not fall at all, implying that, even while a larger share of low-income families made it above the poverty line, they failed to gain on the median family and thus made no relative progress. Since the early 1980s, over a fifth of the population has remained below half the national median.

**FIGURE 5G** Percent of poor below half the poverty line, 1975-2001

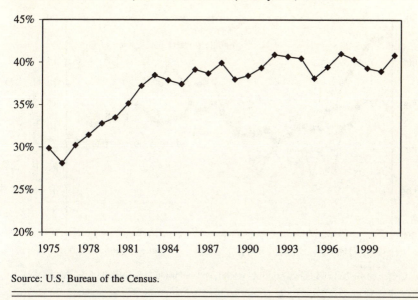

Source: U.S. Bureau of the Census.

The share of the population below twice the poverty threshold is also illustrated in Figure 5F. This value—$35,200 for a family of four in 2000—is quite close to values derived from research on family budgets, which attempt to measure how much income families need to meet their basic needs for housing, food, health care, child care (if they are working), and other necessities. While the family budgets are much more detailed than the poverty measures and tend to be geographically specific (since costs vary across place), "twice the poverty line" is a simple proxy for this concept.

By this measure, an average of about one-third of the population has been poor or near-poor since the mid-1970s. As might be expected—since this group contains more working families than are in the poverty population—the twice-poverty measure moves cyclically and is more responsive to economic growth than the overall rate. For example, while official poverty fell 3.8 points by 2000 from its 1993 peak, the two-times poverty rate fell by 6 points, to a historic low of 29.2%.

Since a poverty threshold is a fixed-income level, families are considered poor whether they are one dollar or a thousand dollars below the poverty line. Thus, another useful way to gauge the depth of poverty is the "poverty gap": the average income deficit (the dollar gap between a poor family's income and its poverty threshold) experienced by poor families or individuals.

**FIGURE 5H** Family poverty gap and poverty rates, 1959-2001

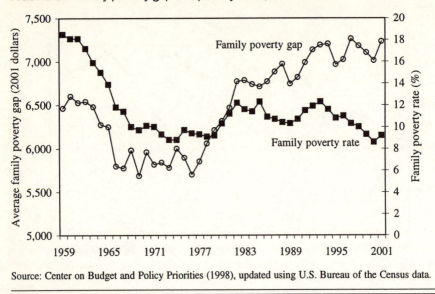

Source: Center on Budget and Policy Priorities (1998), updated using U.S. Bureau of the Census data.

**Figure 5H** plots both family poverty rates and the average family poverty gap. Over the 1960s through the mid-1970s, both the rate of poverty rate and the poverty gap declined, meaning that fewer families were poor and, of those who were, they were on average less poor over time. The strong labor market, along with the expansion of cash transfers over this period, including both Social Security (which significantly reduced the poverty of the elderly) and welfare benefits, contributed to these trends. As shown in **Table 5.6**, the average family poverty gap fell 1.6% annually over this period.

Both family poverty and the poverty gap rose steeply over the recessionary period in the early 1980s, and, as shown in the figure, the two series diverged in the mid-1980s. In fact, the growth rates in the bottom section of the table reveal that the family poverty gap has risen consistently over business cycle peaks (the gap for individuals fell 0.3% annually from 1973 to 1979, but has risen since). Thus, while the 1973 and 2000 poverty rates were about the same (8.8% in 1973 and 8.6% in 2000), the average poor family was over $1,000 (2001 dollars) worse off at the end of the period. A recession-induced expansion of the poverty gap is evident in the last row of the table and in Figure 5H, which show the family poverty gap rising sharply, by 3.1%, and ending close to its historical peak.

Taken in tandem with the fact that a relatively constant share of the popula-

**TABLE 5.6** Average poverty gap, 1967-2001 (2001 dollars)

| Years | Families | Persons not in families |
|---|---|---|
| 1959 | $6,462 | $4,293 |
| 1973 | 5,779 | 3,421 |
| 1979 | 6,210 | 3,440 |
| 1989 | 6,746 | 3,912 |
| 1995 | 6,965 | 4,339 |
| 2000 | 7,011 | 4,510 |
| 2001 | 7,231 | 4,550 |
| *Annual growth rates* | | |
| 1959-73 | -0.8% | -1.6% |
| 1973-79 | 1.2 | 0.1 |
| 1979-89 | 0.8 | 1.3 |
| 1989-2000 | 0.4 | 1.3 |
| 1989-95 | 0.5 | 1.7 |
| 1995-2000 | 0.1 | 0.8 |
| 2000-01 | 3.1 | 0.9 |

Source: Center for Budget and Policy Priorities (1998), updated using U.S. Bureau of the Census data.

tion has incomes below half the poverty line, it is clear that, while poverty has fallen in recent years, it has also deepened. Today's poor families are poorer, on average, than those of years past. To some extent, this is to be expected, given the strong shift of public policy toward work over cash assistance. The families most able to take advantage of both the strong labor market of the latter 1990s and the income supports tied to work, like the EITC, were likely to both climb out of poverty and do so from relatively close to the income threshold. Those left behind are probably the least likely to be able to take advantage of either a strong market economy or work-based supports.

In sum, the official poverty measure is clearly outdated and in need of repair, and it is well within our ability to do a better job of measuring poverty. Furthermore, carefully designed alternative measures show higher levels of poverty than the official approach.

While the latter years of the 1990s saw real progress against poverty, by none of the measures used here can one suggest that we have made great strides over the long term. Why have two decades of growth, interrupted only briefly by recession, failed to drive poverty rates far below levels that prevailed in past decades? We turn next to this important question.

## Poverty, growth, and the inequality wedge

As shown in Figure 5A, despite some periods of intermittent progress, the United States has made few long-term gains against poverty since the mid-1970s. The slowdown in productivity growth that occurred around the mid-1970s has been cited as a major contributor to persistently high poverty, yet, though it slowed, productivity neither stopped growing nor declined after 1973, and average income grew considerably after the mid-1970s. Analysts also point to shifts in family structure and immigration to explain the trend, but, as shown below, while each of these plays a role, they are secondary to the main factor that has created a wedge between economic growth and poverty reduction since 1973: the rise of income inequality. While it is the case that average incomes grew more slowly after than before 1973, the fact that the growth that occurred was shared unequally meant that incomes at the bottom of the income scale fell (or grew less quickly) than those at the top. This factor, more than any other, has slowed the progress we might have hoped to make over a 27-year period in which the economy expanded significantly.

**Table 5.7** looks at key macroeconomic variables to get a broad picture of the trends in poverty and the economy over two periods: 1959-79, when poverty fell sharply, and 1979-2000 when it hardly changed at all. (This analysis uses 1959-79, rather than the 1959-73 period used throughout, to allow a comparison of equal lengths and to avoid the problem of annualizing series that do not intuitively lend themselves to annualizing. This choice has no effect on the substance of the analysis.) We further divide the 1979-2000 period into two sub-periods to gain insight into the shifts that occurred in the latter 1990s.

Both productivity and real per capita income grew most slowly in the 1979-89 period, although productivity still grew by 15% (1.4% per year) over the 1980s and per capita income grew by 23%. Unemployment fell half a point over the 1980s, which should have lowered poverty, and the share of mother-only families grew much more slowly in the 1980s relative to the earlier period.

Yet poverty rates grew slightly in the 1980s after falling sharply—by close to 11 percentage points—from 1959 to 1979. The culprit, as far as these indicators are concerned, is inequality (as measured by the percent increase in the Gini ratio; see Chapter 1 for more discussion of this measure of income inequality), as what growth there was failed to reach the low end of the income scale. Growing inequality creates a wedge between productivity or average income growth and the incomes of the poor (government transfer policy, discussed below, also played a role here). As discussed in much of the income and wage analysis from earlier chapters, inequality grew historically quickly over the 1980s, and its impact on poverty is evident in the table.

**TABLE 5.7** Changes in poverty rates and various indicators, 1959-2000

| Year | Poverty rates | Annual growth rates | | Unemployment | Gini coefficient** | Mother-only families as share of all families |
| | | Productivity* | Per capita income | | | |
| --- | --- | --- | --- | --- | --- | --- |
| 1959-79 | -10.7 | 2.4% | 2.9% | 0.3 | 1.1% | 4.5 |
| 1979-89 | 1.1 | 1.4 | 2.1 | -0.5 | 9.9 | 1.1 |
| 1989-2000 | -1.5 | 1.7 | 1.7 | -1.8 | 3.5 | 1.6 |
| 1995-2000 | -2.5 | 2.6 | 2.2 | -1.6 | 2.1 | -0.8 |

\* Non-farm business sector.
\*\* The percent change in the Gini coefficient, 1989-2000, includes a downward adjustment for the effect of the top-code change in 1993. Without the adjustment, the change would be 7.2. See table note.

Source: Poverty rates, family share, and Gini coefficients from U.S. Bureau of the Census; productivity, BLS; real per capita income, BEA.

In contrast with the 1980s, the 1995-2000 period looks much more like the 1959-79 period. Productivity grew quickly and unemployment fell sharply to historically low levels. Unlike the earlier period, the share of mother-only families declined slightly. At the same time, inequality rose much more slowly than over the 1980s, growing 2.1% as opposed to 9.9% (on an annual basis, the Gini ratio grew just under half as fast in the latter 1990s than in the 1980s). These factors proved to be a potent recipe against poverty, which fell at about the same annual rate between 1995 and 2000 as in the 20-year period beginning in 1959.

Unfortunately, this latter period was much more short-lived, but the message is clear. For the fruits of faster growth to be shared in such a way as to lower poverty, public policy must focus on low unemployment and on less (or, at worst, slow-growing) inequality.

Much of the analysis so far has emphasized the importance of low unemployment. **Figure 5I** uses the variation in poverty rates and unemployment by state to investigate this relationship in two different periods: the 1980s and the 1990s. Each dot in the figures represents the intersection of a state's change in unemployment and poverty over the particular decade. For example, the dot in the far-right-hand corner of the top figure represents a state in which the unemployment rate grew by about three points and the poverty rate grew by about four points. Each figure also includes a "regression line," which helps to illustrate the relationship between changes in unemployment and poverty.

One might expect that most of the dots would congregate in the lower-left or upper-right quadrants of the graph, the former representing falling unemploy-

**FIGURE 5I** Unemployment and poverty in the 1980s and 1990s

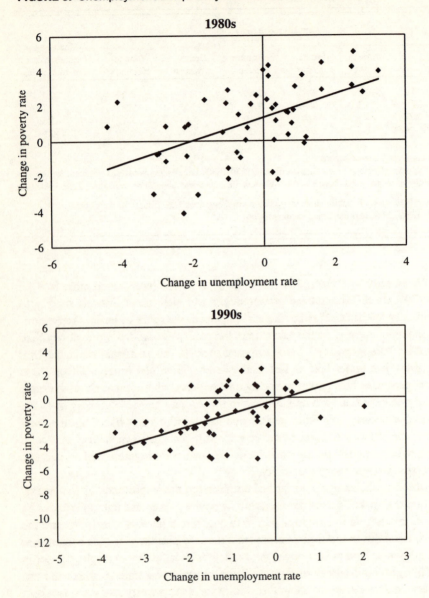

Source: U.S. Bureau of the Census and Bureau of Labor Statistics.

ment and falling poverty and the latter representing rising unemployment and rising poverty. In both figures, this is generally the case, but important differences between the two graphs are worth noting. First, while many states fall in the upper right corner in the 1980s—increases in both unemployment and poverty—the 1990s graph has only three states in that section. Many more states in the latter decade experienced falling unemployment coupled with falling poverty rates. Second, while both graphs have numerous dots in the upper-left section—falling unemployment and *rising* poverty—in the 1990s, these dots are more clustered about the center of the figure, implying smaller changes in both rates.

Finally, the slope of the regression line is steeper in the 1990s than in the 1980s, implying that each point decline in unemployment in the latter decade was associated with a larger decline in poverty than in the earlier period. Though more research is necessary to identify the cause of this increased responsiveness of poverty to falling unemployment, it is likely that the historically low levels of unemployment reached in the 1990s made a difference. In other words, a decline in the unemployment rate from 5% to 4% may lower poverty more than does a decline from 6% to 5%.

### The impact of demographic change

Another explanation for the failure of poverty to fall despite growth cites the increase in family types more vulnerable to poverty. This line of argument typically discounts economic factors, such as inequality or higher unemployment, and emphasizes the increase in the share of families headed by single mothers, for example, since these families have considerably lower income and higher poverty rates than families with two earners (see Chapter 1). This section examines whether there is compelling quantitative evidence for this position.

**Table 5.8** shows the percent of persons in three different family types in the period 1959-2000, along with the poverty rates of persons in those families. Clearly, there has been a shift over time into family types more vulnerable to poverty. For instance, the percentage of persons in married-couple and male-headed families, which have the lowest poverty rates, has consistently fallen, from 85.9% in 1959 to 70.1% in 2000. Conversely, there has been a consistent expansion of female-headed families and an even faster growth of households consisting of single individuals.

By itself, we would expect this pattern of family structure changes to increase poverty rates. Single-parent families typically have only one major earner to depend on, and, in the case of single mothers, are further disadvantaged by the fact that women tend to earn less than men. However, changes in poverty rates within these groups also play a determining role. Growth in vulnerable family types as a share of all families will put upward pressure on poverty rates.

**TABLE 5.8** Changing family structure and poverty, 1959-2000

| Year | Percent of persons in: | | | | Poverty rate of persons in: | | | |
|---|---|---|---|---|---|---|---|---|
| | Female-headed families | Married-couple and male-headed families* | Not living in families | Total | Female-headed families | Married-couple and male-headed families* | Not living in families | All persons |
| 1959 | 8.0% | 85.9% | 6.1% | 100.0% | 49.4% | 18.2% | 46.1% | 22.4% |
| 1969 | 9.0 | 83.7 | 7.3 | 100.0 | 38.2 | 7.4 | 34.0 | 12.1 |
| 1979 | 12.1 | 76.2 | 11.7 | 100.0 | 34.9 | 6.4 | 21.9 | 11.7 |
| 1989 | 13.2 | 72.5 | 14.3 | 100.0 | 35.9 | 7.3 | 19.2 | 12.8 |
| 2000 | 13.6 | 70.1 | 16.4 | 100.0 | 27.9 | 6.3 | 18.9 | 11.3 |
| *Percentage-point changes* | | | | | | | | |
| 1959-69 | 1.0 | -2.3 | 1.3 | | -11.2 | -10.8 | -12.1 | -10.3 |
| 1969-79 | 3.1 | -7.5 | 4.4 | | -3.3 | -0.9 | -12.1 | -0.4 |
| 1979-89 | 1.1 | -3.7 | 2.6 | | 1.0 | 0.9 | -2.7 | 1.1 |
| 1989-2000 | 0.3 | -2.4 | 2.0 | | -8.0 | -1.1 | -0.3 | -1.5 |
| 1959-2000 | 5.6 | -15.9 | 10.3 | | -21.5 | -11.9 | -27.2 | -11.1 |

* From 1979 forward, this group includes a small residual number of persons in unrelated sub-families.

Source: U.S. Bureau of the Census.

But rising relative incomes concurrent with this growth would be a countervailing factor. In fact, the poverty rates for persons by family type show that all family types saw their poverty rates fall over the 1960s and 1970s, with single persons showing the largest drop (12 percentage points in both decades). Note also the decline in the poverty rates of persons in female-headed families of 11.2 points over the 1960s, another 3.3 points over the 1970s, and 8.0 more points over the 1990s, for a cumulative decline of 22.5 points.

What do these trends reveal about the relationship between demographic shifts and changes in poverty rates? The evidence is mixed. On the one hand, it is clear that there has been a compositional shift to families more vulnerable to poverty. However, when the demographic shifts were occurring most rapidly, in the 1969-79 period, the overall poverty rate declined from 12.1% to 11.7%, with declines occurring for each family type but most quickly for those with the highest poverty rates: individuals and those in female-headed families. Conversely, when demographic forces were less poverty inducing over the 1980s, the trend reversed, and poverty grew by one point for those in mother-only families; it also grew about the same amount for the family type least vulnerable to poverty: persons in married-couple families. Thus, while demographic shifts to single-parent families are associated with higher poverty at any point in time, these trends suggest that such shifts might not go far in explaining, for example, why poverty failed to fall much over the 1980s. The question is: how large a part has demographic change played relative to other factors over time?

Before we parcel out the relative contributions of poverty's determinants, one other variable needs to brought into the mix: education levels. Often overlooked, the educational upgrading of heads of families over time has been an important countervailing trend to the shift to lower-income family types. As Americans from all walks of life become more highly educated, they and their families are less likely to be poor (holding all else equal).

This relationship can be seen in **Table 5.9**, which shows the family poverty rates for families with children over the 1969-2000 period by the education level of the family head (top section), along with the shares of families in each category (bottom section). Families headed by persons with higher levels of education are less likely to be poor. Note, for example, that families with children headed by a college graduate have poverty rates between 2.1% and 2.6%. On the other end of the scale, the rates for families headed by someone with less than a high school education (just under a third in 2000) reveal the increased importance of education as an antipoverty tool. Those with the least education were always most likely to be poor, but in 1969 there rates were less than twice the overall average and about 10 times that of families headed by a college graduate; by 2000, the rates for the families headed by high school

**TABLE 5.9** Poverty rates for families with children, by educational level of family head, 1969-2000

| Educational level of family head | Poverty rates | | | | Percentage-point changes | | | |
|---|---|---|---|---|---|---|---|---|
| | 1969 | 1979 | 1989 | 2000 | 1969-79 | 1979-89 | 1989-2000 | 1969-2000 |
| Less than high school | 19.6% | 26.8% | 38.0% | 32.9% | 7.2 | 11.3 | -5.1 | 13.3 |
| High school | 6.9 | 10.5 | 15.3 | 15.0 | 3.6 | 4.8 | -0.3 | 8.2 |
| Some college | 5.1 | 7.1 | 9.9 | 8.6 | 2.0 | 2.8 | -1.3 | 3.5 |
| College degree or higher | 2.1 | 2.5 | 2.6 | 2.5 | 0.4 | 0.1 | -0.1 | 0.5 |
| Total | 10.6 | 12.5 | 15.5 | 12.6 | 1.9 | 2.9 | -2.8 | 2.0 |
| | Percent of poor families | | | | | | | |
| | 1969 | 1979 | 1989 | 2000 | | | | |
| Less than high school | 36.9% | 26.2% | 18.9% | 15.0% | -10.7 | -7.3 | -3.9 | -21.9 |
| High school | 33.9 | 35.0 | 35.6 | 30.7 | 1.1 | 0.6 | -4.9 | -3.2 |
| Some college | 14.6 | 19.5 | 23.0 | 28.4 | 4.8 | 3.5 | 5.4 | 13.7 |
| College degree or higher | 14.5 | 19.4 | 22.6 | 26.0 | 4.9 | 3.2 | 3.4 | 11.4 |
| Total | 100.0 | 100.0 | 100.0 | 100.0 | | | | |

Source: Authors' analysis of March CPS data.

dropouts were about 2.6 times the overall rate and 13 times the college rate. The increasing importance of education in reducing poverty is highlighted in the analysis that follows.

The bottom panel of the table shows the persistent shift toward higher levels of educational attainment by poor families. For instance, over the full 1969-2000 period, there was a 25.1 percentage-point shift out of the bottom two education categories into the "some college" and college graduate categories. The shift out of the least-educated category occurred most quickly over the 1970s. Over the 1990s, the share of poor families headed by a high school dropout fell quickly, but educational upgrading occurred more quickly among those with a high school education (which fell by 8 points) and some college (which grew by 8.5 points). Thus, while family structure shifts may have put upward pressure on poverty rates over time, educational shifts have likely helped to reduce poverty. Simultaneously, as we have stressed throughout, the rate of economic growth and inequality also matter. What's needed is a method to partial out the relative contributions.

**Table 5.10** provides a breakdown, or decomposition, of poverty's growth that separately accounts for these factors (and adds race of the household head). This table separates the growth in poverty rates into three demographic factors—the education level and race of the family head, and family structure—and two economic components—the poverty-reducing effect of overall economic growth and the poverty-increasing effect of growing inequality. Thus, it highlights the relative importance of these factors in the growth of poverty in each time period. If the conventional wisdom is correct—that family structure changes are the key factor breaking the link between economic growth and poverty—then this decomposition should reveal a consistent increase in this factor's role over time. Similarly, the role of economic factors—such as the overall growth of the economy and especially the increase in inequality—should have diminished. In fact, as Table 5.10 shows, the opposite is the case, as the poverty-inducing role of family structure shifts fell steeply over time.

Family structure changes played the largest role in poverty's growth in the 1970s; however, in the 1980s and 1990s, its contribution diminished considerably (from adding 1.9 points in the 1970s to adding 0.7 and 0.3 points in the 1980s and 1990s). Though the poverty-reducing impact of educational upgrading fell by 0.4 points from the 1970s to the latter two decades, it remained a relatively large determinant of poverty outcomes. By the 1990s, the impact of education was four times that of family structure (1.2 compared to 0.3).

Additionally, while family structure was having its most negative impact on poverty's growth, in the 1970s, poverty rates actually fell by 0.5 percentage points, thanks to economic growth that was only partially offset by increasing income

**TABLE 5.10** Impact of demographic and economic changes on poverty rates

| Change | 1969-79 | 1979-89 | 1989-2000 | 1969-2000 |
|---|---|---|---|---|
| **Actual change** | -0.5 | 1.1 | -1.6 | -0.9 |
| **Total demographic effect** | 0.5 | -0.3 | -0.7 | -0.4 |
| Race | 0.3 | 0.3 | 0.3 | 1.0 |
| Education | -1.6 | -1.2 | -1.2 | -4.0 |
| Family structure | 1.9 | 0.7 | 0.3 | 2.9 |
| Interaction | -0.2 | -0.1 | -0.2 | -0.5 |
| **Economic change** | -1.0 | 1.4 | -0.9 | -0.5 |
| Growth | -1.5 | -1.3 | -2.0 | -4.8 |
| Inequality | 0.5 | 2.7 | 1.1 | 4.3 |

Source: Authors' analysis of March CPS data.

inequality (which grew little in this period relative to later periods) and educational upgrading. Poverty rose in the 1980s, and the largest contributor was faster-growing inequality that was only partially offset by overall growth. Over the 1990s, economic growth accelerated and inequality slowed. Combining their disparate effects led to a 0.9-point decline in poverty as the poverty-reducing effects of more education and faster growth combined to outpace the poverty-inducing effects of racial and family structure shifts and more inequality.

**Figure 5J** plots these determinants of poverty from 1969 to 2000. Over the long term, the progress made against poverty has come from more growth and more education. But the figure also reveals that the inequality wedge took back much of the gains from growth. Family structure has played a role—poverty rates would be almost 3 points lower had shifts to more vulnerable family types not occurred. But despite these shifts, by the 1990s this trend added only 0.3 percentage points to the poverty rate.

In fact, the numbers in Table 5.10 suggest that the poverty debate could fruitfully focus less on the problem of single-mother families and turn more of its attention to faster growth, full employment, and less inequality. This is especially so given the fact, as shown in Table 5.8, that the share of persons in female-headed families was essentially unchanged over the 1990s, at the same time that their poverty rates fell steeply.

### The changing effects of taxes and transfers
Another determinant of the poverty rate is the tax and transfer system that serves to collect and redistribute resources throughout the economy. Cash

**FIGURE 5J** Contribution of demographic and economic changes to poverty, 1969-2000

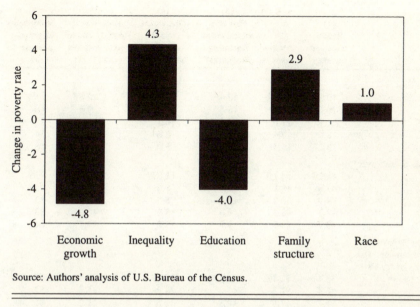

Source: Authors' analysis of U.S. Bureau of the Census.

and near-cash benefits, such as welfare payments or food stamps, increase the resources available to the poor and thus lower poverty. (While the value of food stamps is not counted in the official poverty rate, we correct for that omission below). Payroll taxes paid by low-income workers can raise poverty rates that measure such costs, while EITC benefits can lower poverty. Also, all of these programs vary over time and by family type, so we need to track the trend in their impact on poverty rates for different types of persons.

The impact of the tax and transfer system on poverty is broadly a function of two forces: changes in market-driven poverty rates and changes in the magnitude and incidence of benefits. If the market (pre-tax, pre-transfer distribution) generates less poverty (say, due to stronger and more equal growth), then the transfer system has less work to do to reduce poverty rates. Conversely, when inequality rises and incomes fall, the transfer system must expand if poverty levels are to be maintained, let alone be further reduced.

**Table 5.11** examines the changes in market poverty and the impact of taxes and transfers for various family types from 1979 to 2001 (earlier data are not available). The "All persons" section shows the poverty rate before taxes and transfers; these rates represent the degree of poverty that would exist in the absence of government intervention (18.6% in 2000). Moving left to right, the

**TABLE 5.11** Poverty-reducing effects of transfers, 1979-2001

| Year | (1) Before taxes and transfers | (2) After taxes | (3) Plus non-means tested (including Medicare)* | (4) Plus means tested (including Medicaid)* | (5) Reduction in poverty due to taxes transfers and (1)-(4) | (6) Reduction effective-ness rate (5)/(1) |
|---|---|---|---|---|---|---|
| **All persons** | | | | | | |
| 1979 | 19.5% | 19.3% | 12.4% | 8.9% | 10.6% | 54% |
| 1989 | 20.0 | 20.3 | 13.5 | 10.4 | 9.6 | 48 |
| 1995 | 21.9 | 21.0 | 13.7 | 10.3 | 11.6 | 53 |
| 2000 | 18.6 | 17.6 | 10.8 | 8.6 | 10.0 | 54 |
| 2001 | 19.2 | 18.4 | 11.3 | 9.0 | 10.2 | 53 |
| **Persons 65 and over** | | | | | | |
| 1979 | 54.2% | 54.1% | 15.4% | 12.3% | 41.9% | 77% |
| 1989 | 47.6 | 48.1 | 11.4 | 8.6 | 39.0 | 82 |
| 1995 | 49.9 | 50.2 | 10.3 | 8.5 | 41.4 | 83 |
| 2000 | 48.2 | 48.3 | 9.9 | 8.2 | 40.0 | 83 |
| 2001 | 48.7 | 48.7 | 9.8 | 8.0 | 40.7 | 84 |
| **Persons in female-headed families with children under 18** | | | | | | |
| 1979 | 53.4% | 52.3% | 47.3% | 28.1% | 25.3% | 47% |
| 1989 | 51.4 | 51.1 | 47.0 | 34.9 | 16.5 | 32 |
| 1995 | 51.7 | 47.5 | 44.3 | 30.5 | 21.2 | 41 |
| 2000 | 40.9 | 35.3 | 31.9 | 23.4 | 17.5 | 43 |
| 2001 | 41.1 | 36.5 | 32.8 | 25.3 | 15.8 | 38 |
| **Persons in married-couple families with children under 18** | | | | | | |
| 1979 | 9.4% | 9.1% | 7.3% | 5.2% | 4.2% | 45% |
| 1989 | 10.3 | 10.5 | 9.0 | 6.6 | 3.7 | 36 |
| 1995 | 11.0 | 9.8 | 8.1 | 5.7 | 5.3 | 48 |
| 2000 | 8.6 | 7.3 | 6.0 | 4.6 | 4.0 | 47 |
| 2001 | 8.5 | 7.4 | 6.1 | 4.6 | 3.9 | 46 |

* Includes fungible value of Medicare and Medicaid benefits; see table note.

Source: EPI analysis of U.S. Bureau of the Census, P-60, No. 182-RD, and Ferret table, http://ferret.bls.census.gov/macro/032001/rdcall/2_001.htm.

table introduces different transfers and taxes and shows how poverty would be affected by each. In column 2, for example, the 2000 market poverty rate for all persons fell slightly once taxes (and tax credits) were taken into account. This represents both the poverty-reducing effects of the EITC and the poverty-increasing effects of state taxes, which tend to be regressive. The addition of non-means-tested benefits (column 3), including Medicare (i.e., that portion of

Medicare estimated to increase a family's resources), lowered the rate to 10.8% in 2000. Column 5 totals the effects of government tax and transfer policies, showing, for example, that in 2000 they reduced market-generated poverty by 10.0 points. The final column represents the share of market poverty reduced by government tax and transfer policy.

Market outcomes were worse for all persons in 1989 and 1995 relative to 1979, meaning that the tax and transfer system would have had to work harder to keep poverty from rising. In fact, as seen in column 4, for all persons, poverty rates after taxes and transfers were significantly higher in 1989 than in 1979 (10.4% vs. 8.9%). Column 5 shows that instead of working harder in 1989, transfers reduced poverty one-point less than in 1979. Adding that one point to the half-point difference in market poverty explains the 1.5-point increase observed in Column 4 between 1979 and 1989. Thus, one-third of the increase in this poverty rate adjusted for both market and tax and transfer outcomes is attributable to worse market outcomes and two-thirds to less-effective redistribution. In other words, both factors acted to increase poverty over the 1980s.

The differences between 1995 and 2000 are particularly relevant to shifts in both the economy and poverty policy. Given the strong and relatively equal economic growth over this period, market poverty was significantly lower— 3.3 percentage points—in 2000 than in 1995 (18.6% vs. 21.9%). Yet, taxes and transfers accomplished 1.6 points more poverty reduction in 1995 than in 2000: 11.6% vs. 10.0% (due to the lower base in the latter year, the reduction effectiveness rates are about the same). This diminished role for government was largely due to the decrease in means-tested benefits (primarily welfare and food stamps), which can be observed by moving from column 3 to 4. So, in this period, the market and the transfer system were working at cross-purposes. The 3.3-point fall in market poverty more than explains the 1.7-point decline in adjusted poverty in column 4, since reduced transfers essentially took back 1.6 points of those market gains. In a later section, we further examine the dramatic decline in means-tested cash benefits that occurred over this period.

The second section of Table 5.11 shows the importance of transfers for persons over 65, who have both high rates of market poverty (since few are attached to the labor market) and the highest rates of poverty reduction by far. Market outcomes became less poverty inducing since 1979, and the reduction effectiveness of transfers increased over the 1980s for the elderly while falling for each of the other groups. There are no obvious policy reasons for this change; note that the percentage points of poverty reduction shown in column 5 are similar in each year. Thus, the change in the effectiveness rate appears to be mostly a function of the lower market poverty outcomes after 1979.

Relative to the elderly, taxes and transfers were significantly less effective at reducing the poverty of persons in female-headed families with children. Over the 1979-89 period, market outcomes actually reduced their poverty by 2.0 percentage points, but a fall in benefits led to a post-tax and -transfer poverty rate in 1989 that was 6.8 points higher than in 1979. The reduction effectiveness rate was 15 percentage points lower in 1989 than in 1979. By 2000, female-headed families with children had a much lower rate of market poverty than in 1989 or 1995. Note also that in both 1995 and 2000 the expanded EITC led to increasing reductions in post-tax poverty (column 2). Conversely, the 2000 rates reveal the decline in the poverty-reducing impact of means-tested benefits. In 1979, these benefits reduced poverty rates by 19.2 points (the difference between columns 4 and 3). In 1995, this difference was 13.8, and by 2000 it had fallen to 8.5. In the recession of 2001, a time when the safety net was most needed, means-tested benefits reduced the poverty rates of persons in these family types even less, by 7.5 points. Thus, the reduction effectiveness rate fell from 43% in 2000 to 38% in 2001. It appears that, while the benefits of the higher EITC continued to be effective—note the greater share of poverty reduction after 1995 relative to earlier periods—the loss of welfare benefits associated with welfare reform meant less assistance, and thus less poverty reduction, for vulnerable families in periods of higher unemployment.

Persons in married-couple families with children have the lowest market poverty rates, less than half that of all persons in 2000 (8.6% vs. 18.6%). The expansion of the EITC in the early 1990s clearly reached them as well. In 1989, their rates in columns 1 and 2 are about the same, meaning that, on net, federal and state taxes had little effect on their market poverty rates that year. In 2000, however, their market poverty rate was lowered by 1.3 percentage points. Thus, relative to 1989, persons in these families in 2000 started out with lower poverty rates and were lifted further by favorable tax changes.

## Work and poverty: the policy thrust of the 1990s

Poverty policy, specifically regarding welfare, shifted considerably in the mid-1990s. Even before the passage of the sweeping welfare reform bill 1996, numerous states were already experimenting with a approaches to welfare geared to moving families from the welfare rolls into the labor market. The message that work was a prerequisite for the receipt of public assistance was received and acted upon—and amplified by the strong labor market—by both welfare administrators and recipients.

**Figure 5K** shows the increase in the employment rates of three types of mothers, married, single (divorced, separated, or widowed), and never married, from 1985 to 2000. While all rates trend up, those for married mothers rise slowly relative to the other two groups. In fact, after falling behind married mothers through most of the period, single mothers' employment rates surpass those of married mothers in 1998, and the never-married group, which experienced the largest gains, almost catches up to the others.

This trend had a dramatic impact on the composition of the income of single-mother families. **Figure 5L** shows the earnings and public assistance (means-tested cash benefits, mostly welfare) shares of family income for low-income single-mother families (low income is defined here as the average of the bottom half of the mother-only family income distribution). From 1979 through the late 1980s, incomes of these families came fairly evenly from earnings and public assistance, with each contributing about 35-45% of income (the rest, a consistent share of about 20%, came from various other sources, including other cash benefits, child support, alimony, and interpersonal transfers).

A gap began to open in the early 1990s, and as the decade progressed the gap grew quickly, with a dramatic shift from public assistance to earnings. By 2000, the average public assistance share was about 10%, while the earnings share surpassed 70%. Such surveys as the one used for this figure tend to suffer from underreporting of welfare income, and this problem may have grown over the period of welfare reform. But the divergence of these two income shares is so large that correcting the picture by the amount of underreporting could not possibly change the conclusion that the shift toward earnings and away from benefits has been unprecedented. If a goal of welfare reform was to induce this type of shift, then that goal has been realized.

The problem, however, is that, while these families have more income on average, they are still poor or, with EITC benefits, near poor. **Figure 5M** shows the real average income levels of single-mother families with incomes below the median for that group. Each bar shows the income components noted above plus two other income sources: the value of the EITC that would accompany the average family's earnings for that year, assuming two children, and the market value of food stamps. Average income declined slightly over the 1980s, mostly due to declines in cash welfare benefits and real earnings that were not made up for by a higher value for food stamps and a slightly higher EITC. Welfare income continued to fall through 1995, but earnings grew and, importantly, the EITC was much expanded, growing from $590 to $1,800 (2000 dollars) for two-child families at these earnings levels.

As the previous figure showed, this trend toward less welfare and more earnings grew extremely quickly in the last five years of the 1990s. Earnings

**FIGURE 5K** Employment rates for mothers, 1985-2000

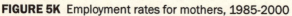

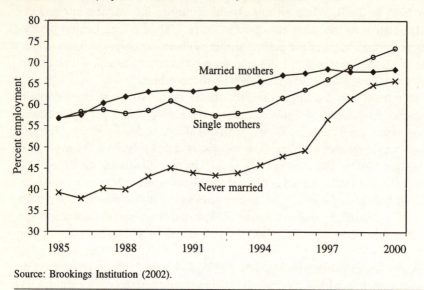

Source: Brookings Institution (2002).

**FIGURE 5L** Income components of low-income single mothers, 1979-2000

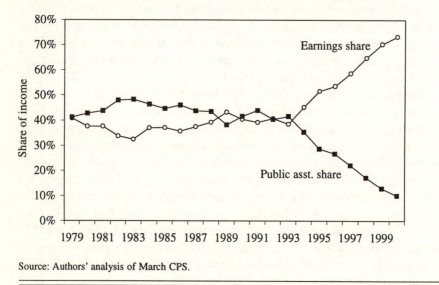

Source: Authors' analysis of March CPS.

**FIGURE 5M** Income by components, low-income single mothers, 1979-2000

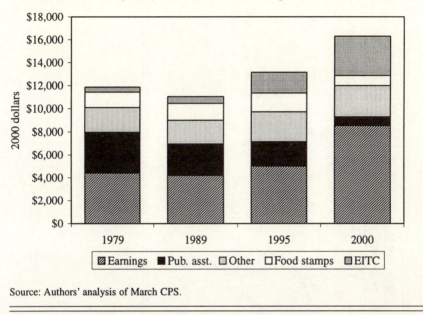

Source: Authors' analysis of March CPS.

among these low-income single-mother families grew by $3,500 and EITC benefits, which are tied to earnings, grew by $1,600. Over the same period, cash welfare benefits fell by about $1,400, and the market value of food stamps fell by $760. The average low-income single-mother family thus ended up with income of $16,300, about $2,400 above the poverty line but still below the level needed to make ends meet, especially considering that this represents the income of a working single parent with two children. Given reasonable assumptions about work expenses, which should be deducted from income before judging poverty status (as in the alternative poverty measure featured in Figure 5D), this family would likely still be poor.

The data in **Table 5.12** show that similar trends affected all prime-age (household head age 25-54) low-income families (since we are interested in labor market activity, elderly families are excluded from this analysis). Over the 1980s average income fell by 8.0% for all low-income prime-age families and by 11.7% for those with children, as declines in earnings and cash assistance were not offset by food stamps. Both annual earnings and public assistance fell between 8% and 15%, but the dollar losses were much greater from earnings, which fell $1,613 for families with children compared to a drop of $170 from cash assistance. Over the 1990s, welfare benefits dropped by over

**TABLE 5.12** Income levels and sources of income, prime-age families (family head 25-54) in the bottom 20th percentile, 1979-2000 (2000 dollars)

| | | | | Percent change | | | Dollar change | | |
|---|---|---|---|---|---|---|---|---|---|
| All prime-age families | 1979 | 1989 | 2000 | 1979-89 | 1989-2000 | 1979-2000 | 1979-89 | 1989-2000 | 1979-2000 |
| Average family income | $16,862 | $15,520 | $17,614 | -8.0% | 13.5% | 4.5% | $-1,342 | $2,094 | $752 |
| Earnings | 12,024 | 11,051 | 13,902 | -8.1 | 25.8 | 15.6 | -973 | 2,850 | 1,877 |
| Cash assistance | 1,542 | 1,320 | 416 | -14.4 | -68.5 | -73.0 | -222 | -904 | -1,126 |
| Food stamps | 719 | 766 | 478 | 6.5 | -37.6 | -33.6 | 46 | -288 | -241 |
| Other* | 2,577 | 2,383 | 2,819 | -7.6 | 18.3 | 9.4 | -195 | 436 | 242 |
| *Prime-age families with children* | | | | | | | | | |
| Average family income | $15,709 | $13,875 | $15,821 | -11.7% | 14.0% | 0.7% | $-1,834 | $1,945 | $112 |
| Earnings | 10,589 | 8,976 | 12,338 | -15.2 | 37.5 | 16.5 | -1,613 | 3,362 | 1,749 |
| Cash assistance | 1,956 | 1,786 | 551 | -8.7 | -69.2 | -71.8 | -170 | -1,235 | -1,405 |
| Food stamps | 899 | 1,013 | 634 | 12.7 | -37.5 | -29.5 | 114 | -379 | -265 |
| Other* | 2,265 | 2,100 | 2,298 | -7.3 | 9.4 | 1.5 | -164 | 198 | 33 |

* Includes other cash benefits, child support, alimony, and interpersonal transfers.

Source: Authors' analysis.

two-thirds for both all prime-age families and those with children, but earnings reversed course sharply, growing 25.8% and 37.5%. Again, while the percent losses were greater for public assistance, the dollar gains from earnings were about twice those of the combined loss of cash assistance and food stamps. (The increase in the "other" category from 1989 to 2000 stems mostly from more Social Security and Supplemental Security Income (SSI), as well as more alimony and child support).

Nevertheless, over the full period from 1979 to 2000, these family types did not end up particularly far ahead. For all, the percent growth was 4.5%; for those with children, income changed little, as earnings growth and benefit losses basically cancelled each other out. The earnings gains of the 1990s were impressive for low-income families but, to pull these families ahead of their level from earlier peaks, these gains from work had to overcome both the steep losses that occurred over the 1980s and the steeper (in percentage terms) losses in cash assistance. The fact that they failed to do so helps explain the lack of dramatic, long-term progress against poverty.

**Table 5.13** broadens the focus to examine not just the incidence of work among the poor but the intensity. The table examines the trend in annual hours worked by poor families from 1979 to 1998 by summing hours of work across poor families and looking at the share of families in each of four hours categories: no work, 1-999 hours, 1,000-1,999, and 2,000 or more. In addition, it includes the average hours worked (including zeros for families with no time in the paid labor market), the average "family wage" (the average of family earnings divided by family hours for families with positive values for both), and the family poverty rate. The so-called "family wage" is not a typical hourly wage measure—unlike the measures shown in Chapter 2, it applies not to a specific person but to a family, wherein one or more persons may have worked at some point during the year in question. We use it here to get a sense of how much more work an average poor family would need to lift its earnings above the poverty threshold.

Note first that, while a minority of poor families work full time (at least 2,000 hours), the share grew in the 1990s. For example, among families with children, the share working full time did not change much over the 1980s (rising slightly from 23.0% to 24.5%) but grew 8.5 percentage points over the 1990s, such that just over a third worked full time in 2000. Particularly large gains of this sort occurred for mother-only families (about a 10-point increase from 1989 to 2000, from 9.5% to 19.4%) and for families headed by a minority. For example, while shares among whites changed very little over the post-1979 period, there was a 10.5-point shift into full-time work by poor Hispanic families, from 29.7% in 1989 to 40.2% in 2000.

**TABLE 5.13** Family work hours and wages among poor families, 1979-98 (percent of poor families in each category)

| | No work | 1-999 | 1,000-1,999 | 2,000+ | Total | Average family hours | Average family wage* (2000 dollars) | Poverty rate |
|---|---|---|---|---|---|---|---|---|
| **All** | | | | | | | | |
| 1979 | 41.7% | 21.2% | 15.7% | 21.4% | 100.0% | 965 | $6.70 | 9.1% |
| 1989 | 40.6 | 19.3 | 17.6 | 22.5 | 100.0 | 1,002 | 5.81 | 10.3 |
| 2000 | 34.0 | 19.2 | 18.5 | 28.4 | 100.0 | 1,132 | 6.62 | 8.6 |
| **Family head 25-54** | | | | | | | | |
| 1979 | 32.5% | 22.4% | 18.5% | 26.6% | 100.0% | 1,175 | $6.46 | 8.9% |
| 1989 | 34.3 | 19.4 | 19.6 | 26.7 | 100.0 | 1,161 | 5.77 | 10.5 |
| 2000 | 25.6 | 18.7 | 21.0 | 34.6 | 100.0 | 1,343 | 6.69 | 8.6 |
| **Families with children** | | | | | | | | |
| *All* | | | | | | | | |
| 1979 | 36.2% | 22.7% | 18.1% | 23.0% | 100.0% | 1,036 | $7.01 | 12.5% |
| 1989 | 36.5 | 20.0 | 18.9 | 24.5 | 100.0 | 1,070 | 5.95 | 15.5 |
| 2000 | 25.3 | 20.5 | 21.3 | 33.0 | 100.0 | 1,297 | 6.72 | 12.6 |
| *Female head of family* | | | | | | | | |
| 1979 | 49.7% | 27.1% | 15.4% | 7.8% | 100.0% | 514 | $6.60 | 39.4% |
| 1989 | 50.8 | 22.7 | 17.0 | 9.5 | 100.0 | 577 | 5.66 | 42.9 |
| 2000 | 32.1 | 24.6 | 23.9 | 19.4 | 100.0 | 935 | 7.02 | 32.4 |
| **By race of family head** | | | | | | | | |
| *White* | | | | | | | | |
| 1979 | 39.1% | 20.3% | 15.8% | 24.7% | 100.0% | 1,126 | $6.26 | 6.1% |
| 1989 | 36.9 | 19.4 | 18.6 | 25.1 | 100.0 | 1,143 | 5.51 | 6.4 |
| 2000 | 37.2 | 20.6 | 16.8 | 25.4 | 100.0 | 1,087 | 6.52 | 5.3 |
| *African American* | | | | | | | | |
| 1979 | 46.1% | 23.7% | 15.5% | 14.7% | 100.0% | 683 | $7.59 | 27.6% |
| 1989 | 48.1 | 20.1 | 16.2 | 15.6 | 100.0 | 723 | 5.97 | 27.9 |
| 2000 | 37.1 | 19.8 | 19.8 | 23.3 | 100.0 | 937 | 7.05 | 18.9 |
| *Hispanic* | | | | | | | | |
| 1979 | 41.9% | 18.8% | 16.0% | 23.3% | 100.0% | 958 | $6.67 | 19.7% |
| 1989 | 36.2 | 16.8 | 17.2 | 29.7 | 100.0 | 1,155 | 6.22 | 23.4 |
| 2000 | 24.3 | 15.9 | 19.5 | 40.2 | 100.0 | 1,418 | 6.51 | 18.5 |

\* "Family wage" is the average of family earnings divided by family hours, calculated only for those families with positive values for both variables. The "average family hours" tabulations include zeros.

Source: Authors' analysis of CPS data.

**FIGURE 5N** Share of poor families with no work, by race/ethnicity, 1979-2000

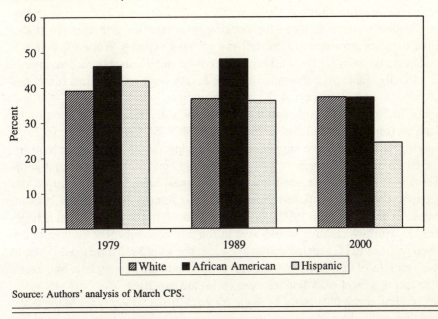

Source: Authors' analysis of March CPS.

With minor exceptions, the shifts over time within the other hours-worked categories are relatively small, i.e., the shares working fewer than 1,000 hours or 1,000-1,999 hours did not grow much (one exception is the 6.9-point growth between 1989 and 2000 in the 1,000-1,999 hours category among single-mother families). Thus, it appears that most of the movement was out of the no-work category, as can be observed by the falling percentages—again, concentrated over the 1990s—in the first column. While about half of single-mother families did not work in the paid labor market at all in 1979 or 1989, that share fell to a third (32.1%) in 2000. The non-working share among prime-age poor families (headed by someone 25-54) fell from about one-third to about one-fourth.

Minority poor families also shifted out of non-work. **Figure 5N** shows that, among poor families in 1979 and 1989, the share of African American non-working families was higher than that of whites, while the Hispanic share was closer to that of whites. But by 2000, the African American and white shares were almost identical, and the Hispanic share was well below both.

These shifts toward more work led to large increases in annual hours for some of these poor families, particularly over the 1990s (Table 5.13). Though the levels of hours worked among poor single-mother families with children remained low even in 2000 (935 per year), the average grew by 358 hours, or

62% over the 1990s, an addition of almost nine weeks of full-time work. For poor families with children, the increase was 227 hours, a 21% increase. One implication of these findings for working poor families with children is that child care is a growing need, as well as a growing expense. While subsidies for child care do exist for the working poor, only a small minority receive them.

Finally, Table 5.13 shows the average family wage in real terms (described above). As would be expected, the levels are extremely low, ranging in 2000 from about $6.50 to $7.00. Although the inflation-adjusted family wage for all poor families (top panel) was lower in 2000 than in 1979 ($6.62 compared to $6.70), it was higher for prime-age, single-mother, and white families. For single mothers, the family wage increased by 24% between 1989 and 2000, a significant jump. Yet despite this increase, their low level of annual hours worked consigns this group to deep working poverty, a condition that persists even with the large increase in hours over the 1990s. In order to make it to the poverty line, a single mother with two children would have to roughly double her the average hours. Even with the EITC supplementing her wage, she would still have to add close to three months of full-time work in order to make it to the poverty line. And again, note that this extra work implies extra child care expenses.

A similar calculus could be made for each of the family types in the table, yielding much the same result. By definition, the working poor earn very low wages. But even with the large increases observed over the 1990s, a significant share of even the prime-age poor do not work (one-fourth in 2000), and, including these non-working families, their average annual hours are far less than those of middle-income families, as shown in Chapter 1. The trends reveal that these families have largely and, in some cases (e.g., single mothers) dramatically responded to both the policy changes and the strong economy of the second half of the 1990s. Yet even with their large percentage gains in hours and wages, poverty rates remain high for some of these groups (32.4% for single mothers; last column of Table 5.13) and not far below the 1979 level for any of them, with the exception of single mothers and African Americans.

One of the main constraints faced by the working poor and near-poor is the conditions in the low-wage labor market. We conclude the poverty analysis with a look at this increasingly important segment of the labor market.

## Poverty and the low-wage labor market

Given the emphasis on work embodied in current policy, and the sharp increases that have occurred in both earnings as share of income and hours worked for many poor and near-poor families, conditions in the low-wage

**FIGURE 50** Share of prime-age workers with full-time/year-round attachment and low earnings, 1974-2000

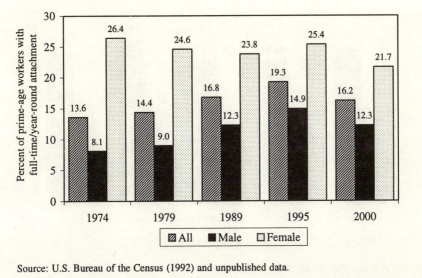

Source: U.S. Bureau of the Census (1992) and unpublished data.

labor market are an ever more important poverty determinant. In this final section, we examine some of the key trends on the characteristics and earnings of low-wage workers.

The next two figures show that even some workers with full-time, year-round labor force attachment earn poverty-level wages. The figures, derived from analysis performed by the Census Bureau, focus on prime-age persons who spent at least 50 weeks of the year at work or looking for work (i.e., in the labor force), worked full time or else part time but involuntarily, and yet had annual earnings too low to reach the poverty line for a family of four, which in 2000 was $16,066 (this threshold is based on the CPI-U-X1).

**Figure 5O** charts the share of these workers, by sex, for the period 1974-2000. The trend shows a gradual increase through 1995 in the proportion earning poverty-level wages. This is particularly the case for men, whose share grew by just under 7 percentage points from 1974 to 1995 before falling 2.6 points from 1995 to 2000, to 12.3%. The steepest growth occurred after 1979, when the wages of males with low earnings fell most steeply (see Chapter 2). In fact, even with their gains of the latter 1990s, the share of low-earning prime-age men still surpassed its 1979 level (12.3% vs. 9.0%).

For women, the share of low earners hovered around 25% through 1995,

351

**FIGURE 5P** Share of workers with full-time/year-round attachment and low earnings, by family type, 1974-2000

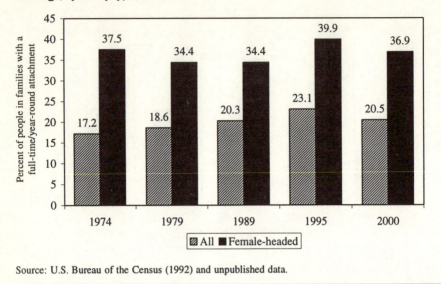

Source: U.S. Bureau of the Census (1992) and unpublished data.

then fell to 21.7% in 2000. Despite the strong growth in both low wages and hours worked from 1995 to 2000, slightly over a fifth of prime-age women (7.8 million) with significant labor force attachment had poverty-level annual earnings in 2000.

**Figure 5P** focuses on low earners (again, with full labor-force attachment) in families with children; families headed by women are shown separately. Note that this group of workers is worse off than those shown in the previous figure (compare the levels in the bars marked "All"), suggesting that families with children are more likely to have lower earnings than the population of all prime-age workers. Families with children that are headed by a female are particularly likely to face low earnings; in 2000, 36.9% of fully attached workers in these families earned poverty-level wages. Between 1974 and 1979, the share of low-earner single mothers fell, from 37.5% to 34.4%. This share remained flat over the 1980s and then rose through 1995. They saw some improvement between 1995 and 2000 (recall from Table 5.13 that their hourly family wage grew strongly over this period), but their low-earning share fell by only 3.0 percentage points.

**Table 5.14** looks at the demographic characteristics of low-wage workers compared to those of the overall workforce in 2001. Low-wage workers, in

**TABLE 5.14** Characteristics of low-wage workers, 2001

|  | Low wage* | Total |
|---|---|---|
| Share of total | 24.4% | 100.0% |
| Number | 28,034,958 | 114,763,673 |
| Average wage | $6.79 | $16.45 |
| **Gender** | | |
| Male | 40.5% | 52.0% |
| Female | 59.5 | 48.0 |
| **Race** | | |
| White | 60.4% | 71.8% |
| Black | 15.4 | 11.8 |
| Hispanic | 19.6 | 11.6 |
| Other | 4.6 | 4.7 |
| **Education** | | |
| Less than high school | 23.9% | 10.5% |
| High school | 37.9 | 31.4 |
| Some college | 24.2 | 21.0 |
| Associate degree | 6.0 | 9.2 |
| College or more | 8.1 | 27.9 |
| **Age** | | |
| 18-25 | 36.9% | 17.3% |
| 26-35 | 20.8 | 24.4 |
| 35 and older | 42.4 | 58.3 |
| **Industry** | | |
| Services | 36.4% | 37.1% |
| Retail trade | 33.2 | 16.0 |
| Wholesale trade | 2.8 | 3.8 |
| Finance | 4.0 | 6.6 |
| Manufacturing | 10.2 | 15.5 |
| Construction | 4.0 | 6.2 |
| Transportation, utilities | 4.0 | 7.7 |
| Government | 2.1 | 5.1 |
| Other | 3.2 | 1.9 |
| **Occupation** | | |
| Services | 30.5% | 13.5% |
| Clerical | 14.6 | 14.9 |
| Managers, professionals | 9.8 | 30.7 |
| Technical, sales | 17.5 | 14.6 |
| Blue collar | 24.0 | 24.7 |
| Others | 3.6 | 1.5 |
| **Union status** | | |
| Union** | 6.7% | 15.2% |
| Non-union | 93.3 | 84.8 |

* Low-wage refers to hourly wage rate necessary to lift a family of four above the poverty line with full-time, full-year work. In 2001, this wage was $8.78.
** Union includes members and workers covered by union contracts.

Source: Authors' analysis of CPS ORG data.

column 1, are defined as those whose hourly wage is less than the wage that would lift a family of four up to the poverty line in 2001, or $8.78 per hour (see Chapter 2 for more extensive analysis of this type).

This group's average wage that year was $6.79, in the same range as the family wages earned by poor families shown in Table 5.13. Comparing the percentages in the two columns reveals categories in which low-wage workers are over-represented. Such workers are disproportionately female, minority, non-college educated, and young. They also are more likely to work in low-wage industries such as retail trade and less likely to work in manufacturing, transportation and utilities, finance, and government (interestingly, the share of low-wage workers in the services industry is about the same as the overall share, due to the varied nature of occupations within this industry—such as security guards and lawyers). By occupation, low-wage workers are over-represented in services, where they staff the low-paying jobs such as cashiers in the retail sector or home health aides in health services. They are least likely to be managers and professionals. Finally, they are significantly less likely to either be union members or covered by union contracts.

**Figure 5Q** shows the trend in the 20th percentile real hourly wage by gender, in 2001 dollars, with the "poverty-level wage" (the poverty threshold for a family of four in 2001 divided by full-time, full-year work, or 2,080 hours) as a reference point. Even with the recent gains over the latter 1990s, the bottom 20% of female wage earners remain far below the poverty wage, while low-wage males surpassed this level only in 2001. Prior to the early 1980s, low-wage men earned well above the poverty wage, but declining real male wages from 1979 through the mid-1990s meant that low-wage male workers were in a deep hole by the time wages reversed course. Female low-wage workers did not experience as large a decline, and their real wages trended up slowly beginning in the mid-1990s. But though they closed part of the gap with low-wage male workers, they still remain both far below the male rate and the poverty-level wage. Note that these low-wage rates for females represent the typical earnings of the working poor (see the family wages in Table 5.13), including single mothers. Such wages are too low to provide for even the basic consumption needs of a working family.

These tables and figures, in tandem with the analysis presented in prior chapters, establish the fact that the poor and near-poor energetically responded to both the strong economy and the work-centered policy changes of the 1990s. They still, however, face considerable constraints. Both their annual and hourly earnings are too low to ensure that these families work their way much above the poverty line, and, even with large increases in employment rates and hours worked per year, the combination of low wages and less than full-time, full-

**FIGURE 5Q** Real hourly wages of low-wage workers (2001 dollars)

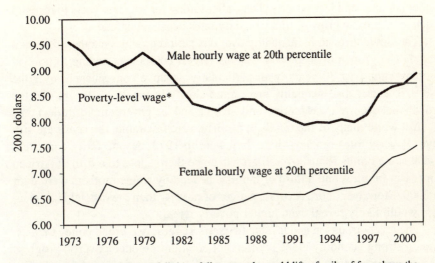

\* $8.70 is the wage level that, at full-time, full-year work, would lift a family of four above the poverty line ($18,104 in 2001).

Source: Authors' analysis of CPS data.

year work means that many of these families will remain near poor at best. Helping these working families leave poverty behind must still be an important goal of social policy.

## Conclusion

Though great progress was made in the latter half of the 1990s in the fight against poverty, the early 2000s recession brought those advances to an end, leaving poverty rates still about where they were a generation ago. Yet there is much to be learned from this period, wherein poverty among some of the most disadvantaged families fell quickly.

The first lesson is that, just as it does for income and wages, low unemployment matters for poverty. The tight labor market of the latter 1990s—particularly the low-wage sector—turned out to be a key determinant of the progress against poverty over these years. And despite its loss of welfare benefits, the average low-income mother-only family fared significantly better in 2000 than at any other point in the past few decades. For these and for many other poor and near-poor families, earnings gains, along with associated higher EITC benefits, led to higher incomes and less poverty. Thus, after failing for so many years to respond much to economic growth, sticky poverty rates became unglued.

The slower growth in inequality over this period provides another important lesson. The growth of inequality was the largest component adding to poverty rates over the past 30 years, with particularly negative consequences over the 1980s. The fact that inequality grew more slowly in the 1990s meant that the growth that occurred was more evenly shared, and the poverty trends reflect this.

Yet while many of the trends in poverty were favorable, the levels are still high. Poverty rates remain where they were in 1973, despite fairly consistent and at some points robust overall growth since then. Close to a fifth of African American families and a third of families headed by single mothers were poor in 2000. Moreover, more accurate gauges of poverty than the official U.S. measure would likely reveal even higher poverty rates.

The recent trends in and levels of poverty suggest two broad policy themes. First, a strong economy alone is often not enough to reduce poverty; progress also requires keeping the labor market at full employment and the inequality wedge at bay. This lesson has particular relevance in the current context given the recession of 2001, which led to higher unemployment and unleashed higher inequality and more poverty.

Second, policies that help to close the gap between the income and needs of working families will continue to be necessary. If the economy allows, the working poor and near poor are, as are most other working families, likely to continue to try to make progress in the labor market. Yet they are pushing against 20 years of wage stagnation or real decline. Even at its best, the low-wage labor market is unlikely to provide many of these workers with the incomes they need to raise their living standards much beyond poverty. Higher minimum wages and increased union representation will help, but ultimately public policy needs to continue down the path of providing work supports—from subsidized child care to expanded tax credits—to low-income working families.

As important as these pro-work policy tools are, it is crucial that public policy not neglect the safety net when the economy weakens. Early experience from the 2001 recession suggests that poverty policy may now be tilting too far in a pro-cyclical direction. That is, the country's emphasis on policies that complement work and its de-emphasis on policies, such as welfare, that do not has reduced the effectiveness of the safety net to catch vulnerable families when the job market contracts.

## CHAPTER 6

# Regional analysis:
# significant variation among the states

Previous chapters have focused exclusively on information of national scope. This chapter examines the state of the economy in each of the nation's regions, Census divisions (groups of states within regions), and states.

A regional focus is important because, as the data below illustrate, there is considerable geographic variation in the economy relevant to working families. The differences are evident both in levels—Southern incomes, for example, are lower than those in the rest of the country—and in trends—income grew more quickly in the 1990s in the South than in the Northeast or West. Moreover, the income growth in the South led to a turnaround in poverty: while Southern poverty rates have historically been the highest in the country, by 2000 they were statistically indistinguishable from rates in the West. A regional analysis can also reveal the economic strengths and weaknesses of specific areas. For example, extreme up-and-down movements in employment resulting from high concentration in one or two industrial sectors may reveal the need to diversify in a particular area.

Essentially, the regional story is a tale of two decades. Much of the national analysis thus far reveals that the 1980s were a relatively weak period for wage and income growth compared the 1990s, especially the later 1990s. However, the regional analysis tells a more complex story. In the Northeast, median family income actually grew more quickly and poverty fell further during the 1980s recovery than in comparable years in the 1990s. Conversely, the impact of the relatively mild (in historical terms) recession of the early 1990s was pronounced in the Northeast, which experienced greater-than-average job and income losses. For most states in the Midwest and South, though, wages, incomes, and employment grew faster in the 1990s than in the 1980s.

**FIGURE 6A** Nominal and price-adjusted median household income relative to U.S. by division, 2000

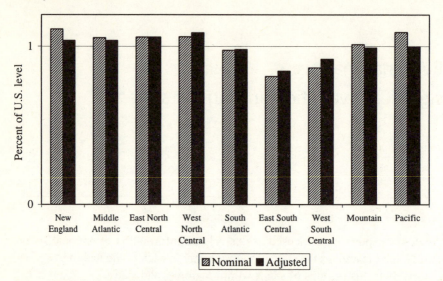

Source: Nominal rate, U.S. Bureau of the Census, income web site; price-adjusted rate, authors' analysis. For detailed information on figure sources, see Figure Notes.

A regional analysis poses numerous measurement difficulties that do not surface in national analyses. A particularly important drawback is the lack of a widely accepted state-by-state measure of prices—a tool that would allow a comparison of what a dollar buys in, say, Mississippi to what it buys in Massachusetts. For the most part, this chapter uses a national inflation measure, which yields numbers that are correct on average but that can overestimate incomes (and underestimate poverty) in states with high prices and underestimate incomes (and overstate poverty) in states with low prices. Several of the analyses below, however, such as the comparison of median household income in 2000 and the examination of poverty, adjust for state-by-state price differences.

## Income

The geographical variation in median household income in 2000 is illustrated in **Figure 6A**, which shows income, both nominal and adjusted for differences in state prices, by Census division as a percent of the overall U.S. household median. Median household incomes in the Northeast, especially in New En-

**FIGURE 6B** Median family income growth, by region, 1953-2000

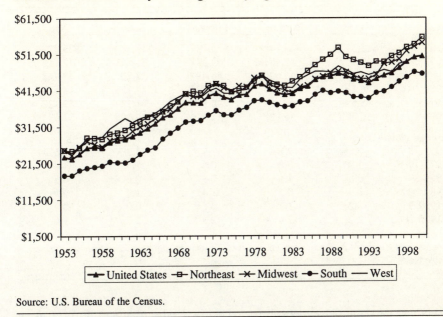

Source: U.S. Bureau of the Census.

gland, are above the U.S. median. The three southern divisions (South Atlantic and East and West South Central) are all below the U.S. level, and there is a large (almost 20%) gap between the more northerly Southern states (South Atlantic division) and the deeper South. In the West, the household median in the Pacific division is 9% above the national median.

The bars on the right side of each division use a price adjustment based on state median housing prices for both owner-occupied and rental housing. (While this approach is not as reliable as a detailed survey of the many consumer goods whose prices vary by state, the Census Bureau has found housing prices to serve as a useful proxy, as housing prices both vary considerably by state and correlate with other interstate price movements.) This adjustment brings all divisions closer to the U.S. level (the 100% line). The largest adjustments occur in New England and the Pacific divisions, where housing prices (as well as most other prices) are well above average. Lower prices in the East South Central and West South Central areas bring relative incomes there closer to the U.S. median.

**Figure 6B**, which illustrates the trend in median income by region from 1953 to 2000, and **Table 6.1**, which examines the peaks of the business cycle (as well as 1995), shows that the recession of the early 1990s, considered a relatively mild one from a national perspective, hit the coasts hardest. (Note

**TABLE 6.1** Median family income by region, 1953-2000 (2000 dollars)

| Year | U.S. | Northeast | Midwest | South | West |
|------|------|-----------|---------|-------|------|
| 1953 | $23,317 | $25,148 | $25,197 | $18,183 | $25,279 |
| 1973 | 40,702 | 43,401 | 43,337 | 35,893 | 42,118 |
| 1979 | 43,311 | 45,600 | 45,487 | 38,807 | 45,748 |
| 1989 | 46,135 | 53,243 | 46,675 | 41,127 | 48,138 |
| 1995 | 45,599 | 49,302 | 48,809 | 41,127 | 47,122 |
| 2000 | 50,890 | 56,128 | 54,576 | 46,009 | 51,034 |
| *Annual growth rates* | | | | | |
| 1953-73 | 2.8% | 2.8% | 2.7% | 3.5% | 2.6% |
| 1973-79 | 1.0 | 0.8 | 0.8 | 1.3 | 1.4 |
| 1979-89 | 0.6 | 1.6 | 0.3 | 0.6 | 0.5 |
| 1989-2000 | 0.9 | 0.5 | 1.4 | 1.0 | 0.5 |
| 1989-95 | -0.2 | -1.3 | 0.7 | 0.0 | -0.4 |
| 1995-2000 | 2.2 | 2.6 | 2.3 | 2.3 | 1.6 |

Source: U.S. Bureau of the Census, income web site. For detailed information on table sources, see Table Notes.

that these data and those that follow, except in the discussion of poverty, use a national rather than a state-specific price index.) Family incomes in the Northeast fell quickly, and did not recover to their pre-recession 1989 level until 1998. Median family income in the South was stagnant from the mid-1980s through the mid-90s. In the latter 1990s, incomes bounced back in the Northeast, growing 2.6%, faster than the national average of 2.2%, while income growth in the West, at 1.6% per year, was comparatively slow. For 1989-2000 overall, annual median family income growth was as slow or slower in the 1990s in these regions (0.5% for both) than in any other period.

One reason for this pattern in the Northeast—and an important factor underlying many regional economic trends—is the industrial composition of jobs there. For example, the financial sector is a large part of the economy of New York and, to a lesser extent, Massachusetts (which also depends heavily on technology), and these states have become particularly vulnerable to shocks in that sector, which is prone to wide cyclical swings and, consequently, exaggerated booms and busts. Jobs in finance, banking, and real estate can be lucrative and create much peripherally related employment (e.g., food services on Wall Street) as well as direct employment, and the downturn of the early 1990s led to considerable retrenchment in the financial sector and thus disproportionately hurt these states and the region. The recession that began in early 2001 shared this characteristic with the last one: it was in part driven by a sharp decline in the value of the stock market. While the available income data extend only to 2000, preliminary evidence suggests that New York again disproportionately felt the brunt of a recession that was billed as relatively mild nationally. Of course, part of this difficulty stems from the terrorist attack of September 11, 2001, but it is still likely that the lack of diversification in terms of the industrial composition of jobs is a problem for New York and for the region.

After stagnating over the early part of the 1990s recovery, median family incomes in the Midwest and South climbed quickly. This too appears to be closely related to the labor market, as unemployment declines and job growth were particularly strong in these areas (discussed below).

Many middle-income families in the Midwest have historically depended on durable-goods manufacturing, like automobiles. Early in the 1990s recovery, manufacturing employment grew quickly in the Midwest, helping to fuel gains in states like Michigan. However, in the late 1990s the fast-growing U.S. trade deficit in manufactured goods led to losses in manufacturing employment; in Michigan manufacturing employment fell by 7% between 1999 and 2001. Thus, as in the Northeast, family incomes in the Midwest may grow more slowly in this recovery relative to the last one.

Broadly speaking, the regional pattern shown in Table 6.1 is evident at the state level, shown in **Table 6.2**, which looks at four-person families. (In order to build sample sizes large enough to produce reliable statistics by state, Table 6.2 combines two years of data.) The 1980s cycle was a boom primarily in the Northeast, with annual rates of growth at or close to 3% in New Hampshire, Massachusetts, Connecticut, and New Jersey. Elsewhere, with only a few exceptions, family income growth was either relatively unimpressive—below 1% per year—or, in nine states, even negative. The pattern shifted in the 1990s, however, as income growth rates were much more uniform throughout the country; if anything, the 1980s boom states in the Northeast were laggards. For example, family income grew at least 2% more slowly in the 1990s in Massachusetts and New Jersey.

The acceleration in the latter half of the 1990s is remarkable in that it was so geographically pervasive. Income growth accelerated in almost every state, and most states posted growth rates of about 2% or higher. Labor markets tightened throughout the country as well (discussed below). Productivity grew at about 2% on average over this period and, in tandem with low unemployment, led to the unique period of broad-based income gains.

**Table 6.3** turns from median family income to a comparison of the incomes of the top 20% to the bottom 20% over time. This analysis that provides insight into whether income inequality is growing or diminishing. (In order to build sample sizes large enough to produce reliable statistics by state and by

**TABLE 6.2** Median income, four-person families, by state, 1978-2000 (2000 dollars)

| | Two-year averages | | | | Annual percent change | | |
|---|---|---|---|---|---|---|---|
| | 1978-79 | 1988-89 | 1995-96 | 1999-2000 | 1980s | 1990s | 1995-2000 |
| United States | $49,468 | $54,959 | $56,053 | $62,112 | 1.1% | 1.1% | 2.1% |
| **NORTHEAST** | | | | | | | |
| *New England* | | | | | | | |
| Maine | $40,405 | $50,743 | $52,129 | $57,827 | 2.3% | 1.2% | 2.1% |
| New Hampshire | 49,182 | 64,448 | 61,472 | 69,879 | 2.7 | 0.7 | 2.6 |
| Vermont | 43,679 | 52,894 | 53,599 | 59,388 | 1.9 | 1.1 | 2.1 |
| Massachusetts | 51,107 | 68,904 | 67,328 | 76,061 | 3.0 | 0.9 | 2.5 |
| Rhode Island | 49,433 | 58,291 | 58,332 | 67,601 | 1.7 | 1.4 | 3.0 |
| Connecticut | 53,933 | 71,630 | 71,724 | 80,371 | 2.9 | 1.1 | 2.3 |
| *Middle Atlantic* | | | | | | | |
| New York | $47,087 | $58,798 | $57,306 | $63,141 | 2.2% | 0.6% | 2.0% |
| New Jersey | 54,080 | 72,689 | 70,323 | 78,259 | 3.0 | 0.7 | 2.2 |
| Pennsylvania | 48,562 | 53,875 | 57,980 | 63,478 | 1.0 | 1.5 | 1.8 |
| **MIDWEST** | | | | | | | |
| *East North Central* | | | | | | | |
| Ohio | $50,246 | $54,797 | $56,904 | $60,188 | 0.9% | 0.9% | 1.1% |
| Indiana | 49,877 | 52,449 | 55,595 | 61,282 | 0.5 | 1.4 | 2.0 |
| Illinois | 53,534 | 58,021 | 60,473 | 68,351 | 0.8 | 1.5 | 2.5 |
| Michigan | 53,686 | 57,751 | 60,433 | 68,203 | 0.7 | 1.5 | 2.4 |
| Wisconsin | 51,442 | 54,546 | 57,384 | 66,146 | 0.6 | 1.8 | 2.9 |
| *West North Central* | | | | | | | |
| Minnesota | $52,936 | $57,464 | $61,256 | $69,735 | 0.8% | 1.8% | 2.6% |
| Iowa | 50,108 | 49,256 | 52,889 | 58,973 | -0.2 | 1.7 | 2.2 |
| Missouri | 46,847 | 52,107 | 53,047 | 59,875 | 1.1 | 1.3 | 2.5 |
| North Dakota | 44,307 | 45,521 | 49,270 | 52,927 | 0.3 | 1.4 | 1.4 |
| South Dakota | 41,674 | 43,595 | 48,350 | 54,575 | 0.5 | 2.1 | 2.5 |
| Nebraska | 46,306 | 49,678 | 50,739 | 57,302 | 0.7 | 1.3 | 2.5 |
| Kansas | 49,199 | 50,764 | 52,969 | 57,950 | 0.3 | 1.2 | 1.8 |
| **SOUTH** | | | | | | | |
| *South Atlantic* | | | | | | | |
| District | | | | | | | |
| of Columbia | $43,842 | $54,487 | $57,087 | $63,889 | 2.2% | 1.5% | 2.3% |
| Maryland | 55,669 | 68,358 | 67,630 | 77,440 | 2.1 | 1.1 | 2.7 |
| Delaware | 49,055 | 58,219 | 61,577 | 68,573 | 1.7 | 1.5 | 2.2 |
| Virginia | 50,474 | 60,364 | 57,272 | 67,284 | 1.8 | 1.0 | 3.3 |
| West Virginia | 43,237 | 42,374 | 44,875 | 46,495 | -0.2 | 0.8 | 0.7 |
| North Carolina | 43,564 | 50,768 | 53,523 | 57,601 | 1.5 | 1.2 | 1.5 |
| South Carolina | 44,619 | 48,914 | 50,403 | 57,076 | 0.9 | 1.4 | 2.5 |
| Georgia | 47,655 | 53,864 | 54,163 | 59,613 | 1.2 | 0.9 | 1.9 |
| Florida | 44,863 | 51,445 | 49,556 | 56,398 | 1.4 | 0.8 | 2.6 |

*(cont.)*

**TABLE 6.2** *(cont.)* Median income, four-person families, by state, 1978-2000 (2000 dollars)

| | Two-year averages | | | | Annual percent change | | |
|---|---|---|---|---|---|---|---|
| | 1978-79 | 1988-89 | 1995-96 | 1999-2000 | 1980s | 1990s | 1995-2000 |
| **SOUTH** *(cont.)* | | | | | | | |
| *East South Central* | | | | | | | |
| Kentucky | $42,838 | $45,763 | $47,345 | $52,594 | 0.7% | 1.3% | 2.1% |
| Tennessee | 43,159 | 47,552 | 49,607 | 54,322 | 1.0 | 1.2 | 1.8 |
| Alabama | 42,775 | 46,784 | 48,455 | 52,808 | 0.9 | 1.1 | 1.7 |
| Mississippi | 39,599 | 42,620 | 42,135 | 47,928 | 0.7 | 1.1 | 2.6 |
| *West South Central* | | | | | | | |
| Arkansas | $39,398 | $41,644 | $41,755 | $46,388 | 0.6% | 1.0% | 2.1% |
| Louisiana | 44,902 | 46,073 | 46,141 | 49,235 | 0.3 | 0.6 | 1.3 |
| Oklahoma | 46,112 | 45,688 | 47,227 | 51,238 | -0.1 | 1.0 | 1.6 |
| Texas | 50,629 | 48,405 | 50,245 | 54,297 | -0.4 | 1.0 | 1.6 |
| **WEST** | | | | | | | |
| *Mountain* | | | | | | | |
| Montana | $43,792 | $45,593 | $46,795 | $49,410 | 0.4% | 0.7% | 1.1% |
| Idaho | 45,618 | 44,806 | 47,781 | 51,514 | -0.2 | 1.3 | 1.5 |
| Wyoming | 52,223 | 47,703 | 51,379 | 56,676 | -0.9 | 1.6 | 2.0 |
| Colorado | 54,233 | 54,654 | 57,913 | 65,798 | 0.1 | 1.7 | 2.6 |
| New Mexico | 45,917 | 41,656 | 41,825 | 46,885 | -1.0 | 1.1 | 2.3 |
| Arizona | 50,663 | 51,811 | 49,611 | 55,243 | 0.2 | 0.6 | 2.2 |
| Utah | 47,928 | 48,861 | 50,626 | 58,108 | 0.2 | 1.6 | 2.8 |
| Nevada | 53,673 | 54,335 | 55,952 | 60,545 | 0.1 | 1.0 | 1.6 |
| *Pacific* | | | | | | | |
| Washington | $52,985 | $55,804 | $57,917 | $64,145 | 0.5% | 1.3% | 2.1% |
| Oregon | 52,614 | 51,875 | 51,230 | 57,017 | -0.1 | 0.9 | 2.2 |
| California | 54,725 | 58,011 | 58,333 | 64,213 | 0.6 | 0.9 | 1.9 |
| Alaska | 67,663 | 65,882 | 65,394 | 69,764 | -0.3 | 0.5 | 1.3 |
| Hawaii | 54,361 | 60,130 | 62,388 | 67,252 | 1.0 | 1.0 | 1.5 |

Source: Authors' analysis of U.S. Bureau of the Census, income web site.

income quintile, Table 6.3 combines three years of data.) For the nation as a whole in the 1980s, the income gap between the top 20% and the bottom 20% expanded, from a ratio of 7.4 to 9.3, a growth of 1.9 points. Primarily due to strong income growth at the bottom of the wage scale, the gap grew more slowly (0.7 points) in the 1990s, yet, despite a few years of full employment in the latter half of the decade, inequality still either grew or held steady in most states.

**TABLE 6.3** Income inequality by state:
average income of top 20% relative to bottom 20%

| | Income ratio, top 20%/lowest 20% | | | Changes (top 20%/lowest 20%) | |
|---|---|---|---|---|---|
| | 1978-80 | 1988-90 | 1998-2000 | Late 1970s-late 1980s | Late 1980s-late 1990s |
| **NORTHEAST** | | | | | |
| *New England* | | | | | |
| Maine | 6.6 | 7.6 | 8.3 | 1.0 | 0.8 |
| New Hampshire | 5.6 | 6.9 | 8.2 | 1.3 | 1.3 |
| Vermont | 6.4 | 7.4 | 8.5 | 1.0 | 1.2 |
| Massachusetts | 7.0 | 8.6 | 10.5 | 1.6 | 1.9 |
| Rhode Island | 6.3 | 7.2 | 8.9 | 0.9 | 1.7 |
| Connecticut | 6.1 | 6.2 | 9.4 | 0.1 | 3.1 |
| *Middle Atlantic* | | | | | |
| New York | 7.8 | 10.4 | 12.8 | 2.6 | 2.4 |
| New Jersey | 7.0 | 8.1 | 9.6 | 1.1 | 1.5 |
| Pennsylvania | 6.4 | 7.9 | 8.8 | 1.5 | 1.0 |
| **MIDWEST** | | | | | |
| *East North Central* | | | | | |
| Ohio | 6.4 | 8.3 | 9.7 | 1.9 | 1.4 |
| Indiana | 5.8 | 7.9 | 7.0 | 2.1 | -0.8 |
| Illinois | 7.5 | 9.6 | 9.4 | 2.1 | -0.2 |
| Michigan | 6.6 | 8.9 | 9.2 | 2.3 | 0.3 |
| Wisconsin | 6.1 | 6.4 | 8.2 | 0.3 | 1.7 |
| *West North Central* | | | | | |
| Minnesota | 6.1 | 7.7 | 7.7 | 1.7 | -0.1 |
| Iowa | 5.7 | 6.5 | 7.9 | 0.8 | 1.4 |
| Missouri | 6.9 | 8.9 | 8.7 | 1.9 | -0.2 |
| North Dakota | 7.3 | 6.8 | 8.3 | -0.4 | 1.4 |
| South Dakota | 7.3 | 7.3 | 7.2 | 0.0 | -0.1 |
| Nebraska | 6.6 | 7.0 | 8.0 | 0.4 | 1.0 |
| Kansas | 6.0 | 7.0 | 8.7 | 1.0 | 1.7 |
| **SOUTH** | | | | | |
| *South Atlantic* | | | | | |
| Delaware | 6.6 | 6.7 | 8.4 | 0.1 | 1.7 |
| Maryland | 6.9 | 7.8 | 8.6 | 0.8 | 0.9 |
| District of Columbia | 12.1 | 16.4 | 21.6 | 4.3 | 5.2 |
| Virginia | 7.4 | 9.1 | 9.3 | 1.8 | 0.2 |
| West Virginia | 6.5 | 8.8 | 9.2 | 2.4 | 0.4 |
| North Carolina | 7.2 | 8.4 | 10.0 | 1.2 | 1.7 |
| South Carolina | 7.9 | 9.3 | 8.1 | 1.4 | -1.3 |
| Georgia | 8.1 | 10.3 | 9.1 | 2.2 | -1.1 |
| Florida | 7.9 | 9.1 | 9.4 | 1.2 | 0.3 |

*(cont.)*

**TABLE 6.3** *(cont.)* Income inequality by state: average income of top 20% relative to bottom 20%

| | Income ratio, top 20%/lowest 20% | | | Changes (top 20%/lowest 20%) | |
|---|---|---|---|---|---|
| | 1978-80 | 1988-90 | 1998-2000 | Late 1970s-late 1980s | Late 1980s-late 1990s |
| **SOUTH** *(cont.)* | | | | | |
| ***East South Central*** | | | | | |
| Kentucky | 7.1 | 9.1 | 10.4 | 1.9 | 1.3 |
| Tennessee | 8.1 | 10.3 | 10.5 | 2.2 | 0.2 |
| Alabama | 9.0 | 9.8 | 10.2 | 0.8 | 0.4 |
| Mississippi | 8.9 | 10.9 | 9.4 | 2.1 | -1.5 |
| | | | | | |
| ***West South Central*** | | | | | |
| Arkansas | 8.6 | 9.3 | 8.5 | 0.7 | -0.8 |
| Louisiana | 9.1 | 15.6 | 11.6 | 6.5 | -4.0 |
| Oklahoma | 7.7 | 9.4 | 9.8 | 1.7 | 0.4 |
| Texas | 8.6 | 10.3 | 11.0 | 1.7 | 0.7 |
| | | | | | |
| **WEST** | | | | | |
| ***Mountain*** | | | | | |
| Montana | 7.7 | 7.2 | 8.9 | -0.5 | 1.7 |
| Idaho | 6.3 | 7.1 | 8.5 | 0.9 | 1.4 |
| Wyoming | 5.6 | 6.9 | 7.9 | 1.3 | 1.0 |
| Colorado | 6.8 | 8.5 | 8.0 | 1.8 | -0.5 |
| New Mexico | 8.5 | 10.5 | 9.8 | 2.0 | -0.7 |
| Arizona | 7.3 | 9.2 | 10.0 | 1.9 | 0.9 |
| Utah | 6.0 | 6.0 | 7.0 | 0.0 | 1.0 |
| Nevada | 6.5 | 6.9 | 8.8 | 0.5 | 1.8 |
| | | | | | |
| ***Pacific*** | | | | | |
| Washington | 7.2 | 7.0 | 8.6 | -0.2 | 1.6 |
| Oregon | 6.4 | 7.0 | 10.0 | 0.6 | 3.0 |
| California | 7.6 | 9.8 | 11.0 | 2.3 | 1.2 |
| Alaska | 9.3 | 9.6 | 8.2 | 0.4 | -1.4 |
| Hawaii | 7.0 | 9.1 | 9.6 | 2.1 | 0.5 |
| | | | | | |
| **Total U.S.** | 7.4 | 9.3 | 10.0 | 1.9 | 0.7 |

Source: Economic Policy Institute/Center on Budget and Policy Priorities' analysis of CPS data.

The growth of inequality was widespread over the 1980s. While a few states were untouched, no area of the country bucked the trend. In the 1990s, inequality's growth decelerated in many states in the Midwest and parts of the South, but a number of Northeastern states—Massachusetts, Connecticut, New York, and New Jersey—saw inequality grow at about the same rate as or faster than in the 1980s.

Over the full 20-year period, these inequality ratios grew by five points in New York and by more than three points in Oregon, Massachusetts, California, Ohio, Connecticut, and Kentucky. Only five states—South Carolina, Mississippi, Arkansas, South Dakota, Alaska—saw either declines or increases of less than one. In these cases, strong income growth at the bottom of the income scale in the latter 1990s helped to stop inequality's growth, but for the vast majority of other states, what was dubbed as "the best economy in decades" failed to reverse the trend.

## Labor markets

In terms of employment, industrial composition, unemployment, and wages, the populous coastal states generally fared better in the 1980s than in the 1990s overall, although the latter 1990s saw a geographically pervasive boom. The data available for the downturn in 2001 suggest that, unlike in the last recession, labor markets have been hit hardest in the Midwest and deep South. The New York economy, due in part to the September 11 attacks, also saw larger-than-average losses.

*Employment:* As discussed in Chapter 3, job growth nationwide accelerated in the latter half of the 1990s. **Table 6.4A**, which ranks the states by growth rates over the 1995-2000 period, shows that many Western states, along with Florida and Texas, achieved annual growth rates over 3% over this period.

From 2000 to 2001, when national employment grew by only 0.3%, employment contracted in 20 states, led by Indiana and Michigan, due to manufacturing employment losses. After growing 1.8% per year from 1995 to 2000, employment in New York was stagnant in 2001.

**Table 6.4B** provides more historical data, including employment levels, along with regional and divisional employment counts. The pace of national employment growth was the same in the 1980s and the 1990s, at 1.8% per year. However, job growth was generally faster in the Northeast and Pacific regions over the 1980s and slower in the 1990s. Job growth in the Midwest and the East and West South Central divisions was faster in the 1990s than in the 1980s.

**Table 6.5** shows employment growth by (non-farm) industrial sector between 1979 and 2000 for four states, each of which is representative of its region. In each state, jobs primarily shifted from manufacturing to services, with other shifts rarely amounting to more than a few percentage points (with the exception of government in Michigan and Georgia). The loss of the share of manufacturing jobs runs from 10.9 percentage points in Michigan to 7.4 per-

**TABLE 6.4A** Non-farm payroll employment by state, 1995-2001

| | Percentage change 1995-2000 | | Percentage change 2000-01 |
|---|---|---|---|
| Nevada | 5.5% | Indiana | -2.1% |
| Arizona | 4.5 | Michigan | -1.9 |
| Colorado | 3.8 | Mississippi | -1.7 |
| Utah | 3.4 | South Carolina | -1.3 |
| Florida | 3.4 | Ohio | -1.0 |
| Texas | 3.3 | Alabama | -0.9 |
| Idaho | 3.2 | North Carolina | -0.8 |
| California | 3.1 | Illinois | -0.7 |
| Georgia | 3.0 | Oregon | -0.7 |
| Washington | 2.9 | Iowa | -0.6 |
| New Hampshire | 2.9 | Connecticut | -0.6 |
| Delaware | 2.8 | Tennessee | -0.6 |
| Virginia | 2.8 | Missouri | -0.6 |
| North Carolina | 2.6 | Washington | -0.5 |
| Oregon | 2.5 | Kentucky | -0.4 |
| Oklahoma | 2.5 | Wisconsin | -0.3 |
| South Carolina | 2.5 | Arkansas | -0.2 |
| Minnesota | 2.4 | Delaware | -0.2 |
| Maryland | 2.3 | Minnesota | -0.1 |
| Kansas | 2.3 | West Virginia | -0.1 |
| Maine | 2.3 | New York | 0.0 |
| Massachusetts | 2.2 | Nebraska | 0.1 |
| Nebraska | 2.2 | District of Columbia | 0.1 |
| Kentucky | 2.1 | Vermont | 0.1 |
| New Jersey | 2.1 | Georgia | 0.1 |
| Wisconsin | 2.1 | Pennsylvania | 0.2 |
| Vermont | 2.0 | Virginia | 0.3 |
| Montana | 2.0 | Massachusetts | 0.3 |
| South Dakota | 1.9 | South Dakota | 0.4 |
| New York | 1.8 | Hawaii | 0.4 |
| Michigan | 1.8 | Rhode Island | 0.5 |
| Tennessee | 1.8 | Louisiana | 0.6 |
| New Mexico | 1.8 | Utah | 0.6 |
| Wyoming | 1.8 | North Dakota | 0.6 |
| Missouri | 1.7 | New Jersey | 0.7 |
| Iowa | 1.7 | New Hampshire | 0.8 |
| North Dakota | 1.7 | Maryland | 0.8 |
| Connecticut | 1.6 | Texas | 0.8 |
| Alaska | 1.6 | Colorado | 0.9 |
| Arkansas | 1.6 | Kansas | 0.9 |
| Pennsylvania | 1.6 | Maine | 1.0 |

*(cont.)*

**TABLE 6.4A** *(cont.)* Non-farm payroll employment by state, 1995-2001

| | Percentage change 1995-2000 | | Percentage change 2000-01 |
|---|---|---|---|
| Louisiana | 1.6% | Arizona | 1.0% |
| Nevada | 5.5 | Indiana | -2.1 |
| Rhode Island | 1.6 | Montana | 1.1 |
| Illinois | 1.6 | Oklahoma | 1.3 |
| Ohio | 1.5 | California | 1.4 |
| Indiana | 1.5 | New Mexico | 1.6 |
| Mississippi | 1.4 | Florida | 1.7 |
| Alabama | 1.4 | Idaho | 1.8 |
| West Virginia | 1.4 | Alaska | 2.1 |
| Hawaii | 0.7 | Wyoming | 2.6 |
| District of Columbia | 0.2 | Nevada | 2.6 |
| **Total U.S.** | **2.4%** | | **0.3%** |

Note: Regional sums do not add to U.S. totals due to separate estimation techniques by states and different timing in benchmarking procedures between state and national estimates.

Source: Authors' analysis of BLS data.

centage points in California, with commensurate if not slightly larger gains in services. Though service employment is highly varied in terms of compensation, there is a wide pay gap overall between that expanding service sector and the contracting manufacturing sector. In Michigan, average manufacturing pay was 69% higher than service pay; in New York and California, manufacturing jobs paid at least one-third more than service jobs. Georgia, which houses more low-end manufacturing, had a smaller differential.

*Unemployment rates*: The national unemployment rate hit a 31-year low of 4% in 2000. As **Table 6.6** reveals, this national trend was reflected throughout the states, all of which reached historically low unemployment in 2000. The lowest levels prevailed in the West North Central division of the Midwest, while the largest declines from 1995 to 2000 took place in the Northeast and the West.

Even with these favorable trends in the populous states of the Northeast and West, the fact that they started the boom period of 1995-2000 with high unemployment rates relative to the other regions meant that labor markets in many of these states failed to tighten up as much as elsewhere. In 2000, New York and California's unemployment rates were 4.6% and 4.9%, respectively, well above the national average (California's rate remained high despite a drop

**TABLE 6.4B** Non-farm payroll employment by state, division, and region, 1979-2001 (thousands)

| | 1979 | 1989 | 1995 | 2000 | 2001 | Percentage change | | | |
| --- | --- | --- | --- | --- | --- | --- | --- | --- | --- |
| | | | | | | 1979-89 | 1989-2000 | 1995-2000 | 2000-01 |
| **NORTHEAST** | 20,407 | 23,644 | 23,072 | 25,338 | 25,389 | 1.5% | 0.6% | 1.9% | 0.2% |
| *New England* | 5,394 | 6,569 | 6,326 | 7,017 | 7,031 | 2.0 | 0.6 | 2.1 | 0.2 |
| Maine | 416 | 542 | 538 | 604 | 609 | 2.7 | 1.0 | 2.3 | 1.0 |
| New Hampshire | 379 | 529 | 540 | 622 | 627 | 3.4 | 1.5 | 2.9 | 0.8 |
| Vermont | 198 | 262 | 270 | 299 | 299 | 2.8 | 1.2 | 2.0 | 0.1 |
| Massachusetts | 2,604 | 3,109 | 2,977 | 3,323 | 3,335 | 1.8 | 0.6 | 2.2 | 0.3 |
| Rhode Island | 400 | 462 | 440 | 477 | 479 | 1.4 | 0.3 | 1.6 | 0.5 |
| Connecticut | 1,398 | 1,666 | 1,562 | 1,693 | 1,682 | 1.8 | 0.1 | 1.6 | -0.6 |
| *Middle Atlantic* | 15,013 | 17,075 | 16,746 | 18,321 | 18,358 | 1.3% | 0.6% | 1.8% | 0.2% |
| New York | 7,179 | 8,247 | 7,892 | 8,635 | 8,633 | 1.4 | 0.4 | 1.8 | 0.0 |
| New Jersey | 3,027 | 3,690 | 3,601 | 3,995 | 4,024 | 2.0 | 0.7 | 2.1 | 0.7 |
| Pennsylvania | 4,806 | 5,139 | 5,253 | 5,691 | 5,701 | 0.7 | 0.9 | 1.6 | 0.2 |
| **MIDWEST** | 24,172 | 26,580 | 29,350 | 32,039 | 31,771 | 1.0% | 1.7% | 1.8% | -0.8% |
| *East North Central* | 17,198 | 18,669 | 20,433 | 22,177 | 21,921 | 0.8 | 1.6 | 1.7 | -1.2 |
| Ohio | 4,485 | 4,817 | 5,221 | 5,625 | 5,566 | 0.7 | 1.4 | 1.5 | -1.0 |
| Indiana | 2,236 | 2,479 | 2,787 | 3,000 | 2,938 | 1.0 | 1.7 | 1.5 | -2.1 |
| Illinois | 4,880 | 5,214 | 5,593 | 6,045 | 6,005 | 0.7 | 1.4 | 1.6 | -0.7 |
| Michigan | 3,637 | 3,922 | 4,274 | 4,674 | 4,587 | 0.8 | 1.6 | 1.8 | -1.9 |
| Wisconsin | 1,960 | 2,236 | 2,559 | 2,833 | 2,826 | 1.3 | 2.2 | 2.1 | -0.3 |
| *West North Central* | 6,973 | 7,911 | 8,917 | 9,862 | 9,850 | 1.3% | 2.0% | 2.0% | -0.1% |
| Minnesota | 1,767 | 2,087 | 2,379 | 2,676 | 2,674 | 1.7 | 2.3 | 2.4 | -0.1 |
| Iowa | 1,132 | 1,200 | 1,358 | 1,478 | 1,469 | 0.6 | 1.9 | 1.7 | -0.6 |
| Missouri | 2,011 | 2,315 | 2,521 | 2,749 | 2,732 | 1.4 | 1.6 | 1.7 | -0.6 |
| North Dakota | 244 | 260 | 302 | 328 | 330 | 0.6 | 2.1 | 1.7 | 0.6 |
| South Dakota | 241 | 276 | 344 | 378 | 379 | 1.3 | 2.9 | 1.9 | 0.4 |
| Nebraska | 631 | 708 | 816 | 909 | 909 | 1.2 | 2.3 | 2.2 | 0.1 |
| Kansas | 947 | 1,064 | 1,198 | 1,345 | 1,357 | 1.2 | 2.1 | 2.3 | 0.9 |

*(cont.)*

**TABLE 6.4B** (cont.) Non-farm payroll employment by state, division, and region, 1979-2001 (thousands)

| | 1979 | 1989 | 1995 | 2000 | 2001 | Percentage change | | | |
|---|---|---|---|---|---|---|---|---|---|
| | | | | | | 1979-89 | 1989-2000 | 1995-2000 | 2000-01 |
| **SOUTH** | 28,571 | 35,989 | 40,654 | 46,235 | 46,377 | 2.3% | 2.3% | 2.6% | 0.3% |
| *South Atlantic* | 14,392 | 19,433 | 21,453 | 24,596 | 24,691 | 3.0 | 2.2 | 2.8 | 0.4 |
| Delaware | 257 | 345 | 366 | 420 | 419 | 3.0 | 1.8 | 2.8 | -0.2 |
| Maryland | 1,691 | 2,155 | 2,183 | 2,450 | 2,470 | 2.5 | 1.2 | 2.3 | 0.8 |
| District of Columbia | 613 | 681 | 643 | 650 | 651 | 1.1 | -0.4 | 0.2 | 0.1 |
| Virginia | 2,115 | 2,862 | 3,070 | 3,517 | 3,528 | 3.1 | 1.9 | 2.8 | 0.3 |
| West Virginia | 659 | 615 | 688 | 736 | 735 | -0.7 | 1.6 | 1.4 | -0.1 |
| North Carolina | 2,373 | 3,074 | 3,460 | 3,934 | 3,901 | 2.6 | 2.3 | 2.6 | -0.8 |
| South Carolina | 1,176 | 1,500 | 1,646 | 1,860 | 1,835 | 2.5 | 2.0 | 2.5 | -1.3 |
| Georgia | 2,128 | 2,941 | 3,402 | 3,949 | 3,954 | 3.3 | 2.7 | 3.0 | 0.1 |
| Florida | 3,381 | 5,261 | 5,996 | 7,081 | 7,198 | 4.5 | 2.7 | 3.4 | 1.7 |
| *East South Central* | 5,223 | 6,121 | 7,020 | 7,638 | 7,576 | 1.6% | 2.0% | 1.7% | -0.8% |
| Kentucky | 1,245 | 1,433 | 1,643 | 1,825 | 1,817 | 1.4 | 2.2 | 2.1 | -0.4 |
| Tennessee | 1,777 | 2,167 | 2,499 | 2,729 | 2,712 | 2.0 | 2.1 | 1.8 | -0.6 |
| Alabama | 1,362 | 1,601 | 1,804 | 1,931 | 1,914 | 1.6 | 1.7 | 1.4 | -0.9 |
| Mississippi | 838 | 919 | 1,075 | 1,154 | 1,134 | 0.9 | 2.1 | 1.4 | -1.7 |
| *West South Central* | 8,957 | 10,436 | 12,180 | 14,001 | 14,110 | 1.5% | 2.7% | 2.8% | 0.8% |
| Arkansas | 749 | 893 | 1,069 | 1,159 | 1,156 | 1.8 | 2.4 | 1.6 | -0.2 |
| Louisiana | 1,517 | 1,539 | 1,772 | 1,920 | 1,931 | 0.1 | 2.0 | 1.6 | 0.6 |
| Oklahoma | 1,088 | 1,164 | 1,316 | 1,490 | 1,509 | 0.7 | 2.3 | 2.5 | 1.3 |
| Texas | 5,602 | 6,840 | 8,023 | 9,433 | 9,513 | 2.0 | 3.0 | 3.3 | 0.8 |

*(cont.)*

**TABLE 6.4B** (cont.) Non-farm payroll employment by state, division, and region, 1979-2001 (thousands)

| | 1979 | 1989 | 1995 | 2000 | 2001 | Percentage change 1979-89 | 1989-2000 | 1995-2000 | 2000-01 |
|---|---|---|---|---|---|---|---|---|---|
| **WEST** | 17,276 | 21,845 | 24,036 | 28,131 | 28,431 | 2.4% | 2.3% | 3.2% | 1.1% |
| *Mountain* | 4,414 | 5,621 | 7,054 | 8,489 | 8,597 | 2.4 | 3.8 | 3.8 | 1.3 |
| Montana | 284 | 291 | 351 | 388 | 392 | 0.3 | 2.6 | 2.0 | 1.1 |
| Idaho | 338 | 366 | 477 | 560 | 569 | 0.8 | 3.9 | 3.2 | 1.8 |
| Wyoming | 201 | 193 | 219 | 239 | 246 | -0.4 | 2.0 | 1.8 | 2.6 |
| Colorado | 1,218 | 1,482 | 1,834 | 2,213 | 2,232 | 2.0 | 3.7 | 3.8 | 0.9 |
| New Mexico | 461 | 562 | 682 | 745 | 757 | 2.0 | 2.6 | 1.8 | 1.6 |
| Arizona | 980 | 1,455 | 1,796 | 2,243 | 2,266 | 4.0 | 4.0 | 4.5 | 1.0 |
| Utah | 548 | 691 | 908 | 1,075 | 1,082 | 2.3 | 4.1 | 3.4 | 0.6 |
| Nevada | 384 | 581 | 786 | 1,027 | 1,054 | 4.2 | 5.3 | 5.5 | 2.6 |
| *Pacific* | 12,863 | 16,224 | 16,982 | 19,642 | 19,834 | 2.3 | 1.8 | 3.0% | 1.0% |
| Washington | 1,581 | 2,047 | 2,347 | 2,711 | 2,698 | 2.6 | 2.6 | 2.9 | -0.5 |
| Oregon | 1,056 | 1,206 | 1,418 | 1,607 | 1,596 | 1.3 | 2.6 | 2.5 | -0.7 |
| California | 9,665 | 12,239 | 12,422 | 14,488 | 14,697 | 2.4 | 1.5 | 3.1 | 1.4 |
| Alaska | 167 | 227 | 262 | 284 | 290 | 3.1 | 2.1 | 1.6 | 2.1 |
| Hawaii | 394 | 506 | 533 | 551 | 554 | 2.5 | 0.8 | 0.7 | 0.4 |
| **Total U.S.** | 89,823 | 107,884 | 117,191 | 131,759 | 132,213 | 1.8% | 1.8% | 2.4% | 0.3% |

Note: Regional sums do not add to U.S. totals due to separate estimation techniques by states and different timing in benchmarking procedures between state and national estimates.

Source: Authors' analysis of BLS data.

**TABLE 6.5** Industrial composition shifts in four states, 1979-2000

| | Employment shares | | | Average weekly pay, 2000 |
|---|---|---|---|---|
| | 1979 | 2000 | Change | |
| **California** | | | | |
| Mining | 0.4% | 0.2% | -0.2% | $1,252 |
| Construction | 4.6 | 5.0 | 0.4 | 776 |
| Manufacturing | 20.8 | 13.4 | -7.4 | 1,110 |
| Transportation* | 5.5 | 5.1 | -0.4 | 909 |
| Wholesale trade | 5.8 | 5.6 | -0.2 | 941 |
| Retail trade | 17.2 | 17.1 | -0.1 | 421 |
| Finance** | 6.2 | 5.7 | -0.5 | 1,157 |
| Services | 21.5 | 31.8 | 10.4 | 796 |
| Government | 18.0 | 16.0 | -2.0 | 793 |
| Total | 100.0 | 100.0 | | |
| **New York** | | | | |
| Mining | 0.1% | 0.1% | 0.0% | $1,002 |
| Construction | 2.9 | 3.8 | 0.9 | 842 |
| Manufacturing | 20.8 | 10.2 | -10.6 | 990 |
| Transportation* | 6.0 | 5.0 | -1.0 | 941 |
| Wholesale trade | 6.3 | 5.2 | -1.1 | 1,010 |
| Retail trade | 14.3 | 15.0 | 0.7 | 395 |
| Finance** | 8.4 | 8.7 | 0.2 | 2,088 |
| Services | 22.9 | 35.2 | 12.3 | 736 |
| Government | 18.3 | 17.0 | -1.3 | 788 |
| Total | 100.0 | 100.0 | | |
| **Michigan** | | | | |
| Mining | 0.4% | 0.2% | -0.2% | $876 |
| Construction | 3.8 | 4.4 | 0.6 | 807 |
| Manufacturing | 31.9 | 21.0 | -10.9 | 1,052 |
| Transportation* | 4.4 | 3.9 | -0.5 | 843 |
| Wholesale trade | 4.7 | 5.0 | 0.3 | 952 |
| Retail trade | 16.2 | 18.4 | 2.1 | 333 |
| Finance** | 4.2 | 4.4 | 0.2 | 838 |
| Services | 17.2 | 28.2 | 10.9 | 624 |
| Government | 17.1 | 14.6 | -2.5 | 685 |
| Total | 100.0 | 100.0 | | |
| **Georgia** | | | | |
| Mining | 0.4% | 0.2% | -0.2% | $879 |
| Construction | 4.9 | 5.1 | 0.2 | 654 |
| Manufacturing | 24.8 | 14.8 | -10.1 | 720 |
| Transportation* | 6.4 | 6.7 | 0.3 | 948 |
| Wholesale trade | 7.3 | 6.4 | -0.9 | 987 |
| Retail trade | 15.9 | 18.1 | 2.1 | 350 |
| Finance** | 5.1 | 5.2 | 0.1 | 965 |
| Services | 15.5 | 28.4 | 12.9 | 656 |
| Government | 19.7 | 15.1 | -4.6 | 608 |
| Total | 100.0 | 100.0 | | |

\* Transportation, communications, public utilities.
\*\* Finance, insurance, real estate.

Source: Center on Budget and Policy Priorities.

**TABLE 6.6** Unemployment rates by state, division, and region, 1979-2001

| | 1979 | 1989 | 1995 | 2000 | 2001* | Percentage-point change | | | |
|---|---|---|---|---|---|---|---|---|---|
| | | | | | | 1979-89 | 1989-2000 | 1995-2000 | 2000-01 |
| **NORTHEAST** | 6.6% | 4.5% | 6.0% | 3.9% | 4.4% | -2.1 | -0.6 | -2.1 | 0.5 |
| *New England* | 5.4 | 3.8 | 5.4 | 2.8 | 3.7 | -1.6 | -1.0 | -2.6 | 0.9 |
| Maine | 7.2 | 4.1 | 5.7 | 3.5 | 4.0 | -3.1 | -0.6 | -2.2 | 0.5 |
| New Hampshire | 3.1 | 3.5 | 4.0 | 2.8 | 3.5 | 0.4 | -0.7 | -1.2 | 0.7 |
| Vermont | 5.1 | 3.7 | 4.2 | 2.9 | 3.6 | -1.4 | -0.8 | -1.3 | 0.7 |
| Massachusetts | 5.5 | 4.0 | 5.4 | 2.6 | 3.7 | -1.5 | -1.4 | -2.8 | 1.1 |
| Rhode Island | 6.6 | 4.1 | 7.0 | 4.1 | 4.7 | -2.5 | 0.0 | -2.9 | 0.6 |
| Connecticut | 5.1 | 3.7 | 5.5 | 2.3 | 3.3 | -1.4 | -1.4 | -3.2 | 1.0 |
| *Middle Atlantic* | 7.0% | 4.7% | 6.2% | 4.3% | 4.7% | -2.3 | -0.4 | -1.9 | 0.4 |
| New York | 7.1 | 5.1 | 6.3 | 4.6 | 4.9 | -2.0 | -0.5 | -1.7 | 0.3 |
| New Jersey | 6.9 | 4.1 | 6.4 | 3.8 | 4.2 | -2.8 | -0.3 | -2.6 | 0.4 |
| Pennsylvania | 6.9 | 4.5 | 5.9 | 4.2 | 4.7 | -2.4 | -0.3 | -1.7 | 0.5 |
| **MIDWEST** | 5.5% | 5.4% | 4.6% | 3.7% | 4.6% | -0.1 | -1.7 | -0.9 | 0.9 |
| *East North Central* | 6.1 | 5.7 | 4.8 | 3.9 | 4.9 | -0.4 | -1.8 | -0.9 | 1.0 |
| Ohio | 5.9 | 5.5 | 4.8 | 4.1 | 4.3 | -0.4 | -1.4 | -0.7 | 0.2 |
| Indiana | 6.4 | 4.7 | 4.7 | 3.2 | 4.4 | -1.7 | -1.5 | -1.5 | 1.2 |
| Illinois | 5.5 | 6.0 | 5.2 | 4.4 | 5.4 | 0.5 | -1.6 | -0.8 | 1.0 |
| Michigan | 7.8 | 7.1 | 5.3 | 3.6 | 5.3 | -0.7 | -3.5 | -1.7 | 1.7 |
| Wisconsin | 4.5 | 4.4 | 3.7 | 3.5 | 4.6 | -0.1 | -0.9 | -0.2 | 1.1 |
| *West North Central* | 4.0% | 4.5% | 3.9% | 3.2% | 3.9% | 0.5 | -1.3 | -0.7 | 0.7 |
| Minnesota | 4.2 | 4.3 | 3.7 | 3.3 | 3.7 | 0.1 | -1.0 | -0.4 | 0.4 |
| Iowa | 4.1 | 4.3 | 3.5 | 2.6 | 3.3 | 0.2 | -1.7 | -0.9 | 0.7 |
| Missouri | 4.5 | 5.5 | 4.8 | 3.5 | 4.7 | 1.0 | -2.0 | -1.3 | 1.2 |
| North Dakota | 3.7 | 4.3 | 3.3 | 3.0 | 2.8 | 0.6 | -1.3 | -0.3 | -0.2 *(cont.)* |

**TABLE 6.6** (cont.) Unemployment rates by state, division, and region, 1979-2001

| | 1979 | 1989 | 1995 | 2000 | 2001* | Percentage-point change | | | |
|---|---|---|---|---|---|---|---|---|---|
| | | | | | | 1979-89 | 1989-2000 | 1995-2000 | 2000-01 |
| **MIDWEST** | | | | | | | | | |
| *West North Central (cont.)* | | | | | | | | | |
| South Dakota | 3.5% | 4.2% | 2.9% | 2.3% | 3.3% | 0.7 | -1.9 | -0.6 | 1.0 |
| Nebraska | 3.2 | 3.1 | 2.6 | 3.0 | 3.1 | -0.1 | -0.1 | 0.4 | 0.1 |
| Kansas | 3.4 | 4.0 | 4.4 | 3.7 | 4.3 | 0.6 | -0.3 | -0.7 | 0.6 |
| **SOUTH** | 5.3% | 5.7% | 5.4% | 3.9% | 4.8% | 0.4 | -1.8 | -1.5 | 0.9 |
| *South Atlantic* | 5.5 | 4.8 | 5.1 | 3.6 | 4.6 | -0.7 | -1.2 | -1.5 | 1.0 |
| Delaware | 8.0 | 3.5 | 4.3 | 4.0 | 3.5 | -4.5 | 0.5 | -0.3 | -0.5 |
| Maryland | 5.9 | 3.7 | 5.1 | 3.9 | 4.1 | -2.2 | 0.2 | -1.2 | 0.2 |
| District of Columbia | 7.5 | 5.0 | 8.9 | 5.8 | 6.5 | -2.5 | 0.8 | -3.1 | 0.7 |
| Virginia | 4.7 | 3.9 | 4.5 | 2.2 | 3.5 | -0.8 | -1.7 | -2.3 | 1.3 |
| West Virginia | 6.7 | 8.6 | 7.9 | 5.5 | 4.9 | 1.9 | -3.1 | -2.4 | -0.6 |
| North Carolina | 4.8 | 3.5 | 4.3 | 3.6 | 5.5 | -1.3 | 0.1 | -0.7 | 1.9 |
| South Carolina | 5.0 | 4.7 | 5.1 | 3.9 | 5.4 | -0.3 | -0.8 | -1.2 | 1.5 |
| Georgia | 5.1 | 5.5 | 4.9 | 3.7 | 4.0 | 0.4 | -1.8 | -1.2 | 0.3 |
| Florida | 6.0 | 5.6 | 5.5 | 3.6 | 4.8 | -0.4 | -2.0 | -1.9 | 1.2 |
| *East South Central* | 6.1% | 6.3% | 5.7% | 4.4% | 5.1% | 0.2 | -1.9 | -1.3 | 0.7 |
| Kentucky | 5.6 | 6.2 | 5.4 | 4.1 | 5.5 | 0.6 | -2.1 | -1.3 | 1.4 |
| Tennessee | 5.8 | 5.1 | 5.2 | 3.9 | 4.5 | -0.7 | -1.2 | -1.3 | 0.6 |
| Alabama | 7.1 | 7.0 | 6.3 | 4.6 | 5.3 | -0.1 | -2.4 | -1.7 | 0.7 |
| Mississippi | 5.8 | 7.8 | 6.1 | 5.7 | 5.5 | 2.0 | -2.1 | -0.4 | -0.2 |
| *West South Central* | 4.7% | 6.8% | 5.9% | 4.3% | 4.9% | 2.1 | -2.5 | -1.6 | 0.6 |
| Arkansas | 6.2 | 7.2 | 4.9 | 4.4 | 5.1 | 1.0 | -2.8 | -0.5 | 0.7 |
| Louisiana | 6.7 | 7.9 | 6.9 | 5.5 | 6.0 | 1.2 | -2.4 | -1.4 | 0.5 |
| Oklahoma | 3.4 | 5.6 | 4.7 | 3.0 | 3.8 | 2.2 | -2.6 | -1.7 | 0.8 |
| Texas | 4.2 | 6.7 | 6.0 | 4.2 | 4.9 | 2.5 | -2.5 | -1.8 | 0.7 *(cont.)* |

**TABLE 6.6** (cont.) Unemployment rates by state, division, and region, 1979-2001

| | 1979 | 1989 | 1995 | 2000 | 2001* | Percentage-point change | | | |
|---|---|---|---|---|---|---|---|---|---|
| | | | | | | 1979-89 | 1989-2000 | 1995-2000 | 2000-01 |
| **WEST** | — | 5.3% | 6.6% | 4.6% | 5.2% | n.a. | -0.7 | -2.0 | 0.6 |
| *Mountain* | 5.0% | 5.5 | 4.9 | 3.8 | 4.5 | 0.5 | -1.7 | -1.1 | 0.7 |
| Montana | 5.1 | 5.9 | 5.9 | 4.9 | 4.6 | 0.8 | -1.0 | -1.0 | -0.3 |
| Idaho | 5.7 | 5.1 | 5.4 | 4.9 | 5.0 | -0.6 | -0.2 | -0.5 | 0.1 |
| Wyoming | 2.8 | 6.3 | 4.8 | 3.9 | 3.9 | 3.5 | -2.4 | -0.9 | 0.0 |
| Colorado | 4.8 | 5.8 | 4.2 | 2.7 | 3.7 | 1.0 | -3.1 | -1.5 | 1.0 |
| New Mexico | 6.6 | 6.7 | 6.3 | 4.9 | 4.8 | 0.1 | -1.8 | -1.4 | -0.1 |
| Arizona | 5.1 | 5.2 | 5.1 | 3.9 | 4.7 | 0.1 | -1.3 | -1.2 | 0.8 |
| Utah | 4.3 | 4.6 | 3.6 | 3.2 | 4.4 | 0.3 | -1.4 | -0.4 | 1.2 |
| Nevada | 5.1 | 5.0 | 5.4 | 4.1 | 5.3 | -0.1 | -0.9 | -1.3 | 1.2 |
| | | | | | | | | | |
| *Pacific* | n.a. | 5.2% | 7.3% | 5.0% | 5.5% | n.a. | -0.2 | -2.3 | 0.5 |
| Washington | 6.8% | 6.2 | 6.4 | 5.2 | 6.4 | -0.6 | -1.0 | -1.2 | 1.2 |
| Oregon | 6.8 | 5.7 | 4.8 | 4.9 | 6.3 | -1.1 | -0.8 | 0.1 | 1.4 |
| California | 6.8** | 5.1 | 7.8 | 4.9 | 5.3 | -1.7 | -0.2 | -2.9 | 0.4 |
| Alaska | 9.2 | 6.7 | 7.3 | 6.6 | 6.3 | -2.5 | -0.1 | -0.7 | -0.3 |
| Hawaii | 6.3 | 2.6 | 5.9 | 4.3 | 4.6 | -3.7 | 1.7 | -1.6 | 0.3 |
| | | | | | | | | | |
| **Total U.S.** | 5.8% | 5.3% | 5.6% | 4.0% | 4.8% | -0.5 | -1.3 | -1.6 | 0.8 |

\* These 2001 numbers will be revised in BLS's January 2003 Employment and Earnings report.
\*\* Observation from 1980.
Note: Unemployment rates for 1994 and beyond are not directly comparable to those from earlier years, due to changes in BLS survey methodology.

Source: Authors' analysis of BLS data from Labstat web site.

of almost 3 percentage points between 1995 and 2000). The fact that the early 1990s recession was more severe in these states and that the boom caught on relatively late attenuated their gains over the full recovery.

The last column of Table 6.6 provides information on the geographical impact of the recession on unemployment rates. The impact was particularly negative in the Midwest, due partly to the sharp contraction in manufacturing jobs there. In one year, the 0.9 percentage point decline that occurred over the late 1990s in Midwestern unemployment was reversed. In four larger states— Indiana, Illinois, Michigan, Missouri, and Wisconsin—unemployment increased between 1.0 and 1.7 percentage points. Some Southern states also saw larger-than-average increases, but overall the employment declines in the South in 2000-01 were not large enough to wipe out the gains of 1995-2000.

Nevertheless, national unemployment continued to climb in 2002, despite faster economic growth in 2002 relative to 2001. Thus, for most states, the 2001 unemployment rates shown here are not peaks—in most states, 2002 unemployment will be higher than in 2001.

*Wages:* Nationally, the late 1990s was a period of broad-based wage growth, but real wage gains for low-wage workers (**Table 6.7**) were much greater in the Midwest and South than in the Northeast. Many Midwestern states had real annual growth rates above 2% and even 3%.

In the 1980s, with the exception of moderate growth in most Northeastern states (excepting New York, where low wages were stagnant), low-wage workers lost ground, especially in the Midwest and West. The pattern reversed in the 1990s, with losses in the Northeast and moderate gains elsewhere, and the gains were largely confined to the 1995-2000 period. For the most part, the momentum of the latter 1990s fueled continued low-wage growth in 2001, despite rising unemployment.

The latter 1990s were a unique period for most low-wage workers. Note the extremely wide swing in many states in low-wage trends, from the steep declines of the 1980s to the relatively fast increases of the 1990s, particularly the late 1990s. When the annual wage changes are accumulated over the decade, low-wage workers in many states over the 1980s experienced double-digit real losses in percentage terms. Yet in these same states in the next decade, low-wage workers saw double-digit gains. For example, low wages in Michigan fell 17% over the 1980s and grew 13% in the 1990s; for Wisconsin, the comparable changes are a drop of 14% and a rise of 21%. This pattern prevailed in other states in the South and West as well. Since many low-wage workers are just beginning their careers, these trends imply that those who did so in the 1990s got a much more promising start, at least in terms of wage

**TABLE 6.7** Low wages (20th percentile) by state, 1979-2001 (2001 dollars)

| | 1979 | 1989 | 1995 | 2000 | 2001 | Annualized percent changes | | | | |
|---|---|---|---|---|---|---|---|---|---|---|
| | | | | | | 1979-89 | 1989-2000 | 1995-2000 | 2000-01 | 1979-2001 |
| **NORTHEAST** | $7.90 | $8.24 | $7.96 | $8.29 | $8.59 | 0.4% | 0.1% | 0.8% | 3.6% | -0.4% |
| Maine | 7.09 | 7.76 | 7.11 | 8.06 | 8.25 | 0.9 | 0.3 | 2.5 | 2.4 | -0.7 |
| New Hampshire | 7.64 | 8.70 | 8.11 | 8.76 | 9.00 | 1.3 | 0.1 | 1.6 | 2.7 | -0.7 |
| Vermont | 7.03 | 7.98 | 7.84 | 8.18 | 8.48 | 1.3 | 0.2 | 0.9 | 3.6 | -0.8 |
| Massachusetts | 7.84 | 9.31 | 8.52 | 8.92 | 9.12 | 1.7 | -0.4 | 0.9 | 2.2 | -0.7 |
| Rhode Island | 7.63 | 8.12 | 7.88 | 8.64 | 8.61 | 0.6 | 0.6 | 1.8 | -0.4 | -0.5 |
| Connecticut | 8.20 | 9.65 | 9.01 | 9.35 | 9.82 | 1.6 | -0.3 | 0.7 | 5.0 | -0.8 |
| New York | 7.94 | 8.08 | 7.85 | 8.05 | 8.25 | 0.2 | 0.0 | 0.5 | 2.5 | -0.2 |
| New Jersey | 7.98 | 8.91 | 8.57 | 8.88 | 9.06 | 1.1 | 0.0 | 0.7 | 2.0 | -0.6 |
| Pennsylvania | 7.97 | 7.38 | 7.39 | 7.95 | 8.26 | -0.8 | 0.7 | 1.5 | 3.9 | -0.2 |
| **MIDWEST** | $7.91 | $7.02 | $7.27 | $8.29 | $8.33 | -1.2% | 1.5% | 2.7% | 0.4% | -0.2% |
| Ohio | 7.93 | 7.15 | 7.10 | 8.16 | 8.15 | -1.0 | 1.2 | 2.8 | 0.0 | -0.1 |
| Indiana | 7.63 | 6.77 | 7.28 | 8.40 | 8.52 | -1.2 | 2.0 | 2.9 | 1.4 | -0.5 |
| Illinois | 8.47 | 7.48 | 7.57 | 8.11 | 8.39 | -1.2 | 0.7 | 1.4 | 3.5 | 0.0 |
| Michigan | 8.48 | 7.19 | 7.75 | 8.44 | 8.35 | -1.6 | 1.5 | 1.7 | -1.0 | 0.1 |
| Wisconsin | 7.87 | 6.92 | 7.26 | 8.67 | 8.53 | -1.3 | 2.1 | 3.6 | -1.7 | -0.4 |
| Minnesota | 7.88 | 7.62 | 8.14 | 9.24 | 9.19 | -0.3 | 1.8 | 2.6 | -0.5 | -0.7 |
| Iowa | 7.48 | 6.57 | 7.08 | 8.28 | 8.26 | -1.3 | 2.1 | 3.2 | -0.3 | -0.4 |
| Missouri | 7.39 | 6.71 | 7.04 | 8.42 | 8.28 | -1.0 | 2.1 | 3.6 | -1.7 | -0.5 |
| North Dakota | 7.07 | 6.34 | 6.32 | 7.25 | 7.16 | -1.1 | 1.2 | 2.8 | -1.3 | -0.1 |
| South Dakota | 6.85 | 5.97 | 6.67 | 7.92 | 7.83 | -1.4 | 2.6 | 3.5 | -1.2 | -0.6 |
| Nebraska | 7.27 | 6.50 | 6.88 | 7.69 | 7.83 | -1.1 | 1.5 | 2.2 | 1.9 | -0.3 |
| Kansas | 7.62 | 6.80 | 6.61 | 7.64 | 7.99 | -1.1 | 1.1 | -2.9 | 4.6 | -0.2 |
| **SOUTH** | $7.16 | $6.74 | $6.83 | $7.55 | $7.78 | -0.6% | 1.0% | 2.0% | 3.0% | -0.4% |
| Delaware | 8.06 | 7.90 | 7.69 | 8.32 | 8.47 | -0.2 | 0.5 | 1.6 | 1.8 | -0.2 |
| Maryland | 8.16 | 8.38 | 8.21 | 8.92 | 9.03 | 0.3 | 0.6 | -1.7 | 1.3 | -0.5 |
| District of Columbia | 8.91 | 8.41 | 8.16 | 9.20 | 9.31 | -0.6 | 0.8 | 2.4 | 1.1 | -0.2 |
| Virginia | 7.32 | 7.55 | 7.51 | 8.39 | 8.62 | 0.3 | 1.0 | 2.2 | 2.7 | -0.7 |

*(cont.)*

377

**TABLE 6.7** *(cont.)* Low wages (20th percentile) by state, 1979-2001 (2001 dollars)

| | | | | | | Annualized percent changes | | | | |
|---|---|---|---|---|---|---|---|---|---|---|
| | 1979 | 1989 | 1995 | 2000 | 2001 | 1979-89 | 1989-2000 | 1995-2000 | 2000-01 | 1979-2001 |
| **SOUTH** *(cont.)* | $7.16 | $6.74 | $6.83 | $7.55 | $7.78 | -0.6% | 1.0% | 2.0% | 3.0% | -0.4% |
| West Virginia | 7.50 | 5.75 | 6.38 | 6.86 | 7.11 | -2.6 | 1.6 | 1.4 | 3.6 | 0.2 |
| North Carolina | 7.07 | 6.90 | 7.19 | 8.04 | 7.89 | -0.2 | 1.4 | 2.3 | -1.8 | -0.5 |
| South Carolina | 6.94 | 6.63 | 6.99 | 8.00 | 8.07 | -0.5 | 1.7 | 2.8 | 0.8 | -0.7 |
| Georgia | 7.18 | 7.00 | 7.03 | 7.92 | 8.21 | -0.2 | 1.1 | 2.4 | 3.8 | -0.6 |
| Florida | 7.02 | 6.96 | 6.85 | 7.41 | 7.69 | -0.1 | 0.6 | 1.6 | 3.7 | -0.4 |
| Kentucky | 7.31 | 6.19 | 6.70 | 7.53 | 7.90 | -1.7 | 1.8 | 2.4 | 5.0 | -0.4 |
| Tennessee | 7.09 | 6.46 | 6.92 | 7.67 | 7.82 | -0.9 | 1.6 | 2.1 | 1.9 | -0.4 |
| Alabama | 7.00 | 6.38 | 6.28 | 7.20 | 7.51 | -0.9 | 1.1 | 2.8 | 4.4 | -0.3 |
| Mississippi | 6.74 | 5.54 | 5.94 | 6.90 | 7.09 | -1.9 | 2.0 | 3.0 | 2.7 | -0.2 |
| Arkansas | 6.91 | 5.98 | 6.21 | 7.03 | 7.20 | -1.4 | 1.5 | 2.5 | 2.4 | -0.2 |
| Louisiana | 7.14 | 5.99 | 6.14 | 7.02 | 6.99 | -1.7 | 1.4 | 2.7 | -0.3 | 0.1 |
| Oklahoma | 7.44 | 6.60 | 6.38 | 7.38 | 7.67 | -1.2 | 1.0 | 3.0 | 3.9 | -0.1 |
| Texas | 7.21 | 6.44 | 6.58 | 7.28 | 7.33 | -1.1 | 1.1 | 2.0 | 0.7 | -0.1 |
| **WEST** | $8.17 | $7.46 | $7.17 | $7.93 | $8.06 | -0.9% | 0.6% | 2.0% | 1.7% | 0.1% |
| Montana | 7.28 | 6.36 | 6.67 | 6.78 | 6.96 | -1.3 | 0.6 | 0.4 | 2.5 | 0.2 |
| Idaho | 7.30 | 6.27 | 6.77 | 7.42 | 7.71 | -1.5 | 1.5 | 1.8 | 3.9 | -0.2 |
| Wyoming | 8.11 | 6.57 | 6.50 | 7.17 | 7.54 | -2.1 | 0.8 | 2.0 | 5.2 | 0.3 |
| Colorado | 7.86 | 7.01 | 7.68 | 8.90 | 9.02 | -1.1 | 2.2 | 3.0 | 1.4 | -0.6 |
| New Mexico | 7.16 | 6.09 | 6.73 | 7.12 | 6.95 | -1.6 | 1.4 | 1.1 | -2.3 | 0.1 |
| Arizona | 7.57 | 7.04 | 6.90 | 7.90 | 8.04 | -0.7 | 1.1 | 2.7 | 1.8 | -0.3 |
| Utah | 7.65 | 7.04 | 7.08 | 7.97 | 7.96 | -0.8 | 1.1 | 2.4 | -0.2 | -0.2 |
| Nevada | 7.93 | 7.69 | 7.83 | 8.01 | 8.19 | -0.3 | 0.4 | 0.5 | 2.2 | -0.1 |
| Washington | 8.79 | 7.77 | 7.81 | 8.68 | 8.40 | -1.2 | 1.0 | 2.1 | -3.3 | 0.2 |
| Oregon | 8.48 | 7.58 | 7.56 | 8.10 | 8.29 | -1.1 | 0.6 | 1.4 | 2.4 | 0.1 |
| California | 8.34 | 7.82 | 7.05 | 7.74 | 8.00 | -0.6 | -0.1 | 1.9 | 3.3 | 0.2 |
| Alaska | 11.87 | 10.11 | 9.19 | 9.22 | 9.73 | -1.6 | -0.8 | 0.1 | 5.6 | 0.9 |
| Hawaii | 7.30 | 8.03 | 8.04 | 7.57 | 7.86 | 1.0 | -0.5 | -1.2 | 3.8 | -0.3 |

Source: Authors' analysis of CPS ORG data; see data appendix.

growth if not in terms of wage levels (since low-wage jobs paid less in 1989 relative to 1979, those who began their careers in the 1990s started from a lower base).

Median wages (**Table 6.8**) followed a similar regional pattern to low wages, though their growth was slightly less impressive than that of low wages in the late 1990s boom. For example, median wages grew at a 2.0% annual rate in the Midwest during that period compared to a 2.7% rate for low wage workers (a similar difference prevailed in the West). Also, in 2001, real median wage growth slowed by half nationally, while that of low-wage workers accelerated. Only in the Northeast did median wages continue to grow quickly in 2001 (though some Southern states also saw larger-than-average real gains).

A variety of factors play a role in generating regional differences in wage trends, including state-level demographics (e.g., states with higher levels of immigration might experience slower wage growth than would otherwise have been the case); state policies toward economic development; and industry shifts. But one factor—state variation in unemployment—tends to correlate with other important state-level trends.

**Figure 6C** plots annualized state real wage changes for low-wage workers against changes in state unemployment rates in the 1980s and latter 1990s. An example is Colorado (indicated in the second panel), where unemployment fell about 3 percentage points and low wages grew more than 2% per year. The line through the dots represents the best linear "fit" passing through that particular scatter of dots.

The most interesting feature of the graphs is the different scatter of dots over the two periods. The expectation would be that states that experienced falling unemployment would also be those that experienced faster real wage growth, as tight labor markets in those states bid up wages relative to states with weaker labor markets (e.g., areas of the country where there was an over-supply of low-wage workers relative to the available number of jobs, for example). In these graphs, that would mean that most of the dots would be in the upper left (rising wages and declining unemployment) or lower right (rising unemployment and falling wages) sections. Yet the figure illustrates that this was much more the case in the 1990s than in the prior decade. In the 1980s, many of the states fall in the lower left section, which corresponds to both falling unemployment and declining real wages, or the lower right section: falling real wages and rising unemployment. Over the 1990s, however, the majority of states shift to the upper left quadrant (rising wages/falling unemployment), a minority of states saw both falling unemployment and falling wages, and only one state (Hawaii) had rising unemployment and falling low wages.

Note also that the line is placed higher in the 1990s graph than in the 1980s

**TABLE 6.8** Median wages (50th percentile) by state, 1979-2001 (2001 dollars)

| | 1979 | 1989 | 1995 | 2000 | 2001 | Annualized percent changes | | | | |
|---|---|---|---|---|---|---|---|---|---|---|
| | | | | | | 1979-89 | 1989-2000 | 1995-2000 | 2000-01 | 1979-2001 |
| **NORTHEAST** | $12.20 | $13.50 | $13.16 | $13.59 | $14.10 | 1.0% | 0.1% | 0.6% | 3.7% | -0.7% |
| Maine | 9.74 | 11.04 | 10.63 | 11.35 | 11.89 | 1.3 | 0.3 | 1.3 | 4.7 | -0.9 |
| New Hampshire | 11.07 | 13.17 | 12.51 | 13.51 | 13.77 | 1.8 | 0.2 | 1.5 | 1.9 | -1.0 |
| Vermont | 10.38 | 11.50 | 11.63 | 12.07 | 12.45 | 1.0 | 0.4 | 0.7 | 3.1 | -0.8 |
| Massachusetts | 11.67 | 13.97 | 13.78 | 14.51 | 14.77 | 1.8 | 0.3 | 1.0 | 1.8 | -1.1 |
| Rhode Island | 11.19 | 12.20 | 12.64 | 13.53 | 13.26 | 0.9 | 0.9 | 1.4 | -2.0 | -0.8 |
| Connecticut | 12.40 | 14.57 | 15.13 | 15.40 | 16.15 | 1.6 | 0.5 | 0.3 | 4.9 | -1.2 |
| New York | 12.46 | 13.68 | 13.32 | 13.45 | 13.89 | 0.9 | -0.2 | 0.2 | 3.3 | -0.5 |
| New Jersey | 12.78 | 14.52 | 14.70 | 14.87 | 15.21 | 1.3 | 0.2 | 0.2 | 2.3 | -0.8 |
| Pennsylvania | 12.40 | 11.89 | 11.92 | 12.61 | 13.09 | -0.4 | 0.5 | 1.1 | 3.8 | -0.2 |
| **MIDWEST** | $12.66 | $11.76 | $11.68 | $12.92 | $13.03 | -0.7% | 0.9% | 2.0% | 0.9% | -0.1% |
| Ohio | 12.97 | 11.97 | 11.64 | 12.97 | 12.81 | -0.8 | 0.7 | 2.2 | -1.2 | 0.1 |
| Indiana | 11.82 | 10.93 | 11.07 | 12.32 | 12.76 | -0.8 | 1.1 | 2.2 | 3.6 | -0.3 |
| Illinois | 13.37 | 12.72 | 12.76 | 13.43 | 13.66 | -0.5 | 0.5 | 1.0 | 1.8 | -0.1 |
| Michigan | 13.92 | 12.64 | 12.67 | 13.46 | 13.77 | -1.0 | 0.6 | 1.2 | 2.3 | 0.1 |
| Wisconsin | 12.48 | 11.36 | 11.74 | 12.58 | 12.83 | -0.9 | 0.9 | 1.4 | 2.0 | -0.1 |
| Minnesota | 12.43 | 12.23 | 12.41 | 14.77 | 14.76 | -0.2 | 1.7 | 3.5 | -0.1 | -0.8 |
| Iowa | 11.63 | 10.62 | 10.59 | 12.24 | 12.31 | -0.9 | 1.3 | 3.0 | 0.5 | -0.3 |
| Missouri | 11.57 | 11.01 | 11.21 | 12.78 | 12.96 | -0.5 | 1.4 | 2.7 | 1.4 | -0.5 |
| North Dakota | 10.85 | 9.82 | 9.48 | 10.37 | 10.18 | -1.0 | 0.5 | 1.8 | -1.8 | 0.3 |
| South Dakota | 9.57 | 9.15 | 9.79 | 11.13 | 11.15 | -0.5 | 1.8 | 2.6 | 0.2 | -0.7 |
| Nebraska | 10.92 | 10.03 | 10.32 | 10.93 | 11.41 | -0.8 | 0.8 | 1.1 | 4.4 | -0.2 |
| Kansas | 11.38 | 11.18 | 10.49 | 11.99 | 12.27 | -0.2 | 0.6 | 2.7 | 2.3 | -0.3 |
| **SOUTH** | $10.94 | $10.81 | $10.85 | $11.81 | $12.07 | -0.1% | 0.8% | 1.7% | 2.2% | -0.4% |
| Delaware | 12.18 | 12.59 | 12.21 | 13.39 | 13.92 | 0.3 | 0.6 | 1.9 | 3.9 | -0.6 |
| Maryland | 13.12 | 13.57 | 13.87 | 14.34 | 14.92 | 0.3 | 0.5 | 0.7 | 4.0 | -0.6 |
| District of Columbia | 13.58 | 13.75 | 13.69 | 15.31 | 15.05 | 0.1 | 1.0 | 2.3 | -1.7 | -0.5 |
| Virginia | 11.54 | 12.52 | 11.94 | 13.76 | 14.10 | 0.8 | 0.9 | 2.9 | 2.4 | -0.9 |

(cont.)

**TABLE 6.8** *(cont.)* Median wages (50th percentile) by state, 1979-2001 (2001 dollars)

| | 1979 | 1989 | 1995 | 2000 | 2001 | Annualized percent changes | | | | |
|---|---|---|---|---|---|---|---|---|---|---|
| | | | | | | 1979-89 | 1989-2000 | 1995-2000 | 2000-01 | 1979-2001 |
| **SOUTH** *(cont.)* | | | | | | | | | | |
| West Virginia | $12.77 | $10.10 | $10.52 | $11.10 | $11.17 | -2.3% | 0.9% | 1.1% | 0.6% | 0.6% |
| North Carolina | 9.93 | 10.40 | 10.75 | 11.85 | 11.95 | 0.5 | 1.2 | 2.0 | 0.9 | -0.8 |
| South Carolina | 9.61 | 10.35 | 10.47 | 12.27 | 12.45 | 0.7 | 1.6 | 3.2 | 1.4 | -1.2 |
| Georgia | 10.70 | 11.18 | 11.10 | 11.84 | 12.55 | 0.4 | 0.5 | 1.3 | 6.0 | -0.7 |
| Florida | 10.14 | 10.74 | 10.69 | 11.41 | 11.80 | 0.6 | 0.6 | 1.3 | 3.4 | -0.7 |
| Kentucky | 11.54 | 10.70 | 10.77 | 11.52 | 12.14 | -0.8 | 0.7 | 1.4 | 5.4 | -0.2 |
| Tennessee | 10.41 | 9.92 | 10.46 | 11.77 | 11.62 | -0.5 | 1.6 | 2.4 | -1.2 | -0.5 |
| Alabama | 10.92 | 10.26 | 9.87 | 11.15 | 11.74 | -0.6 | 0.8 | 2.5 | 5.3 | -0.3 |
| Mississippi | 9.24 | 8.89 | 9.51 | 10.62 | 10.92 | -0.4 | 1.6 | 2.2 | 2.8 | -0.8 |
| Arkansas | 9.34 | 9.11 | 9.71 | 10.31 | 10.32 | -0.2 | 1.1 | 1.2 | 0.1 | -0.5 |
| Louisiana | 11.25 | 9.96 | 10.14 | 11.09 | 11.09 | -1.2 | 1.0 | 1.8 | 0.0 | 0.1 |
| Oklahoma | 11.64 | 10.65 | 10.38 | 10.91 | 11.20 | -0.9 | 0.2 | 1.0 | 2.7 | 0.2 |
| Texas | 11.31 | 10.79 | 10.57 | 11.48 | 11.77 | -0.5 | 0.6 | 1.7 | 2.6 | -0.2 |
| **WEST** | $13.14 | $12.91 | $12.20 | $13.04 | $13.22 | -0.2% | 0.1% | 1.3% | 1.4% | 0.0% |
| Montana | 11.88 | 10.30 | 10.27 | 10.30 | 10.22 | -1.4 | 0.0 | 0.1 | -0.8 | 0.7 |
| Idaho | 11.40 | 10.10 | 10.64 | 11.32 | 11.23 | -1.2 | 1.0 | 1.3 | -0.8 | 0.1 |
| Wyoming | 13.43 | 11.32 | 10.77 | 11.18 | 12.00 | -1.7 | -0.1 | 0.7 | 7.4 | 0.5 |
| Colorado | 12.81 | 11.91 | 12.59 | 14.33 | 14.19 | -0.7 | 1.7 | 2.6 | -1.0 | -0.5 |
| New Mexico | 11.45 | 9.94 | 10.41 | 11.15 | 11.08 | -1.4 | 1.0 | 1.4 | -0.6 | 0.1 |
| Arizona | 11.62 | 11.52 | 11.00 | 12.23 | 12.57 | -0.1 | 0.5 | 2.1 | 2.8 | -0.4 |
| Utah | 12.13 | 11.25 | 10.86 | 12.17 | 12.15 | -0.8 | 0.7 | 2.3 | -0.2 | 0.0 |
| Nevada | 11.96 | 12.12 | 11.51 | 11.92 | 12.13 | 0.1 | -0.2 | 0.7 | 1.8 | -0.1 |
| Washington | 13.95 | 13.15 | 12.58 | 13.89 | 13.76 | -0.6 | 0.5 | 2.0 | -0.9 | 0.1 |
| Oregon | 13.25 | 12.59 | 12.20 | 12.55 | 13.37 | -0.5 | 0.0 | 0.6 | 6.5 | 0.0 |
| California | 13.31 | 13.63 | 12.87 | 13.46 | 13.85 | 0.2 | -0.1 | 0.9 | 2.8 | -0.2 |
| Alaska | 18.91 | 16.31 | 15.12 | 15.06 | 15.25 | -1.5 | -0.7 | -0.1 | 1.3 | 1.0 |
| Hawaii | 11.98 | 12.96 | 12.22 | 12.18 | 12.35 | 0.8 | -0.6 | -0.1 | 1.4 | -0.1 |

Source: Authors' analysis of CPS ORG data; see data appendix.

**FIGURE 6C** The relationship between changes in 20th percentile wages and unemployment

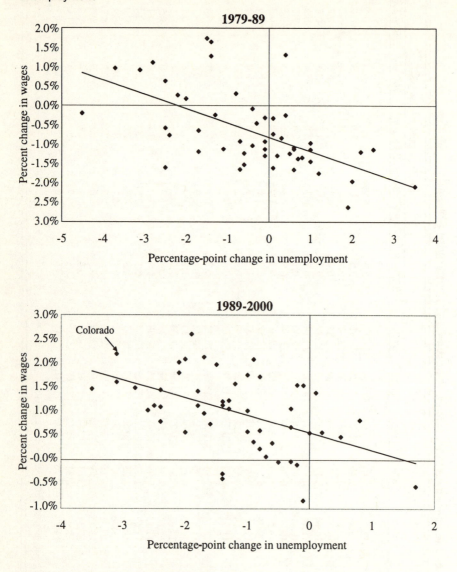

Source: Authors' analysis of CPS ORG data.

graph. This shift implies that the same change in unemployment in either decade led to higher wage growth in the 1990s. For example, a state in which unemployment fell by 2 points in the 1980s would have had a 0.3% annual decline in real 20th percentile wages. In the 1990s, that same decline in unemployment translated into a 1% average increase in real 20th percentile wages.

This return to the expected relationship between falling unemployment and rising wages is one of the tangible benefits of the full employment conditions of the latter 1990s, conditions that were absent over the 1980s. Under these conditions, tight labor markets throughout the country enabled low-wage workers to bid up real wages.

Of course, even with the favorable trends in the 1990s, many disadvantaged workers closed the decade with extremely high rates of joblessness. **Table 6.9** turns to a subset of states for a more refined look at the labor market facing persons whose characteristics—gender, race, education, and age—are associated with less favorable outcomes. (The table pools three years of data to generate larger sample sizes for smaller states). Table 6.9 also includes data for underemployment, a concept that adds both discouraged workers (those who looked for work in the past year but have given up due to perceived slack demand) and the marginally attached (e.g., involuntary part-timers) to the unemployed.

While the overall unemployment rate was 4.2% for the nation in 1998-2000, the unemployment rate for African American men in New York age 16-25 with at most a high school degree (excluding those enrolled in school) was 20.8%, just under five times the national level. The young high school dropouts in these states have particularly high un- and underemployment rates. More than half of the young black women in this group were unemployed in Washington, D.C.; close to 70% were underemployed. In New York, 45.5% of young black males without a high school diploma were unemployed, and just under 60% were underemployed. High school graduates have much lower rates, but their rates are all well above the national average.

Three states have large enough Hispanic samples for this type of analysis. Unemployment for Hispanics without high school diplomas ranged near 20% for females and between 9.4% and 13.7% for males. Though high relative to the national average, these rates are still well below the rates for black high school dropouts in these states. The same differential exists for high school un- and underemployment rates. For example, New York Hispanic males had a 14.7% underemployment rate, compared to 35.4% for comparable African Americans. Thus, while these labor market conditions are particularly unfavorable for young, non-college-educated minorities, they are even worse for blacks than for Hispanics. The fact that this differential is much larger for males than females (in

**TABLE 6.9** Un- and underemployment among African Americans and Hispanics, age 16-25, by gender and education level, 1998-2000

| | Females | | | | Males | | | |
|---|---|---|---|---|---|---|---|---|
| | Unemployment | | Underemployment | | Unemployment | | Underemployment | |
| | Less than high school | High school | Less than high school | High school | Less than high school | High school | Less than high school | High school |
| **African Americans, age 16-25** | | | | | | | | |
| New York | 30.4% | 18.9% | 45.9% | 32.2% | 45.5% | 20.8% | 59.5% | 35.4% |
| Illinois | 37.5 | 25.0 | 51.2 | 37.3 | 39.2 | 21.4 | 54.7 | 32.1 |
| D.C. | 55.0 | 26.2 | 69.4 | 39.4 | 47.6 | 26.0 | 59.6 | 37.6 |
| Georgia | 42.7 | 15.1 | 57.6 | 22.8 | · | · | 43.4 | 24.3 |
| Florida | 27.9 | 15.7 | 42.9 | 26.9 | 31.3 | 14.3 | 41.5 | 23.2 |
| Mississippi | 39.1 | 22.0 | 51.4 | 33.8 | 44.2 | 20.7 | 53.5 | 34.2 |
| Texas | 39.2 | 18.2 | 50.1 | 26.9 | · | 25.7 | 39.3 | 33.9 |
| U.S. | 33.5 | 17.8 | 48.0 | 28.9 | 34.4 | 19.5 | 47.8 | 29.1 |
| **Hispanics, age 16-25** | | | | | | | | |
| New York | 24% | 15.1% | 36.3% | 27% | 13.7% | · | 21.1% | 14.7% |
| Texas | 19.2 | 11.2 | 32.9 | 20.0 | 9.4 | 9.3 | 17.3 | 14.1 |
| California | 19.6 | 9.9 | 34.0 | 21.9 | 12.1 | 9.7 | 22.4 | 17.0 |
| U.S. | 19.7 | 11.1 | 32.0 | 20.6 | 13.2 | 8.8 | 22.3 | 15.2 |

Source: Authors' analysis of CPS data.

**FIGURE 6D** Change in poverty-level wage shares by division, 1979-2000

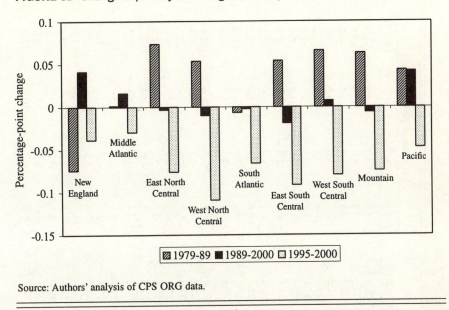

Source: Authors' analysis of CPS ORG data.

New York and Texas, the only states with enough data to compare) suggests that discrimination, which is particularly targeted at young, less-educated black males, may play a role.

## Poverty and low-wage shares

The incidence of poverty and low-wage work varies widely throughout the country. **Figure 6D** shows the changes in poverty-level wage shares (the share of workers earning a wage that, even with full-time, full-year work, cannot lift a family of four above the poverty line) by Census division. The largest decline in the 1995-2000 period occurred in the West North Central division of the Midwest, a drop driven by double-digit declines in Iowa, Missouri, South Dakota, and Kansas (**Table 6.10**). Nearby divisions also saw relatively large declines in poverty-level wage shares during the late 1990s, with smaller declines in the Northeast and Pacific areas.

Remarkably, with the exception of Hawaii, no state saw an increase in poverty-wage jobs (at least by this measure) between 1995 and 2000. As Table 6.10 shows, this trend stands in marked contrast to the experience of the 1980s

**TABLE 6.10** Share of workers earning poverty-level wages, by state, 1979-2001

| | 1979 | 1989 | 1995 | 2000 | 2001 | Percentage-point change | | | |
|---|---|---|---|---|---|---|---|---|---|
| | | | | | | 1979-89 | 1989-2000 | 1995-2000 | 2000-01 |
| **NORTHEAST** | 24.9% | 23.0% | 25.3% | 22.1% | 20.3% | -1.9 | 2.3 | -3.2 | -1.7 |
| *New England* | 26.3 | 18.8 | 23.0 | 19.1 | 17.5 | -7.5 | 4.2 | -3.9 | -1.6 |
| Maine | 38.6 | 29.1 | 35.6 | 25.7 | 22.7 | -9.5 | 6.6 | -9.9 | -3.0 |
| New Hampshire | 28.4 | 19.7 | 25.0 | 19.5 | 17.8 | -8.7 | 5.3 | -5.5 | -1.7 |
| Vermont | 36.5 | 26.2 | 28.5 | 24.1 | 21.9 | -10.4 | 2.3 | -4.3 | -2.2 |
| Massachusetts | 25.2 | 17.0 | 21.3 | 18.6 | 17.0 | -8.2 | 4.3 | -2.7 | -1.6 |
| Rhode Island | 28.4 | 24.9 | 25.4 | 19.5 | 20.4 | -3.5 | 0.6 | -5.9 | 0.9 |
| Connecticut | 22.2 | 15.4 | 19.2 | 16.5 | 14.6 | -6.8 | 3.8 | -2.7 | -1.8 |
| *Middle Atlantic* | 24.4% | 24.5% | 26.1% | 23.2% | 21.4% | 0.1 | 1.6 | -3.0 | -1.8 |
| New York | 24.5 | 23.9 | 26.0 | 24.4 | 22.2 | -0.6 | 2.2 | -1.6 | -2.2 |
| New Jersey | 24.2 | 18.8 | 21.4 | 18.2 | 18.2 | -5.4 | 2.6 | -3.2 | 0.0 |
| Pennsylvania | 24.4 | 29.3 | 29.5 | 24.8 | 22.4 | 5.0 | 0.2 | -4.7 | -2.4 |
| **MIDWEST** | 24.6% | 31.5% | 31.0% | 22.4% | 22.0% | 6.8 | -0.5 | -8.6 | -0.4 |
| *East North Central* | 22.9 | 30.2 | 29.9 | 22.3 | 21.9 | 7.3 | -0.3 | -7.6 | -0.4 |
| Ohio | 23.9 | 30.2 | 31.7 | 23.2 | 23.5 | 6.2 | 1.5 | -8.4 | 0.3 |
| Indiana | 27.6 | 36.7 | 32.7 | 21.8 | 20.9 | 9.1 | -4.0 | -10.9 | -0.9 |
| Illinois | 20.5 | 27.3 | 28.2 | 23.8 | 21.3 | 6.8 | 0.9 | -4.4 | -2.5 |
| Michigan | 20.5 | 28.7 | 27.4 | 21.0 | 21.8 | 8.2 | -1.3 | -6.4 | 0.8 |
| Wisconsin | 25.0 | 32.2 | 31.0 | 19.6 | 20.9 | 7.2 | -1.2 | -11.4 | 1.3 |
| *West North Central* | 29.1% | 34.5% | 33.5% | 22.6% | 22.3% | 5.3 | -1.0 | -10.9 | -0.3 |
| Minnesota | 25.4 | 27.8 | 24.8 | 16.0 | 16.7 | 2.4 | -3.0 | -8.7 | 0.6 |
| Iowa | 28.6 | 37.7 | 35.7 | 23.2 | 22.4 | 9.0 | -1.9 | -12.5 | -0.8 |
| Missouri | 29.9 | 34.6 | 34.7 | 21.5 | 22.5 | 4.7 | 0.0 | -13.1 | 1.0 |
| North Dakota | 35.1 | 42.4 | 44.3 | 35.5 | 35.9 | 7.3 | 1.8 | -8.8 | 0.4 |
| South Dakota | 41.2 | 46.2 | 40.4 | 27.3 | 29.0 | 5.1 | -5.8 | -13.2 | 1.7 |
| Nebraska | 32.0 | 41.0 | 37.5 | 29.2 | 27.2 | 9.0 | -3.5 | -8.2 | -2.0 |
| Kansas | 28.4 | 34.1 | 38.7 | 28.1 | 24.5 | 5.6 | 4.7 | -10.6 | -3.6 |

*(cont.)*

**TABLE 6.10** (cont.) Share of workers earning poverty-level wages, by state, 1979-2001

| | 1979 | 1989 | 1995 | 2000 | 2001 | Percentage-point change | | | |
|---|---|---|---|---|---|---|---|---|---|
| | | | | | | 1979-89 | 1989-2000 | 1995-2000 | 2000-01 |
| **SOUTH** | 33.5% | 36.0% | 35.9% | 28.3% | 27.1% | 2.5 | -0.2 | -7.5 | -1.3 |
| *South Atlantic* | 33.3 | 32.7 | 32.4 | 25.8 | 24.2 | -0.7 | -0.2 | -6.6 | -1.6 |
| Delaware | 24.1 | 25.9 | 27.2 | 22.0 | 21.2 | 1.8 | 1.3 | -5.1 | -0.8 |
| Maryland | 22.4 | 21.7 | 22.7 | 18.2 | 17.2 | -0.7 | 1.1 | -4.5 | -1.0 |
| District of Columbia | 17.1 | 21.6 | 23.5 | 16.8 | 16.5 | 4.5 | 1.9 | -6.7 | -0.3 |
| Virginia | 31.3 | 27.6 | 28.9 | 21.9 | 20.4 | -3.8 | 1.3 | -7.0 | -1.5 |
| West Virginia | 29.3 | 42.3 | 37.7 | 34.6 | 32.1 | 12.9 | -4.5 | -3.1 | -2.4 |
| North Carolina | 37.8 | 36.4 | 33.6 | 25.4 | 25.6 | -1.4 | -2.8 | -8.1 | 0.2 |
| South Carolina | 40.5 | 37.9 | 36.1 | 25.4 | 24.9 | -2.6 | -1.9 | -10.7 | -0.6 |
| Georgia | 34.2 | 33.9 | 33.4 | 26.0 | 22.7 | -0.3 | -0.5 | -7.4 | -3.3 |
| Florida | 37.7 | 35.7 | 36.3 | 30.4 | 28.3 | -2.0 | 0.6 | -5.9 | -2.1 |
| *East South Central* | 36.0% | 41.4% | 39.5% | 30.3% | 28.5% | 5.4 | -1.9 | -9.2 | -1.8 |
| Kentucky | 30.6 | 37.8 | 37.0 | 28.2 | 25.8 | 7.1 | -0.7 | -8.8 | -2.4 |
| Tennessee | 36.0 | 40.6 | 36.0 | 27.3 | 27.5 | 4.6 | -4.6 | -8.6 | 0.1 |
| Alabama | 35.7 | 41.6 | 42.9 | 32.0 | 28.7 | 6.0 | 1.3 | -10.9 | -3.4 |
| Mississippi | 45.5 | 48.3 | 45.1 | 36.9 | 34.8 | 2.8 | -3.2 | -8.2 | -2.1 |
| *West South Central* | 32.3% | 38.9% | 39.6% | 31.6% | 31.2% | 6.6 | 0.7 | -8.0 | -0.5 |
| Arkansas | 42.8 | 46.5 | 42.7 | 35.9 | 33.8 | 3.7 | -3.8 | -6.8 | -2.0 |
| Louisiana | 32.4 | 41.0 | 40.8 | 34.1 | 34.7 | 8.7 | -0.2 | -6.7 | 0.6 |
| Oklahoma | 28.6 | 37.6 | 39.4 | 32.0 | 29.6 | 9.0 | 1.9 | -7.4 | -2.4 |
| Texas | 31.5 | 37.6 | 39.0 | 30.6 | 30.4 | 6.1 | 1.4 | -8.4 | -0.2 |

(cont.)

**TABLE 6.10** (cont.) Share of workers earning poverty-level wages, by state, 1979-2001

| | | | | | | Percentage-point change | | | |
|---|---|---|---|---|---|---|---|---|---|
| | 1979 | 1989 | 1995 | 2000 | 2001 | 1979-89 | 1989-2000 | 1995-2000 | 2000-01 |
| **WEST** | | | | | | | | | |
| *Mountain* | 22.8% | 27.6% | 30.7% | 25.2% | 24.1% | 4.9 | 3.1 | -5.5 | -1.1 |
| Montana | 27.8 | 34.1 | 33.5 | 26.0 | 24.8 | 6.3 | -0.6 | -7.5 | -1.2 |
| Idaho | 30.2 | 39.8 | 40.0 | 38.7 | 36.9 | 9.6 | 0.2 | -1.3 | -1.8 |
| Wyoming | 30.1 | 40.2 | 38.1 | 31.2 | 28.6 | 10.1 | -2.0 | -7.0 | -2.6 |
| Colorado | 23.1 | 35.4 | 38.7 | 32.9 | 28.9 | 12.3 | 3.3 | -5.7 | -4.0 |
| New Mexico | 25.1 | 31.8 | 27.4 | 18.8 | 18.2 | 6.7 | -4.4 | -8.6 | -0.6 |
| Arizona | 31.7 | 42.3 | 38.6 | 32.9 | 33.9 | 10.5 | -3.7 | -5.7 | 1.0 |
| Utah | 29.9 | 32.8 | 35.5 | 26.3 | 24.7 | 2.9 | 2.7 | -9.2 | -1.6 |
| Nevada | 27.5 | 33.4 | 34.8 | 26.1 | 25.8 | 5.8 | 1.4 | -8.7 | -0.3 |
| | 25.0 | 27.8 | 29.5 | 25.5 | 22.8 | 2.8 | 1.7 | -4.0 | -2.7 |
| *Pacific* | 21.2% | 25.4% | 29.6% | 24.9% | 23.8% | 4.3 | 4.2 | -4.7 | -1.1 |
| Washington | 18.7 | 25.8 | 27.5 | 19.5 | 21.7 | 7.1 | 1.6 | -8.0 | 2.2 |
| Oregon | 20.6 | 27.9 | 28.2 | 24.4 | 22.2 | 7.3 | 0.4 | -3.8 | -2.2 |
| California | 21.5 | 25.4 | 30.6 | 26.0 | 24.4 | 3.8 | 5.2 | -4.6 | -1.6 |
| Alaska | 7.4 | 13.5 | 17.2 | 16.9 | 15.3 | 6.1 | 3.8 | -0.3 | -1.6 |
| Hawaii | 27.6 | 24.8 | 25.4 | 27.8 | 25.1 | -2.7 | 0.6 | 2.4 | -2.7 |
| U.S. averages | 27.1% | 30.5% | 31.5% | 25.0% | 23.9% | 3.3 | 1.1 | -6.5 | -1.1 |

Source: Authors' analysis of CPS data.

388

**FIGURE 6E** Poverty rates by region, 1971-2000

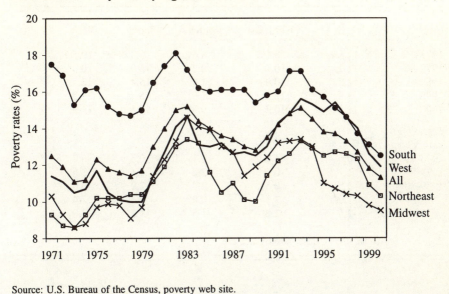

Source: U.S. Bureau of the Census, poverty web site.

and the early 1990s. Low-wage employment rose in 32 states between 1989 and 1995, and in the 1980s, outside of New England, the share of low-wage jobs grew in most states.

**Figure 6E** and **Table 6.11** show regional poverty rates. Variation across regions in the growth rates of low-income jobs led to a significant re-ranking of regional poverty levels. As with income, the poverty data reveal that the only significant poverty reduction over the full decade of the 1990s occurred in the Midwest and South. Higher incomes in the Northeast gave that region the lowest poverty rates in the nation from the mid-1980s to the early 1990s. But by the mid-1990s, as gains for low-income workers weakened in the Northeast compared to other regions, the lowest rates could be found in the Midwest.

Historically, the South has had by far the highest poverty rates in the nation. But with the strong growth in incomes for low-income workers there in the 1990s, Southern poverty rates became statistically indistinguishable for those in the West. In fact, Western poverty rates fell only slightly from 1989 to 2000, by 0.6 percentage points.

The data in **Table 6.12** (which pools two years of data to generate more stable results) reveal the states most responsible for the shifting regional patterns. Poverty rose in the 1990s in some of the more populated New England

**TABLE 6.11** Poverty rates for persons by region, 1973-2000

| Year | U.S. | Northeast | Midwest | South | West |
|------|------|-----------|---------|-------|------|
| 1973 | 11.1% | 8.6% | 8.6% | 15.3% | 10.5% |
| 1979 | 11.7 | 10.4 | 9.7 | 15.0 | 10.0 |
| 1989 | 12.8 | 10.0 | 11.9 | 15.4 | 12.5 |
| 1995 | 13.8 | 12.5 | 11.0 | 15.7 | 14.9 |
| 2000 | 11.3 | 10.3 | 9.5 | 12.5 | 11.9 |
| *Percentage-point changes* | | | | | |
| 1973-79 | 0.6 | 1.8 | 1.1 | -0.3 | -0.5 |
| 1979-89 | 1.1 | -0.4 | 2.2 | 0.4 | 2.5 |
| 1989-2000 | -1.5 | 0.3 | -2.4 | -2.9 | -0.6 |
| 1989-95 | 1.0 | 2.5 | -0.9 | 0.3 | 2.4 |
| 1995-2000 | -2.5 | -2.2 | -1.5 | -3.2 | -3.0 |

Source: U.S. Bureau of the Census, poverty web site.

and Mid-Atlantic states including Massachusetts, New York, New Jersey, and Connecticut, which saw the largest increase in the nation (3.4 percentage points). At the same time, Western and Southern states saw larger-than-average declines. Once again, states in the deep South (the East and West South Central regions) saw particularly large declines (in Mississippi, poverty fell 10.1 percentage points, more than seven times the national average).

Recent experimental work by the Census Bureau on measuring poverty enables an approximation of the impact of interstate price differences on state poverty rates. (This work, while preliminary, is important because it can help to quantify the extent to which poverty is overestimated in states with lower prices and visa versa. Like the index used at the beginning of this chapter, this index is based on housing costs, which both vary considerably by state and are known to correlate with other goods whose prices vary across place.) Differences in state prices lead in some cases to significant differences from the official rate. States with higher-than-average housing costs, such as New York, Massachusetts, New Jersey, and California, all have higher adjusted poverty rates (**Table 6.13**). For example, accounting for price differences in California increases measured poverty there by 3.4 percentage points, adding 1.1 million to the poverty rolls. The opposite trend is evident in lower-cost states. In Alabama, Mississippi, Arkansas, Louisiana, and Oklahoma, for example, price-adjusted poverty rates are between 2.8 and 3.5 points below the official rates, removing over 500,000 from the poverty rolls.

**TABLE 6.12** Poverty by state, 1988-2000, two-year averages

| | 1988-89 | 1999-2000 | Percentage-point change 1988/89 to 1999/2000 |
|---|---|---|---|
| **NORTHEAST** | | | |
| *New England* | | | |
| Maine | 11.8% | 9.5% | -2.3 |
| New Hampshire | 7.2 | 6.4 | -0.7 |
| Vermont | 8.0 | 10.5 | 2.5 |
| Massachusetts | 8.6 | 10.9 | 2.2 |
| Rhode Island | 8.3 | 9.5 | 1.2 |
| Connecticut | 3.4 | 6.8 | 3.4 |
| | | | |
| *Middle Atlantic* | | | |
| New York | 13.0% | 13.7% | 0.7 |
| New Jersey | 7.2 | 7.9 | 0.7 |
| Pennsylvania | 10.3 | 9.1 | -1.2 |
| | | | |
| **MIDWEST** | | | |
| *East North Central* | | | |
| Ohio | 11.5% | 11.0% | -0.6 |
| Indiana | 11.9 | 7.7 | -4.2 |
| Illinois | 12.7 | 10.7 | -2.0 |
| Michigan | 12.6 | 9.8 | -2.8 |
| Wisconsin | 8.1 | 9.1 | 1.0 |
| | | | |
| *West North Central* | | | |
| Minnesota | 11.4% | 6.6% | -4.8 |
| Iowa | 9.8 | 7.3 | -2.5 |
| Missouri | 12.7 | 9.8 | -2.9 |
| North Dakota | 12.0 | 11.6 | -0.4 |
| South Dakota | 13.8 | 8.7 | -5.1 |
| Nebraska | 11.5 | 9.9 | -1.6 |
| Kansas | 9.5 | 10.9 | 1.4 |
| | | | |
| **SOUTH** | | | |
| *South Atlantic* | | | |
| District of Columbia | 16.6% | 14.9% | -1.7 |
| Maryland | 9.4 | 7.4 | -2.0 |
| Delaware | 9.4 | 9.8 | 0.4 |
| Virginia | 10.9 | 7.8 | -3.1 |
| West Virginia | 16.9 | 14.8 | -2.0 |
| North Carolina | 12.4 | 12.8 | 0.4 |
| South Carolina | 16.2 | 11.2 | -5.1 |
| Georgia | 14.5 | 12.0 | -2.5 |
| Florida | 13.0 | 11.5 | -1.5 |
| | | | |
| *East South Central* | | | |
| Kentucky | 16.9% | 12.0% | -4.9 |
| Tennessee | 18.2 | 13.3 | -4.9 |
| Alabama | 19.1 | 14.8 | -4.3 |
| Mississippi | 24.6 | 14.5 | -10.1 |

*(cont.)*

391

**TABLE 6.12** *(cont.)* Poverty by state, 1988-2000, two-year averages

| | 1988-89 | 1999-2000 | Percentage-point change 1988/89 to 1999/2000 |
|---|---|---|---|
| **SOUTH** *(cont.)* | | | |
| *West South Central* | | | |
| Arkansas | 19.9% | 16.3% | -3.7 |
| Louisiana | 23.0 | 18.3 | -4.8 |
| Oklahoma | 16.0 | 14.0 | -2.0 |
| Texas | 17.5 | 14.8 | -2.7 |
| **WEST** | | | |
| *Mountain* | | | |
| Montana | 15.1% | 15.6% | 0.5 |
| Idaho | 12.5 | 13.4 | 0.9 |
| Wyoming | 10.2 | 11.4 | 1.2 |
| Colorado | 12.3 | 8.2 | -4.1 |
| New Mexico | 21.2 | 18.7 | -2.5 |
| Arizona | 14.1 | 12.0 | -2.1 |
| Utah | 9.0 | 7.7 | -1.3 |
| Nevada | 9.7 | 9.9 | 0.2 |
| *Pacific* | | | |
| Washington | 9.2% | 9.8% | 0.6 |
| Oregon | 10.8 | 11.9 | 1.1 |
| California | 13.0 | 13.3 | 0.3 |
| Alaska | 10.7 | 7.9 | -2.9 |
| Hawaii | 11.2 | 10.4 | -0.7 |
| **Total U.S.** | 12.9% | 11.5% | -1.4 |

Source: U.S. Bureau of the Census, poverty web site.

## Conclusion

The national trends in income, wages, employment, and poverty vary extensively by state and region. For example, the 1990s boom took hold more in the Midwest and South than in the rest of the country (though significant gains occurred there as well), leading to faster income growth and bigger poverty declines there. Part of these gains stem from the fact that the early 1990s recession, mild by historical standards, was felt much more acutely in the Northeast and, to a lesser extent, the West.

While labor markets tightened everywhere in the 1990s (particularly in the second half), they tightened the most in the Midwest and the South, helping to fuel some of the impressive trends in income and poverty there. Yet middle- and low-wage workers in almost every state experienced gains in wages and

**TABLE 6.13** Poverty rates, 1999, official and adjusted for state price differences

| | Official rate | Price-adjusted rate | Difference (adjusted minus official) | Effect of adjustment (persons) |
|---|---|---|---|---|
| **NORTHEAST** | | | | |
| Maine | 10.6% | 9.9% | -0.7% | -8,574 |
| New Hampshire | 7.7 | 8.9 | 1.2 | 14,579 |
| Vermont | 9.7 | 9.7 | 0.0 | 0 |
| Massachusetts | 11.7 | 14.0 | 2.3 | 141,276 |
| Rhode Island | 9.9 | 10.4 | 0.5 | 5,319 |
| Connecticut | 7.1 | 8.2 | 1.1 | 37,881 |
| New York | 14.1 | 16.9 | 2.8 | 520,550 |
| New Jersey | 7.8 | 10.5 | 2.7 | 216,964 |
| Pennsylvania | 9.4 | 8.5 | -0.9 | -103,775 |
| **MIDWEST** | | | | |
| Ohio | 12.0% | 10.8% | -1.1% | -126,664 |
| Indiana | 6.7 | 5.7 | -1.0 | -58,571 |
| Illinois | 9.9 | 10.0 | 0.1 | 9,917 |
| Michigan | 9.7 | 9.4 | -0.3 | -30,855 |
| Wisconsin | 8.6 | 8.2 | -0.3 | -18,142 |
| Minnesota | 7.2 | 7.1 | -0.1 | -7,117 |
| Iowa | 7.5 | 5.7 | -1.8 | -50,463 |
| Missouri | 11.6 | 8.5 | -3.1 | -167,230 |
| North Dakota | 13.0 | 10.2 | -2.8 | -16,988 |
| South Dakota | 7.7 | 5.4 | -2.3 | -16,077 |
| Nebraska | 10.9 | 9.2 | -1.7 | -28,594 |
| Kansas | 12.2 | 9.5 | -2.6 | -69,047 |
| **SOUTH** | | | | |
| Delaware | 10.4% | 11.6% | 1.2% | 9,484 |
| Maryland | 7.3 | 7.5 | 0.3 | 13,081 |
| District of Columbia | 14.9 | 17.8 | 2.9 | 15,228 |
| Virginia | 7.9 | 7.9 | 0.0 | 0 |
| West Virginia | 15.7 | 12.7 | -3.0 | -52,878 |
| North Carolina | 13.5 | 11.8 | -1.7 | -130,443 |
| South Carolina | 11.7 | 9.1 | -2.6 | -97,903 |
| Georgia | 12.9 | 11.9 | -1.0 | -81,387 |
| Florida | 12.4 | 12.4 | 0.0 | 4,192 |
| Kentucky | 12.1 | 10.4 | -1.7 | -64,229 |
| Tennessee | 11.9 | 9.7 | -2.2 | -121,562 |
| Alabama | 15.1 | 12.3 | -2.9 | -127,270 |
| Mississippi | 16.1 | 13.1 | -3.0 | -81,949 |
| Arkansas | 14.7 | 11.3 | -3.5 | -88,261 |
| Louisiana | 19.2 | 16.3 | -2.9 | -123,633 |
| Oklahoma | 12.7 | 9.9 | -2.8 | -90,167 |
| Texas | 15.0 | 14.2 | -0.8 | -162,249 |

*(cont.)*

**TABLE 6.13** *(cont.)* Poverty rates, 1999, official and adjusted
for state price differences

| | Official rate | Price-adjusted rate | Difference (adjusted minus official) | Effect of adjustment (persons) |
|---|---|---|---|---|
| **WEST** | | | | |
| Montana | 15.6% | 13.8% | -1.9% | -16,640 |
| Idaho | 13.9 | 11.3 | -2.7 | -33,465 |
| Wyoming | 11.6 | 9.4 | -2.2 | -10,654 |
| Colorado | 8.3 | 9.0 | 0.6 | 26,687 |
| New Mexico | 20.7 | 17.8 | -2.9 | -51,617 |
| Arizona | 12.0 | 11.7 | -0.2 | -11,174 |
| Utah | 5.7 | 5.4 | -0.3 | -5,362 |
| Nevada | 11.3 | 12.5 | 1.3 | 24,569 |
| Washington | 9.5 | 10.4 | 1.0 | 54,231 |
| Oregon | 12.6 | 11.7 | -0.8 | -28,382 |
| California | 13.8 | 17.2 | 3.4 | 1,136,855 |
| Alaska | 7.6 | 8.9 | 1.4 | 8,634 |
| Hawaii | 10.9 | 15.8 | 4.9 | 59,485 |
| **Total U.S.** | 11.8% | 11.9% | 0.1% | 217,608 |

Source: U.S. Bureau of the Census, poverty web site (official rate; see table note for price-adjusted rate).

income and declines in poverty in the latter 1990s, as unemployment fell throughout the country and low-wage labor markets tightened.

Still, as impressive as these gains were, they did not continue long enough to reverse the trend of rising inequality in most states. The gap between those at the top and the bottom of the income scale was significantly higher at the end of the 1990s than in the late 1970s in almost every state.

It is too early (as of this writing) to fully assess the geographical impact of the recession of 2001 and the subsequent slow-growth recovery. It appears, however, that the increase in unemployment and the loss of jobs were greater in the South and Midwest, the areas that most enjoyed the boom of the latter 1990s. In this regard, the pattern of the last recession, in which the East and West Coasts felt the brunt of the downturn, may be shifting.

# International comparisons:
# more inequality, less mobility out of poverty

In the preceding chapters, we judged current economic outcomes using historical data for the United States as a benchmark. In this chapter, we compare the economic performance of the United States to that of 19 other rich, industrialized countries that, like the U.S., belong to the Paris-based Organization for Economic Cooperation and Development (OECD). This analysis, which allows a comparison of the U.S. economy with similar economies facing the same global conditions with respect to trade, investment, technology, the environment, and other factors that shape economic opportunities, provides an independent yardstick for gauging the strengths and weaknesses of the U.S. economy.

Because of high productivity growth and low unemployment in the United States during the 1990s relative to Europe, many have argued that Europe should emulate key features of the U.S. economy, including weaker unions, lower minimum wages, less-generous social benefit systems, and lower taxes. The international comparisons in this analysis can shed light on this ongoing debate about the advisability of exporting this "U.S. model."

Overall the 1990s were a period of slow growth in national income and productivity in most of the OECD economies. In the second half of the 1990s in the United States, however, both national income and productivity growth increased more so than in other OECD countries. But the recent good news for the United States must be considered along with other economic trends. First, income and productivity growth over the last decade have generally trailed the rates obtained in the 1970s and 1980s and are far below those of the "Golden Age" from the end of World War II through the first oil shock in 1973. Second, the above-average income and productivity growth in the United States in the late 1990s came after decades of consistent rankings in the middle or near the bottom among OECD countries since the 1970s. Third, the U.S. economy has consistently produced the highest levels of economic inequality. Moreover, inequality in the United States (along with the United Kingdom) has shown a strong tendency to rise, even as inequality was relatively stable or declining in most of the rest of the OECD. Fourth, poverty is deeper and more difficult to escape in the United States than in the rest of the OECD. The lack of redistributive social policies only exacerbates the high levels of poverty and income inequality in the United States.

## Incomes and productivity: U.S. lead narrows

For the entire post-World War II period, the average standard of living in the United States has been among the highest in the world. **Tables 7.1** and **7.2** summarize data from 1960 through 2000 on the most common measure of average living standards, per capita income, or the total value of goods and services produced in the domestic economy per member of the population. Table 7.1 converts the value of foreign goods and services, measured in foreign currency, to U.S. dollars using the market-determined exchange rate in each year. By this measure, in 1960, the United States had one of the highest standards of living among the 20 countries examined here, trailing only Switzerland, Sweden, and Denmark, and it was well ahead of most of the European economies that were still rebuilding themselves after World War II. Per capita income grew rapidly in the United States in the 1960s and 1970s, but it rose even more rapidly in almost all the other economies. As a result, almost all of the OECD economies narrowed the income gap with the United States. In the 1980s and again in the 1990s, growth in per capita income decelerated sharply throughout most of the OECD, but it held at earlier levels in the United States. In the last decade, growth in U.S. per capita income was above average compared to the other rich countries. By 2000, per capita income in the United States was $36,868 per year, above the non-U.S., population-weighted average of $25,088 but below that of Switzerland ($52,817), Japan ($50,572), Denmark ($43,621), Norway ($42,885), Austria ($37,202), and Germany ($36,943).

Using market exchange rates to convert the cost of goods and services in other countries to a U.S. value can, in some cases, give a misleading picture of relative standards of living. The relatively high level of income in Japan, for example, reflects fluctuations in market exchange rates in response to short-term international capital flows and other macroeconomic factors. However, this does not necessarily reflect long-term differences in national prices and the

**TABLE 7.1** Per capita income, using market exchange rates,*
1960-2000 (2000 dollars)

| Country | Per capita income | | | | Annual growth rates (%) | | |
|---|---|---|---|---|---|---|---|
| | 1960 | 1979 | 1989 | 2000 | 1960-79 | 1979-89 | 1989-2000 |
| United States | $16,283 | $24,011 | $29,272 | $36,868 | 2.1% | 2.0% | 2.1% |
| Japan | 6,780 | 31,338 | 43,006 | 50,572 | 8.4 | 3.2 | 1.5 |
| Germany** | 11,868 | 26,199 | 31,584 | 36,943 | 4.3 | 1.9 | 1.4 |
| France | 11,790 | 23,355 | 28,051 | 32,825 | 3.7 | 1.8 | 1.4 |
| Italy | 9,285 | 15,967 | 20,140 | 23,583 | 2.9 | 2.3 | 1.4 |
| United Kingdom | 11,763 | 16,403 | 20,332 | 24,653 | 1.8 | 2.2 | 1.8 |
| Canada | 12,871 | 18,812 | 22,165 | 25,901 | 2.0 | 1.7 | 1.4 |
| | | | | | | | |
| Australia | $11,679 | $17,785 | $21,362 | $26,637 | 2.2% | 1.8% | 2.0% |
| Austria | 10,498 | 24,764 | 30,072 | 37,202 | 4.6 | 2.0 | 2.0 |
| Belgium | 10,480 | 23,073 | 28,473 | 35,037 | 4.2 | 2.1 | 1.9 |
| Denmark | 16,321 | 31,073 | 35,658 | 43,621 | 3.4 | 1.4 | 1.8 |
| Finland | 13,155 | 22,218 | 30,430 | 36,137 | 2.8 | 3.2 | 1.6 |
| Ireland | 6,191 | 12,060 | 15,696 | 31,816 | 3.6 | 2.7 | 6.6 |
| Netherlands | 12,003 | 23,777 | 27,310 | 35,270 | 3.7 | 1.4 | 2.4 |
| New Zealand | 11,534 | 15,474 | 17,725 | 20,269 | 1.6 | 1.4 | 1.2 |
| Norway | 13,982 | 25,514 | 32,066 | 42,885 | 3.2 | 2.3 | 2.7 |
| Portugal | 2,625 | 8,001 | 10,779 | 14,604 | 6.0 | 3.0 | 2.8 |
| Spain | 5,456 | 12,221 | 15,345 | 19,924 | 4.3 | 2.3 | 2.4 |
| Sweden | 17,365 | 25,204 | 30,695 | 35,402 | 2.0 | 2.0 | 1.3 |
| Switzerland | 25,518 | 42,821 | 50,538 | 52,817 | 2.8 | 1.7 | 0.4 |
| | | | | | | | |
| Average excluding U.S. | $10,104 | $20,880 | $26,062 | $25,088 | 4.5% | 2.3% | 1.7% |

* At the price levels and exchange rates of 1995 except 1960, which is calculated at 1990 exchange rates.
** Eastern and western Germany.

Source: Authors' analysis of OECD (1999a, 2001a) data. For detailed information on table sources, see Table Notes.

relative standard of living in Japan and the United States. In reality, prices vary considerably across countries. For example, land and housing prices are generally much lower in the wide-open United States, Canada, and Australia than they are in more crowded European countries and in Japan. To correct for this shortcoming, Table 7.2 uses an alternative set of criteria for converting the value of each country's goods and services into U.S. dollars. These alternative exchange rates, known as purchasing-power parities (PPPs), are not based on international currency market exchange rates but, rather, on the price of buying an equivalent "basket" of goods and services in all countries. While calculation of PPPs presents many practical and conceptual problems, PPPs are probably a

**TABLE 7.2** Per capita income, using purchasing-power-parity exchange rates, 1970-2000 (2000 dollars)

| Country | Per capita income | | | | Annual growth rates (%) | | |
|---|---|---|---|---|---|---|---|
| | 1970 | 1979 | 1989 | 2000 | 1970-79 | 1979-89 | 1989-2000 |
| United States | $19,084 | $24,011 | $29,272 | $36,868 | 2.6% | 2.0% | 2.1% |
| Japan | 12,875 | 17,345 | 23,803 | 27,990 | 3.4 | 3.2 | 1.5 |
| Germany* | 14,457 | 18,628 | 22,456 | 26,267 | 2.9 | 1.9 | 1.4 |
| France | 13,979 | 18,046 | 21,674 | 25,363 | 2.9 | 1.8 | 1.4 |
| Italy | 12,739 | 16,776 | 21,161 | 24,779 | 3.1 | 2.3 | 1.4 |
| United Kingdom | 12,984 | 15,896 | 19,702 | 23,889 | 2.3 | 2.2 | 1.8 |
| Canada | 16,544 | 21,832 | 25,723 | 30,060 | 3.1 | 1.7 | 1.4 |
| Australia | $16,019 | $18,640 | $22,391 | $27,918 | 1.7% | 1.9% | 2.0% |
| Austria | 13,176 | 18,179 | 22,075 | 27,310 | 3.6 | 2.0 | 2.0 |
| Belgium | 14,171 | 18,513 | 22,845 | 28,111 | 3.0 | 2.1 | 1.9 |
| Denmark | 17,647 | 20,683 | 23,735 | 29,036 | 1.8 | 1.4 | 1.8 |
| Finland | 12,609 | 16,551 | 22,670 | 26,922 | 3.1 | 3.2 | 1.6 |
| Ireland | 8,782 | 11,851 | 15,425 | 31,267 | 3.4 | 2.7 | 6.6 |
| Netherlands | 15,390 | 18,831 | 21,629 | 27,934 | 2.3 | 1.4 | 2.4 |
| New Zealand | 15,164 | 16,072 | 18,410 | 21,052 | 0.6 | 1.4 | 1.2 |
| Norway | 12,269 | 17,676 | 22,217 | 29,711 | 4.1 | 2.3 | 2.7 |
| Portugal | 7,404 | 10,153 | 13,679 | 18,533 | 3.6 | 3.0 | 2.8 |
| Spain | 9,789 | 12,483 | 15,673 | 20,351 | 2.7 | 2.3 | 2.4 |
| Sweden | 15,965 | 18,481 | 22,508 | 25,959 | 1.6 | 2.0 | 1.3 |
| Switzerland | 23,581 | 25,180 | 29,718 | 31,058 | 0.7 | 1.7 | 0.4 |
| Average excluding U.S. | $13,528 | $17,388 | $21,800 | $25,713 | 2.9% | 2.3% | 1.7% |

* Eastern and western Germany.

Source: Authors' analysis of OECD (2001a) data.

reasonable indicator of the relative price of consumption and arguably a better measure of relative living standards than market exchange rates.

When per capita income is measured on a PPP basis, as compared to market exchange rates, the United States appears to provide an average standard of living that is well above that of the rest of the OECD economies. This ranking suggests that consumption goods (housing, food, transportation, clothing, and others) are generally cheaper in the United States than in the other economies, and these lower prices help to raise the standard of living in the U.S. relative to other "more expensive" economies. However, it is worth noting that PPPs do not account for the cost of non-market social goods, such as education, health care, or child care, which are much lower in many European countries relative to the United States.

**TABLE 7.3** Income and productivity levels in the OECD, 1950-99

| Country | GDP per hour worked, United States = 100 | | | | | |
|---|---|---|---|---|---|---|
| | 1950 | 1960 | 1973 | 1989 | 1995 | 2001 |
| United States | 100 | 100 | 100 | 100 | 100 | 100 |
| Japan | 21 | 27 | 54 | 68 | 73 | 72 |
| Germany | - | - | - | 89 | 93 | 90 |
| West Germany* | 50 | 64 | 87 | 108 | 110 | 109 |
| France | 52 | 60 | 82 | 110 | 113 | 106 |
| Italy | 42 | 40 | 67 | 83 | 91 | 84 |
| United Kingdom | 69 | 58 | 66 | 78 | 83 | 82 |
| Canada | 90 | 86 | 87 | 84 | 85 | 79 |
| Australia | 81 | 75 | 73 | 77 | 81 | 83 |
| Austria | 35 | 44 | 66 | 83 | 87 | 91 |
| Belgium | 54 | 52 | 74 | 101 | 107 | 107 |
| Denmark | 66 | 63 | 84 | 90 | 96 | 91 |
| Finland | 39 | 41 | 64 | 75 | 82 | 85 |
| Ireland | 32 | 29 | 42 | 68 | 78 | 94 |
| Netherlands | 77 | 81 | 103 | 108 | 108 | 101 |
| New Zealand | - | - | - | 68 | 66 | 61 |
| Norway | 56 | 60 | 73 | 100 | 114 | 112 |
| Portugal | 20 | 24 | 42 | 47 | 51 | 51 |
| Spain | 26 | 27 | 54 | 77 | 82 | 73 |
| Sweden | 62 | 61 | 80 | 81 | 84 | 82 |
| Switzerland | 83 | 79 | 88 | 86 | 85 | 82 |
| Average excluding U.S. | 47 | 49 | 70 | 83 | 87 | 84 |

* Levèl for West Germany 2001 imputed based on Germany/West Germany productivity ratio in 1997.

Source: Authors' analysis of University of Groningen (2002) data.

The pattern of growth in per capita income is similar regardless of whether PPPs or market exchange rates are used. Across many of the economies examined in Table 7.2, growth in per capita income decelerated sharply in the 1980s and again in the 1990s. The U.S. growth rate remained fairly constant from the 1980s to the 1990s, and at 2.1% it was higher than the non-U.S. average from 1989 to 2000.

The main determinant of an economy's current and future standard of living is the level and rate of growth of productivity—the value of goods and services that the economy can produce on average in an hour of work. Productivity is, therefore, the starting point in any explanation of differences in the level and growth of income across countries. **Table 7.3** presents other nations' productivity levels as a percentage of the U.S. level. In 1960, the U.S. economy was far more productive than the others, producing almost four times more goods and services in an hour than Japan and almost twice as much in an hour as France or the United Kingdom. The nearest competitors were other economies that had escaped massive dislocation during World War II: Canada (86% of the U.S. level), Australia (75%), the Netherlands (81%), and Switzerland (79%). Between 1960 and 2001, all of the economies narrowed the productivity gap with the United States, and five of the economies—Norway (112%), western Germany (109%), Belgium (107%), France (106%), and the Netherlands (101%)—exceeded U.S. productivity levels in 2001.

The pattern of productivity growth, summarized in **Table 7.4** and **Figure 7A,** closely resembles that of per capita income. The first key feature of productivity growth is the dramatic slowdown after the mid-1970s: growth was much more rapid in the 1960s than it was in the 1980s and 1990s. A second key feature is the comparably poor performance of the United States before growth rebounded between 1995 and 2000. (The estimate for the United States for the period 1979-2000, taken from the OECD, is slightly lower than the official U.S. government rate because the estimates in Table 7.4 do not take into account recent changes in the method that the Bureau of Labor Statistics uses to calculate labor productivity. The figures here, however, are comparable across countries.)

Economists excused the poor U.S. performance prior to 1995 by arguing that it is much harder to lead than to follow, to innovate than to imitate. In this view, productivity growth was faster outside the United States because other economies were engaged in a constant game of catch-up in which they rapidly assimilated technological improvements pioneered in the United States. While this view may have made sense as late as the 1960s or 1970s, the data on productivity levels in Table 7.3 suggest that, by the end of the 1990s, several European economies had matched or exceeded U.S. productivity levels, and many others had narrowed the gap considerably—even with the relatively rapid productivity gains of the late 1990s in the United States. The ability of Belgium, France, western Germany, the Netherlands, and Norway to reach U.S. productivity levels in the 1990s suggests that these countries' comprehensive welfare and collective-bargaining systems have not stymied income growth or improvements in economic efficiency relative to the more free-market-oriented United States.

Some economists have also dismissed the evidence of high European productivity levels as simply a by-product of high European unemployment rates. These economists argue that low-productivity workers find jobs in the low-unemployment United States, thus pulling down the average productivity level

**TABLE 7.4** Labor productivity* growth per year in the OECD, 1960-2000

| Country | 1960**-73 | 1973-79 | 1979-89 | 1989-95 | 1995-2000 |
|---|---|---|---|---|---|
| United States | 2.6% | 0.3% | 1.2% | 1.2% | 2.2% |
| Japan | 8.4 | 2.8 | 2.8 | 1.2 | 1.2 |
| Germany*** | 4.5 | 3.1 | 1.8 | 2.3 | 1.1 |
| France | 5.3 | 2.9 | 2.5 | 1.7 | 1.4 |
| Italy | 6.4 | 2.8 | 1.9 | 2.1 | 1.1 |
| United Kingdom | 4.0 | 1.6 | 1.8 | 1.8 | 1.2 |
| Canada | 2.5 | 1.1 | 1.0 | 1.3 | 1.7 |
| Australia | 3.0% | 2.5% | 1.1% | 1.7% | 2.5% |
| Austria | 5.9 | 3.1 | 2.4 | 2.4 | 2.4 |
| Belgium | 5.2 | 2.7 | 2.6 | 1.6 | 2.0 |
| Denmark | 3.9 | 2.3 | 1.4 | 2.5 | 2.3 |
| Finland | 5.0 | 3.2 | 3.4 | 3.5 | 3.0 |
| Ireland | 4.8 | 4.3 | 4.1 | 3.3 | 4.2 |
| Netherlands | 4.8 | 2.6 | 1.5 | 1.5 | 1.0 |
| New Zealand | 2.1 | -1.1 | 1.9 | 0.0 | 1.5 |
| Norway | 3.8 | 2.7 | 1.0 | 2.8 | 1.3 |
| Portugal | 7.5 | 0.5 | 2.1 | 1.5 | 2.1 |
| Spain | 5.9 | 2.8 | 2.9 | 2.7 | 0.9 |
| Sweden | 3.7 | 1.4 | 1.8 | 3.0 | 2.0 |
| Switzerland | 3.3 | 0.8 | 0.2 | 0.1 | 1.2 |

\* Business sector
\*\* Or earliest available year: 1961 for Australia and Ireland; 1962 for Japan and the U.K.; 1964 for Spain; 1965 for France and Sweden; 1966 for Canada and Norway; 1967 for New Zealand; 1969 for the Netherlands; and 1970 for Belgium.
\*\*\* First two columns refer to western Germany.

Source: OECD (1998, 2001d).

of the U.S. economy. Indeed, in Europe, which generally has higher unemployment rates than the United States, low-productivity workers are less likely to work and therefore don't pull down average productivity levels. This argument, however, has several flaws. First, two of the European economies in Table 7.3 with productivity levels above the U.S. level—the Netherlands and Norway—actually have *lower* unemployment rates than the United States. (See Table 7.20, which shows that, in 2000, the unemployment rate was 2.4% in the Netherlands and 3.6% in Norway.) The very low unemployment rates in these countries did not prevent them from achieving high productivity levels. Second, in the U.S. in the late 1990s, even as the unemployment rates of low-skill workers fell to historic lows, productivity rose. Third, in the Euro-

**FIGURE 7A** Productivity growth rates, 1960-2000

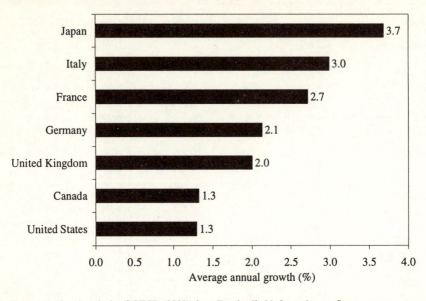

Average annual growth (%)

Source: Authors' analysis of OECD (2002) data. For detailed information on figure sources, see Figure Notes.

pean economies that do have high unemployment rates, an important share of unemployed workers has mid- to high levels of formal education. (See, for example, Table 7.21 and the related discussion.) This suggests that unemployed workers finding work would not have a significant negative impact on average productivity. Even if currently unemployed workers had zero productivity, however, their inclusion in the workforce would not substantially alter the picture in Table 7.3. Take the case of France, with a 2001 productivity level 106% that of the United States. In that same year, the unemployment rate in France was 8.6%, about 3.8 percentage points above the 4.8% rate in the United States. If we lowered the French unemployment rate to be equal to that of the United States, and assigned these formerly unemployed workers to jobs with zero productivity, the relative productivity level in France would fall from 106% of the U.S. level to roughly 102%, and thus France would still maintain its productivity advantage. It is also worth noting that France achieved its relatively high productivity even as it lowered the standard work week.

**TABLE 7.5**  Real compensation growth per year in the OECD,* 1979-2000

| Country | 1979-89 | 1989-95 | 1995-2000 |
|---------|---------|---------|-----------|
| United States | -0.3% | 0.1% | 1.6% |
| Japan | 1.4 | 0.4 | -0.3 |
| Germany** | 1.2 | 1.5 | -0.3 |
| France | 1.0 | 0.3 | 0.7 |
| Italy | 1.4 | 0.7 | -0.1 |
| United Kingdom | 2.1 | 1.4 | 1.7 |
| Canada | 0.5 | 0.3 | 1.9 |
| Australia | 0.4% | 0.3% | 1.7% |
| Austria | 1.9 | 1.5 | 0.6 |
| Belgium | 0.7 | 2.2 | 1.0 |
| Denmark | 0.2 | 1.5 | 1.3 |
| Finland | 3.0 | 1.4 | 1.6 |
| Ireland | 1.7 | 1.3 | 1.9 |
| Netherlands | 0.0 | 0.5 | 0.7 |
| New Zealand | 0.1 | -1.6 | 1.0 |
| Norway | 0.4 | 1.2 | 2.2 |
| Portugal | 0.0 | 3.3 | 2.3 |
| Spain | 0.1 | 3.2 | 0.8 |
| Sweden | 1.3 | 0.5 | 3.7 |
| Switzerland | 1.6 | 0.4 | 1.0 |
| Average excluding U.S. | 1.1% | 1.0% | 0.6% |

\*  Compensation per employee in business sector.
\*\* Growth rate for western Germany 1979-91; eastern and western Germany 1992-2000.

Source: Authors' analysis of OECD (2001d) data.

## Workers' wages and compensation: unequal growth

Wages and other work-related benefits are by far the most important source of income for the vast majority of people in the United States and the other countries analyzed here. The level, growth, and distribution of wages and benefits are therefore important starting points for international economic comparisons. **Table 7.5** shows the inflation-adjusted annual growth rate of total compensation (wages plus fringe benefits) in the private sector for 20 countries in the 1980s and 1990s. In both decades, growth rates varied considerably across countries. In the 1980s, the United States put in the worst performance, with average compensation falling about 0.3% per year; compensation grew most in Finland (3.0% per year) and the United Kingdom (2.1% per year). In the early 1990s,

**TABLE 7.6** Relative hourly compensation of manufacturing production workers, 1979-2000, using market exchange rates (U.S. = 100)

| Country | Hourly compensation | | |
| --- | --- | --- | --- |
| | 1979 | 1989 | 2000 |
| United States | 100 | 100 | 100 |
| Japan | 60 | 88 | 111 |
| Germany* | 124 | 123 | 121 |
| France | 85 | 88 | 83 |
| Italy | 78 | 101 | 74 |
| United Kingdom | 63 | 74 | 80 |
| Canada | 87 | 103 | 81 |
| Australia | 83 | 87 | 71 |
| Austria | 88 | 99 | 98 |
| Belgium | 131 | 108 | 106 |
| Denmark | 116 | 101 | 103 |
| Finland | 83 | 118 | 98 |
| Ireland | 54 | 67 | 63 |
| Netherlands | 126 | 105 | 96 |
| New Zealand | 52 | 54 | 41 |
| Norway | 114 | 128 | 111 |
| Portugal | 19 | 21 | 24 |
| Spain | 59 | 63 | 55 |
| Sweden | 125 | 122 | 101 |
| Switzerland | 117 | 117 | 107 |
| Average excluding U.S. | 82 | 93 | 95 |

* Western Germany.

Source: Authors' analysis of BLS (2001a) data.

average compensation growth in the United States became barely positive, with an annual growth rate of 0.1%. In most economies in the early 1990s, total compensation grew more rapidly than in the United States. By the late 1990s, however, tight labor markets in the United States allowed wages to rise alongside productivity. Between 1995 and 2000, average compensation grew by 1.6% per year in the United States, far higher than the average of 0.6% but lower than in seven other countries. In three countries, Germany, Japan, and Italy, compensation growth was slightly negative over these five years.

The most extensive international data on compensation covers the narrower group of workers in manufacturing, which includes between 12% and 20% of employed workers on average across the OECD. **Tables 7.6** and **7.7** compare

**TABLE 7.7** Relative hourly compensation of manufacturing production workers, 1979-2000, using purchasing-power parities (U.S. = 100)

| Country | 1979 | 1989 | 2000 |
|---|---|---|---|
| United States | 100 | 100 | 100 |
| Japan | 49 | 61 | 79 |
| Germany* | 86 | 111 | 127 |
| France | 66 | 86 | 89 |
| Italy | 87 | 100 | 97 |
| United Kingdom | 62 | 76 | 81 |
| Canada | 81 | 92 | 102 |
| | | | |
| Australia | 71 | 79 | 94 |
| Austria | 72 | 92 | 108 |
| Belgium | 91 | 107 | 126 |
| Denmark | 71 | 78 | 96 |
| Finland | 59 | 80 | 102 |
| Ireland | 50 | 65 | 72 |
| Netherlands | 87 | 101 | 114 |
| New Zealand | 55 | 56 | 61 |
| Norway | 70 | 90 | 91 |
| Portugal | 31 | 34 | 40 |
| Spain | 58 | 70 | 75 |
| Sweden | 78 | 88 | 96 |
| Switzerland | 75 | 87 | 96 |
| | | | |
| Average excluding U.S. | 68 | 83 | 93 |

* Western Germany.

Source: Authors' analysis of BLS (2001b) and OECD (2001f) data.

hourly compensation in manufacturing in 19 OECD countries to the corresponding levels in the United States in 1979, 1989, and 2000. In terms of market exchange rates (which reflect the relative value of American goods, services (including labor), and assets in international markets and thus capture the relative costs to an employer of hiring U.S. labor), seven of the 19 countries had total compensation levels higher than those in the United States. Between 1979 and 2000, manufacturing wages converged closer to the U.S. average: whereas in 1979, eight countries had manufacturing wages within 80% to 120% of the United States, by 2000 12 countries fell within this range.

In terms of purchasing power parities (which better reflect the ability of the compensation levels in each country to guarantee a specific standard of living),

U.S. workers fare better in the international comparison. In 1979, manufacturing compensation on a PPP basis was higher in the United States than in every other country examined here. Only one country, Belgium (91), was within 10% of the U.S. level. All of the economies, however, closed the compensation gap between 1979 and 2000. By 2000, manufacturing compensation in the United States (100) had fallen behind that of western Germany (127), Belgium (126), the Netherlands (114), Austria (108), Canada (102), and Finland (102).

Table 7.8 looks more carefully at growth in manufacturing compensation, on a purchasing power basis, over the periods 1979-89, 1989-95, and 1995-2000. The table examines growth in compensation over the three periods separately for all manufacturing employees and for production workers only. During the 1980s, the United States, at just 0.2% per year, had one of the lowest rates of growth in hourly compensation in manufacturing. Among U.S production workers, real hourly compensation actually fell 0.8% per year, compared to an average growth in the other advanced economies of 1.5% per year. Production worker compensation also fell in France (–1.6% per year), New Zealand (–0.7% per year), and Denmark (–0.1% per year), but rose in every other country examined here. In the early 1990s, the United States turned in one of the worst performances in compensation rates for all manufacturing employees, with a 0.2% per year growth rate (only Sweden was lower at –0.4%). At the same time, compensation for production workers in the United States fell by 0.4% per year. Outside the United States, hourly compensation for production workers grew, on average, 1.3% per year. The late 1990s saw improved wage growth for manufacturing workers overall in the United States, with compensation higher than average at 1.3%. Compensation growth was still slow, however, for production workers at 0.5%, far below the average of 1.1%.

The positive growth rates in hourly compensation for all manufacturing employees (which include both production, or non-supervisory, workers and non-production, or supervisory, workers) and the negative-to-slow growth rates for production workers in the United States through the 1990s are another manifestation of growing inequality in the United States. The majority of manufacturing workers are production workers. The wide disparity between growth in production workers' wages and wages overall means that manufacturing supervisors and other, non-production workers' wages are far outpacing production workers' wages. In short, the hourly compensation data suggest that manufacturing compensation is growing more slowly and more unequally in the United States than it is in other OECD countries.

Table 7.9 uses data on full-time employees in all sectors of the economy to take a broader look at international earnings inequality. The table measures inequality by the ratio of the earnings of high-wage workers (those making

**TABLE 7.8** Annual growth in real hourly compensation in manufacturing in the OECD, 1979-2000

| | 1979-89 | | 1989-95 | | 1995-2000 | |
|---|---|---|---|---|---|---|
| Country | All employees | Production workers | All employees | Production workers | All employees | Production workers |
| United States | 0.2% | -0.8% | 0.2% | -0.4% | 1.3% | 0.5% |
| Japan | 1.8 | 1.4 | 2.7 | 2.7 | 1.0 | 0.9 |
| Germany* | -1.9 | 2.0 | 2.6 | 1.0 | 1.2 | 1.0 |
| France | -1.9 | -1.6 | 1.5 | 0.9 | 1.6 | 1.9 |
| Italy | 4.7 | 5.6 | 1.5 | -0.4 | 0.6 | 0.6 |
| United Kingdom | 4.1 | 2.7 | 2.3 | 0.6 | 1.0 | 1.2 |
| Canada | 6.8 | 6.6 | 1.6 | 1.3 | 0.3 | 0.0 |
| Australia | — | 0.5% | — | 1.4% | — | 1.4% |
| Austria | — | 2.0 | — | 2.0 | — | 1.3 |
| Belgium | 1.3% | 1.0 | 1.5% | 2.3 | -0.1% | 0.9 |
| Denmark** | 0.0 | -0.1 | — | 1.9 | — | 1.9 |
| Finland | — | 3.1 | — | 3.6 | — | 2.0 |
| Ireland | — | 1.9 | — | 1.4 | — | 1.9 |
| Netherlands | 0.9 | 0.5 | 1.1 | 0.6 | 1.1 | 1.1 |
| New Zealand | — | -0.7 | — | -0.4 | — | 1.9 |
| Norway | 1.0 | 1.0 | 1.2 | 0.7 | 2.8 | 2.4 |
| Portugal | — | 1.5 | — | 1.2 | — | 2.4 |
| Spain | — | 1.4 | — | 1.7 | — | 1.4 |
| Sweden | 1.1 | 0.9 | -0.4 | -0.2 | 2.6 | 3.1 |
| Switzerland | — | 1.3 | — | 0.4 | — | 0.0 |
| Average excluding U.S. | 1.8% | 1.5% | 2.1% | 1.3% | 1.0% | 1.1% |

\* Western Germany.
\*\* Number for all workers in second period is 1989-93.

Source: Authors' analysis of BLS (2000a, 2001c) and OECD (2001d) data.

more than 90% of the total workforce) to the earnings of low-wage workers (those making more than only 10% of the workforce). By this measure, the United States has the highest earnings inequality of all OECD countries (4.8 for men and 4.1 for women). Inequality grew in most economies among both men and women. Among men, the ratio of earnings of the 90th-percentile worker to those of the 10th-percentile worker (the "90-10 ratio") increased by an annual rate of 1.4% in the United States. This was surpassed only by Ireland (2.3% per year), New Zealand (2.1% per year), and Italy (1.6% per year), and well above most of the rest of the economies in the table. Among women, inequality in the 90-10 ratio increased most in the United States (1.6% per year), with the United Kingdom next closest (1.2% per year).

**TABLE 7.9** Earnings inequality in OECD countries, 1979-2000

| Country | Years | 90th percentile relative to bottom 10th percentile, latest year available | | Average annual percentage changes | | |
| --- | --- | --- | --- | --- | --- | --- |
| | | | | 90th percentile relative to bottom 10th percentile | | Real wages, lowest decile |
| | | Men | Women | Men | Women | |
| United States | 1979-2000 | 4.8 | 4.1 | 1.4% | 1.6% | -0.8% |
| Japan | 1979-99 | 2.7 | 2.3 | 0.3 | 0.1 | 0.9 |
| Germany | 1984-98 | 2.9 | 2.8 | 0.9 | -0.2 | 1.5 |
| France | 1979-98 | 3.3 | 2.7 | -0.2 | -0.1 | 1.3 |
| Italy | 1986-96 | 2.4 | 2.1 | 1.6 | -0.6 | 1.2 |
| United Kingdom | 1979-2000 | 3.4 | 3.1 | 1.3 | 1.2 | 2.0 |
| Canada | 1981-94 | 3.8 | 4.0 | 0.6 | 0.5 | -0.1 |
| Australia | 1979-2000 | 3.2 | 2.7 | 0.7% | 0.5% | -0.2% |
| Austria | 1996 | 2.9 | 2.3 | - | - | - |
| Belgium | 1985-95 | 2.2 | 2.2 | - | - | 0.6 |
| Denmark | 1980-90 | - | - | - | - | 0.5 |
| Finland | 1980-99 | 2.5 | 2.0 | 0.1 | -0.1 | 2.2 |
| Ireland | 1987-97 | 4.1 | 3.3 | 2.3 | -1.1 | 2.1 |
| Netherlands | 1979-99 | 2.8 | 2.6 | 0.9 | 0.2 | 0.0 |
| New Zealand | 1984-97 | 3.5 | 2.8 | 2.1 | 1.1 | -1.3 |
| Norway | 1980-91 | - | - | - | - | 1.6 |
| Sweden | 1980-98 | 2.3 | 1.9 | 0.6 | 0.7 | 0.5 |
| Switzerland | 1991-98 | 2.4 | 2.4 | 0.8 | -0.8 | - |

Source: Glyn (2001) and authors' analysis of unpublished OECD data.

408

One of the most troubling aspects of U.S. inequality is that it has been driven in part by absolute, not just relative, declines in the standard of living for those at the bottom. The last column of Table 7.9 shows that, despite relatively high levels of average productivity in the U.S. economy, workers at the 10th percentile of the earnings distribution experienced a decline in inflation-adjusted wages of 0.8% per year, more than any other country excluding New Zealand (−1.3% per year). Wages for workers in the lowest decile increased in most other countries, with highs of 2.2% per year in Finland, and 2.1% per year in Ireland, countries with relatively low unemployment.

Inequality in wages by gender has slowed among many countries, but progress stalled during the 1990s. **Figure 7B** shows the gap in pay among men and women across countries. The United States performs relatively well: by 1999, the gender pay gap was 23.5, meaning that, on average, among full-time workers, women earned 23.5 cents less than men for every dollar earned, down from 31.8 in 1985. This relatively small gender gap occurs alongside high employment rates for women in the United States (see Table 7.16). The gender pay gap was smaller in 1999 in six countries, three of which—the Netherlands, New Zealand, and Sweden—had female employment rates similar to those of the United States. Japan stands out as the country with the largest gender wage gap, at 39.2 in 1999. Over the 1990s, progress on closing the gender gap appears to have slowed in most every country, with the gap actually widening in France.

## Household income: unequal growth

The per capita income figures in Tables 7.1 and 7.2 were economy-wide, annual averages. Since individuals make many important decisions about consumption as part of a family or broader household, and since, as we have seen, averages can be deceiving because they mask inequality, international data on the distribution of household income can yield illustrative comparisons.

Since labor compensation accounts for the largest share of household income, the basic pattern of inequality that has occurred with earnings repeats itself here: income inequality is high (and rising) in the United States compared to the rest of the OECD. U.S. inequality yields poverty rates that are higher, and living standards that are lower at the bottom, than those in comparable economies. Moreover, income mobility appears to be *lower* in the United States than in other OECD countries.

Household income in this analysis is measured after taxes and transfers, including refundable tax credits. **Table 7.10** uses two measures of household income inequality for 19 OECD countries. The first measure is the "90-10 ra-

**FIGURE 7B** Gender wage gaps in the OECD,* 1985, 1995, and 1999

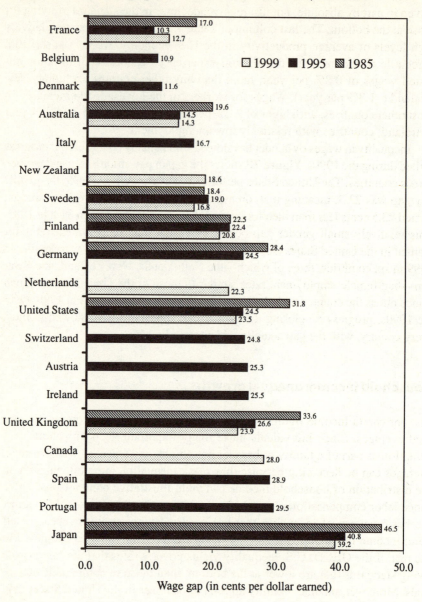

Wage gap (in cents per dollar earned)

* Female median full-time earnings as a percent of male median full-time earnings.

Source: OECD (2001g).

**TABLE 7.10** Household income inequality* in the OECD

| Country | Year | Gini coefficient | Percent of median income | | Ratio of 90th to 10th percentile |
| | | | Low income (10th percentile) | High income (90th percentile) | |
|---|---|---|---|---|---|
| United States | 1997 | 0.372 | 38% | 214% | 5.64 |
| Japan | 1992 | - | 46 | 192 | 4.17 |
| Germany | 1994 | 0.261 | 54 | 174 | 3.18 |
| France | 1994 | 0.288 | 54 | 179 | 3.32 |
| Italy | 1995 | 0.342 | 43 | 201 | 4.68 |
| U.K. | 1995 | 0.344 | 46 | 209 | 4.52 |
| Canada | 1998 | 0.305 | 47 | 184 | 3.90 |
| | | | | | |
| Australia | 1994 | 0.311 | - | - | - |
| Austria | 1995 | 0.277 | 56% | 162% | 2.89 |
| Belgium | 1997 | 0.255 | 59 | 162 | 2.76 |
| Denmark | 1997 | 0.257 | 54 | 155 | 2.84 |
| Finland | 1995 | 0.226 | 59 | 159 | 2.68 |
| Ireland | 1987 | 0.328 | 50 | 209 | 4.20 |
| Netherlands | 1994 | 0.253 | 56 | 171 | 3.08 |
| Norway | 1995 | 0.238 | 56 | 157 | 2.82 |
| Spain | 1990 | 0.303 | 50 | 197 | 3.96 |
| Sweden | 1995 | 0.221 | 60 | 156 | 2.59 |
| Switzerland | 1992 | 0.307 | 54 | 185 | 3.39 |
| | | | | | |
| Average excluding U.S. | | 0.297 | 50% | 187% | 3.83 |

* Income inequality measured as disposable household income per equivalent adult. Income ratios are purchasing-power-parity adjusted from OECD 1996 benchmark.

Source: Authors' analysis of Luxembourg Income Study (2001a) and Smeeding and Rainwater (2001).

tio," which measures how many times more income a household in the 90th percentile has compared to a household in the 10th percentile. The second inequality measure is the Gini coefficient, a special inequality scale ranging from zero (perfect equality of income across households) to one (all income is concentrated at the very top of the income distribution). The United States has by far the most unequal household income by both measures (see also **Figure 7C**). In the United States, a household in the 10th percentile of the income distribution receives just 38% of the income of the median household (the household exactly in the middle of the income distribution). In the other 18 economies, the 10th percentile household receives between 43% (Italy) and 60% (Sweden)

**FIGURE 7C**  Relative income comparisons in the OECD*

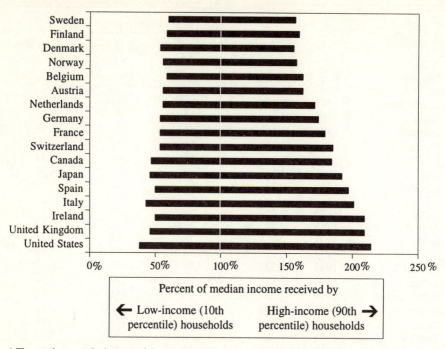

Percent of median income received by

← Low-income (10th          High-income (90th →
percentile) households      percentile) households

\* The gap between the income of the top 10% and the bottom 10% of households in each nation.

Source: Smeeding and Rainwater (2001).

of the median national income. At the other extreme, the 90th percentile household in the United States makes 214% of the median national income, a level matched only by Ireland (209%) and the United Kingdom (209%), with most other countries falling between 155% (Denmark) and 201% (Italy).

The income inequality shown in Table 7.10 compares the position of low- and high-income households relative to the median income in each country. **Table 7.11** and **Figure 7D** compare the incomes of low- and high-income households to the median in the United States, an analysis that illustrates differences in the absolute standard of living of low- and high-income households across countries. Despite the high median income in the United States, inequality in the United States is so severe that low-income households in the United States are actually worse off than in every other country in the table except the United Kingdom and Australia (both of which have lower median household income than the United States and relatively high levels of income inequality). Not surprisingly, high-

**TABLE 7.11** Household income inequality, relative to U.S. median income*

| Country | Year | Low income (10th percentile) | High income (90th percentile) | Ratio of 90th to 10th percentile |
|---|---|---|---|---|
| | | Percent of U.S. median income | | |
| United States | 1997 | 39% | 209% | 5.36 |
| Germany | 1994 | 44 | 139 | 3.16 |
| France | 1994 | 43 | 148 | 3.44 |
| Italy | — | — | — | — |
| United Kingdom | 1995 | 33 | 142 | 4.30 |
| Canada | 1994 | 41 | 167 | 4.07 |
| Australia | 1994 | 34% | 148% | 4.35 |
| Belgium | 1996 | 47 | 153 | 3.26 |
| Denmark | 1995 | 43 | 123 | 2.86 |
| Finland | 1995 | 41 | 110 | 2.68 |
| Netherlands | 1994 | 43 | 133 | 3.09 |
| Norway | 1995 | 50 | 143 | 2.86 |
| Sweden | 1995 | 40 | 103 | 2.58 |
| Switzerland | 1992 | 55 | 185 | 3.36 |
| Average excluding U.S. | | 43% | 146% | 3.49 |

* Percent of overall U.S. 1997 median equivalent income in purchasing-power-parity terms. Income inequality measured as disposable household income per equivalent adult.

Source: Smeeding and Rainwater (2001).

income households are much better off in the United States (209% of the median income) than in the rest of the countries. The next closest is Switzerland, where high-income household are only 185% of the U.S. median.

**Table 7.12** shows that, since the end of the 1970s, income inequality has been growing in most rich, industrialized countries. In absolute terms (see the last column), the annual increase in income inequality has been strongest in the United States and the United Kingdom. Income inequality has grown more slowly in Italy, Australia, Belgium, Germany, Finland, and Norway and has fallen over the same period in Canada, Spain, the Netherlands, France, and Switzerland. Given the lower initial levels of inequality in most countries other than the United States, the absolute increases in other economies represent much larger relative increases in inequality than they would in the United States. Even so, in percentage terms, the United States saw the largest increase in inequality, second only to the United Kingdom and close to Austria.

**FIGURE 7D** Real standards of living in the OECD*

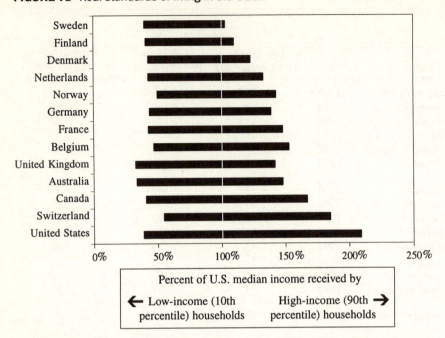

Percent of U.S. median income received by

← Low-income (10th        High-income (90th →
percentile) households     percentile) households

* These relative income measures compare the gap between the top 10% and the bottom 10% of
  household income in each country to the 1997 U.S. median income in purchasing-power-parity terms.

Source: Smeeding and Rainwater (2001).

## Poverty: deeper and more enduring in the United States

Higher inequality in the United States is associated with higher levels of poverty, relative to the rest of the OECD, even though per capita income is high in
the United States. Poverty is also more enduring in the U.S. **Table 7.13** summarizes international data from the 1990s on poverty rates. Following the standard
methodology for international comparisons, the table defines the poverty rate
as the share of individuals receiving 50% or less of the median income in each
country. In the United States, this threshold amounts to an income that is much
higher than the official poverty rate (see Chapter 5). (The data in Table 7.11,
which compare the income of the 10th-percentile household in each country to
the U.S. median income, provide an indication of the absolute standard of living of low-income families across the OECD countries.) Like the official U.S.
definition, the poverty rates in Table 7.13 take into account cash transfers and

**TABLE 7.12** Change in income inequality in the OECD after 1979

| Country | Time period | Change in Gini coefficient* | |
| --- | --- | --- | --- |
| | | Percent change | Percentage point change |
| United States | 1979-97 | 23.6% | 0.071 |
| Germany | 1981-94 | 7.0 | 0.017 |
| France | 1979-94 | -1.7 | -0.005 |
| Italy | 1986-95 | 11.8 | 0.036 |
| United Kingdom | 1979-95 | 27.4 | 0.074 |
| Canada | 1981-98 | 7.4 | -0.032 |
| Australia | 1981-94 | 10.7% | 0.030 |
| Austria | 1987-95 | 22.0 | 0.050 |
| Belgium | 1985-97 | 12.3 | 0.028 |
| Denmark | 1987-97 | 1.2 | 0.003 |
| Finland | 1987-95 | 8.1 | 0.017 |
| Netherlands | 1983-94 | -2.7 | -0.007 |
| Norway | 1979-95 | 6.7 | 0.015 |
| Spain | 1980-90 | -4.7 | -0.015 |
| Sweden | 1981-95 | 11.2 | 0.024 |
| Switzerland | 1982-92 | -0.6 | -0.002 |

* Measured as the relative change in the Gini coefficient, where growth reflects more inequality.

Source: Authors' analysis of Luxembourg Income Study (2001a) data.

are adjusted for family size, but, unlike the U.S. definition, they also account for taxes and tax credits. The United States, with 16.9% of its total population living in poverty, has the highest level of overall poverty among the 19 countries examined here. The next closest is Australia (14.3%), Italy (14.2%), the United Kingdom (13.4%), and Canada (12.8%). The United States is also unique in that it has the highest rate of child poverty (22.3%).

Table 7.13 provides three other definitions of poverty: poor at least once over the three years examined, poor in all three years, and "permanent income poverty," which shows the proportion of people whose average income over the entire three-year period was less than the average of the poverty level over the three years. Individuals who move in and out of poverty but whose incomes do not rise much above the poverty level, will be captured by the permanent income poverty measure. The United States is not much higher than other countries in terms of the proportion of people who were poor at least once over the three-year period. However, the United States has a much higher rate of people

**TABLE 7.13** Poverty rates in OECD countries

| | Poverty line (50% of median)* | | | Poverty over 1993 to 1995 | | |
|---|---|---|---|---|---|---|
| Country | Total population | Children | Elderly | Poor at least once | Always poor | Permanent-income poverty** |
| United States | 16.9% | 22.3% | 20.7% | 23.5% | 9.5% | 14.5% |
| Germany | 7.5 | 10.6 | 7.0 | 19.2 | 4.3 | 8.1 |
| France | 8.0 | 7.9 | 9.8 | 16.6 | 3.0 | 6.6 |
| Italy | 14.2 | 20.2 | 12.2 | 21.5 | 5.6 | 10.4 |
| United Kingdom | 13.4 | 19.8 | 13.7 | 19.5 | 2.4 | 6.5 |
| Canada | 12.8 | 16.3 | 7.8 | 18.1 | 5.1 | 8.9 |
| Australia | 14.3% | 15.8% | 29.4% | - | - | - |
| Austria | 10.6 | 15.0 | 10.3 | - | - | - |
| Belgium | 8.2 | 7.6 | 12.4 | 16.0% | 2.8% | 5.2% |
| Denmark | 9.2 | 8.7 | 6.6 | 9.1 | 0.8 | 1.8 |
| Finland | 5.1 | 4.2 | 5.2 | 25.1 | 6.5 | 12.2 |
| Ireland | 11.1 | 13.8 | 14.4 | 15.3 | 1.3 | 5.3 |
| Netherlands | 8.1 | 8.1 | 6.4 | 12.9 | 1.6 | 4.5 |
| New Zealand | - | - | - | - | - | - |
| Norway | 6.9 | 3.9 | 14.5 | - | - | - |
| Portugal | - | - | - | 24.2 | 7.8 | 13.4 |
| Spain | 10.1 | 12.2 | 11.3 | 21.3 | 3.7 | 8.7 |
| Sweden | 6.6 | 2.6 | 2.7 | - | - | - |
| Switzerland | 9.3 | 10.0 | 8.4 | - | - | - |

\*   Data are from 1987 for Ireland; 1990 for Spain; 1992 for Switzerland; 1994 for Australia, Luxembourg, the Netherlands, France, and Germany; 1995 for Austria, Finland, Norway, Sweden, the U.K., and Italy; 1997 for Belgium, Denmark, and the U.S.; and 1998 for Canada.

\*\*  Permanent income poverty is the proportion of individuals with total income over the three-year period less than the sum of the poverty level over that period.

Source:  OECD (2001e) and Luxembourg Income Study (2000b) data.

who were poor over all three years; at 9.5%, it is over twice as high as most other countries, which range from 0.8% (Denmark) to 7.8% (Portugal). The United States also has the highest rate of permanent income poverty (14.5%). The relatively large numbers of people in poverty for long durations in the United States indicates that mobility out of poverty is more limited here than in other OECD countries.

This observation is confirmed in **Table 7.14**, which shows the probability of entering and exiting poverty and associated changes in family structure and

**TABLE 7.14** Frequency of family and job-related events associated with poverty transitions in the OECD

| | Entries into poverty | Percentage of total entries into poverty associated with: | | | | | | | |
| | Yearly rate of entry | Change in family structure: | | | Fewer workers | Largest decrease in income from: | | | |
| Country | | Total | New child | Separation/divorce | | Earnings | Transfers | Capital and miscellaneous income | Other |
|---|---|---|---|---|---|---|---|---|---|
| United States | 4.5% | 37.5% | 8.8% | 10.9% | 15.0% | 27.6% | 2.8% | 16.5% | 4.2% |
| Germany | 5.1 | 21.6 | (3.0) | 7.2 | 15.9 | 27.2 | 26.0 | 7.5 | 1.9 |
| France | 4.6 | 27.1 | (2.0) | 9.1 | 10.8 | 21.7 | 35.3 | 3.1 | 4.5 |
| Italy | 5.3 | 25.6 | 2.8 | 6.3 | 21.4 | 24.1 | 23.2 | 3.9 | 1.7 |
| United Kingdom | 6.0 | 25.9 | 4.1 | 8.5 | 16.2 | 17.5 | 32.9 | 5.8 | - |
| Canada | 4.8 | 41.2 | 4.3 | 12.6 | 9.3 | 26.1 | 16.9 | 6.4 | - |
| Belgium | 4.7% | 16.5% | - | (4.3)% | 20.7% | 18.1% | 33.3% | 7.2% | - |
| Denmark | 3.1 | 39.0 | - | (7.3) | 15.2 | 13.5 | 26.0 | - | 0.6% |
| Ireland | 5.0 | 32.3 | 5.5% | 5.3 | 21.0 | 17.3 | 22.7 | 5.0 | 1.7 |
| Netherlands | 4.2 | 28.6 | (3.4) | 5.0 | .. | 37.5 | 32.3 | - | 4.4 |
| Portugal | 5.4 | 22.3 | 3.5 | 4.5 | 35.5 | 17.6 | 17.9 | 3.8 | 0.2 |
| Spain | 5.9 | 25.3 | 3.2 | 6.7 | 30.1 | 22.4 | 17.5 | 4.1 | 0.7 |

Note: Values in parentheses are based on less than 30 observations.

(cont.)

417

**TABLE 7.14** (cont.) Frequency of family and job-related events associated with poverty transitions in the OECD

**Exits from poverty**

Percentage of total exits from poverty associated with:

| Country | Yearly rate of exit | Change in family structure: Total | Fewer family members | Marriage | More workers | Largest increase in income from: Earnings | Transfers | Capital and miscellaneous income | Capital and other combined | Other |
|---|---|---|---|---|---|---|---|---|---|---|
| United States | 29.5% | 27.0% | 12.2% | 8.1% | 19.1% | 36.8% | 3.8% | 13.2% | | 0.1% |
| Germany | 41.1 | 11.3 | 4.0 | (2.2) | 21.9 | 26.7 | 32.0 | | 8.1% | - |
| France | 46.9 | 14.4 | 4.6 | 4.4 | 26.9 | 22.4 | 29.6 | 3.1 | | 3.7 |
| Italy | 40.6 | 20.2 | 2.7 | 5.3 | 23.6 | 29.2 | 24.2 | | 2.8 | - |
| United Kingdom | 58.8 | 12.1 | (2.8) | 3.8 | 20.5 | 23.7 | 40.3 | | 3.4 | - |
| Canada | 36.4 | 31.5 | 5.2 | 8.9 | 15.6 | 25.5 | 19.6 | 7.5 | | 0.4 |
| Belgium | 48.2% | 9.9% | - | (3.1)% | 18.2% | 17.0% | 41.5% | | 13.4% | - |
| Denmark | 60.4 | 20.7 | (5.4)% | (7.3) | 16.3 | 29.2 | 27.6 | - | | - |
| Ireland | 54.6 | 20.8 | 5.6 | (4.2) | 27.7 | 20.6 | 29.9 | - | | - |
| Netherlands | 55.7 | 23.6 | 11.7 | 5.4 | .. | 33.2 | 41.2 | - | | - |
| Portugal | 37.0 | 17.6 | 2.9 | (1.6) | 41.2 | 16.0 | 22.0 | 2.4% | | 1.0% |
| Spain | 49.6 | 16.7 | 3.9 | 4.2 | 34.5 | 30.6 | 15.2 | | 2.9 | - |

Note: Values in parentheses are based on less than 30 observations.

Source: OECD (2001e).

income sources. The United States is not much different than other countries in its yearly entry rate into poverty (4.5%), but its exit rate (29.5%) is exceptionally low. Exit rates among other countries range from 36.4% (Canada) to 60.4% (Denmark). Government transfers play a relatively minor role in entry into and exit from poverty in the U.S. but are important in all other countries. In the United Kingdom, the Netherlands, and Belgium, transfers account for two out of five poverty exits, compared to about two out of 70 in the U.S. Conversely, loss of earned income is more likely to push a family into poverty in the United States while increases in earned income are more likely to pull them out of poverty, relative to all other countries. Also, family structure and presence of children play a larger role in entry into and exit from poverty in the United States than in other countries. In the U.S., for example, entries into poverty are more likely to be associated with a new child (8.8%) or separation or divorce (10.2%) than in other countries, and exits from poverty are more likely to be associated with having fewer family members (12.2%) or with marriage (8.1%).

The association of family structure and presence of children with poverty in the United States is related to the relative dearth of "family-friendly" policies in the United States. Though the United States has a high proportion of children in formal child care (**Table 7.15**), a relatively low proportion of children receive publicly supported child care. As the final two columns show, in the United States the government covers a relatively small share of child care costs. Thus, paying for child care presents a financial burden for American families unlike that experienced in many other countries. It is also more difficult for parents to afford time off to care for their children in the United States, since it is one of just three countries (the others are New Zealand and Australia) that does not mandate paid maternity or paternity leave. The majority of workers in the United State are not even eligible for unpaid family leave. In eight countries, 100% of wages are covered during maternity leave, and the leave lasts a minimum of three months. The lack of paid maternity leave is one reason that families in the United States have a relatively high rate of entry into poverty with the addition of a new child.

These and other relatively low expenditures on social welfare are implicated in the high poverty rates in the United States. The diagonal line in **Figure 7E** illustrates how countries with higher cash and near-cash expenditures as a percent of GDP on the non-elderly population have lower poverty rates among children. The United States stands out as the country with the lowest expenditures and the highest child poverty rate. The paucity of social expenditures addressing high poverty and growing income inequality in the United States is not due to a lack of resources; high per capita income and high productivity make it possible for the United States to afford social welfare spending. More-

**TABLE 7.15** Maternity and child care policies in the OECD

| Country | Maternity/child care leave indicators | | | Proportion of young children using formal child care arrangements | | Percentage of children in publicly supported care | | Share of child care costs covered by government | |
|---|---|---|---|---|---|---|---|---|---|
| | Duration of maternity leave (weeks) | Maternity benefits (% of average wages) | Total weeks of maternity/child care leave | Age under 3 | Age 3 to mandatory school age | Age under 3 | Age 3 to mandatory school age | Age under 3 | Age 3 to mandatory school age |
| United States | 0 | 0% | 12 | 54% | 70% | 5% | 54% | 25%–30% | 25%–30% |
| Japan | 14 | 60 | 58 | 13 | 34 | — | — | — | — |
| Germany | 14 | 100 | 162 | 10 | 78 | 2 | 78 | — | — |
| France | 16 | 100 | 162 | 29 | 99 | 23 | 99 | 72–77 | 100 |
| Italy | 21.5 | 80 | 64.5 | 6 | 95 | 6 | 91 | — | — |
| United Kingdom | 18 | 44 | 44 | 34 | 60 | 2 | 60 | — | — |
| Canada | 15 | 55 | 50 | 45 | 50 | 5 | 53 | — | — |

*(cont.)*

**TABLE 7.15** (cont.) Maternity and child care policies in the OECD

| Country | Maternity/child care leave indicators | | | Proportion of young children using formal child care arrangements | | Percentage of children in publicly supported care | | Share of child care costs covered by government | |
|---|---|---|---|---|---|---|---|---|---|
| | Duration of maternity leave (weeks) | Maternity benefits (% of average wages) | Total weeks of maternity/ child care leave | Age under 3 | Age 3 to mandatory school age | Age under 3 | Age 3 to mandatory school age | Age under 3 | Age 3 to mandatory school age |
| Australia | 0 | 0% | 52 | 15% | 60% | — | — | — | — |
| Austria | 16 | 100 | 112 | 4 | 68 | 3% | 80% | — | — |
| Belgium | 15 | 77 | 67 | 30 | 97 | 48 | 82 | 70%–80% | 70%–80% |
| Denmark | 30 | 100 | 82 | 64 | 91 | 21 | 53 | 85 | 85 |
| Finland | 52 | 70 | 164 | 22 | 66 | — | — | — | — |
| Ireland | 14 | 70 | 42 | 38 | 56 | — | — | — | — |
| Netherlands | 16 | 100 | 68 | 6 | 98 | — | — | — | — |
| New Zealand | 0 | 0 | 52 | 45 | 90 | — | — | — | — |
| Norway | 42 | 100 | 116 | 40 | 80 | 20 | 63 | 68 | 68 |
| Portugal | 24.3 | 100 | 128.3 | 12 | 75 | — | — | — | — |
| Spain | 16 | 100 | 164 | 5 | 84 | — | — | — | — |
| Sweden | 64 | 63 | 85 | 48 | 80 | 33 | 72 | 82–87 | 82–87 |
| Switzerland | 16 | — | 16 | — | — | — | — | — | — |

Note: Data for maternity/child care leave are from the latest available year: 1995 for the United States; 1997 for Norway; 1998 for Japan, France, Italy, Austria, Denmark, Finland, Ireland, the Netherlands, New Zealand, and Sweden; 1999 for Canada, Australia, and Portugal; and 2000 for Germany, the U.K., Belgium, and Spain; Switzerland was not available.

Source: OECD (2001e) and Waldfogel (2001).

**FIGURE 7E** Social expenditures vs. child poverty in the OECD

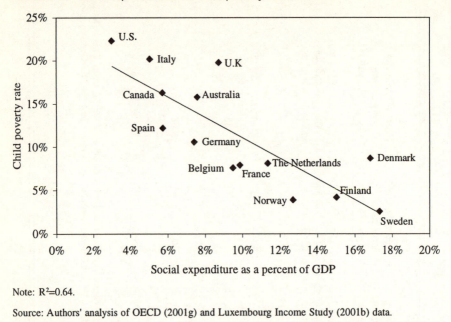

Note: $R^2$=0.64.

Source: Authors' analysis of OECD (2001g) and Luxembourg Income Study (2001b) data.

over, other OECD countries that spend more on both poverty reduction and family-friendly policies have done so while maintaining competitive rates of productivity and income growth. Growth, then, has benefited a broader spectrum of workers in these countries. Although strong growth in the United States over the late 1990s benefited low-wage workers and their families, inequality continued to rise, following its long-term trend. In the United States, growth has generally not been shared equally either in terms of wages paid by firms or through redistributive social policies.

## Employment and hours worked: problems with the U.S. model

The per capita income figures in Tables 7.1 and 7.2 appear, at face value, to be at odds with the international estimates of productivity levels in Table 7.3. Per capita income in the United States—the value of goods and services produced per year per person—is generally much higher relative to the other OECD economies than is the U.S. productivity level—the value of goods and services produced in an one hour of work in the United States. These differences between per capita income and productivity levels stem from two important differences across countries: the share of the total population employed, and the average number of hours worked each year by those with jobs.

The U.S. economy employs a greater share of its working-age population, and its workers work, on average, more hours per year, than is the case in any other rich, industrialized economy. This additional work raises per capita income in the United States relative to other economies with roughly similar productivity levels but lower levels of employment and lower average annual hours worked. Supporters of the U.S. model have long argued that the U.S. ability to generate a greater volume of work, whether measured in terms of number of jobs or hours of work, is a major feature of the U.S. model. To address this contention, this section takes a closer look at international employment rates, average hours worked, and unemployment rates.

The United States indeed employs a greater share of its working-age population (men and women combined) than do any of the 10 countries listed in **Table 7.16** for which comparable data are available. In 2000, the United States employed 71.8% of its male working-age population (second only to Japan with 72.5%) and ranked first with respect to female employment, with 57.7% of women employed. Employment rates can vary because of differences across economies in school enrollment rates for adults, early retirement rates, and women's non-market responsibilities, especially child care.

Table 7.16 shows a different pattern over time for employment rates of men and women. Among working-age men, employment rates fell in every country during the 1980s and in every country except the Netherlands in the 1990s. The decline in male employment rates between 1979 and 2000 was smallest in the United States (–2.0 percentage points) and relatively high in France (–10.6 percentage points), Italy (–9.8 percentage points), Sweden (–9.4 percentage points), and Germany (–8.1 percentage points). Among working-age women, employment rates rose between 1979 and 2000 in every country but Sweden (–1.1 percentage points from a high base in 1979). The largest increases occurred in the Netherlands (22.5 percentage points from a very low base in 1979), Australia (11.9 percentage points), Canada (10.5 percentage points), and the United States (10.2 percentage points).

In 2000, workers in the United States worked, on average, more hours per year (1,877) than workers in any of the other countries, including Japan (1,840 hours), the historic leader in hours worked (**Table 7.17**). Between 1979 and 2000, as nearly every other country reduced its average hours worked per year, the United States increased its average by 32. (Sweden also increased its average hours worked, by 108, but only to a level that kept it next to the bottom in average hours worked per year.)

**TABLE 7.16** Employment rates* in OECD countries

| | 1969 | 1979 | 1989 | 2000 | Percentage-point change, 1979-2000 |
|---|---|---|---|---|---|
| **Male** | | | | | |
| United States | 77.6% | 73.8% | 72.5% | 71.8% | -2.0 |
| Japan | 80.5 | 78.2 | 75.1 | 72.5 | -5.7 |
| Germany** | 78.5 | 69.8 | 65.9 | 61.7 | -8.1 |
| France | 76.5 | 69.6 | 61.2 | 59.0 | -10.6 |
| Italy | 72.4 | 66.3 | 59.9 | 56.5 | -9.8 |
| United Kingdom | 80.0 | 74.5 | 70.4 | 67.5 | -7.0 |
| Canada | 74.9 | 74.3 | 71.7 | 68.3 | -6.0 |
| Australia | 83.2 | 75.3 | 72.1 | 68.7 | -6.6 |
| Netherlands | — | 74.3 | 65.1 | 71.9 | -2.4 |
| Sweden | 77.8 | 73.7 | 70.9 | 64.3 | -9.4 |
| **Female** | | | | | |
| United States | 40.7% | 47.5% | 54.3% | 57.7% | 10.2 |
| Japan | 48.3 | 45.7 | 47.4 | 46.4 | 0.7 |
| Germany** | 38.2 | 38.4 | 39.7 | 44.6 | 6.2 |
| France | 37.7 | 40.5 | 41.2 | 43.9 | 3.4 |
| Italy | 25.1 | 27.3 | 28.6 | 30.5 | 3.2 |
| United Kingdom | 41.1 | 45.3 | 49.1 | 52.6 | 7.3 |
| Canada | 36.2 | 45.6 | 53.9 | 56.1 | 10.5 |
| Australia | 37.7 | 40.7 | 48.8 | 52.6 | 11.9 |
| Netherlands | — | 29.2 | 37.4 | 51.7 | 22.5 |
| Sweden | 47.9 | 57.2 | 61.7 | 56.1 | -1.1 |

\* Total employment as a percentage of working-age population.
\*\* 1979 and 1989 data are for western Germany; 2000 data are for unified Germany.

Source: Authors' analysis of BLS (2001d).

The data on employment rates and average hours worked suggest that more U.S. workers (as a share of the U.S. working population) contribute more hours on average to GDP than is the case in most other OECD countries. European nations, on the other hand, have chosen to take their productivity gains in the form of reduced hours—through shorter workweeks, longer vacations, and earlier retirements. This is an explicit policy choice: France, for example, has reduced its workweek to 35 hours.

The calculations in **Table 7.18** help to reconcile the differences between the U.S. and the other economies' productivity levels, on the one hand, and

**TABLE 7.17** Average annual hours worked in the OECD, 1979-2000

| Country | 1979 | 1990 | 2000 | Change in hours 1979-2000 |
|---|---|---|---|---|
| United States | 1,845 | 1,819 | 1,877 | 32 |
| Japan* | 2,126 | 2,031 | 1,840 | -286 |
| Germany** | 1,969 | 1,598 | 1,480 | -489 |
| France* | 1,806 | 1,657 | 1,562 | -244 |
| Italy* | 1,722 | 1,674 | 1,634 | -88 |
| United Kingdom | 1,815 | 1,767 | 1,708 | -107 |
| Canada | 1,832 | 1,788 | 1,801 | -31 |
| | | | | |
| Australia | 1,904 | 1,869 | 1,860 | -44 |
| Austria | | | | — |
| Belgium | | | | — |
| Denmark | | | | — |
| Finland | 1,837 | 1,763 | 1,721 | -116 |
| Ireland | | | | |
| Netherlands | | | | |
| New Zealand | — | 1,820 | 1,817 | — |
| Norway | 1,514 | 1,432 | 1,376 | -138 |
| Portugal | | | | — |
| Spain | 2,022 | 1,824 | 1,812 | -210 |
| Sweden | 1,516 | 1,546 | 1,624 | 108 |
| Switzerland* | — | — | 1,588 | — |
| | | | | |
| Average excluding U.S. | 1,810 | 1,695 | 1,629 | -215 |

\*   Japan, France, Italy, and Switzerland use 1999 data for 2000.
\*\*  Western Germany for 1979.

Source: OECD (2001e).

their per capita income, on the other. Productivity rates in France, for example, are 123% of the average productivity in OECD countries (column 1), but a smaller-than-average share of the French population works, which reduces per capita income there by 9% relative to the OECD average. Those in France who do work, on average, work fewer hours than the OECD average, which further reduces per capita income in France by 17% relative to the OECD average. As a result, even though French workers are 23% more productive than the average worker in the OECD, France has a per capita income that is 3% lower than the OECD average. The basic lesson of this employment and hours data is that an important portion of the apparently higher standard of living in the United

**TABLE 7.18** Impact of productivity, employment,* and hours differences on relative per capita income, 1997

| Country | Output per hour worked as % of OECD average | Effect of | | Per capita income as % of OECD average |
|---|---|---|---|---|
| | | Employment* | Hours | |
| United States | 120% | -1% | 10% | 129% |
| Japan | 82 | 10 | 14 | 106 |
| Germany | 105 | -5 | -4 | 96 |
| France | 123 | -9 | -17 | 97 |
| Italy | 106 | -11 | -5 | 90 |
| United Kingdom | 100 | -9 | 0 | 91 |
| Canada | 97 | 2 | 2 | 101 |
| Australia | 96 | 0 | 1 | 97 |
| Austria | 102 | -4 | 2 | 100 |
| Belgium | 128 | -5 | -22 | 101 |
| Denmark | 92 | 0 | 11 | 103 |
| Finland | 93 | 0 | -5 | 88 |
| Ireland | 108 | 5 | -18 | 95 |
| Netherlands | 121 | -26 | 0 | 95 |
| New Zealand | 69 | 8 | 2 | 79 |
| Norway | 126 | -17 | 12 | 121 |
| Portugal | 56 | 2 | 2 | 60 |
| Spain | 84 | 13 | -26 | 71 |
| Sweden | 93 | -3 | -1 | 89 |
| Switzerland | 94 | 0 | 17 | 111 |

* Combined effects of differences in unemployment rate, labor force participation rate, and age composition of total population.

Source: Van Ark and McGuckin (1999).

States comes not from working more efficiently than other comparable economies, but simply from working longer.

The capacity of the U.S. economy to sustain high employment rates is an important accomplishment of the U.S. economy. **Table 7.19** attempts to put U.S. job creation into historical and international context. The table shows the annual employment growth rate in 20 OECD economies over three periods, 1979-89, 1989-95, and 1995-2000. Two features stand out. First, the U.S. employment growth rate during the early part of the 1990s (1.0% per year) was slower than in the second half of the 1990s (1.6% per year). This trend was even more pronounced in many other countries: Ireland (with 5.5% employ-

**TABLE 7.19** Employment in OECD countries, 1979-2000

| | Employment (thousands) | | | | Employment change (thousands) | | | Annual growth rate (%) | | |
|---|---|---|---|---|---|---|---|---|---|---|
| | 1979 | 1989 | 1995 | 2000 | 1979-89 | 1989-95 | 1995-2000 | 1979-89 | 1989-95 | 1995-2000 |
| United States | 98,824 | 117,342 | 124,900 | 135,208 | 18,518 | 7,558 | 10,308 | 1.7% | 1.0% | 1.6% |
| Japan | 54,790 | 61,280 | 64,570 | 64,460 | 6,490 | 3,290 | -110 | 1.1 | 0.9 | 0.0 |
| Germany | 26,120 | 27,469 | 35,780 | 36,978 | 1,349 | 8,311 | 1,198 | 0.5 | 4.5 | 0.7 |
| France | 21,395 | 21,842 | 21,908 | 23,375 | 447 | 66 | 1,467 | 0.2 | 0.1 | 1.3 |
| Italy | 20,057 | 20,833 | 19,851 | 20,874 | 776 | -982 | 1,023 | 0.4 | -0.8 | 1.0 |
| United Kingdom | 25,080 | 26,549 | 25,891 | 27,677 | 1,469 | -658 | 1,786 | 0.6 | -0.4 | 1.3 |
| Canada | 10,658 | 12,986 | 13,357 | 14,910 | 2,328 | 371 | 1,553 | 2.0 | 0.5 | 2.2 |
| Australia | 6,079 | 7,715 | 8,219 | 9,048 | 1,636 | 504 | 829 | 2.4% | 1.1% | 1.9% |
| Austria | 3,051 | 3,342 | 3,729 | 3,741 | 291 | 387 | 12 | 0.9 | 1.8 | 0.1 |
| Belgium | 3,660 | 3,670 | 3,715 | 3,973 | 10 | 45 | 258 | 0.0 | 0.2 | 1.4 |
| Denmark | 2,439 | 2,610 | 2,566 | 2,692 | 171 | -44 | 126 | 0.7 | -0.3 | 1.0 |
| Finland | 2,246 | 2,494 | 2,090 | 2,326 | 248 | -404 | 236 | 1.1 | -2.9 | 2.2 |
| Ireland | 1,151 | 1,099 | 1,272 | 1,664 | -52 | 173 | 392 | -0.5 | 2.5 | 5.5 |
| Netherlands | 4,821 | 6,065 | 6,838 | 7,807 | 1,244 | 773 | 969 | 2.3 | 2.0 | 2.7 |
| New Zealand | 1,262 | 1,468 | 1,668 | 1,779 | 206 | 200 | 111 | 1.5 | 2.2 | 1.3 |
| Norway | 1,862 | 2,014 | 2,047 | 2,246 | 152 | 33 | 199 | 0.8 | 0.3 | 1.9 |
| Portugal | 3,854 | 4,377 | 4,382 | 4,877 | 523 | 5 | 495 | 1.3 | 0.0 | 2.2 |
| Spain | 11,902 | 12,260 | 12,049 | 14,446 | 358 | -211 | 2,397 | 0.3 | -0.3 | 3.7 |
| Sweden | 4,180 | 4,466 | 3,986 | 4,159 | 286 | -480 | 173 | 0.7 | -1.9 | 0.9 |
| Switzerland | 3,095 | 3,704 | 3,800 | 3,908 | 609 | 96 | 108 | 1.8 | 0.4 | 0.6 |
| Average excluding U.S. | 25,495 | 27,734 | 29,590 | 30,531 | 2,239 | 1,856 | 941 | 0.8% | 0.9% | 1.2% |

Source: Author's analysis of OECD (2001h).

ment growth), Spain (3.7%), the Netherlands (2.7%), Finland (2.2%), Portugal (2.2%), Canada (2.2%), Norway (1.9%), and Australia (1.9%) all had higher growth rates than the U.S. in the late 1990s. Thus, the U.S. "jobs machine" did not outperform other countries during the last half of the 1990s.

The employment growth data, therefore, suggest that the current U.S. job creation rate is not particularly high either by its own historical terms or when compared with several other economies with different labor market institutions. These job creation data are consistent with the earlier data on employment rates, which showed that the U.S. was not able to prevent the male employment rate from falling in the 1980s and 1990s (though it did a better job than other economies), and that several economies raised their female employment rates by larger margins than did the United States over the same period. The high starting point for female employment rates in the United States played a role in the lagging U.S. performance, as did the lack of adequate policies—such as paid maternity/paternity leave and child care—to address the needs of working women to balance work and family.

**Table 7.20** reports the unemployment rate in 20 OECD countries for 1979, 1989, and 2001. Over the late 1990s, many OECD countries experienced falling unemployment rates. The jobless rate remained low in the United States in 2001 (4.8%), and many other countries had rates at or below 6%—Portugal (4.1%), Denmark (4.3%), United Kingdom (5.0%), Japan (5.0%), Sweden (5.1), and New Zealand (5.3%)—and several had rates even lower—the Netherlands (2.4%), Switzerland (2.5%), Norway (3.6%), Austria (3.6%), and Ireland (3.8%). Higher unemployment in Europe, relative to the United States, is related to the monetary policies of the European Central Bank, the central bank for the 12 European Union countries. Over the late 1990s, due to inflation fears and concerns about strength of the newly introduced euro, the European Central Bank kept interest rates high, even as unemployment was slow to fall.

**Table 7.21** assesses another important claim about the causes of higher European unemployment—that Europe's labor market institutions, such as strong unions, high minimum wages, and generous benefits have priced less-skilled workers out of jobs. If this were the case, we would expect the unemployment rates of less-educated workers and better-educated workers to be relatively close to one another in the United States, where relatively weak unions, low minimum wages, and poor benefits would have less of an effect on the employment prospects of less-educated workers (in other words, compensation can fall so as to promote more jobs for the less skilled). Conversely, we would expect the unemployment rates of less-educated and better-educated workers to be relatively farther apart in Europe, where labor market

**TABLE 7.20** Unemployment rates in the OECD, 1979-2001
(percent of civilian labor force)

| Country | Standardized unemployment* | | |
| --- | --- | --- | --- |
| | 1979 | 1989 | 2001 |
| United States | 5.8% | 5.3% | 4.8% |
| Japan | 2.1 | 2.3 | 5.0 |
| Germany** | 2.7 | 5.6 | 7.9 |
| France | 5.3 | 9.3 | 8.6 |
| Italy | 5.8 | 10.0 | 9.5 |
| United Kingdom | 4.7 | 7.3 | 5.0 |
| Canada | 7.5 | 7.5 | 7.2 |
| Australia | 6.1% | 6.2% | 6.7% |
| Austria | — | — | 3.6 |
| Belgium | 9.1 | 7.5 | 6.6 |
| Denmark | — | 7.4 | 4.3 |
| Finland | 6.5 | 3.3 | 9.1 |
| Ireland | — | 14.7 | 3.8 |
| Netherlands | 5.8 | 6.9 | 2.4 |
| New Zealand | — | 7.1 | 5.3 |
| Norway | 2.0 | 5.0 | 3.6 |
| Portugal | — | 4.9 | 4.1 |
| Spain | 7.7 | 17.2 | 13.0 |
| Sweden | 2.1 | 1.6 | 5.1 |
| Switzerland | — | — | 2.5 |
| Average excluding U.S. | 4.4% | 6.9% | 6.9% |

\* Unemployment based on comparable definitions.
\*\* Western Germany for 1979 and 1989.

Source: OECD (2001e) and (2001h).

institutions would, by conventional thinking, disproportionately hurt job creation for less-educated workers. Yet the data in Table 7.21 run completely counter to this expectation. The unemployment rate for less-than-high-school-educated workers in the United States in 2000 was over four times higher than the rate for college-educated workers. The ratio of less-educated to better-educated unemployment rates was *lower* in every other country examined here. Thus, it appears that Europe's strong labor market institutions have not priced less-skilled workers out of the market. If anything, the European institutions appear to be associated with substantially *lower* relative unemployment rates for less-educated workers.

**TABLE 7.21** Unemployment rates in the OECD by education level, 2000

| | Unemployment rate* | | | Ratio of | |
|---|---|---|---|---|---|
| Country | Less than high school | High school | College | Less than high school/ college | High school/ college |
| United States | 7.9% | 3.6% | 1.8% | 4.4 | 2.0 |
| Japan | 6.0 | 4.7 | 3.5 | 1.7 | 1.3 |
| Germany** | 13.7 | 7.8 | 4.0 | 3.4 | 2.0 |
| France | 13.9 | 7.9 | 5.1 | 2.7 | 1.5 |
| Italy | 10.0 | 7.4 | 5.9 | 1.7 | 1.3 |
| United Kingdom | 8.9 | 4.5 | 2.1 | 4.2 | 2.1 |
| Canada | 9.9 | 5.8 | 3.8 | 2.6 | 1.5 |
| | | | | | |
| Australia | 7.5% | 4.5% | 3.6% | 2.1 | 1.3 |
| Austria | 6.3 | 3.0 | 1.6 | 3.9 | 1.9 |
| Belgium | 9.8 | 5.3 | 2.7 | 3.6 | 2.0 |
| Denmark | 6.3 | 3.9 | 2.6 | 2.4 | 1.5 |
| Finland | 12.1 | 8.9 | 4.7 | 2.6 | 1.9 |
| Ireland | 6.8 | 2.5 | 1.9 | 3.6 | 1.3 |
| Netherlands | 3.5 | 2.1 | 1.8 | 1.9 | 1.2 |
| New Zealand | 7.8 | 3.5 | 3.6 | 2.2 | 1.0 |
| Norway | 2.2 | 2.6 | 1.9 | 1.2 | 1.4 |
| Portugal | 3.6 | 3.3 | 2.8 | 1.3 | 1.2 |
| Spain | 13.7 | 11.0 | 9.5 | 1.4 | 1.2 |
| Sweden | 8.0 | 5.3 | 3.0 | 2.7 | 1.8 |
| Switzerland | 5.0 | 2.0 | 1.3 | 3.8 | 1.5 |
| | | | | | |
| Average excluding U.S. | 9.4% | 5.3% | 3.5% | 2.9 | 1.6 |

\* Standardized rate
\*\* Eastern and western Germany.

Source: Authors' analysis of OECD (2002a).

## Evaluating the U.S. model

The United States suffers from greater earnings and income inequality, higher poverty rates, and lower poverty exits than almost every other OECD economy. Due to the highly unequal distribution of income in the United States, low-wage workers and low-income households are almost universally worse off in absolute terms than their low-wage, low-income counterparts in other, less-affluent OECD countries. Further, American workers work longer hours and have less in the way of social supports for families than do workers in other OECD countries.

Supporters of the U.S. model generally acknowledge the relative inequality in the United States but argue that the model provides greater mobility, greater employment opportunities, and greater dynamism than do more interventionist economies. The evidence, however, provides little support for this view. First, there is less mobility out of poverty in the United States than in other nations. Poverty is deeper and harder to escape in the United States, and much less is available in the way of adequate social policy relative to other OECD countries. Although the gender wage gap is lower, there is much less support for working parents in the United States. The vaunted "flexibility" of the U.S. model serves to benefit mostly employers, not to help employees balance work and family.

Second, U.S. success in employment creation is often exaggerated. U.S. job growth rates in the 1990s were lackluster by its own historical standards and no better than several other OECD countries with different kinds of labor market institutions. In the late 1990s, unemployment was indeed at historic lows in the United States, but it was falling across the OECD, and many countries had jobless rates lower than the U.S. rate. This period was marked not by dramatic changes in labor market institutions or social policy but rather by a favorable macroeconomic climate that led to job, wage, and income growth. Perhaps most importantly, the pattern of unemployment rates in OECD countries is completely inconsistent with the idea that labor market institutions have priced less-educated workers out of jobs: the "flexible" U.S. labor market has the highest relative unemployment rate for less-educated workers among all the OECD countries.

Third, the data on growth rates in per capita income and productivity suggest that, although the U.S. economy has seen increased productivity in the last few years, it has underperformed, relative to other OECD economies, for most of the past 20 years. In the 1980s and the early 1990s, nearly all the OECD economies—including the United States—suffered a dramatic deceleration in the growth rates of both per capita income and productivity. The especially slow growth rates in the United States, however, have allowed all the OECD countries to narrow the U.S. lead; several have eliminated the productivity gap altogether.

The best interpretation of the available international evidence is that, while the late 1990s were a period of low unemployment and overall economic growth, many OECD economies still face labor market challenges. Economic growth and productivity growth rates across the entire OECD are still lower than they were in the 1960s. Inequality has risen sharply, especially in the United States, the United Kingdom, and a few other countries. Social policy has not stepped up to address pressing social needs and the rise in poverty in the United States. Other OECD countries should beware the implications of pursuing similar cutbacks in social spending. The evidence in this chapter, which underscores the diversity of international experience with providing wage, income, and employment security, suggests that those who look exclusively to the United States for solutions will miss a great deal.

# The family income data series

This appendix explains the various adjustments made to the March Current Population Survey data and the methodology used to prepare the data in the tables discussed below.

The data source used for the following tables is the U.S. Bureau of the Census's March Current Population Survey (CPS). Each March, approximately 60,000 households are asked questions about their incomes from a wide variety of sources in the prior year (the income data in the 2001 March CPS refer to 2000). For the national analysis in Chapter 1, we use the data relevant to the year in question. For the state income inequality estimates in Chapter 6 (Table 6.3), we pool three neighboring years of data for each time period of interest. Thus, the first time period, centered on 1979, includes the income data from 1978 to 1980. (These tables were developed jointly with the Center on Budget and Policy Priorities; see Bernstein et al. 2002).

In order to preserve the confidentiality of respondents, the income variables on the public-use files of the CPS are top-coded, i.e., values above a certain level are suppressed. Since income inequality measures are sensitive to changes in the upper reaches of the income scale, this suppression poses a challenge to analysts interested in both the extent of inequality in a given time period and the change in inequality over time. We use an imputation technique, described below, that is commonly used in such cases to estimate the value of top-coded data. Over the course of the 1990s, Census top-coding procedures underwent significant changes, which also must be dealt with to preserve consistency. These methods are discussed below.

For most of the years of data in our study, a relatively small share of the distribution of any one variable is top-coded. For example, in 1989, 0.67%

(i.e., two-thirds of the top 1%) of weighted cases are top-coded on the variable "earnings from longest job," meaning actual reported values are given for over 99% of the those with positive earnings. Nevertheless, the disproportionate influence of the small group of top-coded cases means their earnings levels cannot be ignored.

Our approach has been to impute the average value above the top-code for the key components of income using the assumption that the tails of these distributions follow a Pareto distribution. (The Pareto distribution is defined as $c/(x^{(a+1)})$, where c and a are positive constants that we estimate using the top 20% of the empirical distribution (more precisely, c is a scale parameter assumed known; a is the key parameter for estimation). We apply this technique to four key variables: earnings from longest job, interest, dividend, and rental income. Since the upper tail of empirical income distributions closely follows the general shape of the Pareto, this imputation method is commonly used for dealing with top-coded data (West, undated). The estimate uses the shape of the upper part of the distribution (in our case, the top 20%) to extrapolate to the part that is unobservable due to the top-codes. Intuitively, if the shape of the observable part of the distribution suggests that the tail above the top-code is particularly long, implying a few cases with very high income values, the imputation will return a high mean relative to the case where it appears that the tail above the top-code is rather short.

Polivka (1998), using an uncensored dataset (i.e., without top-codes), shows that the Pareto procedure effectively replicates the mean above the top-code. For example, her analysis of the use of the technique to estimate usual weekly earnings from the earnings files of the CPS yields estimates that are generally within less than 1% of the true mean.

As noted, the Census Bureau has lifted the top-codes over time in order to accommodate the fact that nominal and real wage growth eventually renders the old top-codes too low. For example, the top-coded value for "earnings from longest job" was increased from $50,000 in 1979 to $99,999 in 1989. Given the growth of earnings over this period, we did not judge this change (or any others in the income-component variables) to create inconsistencies in the trend comparisons between these two time periods.

However, changes made in the mid- and latter 1990s data did require consistency adjustments. For these years, the Census Bureau both adjusted the top-codes (some were raised, some were lowered; the new top-codes were determined by using whichever value was higher: the top 3% of all reported amounts for the variable, or the top 0.5% of all persons), and used "plug-in" averages above the top-codes for certain variables. These are group-specific average values taken above the top-code, with the groups defined on the basis of gender, race, and worker status. We found that the Pareto procedure was not feasible with unearned income, given the empirical distributions of these variables, so for March data (survey year) 1996 forward we use the plug-in values. Our tabulations show that, in tandem with the procedure described next regarding earnings, this approach avoids trend inconsistencies.

The most important variable that we adjust (i.e., the adjustment with the largest impact on family income) is "earnings from longest job." The top-code on this variable was raised sharply in survey year 1994, and this change leads to an upward bias in comparing estimates at or around that year to earlier years. (Note that this bias is attenuated over time as nominal income growth "catches up" to the new top-code, and relatively smaller shares of respondents again fall into that category.) Our procedure for dealing with this was to impose a lower top-code on the earnings data that we grew over time by the rate of inflation, and to calculate Pareto estimates based on these artificial top-codes. We found that this procedure led to a relatively smooth series across the changes in Census Bureau methodology.

For example, we find that, while our imputed series generates lower incomes among, say, the top 5% of families (because we are imposing a lower top-code) in the mid-1990s, by the end of the 1990s our estimates were only slightly lower than those from the unadjusted Census data.

**Table 1.20:** Ryscavage et al. (1992) presents the methodology for this table. Following these authors, we capture the impact of demographic changes on household incomes by adjusting the weights of household heads to reflect demographic changes over the time periods shown in the table.

We use the following categories: *education:* high school or less, some college, and college or more; *age:* less than 25, 25-44, 45-64, and 65 and older; *family type:* married-couple households, single-headed households, individuals living alone; *race:* white, non-white.

In order to simulate the income effects of changing shares of the population with these characteristics between $t_0$ and $t_1$, we multiplied each head-of-household's weight by the ratio of the standardized number of households with a particular characteristic in $t_0$ to that in $t_1$. For example, to estimate the effect of the change in the age of household heads over the period 1969-79, we divided the 1979 sample into the age groups noted above, and multiplied the weight of each 1979 householder by the ratio of the weighted number of householders in that cell in 1969 to that in 1979. Both numerator and denominator are standardized by dividing each by the total number of households in their respective years. Finally, to measure the impact of all of the demographic factors taken together, we performed the same exercise but with each representing the intersection of all the variables noted above (e.g., one cell would be non-white, married-couple householders, age 25-34, with four or more years of college).

Two caveats should be noted with this type of analysis. First, due to correlation between some of these characteristics and income levels, there are various interactions between these demographic categories that are not reflected in the table. For example, whites tend to have higher incomes than non-whites, and are also more likely than non-whites to be college educated. Thus, the sum of these two effects—race and education—taken separately are likely to be larger than their combined effect, because the summative approach fails to partial out the correlation.

Second, demographic decompositions such as this one tend to suffer from an endogeneity problem. That is, the exercise assigns causation to the demographic changes under analysis, implying, for example, that the increase in single-parent families led to lower average income levels. It is possible, however, that the causality runs the other way. Say, for example, that income declines stemming from male wage declines have led to an increase in female-headed families. To the extent that this is the case, the contribution of demographic factors will be overstated.

**Tables 1.26–1.33**: The source for these tables is the March CPS datasets described above. The analysis focuses on married-couple families with children, spouse present, where the family head was between 25 and 54 years of age. The distributional analysis places 20% of families, not persons, in each fifth. For tables 1.31-1.33 we add the restriction that neither spouse may be over 54. Also, we found some outlier cases for the 2000 data (from the March 2001 file) that led to non-plausible spikes in trend for the average income or wages in the top fifth (e.g., in Tables 1.29 and 1.30), so for these runs we restricted the sample to the bottom 99%.

Husbands and wives' wages in this analysis (Table 1.30) are constructed differently than in most of the analysis in this book, i.e., they are "hour-weighted" in this section and "person-weighted" elsewhere. Whereas we usually calculate averages by summing the wages and dividing by the weighted number of earners, in this case we calculate annual hours by dividing annual earnings by annual hours. Since earnings levels and number of hours worked are positively correlated, hour-weighted wage levels tend to be slightly higher than person-weighted wages.

Finally, note that in the calculation of income shares in the absence of wives' earnings (Table 1.33), we determine a separate set of quintile cutoffs (based on family income minus wives' earnings) than those for actual shares. This approach simulates one choice of a counterfactual distribution.

**Table 5.10**: The methodology for this decomposition is taken from Danziger and Gottschalk (1995, chapter 5). The change to be explained is the difference in poverty rates between $t_0$ and $t_1$. We first isolate the effect of average income growth by assigning the average growth between the two time periods to all families in $t_0$ and recalculate the poverty rate (we adjust each family's poverty line for the increase in the CPI over this period). This procedure holds the demographic composition and the shape of the income distribution constant in $t_0$ while allowing incomes to grow equally for all families. Thus, the difference between this simulated poverty rate and the actual $t_0$ poverty rate is attributable to the growth in average income.

We repeat this exercise for each demographic group in $t_0$ (we use the three family types in Table 5.8, two races—white and non-white—and three education categories of the family head—less than high school, high school and some college, and college or more). By weighting each of these simulated $t_0$ rates by their $t_1$ population shares, we can simulate a $t_0$ poverty rate that reflects the average income growth and demographic composition of $t_1$. The difference between this simulated rate and the one discussed in the above paragraph gives the contribution of demographic change over the time period. Finally, since this second simulated rate incorporates the mean growth and demographic change between the two periods, but not the change in the shape of the distribution, the difference between this second simulated rate and the actual rate for $t_1$ equals the change in poverty rates attributable to changes in inequality over the two periods.

**Table 6.3:** These data are noted in the above introduction to this section. One other difference in our approach to top-coding here was to estimate separate Pareto means for four different groups of states (for only the variable "earnings from longest job"). We sorted states (including the District of Columbia) into four groups (13 states in three groups and 12 states in one group) based on the share of cases top-coded, and we imputed separate values for each group. Our motivation was to enhance our ability to capture regional variation in income inequality at the top of the income scale.

# Wage analysis computations

*by Danielle Gao*

This appendix provides background information on the analysis of wage data from the Current Population Survey (CPS), which is prepared by the Bureau of the Census for the Bureau of Labor Statistics (BLS). Specifically, for 1979 and beyond, we analyze microdata files provided by BLS that contain a full year's data on the outgoing rotation groups (ORG) in the CPS. (For years prior to 1979, we use the CPS May files; our use of these files is discussed below.) We believe that the CPS ORG files allow for a timely, up-to-date, and accurate analysis of wage trends keeping within the familiar labor force definitions and concepts employed by BLS.

The sampling framework of the monthly CPS is a "rolling panel," in which households are in the survey for four consecutive months, out for eight, and then back in for four months. The ORG files provide data on those CPS respondents in either the fourth or eighth month of the CPS (i.e., in groups four or eight, out of a total of eight groups). Therefore, in any given month the ORG file represents a quarter of the CPS sample. For a given year, the ORG file is equivalent to three months of CPSs (one-fourth of 12). For our analysis, we use a sample drawn from the full-year ORG sample, the size of which ranges from 160,000 to 180,000 observations during the 1979 to 1994 period. Due to a decrease in the overall sample size of the CPS, the ORG has been shrinking since 1994, and our current sample comes in at about 145,000 cases.

Changes in annual or weekly earnings can result from changes in hourly earnings or from more working time (either more hours per week or weeks per year). Our analysis is centered around the hourly wage, which represents the pure price of labor (exclusive of benefits), because we are interested in changing pay levels for the workforce and its sub-groups. We do this to be able to clearly distinguish changes in earnings resulting from more (or less) work rather than more (or less) pay. Most of our wage analysis, therefore, does not take into account that weekly or annual earnings may have changed because of longer or shorter working hours or lesser or greater opportunities for employment. An exception to this is Table 2.1, where we present annual hours, earnings, and hourly weighted wages from the March CPS.

In our view, the ORG files provide a better source of data for wage analysis than the traditionally used March CPS files. In order to calculate hourly wages from the March CPS, analysts must make calculations using three retrospective variables: the annual earnings, weeks worked, and usual weekly hours worked in the year prior to the survey. In contrast, respondents in the ORG are asked a set of questions about hours worked, weekly wages, and (for workers paid by the hour) hourly wages in the week prior to the survey. In this regard, the data from the ORG are likely to be more reliable than data from the March CPS. See Bernstein and Mishel 1997 for a detailed discussion of these differences.

Our subsample includes all wage-and-salary workers with valid wage and hour data, whether paid weekly or by the hour. Specifically, in order to be included in our sub-sample, respondents had to meet the following criteria:

- age 18-64;

- employed in the public or private sector (unincorporated self-employed were excluded);

- hours worked within the valid range in the survey (1-99 per week, or hours vary—see discussion below); and,

- either hourly or weekly wages within the valid survey range (top-coding discussed below).

For those who met these criteria, an hourly wage was calculated in the following manner. If a valid hourly wage was reported, that wage was used throughout our analysis. For salaried workers (those who report only a weekly wage), the hourly wage was their weekly wage divided by their hours worked. Outliers, i.e., persons with hourly wages below 50 cents or above $100 in 1989 CPI-U-X1-adjusted dollars, were removed from the analysis. These yearly upper and lower bounds are presented in **Table B-1**. CPS demographic weights were applied to make the sample nationally representative.

The hourly wage reported by hourly workers in the CPS is net of any overtime, tips, or commissions (OTTC), thus introducing a potential undercount in the hourly wage for workers who regularly receive tips or premium pay. OTTC

**TABLE B-1** Wage earner sample, hourly wage upper and lower limits, 1973-2001

| Year | Lower | Upper |
|------|-------|-------|
| 1973 | $0.19 | $38.06 |
| 1974 | 0.21 | 41.85 |
| 1975 | 0.23 | 45.32 |
| 1976 | 0.24 | 47.90 |
| 1977 | 0.25 | 50.97 |
| 1978 | 0.27 | 54.44 |
| 1979 | 0.30 | 59.68 |
| 1980 | 0.33 | 66.37 |
| 1981 | 0.36 | 72.66 |
| 1982 | 0.39 | 77.10 |
| 1983 | 0.40 | 80.32 |
| 1984 | 0.42 | 83.79 |
| 1985 | 0.43 | 86.77 |
| 1986 | 0.44 | 88.39 |
| 1987 | 0.46 | 91.61 |
| 1988 | 0.48 | 95.40 |
| 1989 | 0.50 | 100.00 |
| 1990 | 0.53 | 105.40 |
| 1991 | 0.55 | 109.84 |
| 1992 | 0.57 | 113.15 |
| 1993 | 0.58 | 116.53 |
| 1994 | 0.60 | 119.52 |
| 1995 | 0.61 | 122.90 |
| 1996 | 0.63 | 126.53 |
| 1997 | 0.65 | 129.54 |
| 1998 | 0.66 | 131.45 |
| 1999 | 0.67 | 134.35 |
| 2000 | 0.69 | 138.87 |
| 2001 | 0.71 | 142.82 |

Source: Authors' analysis.

is included in the usual weekly earnings of hourly workers, which raises the possibility of assigning an imputed hourly wage to hourly workers based on the reported weekly wage and hours worked per week. Conceptually, using this imputed wage is preferable to using the reported hourly wage because it is more inclusive. We have chosen, however, not to use this broader wage measure, because the extra information on OTTC seems unreliable. We compared the imputed hourly wage (reported weekly earnings divided by weekly hours) to the reported hourly wage; the difference presumably reflects OTTC. This comparison showed that significant percentages of the hourly workforce appeared to receive negative OTTC. These error rates range from a low of 0% of the hourly workforce in the period 1989-93 to a high of 16-17% in 1973-88, and persist across the survey change from 1993 to 1994. Since negative OTTC is clearly implausible, we rejected this imputed hourly wage series and rely strictly on the hourly rate of pay as reported directly by hourly workers, subject to the sample criteria discussed above.

For tables that show wage percentiles, we "smooth" hourly wages to compensate for "wage clumps" in the wage distributions. The technique involves creating a categorical hourly wage distribution, where the categories are 50-cent intervals, starting at 25 cents. We then find the categories on either side of each decile and perform a weighted, linear interpolation to locate the wage precisely on the particular decile. The weights for the interpolation are derived from differences in the cumulative percentages on either side of the decile. For example, suppose that 48% of the wage distribution of workers by wage level are in the $9.26-9.75 wage "bin," and 51% are in the next higher bin $9.76-10.25. The weight for the interpolation (in this case the median or 50th percen-

tile) is $\frac{(50-48)}{(51-48)}$ or 2/3. The interpolated median equals this weight, times the width of the bin ($.50), plus the upper bound of the previous bin ($9.75), or $10.08 in this example.

For the survey years 1973-85, the weekly wage is top-coded at $999.00; an extended top-code value of $1,923 is available in 1986-97; a the top-code value changes to $2,884.61 in 1998-2001. Particularly for the later years, this truncation of the wage distribution creates a downward bias in the mean wage. We dealt with the top-coding issue by imputing a new weekly wage for top-coded individuals. The imputed value is the Pareto-imputed mean for the upper tail of the weekly earnings distribution, based on the distribution of weekly earnings up to the 80th percentile. This procedure was done for men and women separately. The imputed values for men and women appear in **Table B-2**. A new hourly wage, equal to the new estimated value for weekly earnings, divided by that person's usual hours per week, was calculated.

In January 1994, a new survey instrument was introduced into the CPS; many labor force items were added and improved. This presents a significant challenge to the researcher who wishes to make comparisons over time. The most careful research on the impact of the survey change has been conducted by BLS researcher Anne Polivka (1996, 1997). Interestingly, Polivka does not find that the survey changes had a major impact on broad measures of unemployment or wage levels, though significant differences did surface for some

**TABLE B-2** Pareto-imputed mean values for top-coded weekly earnings, and share top coded, 1973-2001

| Year | Share | | | Value | |
|------|-----|-----|-------|------|-------|
| | All | Men | Women | Men | Women |
| 1973 | 0.11% | 0.17% | 0.02% | $1,365 | $1,340 |
| 1974 | 0.16 | 0.26 | 0.01 | 1,385 | 1,297 |
| 1975 | 0.21 | 0.35 | 0.02 | 1,410 | 1,323 |
| 1976 | 0.30 | 0.51 | 0.01 | 1,392 | 1,314 |
| 1977 | 0.36 | 0.59 | 0.04 | 1,384 | 1,309 |
| 1978 | 0.38 | 0.65 | 0.02 | 1,377 | 1,297 |
| 1979 | 0.57 | 0.98 | 0.05 | 1,388 | 1,301 |
| 1980 | 0.72 | 1.23 | 0.07 | 1,380 | 1,287 |
| 1981 | 1.05 | 1.82 | 0.10 | 1,408 | 1,281 |
| 1982 | 1.45 | 2.50 | 0.18 | 1,430 | 1,306 |
| 1983 | 1.89 | 3.27 | 0.25 | 1,458 | 1,307 |
| 1984 | 2.32 | 3.92 | 0.42 | 1,471 | 1,336 |
| 1985 | 2.78 | 4.63 | 0.60 | 1,490 | 1,343 |
| 1986 | 0.80 | 1.37 | 0.15 | 2,435 | 2,466 |
| 1987 | 1.06 | 1.80 | 0.20 | 2,413 | 2,472 |
| 1988 | 1.30 | 2.19 | 0.29 | 2,410 | 2,461 |
| 1989 | 0.48 | 0.84 | 0.08 | 2,710 | 2,506 |
| 1990 | 0.60 | 1.04 | 0.11 | 2,724 | 2,522 |
| 1991 | 0.71 | 1.21 | 0.17 | 2,744 | 2,553 |
| 1992 | 0.77 | 1.28 | 0.22 | 2,727 | 2,581 |
| 1993 | 0.86 | 1.43 | 0.24 | 2,754 | 2,580 |
| 1994 | 1.25 | 1.98 | 0.43 | 2,882 | 2,689 |
| 1995 | 1.34 | 2.16 | 0.43 | 2,851 | 2,660 |
| 1996 | 1.41 | 2.27 | 0.46 | 2,863 | 2,678 |
| 1997 | 1.71 | 2.67 | 0.65 | 2,908 | 2,751 |
| 1998 | 0.63 | 0.98 | 0.25 | 4,437 | 4,155 |
| 1999 | 0.71 | 1.12 | 0.21 | 4,464 | 4,099 |
| 2000 | 0.83 | 1.38 | 0.24 | 4,502 | 4,179 |
| 2001 | 0.92 | 1.46 | 0.34 | 4,477 | 4,227 |

Source: Authors' analysis.

sub-groups (e.g., weekly earnings for those with less than a high school diploma and those with advanced degrees, the unemployment rate of older workers). However, a change in the reporting of weekly hours did call for the alteration of our methodology. In 1994 the CPS began allowing people to report that their usual hours worked per week vary. In order to include non-hourly workers who report varying hours in our wage analysis, we estimated their usual hours using a regression-based imputation procedure, where we predicted the usual hours of work for "hours vary" cases based on the usual hours worked of persons with similar characteristics. An hourly wage was calculated by dividing weekly earnings by the estimate of hours for these workers. The share of our sample that received such a wage in the 1994-97 period is presented in **Table B-3**. The reported hourly wage of hourly workers was preserved.

BLS analysts Ilg and Hauzen (2000), following Polivka (1999), do adjust the 10th percentile wage because "changes to the survey in 1994 led to lower reported earnings for relatively low-paid workers, compared with pre-1994 estimates." We make no such adjustments for both practical and empirical reasons. Practically, BLS has provided no adjustment factors for hourly wage trends that we can use—Polivka's work is for weekly wages. More importantly, the trends in 10th percentile hourly wages differ from those reported by Ilg and Hauzen for 10th percentile weekly earnings. This is perhaps not surprising, since the composition of earners at the "bottom" will differ when measured by weekly rather than hourly wages, with low-weekly earners being almost exclusively part-timers. Empirically, Ilg and Hauzen show the unadjusted 50/10 wage gap jumping up between 1993 and 1994, when the new survey begins. In contrast, our 50/10 wage gap for hourly wages falls between 1993 and 1994. Thus, the pattern of wage change in their data differs greatly from that in our data. In fact, our review of the 1993-94 trends across all of the deciles shows no discontinuities whatsoever. Consequently, we make no adjustments to account for any effect of the 1994 survey change. Had we made the sort of adjustments suggested by Polivka, our measured 1990s' fall in the 50/10 wage gap would be even larger and the overall pattern—falling 50/10, rising 90/50, and especially the 95/50 wage gaps—would remain the same.

Demographic variables are also used in the analysis. Our race variable comprises four mutually exclusive categories:

- white, non-Hispanic;

- black, non-Hispanic;

- Hispanic, any race;

- all others.

Beginning in 1992, the CPS employed a new coding scheme for education, providing data on the respondent's highest degree attained. The CPS in earlier years provided data on years of schooling completed. The challenge to make a consistent wage series by education level is to either make the new data consis-

**TABLE B-3** Share of wage earners assigned an hourly wage from imputed weekly hours, 1994-97

| Year | Percent hours vary |
|------|--------------------|
| 1994 | 2.1% |
| 1995 | 2.1 |
| 1996 | 2.5 |
| 1997 | 2.5 |

Source: Authors' analysis.

tent with the past or to make the old "years of schooling" data consistent with the new, educational attainment measures. In prior versions of *The State of Working America*, we achieved a consistent series by imputing years of schooling for 1992 and later years, i.e., making the "new" consistent with the "old." In this version, however, we have converted the "old" data to the new coding following Jaeger (1997). However, Jaeger does not separately identify four-year college and "more than college" categories. Since the wages of these sub-groups of the "college or more" group have divergent trends, we construct pre-1992 wages and employment separately for "four-year college" and "advanced." To do so, we compute wages, wage premiums, and employment separately for those with 16, 17, and 18-plus years of schooling completed. The challenge is to distribute the "17s" to the 16 years (presumably a four-year degree) and 18-plus years (presumably advanced) groups. We do this by using the share of the "17s" that have a terminal four-year college degree, as computed in the February 1990 CPS supplement that provides both education codings: 61.4%. We then assume that 61.4% of all of the "17s" are "college-only" and compute a weighted average of the "16s" and 61.4% of the "17s" to construct "college-only" wages and wage premiums. Correspondingly, we compute a weighted average of 38.6% (or 1 less 61.4%) of the "17s" and the "18s" to construct advanced "wages and wage premiums." Distributing the "17s" affects each year differently depending on the actual change in the wages and premiums for "17s" and the changing relative size of the "17s" (which varies only slightly from 2.5% of men and women from 1979 to 1991).

We employ these education categories in various tables in Chapter 2, where we present wage trends by education over time. For the data for 1992 and later, we compute the "some college" trends by aggregating those "with some college but no degree beyond high school" and those with an associate or other degree that is not a four-year college degree.

# Table notes

**FREQUENTLY CITED SOURCES**

*The following abbreviations are used throughout the table and figure notes.*

**BLS**—Bureau of Labor Statistics.

**CES**—Current Establishment Survey, a survey of U.S. businesses conducted by the BLS.

**CPI**—Consumer price index.

**CPI-U-RS**—Consumer price index for all urban consumers, research series.

**CPS**—Current Population Survey, a survey of U.S. households conducted by the BLS.

**Employment and Earnings**—U.S. Department of Labor, Employment and Earnings, monthly and historical supplements.

**ERP**—President of the United States. Economic Report of the President.

**NIPA**—U.S. Department of Commerce, National Income and Product Accounts.

**ORG**—Outgoing Rotation Group, a segment of the March CPS.

**P-60**—Poverty in the United States. U.S. Department of Commerce, Bureau of the Census.

**SCB**—U.S. Department of Commerce, Survey of Current Business, monthly.

*The following agencies and their respective web sites are referenced throughout the text.*

Bureau of Labor Statistics (BLS)—www.bls.gov
  Current Employment Survey (CES)—http://www.bls.gov/data/home.htm
  Current Population Survey (CPS)—http://www.bls.gov/data/home.htm
Bureau of Economic Analysis (BEA)—www.bea.gov
  NIPA Tables—www.bea.gov/bea/dn/nipaweb/index.asp
U.S. Census Bureau—www.census.gov
  Historical Poverty Tables—www.census.gov/hhes/income/histinc/histpovtb.html
  Historical Income Tables—www.census.gov/hhes/income/histinc/histinctb.html

**INTRODUCTION**

1    *Weekly nominal earnings growth for full-time workers, age 25 and over, by gender.*
    See note to Figure D.

2 *The benefits of full employment.* Productivity growth is for the non-farm business sector and is from the BLS website. Unemployment is also from the BLS website, http://stats.bls.gov/webapps/legacy/cpsatab1.htm. For Census income data, see notes to Tables 1.1 (median) and 1.9 (other percentiles). For wage growth, see note to Table 2.6

## CHAPTER 1

1.1 *Median family income.* Census homepage, Historical Income Tables, Families, Table F-5.

1.2 *Length of time to recovery of median family income after recession.* See note to Table 1.1. Peaks based on National Bureau of Economic Research business cycle dating (http://www.nber.org/cycles.html).

1.3 *Annual family income growth for the middle fifth, unadjusted and adjusted for family size.* The unadjusted (for family size) values come from Census Income Table F-3; however, instead of using the deflator CPI-U-RS (the standard deflator in this edition) we use CPI-U-X1 in order to maintain greater consistency with the growth rates labeled "adjusted for family size." These values are derived by dividing family income by the poverty line, which is deflated using the CPI-U (Census Table F-21).

1.4 *Median family income by racial/ethnic group.* Census homepage, Historical Income Tables, Families, Table F-5.

1.5 *Median family income by age of household head.* Census homepage, Historical Income Tables, Families, Table F-11.

1.6 *Median family income growth by 10-year cohorts, starting in 1949.* Census homepage, Historical Income Tables, Families, Table F-11.

1.7 *Median family income by family type.* Census homepage, Historical Income Tables, Families, Table F-7.

1.8 *Shares of family income going to various income groups and to top 5%.* Census homepage, Historical Income Tables, Families, Table F-2.

1.9 *Real family income by income group, upper limit of each group.* Census homepage, Historical Income Tables, Families, Table F-1.

1.10 *Distribution of tax burdens and income before and after 2001 tax law change.* Gale and Potter (2002), Table 4, p. 85. The post-tax-law-change analysis is evaluated for the fully phased-in tax cut that would occur in 2010 (taken at 2001 income levels), adjusted for inflation to 2001 levels.

1.11 *Effective federal tax rates for all households, by income quintile, using comprehensive household income adjusted for household size.* Congressional Budget Office (2001), Table G-1a, p. 72.

1.12 *The effects of federal tax and income changes on after-tax income shares.* Authors' calculations based on pre-tax adjusted family income and effective tax rates from CBO (2001), Table G-1c, p. 76. The sum of the shares is forced to sum to 100%, which is not the case in the original data due to the exclusion of families and persons with zero or negative income from the lowest quintile and the inclusion of these same families and individuals in the "all" category.

1.13    *Effective tax rates for selected federal taxes.* CBO (2001), Table G-1a, p. 72.

1.14    *Types of federal vs. state and local taxes, as a percent of revenue at each level.* NIPA Tables 3.2 and 3.3.

1.15    *Federal vs. state and local tax revenue as a percent of GDP.* NIPA Tables 1.1, 3.2, and 3.3.

1.16    *Growth of household income inequality using different income definitions and inequality measures.* Census homepage, Experimental Income Measures, Tables RDI-5 and 8.

1.17    *Household income growth, including top 1%, CBO data.* See note to Table 1.11.

1.18    *Income mobility.* Unpublished tabulations of the Panel Study of Income Dynamics by Peter Gottschalk. Family heads are less than 62 years of age over the full period. Quintiles are constructed such that 20% of persons, not 20% of families, are in each group. Quintile cutoffs are income-to-needs ratio, using the official poverty lines, so these rates are adjusted for family-size differences. Family income in 1994 is from the 1995 early release of the Panel Study of Income Dynamics, which does not include Social Security income. However, since the sample selection excludes families where the household head is 63 or over, this omission is unlikely to affect the results.

1.19    *Income mobility over the 1970s and 1980s.* See note to Table 1.16.

1.20    *Impact of demographic change on household income.* See Appendix A.

1.21    *Distribution of families and persons by income level.* Family data are available at the Census homepage, Historical Income Tables, Families, Table F-23. Person data are unpublished tabulations provided by Charles Nelson from the U.S. Bureau of the Census. For this panel, family incomes for different-sized families are made comparable using equivalence scales as in Ruggles (1990), and single individuals are treated as one-person families.

1.22    *Sources of household income by income type.* Unpublished data provided by the Institute on Economic and Tax Policy.

1.23    *Shares of market-based personal income by income type.* From NIPA Table 2.1. Capital gains data are from the Internal Revenue Service Statistics on Income series and include gains as well as losses. The capital gains data for 2000 are an estimate based on the growth in CBO forecasts for capital gains.

1.24    *Shares of income by type and sector.* Based on NIPA Table 1.15. The "corporate and business" sector includes "corporate," "other private business," and "rest of world." The "government/nonprofit" sector includes the household, government enterprise, and government sectors, all of which generate no capital income. Capital income consists of profits, interest, and rental income.

1.25    *Corporate sector profit rates and shares.* Uses capital income and tax data from NIPA Table 1.16. "Pre-tax profit rates" are the sum of corporate profits with inventory valuation and capital consumption adjustments and net interest (lines 9 and 17) as a share of corporate capital (created by Christian Weller based on methodology presented in Baker (1996)). "After-tax profit rates" account for a tax rate based on the quotient of profit tax liability and corporate profits with inventory valuation and capital consumption adjustments (line 11 and 9). The denominator for "profit share" is capital income as defined above (sum of lines 9 and 17); the denominator for "labor share" is compensation to employees (line 6); the denominator for both is their sum. The "capital-output ratio" is corporate capital divided by capital income (both as defined above).

1.26    *Average weeks worked per year by income quintile, married-couple families with children, head of household age 25-54.* See Appendix A.

1.27    *Average hours worked per year by income quintile, married-couple families with children, head of household age 25-54.* See Appendix A.

1.28    *Average hours worked per year by income quintile, married-couple families with children, head of household age 25-54, by race of family head.* See Appendix A.

1.29    *Average income, married-couple families with children, head of household age 25-54.* See Appendix A.

1.30    *Hourly earnings by husbands and wives, couples with children, head of household age 25-54.* See Appendix A.

1.31    *Annual hours by husbands and wives, prime-age, married-couple families with children.* See Appendix A.

1.32    *Annual hours, wives in prime-age, married-couple families with children, and contributions to change, sorted by husband's income.* See Appendix A.

1.33    *Effect of wives' earnings on income shares of prime-age, married-couple families with children.* See Appendix A.

## CHAPTER 2

2.1    *Trends in average wages and average hours.* Productivity data are from the BLS, and measure output per hour in the non-farm business sector. The wage level data are based on the authors' tabulations of March CPS files using a series on annual, weekly, and hourly wages for wage and salary workers (the sample definition in the CPS ORG wage analysis is used, see Appendix B). The weekly and hourly wage data are "hour weighted," obtained by dividing annual wages by weeks worked and annual hours worked. The 1967 and 1973 values are derived from unpublished tabulations provided by Kevin Murphy from an update of Murphy and Welch (1989). Their values include self-employment as well as wage and salary workers. The values displayed in this table were bridged from CPS 1979 values using the growth rates in the Murphy and Welch series. Hours of work were derived from differences between annual, weekly, and hourly wage trends.

2.2    *Growth of average hourly wages, benefits, and compensation.* These data are computed from the NIPA tables, which are available online. "Wages and salaries" are calculated by dividing wage and salary accruals (Table 6.3) by hours worked by full-time and part-time employees (Table 6.9). "Total compensation" is the sum of wages and salaries, and social insurance. Social insurance is total compensation minus the sum of volunteer benefits (sum of health and non-health benefits, Table 6.11) and wages and salaries. "Benefits" is the difference between total compensation and wages and salaries. These data were deflated using the NIPA personal consumption expenditure (PCE, chain-weighted) index, with health insurance adjusted by the PCE medical care (chained) index (Table 7.5).

2.3   *Growth in private-sector average hourly wages, benefits, and compensation.* Based on employment cost levels from the BLS employment cost index series (March data) for private industry workers. We categorize wages and salaries differently than BLS, putting all wage-related items (including paid leave and supplemental pay) into the hourly wage. Benefits, in our definition, include only payroll taxes, pensions, insurance, and "other" benefits. The sum of wages and salaries and benefits make total compensation. It is important to use the current-weighted series rather than the fixed-weighted series because composition shifts (in the distribution of employment across occupations and industries) have a large effect. Employer costs for insurance are deflated by the medical care component of the CPI-U-RS (unpublished series from Stephen Reed at BLS). All other pay is deflated by the CPI-U-RS for "all items." Inflation is measured for the first quarter of each year.

2.4   *Hourly and weekly earnings of private production and non-supervisory workers.* BLS Current Establishment Survey data. Available online. Deflated using CPI-U-RS.

2.5   *Changes in hourly wages by occupation.* Based on analysis of CPS wage data described in Appendix B.

2.6   *Wages for all workers by wage percentile.* Based on analysis of CPS wage data described in Appendix B.

2.7   *Wages for male workers by wage percentile.* Based on analysis of CPS wage data described in Appendix B.

2.8   *Wages for female workers by wage percentile.* Based on analysis of CPS wage data described in Appendix B.

2.9   *Distribution of total employment by wage level.* Based on analysis of CPS wage data described in Appendix B. The poverty-level wage is calculated using the preliminary estimate of the four-person weighted average poverty threshold in 2001 ($18,104) divided by 2,080 hours and deflated by CPI-U-RS to obtain levels for other years. The threshold is available at the Census web site. We calculated more intervals than we show but aggregated for simplicity of presentation (no trends were lost).

2.10  *Distribution of white employment by wage level.* See note to Table 2.9. These are non-Hispanic whites.

2.11  *Distribution of black employment by wage level.* See note to Table 2.9. These are non-Hispanic blacks.

2.12  *Distribution of Hispanic employment by wage level.* See note to Table 2.9. Hispanics may be of any race.

2.13    *Growth of specific fringe benefits.* Based on NIPA data described in note to Table 2.2 and ECI data described in note to Table 2.3.

2.14    *Change in private-sector employer-provided health insurance coverage.* Based on tabulations of March CPS data samples of private wage-and-salary earners ages 18-64 who worked at least 20 hours per week and 26 weeks per year. Coverage is defined as being included in an employer-provided plan where the employer paid for at least some of the coverage.

2.15    *Change in private-sector employer-provided pension coverage.* See note to Table 2.14.

2.16    *Dimensions of wage inequality.* All of the data are based on analyses of the ORG CPS data described in Appendix B. The measures of "total wage inequality" are natural logs of wage ratios (multiplied by 100) computed from Tables 2.7 and 2.8. The exception is that the 1979 data for women are 1978-80 averages. This was done to smooth the volatility of the series, especially at the 10th percentile. The "between group inequalities" are computed from regressions of the log of hourly wages on education categorical variables (high school omitted), experience as a quartic, marital status, race, and region (4). The college/high school and high school/less-than-high-school premiums are simply the coefficient on "college" and "less than high school." The experience differentials are the differences in the value of age (calculated from the coefficients of the quartic specification) evaluated at 25, 35, and 50 years. "Within-group wage inequality" is measured as the root mean square error from the same log wage regressions used to compute age and education differentials.

2.17    *Change in real hourly wage for all by education.* Based on tabulations of CPS wage data described in Appendix B. See Appendix B for details on how a consistent measure of education was developed to bridge the change in coding in 1992.

2.18    *Change in real hourly wage for men by education.* See note to Table 2.17.

2.19    *Change in real hourly wage for women by education.* See note to Table 2.17.

2.20    *Educational attainment of the workforce.* Based on analysis of CPS wage earners. The data are described in Appendix B. The categories are as follows: "less than high school" is grade 1-12 or no diploma; "high school/GED" is high school graduate diploma or equivalent; "some college" is some college but no degree; "associate college" is occupational or academic associate's degree; "college B.A." is a bachelor's degree; and "advanced degree" is a master's, professional, or doctorate degree.

2.21    *Hourly wages of entry-level and experienced workers by education.* Based on analysis of CPS wage data described in Appendix B.

2.22    *Hourly wages by decile within education groups.* Based on analysis of CPS wage data described in Appendix B.

2.23    *Decomposition of total and within-group wage inequality.* All of the data are from the ORG CPS data sample described in Appendix B. "Overall wage inequality" is measured as the standard deviation of log wages. "Within-group wage inequality" is the mean square error from log wage regressions (the same ones used for Table 2.16). "Between-group wage inequality" is the difference between the overall and within-group wage inequalities and reflects changes in all of the included variables: education, age, marital status, race, ethnicity, and region.

2.24  *Hourly wage growth among men by race/ethnicity.* Based on analysis of CPS wage data described in Appendix B.

2.25  *Hourly wage growth among women by race/ethnicity.* Based on analysis of CPS wage data described in Appendix B.

2.26  *Gender wage ratio.* Uses 50th percentile for Tables 2.7 and 2.8.

2.27  *Impact of rising and falling unemployment on wage levels and wage ratios.* The unemployment rate is from BLS. Wage data are based on analysis of quarterly CPS wage data (see Appendix B). The "simulated effect of change on unemployment" was calculated by regressing the log of nominal wages on lagged wages, unemployment, productivity growth, and seasonal dummies for each included percentile, by gender. Using these models, wages were predicted given a simulated unemployment rate series where in one case the unemployment rate maintained its 1979 level through the third quarter of 1987 (preventing its actual increase), and in the other case maintained its 1995 level through the fourth quarter of 2000 (preventing its actual decrease). "Unemployment contribution to change" shows the wage simulated by the model in the final quarter of the simulation period compared to the actual wage.

2.28  *Employment growth and compensation by sector.* Employment levels by industry are from the BLS Current Establishment Survey (CES). Hourly compensation values are from BLS employment cost levels data for March 2002, except "mining," which is deduced from the ECI data based on other categories and employment shares, and "federal government," which is derived based on ratios computed from NIPA compensation data.

2.29  *Employment growth by sector.* Based on data in Table 2.28.

2.30  *The effect of industry shifts on the growth of the college/high school wage differential.* The industry shift effect is calculated from estimated college/high school wage differentials using the model described in the note to Table 2.16, "industry composition actual," and a model that adds a set of industry controls (12), which gives "industry composition constant." The difference in the growth of these estimates is the industry shift effect.

2.31  *Net trade in U.S. manufactures by skill intensity and trading partner.* Cline (1997), Table 4.3, p. 188.

2.32  *Trade-deficit-induced job loss by wage and education level.* Scott et al. (1997), Tables 1 and 2.

2.33  *Effect of changes in prices of internationally traded manufactured goods on wage inequality.* Schmitt and Mishel (1996), Table 9.

2.34  *Legal immigrant flow to the United States.* The immigration figures are from the Immigration and Naturalization Services *Fiscal Year 2000 Statistical Yearbook*, Table 1. Population and foreign-born data were obtained from the Census web site.

2.35   *Educational attainment of immigrant and native men.* Borjas (1999), Table 2-1, p. 21.

2.36   *Union wage and benefit premium.* Employment cost index pay-level data in *Employer Costs for Employee Compensation,* March 2001, Table 13, for private industry. Regression-adjusted union effect from Pierce (1998), Tables 3, 4, and 5. Wages are defined differently in the top and bottom panels, as Pierce follows the BLS definitions while the upper panel defines wages to include paid leave and supplemental pay (as described in note to Table 2.3). Pierce's estimates are based on regressions on ECI microdata for 1994.

2.37   *Union wage premium by demographic group.* "Percent union" is tabulated from CPS ORG data (see Appendix B) and includes all those covered by unions. "Union premium" values are the coefficients on union in a model of log hourly wages with controls for education, experience as a quartic, marital status, region, industry (12) and occupation (9), and race/ethnicity and gender where appropriate.

2.38   *Union premiums for health, retirement, and paid leave.* Buchmueller, DiNardo, and Valletta (2001).

2.39   *Effect of deunionization on male wage differentials.* This analysis replicates, updates, and expands on Freeman (1991), Table 2. The analysis uses the CPS ORG sample used in other analyses (see Appendix B). The year 1978, rather than 1979, is the earliest year analyzed because we have no union membership data in our 1979 sample. The "union wage premium" for a group is based on the coefficient on collective bargaining coverage in a regression of hourly wages on a simple human capital model (the same one used for estimating education differentials, as described in note to Table 2.17), with major industry (12) and occupation (9) controls in a sample for that group. The change in union premium across years, therefore, holds industry and occupation composition constant. "Percent union" is the share covered by collective bargaining. Freeman's analysis assumed the union premium was unchanged over time. We allow the union premium to differ across years so changes in the union effect are driven by changes in the unionization rate and the union wage premium. The analysis compares the change in the union effect on relative wages to the actual change in relative wages (regression-adjusted with simple human capital controls plus controls for other education or occupation groups).

2.40   *Effect of unions on wages, by wage fifth.* From Card (1991), Table 8. The effect of deunionization is the change in union coverage times the union wage premium.

2.41   *Value of the minimum wage.* Historical values of minimum wage from Shapiro (1987), p. 19. Deflated using CPI-U-RS.

2.42   *Characteristics of minimum wage and other workers.* Bernstein and Schmitt (1998), Table 1.

2.43   *Impact of lower minimum wage on key wage differentials among women.* The impact of the change in the minimum wage since 1979 is based on comparing the actual changes from 1979 to simulated wage distributions in 1989 and 1997 where the real value of the minimum wage in 1979 is imposed on the data. This analysis is based on the CPS ORG data described in Appendix B. The simulated microdata are obtained by setting the hourly wages of those in the "sweep" (earning between the current minimum wage and the 1979 value) at the 1979 value (inflation-adjusted by CPI-U-RS) of the minimum wage. Those earning less than the legislated minimum wage were assigned a wage at the same proportionate distance to the 1979 level as they were to the existing minimum. In 1997, the existing minimum was based on a weighted average by month of the prevailing minimum of $4.75 for nine months and $5.15 for three months. The counterfactual returns to education were estimated on the simulated microdata with a simple human capital model and compared to the actual change (based on the same model) presented in Table 2.17. The other wage differentials are based on logged differentials computed from the actual and simulated microdata. The shares earning less than the 1979 minimum are computed directly from the data.

2.44    *Distribution of minimum wage gains and income shares by fifth for various household types.* Bernstein and Schmitt (1998), Table 2.

2.45    *Decomposition of growth of male college/non-college wage premium by occupation.* This decomposition starts from the fact that the college/non-college wage differential in any year is a weighted average of the college wage premium specific to each occupation (e.g., college-educated scientists relative to all non-college workers) and the weight of the occupation (its college employment) in total college employment. Changes in the college/non-college wage differential can therefore be decomposed into changes in occupational weights (e.g., the expansion of an occupation with a higher-than-average premium expands the differential) and changes in occupation premiums. This analysis is based on a regression of log hourly wages on a simple human capital model (see note to Table 2.17) with one education categorical variable— college graduate—interacted with a dummy variable for each occupation group. The sample is described in Appendix B of the last version of this book (the main difference being the definition of college graduates). For this analysis, those with more than a college degree are excluded. Estimates for 1979, 1989, and 1997 were used for the decomposition.

2.46    *Decomposition of growth of female college/non-college wage premium by occupation.* See methodology described in note to Table 2.45.

2.47    *Use of computers at work.* Card and DiNardo (2002).

2.48    *Executive annual pay.* The 1992-2001 data are from a *Wall Street Journal*/William M. Mercer survey (of 350 large companies) of CEO compensation. "Realized direct compensation" includes salary, bonus, gains from options exercised, value of restricted stock at grant, and other long-term incentive award payments. "Cash compensation" data, also from Mercer, go back to 1989. The average compensation for 1989 is backed out of the 1995 data by extrapolating the 1989-95 trend in the Pearl Meyer/*Wall Street Journal* data.

2.49    *CEO pay in advanced countries.* Total CEO compensation in dollars and the ratio of CEO to production-worker pay are from Towers Perrin (1988 and 2001).

**CHAPTER 3**

3.1    *Unemployment rates.* BLS (2002a), Table A-1.

3.2    *Change in monthly unemployment rates over recessions.* Monthly seasonally adjusted unemployment data are from BLS (2002a), Tables A-1 and A-2.

3.3    *Underemployment.* Quarterly non-seasonally adjusted civilian labor force and unemployed data from BLS (2002a), Table A-8. Discouraged workers are individuals not in the labor force who wanted a job, had searched for work in the previous year, or were available to work but were not actively searching for work because of "discouragement over job prospects." "Other marginally attached" individuals are in identical circumstances, but are not actively searching for work for reasons other than discouragement, including family responsibilities, school or training commitments, or ill health or disabilities. "Involuntary part-time" workers cite "economic reasons" for working fewer than 35 hours per week.

3.4    *Effect of a 1% higher unemployment rate on mean annual earnings, mean annual income, and share of total family income, by family income quintile.* Bartik (2002).

3.5    *Employment growth.* Total employees on non-farm payrolls taken from the BLS establishment survey as reported in BLS (2002b), Table B-1. Total civilian employment, civilian non-institutional population, and civilian labor force participation rate from the Current Population Survey of households as reported in BLS (2002a), Table A-1. Hours worked by full-time and part-time employees from NIPA (2002) Table 6.9B, and full-time equivalent employees from NIPA (2002) Table 6.5C.

3.6    *Employment rates.* Monthly seasonally adjusted data are from BLS (2002a), Table A-2.

3.7    *Change in monthly employment rate over recessions.* Monthly seasonally adjusted data are from BLS (2002a), Table A-2.

3.8    *Percent change in monthly employment by industry over recessions.* Monthly seasonally adjusted data are from BLS (2002b), Table B-1.

3.9    *Percent change in monthly employment by occupation over the business cycle.* Monthly seasonally adjusted data are from BLS (2002a), Table A-4.

3.10    *Hours worked, part time and overtime, by industry.* Golden and Jorgensen (2002), Table 1, p. 6.

3.11    *Multiple job holding.* Data from 1994 to 2001 are from BLS (2002a), Table A-10. All figures are for May of the given year. Previous years' data for number of multiple job holders and multiple job holding rate was provided by BLS staff. Data for the reasons for multiple job holding are from previous *State of Working America* analysis of the May Current Population Survey supplement data.

3.12    *Workers feeling overworked.* Galinsky, Kim, and Bond (2001), Table 2, p. 19.

3.13    *Worker participation in retirement and health care benefits by industry.* Health care and retirement benefits are from BLS (2001), Table 1, p. 4. Health care costs are from Table 6, p. 9. Change in employment and earnings are from BLS (2002b). Change in employment from Table B-1, and change in earnings from Table B-4.

3.14  *Percent of workers with access to leave and family-related benefits by industry.* BLS (2001), Table 3, p. 6.

3.15  *Fringe benefits for workers in medium and large private establishments.* Data for 1997 are from BLS (1997), Table 3, p. 8. Data from earlier years are from the same survey and were provided by BLS staff. All 1979 data are for 1979 or earliest year possible.

3.16  *Employed workers by work arrangement.* Data for 1997 though 2001 are from Wenger (2002). Data for 1995 are from Kalleberg et al. (1997), Table 1, p. 9.

3.17  *Characteristics of nonstandard workers.* Wenger (2002).

3.18  *Wages of nonstandard workers, compared to regular full-time workers, by sex and work arrangement.* Wenger (2002).

3.19  *Health and pension coverage by nonstandard work arrangement.* Wenger (2002).

3.20  *Common reasons for nonstandard employment.* Wenger (2002).

3.21  *Workers preferring standard employment by type of nonstandard work arrangement.* Data for 1995 are from Kallenberg et al. (1997), Table 36, p. 61. Data for 2001 are from Wenger (2002), Table 12.

3.22  *Non-agricultural employment by full-time and part-time status.* Data are BLS (2002b) web site, Table A-4. Note that the definition of part time used here differs from the earlier analysis of nonstandard work. Here, part-time workers include any of the work types in the earlier table, including temps and the self-employed who work part-time schedules. In the earlier tables a temp or self-employed worker who generally worked part time would have been classified as a temp or as self-employed regardless of hours. This explains the much smaller share of part-timers in Table 3.14.

3.23  *Employment in personnel services industry.* BLS (2002b).

3.24  *Self-employment.* Data for self-employed workers are from BLS (2002b), Table A-4. Self-employment data are divided by total payroll employment from BLS (2002b), Table B-1.

3.25  *Job stability of white men.* Bernhardt, Morris, Handcock, and Scott (2001).

3.26  *Median years of job tenure by age.* Data from 1963 to 1996 are from Aaronson and Sullivan (1998), Figure 2, p. 21. Numbers corresponding to figure provided by Daniel Aaronson and Ann Ferris. More recent data are from BLS (2002d), Table 1.

3.27  *Share of employed workers in long-term jobs.* Farber (1997b), Table 1, p. 29.

3.28  *Labor market transitions.* Stewart (2002), Figures 1, 2, and 3, p. 31.

3.29  *Employment retention over the 1990s.* Boushey (2002).

3.30  *Rate of job loss by reason.* Farber (1998), Appendix Table 3, p. 12.

3.31 *The costs of job loss.* Percent out of work from Farber (1997a), Table 6, p. 49, last row; post-displacement change in earnings from Farber (1997a), Table 10, p. 55; post-displacement change in earnings compared to continuously employed from Farber (1997a), Table 14, p. 62; health insurance coverage from Gardner (1996), Table 6, p. 53.

3.32 *Perceptions of job security.* Aaronson and Sullivan (1998) analysis of 1997 General Social Survey data, Figure 6, p. 30. Numbers corresponding to figure provided by Daniel Aaronson and Ann Ferris.

## CHAPTER 4

4.1 *Distribution of income and wealth.* Unpublished analysis of Survey of Consumer Finances (SCF) data prepared in May 2000 by Edward Wolff for the Economic Policy Institute.

4.2 *Growth of household wealth.* Net worth and asset data are from the Federal Reserve Bank (2001a), Table Б.100, p. 94. Nonprofit organizations, a small component judging from the breakout on tangible assets, were included because the Federal Reserve does not give breakouts for financial assets. Data were converted to real dollars using the CPI-RS. The number of households is based on Census Bureau (2000b), Table HH-1. We used the number of families in 1950 for the number of families in 1949.

4.3 *Share of aggregate net worth by income quintile.* Data are from Maki and Palumbo (2001), Appendix B. Maki and Palumbo construct a database using household data in the SCF and aggregate data from the Flow of Funds Accounts so that they can estimate wealth after 1998, the most recent year available from the SCF data.

4.4 *Changes in the distribution of household wealth.* See note to Table 4.1.

4.5 *Change in average wealth by wealth class.* See note to Table 4.1.

4.6 *Wealth by race.* See note to Table 4.1.

4.7 *Households with low net wealth.* See note to Table 4.1.

4.8 *Distribution of asset ownership across households.* Poterba (2000), Table 2.

4.9 *Share of households owning stock.* See note to Table 4.1.

4.10 *Household assets and liabilities by wealth class.* See note to Table 4.1.

4.11 *Concentration of stock ownership by income level.* See note to Table 4.1.

4.12 *Home ownership rates, by race and income.* Authors' analysis of published Bureau of Census (1973-2001) data from the American Housing Survey. Home ownership by race and for all Americans for 1999 and 2001 is taken from Housing Vacancy Survey (2001), Table 20. Other years' data are taken from the American Housing Survey. Average home ownership rates by income quintile estimated using ownership rates and population shares by discrete income categories. These data are taken from American Housing Survey (1999), Table 3-12.

4.13    *Retirement income adequacy.* Wolff (2002), Table 20.

4.14    *Household debt, by type.* Debt data taken from Federal Reserve Board (2001a), Table B.100 and Table L.218 and compared to personal income data from Economagic (2002). These data were converted to 2001 dollars using CPI-RS.

4.15    *Household debt service burden.* Quarterly data from Federal Reserve Board (2001b) converted to annual data by taking annual averages.

4.16    *Household debt service as a share of income, by income level.* Kennickell, Starr-McCluer, and Surette (2000), Table 14, pp. 24-5.

4.17    *Households with high debt burdens, by income level.* See note to Table 4.16.

4.18    *Households late paying bills, by income level.* See note to Table 4.16.

4.19    *Debt burdens among bachelor's degree graduates who took out student loans.* Choy and Carroll (2000), Tables 9 and 16. Dollar values are 2000-01, adjusted using the CPI-RS for the school year (September through May).

## CHAPTER 5

5.1     *Percent and number of persons in poverty.* Census homepage, Historical Poverty Tables, Persons, Table 2.

5.2     *Persons in poverty, by race/ethnicity.* See note to Table 5.1.

5.3     *Percent of children in poverty, by race.* Census homepage, Historical Poverty Tables, Persons, Table 3. Data on children under 6 from FERRET Poverty Table 1 for 2001 and from P-60 poverty publications for earlier years.

5.4     *Family poverty, by race/ethnicity of family head and for different family types.* Census homepage, Historical Poverty Tables, Persons, Table 4.

5.5     *Poverty rates and distribution of the poor, official and alternative measures.* U.S. Bureau of the Census, P60-216, Tables 4.1 and 4.2. Of the numerous alternative measures developed by the Census Bureau, we choose to use measure DCM1/U. The main difference between this and some other measures is the method used to value child care expenditures. This method assigns 85% of the median annual child care expenditures to working families with children under 12. The child care costs are based on data from the 1993 SIPP, updated by the CPI for child care and nursery school.

5.6     *Average poverty gap.* Center on Budget and Policy Priorities (1998), updated with U.S. Bureau of the Census, March CPS, FERRET Table 20.

5.7     *Changes in poverty rates and various indicators.* "Poverty rates": see note to Table 5.1; "productivity": BLS, measures of output per hour in the non-farm business sector; "per capita income": NIPA Table 2.1; "unemployment": BLS, monthly CPS; "Gini coefficient": U.S. Bureau of the Census, Historical Income Tables, Families, Table F-4, see note to Figure 1G; "mother-only families as a share of all families": see note to Table 5.8.

5.8    *Changing family structure and poverty.* U.S. Bureau of the Census, P60-214, Appendix Table A-1.

5.9    *Poverty rates for families with children, by educational level of family head.* Authors' analysis of March CPS data.

5.10   *Impact of demographic and economic changes on poverty rates.* See Appendix A.

5.11   *Poverty-reducing effects of transfers.* U.S. Bureau of the Census, P-60, No. 182-RD, and the FERRET, Experimental Measures of Income and Poverty, Table 2.

5.12   *Income levels and sources of income, prime-age families (family head 25-54) in the bottom 20th percentile.* Authors' analysis of March CPS data.

5.13   *Family work hours and wages among poor families.* Based on analysis of March CPS data. Work hours are pooled across families, and include family members with zero hours. The wage calculation is made only for families with positive values on both variables.

5.14   *Characteristics of low-wage workers.* Authors' analysis of CPS ORG data; see Appendix B.


## CHAPTER 6

6.1    *Median family income by region.* Census homepage, Historical Income Tables, Families, Table F-6.

6.2    *Median income, four-person families, by state.* Census homepage, Income, four-person median family income.

6.3    *Income inequality by state: average income of top 20% relative to bottom 20%.* From Bernstein et al. (2002). See Appendix A for discussion of methods.

6.4A   *Non-farm payroll employment by state.* BLS, available online (see Current Employment Statistics survey).

6.4B   *Non-farm payroll employment by state, division, and region.* See note to Table 6.4A.

6.5    *Industrial compositions shifts in four states.* Unpublished tabulations provided by Robert Zahradnik of the Center on Budget and Policy Priorities, using BLS establishment data for the employment data and ES-202 for average weekly pay.

6.6    *Unemployment rates by state, division and region.* BLS homepage, detailed statistics, local area unemployment statistics.

6.7    *Low wages (20th percentile) by state.* Based on analysis of CPS wage data as described in Appendix B.

6.8    *Median wages (50th percentile) by state.* See note to Table 6.7.

6.9    *Un- and underemployment among African Americans and Hispanics, age 16-25, by gender and education level.* Authors' analysis of basic CPS data.

6.10   *Share of workers earning poverty-level wages, by state.* Based on analysis of CPS
       wage data as described in Appendix B. The percentage of workers who earned less
       than or equal to the hourly wage needed to reach the poverty threshold if working
       full-time over the course of a year (2,080 hours). The poverty threshold for a family
       of four ($18,104 in 2001) is a preliminary weighted average and is available online
       (see Census Homepage, Poverty, Poverty Thresholds).

6.11   *Poverty rates for persons by region.* Census homepage, Historical Poverty Tables,
       Persons, Table 9.

6.12   *Poverty by state, two-year averages.* Census homepage, Historical Poverty Tables,
       Persons, Table 21. Two-year averages are used to reduce statistical error induced by
       the small samples in some states.

6.13   *Poverty rates, official and adjusted for state price differences.* See note to Table 6.1
       for "official" rate. "Adjusted" rate is based on experimental state deflators provided
       by Kathleen Short of the U.S. Bureau of the Census.


**CHAPTER 7**

7.1    *Per capita income, using market exchange rates.* GDP per capita for 1960 is from
       OECD (1999a), Table 20, p. 146, converted to 2000 dollars (from 1990 dollars in
       original) using the CPI-U-X1 from *ERP* (2002), Table B-60, p. 376. GDP per capita
       for the other years is taken from OECD (2001a), Table A9, p. 322, converted to 2000
       dollars (from 1995 dollars in original). Average excluding the United States is
       weighted using national populations for 1999 from OECD (2001b), *OECD in Figures,*
       Table 1, page 6.

7.2    *Per capita income, using purchasing-power-parity exchange rates.* GDP per capita
       for all years is taken from OECD (2001a), *National Accounts: Main Aggregates,
       Volume 1,* Table B7, p. 338, converted to 2000 dollars (from 1995 dollars in original)
       using CPI-U-X1 from *ERP* (2002).

7.3    *Income and productivity levels in the OECD.* GDP data taken from University of
       Groningen (2002), GDP per Capita table, and indexed relative to U.S. data for the
       same year.

7.4    *Labor productivity growth per year in the OECD.* The data in the first two columns
       are taken from OECD (1998), Annex Table 59, p. 284, and begin in 1960 or earliest
       available year (see note in Table 7.4). Data from 1985 to 2000 were taken from
       OECD (2001d), Annex Table 13, p. 217. Data for 1979 to 1985 were calculated from
       the Source OECD (2002) Economic Outlook Database, and the table Labour
       Productivity in the Business Sector. Population (1999) weighted average.

7.5    *Real compensation growth per year in the OECD.* Nominal compensation per
       employee in the business sector for years 1985 to 2000 is from OECD (2001d),
       Annex Table 12, p. 216. Data for 1979 to 1985 are from OECD (1999), Annex Table
       12, p. 206. The data were deflated by changes in consumer prices from OECD (2001d),
       Annex Table 16, p. 220. Population (1999) weighted average.

7.6 *Relative hourly compensation of manufacturing production workers, using market exchange rates.* Index of hourly compensation costs for production workers in manufacturing from BLS (2001a), Table 1. Population (1999) weighted average.

7.7 *Relative hourly compensation of manufacturing production workers, using purchasing power parities.* Hourly compensation costs in national currency for production workers in manufacturing from BLS (2001b), Table 3, converted to U.S. dollars using purchasing power parities for GDP from OECD (2001f). Population (1999) weighted average.

7.8 *Annual growth in real hourly compensation in manufacturing in the OECD.* Compensation for all workers in manufacturing is hourly compensation in manufacturing, on a national currency basis, from BLS (2000a), Table 7; The hourly compensation in manufacturing data refer to employees (wage and salary earners) in Belgium, Denmark, Italy, and the Netherlands, and to all employed persons (employees and self-employed workers) in the other countries. Compensation for production workers is hourly compensation costs in national currency for production workers in manufacturing from BLS (2001c), Table 4. Data for 1979 and 1989 are from BLS (2000c), and data for 1995 and 2000 are taken from BLS (2001c). Both are deflated using consumer price indexes derived from OECD (2001d), Table 16, p. 220. Population (1999) weighted average.

7.9 *Earnings inequality in OECD countries.* Data for the last three columns are taken from Glyn (2001), Table 1, p. 4. Real wage deciles are calculated for the last year available, which is the last number in the "years" column. These data are calculated from the unpublished OECD Wage Dispersion Database.

7.10 *Household income inequality in the OECD.* Data for the Gini coefficients are taken from the Luxembourg Income Study Website (2001a). Data for the percentile ratios are taken from Smeeding and Rainwater (2001), Figure 1. Population (1999) weighted average.

7.11 *Household income inequality, relative to U.S. median income.* Data are from Smeeding and Rainwater (2001), Figure 2. Household income at the 10th and 90th percentiles in each country is compared to median income.

7.12 *Change in income inequality in the OECD after 1979.* Data are from the Luxembourg Income Study Website (2001a). Calculations were made by dividing and subtracting the earliest year (after or during 1979) by the year closest to the present.

7.13 *Poverty rates in OECD countries.* Data for poverty for the total population, children, and the elderly are from the Luxembourg Income Study website (2000b). The rest of the data are from OECD (2001e), Table 2.1, p. 45. The OECD data are taken over a three-year period, whereas the data from the LIS (2000b) are for one year only.

7.14 *Frequency of family and job-related events associated with poverty transitions in the OECD.* Data are from OECD (2001e), Table 2.2, p. 50; Table 2.4, p. 56; and Table 2.6, p. 58.

7.15 *Maternity and child care policies in the OECD.* Data for proportion of young children using formal child care arrangements and maternity/child care leave indicators are from OECD (2001e), Table 4.7, p. 144. Data for percentage of children in publicly supported care and share of child care costs covered by government are taken from Waldfogel 2001, Table 2, p. 105.

7.16 *Employment rates in OECD countries.* BLS (2001d), Table 5. pp. 22-3.

7.17 *Average annual hours worked in the OECD.* OECD (2001e), Table F, p. 225. Population (1999) weighted average. Hours are calculated as the total number of hours worked over the year divided by the average numbers of people employed. The data are intended for comparisons of trends over time. Data for Japan include only establishments with five or more regular employees.

7.18 *Impact of productivity, employment, and hours differences on relative per capita income.* Van Ark and McGuckin (1999), Table 1, pp. 33-41. The data in Table 7.19 differ from those in Tables 7.17 and 7.18 and are therefore not directly comparable. In Table 7.19, for example, Japanese employment rates and hours worked appear to be higher than in the United States. Despite some minor inconsistencies, we believe that the exercise in Table 7.19 provides a helpful illustration of the impact of international differences in employment rates and hours worked.

7.19 *Employment in OECD countries.* All data are taken from OECD (2001h), Civilian Employment table, p. 20. Population (1999) weighted average.

7.20 *Unemployment rates in the OECD.* Data for 1979 and 1989 are from OECD (2001e), Table A, pp. 208. Data for 2001 are from OECD (2001h), Basic Structural Statistics table, p. 268. Population (1999) weighted average.

7.21 *Unemployment rates in the OECD by education level.* OECD describes educational categories as: "less than upper secondary," "upper secondary," and "tertiary." OECD (2001e), Table D, pp. 222-223. Population (1999) weighted average.

# Figure notes

## INTRODUCTION

A    *Effects of higher unemployment on size of civilian labor force.* See note to Figure 3D

B    *Payroll employment growth during three recent recessions, from unemployment's low point.* Payroll employment data are from the BLS web site, http://stats.bls.gov/webapps/legacy/cesbtab1.htm.

C    *Growth in nominal average hourly earnings, by quarter.* Hourly wage growth among production, non-supervisory workers are from BLS, http://stats.bls.gov/webapps/legacy/cesbtab3.htm.

D    *Growth in nominal earnings (first half to first half).* Nominal weekly earnings of full-time workers are derived from various issue of the BLS publication, "Usual Weekly Earnings of Wage and Salary Workers," found at http://stats.bls.gov/news.release/wkyeng.toc.htm. Note that these data are for workers 25 and above.

## CHAPTER 1

1A    *Real median family income.* See note to Table 1.1.

1B    *Median family income over the 1980s and 1990s.* See note to Table 1.1

1C    *Average number of persons per family.* Census homepage, Historical Time Series, Households, Table HH-6.

1D    *Ratio of black and Hispanic to white median family income.* See note to Table 1.4.

1E    *Median family income by age of household head.* See note to Table 1.5.

1F    *Low-, middle-, and high-income growth.* See note to Table 1.9.

1G    *Family income inequality, Gini coefficient.* Census homepage, Historical Income Tables, Families, Table F-4. The steep jump in the figure in 1993 is in part due to the lifting of the Census top-codes. In order to discount this change, we ran a time series regression with a dummy variable for the 1993-2000 period. The regression uses the state-space model approach, described in Koopman et al. 2000. STAMP software was used to run the structural model, with a fixed-level, stochastic slope and AR(1) terms to model the unobserved trend and cycle components.

1H    *Ratio of family income of top 5% to lowest 20%.* Census homepage, Historical Income Tables, Families, Table F-3.

1I    *Family income growth by quintile.* See note to Figure 1H.

1J    *Effective federal tax rate for family of four.* Department of the Treasury (1998), Table 4.

1K    *Average real adjusted gross income, top 1% to bottom 50%.* Authors' compilation of IRS data provided by the Center on Budget and Policy Priorities.

1L    *Income and consumption inequality, Gini coefficients indexed to 1981.* Johnson (2001). Consumption in the figure is measured as "consumption expenditures," the money spent by families on current consumption. This measure differs from economic consumption because it does not reflect the flow of services created by the consumption of durable goods.

1M    *Percent staying in same fifth in each pair of years.* Gottschalk and Danziger (1998).

1N    *Impact of demographic change on household income, by fifth.* See note to Table 1.20.

1O    *Income shares in the corporate sector.* See note to Table 1.24.

1P    *Pre- and post-tax return to capital.* See note Table 1.25

1Q    *Changes in unemployment and income during recent recessions and recoveries.* Income data from same source as Table 1.9; unemployment data from BLS website.

1R    *Impact on family income of a 1% decline in unemployment, by year of recovery.* Hines et al. (2001), Table 10.5.

1S    *Contribution of wives' earnings to family income.* Hayge (1993) and unpublished updates provided by Hayge.


## CHAPTER 2

2A    *Hourly wage and compensation growth for production/non-supervisory workers.* See note to Table 2.4. Hourly compensation was estimated based on multiplying hourly wages by the ratio of compensation to wages for all workers in each year. The compensation/wage ratio is drawn from the NIPA data used in Table 2.2. The compensation/wage ratio for 2001 was an estimate based on the previous year.

2B    *Changes in real hourly wages for men by wage percentile.* See note to Table 2.7.

2C    *Changes in real hourly wages for women by wage percentile.* See note to Table 2.8.

2D    *Share of workers earning poverty-level wages, by gender.* See note to Table 2.9

2E    *Share of workers earning poverty-level wages, by race/ethnicity.* See note to Table 2.9

2F    *Private-sector employer-provided health insurance coverage.* See note to Table 2.14.

2G    *Share of pension participants in defined-contribution and defined-benefit plans.* U.S. Department of Labor (2001-02), Table E4b.

2H    *Men's wage inequality.* Based on ratios of wages by decile in annual data presented in Table 2.7.

2I    *Women's wage inequality.* Based on ratios of wages by decile in annual data presented in Table 2.8.

2J    *95/50 percentile wage ratio.* Based on ratios of wages by decile in annual data presented in Tables 2.6, 2.7, and 2.8.

2K    *College/high school wage premium.* Differentials estimated with controls for experience (as a quartic), region (4), marital status, race/ethnicity, and education, which is specified as dummy variables for less than high school, some college, college, and advanced degree. Estimates were made on the CPS ORG data as described in Appendix B, and presented in Table 2.16.

2L    *Productivity and hourly compensation growth.* Average hourly productivity and compensation are for the non-farm business sector and available from the BLS web site (see major sector productivity and cost index). The compensation series is deflated by the CPI-U-RS. The median compensation of female, male, and all workers is derived by multiplying the compensation/wage ratio (based on the NIPA data discussed in the note to Table 2.2) by the real median wage series for each in Tables 2.6, 2.7, and 2.8.

2M    *Entry-level wages of male and female high school graduates.* See note to Table 2.21.

2N    *Entry-level wages of male and female college graduates.* See note to Table 2.21.

2O    *Gender wage ratio by percentile.* The gender wage ratio is calculated by dividing the female wage by the male wage at the respective wage level. See note to Tables 2.6, 2.7, and 2.8 for wage derivations.

2P    *Unemployment.* The unemployment rate is available at the BLS website (see Current Population Survey).

2Q    *Outsourcing.* Feenstra and Hanson (2001).

2R    *Union membership in the United States.* Hirsch and Macpherson (1997) and BLS (Employment and Earnings).

2S    *Real value of the minimum wage.* Series compiled by authors and deflated using CPI-U-RS.

2T    *Ratio of CEO to average worker pay.* Calculated by dividing the CEO average annual pay (see note to Table 2.48) by production non-supervisory workers' average annual pay (hourly average multiplied by 2,080 multiplied by the compensation/wage ratio discussed in note to Table 2.2). The production non-supervisory worker's average hourly pay is available online from the BLS (see Current Establishment Survey).

## CHAPTER 3

3A    *Unemployment rate and its trend.* Authors' calculation for trend of annual unemployment data (using Hodrick–Prescott filter) from BLS (2002a), Table A-1.

3B  *Percentage-point change in unemployment during recession, by educational status.* BLS (2002a), Table A-3.

3C  *Share of unemployed men and women who have been unemployed more than 26 weeks.* BLS (2002a), Table A-6.

3D  *Effects of higher unemployment on size of civilian labor force.* We forecast the seasonally adjusted BLS (2002a) quarterly civilian labor force data using a structural model as described in Koopmen et al. (2000), including an AR(1) term. The model ran through the first quarter of 2000, and we forecast through the first quarter of 2002.

3E  *Family income gained by quintile due to lower unemployment (falling to 4.0% rather than remaining at 5.6%) between 1995 and 2000.* Bartik (2002).

3F  *Labor force participation rates by gender.* BLS (2002a), Table A-2.

3G  *Labor force participation rates for women by race/ethnicity.* See note to Figure 3F.

3H  *Labor force participation rates for men by race/ethnicity.* See note to Figure 3F.

3I  *Employment losses by industry in three most recent recessions.* Monthly seasonally adjusted data are from BLS (2002b), Table B-1.

3J  *Employment change over 2000-02 recession.* Monthly seasonally adjusted data are from BLS (2002b), Table B-1.

3K  *Employment change over 1990-92 recession.* See note to Figure 3J..

3L  *Peak overtime hours and change in employment level in manufacturing across recent economic expansions.* Hetrick (2000), Table 2, p. 30-3.

3M  *Employer-provided health insurance and monthly employee contribution for workers in medium and large establishments.* BLS (1997) data and unpublished BLS data. For family coverage, the 1979 data are from 1980. The average amount paid is CPI-RS for medical care, 2001-adjusted dollars.

3N  *Responsibility for determining own hours of work, by family type.* McCrate (2002), Figure F, p. 8.

3O  *Employment in temporary help industry as percent of total employment.* Data on temporary help industry employment (SIC code 7363) and total employment are from the BLS (2002b) web site.

3P  *Job leavers as share of unemployed.* Data on job leavers and total unemployed are from BLS web site (2002a), Table A-7. Following Polivka and Miller (1995), figures for 1994-2001 have been divided by 0.866 to make them comparable to earlier years.

# CHAPTER 4

4A    *Net worth of "Forbes 400" wealthiest individuals.* Broom and Shay (2000), Table 2, p. 15.

4B    *Growth of U.S. stock market.* Standard & Poor's composite index from *ERP* (2002), Table B-95, p. 430, deflated by the CPI-U-RS.

4C    *Distribution of growth in stock market holdings, by wealth class.* See note to Table 4.8.

4D    *Average homeownership rates.* Yearly average of data published by the Current Population Survey/Housing Vacancy Survey (2001), Historical Tables, Table 14, Homeownership Rates for the U.S. and Regions.

4E    *Average rate of home ownership, by income quartile.* See note to Table 4.10.

4F    *Change in mean retirement wealth by wealth class, age 47 and over.* Wolff (2002), Table 9, p. 26.

4G    *Debt as a percentage of disposable personal income.* See note to Table 4.12.

4H    *Distribution of growth in debt.* See note to Table 4.8.

4I    *Consumer bankruptcies per 1,000 adults.* Data on consumer bankruptcies from the American Bankruptcy Institute web page (2002), U.S. Bankruptcy Filings table. Data on adult population from *ERP* (2002), Table B-34, p. 361.

4J    *Annual growth rates in average tuition and fee charges.* Average tuition and fees data by institution type (public and private two- and four-year institutions) are from the College Board (2001a), Table 5, p. 8. Student enrollment data from 1985 are used for the years 1988, 1987, and 1986, when such data were not available. Similarly, student enrollment data from 1979 were used for 1980.

4K    *Annual growth rates in the share of family income required to pay for tuition at the average college.* Average tuition is a student-weighted average, constructed by weighting tuition data by the number of students in each institution type. These data are from the Census (2000a), Table A7. Average tuition (public and private two- and four-year institutions) is then divided by average family income by quintile. Charts by institution type were taken from the National Center for Public Policy and Higher Education (2002), Figures 1 and 2, p. 5. Family income data were taken from the Census (2002), Table F-3, and divided by the average tuition to calculate the share of family income required for tuition.

4L    *Financial aid awarded to postsecondary students (per student).* Aid for each source of aid was taken from the College Board (2001b), Table 2, p. 7, and based on Figure 1 on the cover page. This aid was divided by total number of students, taken from Census (2000a) data (see notes on missing data from Figure 4J). Unsubsidized loans include unsubsidized loans from both the Ford Direct Loans and Family Federal Loans, and loans from SLS and PLUS. Subsidized loans include subsidized loans from both the Ford Direct Loans and Family Federal Loans. Other aid includes Federal Campus Based, Other Federal Programs, State Grant Programs, Pell Grants, Nonfederal Loans, and Institutional and Other Grants.

4M    *Cumulative amount borrowed by seniors who ever received student loans.* Dollar values are 1999-2000-adjusted using the CPI-RS for the school year (September through May). Data are from the National Center for Education Statistics (2000) website, update to the supplemental tables, Table 2.9.

## CHAPTER 5

5A    *Poverty rate.* See note to Table 5.1.

5B    *Poverty rate over 1980s and 1990s business cycles.* See note to Table 5.1.

5C    *Poverty rates by race/ethnicity.* See note to Table 5.2.

5D    *Official vs. alternative poverty measures.* See note to Table 5.5.

5E    *Poverty rates by price index.* For CPI-U-based poverty rate, see note to Table 5.1. The CPI-U-X1-based poverty rate is available at the Census homepage, Historical Poverty Tables, Poverty by Definition of Income, RDP-3. The CPI-RS measure was calculated by authors using March CPS data.

5F    *Various measures of poverty.* Poverty, one-half poverty, and twice poverty, see note to Table 5.1; one-half median income from unpublished tabulations provided by Charles Nelson of the Census Bureau.

5G    *Percent of poor below half the poverty line.* See note to 5F.

5H    *Family poverty gap and poverty rates.* See notes to Tables 5.4 and 5.6.

5I    *Unemployment and poverty in the 1980s and 1990s.* See notes to Table 5.1 and 5.7. In order to control for the volatility of the data, two-year averages were used (1978-79, 1988-89, and 1999-2000) to calculate the change over the 1980s and 1990s.

5J    *Contribution of demographic and economic changes to poverty.* See note to Table 5.10.

5K    *Employment rates for mothers.* Brookings Institution (2002).

5L    *Income components of low-income single mothers.* Authors' analysis of March CPS. All values except EITC derived from March CPS data; EITC value is based on actual earnings but takes benefits from EITC schedule assuming more than one child.

5M    *Income by components, low-income single mothers.* See note to Figure 5L.

5N    *Share of poor families with no work, by race/ethnicity.* See note to Table 5.13.

5O    *Share of prime-age workers with full-time/year-round attachment and low earnings.* Data for 1974-89 from P60-178, Table 3. Later data provided by Charles Nelson, U.S. Bureau of the Census.

5P    *Share of workers with full-time/year-round attachment and low earnings, by family type.* See note to Figure 5O.

5Q    *Real hourly wages of low-wage workers.* Wages are based on analysis of CPS wage data as described in Appendix B. The poverty-level wage is the wage that, at full-time, full-year work, would lift a family of four above the poverty line. This equals $8.70 in 2001 dollars.

## CHAPTER 6

6A    *Nominal and price-adjusted median household income relative to U.S. by division.* Census homepage, Historical Income Tables, Households, Table H-7. The price-adjusted series was deflated using a regional deflator based on housing costs and derived as follows. We used state median values of rented or owner-occupied housing from the American Community Survey (ACS, published data), along with the shares of persons who rent or own by state. Using these values we derived a population-weighted value of median annual housing expenditures (with the weights being the relative shares of renters and owners). This value for each state was divided by the national value. This value represents the state median housing cost relative to the national median.

   This value needs to be further adjusted for the share of consumption spent on housing. To do so, we took the average consumption share on both rental and owner-occupied housing (a national value taken from published Consumer Expenditure Survey data), again weighted by the relevant state shares. Multiplying the rental index value discussed above by this weighted consumption share provides an index number of the housing consumption by state, relative to the nation. Finally, we added this value to one minus this value (representing relative consumption on other items) to derive a state deflator. These deflators are weighted up to the divisional level using state population as a share of divisional population.

   An example should help to clarify. For Alabama, the median owner-occupied house was worth $85,349 in 2000 according the ACS; rental housing was $447/month. The national values were $120,162 and $612, respectively. Using the relevant population shares, the housing cost value for Alabama was $65,655, while the national value was $84,832. Thus, Alabama housing relative to the U.S. was 0.774. According to the CES, middle-income families (nationally) spent 15% of their expenditures on owner-occupied housing and 24.5% on rental housing. Weighting these by the relevant population share for Alabama yields 0.173. The price index for Alabama, then, is (.774*.173)+(1-.173)=0.961.

6B    *Median family income growth by region.* See note to Table 6.1.

6C    *The relationship between changes in 20th percentile wages and unemployment.* See note to Table 6.7 and 6.6 for 20th percentile wages and unemployment, respectively. Wages and unemployment changes are calculated as annual percentage changes and percentage-point changes, respectively. The trend lines are calculated by regressing the change in poverty on the change in unemployment.

6D    *Change in poverty-level wage shares by division.* See note to Table 6.10.

6E    *Poverty rates by region.* See note to Table 6.11.

**CHAPTER 7**

7A   *Productivity growth rates.* See note to Table 7.4.

7B   *Gender wage gaps in the OECD.* Data are from OECD (2001g), *Society at a Glance 2001,* Annex Table B4. Note that the data for the chart appear only in the web version, not in the book itself.

7C   *Relative income comparisons in the OECD.* Data are from Smeeding and Rainwater (2001), Figure 1.

7D   *Real standards of living in the OECD.* See note to Table 7.12.

7E   *Social expenditures vs. child poverty in the OECD.* Data on child poverty are from the Luxembourg Income Study website (2000b) and are taken for the latest year possible (see Table 7.13 for details). Data for social expenditures are calculated from OECD (2001g) Annex Table B6. Note that, like Figure 7D, the data for the chart appear only in the web version, not in the book itself. The data are from 1997, and are calculated by adding the income support to the working population column to the other social services column. Graph inspired by Brookings Institution (2002).

# Bibliography

Aaronson, Daniel, and Daniel G. Sullivan. 1998. The Decline of Job Security in the 1990s: Displacement, Anxiety, and Their Effect on Wage Growth. *Economic Perspectives*, First Quarter, pp. 17-43.

American Bankruptcy Institute. 2002. *U.S. Bankruptcy Filings 1980-2001*. Alexandria, Va.: American Bankruptcy Institute. <http://www.abiworld.org>

Bajika, Jon, and C. Eugene Steuerle. 1991. Individual Income Taxation Since 1948. *National Tax Journal*, 44(4): 451-75.

Baker, Dean. 1996. "Trends in Corporate Profitability: Getting More for Less?" Technical Paper. Washington, D.C.: Economic Policy Institute.

Bartik, Timothy J. 2002. <http://www.upjohninst.org>

Bernhardt, Annette, Martina Morris, Mark S. Hancock, and Marc A. Scott. 1998. "Trends in Job Instability and Wages for Young Adult Men." Institute on Education and the Economy, Working Paper No. 8. Columbia University.

Bernhardt, Annette, Martina Morris, Mark S. Handcock, and Marc A. Scott. 2001. *Divergent Paths: Economic Mobility in the New American Labor Market*. New York: Russell Sage Foundation.

Bernstein, Jared, Elizabeth McNichol, Heather Boushey, and Robert Zahradnick. 2002. *Pulling Apart: A State-by-State Analysis of Income Trends*. Washington, D.C.: Center on Budget and Policy Priorities and Economic Policy Institute.

Bernstein, Jared, and John Schmitt. 1998. "Making Work Pay: The Impact of the 1996-97 Minimum Wage Increase." Washington, D.C.: Economic Policy Institute.

Borjas, George J. 1999. *Heaven's Door*. Princeton, NJ: Princeton University Press.

Boushey, Heather. 2002. "Employment Duration and Wage Growth Over the 1990s Boom." Washington, D.C.: Economic Policy Institute.

Brookings Institution. 2002. *Welfare Reform & Beyond*. Washington, D.C.: Brookings Institution. <http://www.brookings.edu/dybdocroot/wrb/resources/facts/pres_200202.htm>

Broom, Leonard, and William Shay. 2000. "Discontinuites in the Distribution of Great Wealth: Sectoral Forces Old and New." Paper prepared for the Conference on "Saving, Intergenerational Transfers, and the Distribution of Wealth" at the Jerome Levy Economics Institute, Bard College, June 7-9, 2000.

Card, David. 1991. "The Effect of Unions on the Distribution of Wages: Redistribution or Relabelling?" Working Paper No. 287. Princeton, N.J.: Department of Economics, Princeton University.

Center on Budget and Policy Priorities. 1998. *Poverty Tables*. Washington, D.C.: CBPP.

Choy, Susan P., and C. Dennis Carroll. 2000. *Debt Burden Four Years After College*. Washington, D.C.: U.S. Department of Education, Office of Educational Research and Improvement, National Center for Education Statistics.

Cline, William R. 1997. *Trade and Income Distribution*. Washington, D.C.: Institute for International Economics.

College Board. 2001a. *Trends in College Pricing*. New York, N.Y.: College Board. <http://www.collegeboard.com/press/cost01/html/TrendsCP01.pdf>

College Board. 2001b. *Trends in Student Aid*. New York, N.Y.: College Board. <http://www.collegeboard.com/press/cost01/html/TrendsSA01.pdf>

Conference Board. 1997. "Perspectives on a Global Economy: Understanding Differences in Economic Performance." Report Number 1187-97-RR. New York: Conference Board.

Conference Board. 1999. "Perspectives on a Global Economy: The Euro's Impact on European Labor Markets." Report Number 1236-99-RR. New York: Conference Board.

Congressional Budget Office. 1998. *Estimates of Federal Tax Liabilities for Individuals and Families by Income Category and Family Type for 1995 and 1999*. Washington, D.C.: Congressional Budget Office.

Congressional Budget Office. 2001. *Effective Federal Tax Rates, 1979-1997*. Washington, D.C.: Congressional Budget Office. <http://www.cbo.gov/showdoc.cfm?index=3089& sequence=0>

Danziger, Sheldon, and Peter Gottschalk. 1995. *America Unequal*. New York, N.Y.: Harvard/Russell Sage Foundation.

Duncan, Greg, et al. 1991. "Poverty and Social Assistance Dynamics in the United States, Canada and Europe." Paper presented at the Joint Center for Political and Economic Studies Conference on Poverty and Public Policy, Washington, D.C.

Economagic. 2002. *Economic Time Series Page*. Washington, D.C.: Economagic.com. <http://www.economagic.com/>

*Economic Report of the President*. Annual. Washington, D.C.: U.S. Government Printing Office.

Employment Benefit Research Institute. 1998. Agenda background material for "The National Summit on Retirement Savings," Washington, D.C., June 4-5.

Farber, Henry S. 1997a. *The Changing Face of Job Loss in the United States, 1981-95*. Princeton, N.J.: Princeton University.

Farber, Henry S. 1997b. "Trends in Long Term Employment in the United States, 1979-96." Industrial Relations Section Working Paper No. 384. Princeton, N.J.: Princeton University.

Farber, Henry S. 1998. "Has the Rate of Job Loss Increased in the Nineties?" Industrial Relations Section Working Paper No. 394. Princeton, N.J.: Princeton University.

Federal Reserve Board. 2000. "Recent Changes in U.S. Family Finances: Results From the 1998 Survey of Consumer Finances." *Federal Reserve Bulletin.* January 2000, pp. 1-29.

Federal Reserve Board. 2001a. *Flow of Funds Accounts of the United States: Annual Flows and Outstandings.* Washington, D.C: Board of Governors of the Federal Reserve System. <http://www.federalreserve.gov/releases/Z1/Current/data.htm>

Federal Reserve Board. 2001b. *Household Debt-Service Burden.* Washington, D.C: Board of Governors of the Federal Reserve System. <http://www.federalreserve.gov/releases/housedebt/default.htm>

Freeman, Richard. 1991. "How Much Has De-unionization Contributed to the Rise in Male Earnings Inequality?" National Bureau of Economic Research, Working Paper No. 3826. Cambridge, Mass.: NBER.

Freeman, Richard. 1995. The Limits of Wage Flexibility to Curing Unemployment. *Oxford Review of Economic Policy* 11(1): 63-72.

Freeman, Richard. 1997. "Low Wage Employment: Is More or Less Better?" Harvard University, unpublished paper.

Freeman, Richard. 1998. "The Facts About Rising Economic Disparity." In James A. Auerbach and Richard S. Belous, eds., *The Inequality Paradox: Growth and Income Disparity.* Washington, D.C.: National Policy Association.

Gale, William G., and Samara R. Potter. 2002. *An Economic Evaluation of the Economic Growth and Tax Relief Reconciliation Act of 2001.* Washington, D.C.: Brookings Institution. <http://www.brookings.edu/views/articles/gale/200203.htm>

Galinsky, Ellen, Stacy Kim, and James Bond. 2001. *Feeling Overworked: When Work Becomes Too Much.* New York, N.Y.: Families and Work Institute.

Gardner, Jennifer M. 1995. Worker Displacement: A Decade of Change. *Monthly Labor Review* 118(4): 45-57.

Glyn, Andrew. 2001. "Inequalities of Employment and Wages in OECD Countries." Oxford University, Department of Economics. Unpublished paper.

Golden, Lonnie, and Helene Jorgensen. 2002. *Time After Time: Mandatory Overtime in the U.S. Economy.* Washington, D.C.: Economic Policy Institute. <http://www.epinet.org/briefingpapers/120/bp120.pdf>

Gottschalk, Peter, and Sheldon Danziger. 1998. "Family Income Mobility—How Much Is There and Has It Changed?" In James A. Auerbach and Richard S. Belous, eds., *The Inequality Paradox: Growth of Income Disparity*. Washington, D.C.: National Policy Association.

Gottschalk, Peter, and Timothy M. Smeeding. 1997. "Empirical Evidence on Income Inequality in Industrialized Countries," Luxembourg Income Study Working Paper No. 154.

Hayghe, Howard V. 1993. Working Wives' Contributions to Family Incomes. *Monthly Labor Review* 116(8): 39-43.

Hetrick, R. 2000. "Analyzing the Recent Upward Surge in Overtime Hours." *Monthly Labor Review*. Washington, D.C.: U.S. Government Printing Office.

Hines, James R., Hilary Hoynes, and Alan Krueger. 2001. "Another Look at Whether a Rising Tide Lifts All Boats." In Alan Krueger and Robert Solow, eds., *The Roaring 1990s*. New York, N.Y.: Russell Sage Foundation and The Century Foundation.

Hirsch, Barry T., and David A. Macpherson. 1997. *Union Membership and Earnings Data Book: Compilations from the Current Population Survey (1997 Edition)*. Washington, D.C.: Bureau of National Affairs.

Johnson, David S. 2001. "Using Expenditures to Measure the Standard of Living in the United States: Does It Make a Difference?" Paper prepared for the conference, "What Has Happened to the Quality of Life in American and Other Advanced Industrialized Nations?" Jerome Levy Economics Institute of Bard College, June 6-7.

Kalleberg, Arne, Edith Rasell, Naomi Cassirer, Barbara F. Reskin, Ken Hudson, David Webster, Eileen Appelbaum, and Robert M. Spalter-Roth. 1997. *Nonstandard Work, Substandard Jobs*. Washington, D.C.: Economic Policy Institute.

Kennickell, Arthur B., Martha Starr-McCluer, and Brian J. Surette. 2000. *Recent Changes in U.S. Family Finances: Results From the 1998 Survey of Consumer Finances*. Federal Reserve Bulletin, Vol. 86 (January), pp. 1-29. <http://www.federalreserve.gov/pubs/oss/oss2/98/scf98home.html>

Kominski, Robert, and Eric Newburger. 1999. "Access Denied: Changes in Computer Ownership and Use: 1984-97." Unpublished paper, Census Bureau (August).

Koopman, Siem Jan, Andrew C. Harvey, Jurgen A. Doornik, and Neil Shephard. 2000. *STAMP Manual*. London, U.K.: Timberlake Consultants Ltd.

Leete-Guy, Laura, and Juliet B. Schor. 1992. *The Great American Time Squeeze: Trends in Work and Leisure, 1969-89*. Washington, D.C.: Economic Policy Institute.

Luxembourg Income Study. 2001a. *Income Inequality Measures*. Luxembourg: Luxembourg Income Study. <http://lisweb.ceps.lu/keyfigures/ineqtable.htm>

Luxembourg Income Study. 2001b. *Relative Poverty Rates for the Total Population, Children and the Elderly.* Luxembourg: Luxembourg Income Study. <http://lisweb.ceps.lu/keyfigures/povertytable.htm>

Maki, Dean M., and Michael G. Palumbo. 2001. *Disentangling the Wealth Effect: A Cohort Analysis of Household Saving in the 1990s.* Washington, D.C.: Federal Reserve Board, No. 21.

McCrate, Elaine. 2002. *Working Mothers In a Double Bind.* Washington, D.C.: Economic Policy Institute. <http://www.epinet.org/briefingpapers/124/124.pdf>

Mishel, Lawrence, and Jared Bernstein. 1994. "Is the Technology Black Box Empty? An Empirical Examination of the Impact of Technology on Wage Inequality and the Employment Structure." Presented to the Labor Economics Workshop, Harvard University. Unpublished paper.

Mishel, Lawrence, and Jared Bernstein. 1996. "Did Technology's Impact Accelerate in the 1980s?" Paper presented at the Industrial and Relations Research Association meetings, San Francisco, Calif., January.

Mishel, Lawrence, and Jared Bernstein. 1998. Technology and the Wage Structure: Has Technology's Impact Accelerated Since the 1970s? *Research in Labor Economics.* Vol. 17, pp. 305-355.Mishel, Lawrence, and Ruy Teixeira. 1991. *The Myth of the Coming Labor Shortage: Jobs, Skills, and Incomes of America's Workforce 2000.* Washington, D.C.: Economic Policy Institute.

Muñoz de Bustillo, Rafael and Rafael Bonete. 2000. *Introducción a la Unión Europea: un análisis desde la economía.* Madrid, Spain: Alianza Editorial.

Murphy, Kevin, and Finis Welch. 1989. "Recent Trends in Real Wages: Evidence from Household Data." Paper prepared for the Health Care Financing Administration of the U.S. Department of Health and Human Services. Chicago, Ill.: University of Chicago.

National Association of Colleges and Employers. Various years' September issues. *Salary Survey.* Bethlehem, PA: National Association of Colleges and Employers.

National Center for Public Policy and Higher Education. 2002. *Losing Ground: A National Status Report on the Affordability of American Higher Education.* San Jose, Calif.: National Center for Public Policy and Higher Education.

National Research Council. 1995. *Measuring Poverty: A New Approach.* Washington, D.C.: National Research Council.

Neumark, David, Daniel Polsky, and Daniel Hansen. 1997. "Has Job Stability Declined Yet? New Evidence for the 1990s." Working Paper No. 6330. Cambridge, Mass.: National Bureau of Economic Research.

OECD (Organization for Economic Cooperation and Development). 1998. *Economic Outlook.* Paris: OECD.

OECD. 1999a. *National Accounts of OECD Countries. Main Aggregates Volume I. 1960-1996.* Paris: OECD.

OECD. 1999b. *Economic Outlook.* Paris: OECD.

OECD. 2001a. *National Accounts of OECD Countries. Main Aggregates Volume I. 1989-2000.* Paris: OECD.

OECD. 2001b. *OECD in Figures.* Paris: OECD.

OECD. 2001c. *OECD Science, Technology and Industry Scoreboard 2001: Towards a Knowledge-Based Economy.* Paris: OECD. <http://www1.oecd.org/publications/e-book/92-2001-04-1-2987/>

OECD. 2001d. *Economic Outlook.* Paris: OECD.

OECD. 2001e. *Employment Outlook.* Paris: OECD.

OECD. 2001f. *Purchasing Power Parities (PPPs) for OECD Countries 1970-2001.* Paris: OECD. <http://www.oecd.org/EN/document/0,,EN-document-0-nodirectorate-no-1-9066-0,00.html#title5>

OECD. 2001g. *Society at a Glance, 2001.* Paris: OECD. <http://www.oecd.org/EN/document/0,,EN-document-211-5-no-1-22006-0,00.html>

OECD. 2001h. *Main Economic Indicators.* Paris: OECD.

OECD. 2002. *Source OECD Website: The OECD Online Library of Book, Periodicals, and Statistics.* Paris: OECD. <http://www.sourceoecd.org/content/html/index.htm>

Oxley, Howard, Thai-Thanh Dang, and Pablo Antolin. 1999. "Poverty Dynamics in Six OECD Countries." Paper presented at the European Economic Association Annual Congress, September.

Pierce, Brooks. 1998. "Compensation Inequality." U.S. Department of Labor, Bureau of Labor Statistics, Washington, D.C. Manuscript.

Polivka, Anne E. 1998. "Using Earnings Data for the Current Population Survey After the Redesign." Working Paper No. 306. Washington, D.C.: U.S. Bureau of Labor Statistics.

Polivka, Anne E., and Stephen M. Miller. 1995. "The CPS After the Redesign: Refocusing the Economic Lens." Washington, D.C.: Bureau of Labor Statistics. Unpublished paper.

Poterba, James M. 2000. "Stock Market Wealth and Consumption." *Journal of Economic Perspectives* 14(2): 99-118.

Rose, Stephen J. 1995. *Declining Job Security and the Professionalization of Opportunity.* Research Report No. 95-04. Washington, D.C.: National Commission for Employment Policy.

Ruggles, Patricia. 1990. *Drawing the Line: Alternative Poverty Measures and Their Implications for Public Policy.* Washington, D.C.: Urban Institute.

Ryscavage, Paul, Gordon Green, Edward Welniak, and John Coder. 1992. *Studies in the Distribution of Income*. U.S. Department of Commerce, Bureau of the Census, Series P-60, No. 183. Washington, D.C.: U.S. Government Printing Office.

Schmitt, John, and Lawrence Mishel. 1996. "Did International Trade Lower Less-Skilled Wages During the 1980s? Standard Trade Theory and Evidence." Technical Paper. Washington, D.C.: Economic Policy Institute.

Scott, Robert E., Thea Lee, and John Schmitt. 1997. "Trading Away Good Jobs: An Examination of Employment and Wages in the U.S., 1979-94". Briefing Paper. Washington, D.C.: Economic Policy Institute.

Sekscenski, Edward S. 1980. "Women's Share of Moonlighting Nearly Doubles During 1969-79." *Monthly Labor Review* 103(5).

Shapiro, Isaac. 1987. *No Escape: The Minimum Wage and Poverty*. Washington, D.C.: Center on Budget and Policy Priorities.

Smeeding, Timothy M. 1997. "Financial Poverty in Developed Countries: The Evidence from LIS," Luxembourg Income Study Working Paper No. 155.

Smeeding, Timothy, and Lee Rainwater. 2001. "Comparing Living Standards Across Nations: Real Incomes at the Top, the Bottom, and the Middle." Working Draft Paper. Luxembourg: Luxembourg Income Study.

Stewart, Jay. 2002. "Recent Trends in Job Stability and Job Security: Evidence From the March CPS." Working Paper 356. Washington, D.C.: Bureau of Labor Statistics. <http://www.bls.gov/ore/pdf/ec020050.pdf>

Stinson, John F., Jr. 1986. "Moonlighting by Women Jumped to Record Highs." *Monthly Labor Review* 109(11).

Towers, Perrin and Company. Various years. *Worldwide Total Remuneration*.

University of Groningen and The Conference Board. 2002. *GGDC Total Economy Database, 2002*. <http://www.eco.rug.nl/ggdc>

U.S. Department of Commerce, Bureau of the Census. 1999. *American Housing Survey for the United States*. Washington, D.C.: U.S. Government Printing Office. <http://www.census.gov/hhes/www/housing/ahs/ahs99/ahs99.html>

U.S. Department of Commerce, Bureau of the Census. Current Population Reports. Various dates. *Marital Status and Living Arrangements*. P-20 Series. Washington D.C.: U.S. Government Printing Office.

U.S. Department of Commerce, Bureau of the Census. Current Population Reports. Various dates. P-60 Series. Washington, D.C.: U.S. Government Printing Office.

U.S. Department of Commerce, Bureau of the Census. Current Population Reports. 1990. *Trends in Income, by Selected Characteristics: 1947 to 1988*. P60 Series, No. 167. Washington, D.C.: U.S. Government Printing Office.

U.S. Department of Commerce, Bureau of the Census. Current Population Reports. 1991. *Trends in Relative Income: 1964 to 1989.* P60 Series, No. 177. Washington, D.C.: U.S. Government Printing Office.

U.S. Department of Commerce, Bureau of the Census. Current Population Reports. 1995. *Household and Family Characteristics.* P20 Series. Washington, D.C.: U.S. Government Printing Office.

U.S. Department of Commerce, Bureau of the Census. Current Population Reports. 1996. *A Brief Look at Postwar U.S. Income Inequality.* P60 Series, No.191. Washington, D.C.: U.S. Government Printing Office.

U.S. Department of Commerce, Bureau of the Census. Current Population Reports. 1997. *Money Income in the United States: 1996.* P60 Series, No.197. Washington, D.C.: U.S. Government Printing Office.

U.S. Department of Commerce, Bureau of the Census. Current Population Reports. 2000a. *School Enrollment—Social and Economic Characteristics of Students.* Washington, D.C.: U.S. Government Printing Office. <http://www.census.gov/population/www/socdemo/school.html>

U.S. Department of Commerce, Bureau of the Census. Current Population Reports. 2000b. *Families and Living Arrangements.* Washington, D.C.: U.S. Government Printing Office. <http://www.census.gov/population/www/socdemo/hh-fam.html>

U.S. Department of Commerce, Bureau of the Census. Current Population Reports. 2002. *Historical Income Tables.* Washington, D.C.: U.S. Government Printing Office. <http://www.census.gov/hhes/income/histinc/f03.html>

U.S. Department of Commerce, Bureau of the Census. Housing Vacancy Survey. 2001. *Housing Vacancies and Homeownership Annual Statistics: 2001.* Washington, D.C.: U.S. Government Printing Office. <http://www.census.gov/hhes/www/housing/hvs/annual01/ann01t20.html>

U.S. Department of Commerce, National Telecommunication and Information Administration. 2000. *Falling Through the Net: Defining the Digital Divide.* Washington, D.C.: Government Printing Office. <http://www.ntia.doc.gov/ntiahome/fttn00/charts00.html#t31>

U.S. Department of Education, National Center for Education Statistics. 2000. *National Postsecondary Student Aid Study, 1989-90, 1992-93, 1995-96, 1999-2000.* Washington, D.C.: U.S. Government Printing Office. <www.nces.ed.gov/pubsearch/pubsinfo.asp?pubid=2000151>

U.S. Department of Labor, Bureau of Labor Statistics (BLS). 1997. *Employee Benefits in Medium and Large Private Establishments, 1997.* USDL: 99-02. Washington, D.C.: Bureau of Labor Statistics. <http://www.bls.gov/news.release/ebs3.toc.htm>

U.S. Department of Labor, BLS. 2000. *International Comparisons of Hourly Compensation Costs for Production Workers in Manufacturing, 1975-1998.* Washington, DC: Bureau of Labor Statistics. <http://stats.bls.gov/news.release/ichcc.toc.htm>

U.S. Department of Labor, BLS. 2001. *Employee Benefits in Private Industry, 1999.* Washington, D.C.: Bureau of Labor Statistics. <http://www.bls.gov/news.release/ebs2.toc.htm>

U.S. Department of Labor, BLS. 2001a. *International Comparisons of Hourly Compensation Costs for Production Workers in Manufacturing, 1997-2000.* Washington, D.C.: Bureau of Labor Statistics. <ftp://ftp.bls.gov/pub/special.requests/ForeignLabor/supptab.txt>

U.S. Department of Labor, BLS. 2001b. *International Comparisons of Labor Productivity and Unit Labor Costs in Manufacturing, 2000.* Washington, D.C.: Bureau of Labor Statistics. <ftp://ftp.bls.gov/pub/special.requests/ForeignLabor/flsprodyt07.txt>

U.S. Department of Labor, BLS. 2001c. *International Comparisons of Hourly Compensation Costs for Production Workers in Manufacturing, 2000.* Washington, D.C.: Bureau of Labor Statistics. <http://stats.bls.gov/news.release/ichcc.toc.htm>

U.S. Department of Labor, BLS. 2001d. *Comparative Civilian Labor Force Statistics, Ten Countries, 1959-2001.* Washington, D.C.: Bureau of Labor Statistics. <ftp://ftp.bls.gov/pub/special.requests/ForeignLabor/flslforc.txt>

U.S. Department of Labor, BLS. 2002a. *Current Population Survey.* Washington, D.C.: Bureau of Labor Statistics. <http://www.bls.gov/cps/home.htm>

U.S. Department of Labor, BLS. 2002b. *Current Employment Statistics.* Washington, D.C.: Bureau of Labor Statistics. <http://www.bls.gov/ces/home.htm>

U.S. Department of Labor, BLS. 2002c. *Employee Tenure.* Washington, D.C.: Bureau of Labor Statistics.

U.S. Department of the Treasury, Internal Revenue Service. 1998. *Publication 15, Circular E, Employer's Tax Guide.* Washington, D.C.: Internal Revenue Service.

U.S. Department of the Treasury, Office of Tax Analysis. 1998. *Average and Marginal Federal Income, Social Security, and Medicare Tax Rates for Four-Person Families at the Same Relative Positions in the Income Distribution, 1955-99.* Washington, D.C.: U.S. Department of the Treasury.

Van Ark, Bart, and Robert H. McGuckin. 1999. "International Comparisons of Labor Productivity and Per Capita Income." *Monthly Labor Review,* July. <http://www.bls.gov/opub/mlr/1999/07/contents.htm>

Waldfogel, Jane. 2001. *International Policies Toward Parental Leave and Child Care.* Los Altos, Calif.: Future of Our Children. <http://www.futureofchildren.org/information2826/information_show.htm?doc_id=79378>

Wenger, Jeffrey. 2001. "The Continuing Problems With Part-Time Jobs." Issue Brief. Washington, D.C.: Economic Policy Institute. <http://www.epinet.org/Issuebriefs/ib155ib155.pdf>

Wenger, Jeffery. 2002. Unpublished tables on nonstandard work. Washington, D.C.: Economic Policy Institute.

West, Sandra A. (Undated). "Measures of Central Tendency for Censored Earnings Data From the Current Population Survey." Unpublished Bureau of Labor Statistics report.

Wolff, Edward N. 1992. "Changing Inequality of Wealth." Paper presented at the American Economic Association Meetings, Boston, Mass., January.

Wolff, Edward N. 1993. "The Rich Get Increasingly Richer: Latest Data on Household Wealth During the 1980s." Briefing Paper. Washington, D.C.: Economic Policy Institute.

Wolff, Edward N. 1994. Trends in Household Wealth in the United States, 1962-1983 and 1983-1989. *Review of Income and Wealth,* Series 40, No. 2.

Wolff, Edward N. 1996. "Trends in Household Wealth During 1989-1992." Paper submitted to the Department of Labor. New York, N.Y.: New York University.

Wolff, Edward N. 2002. *Retirement Insecurity: The Income Shortfalls Awaiting the Soon-to-Retire.* Washington, D.C.: Economic Policy Institute.

# Index

Aaronson, Daniel, 263
African Americans, *see* Blacks
Alternative income definitions, 68–75
Alternative measurements
  income, 68–75
  poverty, 319–29
Asians, wage growth of, 170–71
Assets
  home ownership, rates of, 277–78,
    289–92
  net worth defined, 278–79
  overall trend, 289–92
  retirement wealth, 292–93
  stocks, 286–89
Average family
  federal tax rates, 63–64
  income, 4–5
  international comparison of incomes,
    409–13
  unemployment's impact on, 226

Bankruptcy rates, personal, 278, 302
Blacks
  employment rates by wage level, 136–
    41
  health benefit coverage, 146
  home ownership, rates of, 290–92
  household wealth, 283
  income growth, 5, 33–34, 40–43
  labor force participation rates, 229
  longer working hours, 26, 34, 101–3
  low-wage earners, proportion of, 136–41
  low, zero or negative net worth, rates
    of, 284–85

*Blacks (cont.)*
  nonstandard work arrangements
    among, 252
  pension plan coverage, 146
  poverty rates, 11, 24, 313–17
  stock ownership, rates of, 286–87
  unemployment rates, 218–20, 221–22
  unionization among, 191
  wage growth analyzed by race, 170–71
  wage trends for, 383–85
  workplace computer use, rate of, 211–
    12

Capital income increase
  labor income compared, 84–93
  trend, 86–94
Child poverty rates, 11, 316–17, 415
College-educated workers
  entry-level wages, 163–65
  international comparisons, 428–29
  longer working hours, 26, 100–101
  wage differential, 80, 154, 158–62,
    178–80, 207–10
Comprehensive income defined, 68–69
Consumer Expenditure Survey, 74
Consumer Price Index, 31, 324
Contingent jobs, 250–51
Corporate income taxes, 66
Corporate profits, 90–94
  constant profit share defined, 93
  profit rates and capital's share of
    income distinguished, 91–92
  rates at business cycle peaks, 92

# About EPI

**The Economic Policy Institute** was founded in 1986 to widen the debate about policies to achieve healthy economic growth, prosperity, and opportunity.

Today, despite a recent period of rapid growth in the U.S. economy, inequality in wealth, wages, and income remains historically high. Expanding global competition, changes in the nature of work, and rapid technological advances are altering economic reality. Yet many of our policies, attitudes, and institutions are based on assumptions that no longer reflect real world conditions.

With the support of leaders from labor, business, and the foundation world, the Institute has sponsored research and public discussion of a wide variety of topics: trade and fiscal policies; trends in wages, incomes, and prices; education; the causes of the productivity slowdown; labor market problems; rural and urban policies; inflation; state-level economic development strategies; comparative international economic performance; and studies of the overall health of the U.S. manufacturing sector and of specific key industries.

The Institute works with a growing network of innovative economists and other social science researchers in universities and research centers all over the country who are willing to go beyond the conventional wisdom in considering strategies for public policy.

Founding scholars of the Institute include Jeff Faux, distinguished fellow and former president of EPI; Lester Thurow, Sloan School of Management, MIT; Ray Marshall, former U.S. secretary of labor, professor at the LBJ School of Public Affairs, University of Texas; Barry Bluestone, Northeastern University; Robert Reich, former U.S. secretary of labor; and Robert Kuttner, author, editor of *The American Prospect,* and columnist for *Business Week* and the Washington Post Writers Group.

For additional information about the Institute, contact EPI at 1660 L Street NW, Suite 1200, Washington, DC 20036, (202) 775-8810, or visit www.epinet.org.

# About the authors

**LAWRENCE MISHEL** is president of the Economic Policy Institute and was the research director from 1987 to 1999. He is the co-author of the previous versions of *The State of Working America*. He holds a Ph.D. in economics from the University of Wisconsin, and his articles have appeared in a variety of academic and non-academic journals. His areas of research are labor economics, wage and income distribution, industrial relations, productivity growth, and the economics of education.

**JARED BERNSTEIN** joined the Economic Policy Institute as a labor economist in 1992 and is currently the director of the Living Standards Program and co-director of research. Between 1995 and 1996, he held the post of deputy chief economist at the U.S. Department of Labor, where, among other topics, he worked on the initiative to raise the minimum wage. He is co-author of five previous editions of *The State of Working America* and co-author (with Dean Baker) of the forthcoming book *The Benefits of Full Employment and the Costs of Not Being There*. He specializes in the analysis of wage and income inequality, poverty, and low-wage labor markets, and his writings have appeared in popular and academic journals. Mr. Bernstein holds a Ph.D. in social welfare from Columbia University.

**HEATHER BOUSHEY** is an economist at the Economic Policy Institute, where she conducts research on labor markets. She is co-author of *Hardships in America: The Real Story of Working Families*, and her articles on gender and racial inequality, unemployment and wages, and employment retention have appeared in academic journals and the popular press. She has testified before Congress and authored numerous reports and commentaries on the effectiveness of the 1996 welfare reform law. Ms. Boushey received her Ph.D. in economics from the New School for Social Research in 1998 and her B.A. from Hampshire College.